The Christian Theological Tradition

THIRD EDITION

The Christian
Theological Tradition

UNIVERSITY OF ST. THOMAS

General Editors

Catherine A. Cory   **Michael J. Hollerich**

Contributors
Catherine A. Cory
David S. Cunningham
Rev. Patrick D. Gaffney C.S.C.
Michael J. Hollerich
David G. Hunter
Rev. J. Michael Joncas
Shirley E. Jordon
Anne H. King
Terence L. Nichols
David Penchansky
Rev. Thaddeus J. Posey, OFM Cap.
Rev. David W. Smith
John Smithe
Edward Ulrich

PEARSON

Prentice
Hall

Upper Saddle River, New Jersey

Library of Congress Cataloging-in-Publication Data
The Christian Theological Tradition / general editors, Catherine A. Cory, Michael J. Hollerich;
contributors, Catherine A. Cory . . . [et al.]. — 3rd ed.
   p. cm.
   Includes bibliographical references and index.
   ISBN-13: 978-0-13-602832-1
   ISBN-10: 0-13-602832-2
   1. Theology, Doctrinal–History.   2. Catholic Church–Doctrines–History.   3. Christian education—
Textbooks for young adults—Catholic.   I. Cory, Catherine A.   II. Hollerich, Michael J.
   BX1751.3.C48 2009
   230'.2—dc22

                                                                                          2008039862

Senior Acquisitions Editor: Dave Repetto
Project Manager: Sarah Holle
Editorial Director: Leah Jewell
Editor in Chief: Dickson Musslewhite
Editorial Assistant: Pat Walsh
Marketing Manager: Lindsey Prudhomme
Marketing Assistant: Craig Deming
Senior Managing Editor: Mary Rottino
Production Liaison: Fran Russello
Senior Operations Supervisor:
   Brian Mackey
Operations: Cathleen Petersen

Art Director: Jayne Conte
Cover Illustration/Photo: Minnesota Institute
   of the Arts
Manager, Rights and Permissions: Zina Arabia
Manager, Visual Research: Beth Brenzel
Manager, Cover Visual Research & Permissions:
   Karen Sanatar
Image Permission Coordinator: Nancy Seise
Photo Researcher: Francelle Carapetyan
Composition/Full-Service Project Management:
   Jogender Taneja/Aptara®, Inc.
Printer/Binder: RR Donnelley & Sons Company

Credits and acknowledgments borrowed from other sources and reproduced, with permission, in this
textbook appear on page 507.

Pearson Education Ltd., London
Pearson Education Singapore, Pte. Ltd
Pearson Education, Canada, Inc.
Pearson Education–Japan
Pearson Education Australia PTY, Limited

Pearson Education North Asia, Ltd., Hong Kong
Pearson Educación de Mexico, S.A. de C.V.
Pearson Education Malaysia, Pte. Ltd.
Pearson Education, Upper Saddle River, New Jersey

10 9 8 7 6
ISBN-13: 978-0-13-602832-1
ISBN-10:   0-13-602832-2

Contents

Preface   ix

CHAPTER 1   **Introduction**   1
Catherine Cory, Terence Nichols, David Smith, and Jan Michael Joncas

PART I   THE OLD TESTAMENT   *Catherine Cory and John Smithe*   19

CHAPTER 2   **The Primeval Story**   29
John Smithe and David Penchansky

CHAPTER 3   **God's Covenant with Israel**   42
David Smith

CHAPTER 4   **Judges, Prophets, Kings**   60
David Penchansky and John Smithe

CHAPTER 5   **Second Temple Judaism**   74
John Smithe

PART II	THE NEW TESTAMENT *Catherine Cory*	91
CHAPTER 6	**Jesus and the Gospels** *Catherine Cory*	97
CHAPTER 7	**Apostolic Missions** *John Smithe and Catherine Cory*	118
PART III	THE HISTORY OF CHRISTIANITY *Michael Hollerich*	135
CHAPTER 8	**Christianity After the Apostles** *Michael Hollerich*	141
CHAPTER 9	**The Age of the Imperial Church** *Michael Hollerich*	161
CHAPTER 10	**Augustine of Hippo** *David Hunter*	181
CHAPTER 11	**Eastern Christianity** *Jan Michael Joncas*	194
CHAPTER 12	**Islam Past and Present** *Patrick Gaffney*	211
CHAPTER 13	**Christianity in the Early Medieval Period** *Jan Michael Joncas*	235
CHAPTER 14	**Christianity in the High Middle Ages** *Michael Hollerich*	252

CHAPTER 15   Thomas Aquinas   273
              David Smith

CHAPTER 16   Christianity in the Late Medieval Period   288
              Anne H. King

PART IV   THE MODERN PERIOD   Terence Nichols   303

CHAPTER 17   The Renaissance   307
              Terence Nichols

CHAPTER 18   Martin Luther   316
              Shirley E. Jordon

CHAPTER 19   Other Protestant Reformers   332
              David S. Cunningham

CHAPTER 20   The Catholic Reformation   351
              Anne H. King

CHAPTER 21   Global Expansion and the Colonial Churches   363
              Thaddeus Posey

CHAPTER 22   Modern Challenges to Christianity   378
              Terence Nichols

CHAPTER 23   Christianity in America   399
              Michael Hollerich

CHAPTER 24   The Second Vatican Council in Context   422
              Michael Hollerich

CHAPTER 25   **Christianity and the Contemporary Situation**   441
Catherine Cory, Terence Nichols, David Smith, and David S. Cunningham

CHAPTER 26   **Christianity and Interreligious Dialogue**   471
Edward Ulrich

Glossary   484

Copyright Acknowledgments   507

Index   511

Preface

This textbook, *The Christian Theological Tradition*, now in its third edition, has a rich past. The seeds of its creation were planted some eighteen years ago when the Theology Department at the University of St. Thomas in St. Paul, Minnesota, was searching for ways to meet the needs of its large and increasingly diverse undergraduate student body. The result was an introductory level textbook developed and written not by one or two authors but by an entire department, in order that our students might have a common experience of both the richness and the challenges of the Christian theological tradition as its story unfolds throughout history. We are pleased to share with you the fruits of our labors.

We thought you might appreciate hearing the story of how this textbook came to be, because it provides a context for understanding what we were attempting to accomplish by writing it. In the fall of 1990, the Theology Department launched a comprehensive review of its curriculum. That effort became part of a university-wide core curriculum review that was lengthy and sometimes difficult, but always enriching. The department set out to create a new first course in theology, which all undergraduate students would take as part of their general education requirements. This new course was entitled "The Christian Theological Tradition." It was designed to give students a one-semester introduction to the Bible and to major persons, ideas, and events of Christian history with special attention to several important themes of Christian theology. This would be the first of our three-course requirement in the curricular area "Faith and the Catholic Tradition."

The department was convinced of the need for this new first course in theology for at least two reasons. First, our student body was gradually becoming more diverse. In years past, the majority of our students came from local Catholic schools and parishes. Having grown up in what might be termed a Catholic culture, these students shared the same religious vocabulary and common experiences of church and worship, which they also brought to their study of theology. However, in the 1970s and 80s, as Catholics became more integrated into the wider American culture, this Catholic culture became less pervasive. At the same time, our university began to attract more students from other Christian traditions and from other faiths, as well as students with no religious affiliation. They came to us because of the quality of our career preparation programs or because they wanted a values-based education in a safe and respectful environment. But the student body no longer shared the same religious culture. Students had little knowledge about the Bible, the major doctrines of Christianity, the Catholic tradition, or the meaning and significance of various forms of Christian worship. Thus, the course called "The Christian Theological Tradition" was created, in part, to provide our students with the basic theological literacy necessary to engage in meaningful academic discourse about theological issues that impact their lives.

Second, the faculty in our department has had a long-standing commitment to teaching theology through the use of primary texts—not only for majors and minors, but also for students completing undergraduate general education requirements. The reason? Reading a wide range of texts from across the history of the Christian tradition and learning to think critically and write skillfully about these texts is important to a liberal arts education. Therefore the department's first step in crafting this new first course in theology was to develop a list of primary texts. The first list was very long, but eventually the faculty was able to agree upon a modest list of biblical texts including some extended excerpts from the Pentateuch, the prophets, the gospels, and Paul's letters. The list also included some of the most important Christian theological and spiritual writers, such as Irenaeus of Lyons, Augustine, Anselm, Thomas Aquinas, Julian of Norwich, Catherine of Siena, and Martin Luther, as well as excerpts from a number of church councils, including the Second Vatican Council.

As the department prepared to launch this new course, it decided that it needed a textbook to supplement and contextualize its list of primary readings. We considered a number of different textbooks that were available at the time, but we were unable to find something that met all of our needs. Some were too difficult, while others were too simplistic in their approach to the history of Christianity. Some did a good job of presenting the historical information, but did little to promote theological literacy or sketch out a framework for the development of Christian doctrine and spirituality through the centuries. By this time the university-wide curriculum review was well underway, and the Theology Department was busy trying to figure out how it would contribute to the objectives of the new core course curriculum for undergraduates. The university faculty had agreed that the undergraduate general requirements would serve as the foundation for liberal arts learning across the curriculum. Core courses within a particular curricular area would have a certain percentage of common texts to encourage more academic discourse outside of individual classrooms. Core courses would focus on developing critical thinking and writing skills. They would also attend to issues of interdisciplinary learning and cultural diversity. As an academic discipline, theology was well suited to meet these learning objectives, so the department decided that it would design "The Christian Theological Tradition" along these lines. The course would become the one common educational experience of all students who received undergraduate degrees from St. Thomas.

In the summer of 1994, a committee of the Theology Department faculty took on the task of exploring the feasibility of writing a textbook for its new first course, "The Christian Theological Tradition." It was given the charge of developing a book proposal, including a table of contents and some sample chapters, which the department could take up for consideration during the fall semester. The committee had a very productive summer and its members came back to the department energized and excited about the project. Not only did it have a book proposal to present, but it also had several chapters to pilot in the classroom. Faculty volunteered to try out these chapters in their fall sections of "The Christian Theological Tradition" and to solicit feedback from their students. We wanted the textbook to be sophisticated enough to provide our students with tools to successfully grapple with the course's primary texts, but sufficiently lucid and accessible that students could read it on their own without a lot of instructor support. We also wanted the textbook to be comprehensive enough that instructors would have options to develop the course as they wished. Finally, we wanted the textbook to be visually attractive, with an abundance of pedagogical aids, and interdisciplinary in its treatment of various topics. This was no small task for an entry-level textbook! However, the book proposal and the feedback we received on the piloted chapters convinced the faculty that this was a worthwhile venture.

Shortly after the department made its decision to move forward with the textbook project, the book proposal committee of the summer of 1994 became the editorial board for the textbook. Our first task was to secure funding to support the project. St. Thomas had obtained a Bush Foundation grant to support its university-wide curriculum revision, and the Theology Department had the good fortune to receive a portion of that grant to develop the textbook. We also received some funding from the Aquinas Foundation, a university grant program for special projects. Within a couple months, we were ready to begin! Because we are a large department representing a wide range of specializations, it took no time at all to find authors for the textbook's twenty-four chapters. Some were written by individual authors, while others were authored jointly, but all were carefully attended to by the editorial board. Each author prepared a draft of the assigned chapter. Then the editorial board met with the author to offer feedback, suggest additions or changes, and help make connections with other chapters in the textbook, before he or she went back to finish the chapter. In addition, there were numerous consultations in offices and hallways about how to make a particularly difficult topic comprehensible for our undergraduate audience or where to find a fitting illustration for one of the book's chapters. In sum, this textbook was truly a collaborative project.

The chapters of *The Christian Theological Tradition*, so named because it is a companion to the course of the same title, were written between the fall of 1994 and the winter of 1995. The editing was completed by the spring of 1996, and the textbook was in the hands of our students by the fall of 1996. The first iteration of this book was custom published, because we wanted to be sure that we had a free hand in designing it as we wished, but also because it was developed to serve the particular needs of our students. Whatever else came of this project, we wanted never to lose sight of our primary audience, the undergraduates at the University of St. Thomas. They were, and continue to be, our best critics and the source of our ongoing commitment to this course. Much to our surprise, however, faculty at other schools found out about the textbook and asked if they could purchase it for their students. So began our venture into the commercial publishing world. The first commercially published edition of *The Christian Theological Tradition* produced by Prentice Hall became available for student use in the fall of 1999.

Today, we are pleased to say that the textbook is in its third edition. Here is an overview of the changes you will find in this edition:

- New introductory chapter (1), which includes a full treatment of the academic discipline of religious studies;
- New chapters on Islam Past and Present (12), Christianity in America (23), and the Second Vatican Council in Context (24);
- Significantly revised and expanded chapters on Jesus and the Gospels (6), Christianity and the Contemporary Situation (25), and Christianity and Interreligious Dialogue (26);
- Revised and updated chapter content and bibliographies throughout the remainder of the book.

Like the earlier editions, this third edition was done in a spirit of collaboration and with an enduring desire to better serve our students. We hope that it will also serve your educational needs.

ACKNOWLEDGMENTS

We have many, many people to thank for the continued success of *The Christian Theological Tradition* and the course for which it was written. First, we want to thank the editorial board of the first edition and the co-editors of each edition for their significant contributions of time and talent, which was given to reviewing manuscripts, working with authors to clarify key topics and themes, ensuring continuity across the individual chapters, rewriting sections of text, selecting images, creating diagrams and timelines, and writing the glossary. The editorial board for the first edition included Catherine Cory, Michael Hollerich, David Landry, Terence Nichols, and Rev. David Smith, with additional support from Rev. Jan Michael Joncas and Rev. Thaddeus Posey, OFM Cap. The co-editors were Catherine Cory and David Landry. We also want to thank all of our authors, past and present, without which this project would never have come to fruition.

We also extend our gratitude to our university administrators, from our department chairs to the president of the university, who have continued to stand in support of this project over so many years. Thanks also to the Bush Foundation, the Curriculum Review Task Force of the University of St. Thomas, which administered the Bush Foundation grants, and the Aquinas Institute for providing the financial resources to write that first edition. We also thank our colleagues in other departments and programs, whose commitment to the core undergraduate curriculum make all of our work more fruitful. In particular, thanks to Mark Stansbury-O'Donnell of the art history department at the University of St. Thomas, who was willing to engage us in interdisciplinary conversations about theology and art and who helped us select many of the images for this textbook.

Finally, we want to say thank you to the faculty in our Theology Department who continue to devote much time and energy to teaching "The Christian Theological Tradition" and to refining and keeping it relevant for our students over these many years. Remarkably, although we have revised and updated it regularly, we have not lost sight of its original inspiration. Thanks also to our students who engage in this conversation with the Christian theological tradition each semester. Certainly, we are changed by the encounter and we trust that they are as well.

I would like to thank the reviewers of my manuscript for their valuable insights and comments: Joseph Kroger, St. Michaels College, Colchester, VT; Sister Peggy Fanning, St. Johns University, Queens, NY; and Marcia Robinson, Syracuse University, Syracuse, NY.

Catherine Cory and Michael Hollerich
On behalf of the Theology Department
University of St. Thomas
St. Paul, Minnesota

Inspired by Catholic intellectual tradition,
the University of St. Thomas educates students to be morally responsible leaders
who think critically, act wisely, and work skillfully
to advance the common good.
(University of St. Thomas Mission Statement)

Chapter

1
INTRODUCTION

Who are we? Why are we here? How should we act? How should we understand and relate to the world in which we live? Is there a deity, perhaps a power or a personal being, that exists beyond ourselves? If so, how do we relate to this power or personal being?

Everybody, in one way or another, faces questions about the meaning of human existence. The responses people propose to these questions are sometimes organized into a worldview. This worldview provides an overall way of seeing and relating to ourselves, other people, the world in which we live, and possible realities beyond this world. Starting from experience, they ask what that experience means and how it shapes our responses to the people, objects, forces, and events that surround us. Eventually people's responses to these questions coalesce around a set of beliefs, distinctive rituals, and acceptable ways of being in the world, thus creating a worldview. **Religion** is a comprehensive worldview that accounts for these questions of human existence and allows for believing in something beyond the "ordinary"—in God or gods, some unseen power or powers, something beyond human existence.

There are many religions in the world. The most prominent are Christianity, Islam, Hinduism, Buddhism, tribal religions (of Africa, Asia, North America, Australia, etc.), Confucianism, Taoism, Shintoism, and Judaism. Of these Judaism, Christianity, and Islam are **monotheistic** religions, based on a belief in "one God" (*monos* "one" + *theos* "god"). Hinduism, Shintoism, and most tribal religions are usually considered **polytheistic** religions, based on a belief in "many gods" (*polus* "many" + *theoi* "gods"). Perhaps surprising to some, there are forms of Buddhist religion that are **agnostic** (unsure about the existence of God or gods) or **atheistic** (denying that God or gods exist at all). The Jewish, Christian, and Muslim traditions, which are among the most influential in the Western world, believe God to be personal, all-knowing, all-powerful, just, loving, and the creator of everything that exists.

1

However, as stated previously, religion is more than a collection of statements or beliefs about God and the spiritual aspects of reality. It is a comprehensive worldview. It includes experiences, rituals, symbols, institutions, stories, habits, attitudes, and norms of behavior through which human beings, as groups or individuals, relate to the physical, social, cultural, and spiritual world in which they live. How then does one study religion and religious activity? Probably since the dawn of human civilization, people have talked, wondered, and written about religious questions, so this activity is not new. However, the work of people who study religion changes over time because of changing social and cultural conditions that affect the way humans experience their world. For example, a thirteenth-century Korean shaman (healer and intermediary between the earthly and heavenly realms) would have had very different ways of talking about deities and divine powers than did Thomas Aquinas living in Europe in the same time period. Likewise, an eleventh-century Tibetan Buddhist master would have trained the young monks in his care very differently than a Muslim imam or a Jewish rabbi in the present-day United States of America might advise his or her community concerning right living.

Among people of Western cultures, the Age of Enlightenment was a decisive turning point for the study of religion, resulting in entirely new approaches to religious questions and even new kinds of questions. The Age of Enlightenment, in the eighteenth century or perhaps as early as the seventeenth century, represents the beginning of the modern period of history and the emergence of entirely new ways of thinking about God, creation, and the human person. The beginnings of the modern scientific method developed in this period. Great thinkers in the area of philosophy, including Immanuel Kant and René Descartes, turned people's attention to the value of reason and the necessity of empirical evidence as proof for statements of belief. It was no longer acceptable to say that something was true because God had revealed it. Thus, reason and empirical evidence began to dominate discussions about the characteristics of truth, even challenging long-standing religious assertions about the nature of God and God's interactions with the created world.

In the aftermath of the Age of Enlightenment, two modern approaches to the study of religion began to take shape, namely, theology and religious studies. Actually, the academic discipline of theology was already in existence for centuries before the Enlightenment. However, the social and cultural conditions of the Age of Enlightenment and its distinctive worldview forced theologians to rethink the ways they were approaching theological questions. This shift in thinking came about with a great deal of frustration and anxiety, because the Age of Enlightenment appeared to threaten the very existence of religion and religious thinking. In the meantime, some religious scholars began to be more interested in the social and psychological dimensions of religion. Simply stated, instead of asking what we can know about God, they began to ask what humanity's tendency toward religious enagement tells us about the nature of human beings.

This new approach to religious questions eventually gave birth to what we now know as **religious studies**. In content and methodology, religious studies is different from theology. Whereas theology focuses on God and spiritual realities as its subject matter, religious studies focuses on humanity and humans' experience of the divine. Moreover, whereas theologians struggled against the presuppositions and methodologies that characterized Age of Enlightenment thinking, scholars of religious studies embraced this worldview and used its approaches toward the accomplishment of their goal—the scientific study of humanity. Samuel Preus, one of the seminal writers in the religious studies movement, described the positive benefits of this academic discipline, compared to theology, in his 1987 publication entitled *Explaining Religion: Criticism and Theory from Bodin to Freud*:

> The naturalistic approach is at once more modest and more ambitious than the religious one: more modest because it is content to investigate the causes, motivations, meanings, and impact of religious phenomena without pronouncing on their cosmic significance for human destiny; ambitious, in that the study of religion strives to explain religion and to integrate its understanding into the other elements of culture to which it is related. (211; cited in Wiebe 1999, 7)

The phrase *naturalistic approach* refers to religious studies, which is contrasted here with the religious approach, that is, theology.

RELIGIOUS STUDIES AS AN ACADEMIC DISCIPLINE

Intellectual disciplines explore reality from particular perspectives. They employ distinct methods to arrive at their conclusions and a specialized vocabulary to report their conclusions. For example, geology is an intellectual discipline that explores the earth from the perspective of its material composition and transformation, using the methods of natural science; it employs a specialized vocabulary, including terms such as *igneous rock* and *plate tectonics*. Similarly, psychology is an intellectual discipline that explores the human mind and human behavior, using the methods of both the natural and the social sciences.

Although some academic disciplines share certain methods (i.e., ways of approaching the subject matter) and vocabulary, one must be careful not to confuse the methods and vocabulary of the different disciplines. While statistical analysis of human group interaction might be very useful in sociology, it has less value in art history. Musicians, sea captains, and baseball fans all use the term *pitch,* but in widely varying ways. Moreover, one should recognize that each of the disciplines has definite limits. One would not ask a geologist about stock market fluctuations, even though Wall Street is located at a particular site on the globe. Similarly, religious studies has its own methods and vocabulary. These are the tools of the academic discipline.

Anyone who is familiar with religious studies will tell you that there is not one single way to engage this academic discipline. Rather, *religious studies* is an umbrella term that encompasses a variety of social–scientific and philosophical approaches to questions concerning humanity's engagement with religion and religious phenomena. Religious studies scholar Seth Kunin has offered one way to map out the areas under this umbrella in a book entitled *Religious Studies and Theology: An Introduction*, which he coedited with Helen Bond and Francesca Aran Murphy. In it, he surveys the historical development of religious studies in four areas, which he calls theories of religion: psychological, phenomenological, anthropological, and sociological (2003, 32–93). At the risk of oversimplifying a very complex field of study, we will briefly describe each area and provide a few examples of the kind of work being done in these areas.

Psychological Theories of Religion

In general, psychological theories of religion focus on the individual and the individual's experience of religion as a social institution. Some extend their focus beyond the individual to the larger society to which he or she belongs. Scholars who work with these theories see

Figure 1–1 Psychiatrist Sigmund Freud (1856–1939).

religious experience as analogous to other kinds of human experience, except for the fact that the subject of the experience is religious. They also see religious emotions as similar in kind to other emotions except that the object of the emotions is religious. Although some would acknowledge the existence of an external "other" who exerts control on the believer's life, most who espouse these theories argue that this "other" is, in fact, internal and seated in the subconscious or the collective unconscious. Further, they argue that the collective unconscious contains archetypes (e.g., inherited memories or symbolic objects) that become the basis of all religious experiences. Concerned about what religion does, rather than what it is in the abstract, most of these theorists suggest that religion makes it easier or more satisfying for the individual to do what he or she already needs to do for human well-being. Some also argue that religion can contribute to the maturation of human culture (Bond, Kunin, and Murphy 2003, 31–45).

Some of the most notable figures in the history of the development of psychological theories of religion are William James (1842–1910), Sigmund Freud (1856–1939), Carl Jung (1875–1961), and Joseph Campbell (1904–1987). A brief excerpt from Carl Jung's *Psychology and Religion* illustrates what is distinctive about this approach to the study of religion.

Figure 1–2 Psychologist Carl Jung (1875–1961).

Religion appears to me to be a peculiar attitude of the human mind, which could be formulated in accordance with the original use of the term "religion," that is, a careful consideration and observation of certain dynamic factors, understood to be "powers," spirits, demons, gods, laws, ideas, ideals, or whatever name man has given to such factors as he has found in his world powerful, dangerous, or helpful enough to be taken into careful consideration, or grand, beautiful, and meaningful enough to be devoutly adored and loved. . . . I want to make clear that by the term "religion" I do not mean a creed. . . . The psychologist, in as much as he assumes a scientific attitude, has to disregard the claim of every creed to be the unique and eternal truth. He must keep his eye on the human side of the religious problem, in that he is concerned with the original religious experience quite apart from what the creeds have made of it. (Jung 1938, 5–7)

Phenomenological Approaches to Religion

In philosophical circles, the word *phenomenology* describes the study of things as they are perceived by the senses. Scholars who take a phenomenological approach to religious studies seek to describe and classify common observable elements of various religions so that they can better understand the form and structure of religion. In other words, they are looking for patterns of ideas or structures that form the bases of all religions. Therefore, this approach could be described as comparative studies in which the investigator looks for what is universal and/or essential in this phenomenon that we call religion. However, in order to arrive at the universal or essential dimensions of religion, individual aspects of a particular religion are often stripped of their specific cultural contexts. Thus, a particular person's reflection on his or her religious experience will likely not correspond exactly with scholarly descriptions of the phenomenon of religion even though they build their model of religion using patterns of observable data (Bond, Kunin, and Murphy 2003, 45–53).

Seth Kunin identifies W. Brede Kristensen (1867–1953), Mircea Eliade (1907–1986), and Ninian Smart (1927–2001) as three of the most notable figures in the history of the development of phenomenological approaches to the study of religion (Bond, Kunin, and Murphy, 2003, 45–53). The following is a brief description of Ninian Smart's Seven Dimensions of Religion (1989, 10–21).

1. *Experiential/Emotional.* There are certain experiences that seem to give rise to religion: encountering natural or supernatural forces that produce a sense of fear or awe, contemplating one's own death, having an "otherworldly" vision, encountering a person who seems to possess the key to salvation or personal happiness, feeling united with all of reality, or experiencing very strong emotions (such as at the birth of a child or the death of a loved one).
2. *Social/Institutional.* People who have these experiences seek out others with similar experiences and form groups for support. Gradually, these groups grow in size and complexity and, as a consequence, require organizational structures to keep them functioning effectively.
3. *Narrative/Mythic.* In the group, people pass on their experience in stories. In many cases, these stories are eventually collected in written form and become the sacred texts of the religion—their scriptures.
4. *Doctrinal/Philosophical.* As people ask questions about the experiences and the stories, they explain them rationally, as best they can. Some meanings cannot be expressed rationally but must remain as expressed in the stories themselves.
5. *Practical/Ritual.* If the group understands their experiences to relate to powers or beings beyond visible, everyday reality, they work out concrete ways of relating to those powers or beings (for example, liturgy or worship). They also work out formalized ways of relating to people and things that are part of their everyday lives.
6. *Ethical/Legal.* The group decides what actions and way of life are appropriate to their experiences and their understanding of those experiences. They also develop laws to govern the community they have formed.
7. *Material/Artistic.* In living out the preceding six dimensions, the group produces material things (buildings, songs, art objects) in a way that is expressive of and appropriate to their experiences and their understandings of those experiences.

These dimensions are not independent units of a religion, in the sense that they can be treated separately from one another. Rather, they are facets or aspects of a religion that are interrelated and interact with one another.

Smart's Seven Dimensions of Religion provide us with one useful way of thinking about the phenomenon of religion. However, approaches such as this one can also mask important differences within a religion and among different religions. Let us take Christianity as an example. Although all Christians profess faith in Jesus Christ, there are considerable differences among the various forms of the Christian religion, just as there are considerable differences between Christianity and other world religions. Related to the *experiential/emotional* dimension, some Christians can be described as "world embracing," because they find a kind of compatibility between the Christian worldview and the values of the dominant culture. Others, like contemplative monks, are sometimes described as "world rejecting," because they live a way of life that is different from the dominant culture in order to seek God in solitude. Still others, like social activists, can be described as "world trans-forming," because they seek to change the dominant culture to make it conform better to Christian values. Related to the *social/institutional* dimension, some Christian traditions, such as the Roman Catholic tradition and Orthodox traditions, tend to be hierarchically structured with bishops, priests, deacons, and so on, in positions of leadership. Others, like the Society of Friends, or Quakers, consider everyone in the group to have the same status.

With respect to the *narrative/mythic* dimension, all Christians would claim the Bible as sacred scripture. However, certain groups of Christians disagree over the status of some books of the Bible. They would also vary in their judgments concerning other types of Christian literature. Related to the *doctrinal/philosophical* dimension, disagreements among Christian churches on statements of belief can be especially fierce. For example, in past centuries, there have been intense arguments about what God has or has not revealed, how to interpret the Bible, how Christianity ought to relate to other world religions, and whether a certain course of action is faithful to the vision of Jesus.

The most visible differences among religions may be observed in the *practical/ritual* dimension: for example, the use of incense at an Orthodox liturgy, extensive preaching in a Presbyterian worship service, and the practice of speaking in tongues at a charismatic revival. Related to the *ethical/legal* dimension, Christian churches differ on such concrete issues as the morality of the death penalty, how a society is to spend its taxes, whether Christians can serve in the military, or whether abortion is permissible under any circumstances. Finally, Christians differ in terms of the *material/artistic* dimension of religion. Some Christians will build towering and elaborate Gothic cathedrals while others will erect plain structures like the wooden, white-washed congregational churches found in the small towns of New England. Some Christians will vocalize Gregorian chants, others vigorously sing Lutheran chorales, while others will sway to the sound of spirituals.

In sum, phenomenological approaches to the study of religion can help us understand the patterns of ideas or structures that form the bases of all religions, but they do not help us recognize and appreciate the distinctive characteristics of individual religions.

Anthropological Theories of Religion

The term *anthropology* describes the study of humankind with special attention to human culture and the progress or development of human society. Anthropological theories of religion tend to focus on aspects of religious experience that are culturally conditioned. Ritual (symbolic action), rites of passage, myths, and religious symbols are perhaps the most significant. Contemporary anthropologists acknowledge that this approach to the study of religion was sidetracked for a while by mistaken assumptions that so-called primitive religions had to be treated differently than modern religions and that modern Western religions represented a high point in the evolution of culture and therefore were

Figure 1–3 Cultural anthropologist Mary Douglas (1921– 2007).

superior to other religions. Today, however, a more comprehensive approach is favored with the result that religions of all cultures are analyzed using the same methods and theories. Unlike psychological theories of religion, anthropological approaches give much more attention to the social dimensions of religion—in particular, the status of the individual in relationship to the whole and the group's ability to exert control on the individual. Also, like phenomenological approaches to religion, anthropological approaches take on the appearance of comparative studies. In this case, the investigator looks for what is universal and/or essential in various cultural expressions of religious experience (Morris 1987).

Some of the major figures in the history of the development of anthropological theories of religion are Edward Tylor (1832–1912), James Frazer (1854–1951), Lucien Lévy-Bruhl (1857–1939), Emile Durkheim (1857–1917), E. E. Evans-Pritchard (1902–1973), A. R. Radcliffe Brown (1881–1955), and Claude Lévi-Strauss (1908–). Another well-known anthropologist, Mary Douglas, provides us with this commentary on the symbolic structures of purity and impurity (i.e., what is sacred and what is not), which she compares to ancient and modern cultures' treatment of dirt:

> The more we know about primitive religions the more clearly it appears that in their symbolic structures there is scope for meditation on the great mysteries of religion and philosophy. Reflection on dirt involves reflection on the relation of order to disorder, being to non-being, form to formlessness, life to death. Wherever ideas of dirt are highly structured their analysis discloses a play upon such profound themes. This is why an understanding of rules of purity is a sound entry to comparative religion. (Douglas 1966, 7)

Thus something as seemingly insignificant as dirt becomes the key to unlocking the significance of important universal religious themes.

Sociological Theories of Religion

The distinction between anthropological and sociological theories of religion is somewhat artificial, because both belong to the social sciences, and scholars of one approach freely employ the methods and theories of the other. However, because scholars associated with these two approaches have also developed their own sets of presuppositions and their own research literature, we will treat them separately here.

Sociological theories of religion focus on the practice of religion, that is, what people do when they put their religious beliefs into action and relate to others in society. Therefore, to some extent at least, sociological theories of religion give attention to the ethical dimensions of religion. They also tend to be more concerned about religion's effect on group order and group identity than the individual's religious experience. In particular, sociologists of religion are interested in religion's role in maintaining social order and the ways in which it can be an agent of social change. They are also interested in the ways that society shapes religious practice over time. Topics that are typically addressed by sociologists of religion today pertain to relationships between race and religion, gender and religion, and social class and religion. They also address questions involving **pluralism** (the presence of different religious or cultural groups within a single society), **secularism** (the belief that religion has no place in the civic or political realm), and the relationship between religion and culture (Christiano, Swatos, and Kivisto 2002).

Some of the more important figures in the development of sociological approaches to religion include Auguste Comte (1798–1857), Alexis de Tocqueville (1805–1859), Karl Marx (1818–1883), Emile Durkheim (1858–1917), Henri Bergson (1859–1941), Max Weber (1864–1920), and Peter Berger (1929–). In the following excerpt, observe how Berger uses sociological concepts and terminology to write about religion in a pluralistic society. He begins with the observation that religion, as a social institution, has always been influenced by ordinary activities and trends in society:

> Religion has always been susceptible to highly mundane influences, extending even to its most rarified theoretical constructions. The pluralistic situation, however, introduces a novel form of mundane influences, probably more potent in modifying religious contents than such older forms as the wishes of kings or the vested interests of classes—the dynamics of consumer preference.
>
> To repeat, the crucial sociological and social-psychological characteristic of the pluralistic situation is that religion can no longer be imposed but must be marketed. It is impossible, almost a priori, to market a commodity to a population of uncoerced consumers without taking their wishes concerning the commodity into consideration. . . .
>
> This means, furthermore, that a dynamic element is introduced into the situation, a principle of changeability if not change, that is intrinsically inimical to religious traditionalism. In other words, in this situation it becomes increasingly difficult to maintain the religious traditions as unchanging verity. (Berger 1967, 145)

Examples of sociological terminology employed in this excerpt include *commodity*, *consumer preference*, *population*, and *marketing*. In the contemporary situation where religious pluralism is common, Berger argues that religion is affected by consumer preference, in this case, the freedom of people to choose among a variety of religions and religious experiences based on personal preference. Further, Berger argues, because people in a consumer culture do not feel compelled to accept or maintain commitments of loyalty to a particular religion, religion must be marketed. However, when something is marketed, the product needs to be changeable. If large, blue, plastic "thingamajigs" do not sell well in the U.S. market, the marketer needs to be able to change the color, size, or even function and substance of the thingamajig to make her product successful. In most cases, such changes are considered an inevitable part of doing business. But when consumer preference is applied to religion, its impact is dramatic. Suddenly, religious traditions, which once were described as universal or everlasting truths, can no longer bear the weight of such claims. In a pluralistic, consumer-driven culture, some might even argue that particular religions have no right to make any claims of absolute truth. In simple terms, this is Berger's sociological analysis of the challenges faced by religion in a pluralist society.

THEOLOGY AS AN ACADEMIC DISCIPLINE

Unlike the academic discipline of religious studies, which examines religion from the perspective of human experience, **theology** explores religion from another perspective, namely God as ultimate ground and goal of all reality. The term *theology* comes from two Greek words: *theos*, meaning "God" or "the divine," and *logos*, meaning "discourse," "teaching," or "word." Thus theology is "the study of God" or "discourse concerning the divine." St. Anselm (d. 1109) defined theology as "faith seeking understanding." In the case of Christian theology, it is the attempt to understand better the object of faith, namely, the God of Jesus Christ and God's will for humanity and the rest of creation. As an academic discipline, theology involves careful examination and analysis of the **doctrines** (official religious teachings) and practices (ways of relating to God and to the world), bringing reason to bear on faith. Theology draws upon sources, which it considers authoritative, and employs methods and approaches that are comparable to those used in other academic disciplines. Over the centuries it also has developed a specialized vocabulary to clarify its questions and articulate its responses in its exploration of God and the rest of reality in the light of God.

The major difficulty for understanding theology as an intellectual discipline comes from the fact that God is not available for human investigation in the same way that the earth is available for a geologist, reports of dreams and neurotic behavior are available for a psychologist, or musical scores or field recordings are available for a musicologist. Theology's prime subject matter will always remain elusive and mysterious. But this does not mean that theology cannot exist as an intellectual discipline. "The past" is elusive and mysterious, but it can be explored by historians; "love," "courage," and "justice" are also elusive and mysterious, but they can be explored by philosophers and poets. Thus theologians assert that God and reality understood in the light of God can be investigated, though the sources and methods appropriate for this investigation will be different from those used in other disciplines.

Let us begin our overview of theology with two concepts that are central, but not exclusive, to Christian theology. These are revelation and faith. Were we to talk about Jewish theology or Muslim theology, for example, we might refer to these same two concepts. They are noteworthy because scholars' acceptance of revelation and faith as legitimate subjects of inquiry, albeit not measurable by scientific standards, help to highlight the differences between the academic disciplines of theology and religious studies.

Revelation

Most of the monotheistic and polytheistic world religions claim not only that God (or the gods) exist, but also that our knowledge of God (or the gods) depends, not solely on human reason, but also on **revelation**, that is, the deliberate self-disclosure of God (or the gods) to humanity. More specifically, from the perspective of the monotheistic world religions, revelation is a term that refers both to God's act of disclosing God's self to believers and to the content of that revelatory act—that is, revelation about the true nature of God, humanity, and the created order, as well as God's will for humanity and the rest of God's creation.

Christian theologians distinguish between general and special revelation. General revelation is given to all human beings. The means by which general revelation takes place include nature and conscience. From a Christian perspective, nature—the people and things with whom we have contact in the world—is said to reveal God in a general sense because, although it points beyond itself to a creator, this revelation is partial and imperfect: We cannot tell from nature that the Creator is a personal Being or that the creator cares for us as individuals. The human conscience—which we can describe informally as a kind of intuitive, inner sense of what is right and wrong, or a recognition of a fundamental moral law—is also said to reveal God. However, the revelation given through conscience is also partial and imperfect: It can be severely distorted by social pressures in cultures where, for example, theft or killing is honored or human sacrifice is practiced.

In contrast, special revelation is given to particular groups of human beings. The means by which special revelation takes place include prophecy, mystical experience, and history. Prophecy refers to God's communication through a chosen spokesperson: the prophet. Mystical experience describes the direct and individual contact that a human might have with a transcendent power (God, an angel, or other heavenly being); it may be expressed in visions (things seen), locutions (things heard), dreams, and the like. For Christians, personal encounter with Jesus Christ through the power of the Holy Spirit is viewed as the premiere form of special revelation.

For some faith traditions, special revelation is understood to be communicated through human history, because it is the site for God's contact with and intervention on behalf of humanity. For example, Jews point to God's actions in rescuing slaves from bondage in Egypt as a revelatory event. Christians describe Jesus as the fullness of revelation and the life of Jesus as *the* revelatory event. Muslims point to Muhammad as the last and most important of God's prophets and to his visions as the final and perfect revelation of God to human beings. These visions, which were received through the angel Gabriel, are compiled in the Qur'an. All of these examples are instances of special revelation in history.

Finally, we can speak of personal revelation. Unlike special revelation, which is a public revelation given for the sake of a particular group of people, a personal revelation is a private revelation granted to a single individual to fulfill a specific need or address a particular issue. Individual faith traditions have different processes and criteria for testing the authenticity of these personal revelations, but most tend to proceed with caution. On the one hand, they want to affirm that God's revelation can come through many different avenues. On the other, they are suspicious of private or personal revelations that appear to contradict or challenge the doctrines or approved practices of their faith tradition.

One of the most important sources of special revelation is sacred scripture. It contains special revelation that has been handed down to later generations both by word-of-mouth and in written form. This is known in theology as oral and written tradition (from the Latin word *tradere,* "to hand on"). For Jews, Tanakh (later called the Old Testament by Christians) is the record of oral and literary traditions comprising the special revelation granted to them. Christians, recognizing the revelatory character of this material, incorporated it into their Bible, which also includes records of oral and literary traditions about Jesus of Nazareth and his earliest followers (later called the New Testament). Muslims accept the sacred books of both Jews and Christians as the word of God, albeit corrupted in its transmission from the time it was first revealed. However, for the followers of Islam, the Qur'an holds pride of place as the collection of directly dictated revelations given to the prophet Muhammad. He is not the author of the Qur'an in any sense, only its transmitter.

Revelation is enshrined in the practices of communal worship. Thus, people learn about aspects of revelation from hymns, from the prayers and readings that are recited during worship, and from the biblical stories that are recalled and retold in the worship services. Revelation may also be confirmed in the lives of those who are held to be exemplars of the way of life that is espoused by a particular faith tradition. In some faith traditions these persons are called saints (literally, "holy ones"). Thus, we can see how special revelation is handed down in a variety of ways: oral teaching, written scriptures, worship and devotional practices, the lives of those whom the community holds up as role models, and in the ongoing life of the community itself.

Faith

Many people think that faith refers only to the sets of beliefs that one holds. However, like revelation, faith has many aspects. We can talk about faith in at least four ways: (1) as belief in or acceptance of a set of truths, (2) as trust, (3) as action or practice, and (4) as personal insight or experience of the divine. Christian **faith**, which is a response to revelation, begins with belief in God and in God's son, Jesus Christ. Thus, in many Christian denominations, persons who present themselves for Baptism and admission to the church are expected to recite a creed (a statement of belief) before being baptized. In denominations that practice infant Baptism, an adult sponsor recites a creed on the child's behalf. But proclaiming statements of belief is only the beginning. Faith also involves trust in God and Jesus. The word *trust* carries connotations of commitment to or reliance on another. Therefore it has a distinctively personal or relational quality. Through faith believers commit themselves wholeheartedly to the vision of reality and the promise of fulfillment manifest in the Christian revelation.

Trust and commitment to God should also lead to action that will further God's presence in the world: One must practice what one preaches by carrying on works of justice and charity. This kind of faith-in-action is not optional for the believer, and therefore is sometimes described in terms of obedience to God's will. Finally, through belief and trust in God and obedience to God's will in one's life, faith is deepened as one gradually develops a personal insight or experience of God, which is similar to personal revelation.

Subdivisions of Christian Theology

Academic disciplines normally divide their investigations among a variety of specializations. Some sociologists study family interactions; others criminal behavior; still others trends in urban, suburban, and rural populations. In the discipline of business, one can specialize in a variety of fields, such as accounting, marketing, finance, or management. Similarly, the investigations of theology are divided among various specializations. Traditionally, theology has been divided into four major categories.

Biblical studies focuses on the written documents found in the Bible and the literature that is contemporaneous with it. Biblical scholars usually specialize in either the Old Testament or the New Testament. They investigate how these documents were formed, how they were selected to be part of the Bible, what they meant to the original authors and audience, and how they make meaning today. Biblical theologians also explore what these sacred texts might mean for contemporary belief and practice and how they constitute God's revelation to humanity. The Bible has been called the "soul of theology," because Christians claim the Bible as a primary source for coming to know God and God's relation to the world and humanity. Therefore, Christian theologians, whatever their subdiscipline, regularly begin with the Bible when they address questions of theology.

Historical theology investigates how Christian faith developed in the various periods of history after the biblical era. It focuses on how Christian beliefs and practices were shaped by persons and events of different historical periods and how Christianity sees itself in relationship to other social, cultural, and political movements of the time. Historical theologians usually specialize in a particular period, for example, ancient Christianity (the "patristic" era), medieval Christianity, the Reformation, or the modern period.

Systematic theology studies the basic formulations of Christian belief (called dogmas or doctrines) and how they relate to one another. Employing the information gained in biblical and historical theology, systematic theologians try to understand the realities affirmed in Christian teaching and attempt to express them in language understood by contemporary believers. Systematic theologians may treat such subjects as the Trinity (the three-in-oneness of God), Christology (the person and the work of Jesus Christ), theological anthropology (how human beings are viewed in relation to God), or ecclesiology (the meaning and mission of the church).

Moral theology focuses on the values arising from the Bible and Christian beliefs and practices and attempts to identify the behaviors that are congruent and incongruent with these values. Moral theology has both individual and social dimensions, because it addresses issues such as character formation, growth in holiness, and virtues and vices, as well as right relations in international affairs, human rights, and social justice. Moral theologians attempt to determine what ought to be done in light of the findings of biblical, historical, and systematic theology.

Other Categories of Theological Inquiry

As the needs and interests of faith communities change over time and in different historical and cultural contexts, so does the academic discipline of theology. Here are just a few examples of new categories of theological inquiry that have been added in the past century.

Practical theology attempts to interrelate abstract theological concepts with particular concrete situations encountered by individuals and communities of faith through a process of theological reflection. More than simply application of theological principles, the task of practical theology is to extend the circle of those who do theology to the church community itself with the goal of transforming faith communities and the world in which they live. Closely related, in methodology at least, is **pastoral theology**, which trains people to minister to communities of faith through activities like preaching, teaching, spiritual direction, and counseling and advocacy for persons in need.

Sacramental theology, also known as liturgical theology, focuses on the study of Christian worship. Sacramental theology was once a part of systematic theology, but as it began to be recognized as a distinct specialization within theology its interdisciplinary character became more evident. Today, it draws upon biblical studies to investigate the scriptural foundations of the sacraments and upon historical theology to gain theological insights concerning the development of worship forms from the period of the early church to the present. It also draws upon philosophy and anthropology to learn how the words and symbols of religious ritual create meaning for those who participate in worship. The goal of sacramental theology is to enhance the faith community's understanding and appreciation of Christian worship.

Spirituality investigates various forms of prayer and religious practice that orient persons toward God (or the divine) and that direct the way they live in the world. In the area of Christian spirituality, scholars trace the development of certain practices like asceticism (denying the body of physical pleasures in order to focus oneself on God) from the time of the early church to the present. They inquire about the distinctiveness of different kinds of spirituality, for example, following the example of Benedict of Nursia (480–543 A.D.) or Francis of Assisi (1182–1226 A.D.), or a spirituality that characterizes a particular Christian tradition, for example, Methodist spirituality or Anglican spirituality. They also investigate systematic questions like the role of the Holy Spirit in orienting a person toward God in prayer.

Comparative theology is, as its name suggests, a comparison of the views of various religious traditions on theological themes like revelation, the nature of God, sin, and salvation. It also examines the different theological methods and resources of the traditions under investigation to better understand how they formulate their theology. Comparative theology is not the same thing as the study of world religions, which we might describe as a historical and cultural investigation into the beliefs and practices of various religions such as Buddhism, Shintoism, or Islam. However, depending on the topic under investigation, it might well include these religious traditions in its dialogue.

Theologians cannot predict what new categories of theology will evolve over time, but certainly there will be others, because one of the primary goals of theology is to respond to the needs of the time and to be a resource to faith communities who seek to understand, in their own place and time, what it is that they believe and how they ought to live their lives.

WHY LEARN ABOUT RELIGIOUS STUDIES OR THEOLOGY?

Today, with the rapid rise of secularism and religious pluralism, particularly in Western cultures, some people might conclude that religion has become irrelevant or unimportant in contemporary society or that differences in religious worldviews are inconsequential. Others might be frustrated by the fact that it can be difficult to find agreement among theologians or scholars of religion on a given issue, or they might be afraid that the subject matter of religion is just too confusing to those who have never studied it before. As a result, some students wonder whether they would be better off not to study theology or religion at all. What reasons are there for studying religion and theology?

First, most people throughout history have been religious. In all ages except our own (the early twenty-first century), the predominant shapers of beliefs and values have been religious systems, which have usually taught that the supreme good of human beings lies not simply in material prosperity or in unbounded pleasure, but in a proper and harmonious relationship with the unseen spiritual world or ultimate Reality to which religion is a bridge. Even today, a devout Hindu, Christian, Jew, Muslim, or Lakota Sioux would probably agree in this basic belief. Thus, one reason for studying religion seriously and critically is that perhaps the religious claim is true. Perhaps a right relationship with the unseen world of God is as important, or even more important, than material prosperity or pleasure, even though these latter values are the ones stressed by twenty-first century U.S. culture.

Second, many of the students taking this course will probably identify themselves as Christians. However, because we live in a more secular world, educated people today probably know and understand less about their own faith than at almost any other period in Christian history. Understanding the sources, history, and development of Christianity should deepen their understanding of their faith and their own heritage.

Third, much of what is identified as Western civilization has been formed and shaped by the Christian theological tradition. Without knowledge of the Bible and Christian history, much of Western architecture, art, music, poetry, and literature is simply unintelligible.

Fourth, even if one were to decide that God does not exist and that all religious world-views are false, that person will come in contact with other people who believe in the existence of God and who commit themselves to particular religions. Moreover, many of the major struggles that our world faces today involve religion in one way or another. If one expects to interact peacefully and productively with people of diverse backgrounds, it would be helpful, if not necessary, to understand their worldviews.

THE PURPOSE OF *THE CHRISTIAN THEOLOGICAL TRADITION*

The overarching purpose of this textbook is to introduce students to the Christian theological tradition. The term **tradition** should not be understood simply as family or group customs that are passed down from generation to generation. Rather, in a religious sense, it is the accumulated wisdom of the believing community, the church, which is refined over time in its doctrines and celebrated in its worship for the good of its people and all of God's creation. It is conducted within the community of faith and enriched by the experiences and reflections of many persons over many centuries.

Given that our focus is the *Christian* theological tradition, we identify its source, first and foremost, as the word of God revealed in the person of Jesus Christ and in the Christian scriptures, the Bible. Therefore, we will begin our textbook with an introduction to the literature of the Bible, its major themes, and the characters that make its stories come alive for contemporary readers. We will also introduce some strategies for reading the Bible that are consistent with a Christian understanding of revelation as it develops through history and is systematically explored and presented in theology.

Because our focus is the Christian *theological* tradition, this textbook will give considerable attention to the development and articulation of Christian doctrine. An easily accessible and fairly accurate way to describe or understand a religion at any particular point in time is simply to list the major beliefs held by its leaders and practitioners. However, theological inquiry does not take place in a vacuum. Rather, particular theological questions become important in a given place and time because of the situations in which people find themselves. Likewise, the responses of theologians and church leaders, though thoroughly grounded in scripture and tradition, are conditioned by their historical and cultural setting. Therefore, we will survey the Christian theological tradition as it unfolds *historically*. You will be able to read about some of the major people and movements that shaped Christianity from its beginnings in the first decades after the death and resurrection of Jesus to the present, and about those who contributed to its richness and diversity as we know it today. This book will also introduce you to some of Christianity's most important theological literature—the writings of Augustine, Thomas Aquinas, and Martin Luther, to name just a few. Hopefully along the way you also will have opportunities to learn about the goals, tools, and methods of theology.

KEY QUESTIONS AND THEMES

Although *The Christian Theological Tradition* presents itself as a general survey of the history of Christianity and an introduction to its religious literature, there are two overarching sets of questions—questions that almost every religion must address—that govern the selection of topics and themes for each chapter. These are theological anthropology and soteriology.

Theological **anthropology** pertains to the study of human beings in relation to God and God's creation. The nature of human beings is of crucial importance to religion. Here is a sampling of the kinds of questions that theological anthropology addresses: Is there something about human nature that explains things like the persistence of war, oppression, torture, corruption, criminal activity, quarrels, and broken relationships? If so, what is it about humanity that explains these effects, and what is the cause of this situation? Are some humans "good" and others "evil"? If so, how do we distinguish one from the other? How do we account for the fact that people commit evil acts?

Soteriology pertains to the study of salvation. Here are some of the questions that soteriology addresses: If, as most people throughout history have agreed, there is something very wrong with human beings and their interactions in the world, what might be done to respond to this situation? Can we be saved, rescued, or enlightened? What form does the rescue take? Should it be conceived in terms of the development of an authentic humanity in this life, survival of a spiritual soul in heaven, resurrection of the body in a new life, or entry into a mysterious state that is not "existence" and not "nonexistence"? How do we obtain salvation? Can we do it for ourselves, or do we need outside help? What role do success and comfort play in the good human life? What is success? What brings happiness?

In addition to these two overarching sets of questions that govern the selection of materials that are covered in *The Christian Theological Tradition*, this book addresses five themes that are key to the way in which Christianity answers these questions. The five themes are God, creation, revelation, Jesus, and the church. For each theme we have listed some theological questions that relate to it.

1. *God.* Does God exist? If so, what is God like? Is God personal and conscious or some sort of impersonal force? Is God good or evil? Can God be trusted? How much does God know, and how much can God do? Does God interrelate with the world of our experience, and, if so, how? Does God know us personally? Does God care about us? Are we called by God to act justly toward other humans?

2. *Creation.* Was the world we live in created, has it always existed, or did it just happen by the chance interplay of physical forces? Is it even real or just some sort of illusion? Does God interact with the world of our experience in a continuing way? If God created the world, can God do what he wants with it, make changes in it, or work miracles? If God cares about humans, does God have the power to make things turn out well for the humans God favors? Or are God's powers limited?

3. *Revelation.* Has God made an effort to communicate with humans? Does God ask humans to respond in some way? If so, does this revelation take a public form, which those who receive it then pass on to others in an authoritative way? In other words, do other humans have some obligation to believe what certain humans say about what God has revealed to them? Can an individual have visions or other psychic or spiritual experiences, and, if so, what authority do these private revelations have? Does God answer prayers? How should humans pray?

4. *Jesus.* Who is Jesus? Did he actually exist? Is he a human "just like us," or was (is) there something special about him? What significance, if any, does his life have for humans today? Is his significance limited to his wise sayings and the upright moral example he provided? Does he have some role to play in the salvation of human beings? Is he consciously alive somewhere, does he know who we are, and does he want to have a personal relationship with us?

5. *Church.* Is it important for humans to relate to each other and form cooperative associations (churches) as they pursue these questions and seek salvation? Or can we do what needs to be done on our own? Do humans form churches on their own initiative, or is there some sense in which God calls us together? How does God relate to the churches that exist? Are the churches the way they are because God wants them to be like that, or have the churches developed in response to human cultures in a way that might change in the future? How do, or should, different churches relate to each other?

Throughout the textbook, these questions will be addressed with a view to the religious and sociopolitical situations of the historical period being studied. As you read, try to imagine what experiences lie behind the different ways that people at different times and in various places have attempted to answer these questions. Pay special attention to the experiences on which these answers have been based. Then ask whether your worldview has been influenced by similar experiences. Such an exercise can keep the Christian tradition and other traditions you study from becoming just words. We believe that you will find your own curiosity being activated, you will begin to notice new connections between old ideas and experiences and contemporary religious life, you will understand better why other people think the way they do, and perhaps you will better understand and appreciate your own religious worldview.

Key Terms

religion	theology	practical theology
monotheistic	doctrines	pastoral theology
polytheistic	revelation	sacramental theology
agnostic	faith	spirituality
atheistic	biblical studies	comparative theology
religious studies	historical theology	tradition
pluralism	systematic theology	anthropology
secularism	moral theology	soteriology

Questions for Reading

1. What is religious studies, and how does it differ from theology?
2. What are four major theories or approaches to religious studies, and what distinguishes each approach?
3. What are the seven dimensions of religion proposed by Ninian Smart? Explain these categories by relating them to a faith tradition with which you are familiar.
4. What is the distinction among general, special, and personal revelation? What are some of the various ways in which special revelation is thought to occur?
5. Describe the four aspects of faith.
6. What is theology? How does it differ from religious studies?
7. Describe the four traditional subdivisions of theology.
8. What are some of the newer specializations in theology? What are some of the conditions that make it possible to add new specializations?

Works Consulted/Recommended Reading

Berger, Peter L. *The Sacred Canopy. Elements of a Sociological Theory of Religion.* New York: Doubleday, 1967.

Bond, Helen K., Seth D. Kunin, and Francesca Aran Murphy, eds. *Religious Studies and Theology. An Introduction.* New York: New York University, 2003.

Cady, Linell E., and Delwin Brown, eds. *Religious Studies, Theology, and the University. Conflicting Maps, Changing Terrain.* Albany, NY: State University of New York, 2002.

Christiano, Kevin J., William H. Swatos, Jr., and Peter Kivisto. *Sociology of Religion. Contemporary Developments.* Walnut Creek, CA: AltaMira, 2002.

Cipriani, Roberto. *Sociology of Religion. An Historical Introduction.* New York: Aldine de Gruyter, 2000.

Douglas, Mary. *Purity and Danger. An Analysis of Concepts of Pollution and Taboo.* Baltimore, MD: Penguin Books, 1966.

Jung, Carl. *Psychology and Religion.* New Haven: Yale University, 1938.

McGrath, Alister E., ed. *The Blackwell Encyclopedia of Modern Christian Thought.* Oxford: Blackwell Publishers, 1993.

Morris, Brian. *Anthropological Studies of Religion. An Introductory Text.* Cambridge, MA: Cambridge University, 1987.

Musser, Donald W., and Joseph L. Price, eds. *New & Enlarged Handbook of Christian Theology.* Nashville, TN: Abingdon, 2003.

Preus, Samuel. *Explaining Religion: Criticism and Theory from Bodin to Freud.* New Haven, CT: Yale University, 1987.

Rausch, Thomas P. *The College Student's Introduction to Theology.* Collegeville, MN: Liturgical Press/Michael Glazier, 1993.

Smart, Ninian. *The World's Religions.* Upper Saddle River, NJ: Prentice Hall, 1989.

Wiebe, Donald. *The Politics of Religious Studies. The Continuing Conflict with Theology in the Academy.* New York: St. Martin's, 1999.

PART

I

THE OLD TESTAMENT

An examination of the Christian theological tradition must begin with the Bible, for the Bible comprises the sacred texts (or scriptures) of Christianity and hence is the foundation upon which Christianity and much of its theology is built. All Christian churches regard the Bible as revealed or inspired by God, declaring that God is its author, though, as we shall see, not everyone agrees on the manner in which it is inspired. The word **Bible** means "the books." It consists of two major sections, which are traditionally called the Old Testament and the New Testament. Within each section are a number of smaller documents called books. Thus the Bible can be likened to a library of sacred texts for Christian believers.

The list of books contained in the Bible is called a **canon**. But the word *canon* also means "rule" or "measuring stick." Thus the books of the Bible are a measure of faith insofar as they are regarded as authoritative for Christian belief and practice. All Christians refer to their canon of sacred scriptures as the Bible, but as we shall see Christian churches do not all agree on how many books should be included in the canon. How did these different canons originate? Who are the major characters of the Old Testament, and what is the significance of the events that it narrates? What other kinds of literature are contained in the Old Testament? These are some of the questions that will be addressed in this first section of our book. The following section discusses similar topics related to the New Testament.

WHAT'S IN A NAME?

It was not until the third century C.E. that Christians began using the terms *Old Testament* and *New Testament* to describe the two major parts of the Bible, though there was already considerable agreement about which books among those now included in the Old and New Testaments were to be regarded as "scripture." The word **testament** is a synonym for the word *covenant,* which we can define provisionally as "a sacred or formal agreement between

19

two parties" (in this case between God and human beings). Thus, use of the terms *Old Testament* and *New Testament* reflect the Christian belief that God made an earlier covenant with the Jews, which is described in the Old Testament, and a new covenant with the followers of Jesus Christ, which is described in the New Testament.

However, this terminology can be problematic, because some people might conclude that the books of the Old Testament proclaim an *old* covenant, that is, an agreement initiated by God that is no longer valid or has somehow been nullified. But this view is incorrect for at least two reasons. First, the sacred scriptures of Judaism are almost identical to the Old Testament, both of which proclaim a living and enduring covenant between God and God's chosen people, the Jews. Therefore, how can someone say that this first covenant is nullified? Second, although individual Christian churches might come to different conclusions about the meaning of particular biblical texts, all would agree that the books of the Old Testament enjoy the same status within the Bible as do the New Testament books. They are neither less authoritative than the books of the New Testament, nor do they comprise a lesser canon.

What, then, shall we call these two parts of the Bible? One frequently mentioned suggestion is to describe the Bible as the Christian Scriptures. The books that Christians have traditionally called the New Testament would be known as the *Christian Testament*, and the books that have been traditionally called the Old Testament would be named the *Hebrew Scriptures* or the *Hebrew Bible*. This solution resolves the difficulties that arise by labeling the covenant of Judaism as "old." However, one might argue that it goes to the extreme of ignoring entirely the covenant status of the Jewish people, who claim much of this literature as their own sacred canon. Additionally, the term *Hebrew Scriptures* misrepresents this collection of books, because not all of the Old Testament was written in Hebrew nor does it exactly correspond with the scriptures of Judaism. Moreover, some people might mistakenly conclude that Christians do not regard the books belonging to the Hebrew Scriptures as having the same authority as books of the New Testament.

Although other potential solutions have run into similar difficulties, the motive for seeking alternative descriptions of the Old and New Testaments is a positive one: respect for Judaism as the elder brother or sister of Christianity. This textbook will use the terms *Old Testament*, *Hebrew Scriptures*, and *Hebrew Bible* more or less interchangeably, recognizing that, whatever terminology is used, it has its limitations. We should also note that the terms *Old Testament* and *New Testament* need not be problematic as long as we remember that these are distinctively Christian designations and that they represent a Christian perspective on the interpretation of this first testament of the Bible. However, these terms should not be used to deny or downplay the unique and privileged status of God's covenant with Israel, manifested as it is in Judaism today.

HOW THE HEBREW BIBLE CAME TO BE

In large part, the Old Testament was the scripture of the Jews before it became part of the scripture of the Christians. Christianity is an outgrowth of Judaism, and when Christians parted ways with Judaism, one of the things that they retained was their acceptance of the sacred literature that later came to be known as the Old Testament. Of course, Jews do not call it the Old Testament, because for Judaism there is no New Testament to supplement or perhaps supplant it. The Jewish name for these texts is **Tanakh**, which is an acronym for the three parts of the Jewish scriptures: the *Torah* (the Law), the *Nevi'im* (the Prophets), and the *Khetuvim* (the Writings). The Tanakh is also known as the Hebrew Bible.

Most biblical scholars think that the **Torah**—also called the Law or the **Pentateuch**, meaning "five scrolls"—was the first of these three parts of the Jewish scriptures to be developed. Further, they believe that the writing of the Torah took place over a relatively long period of time, beginning with stories and traditions that were passed on orally, some as early as the twelfth century B.C.E., and only much later committed to writing. The theory used to explain this process of retelling, writing, editing, and collecting materials related to the Law is called the **Documentary Hypothesis**. According to this theory, there were at least four different sources or documents that were combined to make up the Torah. These four most commonly accepted sources are the **Yahwist** (dating to the ninth century B.C.E.), the **Elohist** (eighth century B.C.E.), the **Deuteronomist** (seventh–sixth century B.C.E.), and the **Priestly** (sixth–fifth centuries B.C.E.) traditions. By approximately 400 B.C.E., the Law apparently had been accepted as sacred scripture, though we do not know exactly what form it took or what was contained in it. Eventually the books of the Law became the first five books of the Bible: Genesis, Exodus, Leviticus, Numbers, and Deuteronomy.

Calendar Designations B.C.E. and C.E

The abbreviations B.C.E. and C.E. are part of a system of dating frequently used among biblical scholars. For the period before Christ, for which the traditional abbreviation has been *B.C.*, we substitute *B.C.E.*, meaning "before the Common Era." For the period after Christ, for which the traditional abbreviation has been *A.D.* (from the Latin *Anno Domini*, meaning "Year of the Lord"), we substitute *C.E.*, meaning "the Common Era." The new system of dating is an attempt to be sensitive to Jews, Muslims, and other non-Christians who do not believe in Jesus Christ and naturally would not want to have such belief inscribed in their dating system. On the other hand, some theologians argue that, since they are doing *Christian* theology, a specifically Christian system of dating is more appropriate. To honor both concerns, this textbook will use *B.C.E.* and *C.E.* in the chapters devoted to biblical literature, and *B.C.* and *A.D.* for the remainder of the chapters.

The second of the three parts of the Hebrew Bible, the Prophets, underwent a similarly lengthy process of development. Jewish tradition divides the Prophets into two sections: the Former Prophets and the Latter Prophets. The collection called the **Former Prophets**, today also known as Deuteronomistic History (see Chapter 4), includes Joshua, Judges, 1 and 2 Samuel, and 1 and 2 Kings. These books tell the stories of legendary early prophets like Samuel, Nathan, Elijah, and Elisha and of famous (and sometimes infamous) kings like Saul and David. Biblical scholars think that this body of literature was completed sometime between 600 and 440 B.C.E. The collection called the **Latter Prophets** is often further divided into the Major Prophets (Isaiah, Jeremiah, and Ezekiel) and the Minor Prophets (Hosea, Joel, Amos, Obadiah, Jonah, Micah, Nahum, Habakkuk, Zephaniah, Haggai, Zechariah, Malachi), also called the Book of the Twelve.

For the most part, the books of the Latter Prophets were put together by disciples of the prophets who began with traditional stories and the remembered speeches of the prophets and then added their own or other people's interpretations of the prophets' teachings, as well as historical narratives that provide a context for the prophets' teachings. The earliest of these books was written approximately 750 B.C.E., while the last was written approximately 300 B.C.E. About a century later, when the books of the Prophets were beginning to be accepted as sacred scripture, they are mentioned alongside of the Law, described by the phrase "the Law and the Prophets" (2 Macc 15:9). However, we have no way of knowing whether this collection is exactly the same as the list of prophetic books that comprise the Bible today.

The Writings, the third major section of the Hebrew Bible, is a miscellaneous collection of books that were committed to writing sometime between the sixth and second centuries B.C.E., though many of the prayers and proverbs contained in these books might go back as early as the tenth century B.C.E. The author of the Prologue to the Book of Sirach calls them "the other books of our ancestors." Today the Writings include Psalms, Proverbs, Job, a collection of books called the five Megilloth (Song of Songs, Ruth, Lamentations, Ecclesiastes, Esther), Daniel, Ezra/Nehemiah, and 1 and 2 Chronicles. However, most biblical scholars agree that the list of books belonging to the Writings was not fixed until the second century C.E. Thus, Jesus and his disciples, who were first-century Jews, would have understood their scriptures to include the Law and the Prophets. They probably also knew some of the literature that would eventually make up the Writings—the Psalms, for example—but the Tanakh would not take its final form until after many of the books of the New Testament were already written.

How did the Jewish people decide which books should be included in the Tanakh and which should not? That is, what criteria did they use to select the books of their canon? Biblical scholars have proposed a few theories, but the biblical books themselves do not provide many clues, nor do other Jewish writers of the time, except perhaps for one—a Jewish historian of the late first century C.E. named Josephus. In his *Against Apion*, he writes that the Jews' sacred books contain the "record of the whole span of time" and are "rightly believed to be divine" in origin. He adds that they were viewed with such authority that people would hold fast to their teachings even to the point of death (*Against Apion* 1.8; trans. H. St. J. Thackeray, adapted). Using more contemporary language, we might say that Josephus considered these sacred texts to be canonical because they were inspired of God. They were authoritative insofar as their stories reminded the Jewish people of who they are, and their teachings showed them how they ought to live as God's chosen people.

The People: Hebrews, Israelites, and Jews

The people who wrote and collected the books of the Old Testament are known alternately as **Hebrews**, **Israelites**, and **Jews**. This people emerged as an identifiable group around 1200 B.C.E. Over time, they described themselves as both a religious and a national entity. They inhabited the land now known as Israel, they worshiped a God they named **YHWH** (usually pronounced "Yahweh"), and they told stories about their distant origin from a family of Mesopotamian seminomads (Abraham and his descendants). In the Bible, the word *Hebrew* was first used to refer to Abraham (Gen 14:13), but it was more widely used in relation to the history of Israel in Egypt, beginning with Joseph, whom the biblical narrative describes as Abraham's great grandson, and up to the Exodus (Gen 37–50; Exod 1–15; see Chapter 3). However, with only a few exceptions, it is a term used by outsiders; this people usually referred to itself as *Israel* or as the *Israelites.* The term *Israel* is said to derive from a name given to Jacob, whom the biblical narrative describes as the grandson of Abraham (Gen 25:19–35:29). He, together with his twelve sons, became known as the tribal ancestors of the Israelite people. However, as we have already noted, they themselves traced their history back to Abraham.

The terms *Jews* and *Jewish* had a later development. When the kingdom of Israel divided in 922 B.C.E., the northern kingdom was called Israel and the southern kingdom was called Judah, after the Israelite tribe that dominated that region. Two centuries later, the northern kingdom was destroyed, and all that was left was the southern kingdom, Judah, which in turn was destroyed in 587 B.C.E. and its people taken into exile in Babylon (see Chapter 4). During the exile this people gradually established a religious identity apart from the land of their ancestors and, by the end of the exile, their religion had evolved into new forms. This new expression of the Israelite religion is what scholars today call early Judaism. The term *Judaism* comes from the same family of words as *Jew* and *Jewish,* which refer to followers of Judaism and/or members of the ethnic group from which Judaism originated, and which derive from the name of their kingdom of origin, Judah. Like the word *Hebrew,* these terms were most often used by outsiders and not by the Israelite people themselves.

WHICH BIBLE ARE YOU READING?

Anyone who has visited a bookstore to purchase a Christian Bible has probably noticed that there are at least two different versions of the Bible—the Catholic Bible and Protestant Bible. The history of the development of the Bible is lengthy and extremely complex, but the difference between these versions can be summarized in the question, "What books shall we include in the Old Testament?"

The collection of books in the Bible known to Christians as the Old Testament includes a short list of thirty-nine books written mostly in Hebrew but with some sections written in Aramaic, an ancient Semitic language related to Hebrew. Some Christians—Catholics and several Orthodox churches, for example—include an additional seven books, which until recently were thought to have been distinguished from the others by the fact that they were written in Greek and not in Hebrew or Aramaic, the sacred languages of Judaism. Today we know that most of these books also were originally composed in Hebrew and Aramaic. Christians who do not accept these books as part of their canon call them the **Apocrypha** (literally "hidden" books, but they are generally understood as religious writings that are not authoritative for Christian faith and practice). Christians who do accept these books as canon call them **deuterocanonical** books. This does not mean that they comprise a secondary or lesser canon. Rather, the term acknowledges their disputed status over time: Not all Christians have always accepted them as canonical.

To understand how this situation came to be, we need to go back to the period of the early church. Early Christians adopted a Greek translation of the Jewish scriptures, called the **Septuagint**, as their sacred writings even before there was a New Testament. But the Septuagint included several books that did not become part of the Hebrew Bible, namely, Tobit, Judith, 1 and 2 Maccabees, Wisdom, Sirach (also known as Ecclesiasticus), Baruch, and parts of Esther and Daniel. These are the apocryphal or deuterocanonical books.

During the Protestant Reformation in the sixteenth century A.D., the reformers favored the shorter list of books that comprise the Tanakh and chose not to retain the deuterocanonical writings. However, because these disputed books had been read in the churches for a long time, the reformers were not always eager to exclude them altogether. Today, Protestants are accustomed to finding the apocrypha grouped together at the end of the Old Testament. However, the Roman Catholic Church and those Orthodox Christian churches that accept the deuterocanonical books as sacred scripture have them interspersed throughout the Old Testament in their traditional locations.

Thus, it is the canonical status of these seven books and parts of books—variously known as apocryphal or deuterocanonical books—that comes into question when we talk about differences between Catholic and Protestant Bibles. These differences can be summarized as follows:

Canons of the Old Testament

Roman Catholic Bible	Protestant Bible	Hebrew Bible (Tanakh)
1. Genesis	1. Genesis	1. Genesis "In the beginning" (Bereshith)
2. Exodus	2. Exodus	2. Exodus "Names" (Shemoth)
3. Leviticus	3. Leviticus	3. Leviticus "And he called" (Wayiqra)
4. Numbers	4. Numbers	4. Numbers "In the wilderness" (Bemidbar)
5. Deuteronomy	5. Deuteronomy	5. Deuteronomy "Words" (Debarim)
6. Joshua	6. Joshua	6. Joshua (Yehoshua)
7. Judges	7. Judges	7. "Judges" (Shofetim)
8. Ruth	8. Ruth	17. Ruth
9–10. 1 and 2 Samuel	9–10. 1 and 2 Samuel	8. Shemuel
11–12. 1 and 2 Kings	11–12. 1 and 2 Kings	9. "Kings" (Melakim)
13–14. 1 and 2 Chronicles	13–14. 1 and 2 Chronicles	24. "Chronicles" (Dibre Hayamim)
15–16. Ezra and Nehemiah	15–16. Ezra and Nehemiah	23. Ezrah-Nehemyah
17. Tobit	Apocryphal	Noncanonical
18. Judith	Apocryphal	Noncanonical
19. Esther	17. Esther	21. Esther
20. 1 Maccabees	Apocryphal	Noncanonical
21. 2 Maccabees	Apocryphal	Noncanonical
22. Job	18. Job	15. Job (Iyyob)
23. Psalms	19. Psalms	14. Psalms "Praises" (Tehillim)
24. Proverbs	20. Proverbs	16. "Proverbs of" (Mishle)
25. Ecclesiastes	21. Ecclesiastes	19. Ecclesiastes "Preacher" (Qoheleth)
26. Song of Solomon	22. Song of Solomon	18. "Song of Songs" (Shir Hashirim)
27. Wisdom of Solomon	Apocryphal	Noncanonical
28. Sirach (Ecclesiasticus)	Apocryphal	Noncanonical
29. Isaiah	23. Isaiah	10. Isaiah (Yeshayahu)
30. Jeremiah	24. Jeremiah	11. Jeremiah (Yirmeyahu)
31. Lamentations	25. Lamentations	20. Lamentations "How" (Ekah)
32. Baruch	Apocryphal	Noncanonical
33. Ezekiel	26. Ezekiel	12. Ezekiel (Yehezqel)
34. Daniel	27. Daniel	22. Daniel
35. Hosea	28. Hosea	13. "Twelve" (Tere Asar)
36. Joel	29. Joel	" "
37. Amos	30. Amos	" "
38. Obadiah	31. Obadiah	" "
39. Jonah	32. Jonah	" "

40. Micah	33. Micah	" "
41. Nahum	34. Nahum	" "
42. Habakkuk	35. Habakkuk	" "
43. Zephaniah	36. Zephaniah	" "
44. Haggai	37. Haggai	" "
45. Zechariah	38. Zechariah	" "
46. Malachi	39. Malachi	" "

Adapted from Anderson 1966, 4–5.

We have already mentioned that some Orthodox Christian churches (see Chapter 11) accept the deuterocanonical books as part of their canon and others do not. In fact, each has its own rich and complex history when it comes to the development of canon. Some Orthodox churches have canons that go beyond the Hebrew Bible and the deuterocanonical books. Ethiopian Christians, for example, include Jubilees, 1 Enoch, and 4 Ezra and Pseudo-Josephus (Josippon). The Greek Orthodox Church includes 2 Esdras and 3 Maccabees. If you would like to read any of these books, they are available at http://wesley.nnu.edu/biblical_studies/noncanon/pseudepigrapha.htm. They are also published in collections of Old Testament apocrypha such as James Charlesworth's two volume work, *Old Testament Pseudepigrapha*.

THE ISSUE OF INSPIRATION

Jews and Christians read the biblical books in classes and in churches and synagogues, trying to understand and follow their teachings, because they believe that their scriptures contain God's revelation. Christians often refer to the Bible as "the word of God" and say that the Bible is inspired by God. What exactly does all this mean? Jews and Christians believe in the Bible because they think that somehow God speaks through the Bible, that somehow the Bible contains the word of God. However, they do not necessarily believe that God speaks directly in the Bible in the sense that God took pen in hand to write the book of Genesis. They would all agree that God employed human authors to communicate the truths that the Bible contains. However, they do not agree on the extent to which the human authors had freedom to express these truths in their own words. For believers, there is no disagreement that the Bible is inspired by God, but the nature of inspiration or the manner in which inspiration took place is where they disagree.

While there are many views about the nature of the inspiration of the Bible, at the risk of oversimplification we can divide them into three main groups. First, there is the fundamentalist position, which argues that the autograph versions, that is, the original copies of the Bible are fully inspired and without error. They contain not only God's message for humanity, but even the actual words that God wanted revealed to human beings. This view is called **verbal inspiration** and is held by Orthodox Jews and fundamentalist Christians. People who hold this view of inspiration argue that, because the Bible is the word of God and God cannot make mistakes, the Bible must be without error in every sense. This means that God, through the guidance of the Holy Spirit, prevented the human authors of the Bible from making mistakes of theology, history, science, or literary expression. The term used to describe this notion is **biblical *inerrancy*** ("without error").

People who hold this view of inspiration believe that the meaning of a biblical text is directly available to those who read it. The words say what they mean and mean what they say, and there is no need to rely on others to help them understand its meaning. They also believe that the biblical text has direct application to their daily lives and that its message need not (perhaps even ought not) be adapted to the changing social and cultural contexts of our times. For those who prefer clear and unambiguous answers about life's concerns, this approach can be very attractive. However, when it comes to the Bible's statements about creation and the created world, fundamentalists are forced either to deny many of the findings of modern science (for example, the theory of evolution or the belief that the earth is several billion years old) or to produce alternative pseudo-scientific theories that do not disagree with the biblical evidence. They also are placed in the difficult position of having to ignore or otherwise disregard the internal inconsistencies of the Bible, such as multiple and sometimes contradictory accounts of historical events.

On the other end of the spectrum, some people view the Bible as inspiring, insofar as it invites people to a moral way of life and encourages them to wrestle with important questions of human existence. However, they do not accept the possibility that scripture is uniquely inspired by God or that God is its author. One might call this the secular (or nonreligious) view of the Bible. Some people do not believe in God, or they believe in God but do not believe that God reveals God's self to human beings. Alternatively, they might believe that God reveals Himself, but that God did not reveal Himself in these particular books. These people would argue that what we have in the Bible is only what the biblical authors think about God and that God did not have anything to do with the writing of the Bible. Because human beings are limited in their knowledge and tend to make mistakes, there is no guarantee that the Bible contains the truth about God or anything else, for that matter. We can only judge its veracity on a case-by-case basis. Their interest in the Bible is more or less restricted to curiosity about ancient peoples and their literature.

There is a third position, which states that the Bible is inspired of God insofar as it is the "word of God" in the words of human authors. This is the official position of the Roman Catholic Church, as well as a number of Protestant churches. According to this view, God is the author of the Bible in the sense that the Bible contains what God wants us to know about God, God's relationship to the created world, and God's will for humanity, but the human authors were real authors. They used the languages, images, literary forms, and understandings of God and the world that were familiar to them and to the people for whom they were originally writing. God inspired them to write the truth about God and humanity's relationship to God, but the way they expressed these truths and the language and concepts they used to communicate them remain their own.

This middle position has a specific understanding of the revelatory content of the Bible. According to this view, the primary purpose of the Bible is not to convey scientific or historical facts, though it does contain much that is historical, and it does understand God's intentions for human beings to be disclosed in history. Instead, it expresses enduring theological truths. God sees to it that the Bible contains the *truths necessary for our salvation*. However, the human authors expressed these truths by using the means that were available to them at the time, including ancient (and often mistaken) understandings of the rules of science and history, which were commonly accepted at the time. Another way to put this would be to say that God meets us where we are. God did not reveal modern physics and astronomy to the authors of Genesis because no one, not even the biblical writer, would have believed or understood them. Quite simply, the sacred text would have been incomprehensible on these topics.

Thus, according to this view of inspiration, the Bible *can* contain mistakes, at least when it comes to ancient peoples' misconceptions about science, but also as it applies to the human authors' limitations in accurately recounting historical events and the like. However, people who hold this view argue that these mistakes are secondary to the truth that the Bible reveals—truth about God, God's relationship to the created world, and God's will for humanity. One can still speak about the Bible as being without error, but it is without error in the sense that it is a trustworthy guide to salvation. At the heart of this view of inspiration is the belief that Jesus, who is the incarnate (or "enfleshed") Word of God, entered into human history and fully embraced our human existence with all its limitations, even to the point of death. In a similar fashion, sacred scripture is the incarnated word of God, communicated through human authors with their particular worldviews and with all of their limitations. Thus, people who hold this view argue that denying the possibility that God could communicate in this manner also calls into question the incarnation of the Son of God.

The authors of this textbook understand inspiration according to this middle view—that the Bible is the word of God in the words of human authors—and therefore recognize the importance of learning what we can about the literary, historical, and cultural contexts out of which the biblical authors wrote and what they intended to convey to their audiences in order to better interpret the sacred text.

Key Terms

Bible	Elohist tradition	Jews
canon	Deuteronomist tradition	YHWH
testament	Priestly tradition	Apocrypha
Tanakh	Former Prophets	deuterocanonical
Torah	Latter Prophets	Scptuagint
Pentateuch	Hebrews	verbal inspiration
Documentary Hypothesis	Israelites	biblical inerrancy
Yahwist tradition		

Chapter

THE PRIMEVAL STORY

Our examination of the books of the Old Testament begins with Genesis 1–11. These chapters are located at the beginning of the Old Testament, although they were generally not among the first parts of the Old Testament to have been written. The process by which the various parts of the Old Testament were composed, edited, added to, and combined with other parts included rearranging the order of the books and their parts. The end result is that the books are not in chronological order. Nonetheless, the final placement of Genesis at the beginning of the canon and the placement of these eleven chapters at the beginning of Genesis probably reflect the view that these chapters serve as a proper introduction to Israel's salvation story and hence serve as a proper introduction to the salvation story of Judaism's younger sibling, Christianity.

GENESIS' CREATION STORIES

The Bible opens with two accounts of creation, quite different from each other. The first is found in Genesis 1:1–2:3; the second in Genesis 2:4–3:24. The two stories have different styles and vocabulary. For instance, the first story uses the word *Elohim* to designate God, whereas the second uses the word *YHWH* (usually pronounced "Yahweh"). They also differ significantly with respect to the order in which the creation takes place. Further, they vary in their portrayal of God. These traditions probably had independent oral existences—people told the stories from memory and passed them down to their descendants. They were then written down and, some time afterward, were combined into the form that exists today.

These creation stories are two of a collection of stories and genealogies that make up the first eleven chapters of the book of Genesis. Sometimes called the primeval story, they describe the origin of humanity, its relationship to the creator, and how evil entered the world. According to the Documentary Hypothesis (see Part I), the Yahwist (ninth century

B.C.E.) and Elohist (eighth century B.C.E.) sources are interwoven throughout the primeval story (Gen 1–11). The first creation story (Gen 1:1–2:3) is thought to come from the Priestly source (sixth–fifth centuries B.C.E.), while the second (Gen 2:4–3:24) is thought to come from the Yahwist source. This means that the story that is placed first in the Bible was actually written much later than the second story. Perhaps those responsible for the Priestly tradition placed it first in the Tanakh because they appreciated how it dealt with their ultimate beginnings: the creation of the world and the origins of humanity.

Before we can investigate the primeval stories of the book of Genesis, it is necessary to discuss a type of literature called **myth**. The term *myth* is often misunderstood in today's popular culture, because people tend to think of myths as fanciful, fictional stories that have little purpose but to entertain. However, in anthropological terms, myths are those stories that people tell about themselves and their origins in order to teach the most profound truths that the culture holds. These stories are the medium by which the ancient peoples addressed issues that could not be addressed in any other manner. They tell why things are as they are, and they explain the worldview of the people. In religious terms, myths are sacred stories that involve God or gods and their interaction with humanity. Using symbolic imagery, they address our most fundamental religious questions of life—How did we come to be? Why are we here? What is our relationship to God and the rest of creation? How did evil enter the world? What is our destiny? Often situated outside of space and time, these stories help to define the religious community's beliefs about God and God's relationship to the created world.

Similarities with Other Ancient Creation Myths

Genesis 1 offers the culmination of almost a thousand years of theological reflection by the people who claim Elohim as their God. It shows creative use of creation motifs present throughout the ancient Near East. In other words, the biblical authors used the theological language that was current in their own place and time to express their experience of God's creative work. For example, the creation account in Genesis 1 utilizes the technique of creation through speech that is also found in certain Egyptian creation texts. In the *Memphite Theology* the sun god, Ptah, speaks, and the world as we know it comes to be, and this creation is declared as "good." Likewise, the Babylonian creation myth, *Enuma Elish*, contains a similar view of cosmic order that we find assumed in Genesis 1, in particular, a firm dome that separates the waters of chaos from the waters of creation, and Marduk's creation is achieved by imposing order on a chaotic preexistent cosmos. However, in contrast with Genesis 1, these other religions include in their descriptions a polytheistic theology. In the *Memphite Theology*, Ptah first creates other divine beings, and in *Enuma Elish* Marduk is granted kingship over the created world by the other gods. Genesis 1 has a single deity, who remains as the only god at the end of the creation account. This means that Elohim is a single, all-powerful God, without rivals.

In all of these creation accounts, when human creation is included, humans are created last, and their purpose is to serve the divine realm. In *Enuma Elish* they are created out of the blood of a rebellious god; in the Egyptian creation stories humans come from a mixture of divine blood and earthly clay. They are given the "burden" of the lesser gods, so that the gods can now rest from their work. This same theme is reflected in the Priestly account; humans are created in God's image and likeness, that is, made able to rule. It is only then that we get the culmination of creation: God's Sabbath rest. Because humans can now exercise dominion in the place of God, God can rest and be served by humanity. This becomes the basis for Israelite worship life.

The Memphite Theology of Creation

The Memphite god Ptah was considered the greatest of the Egyptian creator gods and one who could create using only thought and speech. The document from which this excerpt is taken dates to approximately 700 B.C.E., but scholars believe it is based on a text that was composed some two thousand years earlier. Compare with Genesis 1:1–2:3, which describes the manner in which Israel's God created the world.

> Thus all the gods were formed and his Ennead [i.e., Ptah's assembly of deities] was completed. Indeed, all the divine order really came into being through what the heart thought and the tongue commanded. Thus the *ka*-spirits were made and the *hemsut*-spirits were appointed, they who make all provisions and all nourishment, by this speech. . . . Thus were made all work and all crafts, the action of the arms, the movement of the legs, and the activity of every member, in conformance with (this) command which the heart thought, which came forth through the tongue, and which gives value to everything. (Pritchard 1958, 2)

Enuma Elish

According to the epic *Enuma Elish,* which may have been composed as early as 2000 B.C.E., the Mesopotamian god Marduk was appointed as champion of a group of deities who were engaged in a battle against the primordial goddess Tiamat and her consort Kingu. After Marduk defeated Tiamat, he created the physical world and human beings to serve the deities. This excerpt describes the creation of humanity. Compare with the Bible's two creation stories, which describe the origin of human beings.

> When Marduk hears the words of the gods,
> His heart prompts (him) to fashion artful works.
> Opening his mouth, he addresses Ea
> To impart the plan he had conceived in his heart:
> "Blood I will mass and cause bones to be.
> I will establish a savage, 'man' shall be his name.
> Verily, savage-man I will create.
> He shall be charged with the service of the gods
> That they might be at ease! . . ."
> Ea answered him, speaking a word to him,
> Giving him another plan for the relief of the gods:
> "Let but one of their brothers be handed over;
> He alone shall perish that mankind may be fashioned. . . ."
> Marduk summoned the great gods to Assembly; . . .
> The Igigi, the great gods, replied to him . . .
> "It was Kingu who contrived the uprising,
> And made Tiamat rebel, and joined battle."
> They bound him, holding him before Ea.
> They imposed on him his guilt and severed his blood (vessels).
> Out of his blood they fashioned mankind.
> He imposed the service and let free the gods.
> (Pritchard 1958, 36–37)

What the Biblical Stories Say About God's Role in Creation

In studying the first creation story in Genesis, people have sometimes asked about the manner in which God created the universe. Did God create the world from previously existing matter, or did God create the world "out of nothing"? It is interesting to note that, before any creative activity, the text says that the earth was "formless" and "darkness covered the face of the deep while a wind from God swept over the face of the waters" (Gen 1:2). Later, in Gen 1:6–7, it says that God separates the "waters" using a dome, but the text never indicates that God created the waters. A chaotic "mess" of wind, darkness, and water seems to exist before God's creative activity, as it is described in Genesis 1. Although subsequent Christian traditions (and some Jewish traditions) affirmed that God created the world using no raw materials, for the Priestly writer it was more important to affirm that God imposed order on the watery chaos. This way of understanding the process of creation suggests that order and structure are pleasing to God. Perhaps the Priestly writer was thereby suggesting that order and structure must also be present in the Israelite religious activities of animal sacrifice and prayer.

In summary, the Priestly account of creation emphasizes the following four points:

1. The creation is regarded as good. The Priestly writer indicates at the conclusion of each act of creation that "God saw that it was good" (Gen 1:10).
2. YHWH is the only God and the source of all creation.
3. The creation must be distinguished from God. The Priestly writer insists that God is completely different and more powerful than the creation.
4. God created the world by *fiat*, that is, by the divine spoken word.

The second account of creation (Gen 2:4–3:24) describes creation as having taken place in a different sequence and time frame than the first account. It answers profound questions regarding the nature of the human person, but it also holds a rather different understanding of God's relationship to the created order. Coming from the Yahwist tradition, Genesis 2:4–3:24 is thought to have been written much earlier than the Priestly account. In contrast to the very abstract and remote God of the Priestly tradition, the Yahwist account portrays God as very humanlike, a concept that is called **anthropomorphism**. God comes down at the pleasant time of the day to commune with the humans and enjoy the garden he has made. The Yahwist writer describes God as fashioning the first humans out of clay, like a potter or sculptor. The second account is much more human centered, focused on the placement of humans within the world.

Many biblical fundamentalists regard the Genesis creation stories as a single story and as a scientifically accurate account of the origin of the universe. The position of the Catholic Church and many other Protestant traditions is that this view represents a misunderstanding of the function of the biblical material. Instead of thinking of the creation accounts as science lessons, these stories argue for a particular understanding of God and God's relationship to the created order. There was no intention on the part of this or any other biblical writer to provide a scientific or historical description of the origin of the universe. Rather, using the medium of myth and the images and manner of expression that were common in their time, the biblical writers were making a theological affirmation that God created the world with no help and no competitors. It is not necessary to argue for a seven-day time frame for creation or reject the theory of evolution in order to assent to this truth.

Figure 2–1 *Creation of the Heavenly Bodies,* mosaic from the cupola of San Marco.

What the Creation Stories Say About the Goodness of Humanity

A major theme of the Genesis creation stories involves the portrayal of human beings in relation to God and the rest of God's creation, or what might be called theological anthropology. There are at least three features to this presentation that should be noted.

First, Genesis 1–3 claims that human beings are created by God and are dependent upon God for their existence. Both creation stories make this point very clearly, and it is a crucial one in both the Jewish and Christian religions. Because human beings are created by God, a certain relationship exists between them that implies particular responsibilities on the part of humans. God is the creator, and human beings are the creatures, or created beings. This creator–creature relationship suggests that human beings by their nature are not independent, autonomous beings who can exist without God, but are dependent beings who are reliant upon God for everything. As a result, human beings should give God thanks and praise for this gift of life.

Second, Genesis 1 suggests that human beings are created in the image of God (see Gen 1:27). There is some kind of resemblance between God and human beings that does not exist between God and other animals. Whether this resemblance is understood in terms of intelligence, power, physical likeness, the ability to reason, or the ability to distinguish right from wrong is not entirely clear. However, it is clear that human beings have a special status in God's eyes, and with this special status come certain responsibilities. God gives human beings "dominion" over the earth and all the other creatures in it. While some have interpreted this to mean that the earth and its resources are given by God to human beings to use and exploit as they see fit, it is probably more accurate to say that because humans resemble God, God entrusts the earth and its resources to the stewardship of human beings, to care for them as God would. God does not give the earth and its creatures to humans to exploit; rather, God entrusts human beings as his representatives to be caretakers of the earth.

Third, Genesis asserts the intrinsic goodness of human beings. Although Genesis 3–11 shows abundantly how human beings are capable of evil acts and wicked behavior, Genesis 1 makes it clear that this is not because human beings were created evil or with some kind of flaw. After God creates human beings, the text notes that "God saw everything that he had made, and indeed, it was very good" (Gen 1:31). This goodness certainly includes human beings. God created human beings for perfection, to live in harmony with God and the other creatures in the world.

GENESIS' STORIES OF HUMAN SIN

In spite of the fact that human beings are created good, Genesis 1–11 teaches that all too often they decide to sin against God and disobey his commands, bringing disastrous consequences upon themselves. How can this be? Although God created human beings to do what is right and be perfect, God also gave human beings free will, that is, the capacity to decide whether to do good or evil.

This point is made most clearly in the mythical story of Adam and Eve, in which God gives Adam and Eve everything they need, and yet they do not seem to be satisfied. Having placed Adam and Eve in the garden, God gives them only one command: not to eat of the tree of the knowledge of good and evil (Gen 2:16–17). However, they allow themselves to be tempted by the serpent (who, contrary to popular opinion, is not identified as Satan or the devil, though later Jewish tradition will make that equation, as we see in Wisdom 2:24), and decide to disobey God and eat the fruit (Gen 3:1–7). They are told by the serpent that they will become "like God," and this provides their motivation for disobedience can be seen in the words of the serpent: "You will not die; for God knows that when you eat of it your eyes will be opened, and you will be like God" (Gen 3:4–5). They eat of the tree because they wish to usurp God's place as creator. Their sin is an act of rebellion against God.

According to Christian interpretation, Adam and Eve's act of rebellion destroys the proper relationship between God and human beings, between the creator and the creatures. The result is that human beings "fall" from the state of perfection intended for them by God into a state of misery and fear. When they hear God walking in the garden, they attempt to hide from him (Gen 3:8). When God confronts them about their wrongdoing, they try to blame someone else (Gen 3:12–13). Finally, God banishes Adam and Eve from the Garden of Eden, and they each are cursed. Eve's curse involves painful childbirth and domination by her husband (Gen 3:16), while Adam's curse involves difficulty in tilling the earth as a farmer (Gen 3:17). Christian theologians refer to this story as the story of **the Fall**, because it tells how human beings lost the state of perfection intended for them before they sinned against the Lord.

The primordial story of humanity's sin does not end with Adam and Eve, however. The rest of Genesis 1–11 continues the story of the Fall, as it tells of how human beings continue to sin more and more seriously, with more and greater curses and punishments being the

Figure 2–2 *Expulsion of Adam and Eve,* mosaic from the cupola of San Marco.

result. Adam and Eve commit a sin of disobedience and are cursed and banished from Eden. Following this, their son Cain murders his brother Abel, a far more serious offense. Cain is exiled from his home and cursed as well (Gen 4:1–16). In the stories following Cain's exile there is even more murder. A man named Lamech sings about murdering a man merely for striking him, and he indicates that blood revenge has increased from sevenfold to seventy-sevenfold (Gen 4:17–24). By the time we reach the Noah stories (Gen 6:9–9:28), there is all manner of sexual immorality and violence being committed by virtually every human being on earth.

Once sin enters the world, the state of human beings declines rapidly, and human beings seem to be helpless to pull themselves out of their miserable condition without God's help. And God "was sorry that he had made humankind on the earth, and it grieved him to his heart" (Gen 6:6). The rest of Genesis will tell the story of how God offers this help and how human beings respond to God's offer. The first is the story of God's promise to Noah after the flood, when God blesses Noah and his family and reestablishes the created order by telling them to "Be fruitful and multiply, and fill the earth" (Gen 9:1), and promises that he will never again destroy the world by flood (Gen 9:8–17).

However, lest you think that humanity is now firmly on the right path, the biblical writer ends this section of Genesis with the story of the Tower of Babel, in which the people once again sinned against God by attempting to build a tower to access God's heavenly dwelling and thereby make a name for themselves (Gen 11:1–9). The Priestly writer uses a long genealogy (Gen 5:1–32) to connect the creation stories to the story of Noah and the flood. The flood story is then followed by more genealogies (Gen 10:1–32) linking Noah to Abraham. Thus, beginning at Genesis 12, the scene is set for the salvation story that unfolds with Abraham, sometimes called the father of Judaism.

Like the creation stories, the primeval sin stories of the book of Genesis have certain similarities with the Egyptian and Mesopotamian myths of the time. For example, in the Mesopotamian creation stories, of which we have several examples, the created order is soon threatened by human action or rebellion. After humanity's rebellion, some of the gods decide that the creation of humans was a mistake and that they must be destroyed, and so they send a flood to wipe them out. However, one family is saved because the father has been warned by another god to build an ark on which both humans and animals can be saved. This is the story of Utnapishtim in the Gilgamesh Epic. Gilgamesh had sought him out to learn the secret of immortality after the death of his friend Enkidu in battle. Thus you can see how the biblical writers were employing some of the same imagery that Israel's neighbors used to answer difficult questions about humanity and its relationship to divinity. If you wish to read the Epic of Gilgamesh you can find it in James Pritchard's *The Ancient Near East,* Vol. I (Princeton, NJ: Princeton University, 1958).

THE GOD OF ISRAEL REVEALED

One of the major functions of Genesis 1–11 is to introduce the reader to the Israelite God, who is known in the Old Testament by several names: Yahweh, Elohim, El Shaddai, and so on. In the original Hebrew Tanakh, God's name is often indicated by four consonants, *YHWH.* The Israelites considered the name YHWH to be too holy to pronounce or say aloud, and even to this day Jews do not pronounce the name of God, instead substituting an expression that means "the LORD." Many modern editions of the Bible observe this practice by printing "LORD" in capital letters wherever God's own name occurs in the Hebrew text.

The peoples of the ancient world held a rich variety of beliefs about the gods, and it is important to understand the beliefs that the Israelites held about their God in the context of this variety. Ancient people disagreed about how many gods there were, whether the gods were good or evil, and the degree to which the gods cared about human beings and interacted with them. Some people believed in male and female deities, while others saw their gods in more impersonal terms, as spiritual or natural forces to be reckoned with. Some religions even proclaimed human leaders, such as emperors and kings, to be gods. The emotions spawned by ancient peoples' experience of the gods ranged from love to terror, and their activity in relation to the gods varied accordingly. Animal sacrifice, human sacrifice, sacrifice of grains and cereals, prayer, and other forms of worship were all common in the religions of the ancient world. Where did the Israelites fit on this spectrum? How did their beliefs about YHWH compare to the beliefs of other religions concerning their gods?

The book of Genesis answers one very important question about Israel's God, namely, how many gods exist? Belief in only one god is known as monotheism, and to many observers this belief in one God who was the creator of all things is the defining characteristic of the Israelite religion. In the ancient Near East, people believed that different gods were associated with every single natural element. For instance, one god was associated with providing the phases of the moon so that humans could mark time. Another goddess was responsible for vegetation that fed wild animals. Among the most popular kinds of gods were sun gods and moon gods, rain (or thunder) gods and earth goddesses. In addition, people believed that the gods oversaw different spheres of human activity, so there was a goddess who protected nursing infants and a god of war. Believers offered prayers and sacrifices to these gods, depending on the activity that they were engaged in.

Any religion that involves belief in many gods is called a polytheistic religion, although there are many different varieties of polytheism. Some ancient people believed that there were many national or territorial gods, with each god having his or her own unchallenged area or sphere of influence. In this view, the Babylonians worshiped the territorial gods of Mesopotamia, while the Egyptians worshiped the gods who oversaw Egypt. Which gods a person worshiped depended upon where one lived or what group one belonged to, since gods would only help "their own" people, or could only help people within certain geographical bounds. Often ancient peoples believed there were many gods, but only one god was best and most powerful.

Although the Israelites became known for their belief in only one God, they were not always monotheistic. Various parts of the Old Testament suggest that in the early stages one or another of the forms of polytheism mentioned above flourished among the Israelites. Genesis 1 represents one of the later stages in the development of the Old Testament, and this text insists upon a strict monotheism. It is clear throughout the creation story that only one God is doing the creating. Moreover, it is clear that the sun and the moon and the other forces of nature are all controlled by YHWH, who created them.

Another attribute of the Israelite God that is revealed in Genesis 1–11 is his power. YHWH's power is shown primarily through the creation of the world. All that YHWH needs to do in order to create is to speak. "Then God said, 'Let there be light'; and there was light" (Gen 1:3). YHWH creates the entire world and not just some portion of it. YHWH creates all of the forces of nature and all living creatures. Nothing that exists is created except by YHWH. YHWH's power is shown not only through creation, however, but also through destruction. Later in Genesis, when YHWH becomes grieved over the evil and wickedness that have pervaded creation, he decides to destroy the world and its inhabitants through a catastrophic flood. The ability to cause this great flood also shows God's power. So great are YHWH's powers that it may be concluded that the Israelite God is in fact all-powerful. Theologians refer to this as God's **omnipotence**.

A third major attribute ascribed to the Israelite God in the book of Genesis is goodness. Many ancient peoples saw their gods as capricious beings whose favor needed constant appeal or as jealous and petty beings who were rather indifferent to human beings and their problems. By contrast, Genesis 1 emphasizes that YHWH is a good God. YHWH's goodness is reflected most of all in the goodness of creation itself. After each of the six "days" of creation, the text emphasizes that God looked upon what had been created, and "God saw that it was good" (Gen 1:12, 18, 21, 25). When YHWH was finished with creation, "God saw everything that he had made, and indeed, it was very good" (Gen 1:31). Hence, YHWH must be a good God, since he created such a good world.

YHWH's goodness is also reflected in other aspects of Genesis 1–11, although it must be acknowledged that the Israelites did not always see YHWH as an exclusively good God. Their belief in God's goodness varied, as did their belief in God's oneness. Still, YHWH's goodness is reflected in the fact that YHWH loves and cares about the creatures in the world, providing them with the things they need to survive and flourish (like food), looking after them, and assisting them when they are in difficulty. YHWH is not indifferent to the plight of human beings, and although he does become angry with human beings at times, he is slow to anger. Theologians refer to this notion of God's goodness as **benevolence**.

Another question that must be addressed in order to understand the Israelite God is the issue of YHWH's gender. Most other ancient religions believed in male and female deities. Often, these religions even told stories in which these gods and goddesses created the world and its inhabitants through sexual activity. There is certainly no sexual activity on God's part in Genesis. In the first creation story (Gen 1:1–2:3), for example, God is portrayed as complete and whole within God's self and not in need of a "partner" to create the world. Does this mean that God is beyond gender? The text is not entirely clear on this point. On the one hand, it is true that the Israelites used exclusively masculine pronouns for God. The reasons for this are complex partly because of the structure of Hebrew language and partly because of the patriarchal nature of Israelite society. However, the Israelite people sometimes also pictured God acting in ways that are nurturing and tender, attributes that were more often associated with female gender than with male gender, and even doing "women's work."

Consider, for example, the second creation story (Gen 2:4–25). After God shaped Adam (Hebrew, meaning "a human") from the dirt (the Hebrew word is *adamah*) and breathed on him to make him a living being (Gen 2:7), God placed him in a garden and provided him with all kinds of plants that were both beautiful to look at and good to eat (Gen 2:8–9). Later we are told that God was concerned for the human being, because he was alone, and set about finding a fitting partner for him (Gen 2:18–22). Finally, after the fall, God is described as making clothes for Adam and his partner, even as they were being driven out of the garden (Gen 3:21). Similar examples can be found throughout the Hebrew Bible.

Language About God

The Judeo-Christian tradition uses various names and descriptions for God. Some of the more popular names for God are *Father* and *King*. Descriptions such as *loving, merciful,* and *all-powerful* are also commonly applied to God. Theologians are careful to point out, however, that these are not literal descriptions of God or proper names. All our language about God is necessarily metaphorical or analogical. An analogy is a comparison between two things that are similar in one respect, but dissimilar in others. For example, if we say, "John is a lion," then we mean that John is similar to a lion in some respects (perhaps he is brave or ferocious) but dissimilar in others (John does not have a long mane or a tail). The same is true when we say, "God is our Father." We are saying that God is like a human father in some respects—God cares for us as a (good) father would, God is the source of life, and so on. But in other respects, God is not like a human father: God is not ignorant or limited or mortal or confined to a body like a human being.

Every positive quality that we ascribe to God comes from the human realm and is drawn from human experience. Therefore, when we apply these terms to God we are speaking analogically. The medieval theologian Thomas Aquinas argued that every positive quality that we ascribe to God—such as goodness, being, life, wisdom, or power—applies in a limited way to creatures, but in an unlimited way to God. God is the perfection of goodness, being, life, wisdom, and power. It takes many analogies to describe God. No one name or description is adequate for God. But even many analogies fall short of a comprehensive description of God. The fullness and mystery of God will always be beyond the reach of human language, because God is infinite, and human language and concepts are finite.

Why is it important to recognize that our language for God is analogous? If we do not, then we mistake God for our *images* of God and end by making God a larger version of ourselves, complete with our prejudices. The problem with this is that we can end in idolatry—worshiping an idol, or image, rather than the living God. Then we will tend to think that God is like us and is perhaps opposed to other people who are not like us. The biggest mistakes in Christian history—that is, wars of religion, inquisitions against heretics, and persecution of non-Christians—have come from the failure to realize that God is greater than our images of God and that God loves even those we do not love. Thus, though we cannot avoid using language or images of God, it is important to be aware that God is beyond our language and images.

A final issue raised by Genesis 1–11 involves God's relationship with human beings. As mentioned earlier, God is portrayed as a loving God who cares about and provides for the creatures God has made. However, the relationship between God and human beings changes somewhat when sin enters the picture. From the point of view of the text, God becomes grieved in the face of human sin, and this reaction results in destruction. This is clear from the way that God reacts to the disobedience of Adam and Eve, the murder of Abel by Cain, and the wickedness of Noah's generation. God punishes Adam and Eve by banishing them from the garden and pronouncing various curses upon them. God punishes Cain by exiling him and cursing the ground that he farms. God punishes the evildoers in Noah's generation by sending the flood to destroy them all.

Many who read the stories of Genesis 1–11 see all this as evidence that YHWH is a wrathful, vindictive God. However, two points must be made about YHWH's behavior in these instances. First, YHWH is portrayed as a just God in these stories. Justice here refers to treating people according to what they merit or deserve. The stories leave no doubt that each of the persons who receive God's punishment deserves it. For example, God sends the flood because "the LORD saw that the wickedness of humankind was great in the earth, and that every inclination of the thoughts of their hearts was only evil continually" (Gen 6:5). Moreover, "the earth was corrupt in God's sight, and the earth was filled with violence" (Gen 6:11). Those who are innocent of any wrongdoing are protected by God; God arranges for them to be rescued from the flood through the building of the ark. In every case in Genesis 1–11, the text emphasizes that those who are punished by God are punished justly.

Second, although YHWH is a just God, YHWH is also merciful. Adam and Eve had been told that they would die if they ate of the fruit of the forbidden tree (Gen 2:16–17), but God did not kill them. YHWH reduced their punishment to banishment from Eden and even provided them with clothing for protection as they departed (Gen 3:21–24). Likewise, God did not kill Cain for murdering Abel but exiled him (Gen 4:11–12). Even as God was pronouncing punishment, YHWH made arrangements for Cain to be protected from anyone who sought to kill him in revenge for Abel's murder (Gen 4:13–16). After the flood, God promised never again to destroy the earth and its creatures, no matter how wicked human beings might become (Gen 9:12–17). Thus is God's mercy shown alongside of God's justice.

Key Terms

myth	the Fall	benevolence
anthropomorphism	omnipotence	

Questions for Reading

1. According to the Documentary Hypothesis, what are the sources for the books of the Pentateuch? Why are there two creation stories in Genesis?

2. In the context of theology or biblical studies, what is meant by myth? How would the recognition that the creation stories are myths affect one's interpretation of the stories?

3. What does Genesis 1–3 tell us about God's role in creation?

4. What does Genesis 1–11 tell us about the nature of human beings?

5. What does Genesis 1–11 tell us about the nature of God and God's relationship to humans?

6. What does it mean, in Genesis 1, to say that humans are made in the image of God?

7. What are some differences between the Israelite idea of God and the ideas of other ancient Near Eastern peoples concerning their gods?

8. What does our knowledge concerning ancient Egyptian and Mesopotamian myths about creation and humanity's relationship with the deities help us understand and appreciate about the primeval stories in the Bible's book of Genesis?

Works Consulted/Recommended Reading

Anderson, Bernhard. *Understanding the Old Testament*. 2nd ed. Upper Saddle River, NJ: Prentice Hall, 1966.

Barton, John, and Julia Bowden. *The Original Story: God, Israel and the World*. Grand Rapids, MI: Eerdmans, 2005.

Birch, Bruce C., Walter Brueggemann, Terence E. Fretheim, and David L. Petersen. *A Theological Introduction to the Old Testament*. Nashville: Abingdon, 2005.

Brown, Raymond E., Joseph A. Fitzmyer, and Roland E. Murphy, eds. *The New Jerome Biblical Commentary*. Upper Saddle River, NJ: Prentice Hall, 1990.

Brueggemann, Walter. *An Introduction to the Old Testament: The Canon and Christian Imagination*. Louisville, KY: Westminster John Knox, 2003.

Ceresko, Anthony R. *Introduction to the Old Testament: A Liberation Perspective*. Maryknoll, NY: Orbis Books, 2001.

Charlesworth, James. *Old Testament Pseudepigrapha*. Garden City, NY: Doubleday, 1983–1985.

Collins, John J. *Introduction to the Hebrew Bible*. Minneapolis, MN: Fortress, 2004.

Crenshaw, James L. *Old Testament Story and Faith: A Literary and Theological Introduction*. Peabody, MA: Hendrickson Publishers, 1992.

Flanders, Henry Jackson, Jr., Robert Wilson Crapps, and David Anthony Smith. *People of the Covenant. An Introduction to the Hebrew Bible*. New York: Oxford University, 1996.

Josephus, Flavius. *Josephus*. Trans. H. St. J. Thackeray. Vol. I: *The Life; Against Apion*. Cambridge, MA: 1961.

McFague, Sallie. *Models of God: Theology for an Ecological, Nuclear Age*. Philadelphia: Fortress, 1987.

Metzger, Bruce, and Roland Murphy, eds. *The New Oxford Annotated Bible with Apocrypha, New Revised Standard Version*. New York: Oxford University, 1991.

Pritchard, James B., ed. *The Ancient Near East*. Vol. I: *An Anthology of Texts and Pictures*. Princeton, NJ: Princeton University, 1958.

Second Vatican Council. *Dei Verbum* (Dogmatic Constitution on Divine Revelation). In *The Documents of Vatican II*. New York: Crossroad, 1989.

Trible, Phyllis. *God and the Rhetoric of Sexuality*. Philadelphia: Fortress, 1978.

GOD'S COVENANT WITH ISRAEL

TIMELINE

3000–2000 B.C.E.	Beginnings of civilization in Mesopotamia (Sumer, Babylonia, Assyria) and in the areas of Syria and Canaan.
c. 1850–1750? B.C.E.	Abraham migrates to Canaan. Beginnings of the patriarchal period.
c. 1700 B.C.E.	The *Enuma Elish* is circulated in Babylonian culture.
c. 1300–1250 B.C.E.	Moses delivers God's people from Egypt in the Exodus. God's covenant people journey to the promised land.

The preceding chapter of this textbook provided us with an overview of Genesis' primordial stories about creation and the origins of sin in the world (Gen 1–11). As we move into the second major section of the book of Genesis (Gen 12–50), we encounter a different kind of literature, namely **legend**. Unlike myths, which often have settings that are outside of space and time and characters that are larger than life, legends are situated in human history and involve characters and events that are part of the historical memories of the people who preserved them. However, even though legends carry more concrete historical recollections than the primordial stories, the primary purpose of legends is not to relate historically accurate details of ancient events. Rather, their purpose is to edify their readers and provide examples of the traditions, values, and ideals that these people hold sacred.

Genesis 12–50 contains legends about the earliest identifiable ancestors of the Israelite people: Abraham and Sarah; Isaac and Rebekah; and Jacob, his wives, and his twelve sons, especially Joseph. It ends with stories about how Abraham's descendants were transplanted to Egypt, where they were eventually enslaved. The second book of the Bible, Exodus, picks up the salvation narrative with Moses, whom YHWH called to lead the Israelites out of slavery in Egypt to the Promised Land. Moses is the one who received the Law from YHWH on Mount Sinai. Through these human persons, YHWH intervened in history on behalf of one particular people, the Israelites. Thus, the stories tell of the Exodus, in which Moses leads the Israelites out of slavery in Egypt. The theological term used to explain this phenomenon of peoplehood is **covenant**, which means "contract" or "agreement." This chapter will provide an overview of two important figures in Israel's covenant history, namely, Abraham and Moses, and one of its central events, Passover. Later inheritors of these stories and traditions, Christians in particular, will understand that God's intervention had a wider purpose than the salvation of Israel alone.

ABRAHAM

Genesis 12–25 tells the story of Abram, the son of Terah, from the land of the Chaldeans, who lived sometime around the end of the nineteenth or beginning of the eighteenth century B.C.E. Abram, whose name would eventually be changed to **Abraham**, first encountered YHWH at Haran in northern Mesopotamia. YHWH spoke to Abram with authority and made a promise to him.

> Now the LORD said to Abram, "Go from your country and your kindred and your father's house to the land that I will show you. I will make of you a great nation, and I will bless you, and make your name great, so that you will be a blessing. I will bless those who bless you, and the one who curses you I will curse; and in you all the families of the earth shall be blessed." (Gen 12:1–3)

This passage introduces several important theological themes associated with the Abraham stories: Abraham's encounter with God, God's promise and Abraham's response (faith), and the notion of covenant.

Abraham's Encounter with God

The stories contained in the book of Genesis were already ancient at the time of their writing. The authors who put these oral traditions into writing understood that God had

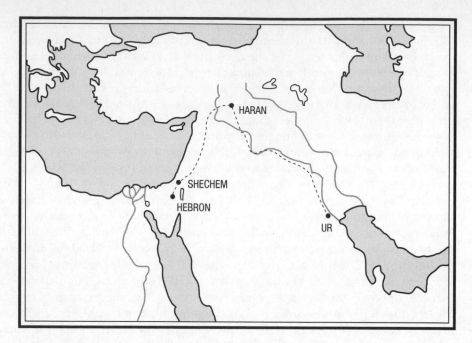

Figure 3–1 The journey of Abraham from Ur to Canaan.

revealed himself to Abram, making him the first **patriarch** (father or founder) of their people. Genesis preserves three versions of the story of Abram's encounter with God (Gen 12:1–9; 15:1–21; 17:1–27). In Genesis 12, the reader is given no information about what Abram's encounter with God was like. We are simply to understand that it was God's initiative to enter into a relationship with him, to establish a new people, and eventually to bring this people into the land that would be known as Israel, then called Canaan.

In Genesis 15, the narrator of the story describes Abram's experience of divine revelation in some detail. YHWH introduced himself as Abram's shield of protection (Gen 15:1). Then, after performing a ritual as YHWH commanded him, Abram fell into a deep sleep, and a deep and terrifying darkness surrounded him, as YHWH spoke to him concerning the future destiny of his descendants (Gen 15:12–16). Finally, Abram saw a vision of a smoking fire pot and flaming torch (Gen 15:17–21). The narrator of the story suggests that it was YHWH who appeared to Abram in the smoking fire pot and flaming torch and he did so in order to make covenant with Abram.

Genesis 17 provides yet another account of YHWH's revelation to Abram. In this account, YHWH introduces himself as God Almighty (Gen 17:1). The divine name is El Shaddai, "the God of the Mountains." The narrator of the story tells us that El Shaddai invited Abram to walk in his presence and that he spoke with him (Gen 17:1–3), making this a direct and personal encounter. Later, YHWH changed Abram's name to Abraham, because he intended to make Abraham "the father of a host of nations" (Gen 17:5). He also talked with Abraham about what was in store for Sarai, Ishmael, and Isaac (Gen 17:15–21), making YHWH a determiner of destinies.

Common to all three of these stories is the belief that YHWH is a personal God who is not only capable of relationship with human beings but who also initiates these encounters.

These stories also make the point that God made God's self known to Abram in history, that is, in Abram's own place and time. Finally, as we shall see, all three stories describe a promise that God made to Abraham and an expectation that Abraham would respond in faith, that is, trusting that God will fulfill the promise.

God's Promise and Abraham's Response

According to the book of Genesis, YHWH offered Abram a vision of a new future, which came in the form of a promise. The promise has several aspects: (1) He will have many descendants (Gen 15:5; 17:2); (2) God will make him a great nation (Gen 12:2; 17:5–6); (3) through him all nations of the earth will be blessed (Gen 12:3); and (4) he will be given a land for his descendants to live in (Gen 12:7; 15:7; 17:8). These ancient traditions are the basis of the Israelite and Jewish convictions that they were God's chosen people living in a Promised Land. Further, YHWH told Abram to trust the promise, to leave his own land and his own people, and to follow the directions that he is given (Gen 12:1, 4). Thus, Abram was challenged to believe what YHWH is saying and to trust that YHWH can bring it about.

However, once Abraham arrived in the land of Canaan, with his wife Sarai, his nephew Lot, and the rest of their clan, his trust was tested, and he did not always respond well. We learn, for example, that he and his kin moved about through the land of Canaan, which was already populated by other peoples, until a famine drove them to Egypt. Because his wife Sarai was very beautiful, Abram feared that the Egyptians would kill him so that the pharaoh could take Sarai into his harem (Gen 12:10–20). Therefore, in order to protect himself, Abram told them that Sarai was his sister. Believing that she was unmarried, the pharaoh took her as his wife, but YHWH rescued her by afflicting the pharaoh and his house with plagues. Later, virtually the same story is repeated with a different king (Gen 20:1–18). In both cases, Abram risked losing Sarai, the one through whom God's promise to Abram would be fulfilled, to save himself.

Genesis contains several other stories about Abraham's failure to trust God's promise. For example, the narrator tells us that Abram thought that YHWH was acting too slowly in fulfilling his promise of a son, so, at the suggestion of Sarai, Abram had sexual relations with her slave girl, Hagar (Gen 15:2-3; 16:1–4). Hagar gave birth to a son named **Ishmael** (Gen 16:15). Under the customs of the time, such a child would still be considered the child of Abram and Sarai. The point of the story is that Abram tried to fulfill God's promise by his own means, but YHWH let Abram know that this was not the descendant through whom the mighty nation would be established (Gen 17:19–22). Instead, YHWH promised Abraham that Sarai, who was already an old woman, would have a son, and God delivered on the promise with the birth of **Isaac** (Gen 17:15–17; 21:1–8). Then, just as everything seemed to be falling into place, YHWH asked Abraham to take Isaac, his son, the only one through whom God's promises could be fulfilled, and offer him as a sacrifice (Gen 22:1–19). Abraham proved his faith and stood ready to sacrifice his son, but the angel of YHWH intervened and provided an animal for Abraham to sacrifice instead.

Whatever his earlier doubts about God's ability to fulfill his promise, Abraham finally demonstrated his total trust in YHWH through his willingness to give up his only beloved son. In a sense, everything in Abraham's life had been leading to this point. The writers of the New Testament—Paul, in particular—will later refer to Abraham as a model of faith, because he "believed the LORD; and the LORD reckoned it to him as righteousness" (Gen 15:6).

Figure 3–2 Mosaic in San Vitale, Ravenna. The illustration in the center describes the scene in which three visitors come to Abraham at the oak of Mamre to announce Isaac's birth. The illustration on the right describes the scene of Abraham's near-sacrifice of Isaac (see Gen 18:1–15 and 22:1–19).

Covenant

In the ancient world, covenants were used for a variety of purposes, including the sealing of treaties and contracts between kings and their subjects. Simply stated, a covenant is a solemn agreement between two parties (individuals or groups) listing their respective rights and responsibilities in the relationship. Because it was sealed with an oath, ancient covenants carried a religious significance—a sense of being guaranteed by God. In the book of Genesis, YHWH is described as confirming his promise to Abraham and his descendants by "making a covenant" with Abraham. In fact, Genesis describes two covenant rituals between YHWH and Abraham. Here is a description of the first one:

> [YHWH] said to [Abram], "Bring me a heifer three years old, a female goat three years old, a ram three years old, a turtledove, and a young pigeon." He brought him all these and cut them in two, laying each half over against the other, but he did not cut the birds in two. And when birds of prey came down on the carcasses, Abram drove them away.
>
> As the sun was going down, a deep sleep fell upon Abram, and a deep and terrifying darkness descended upon him.
>
> When the sun had gone down and it was dark, a smoking fire pot and a flaming torch passed between these pieces. On that day the LORD made a covenant with Abram. (Gen 15:9–13; 17–18)

The detail about YHWH (manifested in the fire pot and flaming torch) passing between butchered animals is very strange to modern readers. The implication of this ritual is that the covenant partners agree to submit to the curse of becoming like the divided animals if they do not adhere to the terms of the covenant. Modern people also sometimes seal solemn promises and agreements with an oath or a ritual. For example, witnesses in court promise to tell the truth "so help me God." The sense of the phrase "so help me God" is that God will punish the one who does not tell the truth. In the quotation above, the animals are split in two, and God passes between them as a promise of God's faithfulness to the covenant he made with Abraham.

A second ritual in the Abraham stories highlights the importance of circumcision as a seal of the covenant between God and Abraham's descendants:

> This is my covenant which you shall keep, between me and you and your offspring after you: Every male among you shall be circumcised. You shall circumcise the flesh of your foreskins, and it shall be a sign of the covenant between me and you. Throughout your generations every male among you shall be circumcised when he is eight days old, including the slave born in your house and the one bought with your money from any foreigner who is not of your offspring . . . So shall my covenant be in your flesh an everlasting covenant. (Gen 17:10–14)

The covenant described in Genesis 15 placed no obligations on Abraham. He simply needed to trust in the promise that God made with him—a promise of many descendants and land for them to occupy. However, in this version, Abraham and his descendants are obligated to perform the ritual of circumcision as a symbol of their acceptance of God's covenant and the responsibilities that come with it. Known as a *bris* or *brit mila*, this ritual continues to be performed today as a visible sign of induction into the everlasting covenant that God made with the Israelites.

JACOB AND THE TWELVE TRIBES OF ISRAEL

Genesis 24–50 goes on to narrate stories about Abraham's descendants, especially Isaac, **Jacob**, and Jacob's twelve sons, who would later be looked upon as the founders of the twelve tribes of Israel. The stories serve several purposes, not least of which was helping the Israelites create a common identity by sharing stories about their origins. They also make a point of establishing just which people are, in fact, descendants and heirs of the promises made to Abraham, including the Promised Land. Thus, the stories describe how some of Abraham's descendants were chosen to inherit the promise, but others were not. In Genesis 12–23, we learned how God chose Isaac, not Ishmael, even though both were Abraham's sons and Ishmael was the firstborn. Here, we learn how God chose Jacob over Esau, even though Esau was the first of the twins born to Isaac and Rebekah (Gen 25:19–26). Through cunning and deceit, Jacob stole the birthright of primary inheritance, which rightfully belonged to Esau, and his dying father's special blessing (Gen 25:27–34; 27:1–40). Thus, against all human standards of justice, Jacob became the inheritor of God's promise to Abraham.

The Genesis stories go on to describe how Jacob himself later became the victim of deceit. Esau was so angry about what Jacob had done to him that he threatened to kill him. Therefore, their mother Rebekah arranged for Jacob to leave the country under the pretense of finding a bride from among their kinfolk (Gen 27:41–28:22). He found the bride he wanted, but then he was shamelessly tricked by his uncle Laban into working an extra seven years and taking an extra wife, in order to obtain his desired bride, Rachel (Gen 29:15–30). Finally, after years in exile and a wrestling match with a mysterious heavenly being, he was able to return to his family and his homeland (Gen 32:1–33:20). It is during this wrestling match that Jacob was given his new name **Israel**, from which the Israelites took their name.

Just who was a legitimate descendant of Abraham was an important question in biblical times, since God's promises were made not to just anyone but specifically to Abraham and his descendants. The importance of descent from Abraham partially explains the frequency with which biblical passages record the genealogies of the characters involved in the story. However, it should be recognized that one did not necessarily need to be from the bloodline of Abraham to claim him as an ancestor and to be considered part of the covenant people. The genealogies did not always reflect biological reality but were often more of a political statement used to indicate inclusion and exclusion within a particular group or tribe. Indeed, the stories of the patriarchs in general are motivated more by political and theological concerns than by the desire to describe history with perfect accuracy.

This is not to say that the stories about the patriarchs have no historical basis. Studies have shown, for example, that customs presupposed in the patriarchal stories accurately fit the period in which the patriarchs are thought to have lived, suggesting that other details of these stories could be historically accurate, as well. On the other hand, modern readers need to know that the writers and readers of the Old Testament understood these stories differently than we often do. For the original writers and readers, the genealogies and stories about the ancestors of tribes and nations were not intended to provide historical documentation of the lives of individuals from the past. Rather, they viewed them as describing, in narrative form, relationships among these tribes and nations as they currently existed. This difference in interpretation reflects the deep cultural differences that exist between the original readers of the Old Testament and modern Western readers.

A Cultural Difference: Genealogies

Among Arabian tribes today, whatever might be the biological reality, all members of a given tribe consider themselves to be descended from the tribe's common ancestors. If strangers join the tribe, they do so "in name and in blood," in a way similar to Western practices of adoption. That is, they take the tribe's ancestors as their own and promise to marry and raise their families within the tribe. The Arabs say that the newcomers have been "genealogized."

When two or more tribes enter into close relationship, for example, a confederation of several tribes or the absorption of a weak tribe by a stronger one, a similar process occurs. If the two tribes are of relatively equal power, they may begin to speak of their common ancestors as brothers and sisters, much as they have now become brothers and sisters by the confederation. If one tribe is dominant over the other, the ancestors' relationship will be spoken of in a way that reflects dominance—for example, as uncle and nephew or father and son.

It is likely that the tribes of the Bible had similar practices. In fact, we can see an example of genealogizing in the Bible itself. In the stories of the conquest of Canaan, Caleb was a member of a tribe foreign to Israel, but he chose to ally himself with Israel and cooperated significantly with the Israelite tribes in the process of spying out and conquering the land (Num 13:30–14:45). As a result, he and his family were genealogized into the tribe of Judah: They were given a share in the tribe's land, and Caleb, despite his actual foreign birth, was from that time on spoken of as a member of the tribe of Judah and as a descendant of Judah, the founder of the tribe.

As the Genesis stories continue, we learn that Jacob (Israel) had twelve sons by his two wives and two of their maids. **Joseph** and Benjamin were the two sons by Jacob's favorite wife, Rachel, and Jacob favored them more than the others (Gen 35:16–26). Jacob's other sons resented the fact that he favored Joseph most of all, so they sold him as a slave to some traders going to Egypt and told Jacob he had been eaten by wild animals (Gen 37:1–36). Forcibly relocated to Egypt, Joseph quickly became very successful under his slave owner, Potiphar, who was an officer of the Egyptian pharaoh. The narrator of the story attributes Joseph's good success to God's protection, saying, "and the Lord was with him" (Gen 39:3). But then Potiphar's wife tried to seduce Joseph, and he was imprisoned on a false charge of attempted rape (Gen 39:7–20). But even in his incarceration, he remained safe, because "the Lord was with him" (Gen 39:21). Eventually Joseph was rescued from prison, after he successfully interpreted for the pharaoh a pair of dreams about an impending famine (Gen 41:1–36). The pharaoh was so grateful to receive Joseph's interpretation that he appointed him to a position of great authority and put him in charge of famine preparations for all the people of Egypt (Gen 41:37–45).

After seven years of prosperity, famine came upon the land just as Joseph had predicted, and people from the surrounding areas were forced to come to Egypt to buy food. Jacob sent his sons also to buy food in Egypt, but he did not allow Benjamin to go, because he was afraid of losing him as he had lost Joseph many years earlier. Thus, the same men who once sold Joseph into slavery were forced to appear before him and beg for food, but they did not recognize who he was (Gen 42:1–8). Joseph did not reveal his identity to them, but instead treated them harshly and even forced one of them to stay behind until they would return with Benjamin (Gen 42:9–28). At first Jacob did not allow it, but as the famine grew more severe he gave in because they had no food (Gen 43:11–15). Joseph treated them well when they returned to Egypt, but when they left to go back home he set up a trap so that Benjamin would be forced to stay behind (Gen 43:16–44:1–13). After much pleading from his brother Judah, Joseph finally revealed his identity, forgave his brothers their earlier wrongdoing, and invited the whole family to resettle in Egypt (Gen 44:14–45:20).

Finally Jacob was reunited with Joseph, his beloved son, and he and his family lived in Egypt and prospered because of their association with Joseph. Eventually Jacob died and, many years later, Joseph died, as well. Before his passing, he told his brothers that God would come and bring them out of Egypt to the land that God had promised to Abraham. He asked only one thing—that they take his bones with them to the land of their ancestors (Gen 50:22–26). Thus the book of Genesis ends on a note of expectation.

MOSES

The second book of the Bible is Exodus, meaning "going out." It picks up Israel's story of salvation where Genesis left off—with the descendants of the twelve brothers of Jacob living in Egypt. They lived there peacefully for several generations, until an Egyptian pharaoh came into power who did not know about Joseph and who was not favorably disposed toward the Israelite people (Exod 1:1–10). He feared their prosperity and their large numbers, and therefore he enslaved them in various work projects. He oppressed them greatly but they continued to prosper, so he treated them even more harshly (Exod 1:11–15). The situation of the Israelite slaves in Egypt was truly desperate! With this scene, the stage is set for the book of Exodus.

The opening chapters of the book of Exodus introduce the reader to **Moses**, who is a central character of the book and the leader of the **Exodus**, the "going out" of the descendants of Jacob from slavery to the Promised Land. It is described as perhaps the most important formative experience of the Israelite people, because from that experience their community and their religion were created. Moses is thought to have lived sometime during the middle part of the thirteenth century B.C.E. According to the book of Exodus, YHWH again took the initiative, this time by calling Moses. YHWH directed and empowered Moses to rescue YHWH's people—the descendants of Abraham—from slavery in Egypt. He led them through the wilderness, established another covenant with them, and settled them successfully in the Promised Land. This new covenant, which they received at Mount Sinai, shaped their religious and community life and acted as their "constitution." (The Sinai covenant still serves today as the constitution of the State of Israel.) Thus, YHWH fulfilled the promises to Abraham expressed in the earlier covenant—that he would have many descendants and a land for them to live in. Perhaps the most well-known feature of this Mosaic (meaning "belonging to or associated with Moses") covenant is the Ten Commandments.

Moses the Prophet

Moses is called a prophet, the first and most important of the great Israelite prophets. The central point of prophecy is that **prophets** are spokespersons for God. The great Israelite prophets, like Moses in the book of Exodus, were called and chosen by God. They were given messages from God to deliver to others, and they experienced a powerful compulsion to convey those messages despite their own fears or misgivings. In a sense, God spoke *through* them to communicate in concrete ways with God's people.

Moses experienced his prophetic call while in exile in a wilderness area called Midian. He had escaped to this land to avoid the wrath of Pharaoh, after killing an Egyptian whom he found beating an Israelite slave (Exod 2:11–15). This day he was shepherding the flocks of Jethro, the priest of Midian, who had befriended him when he first came to Midian and among whose daughters he had found his wife, Zipporah (Exod 3:1; see also 2:15–22). YHWH first attracted Moses' attention by appearing in a bush that was burning but not being consumed by the fire. As Moses came closer to check out this amazing sight, YHWH introduced himself saying, "I am the God of your father, the God of Abraham, the God of Isaac, and the God of Jacob" (Exod 3:6). In other words, this was no new and strange deity who appeared to Moses in the wilderness. Rather, this deity already has a long and storied relationship with the Israelite people. Thus YHWH called Moses, told him that he had heard the cries of his oppressed people, and commanded him to lead YHWH's people out of slavery in Egypt to a land "flowing with milk and honey" (Exod 3:7–8).

God commanded Moses to announce this message to Pharaoh and to the Israelite people. Moses tried to avoid the responsibility, finally asking YHWH to "send someone else," but YHWH would not accept Moses' refusal. Fearful that the people would not listen to him,

Moses asked God what his name was and received that famous and mysterious answer, "I am who am," which, among numerous other explanations, has been variously understood as "I am who exists without being caused by another," "I am who causes to be," or "I am who I am" (Exod 3:13–15). In Hebrew the name is YHWH (Hebrew was written without vowels), but Jews consider the name too sacred to pronounce, substituting instead the word "Lord" (in Hebrew, *Adonai*) wherever the name of YHWH is written. In the Exodus stories about Moses, the writers consistently refer to God as YHWH.

Assisted by his brother **Aaron** the Levite, Moses finally accepted his assignment and returned to Egypt with his message for the ruling pharaoh, who was brutally oppressing the enslaved Israelites (Exod 4:27–31). The message was this: YHWH says, "Let my people go" (Exod 5:1). Thus began a confrontation between Moses and Pharaoh that the book of Exodus portrays as a confrontation between YHWH and the gods of the Egyptians. However, it would be a mistake to conclude from these stories that the Israelite people were entirely monotheistic at this point in their history. At the time of the Exodus, and probably for centuries afterwards, neither the Israelites nor their neighbors thought of YHWH as being the only real God. Rather, the Israelites thought YHWH was the only God *for them* (and often enough they were not faithful even to this conviction). Only much later would they become convinced that their God was the only true God of all.

In order to get the Egyptian pharaoh to release the Israelite slaves, YHWH gave Moses several "magic tricks" and a series of plagues to use against the Egyptians. However, only when God killed all of the Egyptian firstborn did the pharaoh finally release them. In the wilderness, God continued to protect and guide them by providing them with safe passage across the Red (reed) sea, giving them food and water, and finally granting them entrance into the Promised Land. The Exodus stories that describe this confrontation between Moses and the pharaoh, and the events that followed, reveal a number of characteristics of YHWH:

1. YHWH was much more powerful than the Egyptian gods and the gods of the Canaanites.
2. YHWH cared about relieving earthly oppression and providing for material needs; YHWH rescued the Israelites from slavery and settled them in a land that had enough resources to support them.
3. YHWH supported the Israelites in desert places where food and water could not otherwise be found.
4. YHWH was a strong warrior who led Israel in battle against hostile neighbors.

Some modern theologians have drawn attention to these same characteristics of God to challenge churches to work for justice and to counteract the attitude that prevails among some Christians that religious people should only be concerned with life after death. Their argument can be summed up as follows: The Bible shows us that God stands on the side of the poor and oppressed, defending them, and providing for their needs. Therefore we must do the same.

These same Exodus narratives also reveal some interesting characteristics of the Israelites:

1. While they did not enjoy being slaves in Egypt, they were not inclined to try to escape. YHWH and Moses had to push them to cooperate.

2. They did not have much confidence in YHWH's power. They were "slow learners" who kept forgetting how YHWH had just saved them, and they repeatedly failed to trust YHWH's protection.
3. They were constantly grumbling about the hardships they were experiencing and blaming YHWH and Moses for their suffering.
4. Throughout the events of the Exodus, it was YHWH who took all the initiative. Left to themselves, the Israelites probably would have remained where they were, enslaved in Egypt.

Thus the Exodus stories also reveal that YHWH chose the Israelite people not because of their good qualities, but in spite of their "stiff necks" (stubbornness). Why YHWH chose them remained a mystery even to the Israelites themselves. In the New Testament, Paul will remark that other peoples, including Christians, should not feel superior in this respect, since no one is worthy of God's call, and no one has lived up to God's call very well.

The following box summarizes YHWH's conflict with the gods of Egypt. Note how the story is told to show that YHWH is more powerful than the Egyptian gods.

The Ten Plagues

In the book of Exodus, the battle between YHWH and the gods of Egypt is illustrated through a series of ten plagues. At first, the Egyptian magicians could duplicate the plagues Moses was producing (though in an inferior way). But when God sent the third plague they not only failed to duplicate it, they also publicly admitted that YHWH had won the contest. As the plagues went on, other members of the pharaoh's court became convinced that YHWH had won and tried to convince the pharaoh to give up. They also took steps to protect themselves, but the pharaoh held out, making insincere and inadequate promises, only to go back on them again and again. Of course, for the Israelite people, these were not plagues but rather miracles that demonstrated God's care and protection. Here is a summary of the ten plagues.

1. Water into blood (Exod 7:14–24). After Moses turned the water of the Nile River into blood, Pharaoh refused to release the Israelites because his magicians could duplicate the plague.
2. Frogs (Exod 7:25–8:15). After Moses brought swarms of frogs down upon the Egyptians, another plague that the Egyptian magicians could duplicate, Pharaoh promised Moses that if he took away the frogs he would release the Israelites, but he later broke his promise.
3. Gnats (Exod 8:16–19). With the third plague, the Egyptian magicians were unable to keep up and told Pharaoh, "This is the finger of God." But Pharaoh continued to refuse to release the Israelites.
4. Flies (Exod 8: 20–32). The swarms of flies did not affect the land of Goshen, where the Israelites dwelled. YHWH said, "Thus I will make a distinction between my people and your people." Once again Pharaoh broke a promise to release the Israelites long enough to sacrifice to YHWH.
5. Pestilence (Exod 9:1–7). When this plague brought disease upon all the livestock of the Egyptians, YHWH again showed his preference for Israel by sparing their flocks. The pharaoh was not moved.

6. Boils (Exod 9:8–12). The festering boils affected both animals and humans, even the Egyptian magicians, but the pharaoh still refused to release the Israelites.

7. Hail and thunder (Exod 9:13–35). The hail and thunder that affected every region except the land of Goshen were so terrible that the pharaoh immediately summoned Moses and promised to release the Israelites, but he reneged on his promise as soon as the storms ceased.

8. Locusts (Exod 10:1–20). When Moses threatened the Egyptians with clouds of locusts that would devour their crops, the pharaoh agreed to let the men go, but he insisted they leave the women and children behind. This was not acceptable to Moses, and he struck the Egyptians with the plague. The pharaoh beseeched Moses to end the plague and made another promise that he failed to fulfill.

9. Darkness (Exod 10:21–29). After three days of darkness, the pharaoh agreed to let the Israelites go, as long as they left behind all of their livestock, but this was not acceptable to Moses.

10. Death of the firstborn (Exod 11:1–10). YHWH came and struck dead the firstborn of all the Egyptians and their livestock. The Israelites were told to sacrifice a lamb and mark their doors with the blood, so that YHWH would pass over their houses. After the plague, all the Egyptians, mourning their dead, urged the Israelites to go and gave them their valuables. The pharaoh told Moses and the Israelites to go. The next day he changed his mind and pursued them.

One of the most curious features of the story about the confrontation between Moses and the Egyptian pharaoh is the way YHWH "hardens the pharaoh's heart" (e.g., Exod 8:19), thus delaying YHWH's victory and keeping the conflict going. The result of this hardening is to demonstrate YHWH's power more strikingly than would have been the case had the pharaoh been more reasonable. It becomes clear that YHWH has the power to overcome any resistance, no matter how strong it is. At the same time, this feature of the story has raised many questions for later theologians, especially questions about what causes evil and whether humans truly have free will. The problematic character of this story is also reflected in later Jewish traditions: The Passover ritual (Seder), for example, includes the admonition, "Do not celebrate. Egyptians are dying." However, the authors and the original readers of these stories were probably not concerned with these questions and problems. They were just enjoying the story, watching YHWH play with an arrogant pharaoh as a cat might play with a mouse.

Passover

The climax of YHWH's contest with the pharaoh is the tenth plague, the death of the firstborn. Before carrying out this plague, YHWH directed the Israelites to sacrifice a lamb and mark their doorways with the lamb's blood. When the angel came to kill the firstborn and saw the blood-marked doorways, the angel passed over those houses without causing any harm (Exod 12:1–28). The annual feast that later commemorated this event took the name *Passover* from this passing over. Historically, the Passover marked the beginning of the Israelites' Exodus from Egypt and their journey to the Promised Land.

Passage Through the Red Sea

Once they had escaped from Egypt, the Israelites found themselves in a new crisis. The pharaoh had changed his mind again and was pursuing them with his whole army, and they were trapped on the shore of the Red Sea. But YHWH directed Moses to hold up his staff over the waters of the sea, and when he did, YHWH parted the waters so that the Israelites could pass through on dry land. When the Egyptians tried to follow, YHWH let the waters flow back and thus drowned their army.

What kind of miracle had the Israelites witnessed? There are two accounts of this event: a prose account in Exodus 14 and a poetic one in Exodus 15. Exodus 14:21 suggests that YHWH used a physical mechanism to divide the waters—a strong east wind that blew all night. However, the next verse describes an epic heightening of the same event that sounds more directly and flamboyantly miraculous: "the water like a wall to their left and their right" (Exod 14:22). Many scholars suggest that verse 21 is historically more likely, because they can point to another historical occasion when one of the shallow bodies of water in the Northern Sinai was divided by a strong wind, allowing an endangered group to escape. Still, it is likely that those who found themselves in this difficult situation would have considered it a miracle that this event happened just when they needed it. They would not have considered it to be "just a coincidence," even if someone told them that it happened once before only a century earlier.

The poetic description of the escape through the Red Sea in Exodus 15, especially the short form, which is preserved in verse 21, is considered by biblical scholars to be one of the oldest traditions preserved in the Bible:

> The prophetess Miriam, Aaron's sister, took a tambourine in her hand, while all the women went out after her with tambourines, dancing, and she led them in the refrain: "Sing to the Lord, for he is gloriously triumphant; horse and chariot he has cast into the sea." (Exod 15:20–21)

It celebrates the Israelites' rescue as a miracle effected by God and as a cause for great rejoicing.

Wandering in the Wilderness

Once in the wilderness, the Israelites faced new problems. They had no experience of living in such a desolate area. They responded to these challenges by grumbling and blaming YHWH and Moses for their problems. YHWH took care of their needs, but he also showed displeasure at their grumbling and allowed them to suffer for their lack of faith. They grumbled that there was no food: YHWH gave them "manna" (Exod 16:1–36). They grumbled that they wanted meat: YHWH gave them quail (Exod 16:1–36). They grumbled that there was no water: YHWH gave them water from a rock (Exod 17:1–7). At one point, after Moses was absent for a prolonged period, they despaired and turned to the worship of false gods (Exod 32:1–35).

Finally, they grumbled that the inhabitants of Canaan were too strong for them to enter the Promised Land. As punishment, YHWH sent them back into the desert to wander for another forty years until all those who had failed to trust his power had died. YHWH would lead Jacob's descendants into the Promised Land, but not those who had refused to acknowledge YHWH's power (Num 14:1–38). In sum, for the Israelite people the wilderness became a symbol of identity making. It was during this period that YHWH initiated a

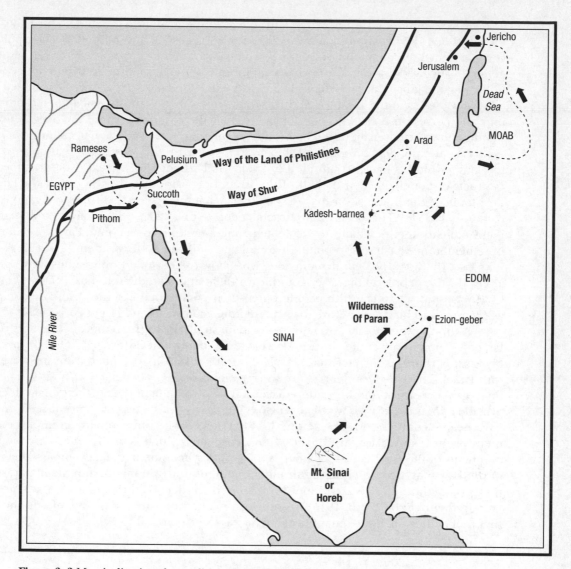

Figure 3–3 Map indicating the traditional route of the Exodus.

covenant with them and revealed himself to them as the God of Abraham, Isaac, Jacob, and Joseph. It was there that YHWH taught them how they should live and how they should relate to God and to one another as God's chosen people.

Covenant at Sinai

The covenant that God made with Moses and the descendants of Jacob on Mount Sinai is similar in form to the political covenants among Israel's neighbors at the time. Some good examples are the Hittite covenants, which began with the king or overlord giving his name and titles of authority. Second, the king recalled his past acts of beneficence on behalf of the vassal, in essence explaining why the vassal ought to accept the covenant with gratitude. Third, the overlord outlined the Treaty obligations between this vassal state and himself. Secular political covenants involved quite a bit of self-interest on the part of the king or overlord. The response generally involved coming to the king's aid in time of need, sending in tribute money, and informing the king of any rebellions being planned. Hittite covenants usually concluded with a list of witnesses to the Treaty, including some of their deities and cosmic powers, and blessings and curses on those who obey or fail to obey the covenant. There was also an understanding that the covenant would be recalled regularly, perhaps in a public reading.

Like the political covenants of the ancient Near East, the Mosaic covenant begins with the king giving his name: "I am the Lord your God" (Exod 20:1). Next, God described his past acts of beneficence on behalf of the Israelites: "who brought you out of the land of Egypt, out of the house of slavery" (Exod 20:2). What follows are the Treaty obligations, the response that YHWH expects of the Israelite people (Exod 20:3–18). Today we call them the Ten Commandments. Finally, the Israelite people were told to celebrate Passover in a ritual of remembrance each year in gratitude for all that God had done for them (Exod 12:24–27). Likewise, the book of Deuteronomy describes how the covenant obligations were spoken aloud for the people so that they could learn them and take them to heart (Deut 5:1) and how Moses saw fit to have the people renew their commitment to the covenant, complete with curses and blessings, before they entered the Promised Land (Deut 29:1–30:20).

Although the Mosaic covenant bears some similarity to the political covenants of the Israelites' neighbors at the time, it also has some important differences. One of the most obvious, perhaps, is the fact that YHWH did not get selfish advantage from this covenant with Israel. The Israelites clearly were the recipients of God's benefaction, and God had little to gain in return. Another difference is that the prologue of the Sinai covenant does not provide a long list of titles ascribed to God, but this is not surprising, since it seems not to have been a common practice among Jewish writers of the time. Finally, an important element of the Exodus account of the Mosaic covenant, which is not found in any political covenants of the Israelites' neighbors, is the cosmic phenomena that accompany the giving of the Law. The people witnessed thunder and lightning, a smoking mountain, and something that sounded like a trumpet blast and concluded (rightly) that God was present among them (Exod 20:18–19). This overlord needed no witnesses from among the pantheon of deities for his covenant because he was the God of all!

The Ten Commandments

Anyone who reads the commandments from the Bible (Exod 20:3–20 or Deut 5:6–21) will notice that they are not numbered. In fact, it is not even clear that there should be exactly Ten Commandments. However, all Christian traditions do identify ten, though Catholic and Lutheran Christian traditions organize them differently than other Protestant traditions and Orthodox Christians do. The traditional Catholic and Lutheran enumeration of the Ten Commandments is listed below. Other Protestant traditions separate the first and second commandments on this list and combine the ninth and tenth into one final commandment.

1. I am the LORD your God, who brought you out of the land of Egypt, out of the house of slavery; you shall have no other gods before me. You shall not make for

yourself an idol, whether in the form of anything that is in heaven above, or that is on the earth beneath, or that is in the water under the earth. (Exod 20:2–4)

2. You shall not make wrongful use of the name of the Lord your God. (Exod 20:7)
3. Remember the Sabbath day, and keep it holy. (Exod 20:8)
4. Honor your mother and father. (Exod 20:12)
5. You shall not murder. (Exod 20:13)
6. You shall not commit adultery. (Exod 20:14)
7. You shall not steal. (Exod 20:15)
8. You shall not bear false witness against your neighbor. (Exod 20:16)
9. You shall not covet your neighbor's house. (Exod 20:17a)
10. You shall not covet your neighbor's wife, or male or female slave, or ox, or donkey, or anything that belongs to him. (Exod 20:17b)

Some who are unfamiliar with the significance of the Mosaic covenant for Israel's salvation story sometimes think of the Ten Commandments as nothing more than a universal set of rules that have been passed down through the ages. Others read the many regulations governing food, work, worship, and other aspects of life contained in the books of Exodus, Leviticus, Numbers, and Deuteronomy and conclude that the Israelite people were obsessed about laws. This is simply not the case. Rather, the commandments are seen as God's desire for the community he has chosen, rescued, and blessed. The people of the covenant kept the laws not primarily to avoid God's anger but rather to show gratitude for what God had done for them. They did not consider the Law of Moses to be a burden but a gift from God. It is a concrete manifestation of the special relationship that YHWH initiated with their community; their faithfulness in obedience to the Law is their grateful response.

Ritual Enactment of the Covenant

Covenants were often sealed or renewed with a **sacrifice**. Animal and vegetable sacrifice was widespread among ancient peoples. A sacrifice was a gift given to God or other spiritual beings, with the understanding that valuable things could be transferred from this world to the spirit world. They thought fire was an appropriate medium for such exchange, since it is capable of turning solid, material things into a substance which the deity could receive and even partake. For example, Judges 13:19–23 describes how Manoah, who later became the father of Samson, made a burnt offering to God. As the fire leapt up into the air, he saw an angel ascending in the flame of the altar, which he understood to be a sign of God's acceptance of the offering. Israelites considered whole burnt offerings to be the best because the entire animal was consumed in the fire and, as the smoke went up into the heavens, the sweet odor would attract God's attention, and God would be pleased.

Ancient worshipers transferred gifts to the spiritual world in order to develop and maintain a relationship with God and spiritual beings. While to some such a sacrifice or gift may take on the appearance of bribery, at its best this giving was an attempt to build and maintain a relationship of caring and trust. People showed their good dispositions to God by offering things of value in the confidence that God, who is good by nature and is now well disposed to them, would meet their needs. They also offered sacrifice in order to show their appreciation for God's free gifts to them by giving God gifts in return.

If one were to create or confirm such a relationship, one must not be cheap or deceitful in one's gifts. The offerings must be "spotless," of good quality, such as one might offer to people of influence in human affairs. "First things" were especially valuable (firstborn animals, the first armful of harvested grain) because the "first" symbolized and stood for the whole. When one offered the "first things," one was symbolically offering everything to God. An extreme example of the importance of offering something of value is Abraham's near-sacrifice of Isaac in Genesis 22. Although YHWH is the one who commanded this sacrifice, Abraham's compliance with the command showed his willingness to risk everything for God, because, if this sacrifice had been carried out, everything Abraham had been living for would have been destroyed. Fortunately, once Abraham showed YHWH that he was willing to carry it out, YHWH proposed an alternative sacrifice.

Exodus 24 describes the ritual sealing of the Mosaic covenant. Animals were sacrificed and their blood collected. Half of the blood was thrown on the altar. Then the Law was read and the people answered, "All the words that the LORD has spoken we will do" (Exod 24:4). Finally, the other half of the blood was sprinkled on the people while Moses said: "See the blood of the covenant that the LORD has made with you in accordance with all these words" (Exod 24:8). The New Testament refers back to this covenant and its ritual enactment when it describes Jesus at the Last Supper—a meal closely connected with the Jewish Passover— taking bread and wine, sharing them with the disciples, and saying:

> This is my body, which will be given for you; do this in memory of me . . . This cup that is poured out for you is the new covenant in my blood. (Luke 22:19–20)

Christians believe that Jesus, in his sacrifice on the cross, offered his life on behalf of humans, and in this offering he became the sacrifice of the new covenant. He asked humans to offer their lives to God in the act of faith by which they are justified.

Key Terms

legend	Isaac	Exodus
covenant	Jacob	prophets
Abraham	Israel	Aaron
patriarch	Joseph	Passover
Ishmael	Moses	sacrifice

Questions for Reading

1. Describe YHWH's promises to Abraham. What is the significance of those promises to the salvation history of the Israelite people?

2. What is a covenant? Describe God's covenant with Abraham and explain how it is similar to or different from the covenant with Moses.

3. What do the Genesis stories reveal about the way in which Abraham is a model of faith?

4. Describe the significance of the Ten Commandments, especially their relationship to the covenant that God made with Moses and the descendants of Jacob.

5. Explain how the ten plagues of the Exodus were, in effect, a contest between YHWH and the Egyptian gods. What role was played by Moses and Aaron, the Egyptian magicians, and the pharaoh?

6. What do the Exodus stories reveal about the nature of God and God's relationship with the Israelite people?

7. Why did ancient peoples offer sacrifices to God or the gods? Why were sacrifices killed or burned up? How do modern people accomplish the same task?

Works Consulted/Recommended Reading

Alt, Albrecht. "The God of the Fathers." In Wilson, trans., *Essays on Old Testament History and Religion*, 1–100.

Batto, Bernard F. *Slaying the Dragon: Mythmaking in the Biblical Tradition*. Louisville, KY: Westminster John Knox, 1992.

Bergant, Dianne. *Israel's Story*. Part One. Collegeville, MN: Liturgical Press, 2006.

Binz, Stephen J. *The God of Freedom and Life: A Commentary on the Book of Exodus*. Collegeville, MN: Liturgical Press, 1993.

Brueggemann, Walter. *An Introduction to the Old Testament: The Canon and Christian Imagination*. Louisville, KY: Westminster John Knox, 2003.

Ceresko, Anthony R. *Introduction to the Old Testament: A Liberation Perspective*. Maryknoll, NY: Orbis, 2001.

Childs, Brevard. *The Book of Exodus*. Philadelphia: Westminster, 1974.

Collins, John J. *Introduction to the Hebrew Bible*. Minneapolis, MN: Fortress, 2004.

Janzen, J. Gerald. *Exodus*. Louisville, KY: Westminster John Knox, 1997.

Metzger, Bruce, and Roland Murphy, eds. *The New Oxford Annotated Bible with Apocrypha, New Revised Standard Version*. New York: Oxford University, 1991.

Mills, Mary E. *Images of God in the Old Testament*. Collegeville, MN: Liturgical Press, 1998.

Pixley, Jorge V. *On Exodus: A Liberation Perspective*. Maryknoll, NY: Orbis, 1987.

Sugirtharajah, Rasiah S., ed. *Voices from the Margin: Interpreting the Bible in the Third World*. Maryknoll, NY: Orbis, 1995.

Teubal, Savina. *Hagar the Egyptian: The Lost Tradition of Matriarchs*. San Francisco: Harper & Row, 1990.

Thompson, Thomas L. *The Historicity of the Patriarchal Narratives*. Berlin, NY: De Gruyter, 1974.

van Seters, John. *Abraham in History and Tradition*. New Haven, CT: Yale University, 1975.

Westermann, Claus. *The Promises to the Fathers: Studies on the Patriarchal Narratives*. Translated by D. E. Green. Philadelphia: Fortress, 1980.

Wilson, R. A., trans. *Essays on Old Testament History and Religion*. Garden City, NY: Doubleday, 1967.

Chapter 4

JUDGES, PROPHETS, KINGS

TIMELINE

c. 1250–1020 B.C.E.	Joshua and the Israelites enter Canaan. The period of the Judges.
c. 1020–1000 B.C.E.	Saul reigns as king of the Israelite people.
c. 1000–961 B.C.E.	David is king of Israel and establishes Jerusalem as its capital.
c. 961–922 B.C.E.	Solomon reigns as king of united Israel and builds the Temple in Jerusalem.
922 B.C.E.	Solomon's kingdom is divided in two: the northern kingdom (Israel) and the southern kingdom (Judah).
c. 750–745 B.C.E.	The prophets Amos and Hosea preach in the northern kingdom of Israel. Assyria becomes a world power.
c. 742–700 B.C.E.	The prophet Isaiah preaches in the southern kingdom of Judah.
721 B.C.E.	The northern kingdom of Israel is defeated by the Assyrians.
c. 626–587 B.C.E.	The prophet Jeremiah preaches in the southern kingdom of Judah. Babylon becomes a world power.
597 B.C.E.	Judah is defeated by Babylon. The Babylonian Exile begins.
597–573 B.C.E.	The prophet Ezekiel preaches in exile in Babylon.
586 (?) B.C.E.	The Jerusalem Temple is destroyed.
c. 540 B.C.E.	The prophet known as Second Isaiah preaches during the exile; Persia becomes a world power.
538 B.C.E.	King Cyrus of Persia issues a decree allowing the people of Judah to return to their homes.
c. 520 B.C.E.	Ezra and Nehemiah begin a religious reform of Judaism. The Temple in Jerusalem is rebuilt.

The Pentateuch ends with an account of the death of Moses and the appointment of Joshua as his successor. The story of Israel's covenant relationship with YHWH does not end here, however, for not all of the promises that God made to Abraham and Moses have yet been fulfilled. In particular, two remain: the promise of possession of the land of Canaan and the promise that Israel will become a "great nation."

This chapter covers the period from the beginnings of the rise of the nation of Israel following the Exodus (thirteenth century B.C.E.) to its fall as a nation (sixth century B.C.E.), when it was conquered by the Babylonians and its people were exiled in Babylon. During this time, we note the establishment of the monarchy, the rise of the institution of prophecy, and the establishment of the centralized Temple in Jerusalem. The books that record the history of this period are classified as the books of the Prophets and are distinguished from the books of the Law (also called the Pentateuch or the Torah). Further, the books of the Prophets are divided into the Former Prophets, which are historical narratives, and the Latter Prophets, which are books that bear the names of actual Israelite prophets and contain their prophecies.

LAW (TORAH)	PROPHETS (NEVI'IM)
Genesis	Former Prophets:
Exodus	Joshua
Leviticus	Judges
Numbers	1–2 Samuel
Deuteronomy	1–2 Kings
	Latter Prophets:
	Isaiah
	Jeremiah
	Ezekiel
	The Twelve (Hosea, Joel, Amos, Obadiah, Jonah, Micah, Nahum, Habakkuk, Zephaniah, Haggai, Zechariah, Malachi)

The books of the Former Prophets are all part of a single, complex, collected work known as the **Deuteronomistic History**, so named because the author(s) were followers of the Deuteronomists, the ones who wrote the book of Deuteronomy in the Law. These books were actually written centuries later than most of the historical period they cover. Although the **Deuteronomistic Historian** (collector and editor of the Deuteronomistic material) provides a great deal of accurate historical information, having gotten his information from various oral and written stories from Israel's early tribal period and from the period of the kings, the main concern of the author was to provide a *theological* interpretation of Israel's history.

At the time the Deuteronomistic Historian was writing, Jerusalem had just been conquered and the Temple had been destroyed by the Babylonians (597–587 B.C.E.). In many ways, these experiences were too painful for the Israelites to comprehend. The experiences created doubt in the minds of some Israelites as to whether the covenant was working and whether YHWH was indeed faithful to the covenant. Thus, the Deuteronomistic Historian retold the history of Israel from the beginning to show that the problem with the covenant was not with YHWH but with Israel. The books continually show how Israel's fortunes were directly correlated to her obedience to the covenant. When the Israelites followed the covenant and kept God's commandments, God was with them and they prospered. When the Israelites abandoned the covenant, breaking the commandments and worshiping other gods, YHWH withheld his protection from them and they were conquered and oppressed by their enemies.

The books of the Deuteronomistic Historian provided a way for Israel to try to make sense out of their experience of loss and abandonment by assuring the readers that God had always remained faithful to his covenant. Their authors sought to explain that even though life for the Israelite people would never again be the same, their God still cared for them and would restore them to their land. Thus, the Deuteronomistic Historian, along with the prophets, emphasized God's faithfulness to the covenant, and the need for Israel to be equally faithful especially by worshiping only YHWH and not any other gods.

JUDGES: CONQUEST AND SETTLEMENT

After the death of Moses, Joshua led the Israelites into the land of Canaan (late thirteenth century B.C.E.). With the help of YHWH, the Israelites were able to conquer the people who occupied this land (although they never gained complete and total control of the entire region), and the Israelites settled in the land of Canaan. At least according to the stories, a major factor in the Israelite victories was the **Ark of the Covenant**. The ark was Israel's most sacred object. On the one hand, the ark served as a *container* for various objects that were sacred to the Israelites, such as the two tablets of the law given to Moses. On the other hand, the ark was viewed as a *throne* on which YHWH sat, invisibly overlooking the people of Israel. The most important feature of the ark was that it was a direct manifestation of God's presence. Wherever the ark went, so went YHWH and so went YHWH's power. For this reason the Israelites sometimes carried the ark into battle during this period of the conquest of Canaan, and the presence of YHWH then ensured an Israelite victory. Eventually, the ark was housed at the national shrine located at Shiloh, before it was moved some centuries later to its final resting place in the Jerusalem Temple.

After the conquest of Canaan, the nation of Israel was established. However, Israel had neither a single leader nor any centralized government. Rather, Israel was a tribal confederacy. The twelve tribes of Israel separated themselves, and each settled in a different portion of the land. Each tribe governed itself and was ruled by elders. The tribes were united only in certain matters of religion and in times of war. At times of national crisis, when the tribes had to act together, a different (but temporary) kind of leader emerged, the **judge** (*shofet* in Hebrew).

The judges were charismatic leaders. This meant that they were chosen by God and endowed with certain gifts that enabled them to lead. One could not decide to become a judge, nor could one be "elected" as a judge. The main purpose of the judges was not to oversee legal disputes. Rather, they were primarily political and military leaders, who also had some religious functions. Perhaps the best translation of *shofet* is "chieftain." According to the book of Judges, a certain pattern established itself in Israelite salvation history. The pattern began with the Israelites failing to observe the terms of the covenant, worshiping other gods, and behaving immorally. YHWH would become angry and withhold his protection from the Israelites, causing them to be afflicted and oppressed by their enemies. The Israelites would then repent of their sins and cry out to God for deliverance. God would heed their call by sending a judge, who would unite the people, call them to a

Figure 4–1 A thirteenth-century French miniature illustrating the festivities that took place when David brought the Ark of the Covenant to Jerusalem.

renewed awareness of their covenant relationship with God, and lead them to military victories over their enemies. Once the judge died, however, the Israelites would fall back into a life of sin.

As the book of Judges progresses, the quality of the judges gradually declines, so that by the end of the book the Israelite society begins to deteriorate. The editor concludes "In those days there was no king in Israel; all the people did what was right in their own eyes" (Judges 21:25). In sum, the Israelite tribal system had degenerated into anarchy.

KINGS: THE DEMAND FOR A MONARCHY

In addition to this internal decline of tribal Israel, an external threat presented the small nation with its most serious crisis. The Philistines, a people who lived on the coast of the Mediterranean Sea near Israel, developed weapons made of iron, and their iron monopoly enabled them to profoundly defeat tribal Israel. This defeat led the Israelites to demand a king from **Samuel**, an Israelite prophet and the last of the judges. Directed by YHWH,

Samuel appointed **Saul**, a young man from the Israelite tribe of Benjamin. Shortly afterward, Saul began to assert his authority over the country and reigned from approximately 1020 to 1000 B.C.E. However, Saul eventually proved unworthy to be king, and he lost the favor of YHWH. Samuel, acting as the agent of YHWH, opposed him and vowed to find a new candidate for the monarchy.

Saul and David

Again under the guidance of YHWH, Samuel immediately found a new candidate for kingship and secretly anointed **David**, a young man from the tribe of Judah, to be king of Israel. However, he could not assume the throne as king of Israel, because Saul was still king. Instead, David attached himself to Saul's royal court, distinguishing himself by defeating the Philistine champion Goliath and leading the Israelite army to one of its few victories against their enemies. Saul became jealous of David and sought to kill him. David was forced to flee.

After a period of instability caused by the conflict between Saul and David and the steady decline of Saul's ability to rule effectively, the Philistines defeated Saul and killed the king and most of his sons. David was quickly made king in the power vacuum that was left by Saul's death, and David reigned as king beginning in approximately 1000 B.C.E. and until his death in 961. David's first recorded royal act was to establish his new capital in **Jerusalem**, which had previously been unconquered by the Israelites. After the conquest, it became known as "the city of David."

David moved the Ark of the Covenant to Jerusalem and established control over the religious apparatus of Israel. From this point on, from the perspective of the Deuteronomistic Historian, most important religious events took place in Jerusalem. Although people continued to practice religion in their own towns and villages, the Deuteronomistic Historian regarded such activity as suspect and even disloyal to YHWH. The reason for this was probably that the religious practice in rural areas tended to blend aspects of other religions and the worship of other gods into authentic YHWH worship, while the Deuteronomistic Historian believed that a pure form of YHWH worship was maintained in Jerusalem.

The Deuteronomistic Historian describes the period of David's rule as a sort of "golden age" of Israelite power, a unique time of divine approval and divine blessing. David's prophet, Nathan, declared that David would establish a dynasty that would never end. Speaking for YHWH, Nathan said, "Your house and your kingdom shall be made sure forever before me; your throne shall be established forever" (2 Sam 7:16). There were many signs of God's approval of David, especially in the military arena. David's forces became dominant in the region. He expanded the outer borders of Israel in every direction (see 2 Sam 8–10 for accounts of some of David's military victories).

However, David's personal fortunes declined in the latter half of his reign. He committed adultery with Bathsheba, the wife of Uriah, one of his military commanders. She became pregnant, and after trying to cover up his deed with deception, the king had Uriah murdered, so he could marry her (see 2 Sam 11). God was displeased at this immoral behavior and, through the prophet Nathan, pronounced a severe punishment on David (see 2 Sam 12). This punishment included the death of the child he conceived with Bathsheba, the curse of continual warfare for his kingdom, and the creation of trouble within David's own house, that is, trouble with his children. One of his sons, Amnon, raped his half sister Tamar, and Amnon was in turn killed by her full brother Absalom (see 2 Sam 13). Absalom then organized a full-scale rebellion against his father, the king. During David's attempt to retake the throne, Absalom was killed. Although David regained his authority, he could not recover from the grief he felt at the loss of his son. "O my son Absalom, my son, my son Absalom! Would I had died instead of you, O Absalom, my son, my son!" (2 Sam 18:33). In spite of all these difficulties, the king was still able to pass on his kingdom, relatively intact, to his son **Solomon**.

Many have noticed the troubling ambiguity of the portrayal of King David in 1 and 2 Samuel. On the one hand, he is portrayed as God's chosen servant, the king appointed by God. Many Israelites knew the story of YHWH's promise to David to always sustain his dynasty. Why then is the close of David's life so sordid? Certainly, there were anti-David factions within Israel who told unpleasant stories about him, and some of these were woven into the Deuteronomistic story. But why? Perhaps the biblical authors sought to teach their readers some moral lessons by recounting the failures of King David. For one thing, it was important for the Israelites to understand that even their kings were subject to the law of YHWH. In many cultures, the kings made the laws and hence were considered above the law. In Israel, the laws did not come from the king, but from God. The story of David and Bathsheba reinforces the point that no one is above the law.

Another point made here is that it is impossible to hide things from God. This is shown in the way in which David tries but fails to cover up his sins. God sees everything (God is all-knowing, or **omniscient**) and God will punish people for their sins. For Jews at this time, rewards and punishments were thought to be meted out in this life, not in the afterlife. The idea of life after death and eternal punishment or reward were concepts not yet known to the Israelites. This is why David is punished not by being sent to hell, but by having his son die and his other children rise up against him. Finally, the story of David's fall from grace provides a warning to all Israelites about how one sin leads to another. David begins with a series of relatively minor indiscretions, but these eventually lead him to the serious sins of coveting, adultery, and murder.

Solomon and the Division of the Kingdom

Solomon received the kingdom from his father, David, and reigned from 961 to 922 B.C.E. Solomon was known for his great wisdom, his large harem (he is said to have had 700 wives and 300 concubines), and for his building projects. Most notably, Solomon built the **Temple** in Jerusalem, which became the center of Israelite religious life. Although he was able to consolidate his father's power, Solomon's abuse of that power (excessive taxation, extensive use of slave labor, neglect of the concerns of the northern tribes) resulted in the division of the kingdom during the rule of his son Rehoboam. The Deuteronomistic Historian claimed that the division of the kingdom was God's punishment for Solomon's sins of idolatry, as Solomon was led in his old age by some of his foreign wives to worship their gods. The northern section of the kingdom split away and established its own government. From this point the northern kingdom is known as **Israel**, and the southern kingdom as **Judah** (from which we eventually get the terms *Jew* and *Jewish*).

The Temple of Solomon in Jerusalem became the central focus of Israelite worship of YHWH, particularly in the south. Although northern shrines were still being built and maintained by the northern kings, the shrine in Jerusalem established itself as vitally important for defining the character of the Israelite faith. A complex order of priests was organized to serve the needs of this massive and ornate construction, and people throughout the nation made pilgrimages to Jerusalem on important holidays to worship YHWH in the Temple. The Temple came to occupy an enormous place in the national religious consciousness, and it was a source of great pride and security to most Israelites. Many Judeans

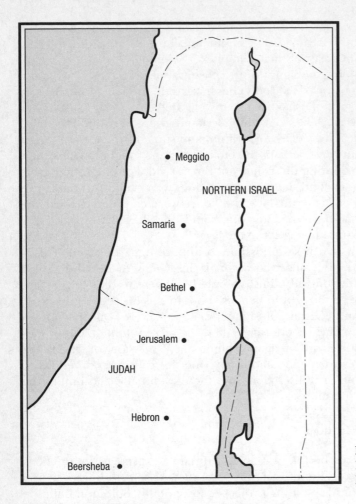

Figure 4–2 The divided kingdom, Judah and Israel, during the reign of Solomon's son, Rehoboam.

felt that as long as they had the Temple in Jerusalem and a son of David sitting on the throne, nothing really bad could ever happen to them.

The primary function of the Temple was to offer animal sacrifices to YHWH. People would bring their livestock offerings to the Temple to be slaughtered by the priests on specially designated altars. Although sacrifices continued in other locations, animal offerings in Solomon's Temple were more important and ultimately, for the Deuteronomistic Historian, the only valid sacrifices. Depending on the nature of the sacrifice, it might be burned completely, shared with the priests, or eaten by the worshiper's family in a sacrificial meal (see Chapter 3 on the nature and function of sacrifice).

PROPHETS

Following David's establishment of a dynasty, the kingship in both Israel and Judah became a hereditary position, passed on from father to son. No longer were kings chosen by God, as Saul and David were. However, another kind of charismatic leader emerged in Israel during the period of the monarchy, a leader called and chosen by God specifically to express God's will and give God's view of the state of the covenant relationship with Israel. These leaders were called the prophets. There were prophets in Israel prior to the monarchy; Moses was certainly a prophet, indeed the greatest of the prophets, and Samuel and Nathan were prophets as well. However, prophets took on a renewed importance in the period of the monarchy. They served as God's representatives in Israel, and their presence was increasingly necessary to provide a counterbalance to the absolute power of the king. For instance, when King David saw a woman who attracted him, what was there to stop him from taking her? What could she do? What could her husband do? After all, he was the king. In Israel, the prophets were there to challenge the power of the king.

The prophets usually had no delegated power within the royal courts of Israel and Judah, but they spoke with a moral authority because their words were believed to be the very words of God. They were not primarily seers who foretold the future, although they did sometimes make such predictions. Prophets are more accurately understood as YHWH's spokespersons. They addressed the events of their societies and acted as emissaries sent by God to the people with a particular message for the present moment in history. Further, like the judges, prophets were charismatic leaders. One needed to be called by God and endowed with special gifts in order to be a prophet.

A crucial focus of the prophets' message was the status of Israel's covenant relationship with God, which determined Israel's political and economic fortunes. Knowing God's "state of mind" allowed the prophets to give advice on political matters, such as whether or not to go to war. If YHWH was looking with favor on Israel, then the prophets assured the Israelites that they could anticipate success. If Israel had violated the covenant, then the prophets foretold that a military defeat would be the result. The prophets also spoke out on social and ethical issues, condemning the social injustice of their own societies, even at great personal cost to themselves. It was the role of the prophets to speak up for the poor, the oppressed, and the powerless in Israelite society. Finally, the prophets also spoke of religious matters. The prophets became the primary proponents of monotheism to people who frequently were attracted to the polytheistic religious beliefs of their cultural neighbors.

The message of the prophets was often a negative, critical one, as they pronounced God's judgment on a sinful nation, group, or individual. Because of this, prophets were often in conflict with the other centers of power in Israel, particularly the king. The political clout of the prophets led some kings to attempt to corrupt the office of prophet. These kings would appoint their own prophets, whose job it was to create the illusion of divine approval for whatever policies they were pursuing. Because of abuses such as these and the fact that some people were simply deluded into believing that God was speaking through them, a distinction had to be made between true prophets and false prophets.

Although it was sometimes difficult for Israelites to tell the difference between true and false prophets until after the fact, there were some hallmarks of a true prophet. One sign of a true prophet was a willingness to stand up to the king. Of course, the prophets did not always disagree with the king, but a prophet who never challenged the king might have been looked upon with suspicion. Some prophets, especially Elijah and Elisha, were said to have the ability to perform miracles, and this would have been a sure sign, as would the ability to predict the future correctly. On the other hand, some people considered it a bad thing that there were prophets on the king's payroll, although not all "court prophets" were false prophets.

The Assyrian Period (Eighth Century B.C.E.)

At various times in the history of the Old Testament, major world powers struggled for dominance of the region of the ancient Near East. Egypt and the two great Mesopotamian powers, Assyria and Babylon, all dominated the region at one time or another, and their power struggles usually involved the land of Israel. In the eighth century B.C.E., Assyria began to assert its dominance in the region. From their capital, Nineveh, on the banks of the Tigris River in what

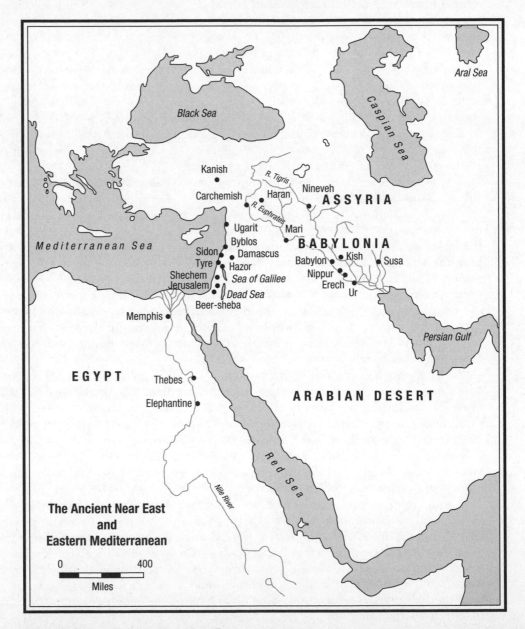

Figure 4–3 Map of the ancient Near East.

is modern-day Iraq, the Assyrians expanded their influence and began to threaten the smaller powers that lay between themselves and Egypt—nations that included Syria, Israel, and Judah. Finally, in 721 B.C.E., the northern kingdom of Israel was conquered by the Assyrians.

The period prior to the conquest was one of unprecedented prosperity for both the northern and southern kingdoms. However, this prosperity brought certain problems with it, and the prophets were quick to identify them. In this time, the cities of the two kingdoms began to take on increasing importance, at the expense of smaller towns and villages. High taxes were imposed on the rural poor to support the lifestyle of urban elite. Previously, under tribal Israel, the difference between the richest and poorest members of the community was relatively small. In the eighth century, however, groups of nobility began to attach themselves to the royal family. These nobles were wealthy rulers and princes who gained and maintained their wealth through their abuse of the poor, especially their rights to ancestral property and to redress in the legal system.

The earliest of the books of the Latter Prophets were written at this time. The Latter Prophets are books that bear the names of the prophets of the eighth to fifth centuries B.C.E. These books consist of various **oracles** (divine pronouncements) by these prophets and biographical stories about these prophets. Most of the prophets (but not all) stood in opposition to the royal administrations under which they lived. They frequently saw their warnings ignored and their admonitions unheeded. Sometimes the kings threw them in jail and threatened to execute them.

Two prophets emerged during the period of prosperity just before the Assyrian conquest and spoke particularly to the northern kingdom regarding the terrible moral illness that threatened to completely overwhelm the nation: the oppression of the poor by the rich. One might imagine how odd such a message would have appeared to Israel's ruling class— telling people who feel secure and complacent that they are in desperate danger. Of course, these prophets were not taken seriously.

The first of these prophets, **Amos** (c. 750 B.C.E.), was not a native of the northern kingdom but rather came up from the south to prophesy in Bethel, the site of one of the royal chapels of the northern king, Jeroboam II. He was commanded by the priests of the temple in Bethel to go back where he came from and prophesy to Judah (Amos 7). But Amos, in the tradition of Israelite prophecy, boldly condemned the social practices of the wealthy in the north, who luxuriated in their wealth and creature comforts and mercilessly oppressed the poor (Amos 6). Amos threatened the northern kingdom with horrible destruction because of its violation of covenant law. In fact, he regarded their mistreatment of the powerless no less a violation of YHWH's laws than if they had worshiped other gods.

The second prophet, **Hosea** (c. 745 B.C.E.), was a northerner who spoke to his own people. He believed that YHWH had commanded him to marry a promiscuous wife, which he did (Hosea 1). His wife Gomer's unfaithfulness helped Hosea portray how God felt about the people's religious unfaithfulness to him. As Gomer treated Hosea, so Israel treated her husband YHWH. Hosea's broken heart paralleled YHWH's pain at Israel's abandonment of God for other gods. Hosea pled with Israel to return to YHWH. First using the image of a marriage relationship, and then the relationship of a parent to a child (Hosea 11), Hosea sought to remind the Israelites of their old memories in an effort to convince them to change their ways.

Both prophets were unsuccessful in truly changing the nature of Israelite society, and in a short twenty-five years, the entire northern kingdom was destroyed by the Assyrians. From the prophets' point of view, this destruction was the judgment of YHWH upon a disobedient nation.

The southern kingdom of Judah, although not conquered by Assyria at this time, was utterly dominated by them both religiously and politically for the next century. However, the Judean people, under the influence of the message of the prophet **Isaiah**, believed that Jerusalem was divinely protected from conquest because of the presence of the Solomonic Temple and the Davidic dynasty—a descendant of David still ruled over Israel.

The Babylonian Period (Seventh to Sixth Centuries B.C.E.)

The final years of the seventh century saw the rise to power of the neo-Babylonian Empire. At first, the Babylonians struggled against the Assyrian Empire, which had been seriously weakened through internal dissension. Although the Egyptian monarch took his troops north to help the Assyrians, the combined efforts of Egypt and Assyria failed to slow the Babylonian juggernaut. Babylon defeated and destroyed Assyrian power, and the pharaoh took his Egyptian army back home in disgrace. The failure of the Assyrians and Egyptians to stop the Babylonians left Judah wide open for conquest.

Jeremiah served as prophet in Jerusalem during this time. As the Babylonians advanced on them, the people felt nervous and flocked to the Temple, chanting over and over, "The Temple of YHWH. The Temple of YHWH. The Temple of YHWH" (Jer 7:4). They believed that the presence of the Temple in Jerusalem would protect them from Babylonian attack. However, Jeremiah threatened them with destruction, telling them that their invocation of the Temple would offer them no help but rather constituted "deceptive words" (Jer 7:26). Jeremiah admonished the people to depend less on their possession of a Davidic monarch and the Solomonic Temple and more on their own adherence to the sacred covenant with YHWH, a covenant that enjoined them to worship YHWH exclusively and to treat their fellow Israelites with justice. Jeremiah also counseled the king to surrender to the Babylonian emperor Nebuchadnezzar. Instead, King Zedekiah tried to flee with his family. The Babylonians apprehended him, murdered his sons in his sight, and then poked out his eyes (2 Kings 25), so that the last sight he saw was that of his dead children. Finally, they destroyed Jerusalem and the Temple, and carried the king and most of the citizens in chains to Babylon.

The Exile (Sixth Century B.C.E.)

The destruction of the Temple and the deportation of many citizens to Babylon—an event known as the **Babylonian Exile**, or simply, the Exile—was an unparalleled disaster for the Jewish people. Thus, the Exile took its place alongside the Exodus from Egypt as one of the defining moments in Israel's history. In fact, the Exile was such a watershed moment that historians and theologians often refer to events and people in Israel's history as being "pre-exilic" or "post-exilic." The Exile came to be understood (through the writings of the prophets and the Deuteronomistic Historian) as the ultimate punishment from God for Israel's failure to uphold the covenant. However, the Exile also represented hope to future generations of Jews, because through that experience Israel renewed its commitment to God and was eventually forgiven and allowed to return to the land. The covenant had not been broken.

The period in which the Judeans were in captivity in Babylon was the first time that they were compelled to maintain their religious identity while separated from the land. The northern kingdom, taken captive by the Assyrians, had not maintained its identity. Those who were deported are no longer known to history, earning them the title of the Lost Tribes of Israel. The newcomers whom the Assyrians settled in their place came to be known as **Samaritans**, from the capital city of Samaria, rather than Israelites, though they would later claim to have maintained older and more authentic Jewish practices than their Judean counterparts. Still, at least according to outside observers, the northern kingdom's population appeared to have turned away from the worship of YHWH and blended in with the religion and culture of their captors.

The Judeans who were exiled in Babylon fared better. The prophets taken into captivity with the other citizens of Judah, most notably, **Ezekiel**, told the people that God had not failed them, when they were defeated by the Babylonians. Rather, YHWH was using the Babylonians to punish them because of their unfaithfulness to the covenant. They remained in Babylon, hopeful that their renewed dedication to the exclusive worship of YHWH and loyalty to the covenant would persuade YHWH to return them to the land of promise. **Second Isaiah** (not the actual prophet Isaiah, but a later author of Isa 40–55), speaking to the Babylonian exiles, encouraged them with the message that YHWH was no longer angry with them and would soon bring them back to Israel in a saving event as miraculous as the Exodus. It was during this period that the Israelites began to place more emphasis on codifying the Law of Moses in written form rather than relying on oral traditions.

The Persian Period (Sixth to Fifth Centuries B.C.E.)

The Babylonian empire was short-lived, crumbling in the late sixth century B.C.E. The Persians (based in what is modern-day Iran) moved in to pick up the pieces. The Persian emperor Cyrus encouraged the various conquered peoples to return to the land of their birth and restore worship of their local gods. The biblical writers attribute Cyrus' edicts to the Spirit of Yahweh, and Second Isaiah actually calls Cyrus God's "anointed" (*messiah*) (Isa 45:1). Perhaps Cyrus felt that getting on the good side of all the local gods would ensure the length and stability of his own reign. In any case, the Judeans who were taken captive by Babylon were given permission to return to Palestine.

Most Judeans, who had been living in Babylonian colonies for upwards of forty years, saw no reason to return. However, a small group of Judean exiles did return, many under the leadership of Ezra and Nehemiah. The returning exiles tried to establish a new society but could maintain only a small area around the rebuilt Jerusalem. The account of this rebuilding effort is found primarily in the biblical books of Ezra and Nehemiah. The returnees rebuilt the walls of the city and after a while rebuilt the Temple. They were especially concerned with ridding the community of foreign elements and establishing religious practice in stricter conformity to their understanding of the covenant, which was laid out in the written scriptures that they had brought back with them from Babylon.

Although those who returned from the Exile tried to reestablish the close connection between the land of Israel and the religion practiced by its inhabitants, there were now so many Israelites settled in various places around the eastern Mediterranean that the nation and the religion could no longer be completely identified. New religious institutions, interpretations of tradition, and scriptures were developed in order to meet the needs of the new situation. These new religious phenomena, combined with ancient traditions, produced a new era in the Israelite faith, called Second Temple Judaism (so called because of the importance of the new, "second" Temple in its functioning). Although the Jews never returned to the splendor and autonomy they enjoyed during the monarchic period, the institutions (Temple, prophecy, monarchy) that had developed during this period were of crucial importance in the subsequent history of Judaism.

Key Terms

Joshua	Jerusalem	Hosea
Deuteronomistic History	Solomon	Isaiah
Deuteronomistic Historian	omniscient	Jeremiah
Ark of the Covenant	Temple	Babylonian Exile
judge (*shofet*)	Israel	Samaritans
Samuel	Judah	Ezekiel
Saul	oracles	Second Isaiah
David	Amos	

Questions for Reading

1. To whom or to what does the term *Deuteronomistic Historian* refer? Describe the Deuteronomistic Historian's message.

2. Explain how tribal Israel was organized. What was the role of the judge (*shofet*)?

3. Describe the circumstances that led to the development of a monarchy in Israel. How would you assess the reigns of Saul, David, and Solomon? Why?

4. What is the nature of the relationship between prophet and king in the history of Israel's monarchy?

5. Describe the message of the prophets Amos and Hosea. What were the social conditions in Israel during their time of ministry?

6. Describe the message of the prophet Jeremiah. What was the historical situation of Judah at the time he proclaimed God's word? Why did Jeremiah attack their faith in the Temple?

7. Describe the impact of the Babylonian Exile and, later, the return from the Exile on the people of Judah and those who came to be known as Jews.

Works Consulted/Recommended Reading

Brown, Raymond E., Joseph A. Fitzmyer, and Roland E. Murphy, eds. *The New Jerome Biblical Commentary.* Upper Saddle River, NJ: Prentice Hall, 1990.

Brueggemann, Walter. *An Introduction to the Old Testament: The Canon and Christian Imagination.* Louisville, KY: Westminster John Knox, 2003.

Ceresko, Anthony R. *Introduction to the Old Testament: A Liberation Perspective.* Maryknoll, NY: Orbis Books, 2001.

Collins, John J. *Introduction to the Hebrew Bible.* Minneapolis, MN: Fortress, 2004.

Dempsey, Carol. *The Prophets: A Liberation-Critical Reading.* Minneapolis, MN: Fortress, 2000.

Emmerson, Grace. *Prophets and Poets: A Companion to the Prophetic Books of the Old Testament.* Nashville, TN: Abingdon, 1997.

Flanders, Henry Jackson, Jr., Robert Wilson Crapps, and David Anthony Smith. *People of the Covenant. An Introduction to the Hebrew Bible.* New York: Oxford University, 1996.

Freedman, David N. *Anchor Bible Dictionary,* 6 vols. New York: Doubleday, 1992.

Hoppe, Leslie. *Priests, Prophets, and Sages. Catholic Perspectives on the Old Testament.* Cincinnati, OH: St. Anthony Messenger Press, 2006.

McCarter, P. K. *1 Samuel.* New York: Doubleday, 1984.

McKenzie, Steven L. "Deuteronomic History." In Freedman, *Anchor Bible Dictionary,* Vol. 2. New York: Doubleday, 1992.

Metzger, Bruce, and Roland Murphy, eds. *The New Oxford Annotated Bible with Apocrypha, New Revised Standard Version.* New York: Oxford University, 1991.

Polzin, Robert M. *Moses and the Deuteronomist.* San Francisco: Harper & Row, 1980.

Chapter

SECOND TEMPLE JUDAISM

TIMELINE

332 B.C.E.	Alexander the Great conquers the Near East and begins the process of Hellenization.
167 B.C.E.	The Maccabeans revolt against the Seleucid king Antiochus IV.
164 B.C.E.	Rededication of the Temple in Jerusalem, commemorated in the festival of Hanukkah.
c. 145 (?) B.C.E.	Beginnings of the Qumran Community.
63 B.C.E.	The Romans conquer Palestine.

After the Persians under Cyrus defeated the Babylonians, the Jews who were exiled to Babylon were allowed to return to Palestine (as the biblical land of Israel would come to be called under Roman occupation). Some Jews remained in Babylon, however. Thus, a distinction is made between Jews who lived in Palestine and Jews who lived outside of Palestine in the **Diaspora** (meaning "dispersion" and referring to those Jews who were "dispersed" through historical circumstances outside the traditional Jewish homeland). The religion of these Palestinian Jews and Diaspora Jews developed in somewhat different ways. For example, Diaspora Judaism centered more on the Torah and the **synagogue** than on the Temple and its sacrifices. Synagogues were buildings where Jews gathered to read and discuss their written scriptures. The increasing importance of following the Law in one's daily life gradually led to the establishment of a synagogue in every town or city with a significant Jewish population. Although being far from the Temple probably forced Diaspora Jews to place more stress on the Torah and the synagogue, the development of the synagogue changed Judaism both inside and outside of Palestine.

MAJOR ELEMENTS OF JEWISH FAITH IN THE SECOND TEMPLE PERIOD

Those Jews who did return to Palestine after the Babylonian Exile (c. 586 B.C.E.) soon set about rebuilding the Temple in Jerusalem, which had been destroyed around 586 B.C.E. This version of the Temple is distinguished from Solomon's Temple and is called the **Second Temple**. Although Judaism in Palestine after the Exile continued to be practiced in many ways that are similar to the preexilic period, there are distinctive elements as well, and so the Judaism of this period, from 520 B.C.E. to 70 C.E., is referred to as *Second Temple Judaism*. Temple sacrifice continued to be a major element of this religion, but in the Second Temple period obedience to the written Law (or Torah) took on increased importance, and one begins to see traces of Jewish belief in a figure called the **messiah**, meaning "anointed one." We will begin this chapter with a closer look at the Temple, the Torah, and the messiah.

Temple

The major way of relating to God in the Jewish religion was through sacrifice. In fact, sacrifice was an important part of almost every ancient religion. Some of these religions offered sacrifices of animals and grain because they felt that they needed to "feed" their hungry gods. It was considered the priest's job to provide this service to the gods to appease them and prevent disaster from befalling the people. However, there is little evidence that the Jews understood their sacrifice as food for YHWH.

The Hebrew Bible gives several reasons for sacrifice. Some sacrifices were understood as gifts to YHWH, in thanksgiving for what he had provided, or as part of a petition for further divine help. Thus, farmers or shepherds would give a portion of their crops and livestock back to God in recognition of the fact that God had given them all that they had. A person who desired some favor from God could also offer a sacrifice. Another purpose of sacrifice was purification or atonement. A person who had sinned against God or their neighbor could atone for their sin through a sacrifice.

The sacrifices that were done by Jews involved grain, incense, and animals. These sacrifices were sometimes burned on an altar. In the case of animal sacrifices, more often the animal would be killed and the blood would be poured out on the foot of the altar. This was particularly the case in sacrifices offered to atone for sins, since the blood was thought to "wash away" the defilement caused by the sin.

There were many elaborate rules for performing sacrifices. These can be reduced to four essential requirements. First, sacrifices could not be done by just anybody. Sacrifices had to be done by the right people, namely the **priests**. The Jews believed that God had set aside a portion of the people of Israel to specialize in making proper sacrifices. Thus, the primary responsibility of the priesthood in Judaism did not involve conducting weekly worship services, but making sacrifices. The priesthood in Judaism was hereditary, traced through the male line. One could not choose to become a priest; one could only be born into the priesthood. There was one priest who exercised leadership over the other priests and was, in fact, the religious leader of the Israelite nation as a whole—the high priest.

Second, sacrifices had to be done at the right time. Although it was true that sacrifices went on almost continually in the Temple, certain times and seasons required particular sacrifices. For example, special sacrifices were always offered on the Sabbath, since this was a day set aside for God. In addition, there were three pilgrimage festivals during the year in which Jewish men were supposed to journey to Jerusalem to make sacrifices. One of these festivals was **Passover**, which commemorated God's rescue of the Israelites from slavery in Egypt, when the angel of death "passed over" the homes of the Israelites that had been marked with lamb's blood and killed the firstborn sons of the Egyptians. At Passover (which corresponded to the spring barley harvest) the people of Israel would sacrifice a lamb in commemoration of this event. The other pilgrimage festivals were **Pentecost** (which corresponded with the spring wheat harvest) and Booths (which corresponded with the autumn olive and fruit harvest). Another day set aside for sacrifice, but not requiring the attendance of all male Jews, was the Day of Atonement, or **Yom Kippur**. On this day each year, the high priest would offer a sacrifice for the sins of the nation as a whole.

Third, sacrifices had to be done with the correct offering. There were certain animals that one could sacrifice (bulls, lambs, pigeons, and turtledoves—animals that were considered "clean") and other animals that one could not sacrifice (pigs, snakes—animals that were considered "unclean"). Moreover, one could not sacrifice just any bull or lamb, but only the firstborn and only an unblemished animal. The firstborn were already thought to belong to God and whatever was offered had to be perfect in every respect.

Finally, sacrifices had to be done at the right place. In Israel's early history, there were a number of altars and shrines at which sacrifices were done. After the building of Solomon's Temple in Jerusalem, however, a king named Josiah eventually centralized all sacrifice in this one location. After that Temple was destroyed, the Jews set about the long, gradual process of rebuilding. At first, the Second Temple was a modest building, not approaching the magnificent structure erected by Solomon. However, in the first century B.C.E., a Jewish king named Herod the Great began a major renovation of the Temple, which (when completed around 66 C.E.) reestablished the Temple in Jerusalem as one of the greatest structures in the ancient world.

The site of the Temple was considered the most sacred ground in the world to Jews. It was here that the divine realm and the human realm intersected. The innermost part of the Temple contained the **Holy of Holies**, where the Ark of the Covenant had been kept and God's presence dwelled. No one ever entered the Holy of Holies except once each year,

Figure 5–1 Model of the Jerusalem Temple (after the renovations of Herod the Great). The model is located at the Holyland Motel in Jerusalem. Photo by Catherine Cory.

when the high priest would enter to offer a sacrifice on the Day of Atonement. On the outside of the Temple was a court where Israel could assemble. The space between the outer court and the Holy of Holies housed the altar where all other sacrifices were conducted. This was a place of intersection between God and Israel, where the priests gave God his animal sacrifices, grain, and incense.

Torah

When Israel was exiled to Babylon and the Temple was destroyed (586 B.C.E.), the Jewish leaders struggled to explain to themselves why Yahweh had allowed these terrible disasters to occur. Their explanation, given to them by God through the prophets, was that they had sinned gravely and thus violated the terms of the covenant. Israel had always believed that God made certain ethical and ritual demands on them as part of the covenant, and the reason for the Exile was their failure to live up to those demands. The answer to the problems of the Jewish people, then, was obvious: a renewed commitment to the terms of the covenant. The Jews in exile rededicated themselves to obedience to God's commands. Part of this effort involved a new emphasis on putting God's laws in writing.

This emphasis continued after the Exile was over. It was during the beginning of the Second Temple period, when the Jews were allowed to return to Palestine and to restore Jerusalem and the Temple, that the last of the four sources that make up the Pentateuch were written. The Priestly Writer and the Deuteronomist are believed to have written in the sixth century B.C.E. Sometime thereafter these sources were combined with the other two documents (the writings of the Yahwist and the Elohist) to form the five scrolls of the Law, what Christians now call the first five books of the Old Testament.

Thus, it is during the Second Temple period that Israel truly established its scriptures, or sacred books. At first these consisted only of the five scrolls of the Law, or the Pentateuch. The Jewish word for "law" is *Torah*, and this word can refer to these five books alone. Eventually, some other books were accepted, at least by some Jews, as sacred scripture as well, and thus the word *Torah* can also refer in a more general sense to all of the books accepted as scripture by Israel. Gradually, the books of the Prophets were included as a second major "section" of the Jewish scriptures, although subordinate in importance to the Law. A third major section, called the Writings, was the last to be written and included in the Jewish canon. This section includes books of prayers and wisdom, teachings such as Psalms and Proverbs, and stories with theological themes such as the book of Job.

For the most part, the writing and editing of all these books took place over very long periods of time, and their inclusion into the Jewish scriptures was a gradual process that inspired a considerable amount of disagreement among the Jews. However, in its final form the Jewish canon consisted of three parts: Law, Prophets, and Writings. This threefold division is often referred to today by the acronym *Tanakh*, which combines the first letters of the Hebrew words for "Law" (*Torah*), "Prophets" (*Nevi'im*), and "Writings" (*Khetuvim*).

Regardless of whether the scriptures were constituted at one historical moment or among one or another Jewish group, all Jews felt themselves to be bound by God's demands as they are expressed in the Torah. Thus, obedience to the Torah took its place alongside Temple sacrifice as the main ways that Jews expressed themselves religiously. In order to be a Jew one needed to be circumcised (if you were male), sacrifice in the Temple at the prescribed times, and follow the Torah in one's daily life (which included following both the ethical guidelines and the special Jewish dietary restrictions called "keeping **kosher**").

Messiah

The Jews believed that they had a covenant relationship with God whereby if they followed the Torah and performed their sacrifices, God would fulfill certain promises to them. God had promised Abraham that his descendants would be numerous, that they would possess the land of Canaan (or Palestine), and that they would form a great nation. For most of their history, it appears that these promises did not come true for the Jews. There is only one period in Israelite history in which the covenant appeared to be working as it really should: the kingdom of David. During David's rule, the Israelites enjoyed unparalleled military success, economic prosperity, and religious unity. However, after David, the kingdom was eventually split in two, and following the split the Jews were conquered successively by the Assyrians, the Babylonians, the Persians, the Greeks, and, finally, the Romans. The Jews suffered terribly under the rule of these foreign powers.

The Jewish explanation for these disasters was always the same. They believed that they must have sinned against the Lord and broken the covenant, which caused God to withdraw

Figure 5–2 Jews gather around the Torah scroll at the Western
Wall of Herod's Temple.

his protection and thus expose the Jews to oppression by foreign powers. The Jews always
blamed themselves, not God, for breakdowns in the proper functioning of the covenant. In
this way of thinking, the solution was equally clear. The way to regain God's favor and
release themselves from bondage to their enemies was to repent of their sins and begin
adhering more precisely to the terms of the covenant.

During these times of oppression the Jewish prophets began to predict that God would
send someone to rescue the Jews from their affliction, just as God had sent Moses to deliver
them from slavery in Egypt, the judges to rescue them from the Philistines, and the prophets
themselves to deliver God's messages. The most common and recent of these manifestations
of God's will were the prophets, but there seems to have been a decline in prophecy starting
in the fourth century B.C.E. Thus, Israel began to hope for a different sort of divine agent. The
figure around whom the Jewish hopes coalesced came to be called the messiah. The word
messiah means "anointed one." The great leaders of Israel's past succeeded, they believed,
because they had been *chosen* by God, and God's election of them was symbolized by the
process of anointing with oil. Thus, by using the term *messiah* the Jews simply expressed their
belief that God would raise up a chosen leader from among the people to save them.

Exactly how God was going to intervene in history to rescue the Jews was a matter of
some disagreement, however. Some believed in a political sort of messiah. They interpreted

2 Samuel 7 to mean that God promised to raise up a descendant of David and reestablish him on the throne of Israel so that David's dynasty would last forever (2 Sam 7:13). God would be like a father to him and he would be like a son to God (2 Sam 7:14). Some of the Psalms of the Hebrew Bible carry similar themes. In Psalm 89, for example, the psalmist appears to remind God of his promise to David and his descendants:

> You said, "I have made a covenant with my chosen one,
>   I have sworn to my servant David:
> 'I will establish your descendants forever,
>   and build your throne for all generations.'" (Psalm 89:3–4; see also Psalm 132:11–12)

Similarly, Psalm 2 describes God as having said about his "anointed," that is, the Davidic monarchy, "You are my son; today I have begotten you" (Psalm 2:7). The psalmist also suggests that the descendants of this dynasty will rule over all the earth not simply over Israel (Psalm 2:8–9). Biblical scholars think that this promise and the themes associated with it became the foundation for Jewish belief in a future messiah who would restore David's dynasty and who would be known (metaphorically) as a son of God.

Other Jews anticipated an **apocalyptic** sort of messiah. The word *apocalyptic* comes from a Greek word meaning "to reveal" or "to uncover," referring to revelations of the heavenly realms and the destiny of this world. Various Jewish apocalyptic groups believed that God would soon bring an end to this evil world, destroying the wicked and establishing a new Paradise for the righteous. Some thought that the messiah would bring all this about. The book of Daniel offers some support for the idea that God would send a heavenly emissary to purge the world of evildoers and rescue the righteous in a battle of cosmic proportions.

> As I watched in the night visions
>   I saw one like a son of man coming with the clouds of heaven
> And he came to the Ancient One and was presented before him.
>   To him was given dominion and glory and kingship,
> that all peoples, nations, and languages should serve him.
>   His dominion is an everlasting dominion that shall not pass away, and his kingship is one that
> shall never be destroyed. (Daniel 7:13–14)

Another Jewish religious text called the Similitudes of Enoch (1 Enoch 37–71) describes a similar scene in which the Righteous One, who is also called the Elect One and the Messiah, will judge the wicked and rescue God's holy ones:

> When the secrets of the Righteous One are revealed,
>   He shall judge the sinners;
> And the wicked ones will be driven from the presence of the righteous and the elect,
>   And from that time, those who possess the earth will neither be rulers nor princes,
> They shall not be able to behold the faces of the holy ones,
>   For the light of the Lord of the Spirits has shined
> Upon the face of the holy, the righteous, and the elect. (1 Enoch 38.3–4; cited in
>   Charlesworth 1983, 30.)

This text, in particular, makes it clear that Jews who awaited an apocalyptic messiah associated his appearance with the end-time punishment of the wicked and rescue of the righteous.

Some Jewish groups expected an end-time messiah who would serve as a priest in God's heavenly temple and have kingly authority. For example, the Jewish religious writing called the Testament of Levi contains this description:

> And then the Lord will raise up a new priest
> to whom all the words of the Lord will be revealed.
> He shall effect the judgment of truth over the earth for many days.
> And his star shall rise in heaven like a king;
> kindling the light of knowledge as day is illuminated by the sun.
> And he shall be extolled by the whole inhabited world. (Test. Levi 18.2–3; Charlesworth 1983, 1:794).

There was at least one Jewish group that expected more than one messiah. For example, scholars of the **Dead Sea Scrolls**, the collection of Jewish religious writings and biblical texts which were preserved at Qumran and discovered only in the past century (1947–1960), think that this Jewish community was waiting for two messiahs—a priest and a king—and an end-time prophet (see the following section titled "Essenes"). These three figures are mentioned in a section of the *Rule of the Community* where community members are commanded to observe carefully all of the laws of Torah:

> They shall deviate from none of the teachings of the Law, whereby they would walk in their willful heart completely. They shall govern themselves using the original precepts by which the men of the *Yahad* began to be instructed, doing so until there come the Prophet and the Messiahs of Aaron and Israel (1 QS 9.9–11; Wise, Abegg, and Cook 1996, 139).

The term *Yahad* refers to the Qumran community. The Messiah of Aaron is a priestly figure (recalling Aaron, the brother of Moses), and the Messiah of Israel is a kingly figure.

There are other passages in the Torah that seem to speak of yet another kind of messiah, although the meaning of these passages is highly controversial. They are the Servant Songs of the Book of Isaiah (Isa 42:1–4; 49:1–6; 50:4–9; 52:13–53:12). The most famous is the fourth Servant Song (Isa 52:13–53:12), which speaks of a **Suffering Servant**, one who takes the sins of other people onto himself and wins forgiveness for them through his suffering. The author of the fourth Servant Song does not reveal the Servant's identity, but most biblical scholars think that the Servant is a metaphor for Israel or at least for a group within Israel that was loyal to God's covenant. He is not being punished for his sin. Rather, he suffers for the sins of others and even dies (Isa 53:8). The kings of the world and all its peoples are then given an opportunity to turn toward God when they observe how much the Servant suffered and how God exalted him for accepting God's will. Christians, of course, pointed to this text to support their belief in Jesus as the suffering messiah. However, nowhere in this text is the servant described as a king or as God's anointed.

In spite of all these apparent references to the messiah in the Hebrew scriptures and other Jewish religious writings, it must be noted that Christians have a tendency to overemphasize the importance of a personal messiah in the Jewish faith, when in fact the level of belief in the messiah varied widely from one Jewish group to another. Some Jews were waiting for the restoration of God's reign on earth, others did not believe in a messiah or messianic age at all, while others may have been familiar with one or more of these messianic expectations but were mostly unaffected by them in their daily lives. A useful comparison might be contemporary Christians who have heard about Christianity's teaching about the return of Christ in the end time. Some eagerly await the event as something that will happen very soon, but many Christians go about the activities of their lives without giving it much thought at all.

JUDAISM IN THE HELLENISTIC AGE

In 336 B.C.E., a young Greek named Alexander took over the throne of Macedonia (in modern Greece) and immediately set about an ambitious program of conquest. Ten years later, Alexander the Great had conquered a substantial part of the known world, including Asia Minor, Syria, Israel, Egypt, and Persia. Alexander's armies reached India before finally refusing to follow him any further. Alexander's plans for the people that he conquered included what was called **Hellenization**. The Greeks' word for their own country is *Hellas*, and to *Hellenize* meant to spread Greek culture or to attempt to turn people into "Greeks." Alexander saw Greek culture as superior to that of other peoples, and his goal was to impose Greek culture on his entire empire, such that people would speak Greek, dress like the Greeks, attend Greek schools, read Greek literature, and worship the Greek gods.

This program of Hellenization created a dilemma for the Jews. On the one hand, some Jews were enthusiastic about the Greek culture and saw this as a way to "blend into" the new empire and avoid further suffering. On the other hand, many Jews were proud of their culture and religion and felt that adopting Greek ways would force them to abandon the true path of Judaism, which would bring God's wrath down upon them even more harshly.

Alexander did not force people to adopt Greek culture, however, and so it was possible for these two groups of Jews to co-exist for a time under Greek rule. This changed in 175 B.C.E., when a new king named Antiochus IV ascended to power and began an effort to force the Jews to become Hellenized. Antiochus prohibited the observance of the Torah and ordered that sacrifices in the Temple be made to the Greek god Zeus instead of to YHWH. These actions enraged the Jews, and, under the leadership of a family called the **Maccabees**, they revolted against Antiochus IV. The Maccabean Revolt began in 167 B.C.E., and by 164 B.C.E. the Jews had retaken Jerusalem and rededicated the Temple to YHWH. Eventually, the Maccabees were able to establish an independent Jewish state once again. The holiday that celebrates the consecration of the Temple following this victory is called **Hanukkah**, or the Festival of Lights. Although many Jews celebrated the stunning victory of the Maccabees over the powerful Greeks, some Jews did not think that the Maccabees should be controlling the Temple and the Jewish state, and they went off into the desert to await God's wrath. They were convinced that the world had become so corrupt that God would surely bring an end to it. This is an example of apocalypticism, a worldview that would become more and more popular in Judaism in the next few centuries.

JUDAISM IN NEW TESTAMENT TIMES

By the middle of the first century B.C.E., the Jews had been conquered again, this time by the Romans. The Jews would continue under Roman domination for several centuries. Judaism at the turn of the millennium was a relatively diverse phenomenon. There were a number of different Jewish groups that had rather different beliefs. Although all Jews agreed on the basic points of Judaism—for example that the way to please God was through Temple sacrifice and obedience to the Torah—different groups of Jews during the first century disagreed on points of emphasis involving Temple, Torah, and Messiah.

Sadducees

Although the Sadducees are mentioned in several historical documents of the Second Temple period, in fact we do not know much about them. However, there is one thing that we know for certain. The **Sadducees** were part of the ruling classes: the priests, the landed nobility, and the major property owners. Because of the Roman policy of allowing local aristocrats to rule their own regions of the empire, the Sadducees occupied some of the major roles of leadership in Judea and Jerusalem, including management of the Temple. Thus, they were both the religious and political leaders of Judaism. The Sadducees also dominated the highest Jewish council in Jerusalem, which was known as the **Sanhedrin**. According to the gospels, Jesus was put on trial before this body.

As members of the ruling aristocracy, the Sadducees were conservative in outlook. They wanted to preserve their power and to maintain the status quo, so they tried as hard as they could to avoid change or reform. To preserve their property and influence, the Sadducees pursued close and cordial ties with the Romans. By contrast, other Jews resented the presence of the Romans in their homeland and actively sought to overthrow the Romans through violent revolution. The Sadducees negotiated certain special privileges for the Jewish people, such as exemption from making sacrifices to the emperor as a god or from military service in the Roman legions, privileges that enabled them (in the Sadducees' view) to continue practicing authentic Judaism.

Temple.   For the Sadducees, Temple sacrifice was the most important aspect of Judaism. This is not surprising, given that the Temple was the source of both wealth and power for the priests who ran it. However, the Sadducees did not support the Temple for purely selfish reasons. All Jews believed that sacrifice was a primary means of relating to God. The Sadducees simply emphasized Temple sacrifice more than any other group. This, too, is not surprising, when we consider that the Sadducees had close associations with the chief priests of the Jerusalem Temple and the captain of the Temple guard (see Acts 4:1; 5:17).

Torah.   The Torah was essential to all Jewish groups, and the Sadducees were no exception. It was in the Torah, after all, that God's demands for sacrifices were set forth. However, in contrast with the Pharisees (see the following section), the Sadducees did not accept as authoritative the collections of traditional (oral) interpretations and legal rulings that had evolved over decades and centuries of studying the Torah. Only the written traditions of the Law, that is, the first five books of the Hebrew Bible, were considered to be authoritative as scripture. The Law was most important to them since it is in the Law that the rules for sacrifice are laid out. They did not accept the Prophets or the Writings as part of the canon. Second, they interpreted the Law very conservatively and were opposed to newer interpretations that appeared to deviate from the literal sense of the Law. One could not add anything to what was in the written text. For this reason the Sadducees did not accept some of the more "recent" ideas in Judaism, such as the notion that the soul survives the body after death, resurrection of the dead and judgment after death, and the existence of angels and spirits.

Messiah.   There is no evidence that the Sadducees believed in a messiah. Although there are no clear reasons for this, it is true that belief in a messiah tends to be more popular among the disenfranchised lower classes than among the ruling upper classes.

Pharisees

The **Pharisees** were also religious leaders, but they were not priests. Rather, they were scholars of the Torah, experts on the written Law and its interpretation. Their practice was rooted not in the Temple but in the synagogue, where the teachers (or rabbis) read from the Torah and presided over subsequent arguments about its meaning and application to present problems and situations. The Pharisees believed strongly that the Torah affected the entirety of human existence, and they sought to develop rules for every area of human life based on the Torah.

Because of their emphasis on behaving in strict accordance with the rules of the Torah, the Pharisees were known for pious living (alms, tithing, prayer, and fasting). The Pharisees also believed that the rules for ritual purity that operated in the Temple should be applied to everyday existence, and so they tried to avoid contact with anything that would make them "unclean." This is why Pharisees did not eat with or associate with tax collectors, prostitutes, or sinners. Some biblical scholars think that the word *Pharisees* (which means "separated ones") derives from the desire of this group not to be contaminated by the uncleanness of others.

Temple.   The Pharisees believed in Temple sacrifice, since it is prescribed in the Torah, which they revered. Likewise, they would have participated in the pilgrimage feasts that brought large crowds to Jerusalem at various times of the year. However, by all estimates, the Pharisees were small in number. Being well educated, they probably were among the social elite, but they did not have the political connections that the Sadducees had. As a consequence, they had little influence on the operations of the Temple or relations with Israel's Roman occupiers.

Torah.   By training and occupation, the Pharisees were interpreters of the Torah, so obviously it was very important to them. They apparently accepted all three parts of the Hebrew Bible, including the Writings, which was still not universally accepted as sacred scripture in the first century C.E. Compared to the Sadducees, the Pharisees were more progressive in their theology, accepting less traditional teachings on a variety of topics, such as reincarnation, immortality of the soul, resurrection of the dead, and the role of fate in people's lives.

The Pharisees were strict interpreters of the Law, but they also tried to apply the Torah to all aspects of daily life. Occasionally, in their studies, they would discover apparently contradictory regulations, or they would encounter laws whose application was ambiguous. Sometimes they would even come across a situation or problem for which there was no answer in the written Torah. The experts among the Pharisees (called *rabbis*, from the Hebrew word meaning "teacher") would attempt to determine how the Law should be interpreted in these particular cases or what regulations should be added to the Law to ensure that the Torah was properly observed. The teachings of the great rabbis on such matters were circulated in oral form from one community to another and from one generation to another. Eventually this oral Torah acquired much the same status as the written Torah, and after some centuries the teachings of the great rabbis were written down. The Mishnah and the Talmud, which are still read, studied, and followed by Jews today, are examples of the practice of preserving the teachings of the great rabbis.

Messiah.   The evidence suggests that the Pharisees believed in a messiah and that the kind of messiah they were expecting was a royal messiah. Some passages in the Torah suggest that God will send a leader like King David to rescue the Jewish people. This leader would unite the Jewish people, lead them to victory over their oppressors, establish Israel as an independent nation, and assume the role of the nation's king. For the Pharisees, and indeed for most Jews who awaited a messiah, the common expectation was of a military/political messiah.

Essenes

The **Essenes** are nowhere mentioned in the New Testament, but biblical scholars know of them from other sources like the first-century Jewish historian Flavius Josephus and from archeological evidence. Apparently there were two kinds of Essenes. The monastic community at Qumran near the Dead Sea is the one with which most people are familiar, because of the Dead Sea Scrolls. This community was thought to have consisted of Jewish males who shared all property in common, took vows of celibacy, and lived an ascetic lifestyle of fasting and meditation. Smaller groups of Essenes lived outside of the Qumran community in the cities and villages of Palestine. According to Josephus, they allowed marriage, but only for the purpose of having children. They owned their own property, but they were also obligated to provide hospitality to fellow Essenes traveling through their village, so perhaps, in some ways, they were like a commune. Both groups, but especially the monastic community, were concerned about ritual purity and strict observance of community rules.

No one knows exactly how the Essenes originated, but they are usually traced back to the Hasideans, a group of pious Jews who supported the Maccabean Revolt in 166 B.C.E. and opposed Jonathan's ascent to the position of High Priest in Jerusalem (152 B.C.E.). Their leader was called the Teacher of Righteousness. Some Qumran scholars think that he had been a priest of the Jerusalem Temple and that he established this community as a protest movement after being ousted from his position in the Temple. The Essenes were highly apocalyptic in their thinking. People who hold apocalyptic views believe that the end time is about to be revealed and that it will include a cataclysmic destruction of the present world order and the triumph of God's holy ones. After the Jewish War and the destruction of the Jerusalem Temple, the Essenes disappeared from history without a trace.

Temple.   The Temple was crucially important to the Essenes, but they did not attend its pilgrimage feasts or participate in its sacrifices. Apparently they thought that the Temple and its leadership were corrupt and, as a consequence, that the sacrifices currently being done in Jerusalem were illegitimate and not acceptable to God. Therefore, they developed their own strict purity regulations and religious rituals, which they performed in the wilderness at Qumran as a protest against the activities of the Jerusalem Temple. Some of these regulations like the *Manual of Discipline* have been preserved among the Dead Sea Scrolls.

Torah.   Included among the Dead Sea Scrolls are fragments of every book of the Bible except the book of Esther. Therefore, scholars are quite certain that the Essenes accepted all three parts of the Hebrew Bible (Law, Prophets, and Writings) as scripture. They were strict interpreters of the scriptures, adhering to the demands of the Torah as thoroughly as possible in their daily lives. They believed that in order to survive the coming apocalypse, they needed to be as pure and holy as possible. This is why they followed the Law so strictly and perhaps also why they withdrew into the desert. Being removed from normal society, they would be less likely to fall into temptation or come into contact with people and things that would make them ritually unclean.

Messiah.   Because of their highly apocalyptic worldview and their perception that the Jerusalem Temple was corrupt, the Essenes had developed some unique views about the coming of the messiah. Essentially, the Essenes believed in two messiahs. The first was a royal messiah who would lead the children of light into battle with the children of darkness and then establish himself as king after the forces of good had vanquished the forces of evil. The second was a priestly messiah who would cleanse the Temple of the illegitimate priests, reestablish the Essenes as the correct priests, and install himself as the new high priest.

Scribes

The word *scribe* denotes an occupation based upon the knowledge of reading and writing. Since most people could not read or write, they relied on the **scribes** to do these things for them. Scribes performed functions that made use of their literacy, such as writing out contracts for people, advising rulers, keeping official records, and taking care of correspondence. Scribes are often associated with the Jewish law, and it is clear that scribes often served as copyists of the Jewish legal traditions; some scribes were legal experts. Scribes did not constitute a coherent, organized group with a consistent point of view, and so were not a group like the Essenes, Pharisees, or Sadducees. However, there were scribes within most of these Jewish groups. Pharisees who interpreted the Torah, for example, must have been scribes.

"People of the Land"

It should be noted that the majority of Jews did not belong to any religious "party" such as the Pharisees, Sadducees, or Essenes. Most members of these groups belonged to the upper classes, comprising perhaps 10 percent of the population and possibly as few as 3 to 5 percent. The remaining 90 to 95 percent were called **People of the Land**, meaning "commoners" or "people of the countryside." Often the term was used in a derogatory manner to refer to the uneducated lower classes. The vast majority of the People of the Land were peasant farmers, though a small number were artisans, while others belonged to the unclean class (those who performed distasteful tasks, such as mining and tanning) and the "expendable" class (the homeless of Jewish society, who survived through begging or stealing).

These people usually did not have the time or the means to concern themselves with the specifics of the interpretation of the Torah, the composition of the priesthood, or the operations of the Temple. Very little is known about them except that the elite among the Jewish people often avoided them or treated them with disdain because they could not or would not adhere to the "rules" of Judaism as strictly as these groups felt they should. A notable exception to this elitism is the Jesus Movement, which was known for welcoming all sorts of "undesirable" people into its ranks. It should be noted, however, that this kind of class discrimination was not unique to Jewish people. Indeed, it was found throughout the first-century Mediterranean world.

The Jesus Movement

Although much more will be said about the development of Christianity in the next chapters, it is important to realize that the first followers of Jesus can easily be understood as members of another group within Judaism, not unlike the Sadducees, Pharisees, and Essenes. In its early decades, Christianity was not a religion separate from Judaism. Early "Christians" (they were not actually called by this name until a few decades after the death of Jesus) still considered themselves Jews, and they continued to observe the religious practices of Judaism—sacrificing in the Temple, obeying the rules of the Torah, being circumcised, and keeping kosher. Christians did have some distinctive attitudes, however, about the Temple, the Torah, and especially the messiah.

Temple.   There is evidence in the gospels to suggest that (like the Essenes) Jesus and his followers were upset about how the Temple was being run. For example, some biblical scholars think that the gospel scene in which Jesus overturns the moneychangers' tables in the Temple and drives out those who are selling animals for sacrifice (Mark 11:15–19 and parallels) indicates that early Christians believed that the Temple had been destroyed because it had become corrupt. However, this did not mean that the Christians abandoned their Jewish roots. The gospels show Jesus as their exemplar: He participated in synagogue services and traveled to Jerusalem for the festivals, as Jewish men were required to do, and in other ways was an observant Jew. The New Testament also presents Jesus's disciples as continuing to teach and preach in the Temple precincts after his death. It seems that what these first Christians wanted was for the Temple to be reformed, not removed from their religion altogether. Thus Christians, like other Jews, struggled to make sense of the destruction of the Temple, and the gospels are in many ways a theological response to this tragic event.

Torah.   Like other Jews, the earliest Christians believed that the Torah was a gift from God. In fact, it was their only scriptures for the first several decades of their existence. These Jesus followers were not required to abandon observance of the rules and regulations of the Torah. In fact, the author of Matthew's gospel describes Jesus's mission in this way: "Do not think that I have come to abolish the law or the prophets; I have come not to abolish but to fulfill" (Matt 5:17). Like the Essenes and the Pharisees, Christians accepted all three parts of the Torah (Law, Prophets, and Writings). On the question of interpreting Torah, the gospels present Jesus as developing case law in much the same way as the Pharisees did. Thus, like the Pharisees, the Christians believed that the written law must be interpreted or supplemented. However, their "supplements" were not limited to the legal judgments of the Pharisees, but they also included the teachings of Jesus. For example, divorce and certain forms of violence or retribution, which were allowed according to the Jewish law, were strongly frowned upon in early Christianity. Another example is the gospels' presentation of Jesus occasionally breaking the rule about not working on the Sabbath when he encountered someone whose life was in danger. Pharisaic teachers cite the principle "Great is human dignity" to allow for such exceptions, and there is no reason to believe that early Christians denied this principle. However, the gospels also associate Jesus' Sabbath healings with the coming reign of God, where there will be no more evil and sickness, and salvation will be available to everyone. Matthew's gospel describes early Christians' view of Sabbath observance this way: "But if you had known what this means, 'I desire mercy and not sacrifice,' you would not have condemned the guiltless. For the Son of Man is lord of the Sabbath" (Matt 12:7–8; cf. Hos 6:6).

Messiah.   Where Christians disagreed most with their counterparts in other Jewish groups was in their belief that the messiah had already come and that this messiah was Jesus of Nazareth. This is the single most important distinguishing feature of early Christianity: The Christians thought that the messiah had already come, while (most) other Jewish groups were still waiting for the messiah. Christians supported their claims that Jesus was the messiah by pointing out how the events of his life fulfilled prophecies in the Torah about the messiah, how he spoke with great wisdom and could perform miracles, and most important of all, how he rose from the dead after being crucified and appeared to his disciples.

Just *what kind* of a messiah Jesus was became a matter of some disagreement among various groups of Christians, but it is clear at least that Jesus did not fit the mold of a political/military messiah that the Pharisees and many other ordinary Jews were expecting. There are other ideas about the messiah expressed in the Torah, and the Christians began to explore them to try to discover who Jesus was and to find evidence to convince their fellow Jews that Jesus was in fact the messiah.

While the understanding of Jesus underwent some significant changes during the first decades of Christianity, one view that was popular among the earliest Christians was that Jesus was an apocalyptic messiah. They believed that Jesus had come once to warn them that the end of the world was near and to instruct them on how to survive the coming apocalypse, and that Jesus would come again soon (the "second coming") to inaugurate the end and to judge the living and the dead. As time went on and Jesus did not return, Christians modified their beliefs about the nearness of the end of the world.

THE JEWISH WAR

The various Jewish groups coexisted more or less peacefully in Palestine until 66 C.E., when war broke out between the Jews and the Romans. Almost all Jews strongly resented the Roman presence in Palestine, and some Jews advocated violent revolt. Minor rebellions had broken out several times prior to 66 C.E. However, a series of events led to the development of a full-blown revolution in 66 C.E., a revolution that was to prove disastrous for the Jewish people.

The revolt was led by the **Zealots**, a group of radical Jews who believed that once the war was started, YHWH would enter it on the side of the Jews and help them defeat the vastly more powerful Romans. Their hopes were not realized, and the Romans quickly and easily defeated the Jews. Thousands of Jews were killed and their leaders crucified. The worst disaster, however, came in 70 C.E., when Jerusalem was destroyed and the Temple burned to the ground. This time the Temple was never rebuilt.

This war proved fateful for most of the various groups within Judaism. Toward the end of the war, a large group of Essenes was accidentally discovered by the Romans in the desert and massacred. Without the Temple, the Sadducees had lost the source of their wealth and power, and for all practical purposes they ceased to exist. The only groups to survive the Jewish War relatively intact were the Pharisees and the Christians. With the Temple gone, however, the Pharisees needed to undertake some major renovations in the Jewish religion. By the end of the first century, the Pharisees had invented a brand of Judaism that relied solely on the Torah and eliminated the practice of sacrifice. This came to be called rabbinic Judaism, and it is the version of Judaism that survives in various forms today.

Key Terms

Diaspora	Holy of Holies	Sadducees
synagogue	kosher	Sanhedrin
Second Temple	apocalyptic	Pharisees
messiah	Dead Sea Scrolls	rabbis
priests	Suffering Servant	Essenes
Passover	Hellenization	scribes
Pentecost	Maccabees	People of the Land
Yom Kippur	Hanukkah	Zealots

Questions for Reading

1. What was the purpose of sacrifice? What kinds of rules did the Jews have about the sacrifices that they conducted?

2. What did the Jewish scriptures consist of? How did these scriptures develop?

3. Explain the development of the concept of the messiah in Jewish thinking and distinguish among the different kinds of messiahs that Jews believed in.

4. What was Hellenization, and how did Jews of the time react to it?

5. Compare and contrast the Sadducees, Pharisees, Essenes, and Christians in terms of their beliefs about the Temple, Torah, and messiah.

6. What happened to each of the Jewish groups following the Jewish War of 66–70 C.E.?

Works Consulted/Recommended Reading

Charlesworth, James H., ed. *The Old Testament Pseudepigrapha*. Vol. 1, *Apocalyptic Literature and Testaments*. New York: Doubleday, 1983.

Jaffee, Martin S. *Early Judaism. Religious Worlds of the First Judaic Millennium*. Bethesda, MD: University of Maryland, 2006.

Murphy, Frederick J. *The Religious World of Jesus: An Introduction to Second Temple Palestinian Judaism*. Nashville, TN: Abingdon, 1991.

Perrin, Norman, and Dennis C. Duling. *The New Testament: An Introduction*. 2nd ed. San Diego: Harcourt Brace Jovanovich, 1982.

VanderKam, James C. *An Introduction to Early Judaism*. Grand Rapids, MI: Eerdmans, 2001.

Wise, Michael, Martin Abegg, Jr., and Edward Cook. *The Dead Sea Scrolls. A New Translation*. New York: HarperCollins, 1996.

PART

II

THE NEW TESTAMENT

The second major section of the Bible is the New Testament. The New Testament has continued to be a very important document for Christians throughout the centuries because it provides the basis for articulating the Christian community's identity and for formulating much of its theology and moral principles. Christians call this section the New Testament because it proclaims the new covenant between God and human beings made possible by the coming of Jesus Christ.

Like the Old Testament or Hebrew Bible, the New Testament is not always an easy document to read and interpret because it is an ancient piece of literature from a culture and historical time period vastly different from our own. At the same time, Christians treat it as a timeless document that has authority to direct and guide their lives. The challenge, then, is to learn how to read and interpret biblical texts as their human authors intended, utilizing a wide range of methods of historical and literary analysis that are available to us today, while also appreciating their enduring character as documents of faith. However, even before we can begin that work, we need to be familiar with the content and organization of the New Testament. Therefore, we will begin with some very basic questions: What kinds of books are contained in the New Testament? How were these books collected into this larger document we call the New Testament?

DIVISIONS OF THE NEW TESTAMENT

The New Testament is usually divided into four sections or subdivisions. The first subdivision consists of four gospels. They are listed here with their most commonly accepted dates of composition. Although the gospels are included first among the books of the New Testament, they were not the first to be written. In fact, Paul's letters, which eventually became part of the New Testament, were written approximately ten to twenty years before the earliest New Testament gospel.

Mark (c. 65–70 C.E.)
Matthew (c. 80–85 C.E.)
Luke (c. 80–85 C.E.)
John (c. 90–100 C.E.)

The gospels tell the story of the life of Jesus and in that sense they are historical documents. However, we should not think of them as having the same goals and purposes as modern histories or biographies. Rather, the gospels are more appropriately understood to be proclamations of faith. The word gospel comes from the Anglo-Saxon *god-spell*, which means "good tidings." The Greek word for gospel is *euangelion*, which means "good message" (of Jesus Christ). The writers of the gospels are called evangelists, that is, "preachers of the good news." The gospels proclaim early Christian communities' faith experience of Jesus as the messiah of God.

The Gospels of Matthew, Mark, and Luke are called synoptic gospels, from the Greek *synoptikos*, which means "seeing the whole together." These gospels tell the same general story about Jesus in the same kind of way and with more or less the same chronology. In fact, in certain parts of the synoptic gospels, the similarities are so pronounced that casual readers might not realize that they are reading a different gospel. However, a careful study of these gospels shows that each has its own unique portrait of Jesus and its own understanding of what it means to be a Jesus follower. The Gospel of John is quite different from the synoptic gospels in terms of style, content, theological perspective, and even chronology, and therefore must be read with different expectations.

The second subdivision of the New Testament is the Acts of the Apostles. This book is a continuation of Luke's gospel, written by the same author. It tells the story of the spread of the "good news" (gospel) of Jesus Christ and the development of early Christian communities from shortly after the death and resurrection of Jesus through the time of Paul's preaching in Rome—the period covering approximately 30 to 64 C.E. Biblical scholars think this book was written in the last quarter of the first century, after the destruction of Jerusalem and the Temple (70 C.E.). Although it reads like a history book, the Acts of the Apostles is not an objective retelling of the story of the beginnings of Christianity. Rather, it gives us a theological interpretation of the events that eventually led to Christianity's identification as a religion separate from Judaism.

The third subdivision of the New Testament consists of twenty-one letters addressed to a variety of Christian churches and individual Christians of the first and early second century C.E. Although thirteen of these letters are attributed to the missionary Paul, perhaps only seven were actually written by him: Romans, 1 and 2 Corinthians, Galatians, Philippians, 1 Thessalonians, and Philemon. Biblical scholars agree that these letters were written between 50 and 60 C.E. The others were likely written by anonymous authors, perhaps later disciples of Paul, to honor his memory: 2 Thessalonians, Ephesians, Colossians, 1 and 2 Timothy, and Titus. Seven more letters are attributed to apostles and early church leaders: James, 1 and 2 Peter, 1, 2, and 3 John, and Jude. One remaining document that bears the title "To the Hebrews" is not really a letter but, because it has traditionally been grouped with the letters, we continue to include it here. Biblical scholars believe that these non-Pauline documents were written between 70 and 125 C.E.

The Book of Revelation (c. 90 to 100 C.E.) makes up the fourth and last subdivision of the New Testament. This book is an apocalyptic account of a divine revelation to a Christian prophet named John. The words *apocalyptic* and *apocalypse* come from a Greek word meaning "to reveal" or "to uncover." Apocalypses consist of collections of symbolic visions and auditions—images and words delivered by an angel or other heavenly being to a human recipient—that appear to be concerned with the imminent destruction of the world and the triumph of God's holy ones. In fact, they address, in highly symbolic language, topics like the sovereignty of God, the composition of the heavenly realm, the final reward of God's holy people, and the punishment of the wicked.

THE QUESTION OF CANON

Another question to be considered as we begin our study of the New Testament is how the New Testament was compiled. When and how did the New Testament come into existence? We know that early Christian communities in the first and second centuries C.E. were reading other religious literature besides the books that eventually found their way into the New Testament. Why did some sacred writings get included in the New Testament while others did not? Answers to questions like these will help us understand the role that the New Testament played in the development of early Christianity and the kind of authority that it continues to have for Christians today.

The term *canon* means "rule" or "standard"—like a measuring stick. This term was first used in early Christian literature to refer to the "rule of faith," that is, the norm or measure of religious truth in the Christian tradition. Most often today, it is used to refer to the collection of authoritative writings of a particular religious group. For example, the canon for Christianity is the Bible. Today the term can also be used in a secular sense to describe the authoritative writings of an academic discipline or a particular period in history. For example, one can talk about the canon of early American literature, meaning a list of writings that literature scholars would agree are the "masterpieces" of this period. When scholars are able to reach consensus on the canon of a particular type of literature or of literature from a particular period, these works are published in an anthology. Two examples are *The Norton Anthology of English Literature* and the *Heath Anthology of American Literature*. By comparison, we might think of the New Testament as an anthology of authoritative religious literature written during the period of early Christianity.

Theory About the Formation of the New Testament Canon

At the earliest stages of Christianity, there was no New Testament at all. Early Christians appropriated the scriptures of Judaism as their own, though sometimes selectively and with different interpretations than some of their Jewish brothers and sisters might have had. Thus, for Jesus and his disciples, as well as the early missionaries of the gospel like Paul and his coworkers, "scriptures" meant Jewish scriptures. By the latter part of the first century and the beginning of the second century C.E., as Christians began to put together their own distinctive scriptures, they did so not all at once, but in stages.

First Stage. People are sometimes surprised to learn that the earliest collections of Christian texts did not include the gospels. Actually, these early collections probably consisted of some of the letters of Paul. In the second letter of Peter (c. 100 to 125 C.E.), the author says, "So also our beloved brother Paul wrote to you according to the wisdom given him, speaking of this as he does in all his letters. There are some things in them hard to understand, which the ignorant and unstable twist to their own destruction, as they do the other scriptures" (2 Pet 3:16). This is our earliest clue that Christians were beginning to collect Christian literature in order to create their own canon. It also suggests that some Christians, at least, were beginning to regard the letters of Paul as having a level of authority comparable to the scriptures of Judaism.

Second Stage.   The Gospels of Matthew, Mark, Luke, and John were not the only gospels being written and read in the first and early second centuries C.E. From early church writers like Clement of Alexandria (wrote 180–200 C.E.), Origen (d. 253 or 254), and Eusebius of Caesarea (d. 339 or 340), we know of the gospel to the Hebrews, the Gospel of the Egyptians, the Gospel of the Ebionites, the Gospel of Peter, and the Gospel of Thomas, to name a few. In other words, there were many so-called gospels (stories of the life of Jesus or collections of his teachings) in the early years of the church, but only four obtained the status of sacred scripture. Our earliest evidence for this canonization process comes from Justin Martyr, writing in the middle of the second century C.E. In his comments on how Eucharist was celebrated in the early Christian churches, Justin mentions that the "memoirs of the apostles" or the writings of the prophets were being read at celebrations of the Lord's Supper, also called Eucharist (*Apology* 1.67). The phrase "memoirs of the apostles" most likely refers to the gospels, and Justin appears to be giving them the same status as the books of the prophets, which were already part of the Jewish scriptures.

A few decades later, Irenaeus (c. 180 C.E.) was apparently the first Christian writer to single out as authoritative the four gospels that would later become part of the New Testament (*Against Heresies* 3.11.8). He also provides evidence that, already in the late second century C.E., people were beginning to distinguish between orthodox and heretical gospels. For example, he dismisses the Gospel of Truth because it "agrees in nothing with the gospels of the apostles" (*Against Heresies* 3.11.9) and he condemns the Gospel of Judas as a "fictitious history" (*Against Heresies* 1.31.1). Likewise, in the fourth century C.E., Eusebius tells us that the Gospel of Peter was banned from some communities because it was considered to contain false teaching about Jesus (*Ecclesiastical History* 6.12).

Third Stage.   Paradoxically, Marcion (c. 140 C.E.), a Christian preacher in Rome, was responsible for the first canon of the New Testament. Christians of his time had inherited the scriptures of Judaism as their sacred writings, but Marcion was troubled by their apparent internal contradictions, which he could not resolve. Likewise, he struggled with what he saw as the Old Testament's portrayal of God as a violent and vengeful God in contrast with his own (Christian) understanding of God as the God of goodness. Further, he understood Jesus Christ to be the Son of the God of goodness and not the messiah of the Jewish God of justice. Thus, he created a very restrictive canon of Christian scriptures that excluded all of the Old Testament scriptures. He also rejected much of Christian literature that had Jewish overtones, accepting only the edited Gospel of Luke and ten of the letters attributed to Paul as his canon. In effect, any text with Jewish overtones was edited or excluded.

The presbyters of the churches in Rome were deeply troubled by Marcion's teachings and held a hearing in which his work was rejected. Marcion's canon also prompted other church leaders to form their own canons or lists of approved books. The most famous of these was the Muratorian canon, an official list of books probably developed in Rome in the latter part of the second century C.E. It included the four gospels, the Acts of the Apostles, thirteen letters attributed to Paul (excluding Hebrews), Jude, 1 John, 2 John, the Wisdom of Solomon (today included in the Old Testament apocrypha or deuterocanonical books), Revelation, and the Apocalypse of Peter (today included among New Testament apocrypha). Other lists or partial lists can be found in the writings of Origen (d. 253 or 254 C.E.), Tertullian (d. 220?), and Eusebius of Caesarea (d. 339/340 C.E.).

The consistent elements in all of the lists that had been compiled in response to Marcion's canon were the four gospels, Acts of the Apostles, and Paul's letters. Bishop Athanasius of Alexandria, in his *Festal Letter* of 367 C.E., was the first to name the twenty-seven books of the New Testament, as we have it today, as canonical. Thus, the canon of the New Testament was created over an extended period of time and from among a wide variety of Christian literature. However, it was not until the Council of Trent in 1546 that the Catholic Church made an official statement listing the books that constitute the canon of the Bible.

The Criteria for Canonicity

Why did some sacred Christian writings get into the New Testament while others did not? Modern biblical scholars cannot fully reconstruct the history of the development of the canon, especially as it relates to the criteria used in this "sorting out" process. Yet, the writings of early church historians and theologians have provided at least a few clues concerning the complexity of the early church's task of identifying a canon of Christian literature.

One criterion that appears to have been used among the early Christian churches was "apostolic origin," meaning that the book could be attributed to an apostle or to a disciple of an apostle. For example, some early church historians and theologians questioned whether the letter to the Hebrews and the book of Revelation ought to be included in the canon because it could not be verified that Paul and John, the son of Zebedee and an apostle of Jesus, were their respective authors. Today, we understand the notion of apostolic authorship in the broadest sense, meaning that the book has some connection to the traditions associated with a particular apostle or the apostles in general.

Other criteria are suggested by early church writers' discussions of the Gospel of Peter. The fragment that is still available to modern readers tells the story of the trial, death, and resurrection of Jesus. It is a strange gospel, complete with enormous angels and a cross that talks. However, the early church historian Eusebius recounts that Bishop Serapion of Antioch (c. 190 C.E.) forbade Christians to read it not because it was historically inaccurate but because some of those who held it as sacred were led into heresy (wrong teaching) by its words.

The wrong teaching, or heresy, to which Serapion referred was docetism, which held that Jesus did not really suffer and die but merely seemed to have done these things. Thus, the exclusion of the Gospel of Peter from the canon of the New Testament appears to have been a question of orthodoxy or right doctrine. However, Serapion's comments suggest two other factors that contributed to the formation of the New Testament canon: the authority of Christian church leaders to determine what was appropriate reading for their Christian communities and the value of a tradition that can trace itself back to the apostles.

Thus, it appears that the authority to decide which books contained sound teaching and which books could be traced back to the apostles was claimed by the bishops of the Christian church. However, the bishops did not simply impose their own preferences on an unwilling church. Some of the bishops resolved the question of canon by asking churches in various regions what books were being read in their worship services. So another criterion for inclusion appears to have been widespread acceptance in the churches. The decisions of the bishops about the canon were not simply their own but appear to have reflected the sentiments of the larger church.

Another factor to be considered in the history of the development of canon is the role of chance. In some cases, individual churches, like the churches of Greece and Asia Minor (modern Turkey), assumed responsibility for collecting sacred documents and distributing them to other churches, thereby ensuring their preservation. Paul's letters are a good example. However, other early Christian literature that might otherwise have been included in the canon of the New Testament simply disappeared for reasons that are unknown to us. Today we have only brief quotations from them or references to them in other early Christian writings.

Chapter

6

JESUS AND THE GOSPELS

TIMELINE

37–4 B.C.E.	Herod the Great is king of Palestine. During his kingship, Herod initiates a major renovation of the Jerusalem Temple.
6–4 B.C.E.	Jesus of Nazareth is born.
4 B.C.E.–39 C.E.	Herod Antipas is king of Galilee and the area to the east of the Jordan River.
26–36 C.E.	Pontius Pilate is procurator in Judea and Samaria.
c. 30 C.E.	The death and resurrection of Jesus.
66–70 C.E.	The Jewish war against Rome.
70 C.E.	The Romans capture Jerusalem and destroy the Temple.
65–70 C.E.	The Gospel of Mark is written.
80–85 C.E.	The Gospels of Matthew and Luke are written.
90–100 C.E.	The Gospel of John is written.

In the early part of the first century C.E., a man named Jesus emerged from the small village of Nazareth in Galilee. This Jesus of Nazareth was a teacher and a miracle worker, and many were drawn to follow him. He began his ministry by proclaiming the nearness of God's kingdom to his Jewish brothers and sisters, and those who became his followers understood him to be the long-awaited Jewish messiah. By all accounts he was an observant Jew: He attended synagogue, went to the pilgrimage feasts in Jerusalem, and otherwise obeyed Torah law. However, some were offended by the sometimes radical nature of his teachings and his controversial interpretations of Jewish law.

Then one year, near the Passover feast, Jesus was arrested in Jerusalem. Charges were made against him, and he was quickly handed over to the Roman authorities for execution. He was crucified, and those who had him arrested probably thought that would be the end of his rabble-rousing, his disciples would scatter, and the people would soon move on to other attractions. However, some women from among his followers began to spread the news that he had been raised from the dead! As Jesus's disciples continued to proclaim the message of Jesus Christ after his death and resurrection, a reform movement was born within Judaism that later spread outward into the Gentile, or non-Jewish, world. This Jesus Movement came to be known as Christianity.

In order to learn more about the Jesus Movement, we will start with the Gospels of the New Testament. Before we begin, however, it is important to note that, among the books of the New Testament, the gospels were not the first to be written. In fact, all of the authentic letters of Paul were written before the first gospel, Mark, was written. Likewise, many of the other books of the New Testament were written by the time the last gospel, John, was written. Why begin with the gospels? Why not read Paul's letters first? Paul, and other New Testament authors like him, assumed that their readers already knew the stories about Jesus's words and deeds, perhaps from the eyewitnesses themselves. But when that first generation of preachers and eyewitnesses passed away, people decided to preserve the stories about Jesus and his teachings in writing. The result was the gospels.

Nearly two millennia later, people who wish to learn about Jesus of Nazareth

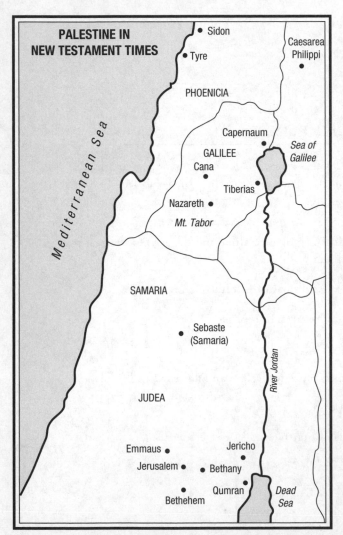

Figure 6–1 Palestine in New Testament times.

Figure 6–2 The Tombs of the Kings in Jerusalem. The entrance to the interior of the tombs was once sealed by a round stone, which can still be seen. The tomb in which Jesus was buried might have looked something like this one. Photo by Catherine Cory, 1985.

obviously cannot sit at the feet of the eyewitnesses, but they can encounter the living Jesus and the witness of his first followers as it is preserved in the gospels. These stories and the teachings of Jesus form the backdrop for the rest of the New Testament, and they are at the heart of the early Jesus Movement. Today, in our religiously and culturally diverse communities, many may not know the gospel stories or their significance for understanding the person and nature of Jesus Christ. This is why we will begin our investigation with the Gospels of the New Testament.

HOW THE GOSPELS CAME TO BE

Whether we are aware of it or not, knowing something about how a book was written helps us understand how to interpret it. This principle also applies to the New Testament gospels. How should we interpret what we read in the gospels? Although they might appear so on the surface, the gospels are not history, strictly speaking. Neither are they biographies, at least not in the modern sense of the word. The Greek word for "gospel," *euangelion*, means "good message" or "good news." As their name suggests, the gospels are proclamations of faith concerning Jesus of Nazareth whom his followers believed was the messiah of God. Although they have individuals' names attached to them—Matthew, Mark, Luke, and John in the case of the New Testament—they were not authored in the same way as books are written today. Instead, they are the result of a somewhat lengthy process of collecting, passing on, recording, and editing the stories and sayings of Jesus into a coherent narrative.

The stages of composition of the gospels can be described briefly as follows: (1) Shortly after the death and resurrection of Jesus, those who had once traveled with him and others who had become preachers of the "good news" began to hand on by word of mouth and in writing stories and sayings concerning Jesus's ministry and teachings. (2) Early Christian communities used these stories and sayings in worship and teaching, in preparation for Baptism, to encourage and console the believers, to resolve controversies, and to admonish the wrongdoers. Gradually, they began to write down these stories and sayings of Jesus. However, as yet there were no written gospels as we know them today. (3) Eventually, the gospel writers began to collect these oral and written traditions, arranging them into a coherent narrative or story of the life, death, and resurrection of Jesus Christ. The authors of the gospels selected and arranged these stories and sayings, with special attention to the particular situation of the communities for which they were writing and to the proclamation of faith that they wanted to make concerning Jesus, the Christ, the messiah of God.

Given the composition history of the gospels, as we have just described it, we cannot talk about the author of a gospel in the same way that we might talk about an author today. For example, today when we pick up a book, we can usually identify its author, determine its intended audience, and learn the date it was published by simply opening its cover. However, the gospels are the products of early faith communities, so we cannot say for certain who actually wrote them down. Further, these authors did not tell us when or for whom they were writing so biblical scholars are left to make educated guesses about these things.

Early Christians attached the titles "Matthew," "Mark," "Luke," and "John" to the New Testament gospels sometime in the second century C.E., in large part owing to the belief that they are based on **apostolic tradition** (the witness of the apostles and early disciples of Jesus). For example, early Christian writers attribute the gospel we now know as the Gospel of Mark to John Mark, a companion of Peter, in Rome. Likewise, the name given to Matthew's gospel is perhaps due to a tradition associated with Papias who was said to have written, "Then Matthew put together the sayings [of Jesus] in the Hebrew dialect and each one translated them as he was able" (Eusebius, *Ecclesiastical History* 3.39.16). The early church had two traditions pertaining to the authorship of John's gospel. One view was that the writer was John, the son of Zebedee, one of the twelve in Mark's gospel. Another view was that his name was John, but that he was not an apostle of Jesus, and that he lived a long life in Ephesus, where he eventually wrote his gospel. The New Testament mentions three times a man named Luke who was a follower of Paul. Based on these three references, some also have concluded that the gospel writer Luke was a physician and a Gentile (non-Jewish) Christian (Phlm 24; Col 4:11–14; 2 Tim 4:11).

Granted that the New Testament gospels are rooted in apostolic tradition, biblical scholars today say that their actual authors are mostly unknown to us. The majority would say that the Gospel of Mark was written between 65 and 70 C.E. by a Gentile Christian. The strong apocalyptic mood of the gospel suggests that the community was enduring some kind of persecution. Concerning the Gospel of Matthew, most say that it was written between 80 and 85 C.E. by an anonymous Jewish Christian author and for a Jewish Christian audience. (Scholars use *Jewish Christians* and *Christian Jews* somewhat interchangeably. Both terms describe Jews who believed in Jesus and participated in the early Jesus movement.) Evidence cited is the large number of references to important Jewish figures and to symbols of the Jewish faith as well as numerous quotations from the Jewish scriptures. Luke's gospel appears to have been written at approximately the same time by a Gentile Christian. In the introduction to his gospel, he indicates that he was not an eyewitness to Jesus's life, but that he had access to traditions, oral or written, from eyewitnesses, and he was aware that others had attempted to write the gospel story of Jesus before him (Luke 1:1–4). Finally, John's gospel appears to have been written approximately 90–100 C.E by a Jewish Christian author and for a community that was suffering persecution at the hands of its Jewish brothers and sisters.

Questions of authorship aside, Christians profess that the gospels tell us the truth about Jesus Christ. As inspired, the gospels are the Word of God, but they are written in the words of their human authors. Therefore, they should be read with an awareness of the historical and political environments in which they were written, the needs of the people for whom they were written, and the literary expressions and cultural practices of the time. Equally important, they should be read as their authors intended—from the perspective of the ending of the story, namely, the death and resurrection of Jesus. The gospels tell the truth about Jesus Christ, but we should not limit the scope of truth by equating it with "historical facts." Rather, for the gospel writers, truth consisted of what their communities of faith had come to know and believe about Jesus's relationship to God the Father and what his life, death, and resurrection meant for the salvation of the world.

The Synoptic Gospels

The gospels of the New Testament provide their readers with four distinctive portraits of Jesus. However, three of these gospels—Matthew, Mark, and Luke—are similar insofar as they tell the same general story of the life and teachings of Jesus Christ and they tell it more or less in the same kind of way. For this reason, they are called **synoptic gospels** from the Greek word *synoptikos*, which means "seeing the whole together." Sometimes the similarities among the three gospels are so striking that one begins to ask, "Who copied whom?" This is called the **synoptic problem**. Stated briefly, the synoptic problem is concerned with the literary relationship among the Gospels of Matthew, Mark, and Luke.

The three gospel versions of the parable of the mustard seed provide an excellent example of the synoptic problem.

Synoptic Versions of the Parable of the Mustard Seed

Matt 13:31–32	**Mark 4:30–32**	**Luke 13:18–19**
He put before them another parable: "The kingdom of heaven	He also said, "With what can we compare the kingdom of God, or what parable will we use for it? It is like a	He said therefore, "What is the kingdom of God like?" And to what should I compare it? It is like a
is like a mustard seed that someone took and sowed in his field; it is the smallest of all the seeds, but when it has grown it is the greatest of shrubs and becomes a tree,	mustard seed, which, when sown upon the ground, is the smallest of all the seeds on earth; yet when it is sown it grows up and becomes the greatest of all shrubs,	mustard seed that someone took and sowed in the garden; it grew and became a tree, and
	puts forth large branches, so that the birds of	
so that the birds of the air come and make nests in its branches."	the air can make nests in its shade."	the birds of the air made nests in its branches."

The literary similarities among the three versions of the parable of the mustard seed are obvious. All three compare the kingdom to a mustard seed that, when it grows, becomes something very large so that the birds of the air can find shelter in it. Moreover, the wording is similar enough to suggest that two, or perhaps all three authors, copied their parable from another written source.

At the same time, a careful analysis of the literary differences among these three versions of the parable of the mustard seed suggests that the individual authors, having a written source in front of them, deliberately altered that source for some reason. Matthew's gospel, for example, refers to the kingdom of heaven, rather than the kingdom of God. Luke's gospel describes the product of the growth of the mustard seed as a tree, while Mark's gospel calls it a shrub. Matthew's gospel identifies it as a shrub and a tree.

The synoptic gospels contain many, many examples of this kind of literary dependence. Early in the last century, biblical scholars set to work trying to discover which of the three synoptic gospels was the earliest and, potentially, the source for the other two. Ultimately the goal would be to learn how these later gospel writers had redacted (edited) their sources and what their redaction process tells us about the gospel writers' worldview and theological perspectives on the life and teachings of Jesus Christ.

The Two-Source Hypothesis

Biblical scholars have investigated a number of solutions to the synoptic problem. Although no one solution accounts for all of the variations in every segment of the synoptic gospels, the most commonly accepted solution is the **Two-Source Hypothesis.** According to this hypothesis, Mark's gospel was written first among the synoptic gospel, perhaps as early as 65 to 70 c.e. Matthew and Luke had access to Mark's gospel when they were composing their own gospels, selecting from it a variety of stories and teachings and following its timeline without much alteration. To account for the fact that the Gospels of Matthew and Luke share a number of stories and sayings of Jesus, which are nowhere to be found in Mark's gospel, proponents of this theory argue that Matthew and Luke also had access to another source, a written document or documents. Biblical scholars have named this hypothetical source **Q**, for the German word *Quelle* ("source"). There have been a number of attempts to reconstruct Q, but no actual copies exist today, and some biblical scholars question whether it ever existed.

The Two-Source Hypothesis solves the synoptic problem by proposing that the writers of the Gospels of Matthew and Luke composed their gospels by drawing from the Gospel of Mark and Q as their primary sources and incorporating other traditional materials known only to their own communities. Matthew's famous Sermon on the Mount (Matt 5:1–7:29) and its parallel Sermon on the Plain from Luke's gospel (Luke 6:17–49) are examples of the material that supposedly belonged to Q. Matthew's stories about the birth of Jesus (Matt 1:1–2:23) represent some of the traditional material known only to the community of Matthew's gospel. Biblical scholars call this material "Special Matthew." Similarly, stories like the Prodigal Son (Luke 15:11–32) and the Good Samaritan (Luke 10:25–37) belong to the traditional material known only to the community of Luke's gospel. This material is known as "Special Luke." Thus, the Two-Source Hypothesis might actually involve four (or more) sources, and it can be diagrammed as follows:

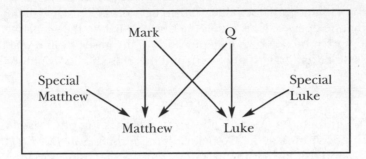

Although the Two-Source Hypothesis is the most widely accepted solution to the Synoptic Problem, it does not explain all of the similarities and differences among the Gospels of Matthew, Mark, and Luke. Therefore, biblical scholars have continued to experiment with alternative theories to describe the literary dependence of the synoptic gospels. If this question is of interest to you, please consult some of the resources listed in the Works Consulted/Recommended Reading section.

The Gospel of John

The Gospel of John is distinctively different from the synoptic gospels in a number of ways. Instead of parables and individual sayings or collections of sayings of Jesus like those found in the synoptic gospels, the Gospel of John contains long discourses or speeches delivered by Jesus in a style that is distinctively Johannine (*adj.;* belonging to or characteristic of the gospel and letters of John). Both the Gospel of John and the synoptic gospels contain miracle stories, but John appears to have known only a few of the same miracle stories found in the synoptic gospels. Two examples are Jesus multiplying loaves and fishes (John 6:1–15; cf. Matt 14:13–21; Mark 6:32–44; Luke 9:10–17) and Jesus walking on water (John 6:16–21; cf. Matt 14:22–27; Mark 6:45–51). At the same time, John incorporates a number of miracle stories that are unique to this gospel. The most famous are the stories about Jesus turning the water to wine at Cana (John 2:1–10) and the raising of Lazarus from the dead (John 11:1–44). Finally, some of the important characters in John's gospel—most notably Nicodemus and the Samaritan woman—are absent from among the synoptic gospels.

Differences such as these have led biblical scholars to conclude that the author of John's gospel may have had access to some of the same oral traditions as those known to the synoptic gospel writers. However, he had not read their gospels. It is even possible that he did not know these other written gospels existed. In sum, the four Gospels of the New Testament provide us with four distinctive portraits of Jesus Christ and this one, the Gospel of John, is the most unique.

FOUR PORTRAITS OF JESUS

An important feature and distinguishing mark of each gospel is its Christology. The word **Christology** derives from two Greek words: *Christos* meaning "the anointed" and *Logos* meaning "word," or in this case "teaching." Hence, Christology is teaching about Jesus as the

Christ. As a theological discipline, Christology concerns itself with the *person* (who he is) and *work* (what he does) of Jesus who is the Christ. What do the gospels tell us about who Jesus is and about what he does? An in-depth study of the gospels will reveal that each gospel paints a somewhat different portrait of Jesus and therefore has its own distinctive Christology.

Mark's Christology

In Mark's gospel, the reader is alerted to the question of Christology even in its opening line: "The beginning of the Gospel of *Jesus Christ, the Son of God*" (Mark 1:1). However, the reader is soon troubled by the narrator's repeated references to Jesus's demand that people not tell anyone about him (Mark 1:44), even when he is about to send his disciples out to preach the good news (Mark 3:13–19) or when he performs a great miracle (Mark 5:21–43). Biblical scholars call this phenomenon the **Messianic Secret**. Does Jesus not want people to know that he is the messiah or the Christ (this Greek title also means "anointed")? If not, why not? The answer to these questions is to be found in the way that the writer of this gospel tells the story of Jesus's life.

There is no simple answer to the Messianic Secret. Perhaps the writer of Mark's gospel wanted to explain in retrospect why it was that some people did not accept Jesus and the message that he came to preach. By giving a backward look into the life and teachings of Jesus, Mark explains that Jesus deliberately kept certain people from hearing and understanding his message. Addressing the disciples, Jesus says, "To you has been given the secret of the kingdom of God, but for those outside, everything comes in parables; in order that they may indeed look, but not perceive, and may indeed listen, but not understand; so that they may not turn again and be forgiven" (Mark 4:11–12).

Another possible explanation for the Messianic Secret is that the writer of Mark's gospel wanted to illustrate in a literary way the forcefulness of the message of Jesus Christ. On one occasion, when Jesus healed a leper (a person with a skin disease), he told the person not to tell anyone about it. Immediately, the person went out and did just the opposite—he went out to proclaim the word about Jesus (Mark 1:40–45). Likewise, at the conclusion of other miracle stories, Mark comments that Jesus's fame continued to spread. It was as if the message of God's kingdom simply could not be silenced.

There is still another possible explanation for Mark's Messianic Secret. This one focuses on the suffering and death of Jesus. Because of texts like 2 Samuel 7, in which the prophet Nathan tells David that an everlasting king would be born from his royal line, many people expected the messiah to be a political leader who would bring together great armies against their enemies. Mark's gospel tells a story that is traditionally called the Confession of Peter, in which Jesus asks his disciples what people were saying about who he was (Mark 8:27–38). Peter responds to Jesus's query with the words, "You are the Messiah" (Mark 8:29). At this point in the story, the reader might expect Jesus to praise Peter for his insight. Instead, Jesus orders Peter and the other disciples not to tell anyone about him (Mark 8:30). Jesus goes on to say, "The Son of Man must undergo great suffering, and be rejected by the elders, the chief priests, and the scribes, and be killed, and after three days rise again" (Mark 8:31). This Jesus tells them openly (Mark 8:32).

Needless to say, this is a very strange story. Peter makes a (true) proclamation about Jesus's identity, and Jesus tells him to keep quiet. Then Jesus tells them some very hard words about what will happen to him, but he has no intention that these words be kept secret. Perhaps Jesus did not want his disciples to identify him as the messiah, because people had the wrong idea of what that meant. Peter apparently had the wrong idea. If he understood what Jesus was saying, he would not have scolded Jesus (Mark 8:32). Or maybe Peter did understand but was unwilling to have his dream shattered: If he follows Jesus, and Jesus's life is destined to end in this way, what is to keep Peter from suffering the same fate? What a troubling paradox! Instead of the glorious and powerful messiah they had long awaited, Jesus would be a messiah who *must* suffer. The Greek word in Mark 8:31 that is translated as *must* means "it is necessary that." In other words, irrespective of what humans thought, it was God's will and desire that the messiah would suffer and die so that he might be raised up "after three days" (Mark 8:31).

From this point onward in the gospel, Mark is consistent in his presentation of Jesus as the suffering messiah. At the conclusion of the story about the two disciples who wanted places of authority in Jesus's coming kingdom (Mark 10:35–45), Jesus declares, "For the Son of Man also came not to be served but to serve, and to give his life as a ransom for many" (Mark 10:45). Later, in the story about the centurion, an officer in the Roman military, who stood guard at Jesus's crucifixion (Mark 15:33–39), proclaims that Jesus is the Son of God. However, the narrator makes it clear that he makes this proclamation as he watches Jesus die (Mark 15:39). Again, Mark's view of the messiah: He is the one who must suffer.

Matthew's Christology

Matthew's gospel contains a rather different and more multifaceted portrait of Jesus as the Christ. First, Matthew uses imagery associated with David, the greatest king of Israel, to describe Jesus as the fulfillment of God's promise to establish an everlasting kingdom through his heir (see 2 Samuel 7). Thus, in the genealogy that introduces the gospel, Jesus is proclaimed as "the Messiah, son of David, son of Abraham" (Matt 1:1). Likewise, Matthew's **infancy narratives** (stories of Jesus's birth and childhood) describe Jesus as having been born in Bethlehem, David's city (cf. Luke 2:4), in fulfillment of a prophecy about a ruler who would arise to shepherd God's people, Israel (Matt 2:5–6; cf. Mic 5:2). This detail is embedded in a longer story about wise men (scholars of the esoteric sciences like astrology and dream interpretation) who had come from the East (probably Persia in modern-day Iran) looking for the newborn king of the Jews, another allusion to the Davidic messiah (Matt 2:1–12).

Second, Matthew uses a variety of images and scripture quotations associated with the Exodus to portray Jesus as a great prophet like Moses. His infancy narratives include a story about how Jesus's family had to flee to Egypt to avoid Herod Antipas who was trying to kill the child Jesus—reminders of the story about the infant Moses's amazing escape from death at the hands of the Egyptian Pharaoh (Matt 2:13–15; cf. Exod 2:1–10). In this context, Matthew claims that the words of the prophet Hosea, "Out of Egypt I have called my son," were fulfilled in Jesus—a clear allusion to the Exodus (Matt 2:15; cf. Hos 11:1). Another Matthean story that is reminiscent of the Exodus is Jesus' stay in the wilderness before he begins his teaching ministry. Unlike the Israelites who failed their test in the desert and grumbled against God, Matthew describes how Jesus succeeded, having defeated the devil in a scripture-based debate in the middle of the wilderness (Matt 4:1–11; cf. Exod 32:1–35).

Again using imagery associated with Moses, Matthew portrays Jesus as the new lawgiver who makes perfect the Law and provides ethical teachings to guide the lives of his followers. This point is demonstrated most clearly in the Sermon on the Mount (Matt 5:1–7:29), the first of five long discourses, which some biblical scholars think were intended to correspond with the five books of the Torah. The setting for Jesus' sermon is an unnamed mountain (Matt 5:1), perhaps to evoke the memory of Mount Sinai, the mountain of revelation from the Exodus story. Jesus sits down (the position of teacher) to deliver God's Law. Beginning with the **beatitudes** (statements that start with the phrase "Blessed are they . . ." or "Blessed are you . . ."), Matthew describes Jesus as teaching a new and more perfect way of keeping the commandments and fulfilling the covenant relationship that had already existed for centuries between God and Moses and the Israelite people.

Another aspect of Matthew's Christology is the notion that Jesus is God's continued presence in the world. Two quotations from Matthew's gospel help to illustrate this theme. The first comes from the beginning of the gospel, where Joseph learns in a dream that his wife Mary is to be the mother of Jesus. The gospel writer adds, "All this took place to fulfill what had been spoken by the Lord through the prophet, 'Look, the virgin shall conceive and bear a son, and they shall name him Emmanuel,' which means God is with us" (Matt 1:22–23; cf. Isa 7:14). The second comes from the concluding scene of the gospel, where the risen Jesus gathers his disciples on a mountain and sends them out to "make disciples of all nations" (Matt 28:19). He encourages them with these words: "And remember, I am with you always, to the end of the age" (Matt 28:20). Thus a prophecy from the opening of the gospel is realized in its final scene: Jesus is Emmanuel (God-with-us). Matthew adds a detail about the disciples' reaction when they saw Jesus on the mountain: "They worshiped him" (Matt 28:17). It is a fitting response, indeed.

Luke's Christology

Luke's gospel has a keen interest in proclaiming God's plan of salvation for all people, especially the poor and dispossessed. Luke's gospel also stresses the essential continuity between Judaism and Christianity by presenting Jesus as the fulfillment of all the promises that God made to Abraham and the Jews in the Old Testament. Luke makes numerous references to Jerusalem because it is the place of the Temple and the place in which God's plan of salvation will be fulfilled through the death and resurrection of Jesus. He also explains the difficulty of a crucified messiah by arguing that the Old Testament prophecies testify to the fact that this messiah was destined to suffer.

What is the best way to describe Luke's distinctive portrait of Jesus? A scene from the gospel that describes the beginning of Jesus's ministry is perhaps the most revealing. Luke says that Jesus, filled with the Holy Spirit, was teaching in the synagogues of Galilee (Luke 4:14–15). When he came to his hometown of Nazareth, he went to the synagogue on Sabbath, as he had done many times in the past (Luke 4:16). When he stood up to do the reading, he was given the Book of Isaiah to read. This is what follows:

He unrolled the scroll and found the place where it was written:

The Spirit of the Lord is upon me,
    because he has anointed me to bring good news to the poor.
    He has sent me to proclaim release to the captives
    and recovery of sight to the blind, to let the oppressed go free,
    to proclaim the year of the Lord's favor.
    And he rolled up the scroll, gave it back to the attendant, and sat down. The eyes of all in the synagogue were fixed on him. Then he began to say to them, "Today this scripture has been fulfilled in your hearing." (Luke 4:17–21; cf. Isa 61:1; 58:6; 61:2)

Thus Luke introduces Jesus, at the beginning of his ministry, as the prophet *par excellence*. He is filled with the Holy Spirit and anointed by God to proclaim the good news to the poor and disadvantaged. His ministry is one of compassion for the "little ones," people who are marginalized from society and otherwise disenfranchised.

As Luke develops the plot of his gospel, he continues to highlight this portrait of Jesus. In Luke's version of the Sermon on the Mount, usually called the Sermon on the Plain (Luke 6:20–49), Jesus blesses the poor and the hungry, but he also warns those who are rich and comfortable that they need to be on the side of the poor, just as God is on the side of the poor. Further, Luke shows Jesus' special concern for the lowest segments of society by incorporating stories that highlight Jesus's compassion for those whom society has rejected. He depicts Jesus going out of his way to associate with tax collectors and sinners. For example, there is the story about Zacchaeus being invited down from his perch in the sycamore tree to meet Jesus (Luke 19:1–10). Luke also portrays Jesus as allowing women to take an active part in his ministry (Luke 8:1–3) and serve in roles traditionally reserved for men (Luke 10:38–42). In sum, Luke presents Jesus, the messiah, as the prophet of justice and compassion.

John's Christology

The portrait of Jesus found in the Gospel of John is very different from those of the synoptic gospels. In its prologue, Jesus is presented as the Word—the Greek term is **Logos**—who came down from the Father to dwell among humanity (John 1:1–18). Like most other introductions, this prologue was probably written after the main part of the gospel, serving to highlight and foreshadow the main themes of the gospel as a whole. Its imagery recalls the literature of the Old Testament and the history of the Jewish people, especially the creation story in Genesis and the covenant imagery of the Pentateuch.

What does it mean to describe Jesus as the Word of God? In addition to its many ordinary and popular meanings, *Logos* is a technical term used in Greek (Stoic) philosophy. It describes the unifying principle of all creation, the power that underlies all of creation, and the principle of order in the universe. For the Stoics, the *Logos* represented the mind of God; they also believed that the human soul contained a spark of the divine *Logos*. Humans can be in harmony with the deity and with creation, because they possess a spark of the same divine *Logos*, which is the mind of God.

Hellenistic Judaism had adopted some of this language about the *Logos* to speak about God and God's relationship to creation. Of particular note is Philo of Alexandria, a first-century Jewish philosopher, who combined the philosophical notion of the *Logos* with the biblical notion of Wisdom, one of the powers of God. In the Old Testament, Wisdom (in Greek the word is *Sophia*) is personified as God's partner in creation, who was with God from the beginning, and who came to dwell with Israel, God's chosen people (Prov 8:22–9:12; Sir 24:1–22; Wis 7:21–8:13). She is the one who teaches those who answer her invitation to be wise in God's ways. Thus, Philo understood the *Logos* to be an intermediary between God and creation, a kind of second god who acted as God's instrument in creation. John uses similar imagery to describe how Jesus is God's Wisdom who came from the Father to dwell with humanity. He is the one who makes the Father known to us (cf. John 1:18). The event in which the divine Word came down from God and took on flesh is called, in theological terms, the **incarnation** (meaning "enfleshment").

This kind of Christology, which describes Jesus as the *Logos* who comes down from heaven to dwell with humankind, is sometimes called high Christology, because it focuses primarily on the divinity of Christ, in contrast to low Christologies that focus first on the humanity of Jesus. John's gospel is also called a three-stage Christology, as the diagram below illustrates.

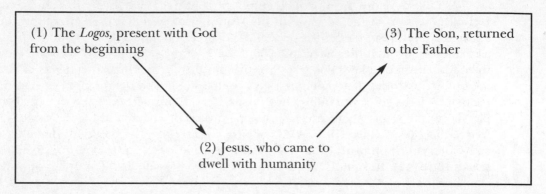

(1) The *Logos*, present with God from the beginning

(2) Jesus, who came to dwell with humanity

(3) The Son, returned to the Father

In addition to its *Logos* Christology, John's gospel is famous for its "I am" sayings. In one incident we hear Jesus declare, "I am" or "I am he," when the Samaritan woman says to him, "I know the messiah is coming" (John 4:25–26). In another, he says, "I am he" or "It is I," when his frightened disciples see him near the boat in the midst of a terrible storm (John 6:20). Though "I am" is translated somewhat differently in these two literary contexts, the words are the same in Greek. Moreover, they are equivalent to the Hebrew YHWH, which is sometimes translated "I am (who am)." This is the divine name, which was revealed to Moses at the burning bush (Exod 3:13–15). John's gospel is replete with words and phrases that have both a plain meaning and a higher symbolic meaning, and this is no exception. In John's gospel, Jesus is the "I am" of God.

John's gospel contains a number of other "I am" sayings, which are longer than the two examples we have already seen. In grammatical terms, these include an object after the subject and verb "I am." Here are some examples:

I am the Bread of Life (John 6:35)
I am the Living Water (John 7:37)
I am the Light of the World (John 8:12)
I am the Door of the Sheep (John 10:7)
I am the Good Shepherd (John 10:11)
I am the Resurrection and Life (John 11:25)
I am the Way, Truth, and Life (John 14:6)
I am the True Vine (John 15:1)

Most of these "I am" sayings depend on imagery of the Hebrew Bible or Jewish feasts for their rich layers of meaning. For example, the "Bread of Life" imagery takes its meaning from the Exodus story in which God gave the Israelites manna from the heavens when they were starving in the wilderness (Exod 16:1–8; cf. Num 11:1–9). The "Living Water" imagery takes its meaning from the Jewish feast of Tabernacles (Booths), in which the priests carried water to the Temple from the nearby Pool of Siloam as a reminder of the water from the rock that God provided to the Israelites during the Exodus (Num 10:2–13).

Figure 6–3 The Samaritan woman meeting Jesus at the well. Sixth-century mosaic from San Apollinare in Classe, Ravenna, Italy.

Although the "I am" sayings are beautifully evocative and poetic, they serve a much greater function in the Gospel of John than simply to delight our senses. On a deeper level of meaning, they explain how it is that Jesus is the **agent of God**. Agency of this sort is difficult for today's readers to appreciate, but first-century peoples would have easily understood, because they saw how the emperor or kings' messengers acted on behalf of their superiors. When the king's messenger came to their village with an order, they listened and obeyed as if the king himself was standing in front of them. They were obligated to honor the messenger in the same way that they would honor the king, because he represented the king in their midst. In the same way, John portrays Jesus as the agent of God. The "I am" sayings of John's gospel describe in words and images how Jesus acted in the world on God's behalf and how he manifests God to the people.

Of course, much more could be said about any one of these portraits of Jesus from the New Testament gospels. Though nearly two millennia old, they continue to inspire Christians and provide them with avenues for encounter with the living Christ. But part of what engages the readers of the gospels is the way that the plot unfolds and the story is told. To better appreciate these aspects of the gospel, we need to focus on their smaller units. Here we will look at two: the parable and the miracle story. They are the subjects of the next section of this chapter.

GOSPEL PARABLES AND MIRACLE STORIES

Biblical scholars study and write a great deal about the smaller units of literature that make up the gospels. They sort these units into categories and analyze their literary forms, they examine how the individual smaller units fit into the larger gospel, and they compare them to other literature of the same period to look for similarities and differences in their form or their usage. They also explore patterns of language and the manner in which readers make sense of individual stories as they progress through the gospels. The goal of this research, of course, is to help the reader better understand and interpret the gospels both as ancient religious literature and as literature that continues to make meaning for the contemporary reader.

The gospels are made up of a number of smaller literary units. For example, careful readers will find collections of sayings attributed to Jesus and longer speeches called discourses. They will also find conflict stories; that is, stories in which Jesus, the protagonist, answers the challenge of his opponents with a pithy saying or a defiant act. These are especially enjoyable because Jesus always wins the debate. The careful reader will also find parables and miracle stories. Perhaps the most common literary forms in the gospel, they are also sometimes the most easily misunderstood by modern readers, because we do not always understand their significance for ancient authors and readers. What follows is a very brief introduction to parables and miracle stories.

The parable is a rather common type of literature associated with ancient teachers. But what are parables? The first thing that often comes to mind for most people is that a parable is a story, and in fact it is. More specifically, a parable is a short fictional narrative with its own plot, setting, and characters. In the case of the gospels, Jesus is the storyteller. Second, in the gospels at least, parables are used to make a comparison. This is why they are often introduced with the phrase, "The kingdom of heaven is like . . ." (Matt 13:44) or with a question, "With what can we compare the kingdom of God, or what parable will we use for it?" (Mark 4:30). Third, as the word itself suggests, a parable is a riddle. That is, it has a surprising or unexpected ending and its meaning is not always obvious. Fourth, parables employ objects or imagery that are part of common life. But this is where modern readers can sometimes misinterpret a parable, because they are unfamiliar with ancient practices of planting crops, fishing, and baking bread.

A parable is usually designed to make a single point about the thing to which it is being compared. Thus, in order to properly interpret the parable, we need to study its literary context–the gospel writer's introduction and concluding remarks concerning the parable. For example, Luke's parable of a woman looking for a lost coin (Luke 15:8–9) could have a number of useful interpretations, but its literary context (Luke 15:1–2, 10) makes the intended message clear: God rejoices with unimaginable joy when a lost sinner is found.

A few gospel parables are much more elaborate and even include their own interpretations. For example, in the parable of the sower (Mark 4:1–20; cf. Matt 13:1–23; Luke 8:4–15), Jesus tells of a farmer who sows seed on the ground. The seed grows in some types of ground, but not in others, and in one type of soil it produces an unbelievably huge harvest. Jesus explains that he is the farmer who sows "the word." The soils, of course, are people who have been exposed to the word of God. Some accept it, at least initially, but then they encounter difficulties that cause them to fall away. Only one type of soil produces good fruit, that is, the hearers of the word who respond with full faith (trust) and go out to proclaim the gospel (good news) of the kingdom of God. In Mark's gospel, these are the "little ones," people whom the larger society might consider to be of no account.

Hopefully these few examples show how important a proper appreciation of parables is for understanding the theological perspectives of the gospels. Likewise, the miracle story is important for conveying certain theological truths of the gospels. Miracle stories are easy to recognize because their structure is simple and straightforward: (1) There is an expression of need; (2) Jesus says or does something to effect the miracle; (3) there is some kind of testimony that the miracle took place. Some are healing miracles: Blind people are able to see (e.g., Mark 10:46–52 and parallels; John 9:1–7); a crippled woman can walk (e.g., Luke 13:10–17); people with leprosy are healed (e.g., Luke 17:11–19). Others are exorcisms: Demons are driven out of people, making them whole again (e.g., Mark 5:1–20 and parallels). Still others are miracles involving nature: Bread and fish are multiplied to feed the crowds (e.g., Mark 8:1–10 and parallels), and Jesus walks on water (Mark 6:45–52 and parallels). There are even a few resuscitations, in which people are brought back from death to life (e.g., Mark 5:21–24, 35–43 and parallels).

Miracle stories can be rather problematic for modern readers who are accustomed to thinking about things like recovery of sight or restoration to health in purely scientific terms. Even more problematic are phenomena like bringing someone back to life or multiplying a few loaves of bread to feed a huge crowd. Science tells us that these things simply cannot happen! In response, some readers of the gospels might argue that the miracles prove Jesus's divinity; Jesus is God, and God can do whatever God wants, even defy the laws of nature. But then how do we explain the New Testament stories about Jesus's followers performing miracles? Peter, for example, is described as healing a crippled man in the Temple area of Jerusalem (Acts 3:1–10), and Paul is described as resuscitating a young man named Eutychus, after he had fallen asleep during one of Paul's speeches. He fell out the window and died! But Paul quickly brought him back to life (Acts 20:7–12). How do we account for their ability to heal people and raise the dead?

Certainly, the gospels' miracle stories demonstrate Jesus' special relationship with God. But is there another reason why the gospel writers included miracle stories in their narratives of the life of Jesus? Mark's gospel suggests one answer to this question. After briefly narrating Jesus's Baptism by John and his testing in the wilderness, Mark describes Jesus as beginning his ministry with these words: "The time is fulfilled, and the kingdom of God has come near" (Mark 1:15). In other words, "Now is the time! God is ready to manifest his concern for God's people and make known his power over evil." Mark follows this proclamation with a long series of miracle stories interspersed with conflict stories. In this context, the miracle stories offer a little preview of God's coming kingdom in which suffering and illness are eradicated. See the next section of this chapter for more on the kingdom of God.

However, John's gospel suggests a rather different function for miracle stories. In this gospel they are called signs, and, as is the nature of signs, they point to something. But to what do they point? John's narration at the end of the first sign, the Wedding Feast at Cana (John 2:1–11), and at the beginning of the last sign, the Raising of Lazarus (John 11:1–54), specifically associates the Johannine miracle stories with the revealing of Jesus's glory. Elsewhere in John's gospel, we learn that Jesus's glorification comes to completion finally in his death and resurrection (see John 12:20–36). In this great act of self-giving, John says, Jesus is glorified and God is glorified in him (John 12:28). In sum, whatever one concludes about the science behind these miracles, the theological message of the miracle story is profound indeed.

Discipleship and the Kingdom of God

All four of the Gospels of the New Testament mention the notion of God's kingdom. In the Gospel of Mark, for example, Jesus's first words of preaching are about the kingdom: "This is the time of fulfillment. The kingdom of God is at hand" (Mark 1:15; cf. Matt 3:2). Where or what is this kingdom of God? Certainly, it is not a geographical space such as we understand the kingdoms of Saudi Arabia or Morocco today. However, it is not to be equated with heaven, either. Perhaps we get a clearer understanding of the concept **kingdom of God** if we think of it in terms of the *reign* of God. The gospels describe the reign of God as something that is manifested in the coming of the Son, in the Spirit's presence among us, and in the conviction that God's grace is greater than all the powers of evil in the world. It signifies a situation in which, by the power of God, good has triumphed over evil and a new world order is established. Thus, the gospels' understanding of kingdom of God has strongly apocalyptic overtones (see Chapter 5).

Further, for Christians, the kingdom of God describes the community's experience of the sovereign power of God manifested in the continuing presence of Jesus. Luke's gospel has two texts that can help us better understand this aspect of the kingdom of God. The first appears in the context of a teaching about the end time:

> Asked by the Pharisees when the kingdom of God would come, [Jesus] said in reply, "The coming of the kingdom of God cannot be observed, and no one will announce, 'Look, here it is,' or, 'There it is.' For behold, the kingdom of God is among you." (Luke 17:20–21)

Luke's point is that the arrival of the reign of God will not be announced with cosmological signs (e.g., earthquake, solar eclipse, falling stars) or by heavenly messengers—in contrast with the view expounded by some contemporary apocalyptic literature—but it will come quietly and suddenly. Indeed, it is already present in the words and deeds of Jesus, but some people refuse to see it.

The second Lukan text that will help us understand the kingdom of God manifested in the continuing presence of Jesus is the famous Emmaus story (Luke 24:13–35). Two disciples are on the way from Jerusalem to a nearby village of Emmaus after Jesus's crucifixion, and suddenly a stranger joins them. They talk about what happened in Jerusalem, but still they do not recognize the stranger until they offer him hospitality—a major theme of Jesus's ministry in Luke's gospel—and he sits at the table with them. Luke continues:

> When he was at the table with them, he took bread, blessed and broke it, and gave it to them. Then their eyes were opened, and they recognized him; and he vanished from their sight. They said to each other, "Were not our hearts burning within us while he was talking to us on the road, while he was opening the scriptures to us?" (Luke 24:30–32)

Earlier, during his last meal with the disciples, the Lukan Jesus said that he would not eat bread again until God's kingdom had come (Luke 22:16). Now, as he eats with them again, the disciples' eyes are opened in the breaking of the bread, and they recognize the risen Jesus in their midst. Their recognition, in turn, prompts them to go out and tell the others—that is, to proclaim the gospel (Luke 24:33–35). Christians, of course, understand the "breaking of the bread" to be a reference to the Eucharist.

As the preceding paragraph suggests, the gospels' understanding of the reign of God is closely related to the notions of discipleship and apostleship. The word *disciple* means "learner," and in the gospels it refers to the people who gathered around Jesus to learn from him. Among this group of disciples were the apostles. The word *apostle* means "one who is sent." These are the ones whom Jesus sent out on a mission to do what he did: to heal the sick, exorcise demons, and preach the kingdom of God (Mark 6:7–13; Matt 10:5–15; Luke 9:1–6). But how does one behave as a disciple of Jesus? Surely it involves more than passively listening to Jesus. One answer is to be found in the synoptic gospels' teaching on discipleship, which Jesus delivers after Peter confessed that Jesus is the messiah. Jesus tells Peter and the other disciples that anyone who wants to be his disciple must be willing to walk in his footsteps and suffer as he will suffer (Mark 8:34–38; Matt 16:24–27; Luke 14:26–27).

Likewise, the parable of the sower (Mark 4:1–9 and parallels) teaches about true discipleship. The interpretation attached to the parable (Mark 4:13–20 and parallels) explains how the seed (the word of God) is scattered on four types of soil: the walking path, rocky soil, thorny soil, and good soil. These four types of soil correspond to four possible responses to the word of God, only one of which (the good soil) bears fruit. It also warns about those things that keep a person from responding in a positive way to the word of God: an excessive concern for riches, approval, or power (the thorny soil); an inability to withstand adversity (the rocky soil); and, worst of all, a refusal even to listen (the walking path). Thus, the parable of the sower teaches that one who wishes to be a Jesus follower must guard against the threats to true discipleship but also must respond positively by hearing the "good news," accepting it, and allowing it to bear fruit in one's life. Those who do this are true disciples.

Mark's gospel describes another attribute of true disciples: They trust in Jesus in spite of their fears. We have already noted that Mark uses miracle stories to demonstrate the coming of God's kingdom and God's power over evil. An example of the latter is the exorcism of a man whom Jesus encountered in the synagogue in Capernaum. As Jesus drives out the demon, he shouts, "What have you to do with us, Jesus of Nazareth? Have you come to destroy us? I know who you are, the Holy One of God" (Mark 1:24). Mark's miracle stories also show the faithful disposition of the recipients of Jesus's miracles. Mark offers these characters as examples of true discipleship. For example, in the story about the healing of a hemorrhaging woman, the woman encounters Jesus in the midst of a crowd and secretly touches him, hoping for a cure. When she is found out, she knelt down before him in fear and trembling and "told him the whole truth" (Mark 5:33). Jesus responds to her, saying, "Daughter, your faith has made you well; go in peace" (Mark 5:34).

By contrast, Mark portrays Jesus's disciples as *negative* examples of discipleship. Although they respond to Jesus's call "immediately" and leave their occupations and families to follow Jesus (Mark 1:16–20), they soon show that they are clueless. Their responses to Jesus and his ministry are characterized by fear and lack of understanding. For example, when the disciples found themselves in a dangerous storm on the sea, while Jesus slept in their boat, they cried out for him to save them. After Jesus calmed the storm, Mark tells his readers, "and they feared a great fear" (see Mark 4:35–41). Later, after Jesus fed 4,000 people with a little bread and fish (Mark 8:1–10), he began warning the disciples about the yeast of the Pharisees, but they were clueless, asking among themselves why Jesus was saying these things (Mark 8:14–16). In response, Jesus chastised them, saying, "Do you still not perceive or understand? Are your hearts hardened? Do you have eyes, and fail to see? Do you have ears, and fail to hear? And do you not remember?" (Mark 8:17–18). Finally, when Jesus was arrested, Mark tells his readers that all of Jesus's disciples deserted him and fled (Mark 14:30). In a word, their fear got the best of them. But all is not lost! After the resurrection, the messenger at the empty tomb has a message for them: They are to go to Galilee where Jesus will see them again (Mark 16:7).

John's gospel also offers negative and positive models of discipleship in the stories and dialogues associated with Nicodemus and the Samaritan woman. Nicodemus, a leader of the Jews and a teacher of Israel, is told that only those who are born from above can enter the kingdom of God, but he clearly does not understand (John 3:3–4). Eventually he fades from the scene, unable to move beyond his initial perception of Jesus as a miracle worker to a fuller recognition of what Jesus was about (John 3:10). By contrast, the Samaritan woman appears somewhat hostile to Jesus when they first meet (John 4:7–12). However, she proceeds, in successive stages, to recognize who Jesus is until finally she returns to her village, saying, "Come and see a man who told me everything I have done. Could he possibly be the Messiah?" (John 4:28–29). The narrator adds, "Many of the Samaritans of that town began to believe in him because of the word of the woman" (John 4:39). Thus, although both misunderstood Jesus's words and failed to understand the significance of his message, at least at first, only one, the Samaritan woman, went out to speak the good news. She is the true disciple of Jesus.

Who gets to be part of God's kingdom? Mark uses the example of little children. Jesus's disciples were trying to turn away the people who were bringing their children to Jesus so that he might bless them, and Jesus intervened saying, "Truly I tell you, whoever does not receive the kingdom of God as a little child will never enter it" (Mark 10:15). In other words, only those who make themselves to be without status or power will be able to receive the gift of participation in the reign of God. Matthew uses the example of separating sheep from goats. Jesus welcomes in those who fed the hungry, gave drink to the thirsty, welcomed the stranger, clothed the naked, cared for the sick, and visited those in prison, because "just as you did it to one of the least of these who are members of my family, you did it to me" (Matt 25:40). In other words, true disciples enjoy a place in God's kingdom, because, even when they are not able to recognize Jesus's continued presence, they act in his name.

Significance of the Death and Resurrection of Jesus

Among all of the events recorded in the gospels, the death and resurrection of Jesus continue to be the touchstone of the Christian faith. Each of the four canonical gospels tells how Jesus was crucified and later raised from the dead. The evidence that the gospel writers provide for Jesus's resurrection varies from one gospel to another, but all include the empty tomb. They also tell of a messenger or messengers sent by God to testify to the fact that Jesus had been raised. Three of the gospels contain stories about the risen Jesus appearing to his followers shortly after his death. Perhaps just as important is the fact that the gospels were written from the perspective of the death and resurrection of Jesus. That is, the gospel writers composed their gospels with the end of the story already in mind, making them truly "good news."

What did these early Jesus followers understand about the significance of a risen messiah? What was their context for understanding what happened to Jesus after his death? Within first-century Judaism, before the death of Jesus, there was already a debate going on about resurrection from the dead. Pharisees believed in it, but Sadducees did not. For those who did believe in resurrection from the dead, it was understood to be one of the ways that God rewarded the righteous ones who had suffered unjustly at the hands of their enemies. The book of Daniel provides a description of this expected resurrection:

There shall be a time of anguish, such as has never occurred since nations first came into existence. But at that time your people shall be delivered, everyone who is found written in the

> book. Many of those who sleep in the dust of the earth shall awake, some to everlasting life, and some to shame and everlasting contempt. Those who are wise shall shine like the brightness of the sky, and those who lead many to righteousness, like the stars forever and ever. (Dan 12:1–3)

But Daniel is writing about the resurrection of the dead in the end time. Moreover, this quotation appears in a section of the book of Daniel that is highly apocalyptic. Thus, Daniel presents the resurrection of the dead as one of the signs that will accompany the end time.

Likewise, the earliest Christians saw Jesus's resurrection from the dead as God's glorious act of vindicating Jesus after his shameful death by crucifixion. Now the world will know that he is God's Righteous One! However, because resurrection of the dead was thought to happen only in the end time, the earliest Christians thought that Jesus's resurrection marked the beginning of the end time. Just as God raised Jesus from the dead, God would soon rescue the rest of God's righteous ones. They needed only to wait for the glorious return of the messiah, at which time the kingdom of God would be fully established for the righteous, and the wicked would be consigned to eternal damnation. Thus, belief in the Second Coming of Christ—the technical term is *parousia*—became an important feature of early Christianity. Indeed, most of the earliest Jesus followers believed that he would return within their lifetimes. Christians today also believe in the *parousia*, though some think it will come soon, while others view it as a more distant future reality.

Baptism and Eucharist in the Gospel Traditions

Baptism and the Eucharist are two of the most important religious rituals for Christians today. Therefore, we should not be surprised to discover that they were also important for Christians of the New Testament period. Unfortunately, the writings of the New Testament tell us little about how Baptism and the Eucharist were actually celebrated, but they do tell us something about their meaning or significance for early Christian communities. For example, an early Christian missionary named Paul wrote about the significance of Christian Baptism by describing it in terms of participation in the death and resurrection of Jesus. Thus, in his letter to the Romans, Paul writes:

> Through Baptism into [Christ's] death we were buried with him, so that, just as Christ was raised from the dead by the glory of the Father, we too might live a new life . . . in Christ Jesus. (Rom 6:4)

Compare this view of Baptism with that of the first letter of Peter, which describes Baptism as the means by which Christians are saved from sin (1 Pet 3:21) and born anew (1 Pet 1:23) to become "a chosen race, a royal priesthood, a holy nation, God's own people" (1 Pet 2:9).

But where did Christians get the idea to use Baptism as a ritual of incorporation into the community of believers? This question is a complicated one, and biblical scholars have not fully decided how this came to be. However, the gospels present John the Baptist as a Jewish prophet who preached a baptism of repentance (Mark 1:4–8; and parallels). Perhaps Christian Baptism has its roots in this Jewish practice. At the same time, the gospels make a distinction between the Baptism of John and the Baptism of the Holy Spirit that Jesus came to bring (Mark 1:7–8; and parallels). Thus, somehow Baptism became for the earliest Christians not only a ritual of repentance but also an initiation into the community of believers and a conferral of the Holy Spirit. Matthew's gospel describes a scene in which the risen Christ commissions his disciples to go out and make disciples of all nations, baptizing them in the name of the Father, of the Son, and of the Holy Spirit (Matt 28:19). Christians today use a similar phrase in their ritual of Baptism.

The word *Eucharist* comes from a Greek word meaning "to give thanks." According to the synoptic gospels, this is what Jesus did when he shared the last meal with his disciples: He broke the bread and blessed the cup of wine and, giving thanks, he gave it to them to drink (Mark 14:22–25 and parallels). This is also what he commanded his disciples to do in memory of him (Luke 22:19). Paul, who gives us perhaps the earliest recorded references to early Christian Eucharist, recalls this same traditional story of the Last Supper:

> I received from the Lord what I handed on to you, namely, that the Lord Jesus on the night in which he was betrayed took bread, and after he had given thanks, broke it and said, "This is my body, which is for you. Do this in remembrance of me." In the same way, after the supper, he took the cup, saying, "This cup is the new covenant in my blood. Do this, whenever you drink it, in remembrance of me." Every time, then, you eat this bread and drink this cup, you proclaim the death of the Lord until he comes! (1 Cor 11:23–27)

Both Paul's teaching on the Eucharist and the synoptic gospels' account of the Last Supper suggest that Eucharist was understood to be a celebration of expectation concerning the return of the messiah and the coming of God's kingdom (see also Matt 26:29, Mark 14:25, and Luke 22:16, 18).

Equally important is the fact that the first Eucharist had its roots in the celebration of Passover, the Jewish feast commemorating the Exodus event. It is a festival of remembrance concerning the loving kindness of God toward his people during their stay in the desert, but it is also a celebration of anticipation when all of God's people will enjoy liberty. According to the synoptic gospels, Jesus's Last Supper with his disciples was the Jewish Passover meal. With that meal, Jesus anticipated his death and reinterpreted the Passover symbols: "This cup that is poured out for you is the new covenant in my blood" (Luke 22:20).

Baptism and the Eucharist continue to hold a significant place in Christian traditions today, at least in part because both rituals are outward signs of that which Christians understand to be a new covenant through Jesus Christ. Through Baptism, Christians give public expression to their identity as people of the new covenant. Through the Eucharist, Christians, in community, celebrate their covenant relationship with God as they await the experience of the fullness of that covenant in God's kingdom.

Key Terms

apostolic tradition	Messianic Secret	kingdom of God
synoptic gospels	infancy narratives	disciple
synoptic problem	beatitudes	apostle
Two-Source Hypothesis	*Logos*	*parousia*
Q	incarnation	
Christology	agent of God	

Questions for Reading

1. Briefly describe what scholars have concluded about the manner in which the gospels came to be written.

2. What is the synoptic problem, and how does the Two-Source Hypothesis provide a possible answer to this problem?

3. Although all four gospels tell the story of Jesus's life, each provides a somewhat different portrait of Jesus. For each gospel, select one key idea that you think best describes its Christology.

4. What is the meaning of the term *kingdom of God*, and how does it relate to the gospel writers' understanding of who Jesus is and what he came to do?

5. What do the gospels say about what it means to be a disciple of Jesus?

6. Explain some of the reasons why the death and resurrection of Jesus was an important event for early Christians and how they made it a central part of their theological reflection on the Christian faith.

7. Although the New Testament tells us little about how early Christians celebrated Baptism and the Eucharist, it does tell us something about the meaning they attached to these rituals. Explain.

Works Consulted/Recommended Reading

Brown, Raymond E. *An Introduction to the New Testament.* New York: Doubleday, 1997.

Duling, Dennis C., and Norman Perrin. *The New Testament: Proclamation and Parenesis, Myth and History.* 3rd ed. Fort Worth, TX: Harcourt Brace, 1994.

Eusebius. *Ecclesiastical History.* Translated by Isaac Boyle. Grand Rapids, MI: Baker Book House, 1990.

Metzger, Bruce, and Roland Murphy, eds. *The New Oxford Annotated Bible with Apocrypha, New Revised Standard Version.* New York: Oxford University, 1991.

Powell, Mark Allan. *Fortress Introduction to the Gospels.* Minneapolis, MN: Fortress, 1998.

Raisanen, Heikki. *The "Messianic Secret" in Mark.* Translated by Christopher Tuckett. Edinburgh: T & T Clark, 1990.

Chapter

7

APOSTOLIC MISSIONS

TIMELINE

c. 4–6 C.E.	Birth of Paul.
30? C.E.	Death of Jesus.
32–33? C.E.	Paul's conversion on the road to Damascus.
37–40 C.E.	A Christian church is established at Antioch.
49 or 50 C.E.	The Jerusalem Conference meets to decide whether Gentile converts must observe Jewish Torah regulations.
49 C.E.	A Christian church is already in existence in Rome.
49–50 C.E.	Paul establishes the church at Corinth.
50–60 C.E.	Paul writes his letters to the churches he founded during his missionary journeys.
58–60 C.E.	Paul is arrested in Jerusalem.
60–61 C.E.	Paul is tried and sent to Rome.
62–64 C.E.	Paul is killed by the Roman emperor Nero.

Although Christians were still a tiny minority in the Roman Empire in 100 C.E., the seeds of Christianity's emergence as the dominant religion in the Mediterranean world were sown by the success of first-century missionaries who spread the word about the crucified and risen Jesus. By the end of the first century, Christian churches thrived in most of the major cities of the Roman Empire. However, because Christianity grew so rapidly in its first decades and with so little institutional control, the religion quickly began to mean different things to different people. The result was that Christianity in the first century was an extremely diverse religious phenomenon, with all sorts of people calling themselves "Christians" but having some very different beliefs and practices.

In spite of the diversity of beliefs and practices in first-century Christian churches, it is possible to see traces of three unifying forces that will manifest themselves in later centuries. (1) Already, from the beginning, the apostles and first followers of Jesus held a place of authority within the churches as teachers and spiritual guides for the Christian communities. Some Christian communities gave to Peter a special status as the first of the apostles. Later, the bishops and leaders of the church would trace the source of their teaching authority back to Peter and the apostles. (2) The early churches also proclaimed the same basic message, namely that Jesus was the messiah and Son of God, the one who was crucified, but also raised from the dead by God's power, so that all who believe might have eternal life. Later, the leaders of these churches used this message to formulate and refine doctrine (teaching) concerning the nature of God, the relationship between God and Jesus, and a variety of other issues that divided the churches. In addition, Christian communities had an intense belief in the power of the Holy Spirit acting in their midst as comforter, inspiration, and guide in the Christian life. (3) Finally, it was during this early period that the books that will later be known as the New Testament were being written. In the centuries that follow, they would become known as the canon, or list of religious documents that are authoritative, for defining the Christian faith and governing its way of life.

THE APOSTLE PAUL

The most prolific of the first generation of Christian missionaries was **Paul**. His importance for the spread of early Christianity is attested to by the amount of space in the New Testament that is devoted to him: Fourteen of the twenty-seven books in the New Testament were included because they were believed to have been written by Paul. Another New Testament book, the Acts of the Apostles, devotes a majority of its pages to describing Paul's missionary activities. These books are the main sources for our understanding of Paul's life and message.

An Overview of Paul's Life

Paul was reportedly born in the city of Tarsus, in Asia Minor (modern Turkey), into a Jewish family that belonged to the party of the Pharisees. Paul's membership in this group meant that he was known for pious behavior and spent a great deal of time studying the Torah. In fact, it seems that Paul surpassed even the other Pharisees in his devotion to the Law, as he says in one of his letters: "I advanced in Judaism beyond many among my people of the same age, for I was far more zealous for the traditions of my ancestors" (Gal 1:14). Although Paul apparently received an outstanding education in the ways of Judaism, his letters also show that he gained a broad knowledge of the Greek language and culture. It is this combination of Judaism and Hellenism in his background that enabled Paul to assume the leadership of Christianity when it was beginning to make the transition from a small Jewish sect to a major world religion.

Little is known of Paul's life prior to his becoming a follower of Jesus, although some scholars theorize that he was a Jewish missionary. In Paul's time, there were many Gentiles who were interested in Judaism, which was attractive to them in large part because of its monotheism and strict ethical code. In the Acts of the Apostles, people who were attracted to Judaism but uncertain whether to become fully Jewish (perhaps because of other Jewish requirements, such as circumcision and the kosher dietary restrictions) are called **God-fearers** (e.g., Acts 10:1–2). They would often attend the synagogue and listen to the readings of the Torah and debates over the Jewish law. They also participated in certain Jewish feasts and other aspects of Jewish life where Gentiles were permitted. Biblical scholars think that the first Gentile Christians came from among these God-fearers. They would have already known the stories of Israel's salvation history, and they would have understood the significance of the Jewish feasts that Christianity eventually expropriated for its own.

We do not know in what capacity Paul first encountered the message about Jesus Christ. However, since the early Jesus Movement was a reform movement within Judaism, it is possible that he learned of it in the synagogues where Jewish-Christian missionaries might have gone to spread their belief that the messiah had come. We also do not know exactly how Paul first received this message, except to say that he was not positively disposed. From the Acts of the Apostles, we learn that he was present as a witness to the killing of a Christian leader named Stephen, who was accused of speaking against the Temple and against Jewish law (Acts 6:13). Later, we learn that he was harassing Jesus followers, breaking into their homes and hauling them off to prison (Acts 8:3). He even solicited a letter from the high priest of the Jerusalem Temple to authorize him to arrest any among the members of the synagogues in Damascus who "belonged to the Way" (Acts 9:1-2).

It was while he was on his way to Damascus that Paul became a follower of Jesus Christ. Paul himself never describes the conversion experience in any detail (see Gal 1:13–17), but the Acts of the Apostles tells us that Paul was blinded by a bright light and he heard a voice from heaven that said, "Saul, Saul, [Paul's Jewish name] why do you persecute me?" Paul answered, "Who are you, Lord?" The voice replied, "I am Jesus, whom you are persecuting" (Acts 9:4–5; cf. Acts 22:4–16; 26:9–18). This experience convinced Paul that Jesus was in fact the messiah. He was led into Damascus, where his blindness was cured, and he was baptized as a Christian by a man named Ananias (Acts 9:8–19).

Evidence for the Events of Paul's Life

Our evidence for certain events in Paul's life, such as the details of Paul's conversion, his participation in the martyrdom of Stephen, and his final arrest and trials, is found only in the Acts of the Apostles. It must be said that the interests of the author of the Acts of the Apostles (also the author of the Gospel of Luke) were more theological than historical. What this means is that Acts is not universally regarded as being a completely reliable source for historical information about Paul or other figures and events in early Christian history. Paul's letters themselves are usually regarded by

Figure 7–1 St. Paul on the road to Damascus.

historians as a more reliable source. Hence, in this overview of Paul's life we rely more on Paul's letters than on Acts, and we attempt to acknowledge those places where evidence is used from the less reliable Acts of the Apostles.

After this revelation, Paul immediately redirected his missionary zeal toward the Christian message. His first journeys were to Arabia (also called Nabataea) and Damascus (Gal 1:17), then to Jerusalem to meet Peter and James (Gal 1:18–19), and later to Damascus (again) and Cilicia (Gal 1:21). There is no record of Paul having any great successes in these areas. At some point Barnabas, a Jewish Christian missionary, brought Paul to Antioch in Syria, where a group of Christian prophets and teachers were gathered. As they prayed, the Holy Spirit spoke, saying, "Set apart for me Barnabas and Saul for the work to which I have called them" (Acts 13:3), and so they were sent off to preach the message of Jesus Christ. As they traveled to various cities throughout the Mediterranean, they first went to the synagogue, where their message met with mixed success among Jews but was enthusiastically received by the Gentile God-fearers (Acts 13:13–14:28).

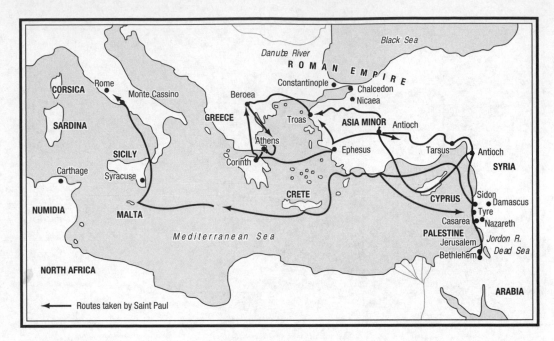

Figure 7–2 Map of Paul's missionary journeys.

As large numbers of Gentiles began to accept the message of Jesus, the question arose as to whether these Gentiles must first become Jews in order to convert to Christianity. Up to this point, the Christian movement had retained all of the requirements of Judaism. Did these Gentiles then also need to become circumcised, follow the Torah, sacrifice in the Temple, and keep kosher? Or was it enough that they believed in Jesus Christ, without taking on the other requirements of the Jewish faith? Paul and Barnabas thought that faith in Jesus Christ was enough and that Gentiles were not required to do such things as becoming circumcised and following the Jewish Law. However, this new gospel created a storm of controversy among Christian Jews (also called *Jewish Christians*) who believed strongly that there could be no compromise about the retention of all the elements of Judaism.

In 49 or 50 C.E. a conference was called to discuss the question of whether Gentiles needed to become Jews in order to convert to Christianity. This meeting is called the **Jerusalem Conference**. Paul and Barnabas attended the conference and defended the position that the Gentiles did not need to follow the Law and become circumcised (Acts 15:2–3, 12; Gal 2:1–3, 5, 7–8). Opposed to them was a group of conservative Jewish Christians who supported requiring all Christians to keep the requirements of Judaism (Acts 15:5; Gal 2:4–5). The leaders who were convened to decide the question were the Jerusalem apostles, led by Peter, John, and James, "the brother of the Lord."

Exactly what happened at the Jerusalem Conference is a matter of some dispute. Paul records that the conference ended with the Jerusalem apostles completely vindicating his gospel and approving unconditionally that he be allowed to preach the message of Jesus Christ to the Gentiles without obligating them to become Jews (Gal 2:9–10). The Acts of the Apostles records more of a compromise, in which Gentiles are released from some of the requirements of Judaism, but not all (Acts 15:19–21). Apparently, the issue was not decided once and for all at the conference, as Paul continued to have difficulty with conservative Jewish Christians who often tried to undermine his subsequent missionary efforts. Sometimes Paul was even forced to confront the same Jerusalem apostles who had given approval for his activities (see Gal 2:11–14).

Whatever the precise outcome of the Jerusalem Conference, Paul felt that he had been given a mandate by God to preach a gospel without the Law and circumcision to the Gentiles. After the conference he began a series of ambitious missionary journeys, which included travels to Cyprus, Asia Minor, Macedonia, and Greece. These journeys were a stunning success. Paul founded numerous churches and made thousands of converts, becoming probably the greatest missionary Christianity has ever seen.

Except for the letter to Philemon, the letters of Paul found in the New Testament are all written to churches or communities of believers. Among those, all except the letter to the Romans are written to churches that he himself founded, and they all contain Paul's specific responses to the questions, needs, and problems of that particular church. After Paul left a community—either because he wanted to continue his missionary work elsewhere or because he was forced by persecution to leave—he would communicate with the church he left behind through hand-delivered letters, especially if he heard that there was some problem or crisis facing the community. Some of these letters survived and were eventually included in the canon of the New Testament.

Paul's Authentic Letters and the Question of Pseudonymity

It must be acknowledged that not all of the letters traditionally ascribed to Paul were actually written by him. One of them (the letter to the Hebrews) does not actually have Paul's name attached to it. Only seven of the other thirteen letters are universally believed by scholars to have been written by Paul (1 Thessalonians, 1 and 2 Corinthians, Galatians, Philippians, Philemon, and Romans). Authorship of the other six letters (2 Thessalonians, Colossians, Ephesians, 1 and 2 Timothy, and Titus) is disputed to varying degrees. Many scholars believe that these letters were written by disciples of Paul in their master's name.

The practice of writing a document with a false name attached is called **pseudonymity**. Today we might be inclined to view pseudonymous works as somehow suspicious or deceptive. However, in the ancient world, and especially when it came to religious literature, writing under a pseudonym was an important way to honor a great and holy person and also to continue his legacy. Therefore, we should not consider the possibility that the New Testament contains pseudonymous letters of Paul as a challenge to their authoritative status. Rather, they are testimony to the success of Paul's work and the acclaim he had earned in the early decades of Christianity.

Paul's missionary activity came to an end when he had journeyed to Jerusalem apparently to deliver a collection he had been taking up to support the church in Jerusalem, which was undergoing some sort of persecution or financial difficulty (see Acts 11:29–30; 24:17; Rom 15:26; 1 Cor 16:1–3; 2 Cor 8:1–15). At first he was greeted warmly, but then he was accused of telling Jews who lived among Gentiles that they were not required to obey

Mosaic law, circumcise their children, or keep other Jewish customs (Acts 21:17–22). Soon a huge riot erupted in the Temple precincts, and Paul was seized by the crowd. As they were trying to kill him, a Roman military tribune noticed what was going on and rescued Paul by arresting him and throwing him in jail (Acts 21:27–38). Eventually he was taken to Rome, where church tradition has it that he was executed by the Roman emperor Nero in approximately 62–64 C.E.

The Authority of Paul as an Apostle

In almost every one of Paul's letters he identifies himself as an apostle. The word *apostle* comes from the Greek word *apostello*, which means, "to send out." An apostle, then, is "one who is sent out." For early Christians the term meant "one who is sent out by Jesus to preach the word about him." Thus, an apostle is distinct from a disciple. The word *disciple* refers simply to a learner or a follower. One could be both a disciple and an apostle (like Peter and John, who both followed Jesus during his lifetime and were sent out by him to preach the gospel, the good news about Jesus Christ, to others), but one could be a disciple without being an apostle. That is, it was quite possible to have been a follower of Jesus but not specifically sent out by him to preach the gospel. It was presumed by many early Christians that in order to be an apostle, one must have known Jesus and been sent out by him to preach during his lifetime.

By this definition, it would be impossible for Paul to be an apostle, because he never knew Jesus during his lifetime. However, Paul claimed that he was an apostle (e.g., Rom 1:1; Gal 1:1), because he had been sent out by Jesus to preach the gospel. How was Paul's apostleship different from that of Peter or the others who walked with Jesus? Paul's mission was not given to him during Jesus's lifetime, but in a revelation that took place after Jesus's death and resurrection.

Paul's revelation-based claim to be an apostle was eventually accepted by the church as a whole, as is attested by the inclusion of Paul's letters in the canon of the New Testament. However, the fact is that Paul often struggled to be accepted as an apostle during his lifetime. In fact, much of the controversy that dogged Paul throughout his career can be attributed to the question of whether or not he was a "real" apostle like Peter and John. Many people were skeptical about his claim to have had a revelation and felt more comfortable with the leadership of people like Peter and John, who had been among Jesus's original twelve disciples and whose apostleship was not in dispute.

An Overview of Paul's Message

It is no easy matter to summarize Paul's message. His letters are often difficult to understand, because they were not written to satisfy the curiosity of future generations, but to meet the concrete needs of particular first-century communities. Nonetheless, Paul's letters are important for describing a number of important themes in Christian theology.

Many scholars and church leaders have located the "center" of Paul's theology in the principle of **justification** by faith, which is prominent in the letter to the Galatians and in the letter to the Romans. In both of these letters, Paul argues strongly that one cannot be justified by the works of the Law, but only through faith in Jesus Christ. What does Paul mean by this? One of the meanings of the word *justification* has to do with alignment. If the right-hand margin on a printed page has been made perfectly straight, then it is a justified right margin. If the margin is crooked or ragged, then it is not justified. Hence, justification in general can refer to making straight something that is crooked, or even more generally to fixing or repairing something that is broken. In a religious context, justification refers to one's relationship with God. If this relationship is good (or "straight"), then a person is justified. If this relationship is broken (or "crooked"), then a person is not justified. Hence, justification refers to the state of being in a right relationship with God, and a person who is in right relationship with God is said to be justified.

Both the Jewish and Christian faiths assume that human beings in their present state are not in a right relationship with God. This broken relationship is caused by sin. Human beings sin against God, and this sin creates distance between ourselves and God. We are estranged from God by sin. The question is how to overcome this distance. How can we repair this broken relationship with God? When Paul refers to justification by works and justification by faith, he is speaking of two different and opposing theories about how our broken relationship with God can be repaired.

Justification by Works.   **Justification by works**, which is often thought to be characteristic of traditional Judaism, involves two responses to the question about how humanity can repair its broken relationship with God. First, if our bad relationship with God is caused by sin, then the solution is to avoid sin as much as possible. Judaism holds that God assisted in the avoidance of sin by giving people the Law of Moses to follow. The Law helps people to know what counts as a sin and what does not, what is pleasing to God and what is not. Second, when people do sin, they must try to make up, or atone, for that sin by doing some good deed. In Judaism, for example, one could atone for sin by doing such things as performing sacrifices, fasting, praying, or giving alms (donating money to the poor). These are the works or good deeds prescribed by the Law. At the heart of these two approaches is the notion of covenant. God made a covenant with Israel and gave them the Law of Moses as their obligation to the covenant. Thus, for Israel, keeping the covenant—that is, staying in right relation with God—meant keeping the Law.

Justification by Faith.   **Justification by faith** is the response that Paul supports. He begins by arguing that it is not possible to be justified by works for two reasons. On the one hand, it is impossible for human beings to successfully avoid all sin. Human nature is such that sin is inevitable. Moreover, it is impossible for human beings to "make up" for sins with good deeds. As Paul understands the problem, through sin, humanity has broken covenant with God. Our sins are an affront to God and a breaking of that covenant. Whatever good humans do to try to repair that relationship, they will not be successful, because God is the one who initiated the covenant, and only God can restore it.

Perhaps the two meanings of the Greek verb *dikaioun* ("to justify") can help us understand why Paul argues that a person can only be justified by faith. One meaning of the word *dikaioun* is "to acquit," as in a court of law. When Paul says that we cannot be justified by our works, he means that if human beings were judged on the merits of their case, according to what we really deserved, no one would be justified. Because of our sinful nature, no one would ever be able to stand as acquitted before God. It is impossible for human beings to use good works to "earn" acquittal. The only way we can be acquitted is if God simply gives it to us as a free gift, in spite of the fact that we do not deserve it. This idea of God's bestowal of a free gift is what theologians mean by **grace**.

The other meaning of *dikaioun* is "to make upright." According to this meaning of the word, someone must act in our behalf to make us upright or to put us in right relationship with God. Paul describes justification as God's free gift, not as something we have earned or deserve. God has given this gift by sending His son, Jesus Christ. For Paul, Jesus's death on the cross functions as a sacrifice that makes us upright, that makes us able to stand before God in right relationship. This understanding of the purpose of Jesus's death—that Jesus died for our sins—is called **sacrificial atonement**. The death of Jesus constitutes, for Paul, God's offer of salvation to human beings. We cannot bridge the gulf between God and ourselves through our own efforts, but we can allow God to bridge this gulf for us.

What, then, does Paul mean when he talks about justification by faith? God's offer of justification in Jesus Christ is a free gift. We cannot bring about our justification by our works. Any good deeds that we could do would not be enough to earn us an acquittal in God's tribunal of justice. However, we can be *made* righteous by accepting in faith the free gifts offered by God. Faith, as Paul understands it, is not confined to a set of beliefs that one learns. Rather, it should be understood as trust. God acts in our behalf to make us upright. We respond in trust, believing that it is true. But this trust does not mean that the Christian sits back and does nothing. For Paul, faith is *active* trust, or trust that manifests itself in the way the believer lives his or her life. He describes it as "faith working through love" (Gal 5:6). The believer demonstrates his or her faith by living the Christian life as an expression of love.

Paul's teaching on justification by faith appears, at first glance, to be fairly straightforward and unambiguous. However, depending on what one understands Paul to be saying (or not saying), his message can have strikingly different ramifications. At the heart of the ambiguity are questions concerning what Paul thinks about sin and how he conceives of human nature. It is unclear from Paul's writings whether or not he thinks that human nature by itself is capable of any good. In his letter to the Romans, for example, he says that humans were made capable of knowing God, but they chose not to—implying their capacity to do good, in spite of their choice to do evil (Rom 1:19). If we assume that Paul had this view of human nature in mind, then we can also argue that Paul would allow for the possibility that, although God justifies, humans can do good deeds that aid in their salvation. However, later, in this same letter, Paul says that human beings by themselves are unable to win the inner war of the spirit (or inner will) over the flesh (Rom 7:14–24). In this way of thinking, humans are simply too sinful by nature to do good.

Because of this ambiguity, Christian denominations have held a variety of interpretations of Paul's principle of justification by faith. In fact, the teaching on justification by faith has been an important point of discussion in Lutheran and Roman Catholic ecumenical dialogue for many years. Most recently, in 1999, these two churches published the *Joint Declaration on the Doctrine of Justification,* which identifies areas of common understanding and explains the differences that still remain in their interpretations of the doctrine of justification by faith. The document notes that they were able to come to these common understandings by using the insights of modern biblical studies and research into the history of the development of doctrine (§2). It is a good example of how communities of faith can come together in dialogue on a matter that they once thought divided them irreparably.

Life in Christ

Although in such letters as Galatians and Romans Paul's major focus is how persons are to be justified, all of his letters together reveal an equal concern for how persons are to live as

Christians. But living the good Christian life does not earn one salvation in Paul's view. Rather, a moral life is the expected response to God's grace in Christ Jesus. This is Paul's command: "You are in Christ, so live in Christ." Thus, Paul's emphasis on "life in Christ" accompanies the theme of justification by faith. Although there are multiple ways to illustrate Paul's teaching on this topic, perhaps three examples will suffice: (1) freedom and love, (2) the activity of the Holy Spirit, and (3) the church as the Body of Christ. We will conclude this section with a brief word on Paul's understanding of Baptism and Eucharist, which are sacramental expressions of the Christian community's life in Christ.

Freedom and Love.   Paul writes at some length about freedom in his letter to the Romans and his letter to the Galatians. In both cases, he closely links freedom from the Law with justification through faith in Jesus Christ. In our contemporary Western culture, we tend to think of freedom as a person's right to do whatever he or she wishes, without limitation, except perhaps the constraint of not harming another. To the uninformed, Paul's "freedom from the Law" can sound quite similar. Apparently some people in the church at Corinth thought so, too, because it seems that they had written to him saying, "All things are lawful for us" (1 Cor 6:12). However, in his response to the Corinthian church he corrects their wrong thinking about freedom by adding, "but not all things are beneficial" (1 Cor 6:12). Elsewhere, he writes about freedom "in regard to righteousness" (Rom 6:20) and freedom from the power of sin, which brings death (Rom 6:7, 22–23).

In order to more fully understand Paul's teaching on freedom and appreciate its implications for the life of the community of faith, we need to be aware that Paul talks about both *freedom from* and *freedom for.* To his way of thinking they are like two sides of the same coin: Those who are justified are freed from slavery to sin so that they can be freed for slavery (or committed service) to God (Rom 6:16–18, 20–22). The imagery is reminiscent of the great covenants of Israelite history. When God justified humanity through the death and resurrection of Jesus, he restored covenant relationship for all who believe (trust) in his name. God's covenant with Moses and the Israelites in the wilderness placed certain obligations on its recipients, namely, the Law. However, Paul says, this restoration of covenant relationship is given as a free gift to all who believe (Rom 3:24).

But the fact that God justifies, as a free gift, all who believe does not mean that no response is needed. Paul uses the phrase "faith working through love" (Gal 5:6) to describe the believers' response to God's gift of justification. Further, he exhorts his communities with these words: "For you were called to freedom, brothers and sisters; only do not use your freedom as an opportunity for self-indulgence, but through love become slaves to one another" (Gal 5:13). Elsewhere in his letters he describes the character of this love. Paul says that love should be genuine. It should be patient and kind, it should not be hurtful or boastful, and it should always rejoice in the truth (1 Cor 13:4–7). Further, the community should be known by their mutual regard for one another, living in harmony, holding up the weak, providing for the needs of those who have less, and giving hospitality to strangers (Rom 12:9–16). If they love one another, then they have fulfilled the whole of the law (Rom 13:8–10; Gal 5:14). This is what it means to live in Christ.

The Activity of the Holy Spirit.   As already noted, most of Paul's letters were written to address specific issues within the communities to whom he was writing. The first letter to the Corinthians is a good example. Based upon several comments in the letter, we can conclude that the Christian community at Corinth enjoyed and perhaps promoted certain gifts of the Holy Spirit such as *glossolalia* (speaking in tongues). Perhaps some even considered themselves to be more spiritual than the others because they possessed such gifts (1 Cor 14:1–12; see also 1 Cor 3:1–3; 4:6–7).

There is plenty of evidence in Paul's letters that he values the gifts of the Holy Spirit. He tells his communities that, through the Spirit, they have become children of God (Rom 8:14–17) and that they ought to "live in the Spirit" (Gal 5:16). He believes that the Spirit helps them in their need and intercedes for them (Rom 8:26–27). He also attributes the various ministries in the community—apostles, teachers, prophets, healers, and other kinds of leadership—to the work of the Holy Spirit (1 Cor 12:8–11, 27–31). However, he cautions the Christian community at Corinth about the use of *glossolalia*. The reason is clear—the gifts of the Spirit are intended for the common good (1 Cor 12:7). Someone who has the gift of speaking in tongues does not benefit the community unless there is someone present who can interpret the strange words. Indeed, those who have the gift of tongues might be tempted to use it to build up themselves (1 Cor 14:1–5). Instead, he prefers that they foster the gift of prophecy, because those who prophesy speak for the "upbuilding and encouragement and consolation" of the church (1 Cor 14:3).

In general, Paul urges those who are eager for the spiritual gifts to "strive to excel in them for the building up of the church" (1 Cor 14:12). And how does a person discern what is the activity of the Holy Spirit and what is not? Paul identifies these virtues as the fruits of the Holy Spirit: love, joy, peace, patience, kindness, generosity, faithfulness, gentleness, and self-control (Gal 5:22–23). Whatever manifests itself in contrary ways does not belong to the Holy Spirit (see, for example, Gal 5:19–21), and the Christian community that manifests the fruits of the Spirit knows that it lives in Christ.

Church as the Body of Christ.   For Paul, God's grace-filled gift, which is effected through Christ's death and resurrection, both reconciles sinners to God and unites all baptized Christians with Christ and with each other to form Christ's body. The source of this unity, Paul believes, is the fact that the Spirit of God dwells in them:

> For just as the body is one and has many members, and all the members of the body, though many, are one body, so it is with Christ. For in the one Spirit we were all baptized into one body—Jews or Greeks, slaves or free—and we were all made to drink of one Spirit. (1 Cor 12:12–13)

How does the Spirit make the church into the one body of Christ? As Paul sees it, the members of the Christian community are not simply committed to one another through friendship or church affiliation. Rather, they are each individually united with Christ through Baptism, making their bond to one another of the highest order—they share the same Holy Spirit. Different members have different gifts, according to God's grace, all for the common good (Rom 12:3–8; 1 Cor 12:4–11). However, no member of the body is more important than the others, and no member of the body is less honorable, and when one member of the community suffers they all suffer (Rom 12:3; 1 Cor 12:22–24). They are all one body, and they must demonstrate the "same care for one another" (1 Cor 12:25). In other words, this notion of the church as Body of Christ is not simply a theoretical concept that captures the imagination of theologians. Rather, it has profound ethical implications for how the Christian community lives in the world.

Baptism and Eucharist in the Pauline Churches.   Life in Christ expresses itself spiritually and sacramentally in Baptism and the Eucharist. Paul taught that in Baptism the believer was incorporated into Christ. The baptized went down into the water in order to be baptized into Christ's death and to be buried with him so that, just as he was raised from the dead, they could walk in the new life of a Christian (Rom 6:1–4). Similarly, Paul saw the Eucharist as a way in which Christians participated in the body of Christ (1 Cor 10:16). Thus, the Eucharist ought to be the source of their unity with other Christians. If it is not celebrated in a way that demonstrates their unity—if the wealthy and privileged of the community do not wait for the poor and allow them to share equally of the Eucharistic table—then eating the bread and drinking the cup of the Lord will be their condemnation (1 Cor 11:17–34). These are harsh words, to be sure, but they make clear Paul's feelings about what it means to live in Christ.

OTHER APOSTOLIC MISSIONS

The growth of Christianity during the first and second centuries was not limited to the cities Paul visited or to the churches that he founded. Rather, it is only the case that we have considerably more information about the Christian communities that Paul founded. This is due in large part to the fact that so many of his letters were preserved among the books of the New Testament. In contrast, there is relatively little information available with which to reconstruct a portrait of early non-Pauline Christian communities (Christian churches not founded by Paul). Yet, Christian literature of a century or two later and early traditions of individual churches suggest that these other churches also have a very long and colorful history, dating back to the first and second centuries of the Common Era of Christianity and Judaism.

From the Acts of the Apostles and the writings of second- and third-century Christian historians and theologians, we can piece together bits of information about Christian communities at Jerusalem, Rome, Alexandria, and Antioch, which, together with Constantinople, come to be identified as the **patriarchal sees** (meaning "head or leading seats") of the early Christian church. These churches become very important players in the history of Christianity in both the East and the West during the next centuries of its development. We will also comment briefly on the variety of Christian churches that emerge in places outside of these central churches.

The Jerusalem Church

The church in Jerusalem was among the more important Jewish Christian communities of the first century C.E. While we do not know when this Jewish community first identified itself as Christian, it appears to have already been firmly established by 48–49 C.E., when Paul and Barnabas went there for a meeting with its leaders concerning the admission of Gentile converts (Acts 15; Gal 2). According to Paul's letter to the churches in Galatia and several references in Acts of the Apostles, the leader of the Christian church at Jerusalem was James, identified as the brother of the Lord (Gal 1:18; 2:9, 12; Acts 12:17; 15:13). This community also gave special honor to the apostles and the presbyters or elders of the community (Acts 15:22).

It appears that the Christian community at Jerusalem retained the practice of circumcision and other legal requirements of Judaism, along with their newly founded Christian beliefs and practices. Further, concerning worship and lifestyle, the Acts of the Apostles describes the Christians at Jerusalem as sharing all things in common, going to the Temple daily, and gathering to "break bread" in their homes (Acts 2:42–47). The breaking of bread is a reference to the celebration of the Eucharist. Acts of the Apostles also tells us that these early Christians were sometimes called "followers of the Way" (Acts 9:2; 16:17; 19:9, 23; 24:14, 22). Historians do not know what happened to this church after the Romans sacked Jerusalem in 70 C.E.

The Church of Rome

Already in the first century B.C.E., there was a large and perhaps influential Jewish community in Rome. Literature and archeological data of the time suggest that by the first century C.E., Rome had a population of approximately 40,000 to 50,000 Jews and ten to thirteen synagogues. Christianity in Rome probably emerged out of these Jewish communities and from among the Gentile "God-fearers" who had attached themselves to their synagogues. Like other Jewish Christian communities, these Christians probably still saw themselves as part of a reform movement in Judaism.

By the time Paul wrote to the Christian communities in Rome, perhaps around 55 C.E., they had undergone some rather significant changes. In Acts of the Apostles, Luke mentions Priscilla and Aquila, a husband-and-wife missionary team who had fled Rome when Emperor Claudius expelled the Jews from Rome in 49 C.E. Apparently, there had been some fighting between Jews and Jewish Christians over teachings about Jesus as the Christ, and Claudius decided to settle the problem by getting rid of the whole lot. Thus, the Christian communities at Rome were left for a time with only their Gentile membership, although some Jewish Christians may have returned after Claudius' death in 54 C.E. At the time of Paul's writing, it appears that Jews and Christians were still fighting, since Paul indicates that Christians in Rome ought to remember their roots and not think themselves better than their Jewish brothers and sisters (Rom 11:17–24).

The Christian communities at Rome appear already to have been strongly established by 49 C.E. Church historians and other writers of the second, third, and fourth centuries associate Peter with its early years, if not with its founding. According to Eusebius, a fourth-century church historian, Peter was martyred in Rome, in approximately 64 C.E.

The Church at Antioch in Syria

From Paul's letter to the churches in Galatia and from several references in Acts of the Apostles, we know that there was a Christian community at Antioch in Syria rather early in the first century C.E. (Acts 11:19–20; Gal 2:12). Acts of the Apostles indicates that the Jerusalem church sent Barnabas to help shepherd the church at Antioch even before Paul began his missionary activity, approximately 37 to 40 C.E. (Acts 11:19–25). Like the Christian communities founded in Jerusalem and Rome, the initial thrust of Christian missionary activity in Antioch appears to have been among its Jewish communities. Gentiles, however, were also joining their church. Acts of the Apostles notes that it was at Antioch that the name Christian was first used (Acts 11:27).

Syria is also the likely home of an early Christian writing called the *Didache* or "The Teaching of the Twelve Apostles," believed to have been written in the late first century or early second century C.E. Its catechetical section (teachings about the Christian way of life) has many parallels with the Gospel of Matthew, which may also have originated in Syria. Its liturgical section (teachings about the right ways to worship) highlights the importance of Baptism and the Eucharist for Christian communities. It also reflects a church organization that held the Christian prophet in a place of honor and authority within its Christian communities. Acts of the Apostles also mentions the presence of Christian prophets in Antioch (Acts 13:1).

Christianity in Alexandria and Egypt

In addition to the churches of Jerusalem, Rome, and Antioch, Acts of the Apostles offers a few other very tentative clues about the spread of Christianity elsewhere during the first century C.E. For example, Acts of the Apostles mentions a certain Apollos from Alexandria in Egypt who was "both an authority on scripture and instructed in the new way of the Lord" (Acts 18:24–25). Apollos, a Jew, became a Christian and embarked on his own missionary ventures. Paul mentions him in relation to his preaching in Corinth (1 Cor 1:12; 3:5–9). Along with Athens and Antioch, Alexandria was one of the primary centers of Hellenistic culture prior to the beginnings of Christianity in the first century C.E. In particular, it was noted for its philosophers and students of Plato's writings.

Although no written evidence exists concerning the origins of the Christian church at Alexandria and the Nile valley, it must have been established fairly early, because Christian writers of the second century were arguing against certain other teachers from this place, whom they labeled as Christian heretics (teachers of false doctrine). Among some of Alexandria's famous Christian writers are Clement of Alexandria, Origen, and Athanasius. All three figure predominantly in the articulation of Christian teaching as it develops through the fourth century.

Christianity in Ethiopia, Edessa, Adiabene, and Beyond

Acts of the Apostles tells of the conversion of another early Christian, an official from the court of the queen of Ethiopia who, while on his return trip from pilgrimage to Jerusalem, was baptized by Philip (Acts 8:26–40). Again, written history is mostly silent about early beginnings of the Christian church in Ethiopia, although Rufinus, another fourth-century church historian, claims that King Ezana converted to Christianity in the mid-fourth century, making his kingdom of Aksum a Christian nation. He also tells about Frumentius, a Syrian by birth and a one-time slave in Ethiopia, who was ordained by Athanasius of Alexandria to serve the church in Ethiopia (*Ecclesiastical History* I, 9–10). This ordination created a special bond between the two churches of Alexandria and Ethiopia, a bond that endured through much of their history into the modern period.

The Ethiopian Christian church preserves among its early traditions some interesting answers to questions for which written history is otherwise silent. For example, the Ethiopian church holds within its traditions the name of the eunuch baptized by Philip on the road to Gaza, identifying him as Juda, also called Djan Daraba. They also claim within their tradition the identity of one of the three wise men who, according to Matthew's gospel, went to Bethlehem to worship the child Jesus, namely, King Bazan (Balthazar) who ruled Ethiopia for seventeen years at the turn of the era.

There are numerous other traditions concerning the apostles and the expanse of their missionary activity in the first centuries of Christianity. In his *Ecclesiastical History*, Eusebius indicated that the apostles were scattered over the whole world and that their influence could be felt in different areas: Thomas in the region of the Parthians; John in Asia; Peter

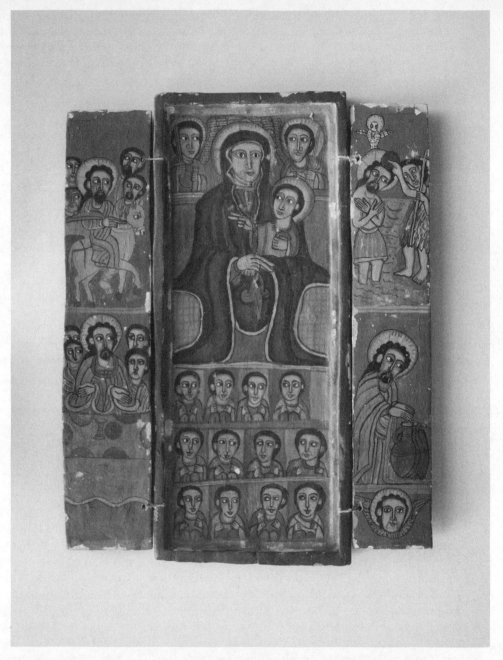

Figure 7–3 Ethiopian icon of Mary and the Child Jesus. University of St. Thomas Permanent Art Collection. This triptych demonstrates influence of Jesuit missionaries who explored this area in the seventeenth century. The center upper panel shows the Virgin Mary dressed in blue and holding a handkerchief, following an example from Santa Maria Maggiore in Rome. The apostles are depicted in the center lower panel, and scenes from the life of Christ are illustrated in the outer panels.

Figure 7–4 Map of the expansion of Christianity at the end of the first century C.E.

in Pontus, Galatia, Cappadocia, Bithynia, and Rome; and Andrew in Scythia (*Ecclesiastical History* III.I.1). Gregory of Nazianzus wrote that Thomas also preached the gospel in India and was martyred there (*Orations* 25).

Two other locations are worthy of brief mention in the early history of Christianity: Adiabene in Persia and Edessa in Eastern Syria. Again, our information is sparse. However, Christianity is believed to have come to Adiabene at the end of the first century through the preaching of Addai. His Christian missionary activity supposedly followed upon an earlier Jewish mission in which Izates, the king of Adiabene, and his mother, Queen Helena, were converted to Judaism. Tradition has it that both were buried in Jerusalem.

The Christian church at Edessa also claimed Addai as its founder. Eusebius tells of a tradition in which King Abgar, who had been very ill and who had heard about Jesus's miracles, received a letter from Jesus delivered by one of Jesus's disciples who also healed him of his illness. Later, Thomas sent Thaddeus to his city to teach about Christ (*Ecclesiastical History* I.13). This tradition is especially important to the Armenian church, which claims its origin through the apostle Thomas.

In sum, although reliable information about the first hundred years of Christianity is very sketchy, we can see several important trends developing in its history. We can see that early Christianity spread very rapidly, especially among the larger centers of culture and trade. It grew and developed in a rather charismatic fashion, without much institutional control, and it gave birth to diverse and distinctive communities, all of whom called themselves Christian. Thus, for each of these communities, their Christian identity meant something quite different from other Christian communities. This early history helps us to understand why the major thrust of the next period in early Christian history must be, of necessity, the articulation and clarification of Christian doctrine or teaching.

Key Terms

Paul
God-fearers
Jerusalem Conference
pseudonymity

justification
justification by works
justification by faith
grace

sacrificial atonement
glossolalia
patriarchal sees

Questions for Reading

1. Why was there so much diversity in early Christian beliefs and practice? What elements of early Christianity would later be used to unify the church?

2. Give an account of Paul's activities prior to his becoming a follower of Jesus Christ, and explain how he eventually came to follow Jesus.

3. What was the issue addressed at the Jerusalem Conference, and how was it resolved?

4. Define the term *apostle*, distinguishing it from the term *disciple*, and explain why Paul had difficulty being accepted as an apostle in his lifetime. Is he ever recognized as an apostle by the church?

5. Explain the difference between justification by works and justification by faith. Which does Paul prefer? Why?

6. Explain Paul's understanding of the church as Body of Christ.

7. Name the four major non-Pauline Christian churches of the first and second centuries C.E. and the New Testament apostles or preachers associated with them. Which, if any, originated as Jewish Christian communities?

Works Consulted/Recommended Reading

Bornkamm, Gunther. *Paul.* New York: Harper & Row, 1971.

Cousar, Charles. *The Letters of Paul.* Nashville, TN: Abingdon, 1996.

Daniélou, Jean, and Henri Marrou. *The First Six Hundred Years. The Christian Centuries*, Vol. 1. New York: Paulist Press, 1964.

Di Berardino, Angelo, ed. *Encyclopedia of Early Christianity.* Translated by Adrian Walford. New York: Oxford University, 1992.

Malina, Bruce, and John Pilch. *Social-Science Commentary on the Letters of Paul.* Minneapolis, MN: Fortress, 2006.

Metzger, Bruce, and Roland Murphy, eds. *The New Oxford Annotated Bible with Apocrypha*, New Revised Standard Version. New York: Oxford University, 1991.

Official Dialogue Commission of the Lutheran World Federation and the Vatican. "Joint Declaration on the Doctrine of Justification." *Origins* 28 (1998) 120–127.

Perrin, Norman, and Dennis C. Duling. *The New Testament: An Introduction.* 2nd ed. San Diego: Harcourt Brace Jovanovich, 1982.

Roetzel, Calvin. *The Letters of Paul: Conversations in Context.* Louisville, KY: Westminster John Knox, 1998.

PART

III

THE HISTORY OF CHRISTIANITY

SCRIPTURE AND TRADITION

Christianity is first of all based on belief in a person, Jesus Christ, rather than on belief in a book. The priority of the person to the book was vividly stated already in the early second century in a letter written by Ignatius, bishop of Antioch: "When I heard some people say, 'If I don't find it in the original documents [i.e., the Jewish scriptures that Christians would eventually call the Old Testament], I don't believe it in the gospel,' and when I said in response to them, 'But it *is* written,' they answered me, 'That begs the question.' But as far as I am concerned, *Jesus Christ* is the original 'documents,' his cross and death and resurrection are the inviolable 'documents,' and the faith which comes through him" (*Letter to the Philadelphians* 8:2, trans. M. J. Hollerich). Ignatius meant that it was faith in Jesus Christ, as passed on by tradition, which allowed for the proper understanding of "the original documents," meaning the scriptures Christians inherited from Judaism.

There is an important sense, however, in which Christianity, like Judaism before it and Islam after it, can also be called a "religion of the book." Parts I and II of this textbook have explored the character of the Christian sacred book, the Bible. All Christian churches accept the Bible as the revealed word of God, even if they do not agree on the precise list of books to be included in the Old Testament. During the second and third centuries, Christians gradually came to agree that God's public revelation in Christ ended with the death of the apostolic generation. The canon was therefore "closed," and no new books were considered for inclusion in the New Testament. The biblical canon of Old and New Testaments has *remained the only universally accepted standard* for defining the character of Christianity.

With the passage of time, however, a religion of the book faces a problem. In new historical circumstances, new problems and issues will arise that are not addressed at all (at least not directly) in the sacred texts. These new experiences will require new insights into

135

the written revelation. The canonical texts need to be interpreted so that they speak to the challenges of the contemporary world and address the needs and problems of contemporary Christians. But that raises the further problem of conflict in interpretation. Disagreements about the meaning of the canonical text may require invoking another standard or authority outside of scripture, if the disagreement is to be resolved.

Moreover, even if there were no gaps in the answers provided by the Bible to the questions of Christian life, there would still be a role in Christianity for ideas, writings, and thoughts that are not biblical in their origins. The canonical text needs to be brought alive if it is to energize the faithful. Human creativity continues to invent new symbols, literary forms, prayers and ceremonies, role models for Christian life, ways of organizing the community, and innovations of many other kinds to nurture and refresh the religion.

For all of these reasons, Christianity (like Judaism and Islam) has found it necessary to supplement the original revelation with **tradition,** which effectively mediates or communicates the written revelation to later generations. Tradition here refers to the accumulated wisdom of the church's teachers, whereby the faith derived from the scriptures, contained in the creeds, and expressed in the liturgy, is passed on and interpreted for contemporary believers. All Christian churches employ tradition in at least some sense of the word. However, they don't all agree on just how important and authoritative tradition is. The most serious division is between Catholic and Orthodox churches, on the one hand, and Protestant churches on the other. Catholics and Orthodox hold that scripture and tradition are in *continuity* with one another, and hence that tradition is also an authoritative source for Christians asking questions about behavior and belief. Catholics and Orthodox also agree that tradition is equal or nearly equal in importance to the Bible. Protestant forms of Christianity are more skeptical about the authority of tradition and attempt to place much less emphasis on it. In practice, however, the different Protestant churches have all developed some form of tradition, creating a wide variety of solutions for dealing with historical change and development.

The rest of this book is devoted to telling the story of the history of Christianity from the time of Christ up to the present. This historical approach has been chosen for three reasons. First, narrative (the telling of stories) is typical of the Bible's own approach to revelation. Second, especially since the conversion of the Roman Empire, Christianity has been an inseparable element of the history of Western civilization, understood in the broadest sense (though, as we will see, Christianity also has a highly important history outside Western civilization as well). Since the history of the church is so much a part of the history of the Western world (and vice versa), it is valuable for students to know this history. Finally, a historical approach seems the fairest and most efficient way to illustrate both the continuity and the diversity of Christianity. In order to explain best how groups of Christians came to differ from one another—and how Christians continue to agree on some fundamental things—it is necessary to show the origins of the disagreements and the process by which agreements were reached.

THE DIVISIONS OF CHRISTIAN HISTORY

It is customary to divide the history of Christianity into three different periods, each of which has been marked by the differentiation of new types of Christianity:

The Early Christian or "Patristic" Period (Second to Fifth Centuries)

During its early years, Christianity grew away from its Jewish roots and spread throughout the Roman Empire. Christianity developed the institutions, doctrines, and practices that gave it its classic shape. During the fourth century, the church underwent a momentous change—from a persecuted minority to the established religion of the state. Theological disagreements and cultural divisions with their roots in the councils of the fourth and fifth centuries would eventually lead several Christian churches in the Middle East to separate from the rest of the Christian tradition. The history of this period is covered in Chapters 8 to 11.

The Medieval Period (Sixth to Fifteenth Centuries)

This period is marked by major geographical shifts in the Christian world. In the fifth century, the Roman Empire in the West was replaced by a series of Germanic kingdoms, and Western Christianity, led by the pope of Rome, shouldered the burden of rebuilding civilization on a Christian foundation. After the seventh century the spread of Islam, the third great monotheistic faith, caused Christianity to lose most of North Africa, the Middle East, and even parts of Europe. The Christianity that had existed in the Eastern (Greek) and Western (Latin) halves of the Roman Empire split permanently into Orthodox and Catholic versions of Christianity. The medieval period came to a close with Catholic Christianity locked in crisis and seeking to reform itself. At the same time, the cultural movement of the Renaissance was renewing European culture and moving it toward a new stage of human self-awareness. The history of this period is found in Chapters 11 to 16.

The Modern Period (Sixteenth to Twenty-First Centuries)

The modern period may be subdivided into the Reformation and post-Reformation periods.

1. The Reformation (sixteenth to seventeenth centuries). Frustrated tensions for reform finally split Western Christianity into Roman Catholicism and the various types of Protestant Christianity. The result was the destruction of the old internationalist ideal of Christianity ("Christendom") and its replacement by nationalized state churches. The Protestant reforming vanguard was led by Martin Luther in Germany and Ulrich Zwingli and John Calvin in Switzerland. They became the architects of the Lutheran and the Reformed types of Protestantism, respectively. In England King Henry VIII withdrew the English (Anglican) church from communion with the pope; this began a turbulent century and a half during which English monarchs tried unsuccessfully to impose a single version of Christianity. On the continent smaller numbers of Christians sought an even more radical reform by withdrawing from participation in the state and returning to the voluntary status of Christianity prior to Constantine. Catholicism itself engaged in a renewal movement known as the Catholic Reformation, partly in response to the challenges posed by the Protestant reform movements. The Reformation period is discussed in Chapters 17 to 20.

2. Post-Reformation (seventeenth to twenty-first centuries). From the end of the fifteenth century, the dawning of the age of world exploration and of European colonialism had already seen Christianity spread (largely in its Catholic form) by force and by persuasion westward to the Americas and eastward to India and the Far East. In the seventeenth

and eighteenth centuries, European Protestantism also began to contribute to the globalization of Christianity. The post-Reformation era is marked by the developments that have created the modern world: the scientific revolution; the Enlightenment; the rise of the sovereign nation-state; the separation of church and state and other forms of secularization; modern movements of emancipation, such as the abolition of serfdom and slavery, and equal rights for women; the spread of democratic political systems; urbanization and industrialization; the rollback of European colonialism around the globe; increasing globalization through trade, manufacturing, communication, and migration; and continual intellectual challenges from modern science, philosophy, and history. The history of Christianity in the post-Reformation period is dealt with in Chapters 21 to 26.

THE GENEALOGY OF CHRISTIANITY

Because one reason for studying Christian history is to understand the reasons why there are different groups of Christians today, and because so much of this history is precisely concerned with conflicts and schisms between different groups of Christians, it might be useful to have a preview of this aspect of Christian history before we begin. The following chart is a sketch of the Christian family tree from the time of the early church up to the modern period. It is intended to highlight the major forks in the road and to indicate, in a very schematic way, the genetic affiliation of the main branches of the Christian family. The chart ends with the eighteenth century, when the secularization of the state got underway, beginning in post-revolutionary America. The separation of church and state was in effect a deregulation of religion. It led to intense religious competition and the rise of many new churches, especially in America, which has been a spiritual greenhouse for the production of new strains of Christianity (see Chapter 23).

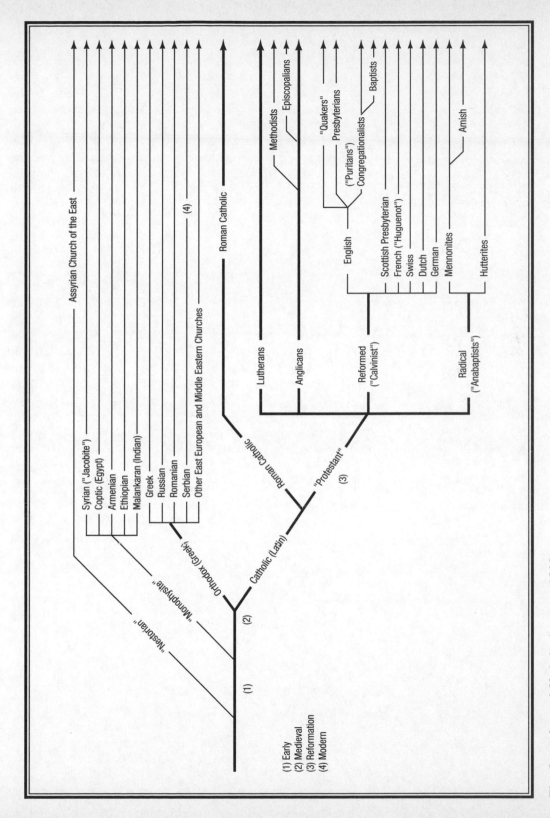

The Genealogy of Christianity up to 1800

Chapter

CHRISTIANITY
AFTER THE APOSTLES

TIMELINE

A.D. 70	Destruction of Second Temple during Jewish revolt.
c. A.D. 90	Expulsion of Christian Jews from synagogues.
c. A.D. 165	Justin is martyred in Rome.
c. A.D. 178	Irenaeus is elected bishop of Lyons. Writes *Against Heresies*, first work of Christian theology.
c. A.D. 190	Clement teaches at Alexandria.
A.D. 202–203	Perpetua and companions martyred at Carthage.
A.D. 250	Emperor Decius imposes first universal persecution.
c. A.D. 253	Death of Origen of Alexandria.
A.D. 303	Emperor Diocletian begins the last persecution, which lasts until 313, with a temporary toleration in 311.
A.D. 306	Constantine named emperor by his father's troops.

This chapter treats the historical and theological developments of early Christianity. However, the term "early Christianity" is imprecise. One could define it as the six hundred years separating Jesus from Muhammad (d. A.D. 632). This book will limit "early Christianity" to the time between the writing of the New Testament books—as late as c. A.D. 100—and the Council of Chalcedon, which met in A.D. 451. This period is also called the **patristic era,** because the major orthodox writers of the time are known as the Fathers (*patres* in Latin) of the church. In several branches of the Christian tradition (mainly Catholic, Orthodox, and Anglican), the patristic writings have a special prestige because of their role in shaping the Christian tradition.

During the patristic period Christianity assumed many of the classical features that mark it as a distinct religion separate from Judaism: its biblical canon, with a Christian New Testament that complemented the Jewish scriptures, now known as the Old Testament; its fundamental doctrines of God and of Jesus Christ; and its basic organizational structure, especially the office of the bishop. This chapter will present developments prior to the conversion of Constantine, when Christianity finally gained legal toleration. Chapter Nine will study Christianity's experience under Christian Roman emperors.

THE SPREAD OF CHRISTIANITY IN THE PATRISTIC ERA

During the second and third centuries, Christianity developed its distinctive religious identity. Three circumstances shaped this development: the gradual break with Judaism; the delay in Christ's return; and Christianity's encounter with the Greco-Roman world.

Christianity's Break with Judaism

The earliest followers of Jesus did not see Christianity as a separate religion but as a sect or reform movement within Judaism. Judaism in the first century A.D. was able to accommodate a fair amount of diversity within itself. Christians saw themselves as one group within Judaism, but distinct from other Jews because they believed that Jesus was their long-awaited messiah. The status of Jesus's followers within Judaism began to change, however, after the failure of the great Jewish revolt of A.D. 66 to 70. During the Romans' capture of Jerusalem in A.D. 70, the Temple was destroyed. It was never rebuilt. Because the Temple was the only place where valid sacrifices could be offered, the destruction of the Temple meant the end of the sacrificial cult and the decline of the priestly class which had maintained the Temple liturgy. Groups like the Sadducees and the Essenes gradually disappeared from Jewish life: the Sadducees because of their link with the Temple and its priesthood, the Essenes because the Romans destroyed their major community at Qumran. The role of the Pharisees was gradually taken over by rabbis who set in motion a redefinition of Judaism that eventually produced the Mishnah (interpretations of Jewish scripture) and the Talmud (discussions of the Mishnah and case law related to interpretations of the Torah), both of which are currently part of the Jewish canon.

This redefinition of Judaism resulted in a tightening of its boundaries, as a result of which Christian Jews appear to have been expelled from Jewish community life sometime in the 90s. Perceived by the Roman state as rebels against their own religious tradition, Christians lost the legal toleration that Judaism had traditionally enjoyed and became vulnerable to persecution. At the same time, the increase of Gentile conversions meant that Jewish

Christians were gradually outnumbered in a movement they themselves had started. Christians began to think of Jews as "other" and of themselves as "the true Israel." Probably by the middle of the second century, we can speak of "Judaism" and "Christianity" as distinct and opposed religions. But even then, the Christian teacher Justin, a second century Christian philosopher (often called Justin Martyr because he was executed by the Roman state in 165) admitted that Christians who observed Mosaic practice could be saved, provided that they did not insist on other Christians doing so as well (Justin, *Dialogue with Trypho*, 47).

The Delay of Christ's Return

The earliest Christians believed that Christ's resurrection was a sign of the beginning of the end of time, which would be completed very soon when Christ returned in glory. However, when the first generation of Christians began to die, those who were left had to deal with the unexpected delay. It became necessary to ensure the safe transmission of their tradition for the interim period, however long that might be. Moreover, some Christians thought that the second coming was delayed because the church had not completed the task that Christ had given to it: to spread the gospel to the whole world. The delay therefore led Christians to pursue their missionary activities with great zeal. They took the risen Christ's commission to preach the gospel to all nations (Matt 28:19) and turned the movement outwards to the larger **pagan** (meaning everyone that was neither Christian nor Jewish) world of the Roman Empire. There Christians encountered significant challenges, such as the intellectual tradition of Greek philosophy, the opposition of the Roman state, and the rich diversity of the empire's many religions.

The Move into the Greco-Roman World

The risk of persecution did not keep Christians from spreading their message and winning converts. By the end of the third century, Christian communities existed from Spain in the West to Mesopotamia in the East, and even as far as Persia, beyond the Roman Empire's eastern frontier. This geographic spread covered three main linguistic environments: Latin in the Western Roman world; Greek in most of the Eastern Roman world; and Syriac in scattered parts of the East. Although Greek was the dominant language, each of these geographic areas eventually produced its own Christian literature, beginning with translations of the Bible.

The Christian message circulated by word of mouth, household connections, streetcorner preaching, public lectures, and the spectacular form of witnessing known as martyrdom (see the following paragraphs). Roman cities were highly competitive religious "free markets," in which many cults and religions contended for the attention and support of followers. There were the official cults of the cities, devoted to the traditional Olympian gods and to local deities who were identified with them. There were the tribal and national gods of the many ethnic groups absorbed into the empire. For those who sought answers for more personal needs, there were shrines and oracles that offered healing and divine counseling for the insecurity and grief of daily life: worries about health, love, fertility, money, work, and the like. The huge popularity of magic and also of astrology seems to reflect a widespread fear that dark spiritual forces ultimately dictated human destiny.

Another form of more personal religious experience was the **mystery religions,** so called because they relied on initiating converts into secret rituals and mysteries (the word comes from Greek *mystês*, meaning "initiate") about a particular god or goddess. The mystery

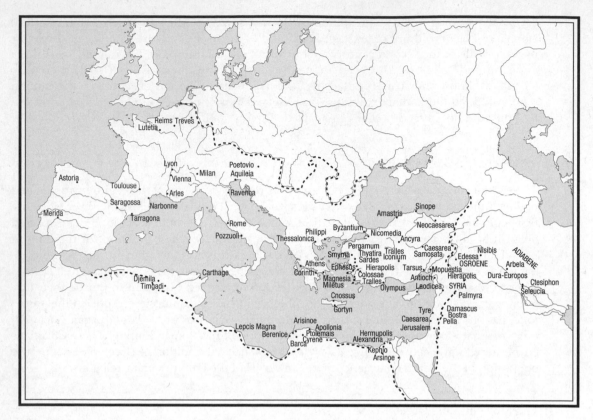

Figure 8–1 Extension of Christianity at the middle of the third century.

religions shared certain features in common with Christianity: initiation and purification rituals that symbolically expressed death and rebirth, intense emotional experiences, divine revelations, membership in a privileged group, sacred meals, professional priest-hoods and grades of membership, and personal devotion to a single deity. Several examples include Mithraism, the cult of Isis, the cult of Dionysus, and the Eleusinian Mysteries. Mithraism was inspired by the ancient Persian god Mithra. The cult, practiced in caves or underground chambers, was only open to men and was especially popular in the Roman army. Mithras, to use his Roman name, was closely identified with the sun, either as his divine companion or actually as the same divine person; both of them were called *Invictus* ("Unconquered"), and the god's birthday on December 25, the Roman winter solstice, made that date an appealing choice when Christians were establishing an anniversary for the birth of Christ, the "Sun of Righteousness" (cf. the book of Malachi 4:2).

The mysteries of the goddess Isis spread devotion to her far beyond her homeland in Egypt, as evidenced by the many poems written in praise of her virtues. In this example she is credited with a universal authority, with the establishment of human culture, and even with creation itself (thus absorbing functions traditionally claimed by other divinities):

I am Isis, the mistress of the whole land... I am she who discovered fruit on behalf of human beings... I am she who separated the earth from heaven... I discovered navigation... I have shown mortals the initiations [*mysteries*]. I have taught them to honor the images of the gods... I have established language for Greeks and for barbarians... I am she who is called the legislator. (Cited in Klauck 2000, 132)

Images of Isis nursing her infant son Horus resemble later Christian representations of the Mother of God nursing the child Jesus.

The wild rites—*orgies* was the term that was used—associated with the mysteries of Dionysus, the Greek god of wine and fertility, have given us the word *bacchanalia*, from *Bacchus,* Dionysus' alternative name. Wall paintings of what appear to be Dionysian ceremonies were discovered in a villa at Pompeii, the Italian city buried by the eruption of Mt. Vesuvius in A.D. 79.

The mysteries of the goddess Demeter and her daughter Persephone were celebrated at Eleusis, outside Athens, the only mystery religion that was restricted to a single site.

Despite the superficial resemblances between Christianity and the mysteries, there were even more notable differences. The Christian clergy were an actual confederation that linked communities all over the empire; the Christian rituals required a far more rigorous moral discipline than the pagan mysteries; the Christian sacramental enactment of death and rebirth was based on events that had happened in recent historical time, not in some distant, mythic time; and, most importantly, the Christian deity required exclusive loyalty ("no man can serve two masters," as Jesus had said in the Sermon on the Mount, Matt 6:24) that forbade participation in any other cult—pagan religions in general had no such prohibition against multiple memberships.

Sometimes the mystery religions disclosed the prospect of an afterlife. Mithraism, for example, appears to have taught the ascent of the soul through the heavenly spheres, and the Eleusinian mysteries, which spoke of Persephone's annual return from her months of captivity in the underworld (originally reflecting vegetation myths and rituals), seem to have held out the hope of a better destiny beyond the grave ("the Elysian fields"). But it is difficult to tell how literally we should understand the language of "rebirth" in accounts of the mysteries. Did rebirth merely entail an enlarged emotional experience or insight into life here and now? Or was it really believed to pave the way for personal existence after death? If a generalization must be made, the impression is that the pagan world was skeptical or at best vague about the afterlife, with an important exception being those who had been educated in the Platonic philosophical tradition.

Christian converts seem to have been seeking the same things that drew people to other religions and cults: the desire for healing from physical and spiritual ills, the need for advice and counsel, the promise of fellowship and mutual support, and the desire to know one's destiny in a mysterious and threatening universe. Christianity answered these various needs in a uniquely potent and comprehensive way. Christians were widely known and admired for helping and supporting each other in their community life. They were also known for their single-minded devotion to Jesus Christ as savior and Son of God, an exclusive loyalty that was a prime mover behind the persecutions. A chief sign of Christians' zeal was the extravagant courage with which their martyrs faced death, based on their belief in the resurrection of Jesus. As opposed to the cosmic determinism that so many ancient people felt looming over them, early Christianity stressed human free will, responsibility, and ultimate redemption, not just for a few initiates or philosophical supermen, but for all men and women, however humble their station, who embraced Jesus's way of life and the church's sacramental rebirth. There was nothing in paganism to match this.

Figure 8–2 Christ portrayed as a seated philosopher. Fourth century A.D.

Figure 8–3 Christ as good shepherd. Third century A.D.

Portrayals of Christ in Christian Art

Despite the focus of Christian faith on the person of Jesus, it is interesting to note that no actual likeness of him survives. Christians at first were reluctant to use paintings or statues of any kind, for fear of committing the sin of idolatry. This reluctance began to disappear in the fourth and fifth centuries, as more and more people became Christians. However, even before that time Christians used paintings to decorate walls of tombs and house churches. Likenesses of Jesus were first adopted from generic pagan models that were compatible with Christian ideas about Jesus: the Good Shepherd and the philosopher–teacher being favorite types.

Figure 8–2 shows a statue of Christ as a seated philosopher, dated mid-fourth century. He is often represented in Christian art as a philosopher teaching the true philosophy of Christianity to his disciples.

Figure 8–3 shows Christ as the good shepherd, from a late third-century sarcophagus.

Late in the fourth century, the first depictions of Jesus with long hair and beard begin to appear (see Figure 9–2 on page 172). After A.D. 500 in the Greek-speaking East, Jesus is always represented with a beard, though in the West the youthful unbearded type survived for centuries. Also in the fourth century, Jesus is shown more frequently as reigning in heavenly majesty, either giving the Law to his earthly representative, St. Peter, or receiving honor from the angels and saints. Representations of Christ on the cross are not found until the fifth century. Before that time Christians tended to use a bare cross.

Figure 8–4, from the sixth-century Basilica of San Vitale in Ravenna, shows Jesus sitting on the orb of the world, attended by angels and receiving the martyr's crown from St. Vitalis. The figure on the right is the bishop who built the church.

Figure 8–4 Christ seated on the orb of the world. Sixth century A.D., San Vitale in Ravenna.

ROMAN ATTITUDES TOWARD CHRISTIANITY

The Roman Empire did not have an official "state" religion in the sense of one single faith to which everyone had to belong, even though many of the cults, temples, and priesthoods received public funding and support. It should be remembered that "paganism" was not a religion per se but a catch-all term for all Greco-Roman religions that were neither Jewish nor Christian. The Roman policy towards religion was inclusive and pragmatic: To tolerate as many gods as possible, so that at all times someone, somewhere was sure to be paying the worship which a particular deity wanted—otherwise, gods who were ignored might inflict their wrath on the empire. "Religion" was primarily a pattern of ritual interaction between human beings and the invisible powers that actually governed the world. But religion was also crucial for shaping personal and social behavior: Because most human beings aren't philosophers, religion was the most likely way the Masses were going to learn their morality, and a diversity of religions fit the diversity of the Roman Empire's approximately sixty million inhabitants. Furthermore, religious myths, beliefs, rituals, and symbols were embedded in every aspect of the empire's public life, from its art, architecture, and literature to its economics and politics: Anyone who refused to recognize the empire's gods in some form or other was undercutting, not just belief in the gods, but a broad consensus underlying politics and culture as well. They instantly made themselves outcasts. Even at that, persecution was usually a last resort. The empire did not have the police force or the bureaucracy to indulge casually in religious manhunts.

One apparent exception to this generally tolerant posture was the **imperial cult,** or worship of the emperor. But even that was in principle voluntary, and it was certainly not exclusive. The imperial cult was both genuinely political, being a public demonstration of loyalty to the emperor, and genuinely religious, since it consisted of temples, feast days, sacrifices, and priesthoods. The extent to which people really thought of the emperor as a divinity on earth is unclear. Technically a reigning emperor was "a son of a god" in the sense that he had been adopted by his predecessor, who in turn had been declared *divus* (divine) by decree of the Senate after his death. Most often the imperial cult represented worship not of the emperor in his own person but of his *genius* or *tychê* (Greek for "fortune"), a guiding and protecting spirit rather like what Christians call a guardian angel. But no doubt many did think of the emperor as a kind of earthly god, especially if we remember that the pagan world recognized various levels or degrees of divinity. Jews were not expected to participate in the imperial cult and were allowed instead to offer prayers on his behalf in their synagogues (and sacrifices in the Temple when the Temple still existed). Judaism's and the Jewish people's antiquity earned the Romans' reluctant respect and toleration. Christians on the other hand gained no such respect. Having split off from the Jews, they were seen as rebels against the traditions of their ancestors—a serious charge in a culture that prized tradition, the *mos maiorum* ("the ways of the ancestors"), as the surest benchmark of truth. Nor did it help that their founder was known to have been executed by the Roman government. Once the empire decided that Christians deserved punishment, participation in the imperial cult was used to test an accused person's loyalties.

Prior to the third century, persecutions were sporadic and local affairs mainly inspired by popular prejudice against Christians, though they were no less bloody for being occasional (the testimony of historically authentic martyr acts, such as *The Martyrdom of Perpetua and Felicity*, shows this vividly). This changed in 250, when the emperor Decius (249–251) targeted the Christian church for the first truly universal persecution. His motive is uncertain, but he probably wanted to return the empire to traditional beliefs and customs, as a

Figure 8–5 A second-century pagan graffito of a Christian worshiping a crucified ass. The inscription reads, "Alexamenos worships god."

way of unifying the empire and pleasing the gods at a time when the empire was under great stress. Under the emperor's orders, local examining boards issued certificates to all Roman citizens to verify that they had offered sacrifice to the emperor's image. Christians who died for their faith rather than offer sacrifice were called **martyrs** (Greek for "witnesses"). Their bodily remains were venerated as holy **relics** and the anniversaries of their deaths were celebrated annually (the origin of saints' feast days). Those who were arrested and stood firm but were not put to death were called **confessors** for having confessed their faith publicly; they enjoyed great prestige in the churches and sometimes claimed the right to forgive sins. Those Christians who did offer sacrifice in the persecution of A.D. 250 created a crisis afterwards when they regretted their sin of **apostasy** (falling away from the faith) and pleaded to be re-admitted to communion with their Christian brothers and sisters. The bishops and their clergy were hard pressed to find a middle way between the "rigorists" (very strict Christians), who wanted to deny any forgiveness to those who had lapsed into apostasy, and those, like some of the confessors, who wanted to extend forgiveness immediately and to do so on their own authority, not that of the bishop.

According to Christian authors, the most frequent Roman charge against Christians was atheism. The accusation did not mean that Christians denied the existence of God as such, but rather that they denied everyone *else's* gods except their own. Christians said publicly that the gods were demonic deceptions and that worshiping them was idolatry. That undercut Roman religious policy as previously described, which depended on a broad consensus about religion, morality, and the state.

Pagans, especially pagan intellectuals, had other objections to Christianity. They resented the claim (made of course by Jews as well) that God had revealed himself uniquely in the history of a particular people, the people of Israel. Such a concept of revelation seemed narrow and bigoted. Furthermore, Christianity claimed that this special relationship with one people culminated in God's appearance in human form, as a man who had been subjected to a shameful death as a criminal. While some pagan critics admired Jesus personally, they were offended by the Christian belief that he was divine. The first Roman eye witness to Christianity that we have, the Roman official Pliny the Younger's celebrated letter to the emperor Trajan, written around A.D. 112, says that they "sang hymns to Christ as to a god." Enlightened pagans believed in a single supreme being who existed at the top of a pyramid of lower divinities, the many gods of polytheism, who acted as his subordinates in the divine government of the universe. A monotheism of this sort was compatible with polytheism. But belief in the full divinity of Jesus implied that there could be *two* such supreme gods. Furthermore, the very idea of a divine incarnation (God taking on human flesh) was thought to be unworthy of God. Pagan thinkers influenced by the philosophy of Plato believed that the spiritual was inherently superior to the material, so they found the doctrines of incarnation and resurrection unbelievable and even offensive. Christians were regarded as gullible because they emphasized faith more than knowledge. They were also accused of political irresponsibility for refusing to hold office or to serve in the military. Christians' refusal to kill even in war seemed dangerous and foolish to an empire with enemies on its borders.

THE APOLOGISTS AND THE DEFENSE OF CHRISTIANITY

Christian writers called the **apologists** (the word means "defenders") tried to respond to Roman criticisms of Christianity. They insisted that Christians were loyal citizens who prayed for the emperor when he engaged in just wars, even though they themselves refused to fight in them (cf. Origen, *Against Celsus* 8.73–75). They also attempted to explain, in imagery and terminology that made sense to pagans, what it was that Christians believed and how they lived their lives.

The most important accomplishment of the apologists of the second and third centuries was the development of the *Logos* theology, by which the apologists established a link between pagan philosophy and Christian theology. The Greek word *logos* can mean two things: (1) spoken or written word and (2) internal reason or mind. As spoken or written word, the *Logos* could stand for God's Word in the scriptures and in their proclamation. As reason or mind, the *Logos* could also be identified as the divine Mind, which Greek philosophers like Plotinus (A.D. 204–270) saw as a secondary divine principle that contained God's "thoughts," the Ideas that were the eternal patterns of everything that exists. (Later, in his book *Confessions*, St. Augustine would recognize the parallels, but also the profound differences, between Plotinus and the Christian doctrine of God—see Chapter Ten in this book and *Confessions* 5.9). Christians identified this divine *Logos* with Jesus, who according to the Gospel of John was with God in the beginning as God's agent in creation (1:1–3), was the true light who enlightens everyone (1:9), and became human and dwelt among us (1:14). The apologists saw the pagan acceptance of the *Logos* principle as a preparation for receiving the message about Jesus Christ. Since Jesus was divine Reason incarnate, the apologists could argue that the Christian life was based on reason, and all who lived according to reason already had a limited knowledge of God. In the words of Justin Martyr:

> We have been taught that Christ is the first-born of God, and we have already mentioned that he is the *Logos* of which the entire human race has a share and in whom they participate. Those who lived according to reason are Christians, even though they were regarded as atheists. Examples of these among the Greeks include Socrates, Heraclitus, and others like them. Among the barbarians they include Abraham, and Hananiah, Azariah, and Mishael [*see Daniel 1:6–7*], and Elijah, and many others whose names and deeds it would take too long to list. Those who existed before the time of Christ and who did *not* live according to reason could therefore be called "non-Christian" [*in Greek "achrêstos" means "useless" but could also reflect a pun by Justin, because the Greek pronunciation would have sounded much like "christos" and might suggest "not Christ" or "non-Christian" to readers*] and hostile to Christ, and the murderers of those who *do* live according to reason; those who in the past lived according to reason and those who do so now are Christians, with a right to live free from fear and disturbance. (*First Apology* 46.2–4, trans. M. J. Hollerich)

THE DEVELOPMENT OF CHRISTIAN DOCTRINE

To a degree that is unique among the world's religions, the history of Christianity has been preoccupied with debates about **orthodoxy,** or correct doctrine. The factors that guided the development of orthodox Christian doctrine were many: the church's preaching, its biblical interpretation, its standards of discipleship, its communal life and ministry, its central rituals of Baptism and the Eucharist, and its prayers and hymns. These different aspects of Christian life all served as carriers of the faith in Jesus as Savior and Son of God. They made up a tradition that Christians believed was the work and witness of the Spirit of God, poured out through Jesus's death and resurrection. The early Christian period was especially concerned with establishing the orthodox doctrines of the Trinity and the incarnation.

A look at the development of the doctrine of the **Trinity** (according to which the one God exists as three distinct "persons," the Father, the Son, and the Holy Spirit) shows how orthodox doctrine was determined by factors such as evidence from the Bible and the assumptions inherent in Christian rituals. Christians saw that the idea of the Trinity is found throughout the New Testament. The New Testament describes the God of Israel, whom Jesus called "Father"; Jesus himself, who is both Son of God, the Word made flesh (John 1:14), and the Son of Man who died as a ransom for many (Mark 10:45); and the Spirit who is God's powerful presence among believers after Jesus's ascension (Acts 2). In terms of Christian rituals, the Baptismal formula also revealed the threefold character of God, because the Christian was initiated in the name of the Father, the Son, and the Holy Spirit (Matt 28:19). Baptized Christians were understood to be sealed with the Spirit, which was the cause of holiness in the church. Likewise, the structure of early Christian **creeds,** or short summaries of belief, which originated as Baptismal instructions, reflected this trinitarian focus. They are usually divided into three sets of clauses dealing with the Father, the Son, and the Spirit, respectively. The fourth-century church would formally define the Trinity as three persons sharing one divine nature (Chapter Nine).

The doctrine of the incarnation (meaning "taking on flesh") is concerned with the belief that Jesus Christ is the eternal Son of God who took on flesh for our sake. Christians always believed that Jesus must therefore be both human and divine in some sense. But they disagreed about precisely *how* he was both human and divine. In certain respects many Christians found it a little easier to grasp his spiritual and divine aspect than his fleshly and human one. The sacrament of the Eucharist helped ensure that Christians did not lose sight of the reality of Jesus's human embodiment. That is because Christians were taught to believe that they became truly united with Jesus in the Eucharistic bread and wine. Early descriptions of the Eucharist can be startlingly realistic in the way they equate the elements of bread and wine with the flesh and blood of Christ. Already around the year A.D. 110, Ignatius of Antioch had called the Eucharistic bread "the medicine of immortality" (*Letter to the Ephesians* 20.2), meaning that it was food that nourished eternal life in the believer. Here is how Justin Martyr described it in a famous passage from his *First Apology*, written in the mid-second century:

> Among us this food is called *Eucharist*...[W]e do not receive it as if it were ordinary bread or ordinary drink. But just as Jesus Christ our Savior, when he was made flesh by the Word of God, took on flesh and blood for the sake of our salvation, in the same way, so we have been taught, this food, once it has been consecrated by the word of prayer that comes from him, and which nourishes our flesh and blood by digestion, is also the flesh and blood of that Jesus who was himself made flesh (*First Apology* 66.1–2, trans. M. J. Hollerich).

Early Christianity, especially in its first hundred and fifty years, exhibited considerable diversity. There were various approaches as to how communities should be organized, how Christians ought to live, what biblical books they should accept, and what they ought to believe. The diversity perhaps reflected the speed with which Christianity spread, the new challenges awaiting the movement once it outgrew its Jewish matrix, and the adjustment to the delay in Christ's return. In such unsettled conditions we should not be surprised that there was a degree of trial and error.

By the end of the second century, this diversity was giving way to a greater uniformity, as the main standards of **catholic** (the word simply means "universal") Christianity became recognized: (1) agreement on the core books of the New Testament and on the necessity of retaining the Jewish scriptures; (2) the development of short summaries of beliefs called creeds, which were used to instruct candidates for Baptism; and (3) the universal acceptance of the office of the **bishop** (from a Greek word meaning "overseer") as the leader of the local Christian community. To these we may add (4) the sacramental life of the Christianity (see previous paragraphs on the doctrinal implications of Baptism and the Eucharist). These four elements—canon, creed, **episcopacy** (government by bishops), and liturgy—consolidated Christianity's identity in a compact and durable form that would enable it to survive the eventual collapse of the whole ancient world in which it had come into being.

THE GNOSTIC CHALLENGE

The opposite of orthodoxy is **heresy** (false teaching). The word comes from a Greek word that means "choice" or "faction." Originally it applied either to political factions or to the various schools or sects of ancient Greek philosophy which a student could choose to join. Christianity too had its separate schools and teachers. During the second-century shakeout of belief and practice, teachers and bishops had to distinguish differences of opinion that were acceptable from those they rejected as heretical.

The most important second- and third-century heretical movement was **gnosticism.** It takes its name from the Greek word *gnosis*, meaning "knowledge," because its adherents claimed to possess a special secret knowledge that was known only to them. In the Bible, faith, meaning trust and belief in God, matters more than knowledge, and Abraham would be an exemplary figure. But as we saw above, knowledge and reason are what counted in the classical philosophical tradition, in which Socrates is the ideal type. Christians who were attracted to gnosticism were often those who wished for more satisfying answers to questions about the origin of evil and the imperfections of the material world and of the human body in comparison to the spiritual world, which was especially an issue for anyone conversant with Plato's philosophy. Gnosticism also appealed to those who were critical of various aspects of the Bible: the sometimes crude and capricious ways in which God is represented as acting, his changeability of mood, the uneven moral behavior of many prominent figures in the Bible, and, perhaps most of all, the obvious differences between the Old Testament and the New. (Problems like these will crop up again when Augustine explains the appeal which the gnostic-like religion of the Manichees had for him; see Chapter Ten.)

It is not easy to describe accurately the confusing variety of teachers, books, and ideas that ancient and modern observers think of as "gnostic." Older descriptions of the movement had to rely largely on what the orthodox opponents of the gnostics said about them. A more direct understanding of gnosticism became possible after a collection of ancient treatises, most of them gnostic in character, was discovered in Egypt in 1945. The books were written in Coptic (the popular language of Egypt) but are believed to be translations of writings originally in Greek. In their present form they are dated to the late fourth century A.D., though many of the Greek originals may go back to the second century A.D.

The "knowledge" of the human situation claimed by the gnostics is expressed in this often-quoted second century statement: "[It is] the knowledge of who we were, what we have become; where we were, where we have been thrown; where we are hastening, from where we are redeemed; what birth is, what rebirth is" (preserved in Clement of Alexandria,

Excerpts from Theodotus 78.2, trans. M. J. Hollerich). According to one recent study (Markschies 2003), a catalog of the knowledge thus claimed typically included elements such as the following:

- the extreme other-worldliness of God, who is unknown to us;
- the existence of a whole series of intermediary semi-divine principles (often called *aeons* in gnostic texts) who separate God from the rest of reality;
- the experience of the created world as evil and wretched, and of the misery of human life in it;
- the introduction of a different and inferior deity, thought of as ignorant or even as evil, who is the actual creator of our world and is equated with the creator God of the Old Testament;
- the blaming of the chain of events that creates our world on some kind of fault or fall in the heavenly realm itself (thus in the gnostic scenario the biblical sequence of creation-then-fall is actually reversed and becomes fall-then-creation);
- the fall of some of the divine substance from the heavenly world into one particular class of human beings in this world, in whom alone it slumbers and from whom it must be liberated;
- and the need for a heavenly messenger who brings the needed awakening and knowledge that enables the liberation, and who then returns to the heavenly realm.

Gnosticism was thus typically marked by a strong dualism: two divine beings, two realities (spiritual and material), and two classes of human beings (those with the divine spark and those without it).

For orthodox Christians, there were obvious problems with such a set of beliefs, above all the rejection of the creator God of the Old Testament as a different divine being from the God of Jesus. Orthodox Christians also could not accept the common corollary that Jesus Christ himself was not truly human but a purely spiritual being who only used a body that was not to be identified with himself. The doctrine that Jesus only appeared to be human and to suffer and die is called **docetism** (from a Greek word that means "appearance"). Some gnostic texts regard the suffering as real, but still seem to separate the person who suffers from the Christ who is the actual heavenly messenger. (The closer gnostic texts come to mainstream Christianity, the more they tend to take the reality of Jesus's suffering and death seriously.) Gnostic denial of Jesus's real embodiment also entailed doubts about his resurrection: Because it was the spirit which mattered, not the body, the resurrection was understood symbolically as the gnostic's rebirth. Finally, gnostic speculation divided the human race into two predetermined classes of people, those who would be saved and those incapable of salvation (versions of gnosticism associated with the Christian gnostic teacher Valentinus added a third category, those human beings who might be saved, but only for a lower order of salvation).

Sometime around A.D. 180, **Irenaeus of Lyons,** bishop of the Christian community in Lyons in southern Gaul (modern-day France), wrote a lengthy work called *Against Heresies,* primarily in response to gnosticism. Irenaeus is our foremost witness to mainstream Christianity in the second century. His defense of orthodox teaching—he called it "the apostolic tradition"—focused on the fourfold elements of catholic (i.e., universal) Christianity mentioned previously: canon, creed, episcopate, and liturgy. Irenaeus was the first early Christian writer to mention all four canonical gospels as a set. Besides written scriptures, he also stressed the oral tradition of apostolic teaching. He called it "the rule of truth," and in his descriptions it sounds like a type of creed used to prepare people for Baptism (see e.g., *Against Heresies* 1.9.4, 1.22.1, 3.2.1, 3.11.1, etc.). Irenaeus understood this creed to be a measure by which orthodoxy is determined. Thus he made an explicit contrast between the rule of truth, which is public and everywhere the same, and the teachings of the gnostics, which are esoteric and contradictory.

Irenaeus pointed to the bishops as the authorized preservers of the apostolic tradition, because they stood in a living chain that went back to Jesus' first followers. This claim, he said, was open to verification by anyone who wished to examine it. All they had to do was trace the succession of the bishops of a given church back to the apostles. Interestingly, he singled out the church in Rome ("greatest and oldest," he called it) as a special reference point for the apostolic tradition, because of its "foundation" by two apostles, Peter and Paul (by which he meant the fact that they were buried in Rome). In a passage whose exact meaning has been debated, he appears to say that every authentic church must be in agreement with the apostolic tradition as preserved in Rome (Irenaeus, *Against Heresies* 3.3.2), though any church with an apostolic foundation will also have the same apostolic tradition (e.g. Ephesus in Asia Minor, where the apostle John lived).

Against gnostic dualism, Irenaeus consistently emphasized *unity*. Creator and Redeemer were one: The God who created the world is the same God who redeems it, instead of positing two opposed gods. Jesus Christ was one person, both human and divine, rather than a disembodied spiritual messenger who only appeared to take on flesh. The human race was one: fallen in Adam and redeemed in Christ, not divided into those who can be saved and those who cannot. The Old and the New Testaments were a single Bible, in which God's plan for redemption—what Irenaeus called God's "dispensations" or his "economy" of salvation—was disclosed progressively by degrees. Irenaeus was so convinced of the goodness of the created though fallen world, including our bodies, that he interpreted "heaven" as a transformed earth: In language that somewhat embarrassed Christians more inclined to Plato's ideas about the superiority of the spiritual realm, Irenaeus talked about the restored and renewed world in highly materialistic terms (e.g., *Against Heresies* 5.33.3–4). Even the gap between God and humanity was now bridged: When Irenaeus asked, "How could humanity cross over to God, if God had not crossed over to humanity?" (*Against Heresies* 4.33.4, trans. M. J. Hollerich), he was laying the basis for the Christian doctrine of the "divinization" of humanity, or *theôsis* in Greek, which has been so important in the Eastern Christian tradition (see Chapter 11). For Irenaeus, the redemption won by Jesus was really a **recapitulation,** a repetition or "doing-over" of all that had gone wrong in human history beginning with the Fall, a history that was now going to return to the pure condition in which it had begun.

THE BIRTH OF THEOLOGY

We have thus far spoken about doctrine or teaching more than about theology as such. The word *theology* literally means "discourse or talk about God." Its origin is in Greek philosophy. The Platonic tradition saw theology as a *mythic* way of talking about the gods and their relation to the world, understanding *myth* in the sense of symbolic stories that should not be taken literally. Aristotle saw theology as the *rational* knowledge of God and a branch of metaphysics (in Aristotle's philosophy, metaphysics is the understanding of first principles or ultimate reality). The Stoics gave the most prominent attention to theology, which they divided into three subcategories: mythic (by which they meant the traditional stories about the gods as found in classical literature), physical or natural (meaning rational knowledge about the divine as known from the character of the world), and political (meaning the knowledge of the gods mandated by the city and preserved by the priests and the public cult).

Christian authors were slow to adopt the word for themselves. In Christian usage to *theologize* meant first of all to ascribe divinity to the Son and the Holy Spirit; second, it meant describing the descent of divinity to our world in the incarnation. Then it was extended to mean praise of God, as in the liturgy, or mystical knowledge of God, as in the search for union with God—in this sense *theology* meant something more like prayer than reflection or argument. The people who "did" theology were originally Christian teachers, often lay people, especially if they had had some training in philosophy and rhetoric. Such teachers were sometimes independent practitioners who functioned like what we might call consultants. After Christianity was legalized in the fourth and fifth centuries, theology came more under the control of the institutional church and its clergy. At the same time, the rise of the monastic movement (Chapter Nine) provided a setting for theology different from that of the bishops and their priests.

Early Christian theological literature was devoted first of all to commentary and preaching on God's revelation in the Bible. Other subjects that were treated included the defense of the faith against both pagans and Jews, and doctrinal controversies within the church. Most early Christian literature, however, was written to meet various practical needs of Christian life and scarcely qualifies as theology. The manuals modern scholars call church orders, the oldest of which is the **Didache** or "The Teaching of the Twelve Apostles" (parts of it probably go back to the end of the first century), dealt with issues of church government, worship, and discipline. Christians liked to read inspirational stories about the first generation of Christians, which led to the production of apocryphal acts of Peter, Andrew, John, Thomas, Paul (who is described as traveling with a woman companion named Thecla), and others, on the analogy of the New Testament's Acts of the Apostles. Hagiography, or the writing of the lives of saints, began with the acts of Christian martyrs, some of which, like the *Martyrdom of Perpetua and Felicity*, have a sound historical foundation. There was instructional literature to prepare people for Baptism. Beginning with Athanasius' *Life of Antony*, the monastic movement of the fourth and fifth centuries would produce a rich literature of spiritual advice avidly read by lay people as well as monks.

Theology in the sense of a reasoned examination of revelation required a philosophical education that few Christians had before the fourth century. In the second and third centuries Christian intellectual leadership was to be found in Alexandria in Egypt, which had long been the greatest center of scholarship in the ancient world. It was the home of the Library of Alexandria, with its enormous book collection, and the Museum of Alexandria, a center for study and lecturing. If Christians in Alexandria were to compete with pagans on an equal footing, they, like the Jewish community that preceded them, could not afford to ignore the role of study and learning in theology. It is probably not an accident that many of the Christian gnostics of whom we have knowledge originally came from Alexandria.

The focus of Christian scholarship in Alexandria was the Catechetical School (so named from a Greek word meaning "instruction"), which was both an instructional program for new Christians and an academy for more advanced studies. Two of the most important and creative early Christian theologians, Clement of Alexandria (mid-2nd century–c. 215) and **Origen of Alexandria** (c. 185–c. 253), served as directors of the school. Clement was very well read in Greek philosophy and Greek literature in general. Origen achieved extraordinary fame for his learning, his productivity, and his holiness. The Christian historian Eusebius of Caesarea reports that even pagan rulers wished to meet him—Julia Mamaea, mother of the Roman emperor Severus Alexander (222–235), invited Origen to visit her in Antioch. Pagan intellectuals read his books and attended his lectures. Christian bishops allowed him to preach in their presence, even though he had not been ordained, and enlisted him as a theological expert to cross-examine bishops whose orthodoxy was in question. As a beloved teacher, he inspired a generation of students who went on to become missionaries, bishops, and theologians in their own right. Wealthy lay people generously supported his scholarly labors. He taught and wrote in Alexandria until 231, when he had a serious falling out with Demetrius, the bishop of Alexandria, because bishops in Palestine had ordained Origen as a priest without Demetrius' permission. As a result, Origen spent the last two decades of his life in Caesarea in Palestine. It has been estimated that his *Hexapla* was the longest book ever written in the ancient world. It consisted of the Old Testament written out in six parallel columns (hence the name, meaning "sixfold"): the Hebrew original, the Hebrew written in Greek letters (presumably so that it could be pronounced by someone who didn't know Hebrew), the Septuagint (the Greek translation of the Hebrew Bible that had become the church's Old Testament), and at least three other Greek translations. The purpose of this mammoth work was to correct mistakes that had crept into the manuscripts of the church's Greek Bible, and to give access to the Hebrew original for Christian scholars and for debates with Jews.

Origen believed that the theologian had a calling from the Holy Spirit. Though everyone was obliged to accept what apostolic tradition taught, he believed that theologians were called to investigate subjects that apostolic tradition had not already defined. In this way, members of the church who were endowed with intellectual talent and had advanced in personal holiness could arrive at a deeper understanding of the church's faith beyond that held by simple believers. Origen left the Christian tradition with a massive intellectual and spiritual legacy. In the area of biblical interpretation, he pioneered in the writing of line by line biblical commentaries. His use of the **allegorical** method (looking for hidden spiritual meanings beneath the bare literal meaning of the text) was especially influential and would eventually help Augustine get around some of his objections to the Bible (see *Confessions* 5.14.24). Likewise, his homilies were copied and circulated everywhere. Works of spirituality such as *On Prayer* and his commentary on the Song of Songs from the Bible have exerted a permanent influence on Christian teaching about the soul and its relationship with God.

Two of Origen's works deserve special mention. His *Against Celsus*, written late in his life, is a lengthy response to the first serious non-Christian critique of Christianity of which we have record. Along with Augustine's *On the City of God*, it is one of the two most important apologies from the early Christian period. Indeed, of early Christian authors only Augustine can match Origen for his lasting influence on the whole scope and breadth of the Christian tradition. The other book is a product of Origen's youth, the treatise called *On First Principles*, a bold exposition of Christian doctrine that could be called the first Christian systematic theology. The original version of the book is partially lost because some of Origen's ideas (such as the preexistence of souls, the idea that human souls existed in heaven before they were born into bodies, which had been an acceptable hypothesis in Origen's own time) were condemned as heretical long after his death. Enough survives in

Latin translation and from the Greek original to give a good idea of its contents. It was a highly creative interpretation of Christian teaching, with the help of Platonic philosophy, for the purpose of defending scripture and apostolic tradition and addressing the questions of educated Christians.

CHRISTIAN LIFE AND COMMUNITY

Standards of membership in the early Christian churches were at first very high because the church was thought of as an ark of the saved, the only refuge in a drowning world. The *Didache*, for example, is an excellent witness to the Christian commitment to high moral standards and the expectation that the church would be a community of saints— though even then, in the early second century, we can see evidence that the community that kept the *Didache* had to worry about prophets who were quick to ask for money and about people who were taking advantage of Christian almsgiving (charity). A prospective convert underwent years of preparation before being judged fit for Baptism. Certain occupations were forbidden, especially if they involved bloodshed (such as being a gladiator), illicit sexual activity, and pagan religious ceremonies. There was also a prohibition against careers in teaching, because the myths about the gods were taught in school. As noted above, military service was consistently frowned on because of the Christian rejection of bloodshed and the oath of loyalty taken by soldiers. In some Christian sources, such as the third-century church manual known as the *Apostolic Tradition* and traditionally attributed to Hippolytus of Rome (d. 235), military service was regarded as a disqualification for Baptism:

> A soldier in command must be told not to kill people; if he is ordered to do so, he shall not carry it out. Nor should he take the oath. If he will not agree, he should be rejected. Anyone who has the power of the sword, or is a civil magistrate wearing the purple, he should desist, or he should be rejected. If a catechumen or a believer wishes to become a soldier, they should be rejected, for they have despised God. (*Apostolic Tradition* 16:8–10, trans. A. Stewart-Sykes)

Despite such an explicit prohibition, it is clear that Christians were already serving in the Roman army. The rationale for this change is uncertain, but it may have been based on Christian respect for the empire's role as protector and peacekeeper. Christians would eventually find justification in New Testament passages such as John the Baptist's words to soldiers, "Be content with your wages" (Luke 3:14; the point is that he did not tell them to resign their commission), Peter's Baptism of the Roman centurion Cornelius (Acts 10), or Paul's description of the one who bears the sword as "the servant of God to execute his wrath on the wrongdoer" (Rom 13:4).

By the third century, the growing number of Christians seems to have caused a decline in standards. Origen complained about this decline, and the large number of lapsed Christians (those guilty of apostasy) in the Decian persecution (250) confirms his pessimism. There were heated debates over what to do with those who failed to live up to the promises of their Baptism. Some Christians went so far as to deny that the church had the right to forgive serious sins after Baptism; they thought their severity was justified by the New Testament itself (cf. Hebrews 6:4–6). The most common practice seems to have been to allow repentant sinners a one-time chance for forgiveness for serious sin after Baptism. By the fourth century, after the conversion of the Roman emperor Constantine, the problem of diluted standards would become even greater.

The fellowship of the bishops was the chief institutional expression of the churches' catholicity or universality. At the same time, the bishop was the overseer of a local church or group of churches. The blend of local and universal was symbolized by the fact that the bishop was elected locally by the board of priests or presbyters (elders), with the consent of the laity, but could not be consecrated as a bishop without the cooperation of several other bishops. Bishops were regarded in principle as equal, all being successors of the apostles, but bishops in larger cities naturally carried more weight than those in small towns. A few bishops, chiefly Rome, Alexandria, and Antioch, enjoyed exceptional influence and prestige.

The bishops exercised primary control over the teaching and governing aspects of the church. They also presided at the Eucharist. However, they did not enjoy a complete monopoly of authority. By virtue of their Baptism, all Christians were thought eligible to enjoy the gifts of the Spirit, such as prophecy. Although prophecy gradually waned as a force in community life, it probably lasted longest in North Africa. The *Didache* shows a very early state of affairs when traveling prophets, teachers, and "apostles" outranked local bishops and deacons. Likewise, the charismatic authority (meaning authority freely granted by the Spirit) of martyrs and confessors was a powerful force in church life, as we can see in *The Martyrdom of Perpetua and Felicity*. According to Origen, Christian teachers also possessed a charismatic authority based on the gifts of wisdom and holiness.

Christian churches kept in touch through official letters called *letters of peace*, through the travels of business people and other folk, and through regular meetings with neighboring churches on matters of common interest. As the church's organization grew, it took on the character of a state within the state. The churches were strengthened by the belief that they were the earthly extension of a community that existed in heaven as well: As St. Paul wrote, "Our commonwealth is in heaven" (Phil 3:20). Besides the communion they shared with their sister churches around the Roman world, Christian churches were thus linked spiritually to the angels and martyred saints who praised God in heaven. This "communion of saints," as it was called in early Christian creeds, was experienced in the liturgy and in prayer, with the angels being thought of as individual protectors and co-worshipers with the church on earth. When persecution failed to crush this alternative society, the way was open in the fourth century for the Roman Empire to win over Christianity by merging with it rather than by trying to destroy it.

Key Terms

patristic era	apologists	gnosticism
pagan	orthodoxy	docetism
mystery religions	Trinity	Irenaeus of Lyons
imperial cult	creeds	recapitulation
martyr	catholic	*Didache*
relics	bishop	Origen of Alexandria
confessors	episcopacy	allegorical
apostasy	heresy	

Questions for Reading

1. What effect did the fall of Jerusalem in A.D. 70 have on the Christian movement?

2. What sorts of motives seem to have attracted converts to Christianity during the second and third centuries?

3. Why did the Roman Empire persecute Christians? What kinds of objections did pagans raise against Christianity?

4. How did the *Logos* theology help the apologists defend Christianity?

5. What were the most important factors in the formation of orthodox Christian doctrine? (Illustrate with specific reference to Baptism and the Eucharist.)

6. By the end of the second century, a universal (catholic) Christian consensus was beginning to take shape. What were the four main elements that helped to consolidate Christianity's identity?

7. What are the doctrines about God, creation, humanity, and redemption that are regarded as broadly typical of gnosticism?

8. How did the theology of Ireneaus of Lyons respond to gnostic dualism?

9. According to Irenaeus, how are we able to identify and know what apostolic tradition is?

10. How did Origen of Alexandria see the calling of the theologian, in relation to the apostolic tradition of the church? List some of Origen's lasting contributions to the Christian tradition.

11. The bishop played the key role in the life of the local Christian community and also served as the main link to Christian communities elsewhere. What were his local responsibilities? What other types of authority existed in Christian communities?

Works Consulted/Recommended Reading

Bauer, Walter. *Orthodoxy and Heresy in Earliest Christianity.* 2nd ed. Translated by Georg Strecker. Philadelphia: Fortress, 1971.

Chadwick, Henry. *The Church in Ancient Society: From Galilee to Gregory the Great.* New York: Oxford University, 2001.

———. *The Early Church.* Vol. 1 of *Penguin History of the Church.* New York: Penguin Books, 1993.

Crouzel, Henri. *Origen: The Life and Thought of the First Great Theologian.* Translated by A. S. Worrall. San Francisco: Harper & Row, 1989.

Daniélou, Jean, and Henri Marrou. *The First Six Hundred Years.* Vol. 1 of *The Christian Centuries: A New History of the Catholic Church.* Translated by Vincent Cronin. New York: McGraw-Hill, 1964.

———. *From Shadows to Reality: Studies in the Biblical Typology of the Fathers.* Translated by Dom Wulstan Hibberd. Westminster, MD: Newman, 1960.

———. *A History of Early Christian Doctrine before the Council of Nicaea.* 3 vols. Translated by John A. Baker. London: Darton, Longman, and Todd, 1964–77.

Dodd, E. R. *Pagan and Christian in an Age of Anxiety.* New York: W. W. Norton, 1970.

Eusebius of Caesarea. *The History of the Church: From Christ to Constantine.* Translated by G. A. Williamson. Rev. ed., Andrew Louth. Penguin Classics, 1990.

Grafton, Anthony, and Megan Williams. *Christianity and the Transformation of the Book: Origen, Eusebius, and the Library of Caesarea.* Cambridge, MA: Harvard University, 2006.

Grant, Robert M. *Augustus to Constantine: The Thrust of the Christian Movement into the Roman World.* New York: Harper and Row, 1970.

Hippolytus. *On the Apostolic Tradition.* Translated by Alistair Stewart-Sykes. Crestwood, NJ: St. Vladimir's Seminary, 2001.

Jensen, Robin Margaret. *Understanding Early Christian Art.* London and New York: Routledge, 2000.

Kelly, J. N. D. *Early Christian Creeds.* 3rd ed. New York: Longman, 1972.

———. *Early Christian Doctrines.* New York: Harper and Row, 1960.

Klauck, Hans-Josef. *The Religious Context of Early Christianity: A Guide to Graeco-Roman Religions.* Translated by Brian McNeil. Edinburgh: T. and T. Clark, 2000.

Kugel, James L., and Rowan A. Greer, *Early Biblical Interpretation.* Library of Early Christianity. Philadelphia: Westminster, 1986.

Lane Fox, Robin. *Pagans and Christians.* New York: Alfred A. Knopf, 1987.

Markschies, Christoph. *Gnosis: An Introduction.* Translated by John Bowden. London and New York: T. and T. Clark, 2003.

Origen. *Contra Celsum.* Translated by Henry Chadwick. Cambridge: Cambridge University, 1986.

Pelikan, Jaroslav. *The Emergence of the Catholic Tradition (100–600).* Vol. 1 of *The Christian Tradition: A History of the Development of Doctrine.* Chicago: University of Chicago, 1971.

Richardson, Cyril C., trans. *Early Christian Fathers.* New York: Macmillan, 1970.

Robinson, James M., ed. *The Nag Hammadi Library in English.* 4th rev. ed. Leiden and New York: E. J. Brill, 1996.

Rudolph, Kurt. *Gnosis: The Nature and History of Gnosticism.* Translated by R. McLachlan Wilson. San Francisco: Harper & Row, 1987.

Sanders, E. P., ed. *The Shaping of Christianity in the Second and Third Centuries.* Vol. 1 of *Jewish and Christian Self-Definition.* Philadelphia: Fortress, 1980.

Snyder, Graydon F. *Ante Pacem: Archaeological Evidence of Church Life before Constantine.* Macon, GA: Mercer University, 1985.

Swift, Louis J. *The Early Fathers on War and Military Service.* Message of the Fathers of the Church, 19. Wilmington, DE: Michael Glazier, 1983.

Trigg, Joseph Wilson. *Origen: The Bible and Philosophy in the Third-Century Church.* Atlanta: John Knox, 1983.

Wilken, Robert L. *The Christians as the Romans Saw Them.* New Haven, CT: Yale University, 1984.

Chapter

THE AGE OF THE IMPERIAL CHURCH

TIMELINE

A.D. 251–356	Lifetime of Antony of Egypt, traditional founder of monastic way of life.
A.D. 306	Constantine is named emperor by his father's troops.
A.D. 312	Battle of the Milvian Bridge. Constantine said to have received a vision in which he was told to place the "heavenly sign of God" on his soldiers' shields.
A.D. 313	Edict of Milan announces universal religious toleration and the restoration of seized property to the Christian churches.
A.D. 325	The first ecumenical council is held at Nicaea, defining the full divinity of the Son of God and condemning the teachings of Arius as heresy.
A.D. 328	Athanasius becomes bishop of Alexandria.
A.D. 380	Emperor Theodosius I makes orthodox Christianity the sole legal religion of the Roman Empire.
A.D. 381	The Nicene Creed is confirmed and expanded at the Council of Constantinople.
A.D. 431	The teachings of Nestorius are condemned as heresy, and Mary is declared to be the Mother of God at the Council of Ephesus.
A.D. 451	The Council of Chalcedon issues a definition of faith concerning the doctrine of the incarnation.

During the course of the fourth century, Christianity underwent a great reversal in its relationship with the Roman Empire. From 303 to 313 it endured the last and most prolonged of the persecutions. But shortly after this, the conversion of the emperor **Constantine** (reigned 306–337) inaugurated a new era in which Christianity won legal toleration and eventual establishment as the empire's official religion. Christianity had begun as a Jewish splinter group looking forward to Jesus's second coming and the full realization of the kingdom of God. Now it embarked on its long career as an established religion approved and promoted by the state. The union of church and state profoundly influenced Christianity. This chapter discusses Constantine's conversion and the transformation of Christianity into an "imperial church" (the church of the Roman Empire), the church councils and doctrinal developments of the period, and important trends in Christian life. The next chapter will be devoted entirely to St. Augustine of Hippo (354–430), the theologian whose ideas most fully reflected Christianity's transition to becoming a state church.

CONSTANTINE AND HIS LEGACY

Rise to Power and Religious Policies

Constantine came to power at a time when the Roman Empire was divided into sections ruled by an imperial board or college. This system was invented by the emperor Diocletian (reigned 284–305), who restored the empire to stability after it almost collapsed in the late third century A.D. In 303 Diocletian inflicted a brutal persecution on Christianity. He did so because he wanted to make the empire's peoples return to traditional Roman values, to secure the good will of the gods, and to ensure the loyalty of the army. (Despite the church's prohibitions against bloodshed mentioned in Chapter Eight, Christians were serving in the Roman army by the third century.) Although the persecution failed, it left the churches bitterly divided over what to do with those who had lapsed in their faith during the persecution, just as had happened in the third century persecutions (see Chapter Eight). Schisms broke out in Egypt and in North Africa; in the latter area Christians in the Donatist movement refused to accept sacraments from Catholic clergy whom they accused of betraying the faith during the persecution (see Chapter Ten).

Constantine's father had been one of three co-rulers with Diocletian. When his father died in 306, Constantine succeeded him. For the next six years he fought for control of the Western half of the empire. The crucial battle came in 312, when he defeated his last Western rival at the Milvian Bridge outside of the city of Rome. Before the battle he became convinced that he would achieve victory with the help of the Christian God. According to the earliest account, he had a dream in which he was told to place the "heavenly sign of God" on the shields of the soldiers. The "sign" was probably the cross, though it has also been construed as the "Chi-Rho," a monogram consisting of the first two letters of the Greek spelling of Christ's name (the Greek letters *chi* and *rho,* which look like our *x* and *p,* superimposed on one another; it was later featured on Constantine's standards and on his battle helmet).

Figure 9–1 The Chi-Rho, a monogram for the name of Christ, which the emperor Constantine used on his royal standards and battle gear.

A later account by his biographer, the church historian Eusebius of Caesarea (c. 260–339), says that he had a daytime vision of a cross of light above the sun, with the words "By this, conquer," followed by a dream in which Christ told him to put the sign he had seen as a protection in battle (Eusebius, *Life of Constantine* 1.28–32). The following year he and his Eastern counterpart, the emperor Licinius, agreed to announce universal religious toleration and the restoration of seized property to the Christian churches, a decision traditionally known as the Edict of Milan (313). Constantine later went to war with Licinius and defeated him in 324, thus uniting the whole empire under his sole rule until his death in 337.

Modern historians have argued about whether Constantine was really a Christian. During the decade after 312, the evidence of his official coins (a traditional way for emperors to advertise their allegiances) is ambiguous. Some coins represent him under the sponsorship of the "Unconquered Sun," a pagan form of monotheism especially popular in the army—but also a religion less offensive to Christianity than polytheism. Nevertheless, after 312 Constantine produced a constant flow of letters and decrees that demonstrate his deep involvement in the affairs of the Christian church, even though he was not baptized until just before he died. He called church councils and enforced their decisions by exiling dissenters and burning condemned books. He subsidized the construction of new churches, especially in Palestine, which became a Christian "holy land" from this time forward. He gave large grants of money to the churches for their charitable work. He made his new Eastern capital of Constantinople, founded on the site of the ancient city of Byzantium, into an explicitly Christian city.

Christianity represented for Constantine, above all, a divine guarantee of victory over evil. That is why he adopted the Chi-Rho and the cross as imperial symbols. He believed that God had chosen him for a special mission to bring the Roman Empire to Christianity, in return for which God would bless his reign and give the empire peace and prosperity. Upon the triumphal arch of the magnificent church he built over the grave of St. Peter, Constantine inscribed the following grateful dedication to Christ: "Since under your leadership the Empire rose once again triumphant to the stars, Constantine the Victor has founded this audience hall in your honor."

Constantine saw the Christian church as providing heavenly support for the Roman Empire through the prayers of its clergy, and a common religion to hold its diverse peoples together, even though Christians were still just a small proportion of the population. To realize these goals, he gave the clergy important benefits, such as tax exemption and the power to act as judges in civil lawsuits. To a certain extent Christian values influenced his laws, though an enactment like making Sunday, "the day of the Sun," a day of rest was the kind of ambiguous act that could please both Christians and non-Christians. He confiscated the wealth of pagan temples, ended their state subsidies, and imposed certain restrictions on Jews. Nonetheless, he never revoked the Edict of Milan. It was his successors, especially **Theodosius I** (reigned 379–395), who made Christianity the sole legal religion of the empire.

Constantine's Impact on the Development of Christianity

The reign of Constantine left a lasting impression on Christianity. First, Constantine established the practice of calling an **ecumenical** or **general council**, a universal gathering of Christian bishops, to resolve urgent issues affecting the whole church. These councils and their decrees were crucial to the development of Christianity from the fourth century on. Second, his conversion and his policies as emperor greatly increased the rate of conversion to Christianity, although contemporary observers like Eusebius admitted that many of these conversions were politically motivated. Third, Constantine founded the city of **Constantinople**, which can be seen as a symbolic beginning of the Byzantine Empire, the name that historians give to the continuation of the Roman Empire in the East. The Byzantine Empire lasted for over a thousand years and served as a Christian barrier against Muslim expansion until the Ottoman Turks (adherents of Islam) finally captured Constantinople in 1453. This Christianized Eastern Roman Empire became the center of what we now call Eastern Orthodox Christianity (Chapter 11).

Moreover, Constantine inaugurated a model of Christian kingship in which the king receives his authority to rule directly from God, not from an institution such as the church. According to Eusebius the emperor once said to him, "You are bishops of those within the Church, but I am perhaps a bishop appointed by God over those outside [the church]" (*Life of Constantine* 4.24). Constantine was making an analogy between the bishops' oversight of the church—the word *bishop* means "overseer"—and his own divinely ordained oversight of the empire as a whole. In his view the emperor was not supposed to take over the spiritual work proper to the church, but to enable the church to perform its divine tasks rightly. This type of Christian kingship was imitated by Byzantine emperors, by many Western kings and emperors in the medieval period and, in some cases, even into the modern period.

Finally, Constantine inspired the growth of a Christian devotion to the Roman state as an institution willed by God. Henceforth, Christians demonstrated their patriotism by holding public office and serving in the army. This Christian patriotism can be seen in both a positive and a negative light. In a positive sense it reflected a deepened awareness of civic responsibility. To Christians like Eusebius, it seemed logical that Christians should not flee from the world but should seek to exercise power on behalf of the church and the gospel. Eusebius went so far as to describe the Roman Empire and its government as an image of God's heavenly government (see his *Oration in Praise of Constantine*, given on the thirtieth anniversary of Constantine's reign). This new patriotism and civic involvement provided an answer to pagan critics who had accused Christians of shirking their public duties while enjoying the benefits and protection of the Roman Empire.

To justify the duty to defend the state, Christians could appeal to many texts in the Bible, such as Romans 13:1–7 ("Those authorities that exist have been instituted by God . . ."), which recognized that all earthly power is under God's direction and is answerable to God. Some Christian writers, such as St. Augustine, distinguished individual killing from the publicly authorized use of the sword on behalf of the community (see *On the City of God* 1.21 and 19.7). Augustine and St. Ambrose, archbishop of Milan from 374 to 397, helped to form a Christian version of "just war theory" by adapting traditional Roman criteria for deciding when and how to wage war justly.

On the negative side, Christianity's alliance with the state created some problems, too. Emperors were always tempted to overstep their limits and intervene in church affairs. Moral responsibility for the actions of a supposedly Christian state exposed Christians to new tests of their consciences. Hadn't Jesus said to Pontius Pilate, "My kingdom is not from this world" (John 18:36)? Was the abandonment of Jesus's prohibition of bloodshed actually justified? In later centuries some Christian churches like the Mennonites and the Quakers would reject Christian participation in war as incompatible with the teachings of Jesus in the Sermon on the Mount. Another issue was the possible corruption of the church. Wealth and political influence threatened the integrity of the church's government. Bishops were tempted to switch from one city to another in the hope of increasing their power and influence, and church laws against this practice were widely ignored. There was also a growing tendency to equate Christianity with the civilization of the Roman Empire, when in fact many Christians already lived outside of the empire. Constantine's conversion, for instance, exposed Persian Christians across the eastern border to persecution as suspected traitors. Finally, there was the ominous beginning of religious coercion, as the institutional church used its privileged position within the state to persecute heretics and unbelievers. Under the Christian emperors, Jews would gradually lose many of the legal protections and exemptions they had enjoyed earlier under the pagan emperors.

DOGMATIC DEVELOPMENT: TRINITY AND INCARNATION

The most significant theological achievement of the fourth and fifth centuries is the defining of the dogmas of the Trinity and the incarnation, the complementary Christian doctrines about God that distinguish Christianity from all other religions. A **dogma** is a religious teaching based on divine revelation and defined by the church. Why were these important dogmas not defined until centuries after Jesus's death? Although the basic shape of the Christian doctrine of God had been in place from the beginning, precise definitions were still lacking and numerous important issues were unresolved, including some that were as yet hardly recognized as problems, such as the full humanity and divinity of Christ. A good deal of theological trial and error was necessary before consensus was possible.

One should also remember that until the fourth century, there was no church structure that spoke effectively for everybody. The solution to this problem was the development of ecumenical councils. However, even the councils were not perfect institutions. The emperors often influenced church councils, since they now had a big stake in the outcome. Church rivalries also played a role. As a result, only a few of the councils held during these years are recognized today as ecumenical (or worldwide). The process by which later tradition chose to accept or reject these early councils resembles somewhat the sifting process that produced the canon of the Bible. Reasons for not accepting a council could include its adoption of false doctrines, an attendance list that did not adequately represent the universal church, or the use of excessive political and social pressure on the bishops' deliberations. Of the councils that were held in the fourth and fifth centuries, those which Catholics, Eastern Orthodox, and most mainstream Protestants accept are the ones that met at Nicaea (325), Constantinople (381), Ephesus (431), and Chalcedon (451).

Nicaea (325)

It was noted earlier that ecumenical councils were called to address urgent issues affecting the whole church. The issue that provoked the Council of Nicaea was the teaching of **Arius**, a priest from Alexandria in Egypt, about the relation between God and his Son. The prologue of John's gospel (John 1:1–18) and the theologians of the second and third centuries had recognized a distinction between God and his Word, between the Father and the Son. Arius argued that only God the Father could be called God in the full sense of the word. Only the Father could be said to be *without beginning*; all else had a beginning, including the Son, or the Word. The Son was a "second-class" god who was necessary in order to be the link between the truly transcendent God and the rest of the universe, both in creating the world and in redeeming it. Since the transcendent God could not interact directly with the world in order to redeem it, redemption would be the mission of a subordinate divine being, the Son or Word.

Arius appealed to the Bible to support his position. Proverbs 8:22, for example, speaks about God's Wisdom as though it were an actual entity distinct from God: "The Lord created me at [*or "as"*] the beginning of his work, the first of his acts of long ago." Christians applied this passage to Jesus, whom they thought of as "the wisdom of God" (1 Cor 1:24), but Arius understood it to mean that the Son of God actually had a beginning, that there was a "time," so to speak, when he did not exist.

Arius' critics strongly objected to this teaching because it turned the Son of God into a being so much less than God as to be virtually a creature himself. Unfortunately, the Bible could not be quoted to prove decisively that Arius was wrong. The Gospel of John played a central role in Christian understandings of Jesus's divinity and humanity, but both sides could find support for their positions. John 14:28 has Jesus say, "The Father is greater than I," which is capable of an Arian interpretation. However, John also has Jesus say, "The Father and I are one" (John 10:30), and "Whoever has seen me has seen the Father" (John 14:9). **Athanasius of Alexandria**, bishop or patriarch of Alexandria from 328 to 373, made the anti-Arian case most forcefully. According to Athanasius, the heart of the Bible's teaching is that in Christ human beings could see the true God, not a subordinate or an underling: "For in him [Christ] all the fullness of God was pleased to dwell, and through him God was pleased to reconcile to himself all things, whether on earth or in heaven, by making peace through the blood of his cross" (Col. 1:19–20). No subordinate God was necessary to protect true divinity from contact with the world. Only the one true God could save us; anything less put our salvation in doubt. There was never a time when the Father was not the *Father*, when the Son did not exist. They are co-eternal.

At the **Council of Nicaea** the bishops indicated their opposition to Arianism by approving a creed, or statement of beliefs. This statement of beliefs came to be called the Nicene Creed. In it the bishops adapted an already existing creed by inserting a few phrases designed to link Father and Son as closely as possible and hence to express their opposition to the position of Arius, who separated the Father and the Son by denying the true divinity of the Son. Most importantly, they asserted that the Son is "one in being with the Father." Unfortunately, the Greek word that the bishops used for "one in being"—*homoousios* (literally, "of the same substance")—created problems. It could be misunderstood in a materialist sense, as if God were "stuff" that could be divided, or even taken to mean that Father and Son were simply the *same* being. Besides being philosophically suspect in the eyes of many educated bishops, the word also did not come from the Bible, whereas earlier creeds had consisted of biblical language and images. On top of that, the word had previously been found mostly among gnostic writers. As a result, rather than settling things, Nicaea provoked decades of controversy, made all the worse by the shifting opinions and policies of the emperors themselves.

Constantinople (381)

After a half century of strife, the decision of the Council of Nicaea was ratified once and for all when the new emperor, Theodosius I, recognized it as the law of the empire. The celebrated edict of 380 known as *Cunctos Populos* ("All the peoples") not only mandated the creed of Nicaea but also named the bishops of Rome and Alexandria as the judges of orthodox doctrine. *Cunctos Populos* was followed in 391 by a sweeping edict against paganism. The reign of Theodosius was thus the time when Christianity really became the sole legal religion of the empire.

Emperor Theodosius the Great's Decree on Orthodoxy and Heresy, *Cunctos Populos*

It is Our Will that all the peoples who are ruled by the administration of Our Clemency shall practise that religion which the divine Peter the Apostle transmitted to the Romans . . . this is the religion that is followed by the Pontiff [Pope] Damasus and by Peter, bishop of Alexandria, a man of apostolic sanctity; that is, according to the apostolic discipline and the evangelic doctrine, we shall believe in the single Deity of the Father, Son, and Holy Spirit, under the concept of equal majesty and of the Holy Trinity. We command that those persons who follow this rule shall embrace the name of the Catholic Christians. The rest, however, whom We adjudge demented and insane, shall sustain the infamy of heretical dogmas, their meeting places shall not receive the name of churches . . ." (*Theodosian Code* XVI.1.2, cited in Stevenson 1989, 150)

At Theodosius' instigation a council of bishops met in the Eastern capital of Constantinople in 381. At this **Council of Constantinople**, the Nicene Creed was confirmed and expanded. The expansions were designed to clarify the Council of Nicaea on a point that had only recently become a disputed issue, the full divinity of the Holy Spirit. Nicaea had ended its creed rather abruptly by saying only, "And we believe in the Holy Spirit." The article on the Holy Spirit was now expanded with new clauses that recognized the Spirit's traditional functions of inspiration ("spoke through the prophets") and sanctification ("giver of life," in the sense of being the redeeming presence of God's grace within believers). The new clauses also asserted that the Father is the source of the Spirit and that the Spirit is accorded worth and dignity equal to that of the Father and the Son.

This amended form of the Nicene Creed has become the most universally accepted benchmark of the Christian faith outside of the Bible itself. Because it is the product of two councils, not just one, its proper name is the Nicene–Constantinopolitan Creed. With the exception of the dispute between Western and Eastern Christians over the "procession" of the Holy Spirit from the Father (see Chapter 11), this is essentially the wording of the creed as it is recited in churches today:

> We believe in one God, the Father, almighty, maker of heaven and earth, and of all things visible and invisible.
>
> And in one Lord Jesus Christ, the only begotten Son of God, begotten from the Father before all ages, light from light, true God from true God, begotten not made, of one substance with the Father, through whom all things came into existence, who because of us men and because of our salvation came down from heaven, and was incarnate from the Holy Spirit and the Virgin Mary and became man, and was crucified for us under Pontius Pilate, and suffered and was buried, and rose again on the third day according to the scriptures, and ascended to heaven and sits on the right hand of the Father, and will come again with glory to judge living and dead, of whose kingdom there will be no end.

And in the Holy Spirit, the Lord and life-giver, who proceeds from the Father, who with the Father and the Son is together worshipped and together glorified, who spoke through the prophets; in one holy catholic and apostolic church. We confess one baptism for the remission of sins; we look forward to the resurrection of the dead and the life of the world to come. Amen. (Cited in Kelly 1972, 297–298)

This clarification of the original creed of Nicaea reflects important theological advances made by Basil of Caesarea (330–379), his brother Gregory of Nyssa (331/40–c. 395), and Basil's friend Gregory of Nazianzus (c. 329–390). These three are often referred to as the **Cappadocian Fathers**, because they came from the central region of Asia Minor known as Cappadocia. They represent the highest point of advance in the long process by which ancient Christianity gradually appropriated Greek philosophical ideas and incorporated them into Christianity.

Where development of the doctrine of the Trinity is concerned, the Cappadocians were responsible for several accomplishments. First, they distinguished the meaning of abstract terms such as *person* and *substance* as applied to the Trinity. Henceforth everyone agreed to say that the divine substance was the *nature* that Father, Son, and Spirit have as God, no one of them more so than the others. But this divine substance, the Godhead, has three distinct and separate manners of being. Each of these is really and truly God and hence can be called a *person,* marked by its distinctive qualities. Though these qualities do make for an ordering of the three, this is simply in respect to their particular qualities (for example, the Father begetting the Son, or the Spirit being sent by the Father) and not in respect of their divinity. One person of the Trinity is not "more God" than another.

Second, the Cappadocians clearly recognized that all language about God could only be an analogy, not a literal description of what God really was. God in God's own nature, they insisted, was unknowable; we know God only from God's effects recorded in the Bible and seen in the world. The gender-free language in the previous sentence reflects the Cappadocians' recognition that, unlike the gods and goddesses of pagan mythology, the true God was beyond such distinctions.

Third, they admitted that the Bible alone might not be a sufficient standard for defining the full divinity of the Spirit. The Bible needed to be supplemented by the evidence of the church's tradition, such as the trinitarian character of the baptismal ritual, in which people are baptized "in the name of the Father and of the Son and of the Holy Spirit." In other words, the Cappadocians recognized that what Christians believed had to be consistent with the way they worshiped. Gregory of Nazianzus even suggested there had been a gradual revelation of the reality of the Trinity, with the process beginning in the Old Testament and extending beyond the New Testament into the life and experience of the church. In each period God had disclosed as much as, but not more than, people were prepared to receive.

Ephesus (431) and Chalcedon (451)

Christians had always confessed Jesus Christ to be both human and divine. However, the divine aspect tended to receive greater emphasis. Once the Council of Nicaea had firmly established that his divinity was the same as that of God the Father's, Christians were forced to think more carefully about the incarnation (John 1:14: "And the Word became flesh.") of this fully divine Son. What did it mean to say that the one true God had taken on flesh and suffered and died for human beings? Did this mean for example that God as God had really suffered and died? How could God be said to die? Educated Christians accepted the philosophical axiom that God was *impassible*, meaning that God could not suffer or change.

The problem was even more complex, however. It seems that many theologians, including Athanasius, understood the incarnation to consist of the union of the *Logos* or Son of God with a human body but not with a human soul. In other words, the *Logos* took the place of Christ's human soul. Athanasius, for instance, often described the flesh of Christ—and the Gospel of John had explicitly mentioned only the flesh in the incarnation—as an instrument that the *Logos* had assumed in order to reveal Himself to human beings and to renew our nature. This view of the incarnation made it easier to see how divine and human could be joined in one person. But it seems to express a deficient view of the humanity with which God was united, as though Christ's human flesh were all that he had in common with us. After a theologian named **Apollinaris of Laodicaea** taught explicitly that Christ had no human soul, other Christians repudiated his model of the incarnation because they believed that Christ had redeemed *all* of human nature. Gregory of Nazianzus gave a classic expression to the doctrine that Christ took on a complete human nature when he said, in his *First Letter to Cledonius*, "For that which He [Christ] has not assumed, he has not healed." What was not assumed [by the Word in the incarnation] was not saved. Humanity's sinfulness was not a function of the flesh alone but of the whole person, soul and body, and so it was the whole of human nature that Christ had come to save.

Gregory saw that Christ needed to have had a complete human nature for human beings to be saved by him, but it remained difficult to see how divinity and humanity could coexist in a single person. Two broadly different approaches to the problem emerged in the fifth century. The chief concern of the "School of Antioch," as theologians in Syria came to be called collectively, was to protect the integrity of each aspect of the incarnation, the divine and the human: On the one hand, the *Logos'* full divinity had to be protected from having inappropriate contact with the reality of time and space; and on the other hand, the gospel testimonies to Jesus's full humanity (his birth from Mary, his growth in knowledge, his temptations, his suffering and death, etc.) had to be respected. Therefore, Antiochene theologians often spoke as though the Word had assumed a complete human being, or of the Word's "indwelling" of Christ's human nature. Either way, the union of the two could seem more like a divine–human partnership rather than a true unity of subject.

That at any rate was the fear of their opponents, the School of Alexandria: They thought that the Antiochenes risked dividing the incarnate Christ into two separate realities, indeed into two persons. Alexandrian theologians took the divine–human fact of the incarnation as their starting point. From the instant of his conception Jesus had been both God and man. Divinity and humanity were so indissolubly joined that they could only be distinguished in thought, but not as separately existing realities in the incarnation. The real subject of all the actions reported of Jesus in the gospels was the Word of God, but the Word *incarnate*, that is, personally united with a human nature in a *single* reality. This human nature was indeed complete so far as soul and body were concerned. But it lacked a human personal "identity," to use modern language. All of Jesus's human experiences were truly human, including his interior mental and emotional life, but they were all referred to the Word, who claimed them as his own. The result was to make Jesus's limitations seem as though the Word had merely consented to them, rather than experienced them as real. It is important to note that Alexandrian emphasis on the Word as the subject of the incarnation was deeply rooted in the faith of ordinary Christians, who believed they shared Christ's divinity when they were united with him in the Eucharist. The great Alexandrian spokesman Cyril of Alexandria (c. 375–444) made this Eucharistic connection explicit in his *Third Letter to Nestorius*, an Antiochene theologian who became patriarch of Constantinople in 428:

> We must necessarily add this: Proclaiming the death in the flesh of the unique Son of God, that is, Jesus Christ, and confessing his return to life from the dead, and his reception into heaven, we celebrate the unbloody service [worship] in the churches. So we approach to the mystical gifts and are sanctified, becoming partakers of the holy flesh and the honorable blood of Christ the Saviour of us all, not receiving it as ordinary flesh—God forbid—nor as that of a man sanctified and conjoined with the World by a unity of honor, or as one who had received a divine indwelling, but as truly life giving and the Word's own flesh. (Cyril, *Third Letter to Nestorius* 7, cited in Hardy 1954, 352)

The Christological controversy between Antioch and Alexandria came to a head when **Nestorius** (patriarch of Constantinople 428–431, d. 451) began to preach that it was inappropriate to call Mary the Mother of God (in Greek, *Theotokos*, "the Godbearer"), on the grounds that God could not be said to have been born. Nestorius held that at best Mary was only the Mother of Christ, meaning of his humanity. Nevertheless, at the **Council of Ephesus** in 431, Mary was declared to be the Mother of God, and Nestorius was deposed from office and condemned for heresy. Today scholars tend to doubt that Nestorius actually taught the view for which he was condemned, namely, that there were two distinct persons in the incarnation, one divine and the other human. But the turbulence and bitterness of the council's proceedings, inflamed by church rivalries, did not make for a charitable discussion of views.

The Council of Ephesus did not bring an end to the agitation over Jesus's humanity and divinity. Twenty years later a new emperor was persuaded to convene another assembly. The canons and definition of the **Council of Chalcedon** (451) represent the decisive stage in the development of the early Christian doctrine of Christ. Here is the central portion of the council's definition of the incarnation:

> Wherefore, following the holy fathers [of Nicaea, Constantinople, and Ephesus], we all with one voice confess our Lord Jesus Christ one and the same Son, the same perfect in Godhead, the same perfect in manhood, truly God and truly man, the same consisting of a reasonable soul and a body, of one substance with the Father as touching the Godhead, the same of one substance with us touching the manhood, "like us in all things apart from sin" (Heb 4:15); begotten from the Father before the ages as touching the Godhead, the same in the last days, for us and for our salvation, born from the Virgin Mary, the Theotokos, as touching the manhood, one and the same Christ, Son, Lord, Only-begotten, to be acknowledged in two natures, without confusion, without change, without division, without separation; the distinction of natures being in no way abolished because of the union, but rather the characteristic property of each nature being preserved, and concurring into one person and one subsistence, not as if Christ were parted or divided into two persons, but one and the same Son. (Cited in Stevenson 1989, 337)

The bishops tried to pacify the warring factions by a balanced statement that drew on both Antiochene and Alexandrian traditions and phrasing. The controversial phrase "acknowledged in two natures" was Antiochene in origin. A key Western contribution, where the duality of the natures was also important, was a long letter (traditionally called the *Tome*) that Pope Leo of Rome sent to the Council. From Leo's letter the fathers took the formulation "the characteristic property of each nature being preserved and concurring . . . in one person." But the bulk of the actual wording came from Cyril of Alexandria's Second and Third Letters to Nestorius. Those letters, along with Leo's *Tome* and a document called *The Formula of Reunion* from the church of Antioch, were then read into the record at the Council. The resulting definition was thus truly ecumenical. Nevertheless, dissenters from Chalcedon's definition believed that it betrayed the genuine teaching of Cyril of Alexandria. The most they would concede was that Christ was from or out of two natures, but after his incarnation they insisted on speaking of only one nature, meaning "nature" in the sense of a single reality. As a result, those who accepted Chalcedon called those who rejected it **monophysites** (from Greek *monos*, "single" or "sole," and *physis*, "nature," hence "believers in a single nature").

The Councils of Nicaea, Constantinople, Ephesus, and Chalcedon marked the greatest institutional and doctrinal unity that the Christian tradition has ever achieved. Ironically, the latter two councils also led to the first permanent schisms (splits) in the church. Those whose views were condemned at Ephesus as Nestorian were eventually forced to move across the eastern border into Persian territory. Over the next thousand years they spread as far east as China and India, though their numbers today are vastly reduced (see Chapter 11). The Council of Chalcedon caused even greater damage to Christian unity. Several modern Christian churches in the Middle East and in Africa originated as a result of their protests against the Council of Chalcedon's definition of the two natures in Christ (see Chapter 11).

THE LIFE OF THE CHURCH

The fourth and fifth centuries saw important developments in other areas besides politics and theology. Three of these include the consolidation of the church's universal government, the rise of monasticism, and trends in liturgy and church design.

Church Government

Until the fourth century, Christianity had consisted of a confederation of local churches linked by a common faith and the fellowship of the bishops. In theory all bishops were equal successors of the apostles, but in reality the bishops of the larger cities dominated. The Council of Nicaea recognized regional spheres of interest centered in Rome, Alexandria, and Antioch (the largest cities in the empire), with Jerusalem enjoying an honorary status as the historic mother church of Christianity. To these four was soon added Constantinople, the new Eastern capital. Four of these cities were located in the Eastern part of the Roman Empire (Antioch, Alexandria, Jerusalem, and Constantinople), with only one in the West (Rome). The bishops of these cities eventually gained the honorary title of **patriarch**. The idea later developed in the Eastern churches that the five patriarchs should share spiritual jurisdiction as a committee or college. Such a system never got much beyond the level of theory, however, mainly because of rivalry among the patriarchs.

Figure 9–2 A relief on a sarcophagus, or stone casket, dating from about 380, which has the very common artistic theme of Christ handing Peter the Law in the form of a scroll; Peter is holding a cross, broken at the top, in token of Christ's prediction in John 21:18–19 that Peter would die a martyr's death.

The Roman church represented a special case in that it was the only church with a convincing claim to *primacy* (literally, being first). Rome's unique prestige was based mainly on its possession of the tombs of both Peter and Paul and on its location in the capital of the empire. Moreover, the Roman church and its bishop had always shown a strong sense of responsibility for the Christian churches as a whole. In the fourth century, Eastern bishops and theologians looking for support abroad often went to Rome as a refuge and a court of appeal, although the Easterners never accepted that the bishop of Rome had the right to intervene in their affairs without being asked first. The bishop of Rome eventually came to be called the **pope**. (The word comes from the Latin *papa*, meaning "father," and originally could be applied to other bishops as well; the head of the Coptic Orthodox Church in Egypt still claims it as a title.) A major concern for the bishop of Rome was the growing ambition of the church of Constantinople; according to certain conciliar canons (statements issued by church councils) that the Roman church has never accepted, Constantinople possessed an authority second only to that of Rome's. This claim to authority was made on the frankly secular and political ground that, as the Eastern capital, it was the "new Rome."

The sermons, letters, and decrees of Pope Leo I (reigned 440–461) expressed many of the ideas that have remained basic to the **papacy** (the government of the pope) ever since: Peter was the chief or prince of the apostles; he was divinely commissioned to rule the church at the center of the empire; the pope is the direct successor of Peter, "the door-keeper of the kingdom of heaven," as Leo called him (see Matt 16:15–19); and the pope's authority is grounded not in his personal merit but in the merits of Peter.

Peter's Confession According to Matt 16:15–19

[Jesus] said to them, "But who do you say that I am?" Simon Peter answered, "You are the Messiah, the Son of the living God." And Jesus answered him, "Blessed are you, Simon son of Jonah! For flesh and blood has not revealed this to you, but my Father in heaven. And I tell you, you are Peter, and on this rock I will build my church, and the gates of Hades will not prevail against it. I will give you the keys of the kingdom of heaven, and whatever you bind on earth will be bound in heaven, and whatever you loose on earth will be loosed in heaven."

These ideas concerning papal primacy would not be fully applied even in the West until the Germanic invasions and the conquests of Islam radically reshaped the Christian map and left the papacy largely in a world of its own. They were, however, never fully accepted in the East. Although Eastern Christians did not view the primacy of Rome the same way that Westerners did, the acceptance of Leo's *Tome* at the Council of Chalcedon testifies to the regard in which the Eastern bishops held the Roman church: "Peter has spoken through Leo," they cried. They did not mean that Leo's teaching was true just because it was Leo who had said it; rather that in their judgment Leo had correctly expressed the faith that they too held, for they also shouted out, "Cyril [of Alexandria] so taught . . . Leo and Cyril taught the same thing." In the Christian East (but also in the West) a common interpretation of Peter's confession of faith in Matt 16:16–19 was that the "rock" (*petra* in Greek) on which Jesus founds the church was not so much the *person* of Peter as his faith in Christ, which was professed by all. Eastern Christianity has traditionally seen the Roman bishop as, at best, "the first among equals," meaning that he has a unique spiritual prestige, a primacy of honor, but not a right of command or jurisdiction over other patriarchs.

Monasticism and the Ascetical Movement

The fourth century also saw the rise of monasticism and of the ascetical movement in the Eastern Roman Empire. **Asceticism** refers to the training or discipline of the passions and the appetites. **Monasticism** refers to the way of life of monks, who separate themselves from society to pray for the world. The word **monk** comes from the Greek word *monachos*, meaning "a single or a solitary person." It was coined in the fourth century as a name for the many men and women who had begun to withdraw to secluded desert regions to lead lives of prayer and spiritual discipline. It is not a coincidence that this became popular just about the time when Christianity was winning acceptance by the Roman Empire. The monastic life replaced martyrdom as the model of Christian perfection.

Tradition credits **Antony of Egypt** (251–356) with being the father of Christian monasticism. According to the *Life of Antony* written by Athanasius of Alexandria, Antony chose to change his life when he heard the gospel story of Christ's counsel to the rich young man: "If you wish to be perfect, go, sell your possessions and give the money to the poor . . . then come, follow me" (Matt 19:21). His basic motive was thus the full discipleship of Christ and his command to be perfect (Matt 5:48). The monk struggled to subdue human appetites and passions of all kinds (for food, for possessions, for comfort, for freedom, for sexual union, and so on), for the sake of restoring the original innocence of humanity before the Fall. In the eyes of these early monks, the struggle for perfection required a departure from the normal life of the world, either through enclosure (hence the term *cloister*) or through actual withdrawal into the desert. In fact, devout groups of Christian men and women were already practicing asceticism within church communities long before Antony; his main innovation was physical seclusion.

Despite the desire for separation from the world, monks aspired to support themselves and to work for the good of others. They did not coldly leave the rest of humanity to its fate. Monks often remained close enough to towns and villages to serve as advocates for those in need, to proclaim Christ's message to the high and the mighty, to heal the sick and counsel the troubled, and above all to serve as an example to others. Ordinary Christians saw them as living links to heaven. Even the pillar saints of Syria, who mounted columns in order to withdraw from society, were pursued into the desert by pilgrims and by communities of monks who settled around them. Christian asceticism was not a condemnation of the world as such but a personal struggle against the reign of sin and of the demons in the soul. Therefore, the movement did not condemn Christians who continued to live in the world nor did it protest against the conversion of the empire to Christianity. Although monasticism had a generally positive impact on both the monks and those whom they served and for whom they prayed, examples of destructive fanaticism were not unknown. Monks occasionally inspired mob violence against pagans and pagan shrines or pursued ascetical self-denial in extreme forms, such as the wearing of chains.

The primary model for the monastic life was Jesus himself, who was unmarried, had no permanent home, and said no human obligation should stand in the way of the kingdom of God. Other important New Testament models included the ascetical prophet John the Baptist, and also Paul, who seems not to have been married and who recommended virginity as superior to marriage (see 1 Cor 7:8). Another biblical inspiration was the communal sharing of property in the Jerusalem church (Acts 2:44–45). There were also antecedents in Judaism, such as the Essene monasticism of Qumran, where celibacy for some and community ownership of goods were practiced, and the communities of Jewish contemplatives in Egypt described by Philo of Alexandria. There were pagan ascetics, too, influenced by philosophical ideas of the superiority of the spiritual realm over the material. The ascetical life appealed to many high-minded pagans as well as to Christians.

Alongside the hermit or solitary type of monasticism, there were also communities of monks. This kind of monasticism is called **cenobitic monasticism** from the Greek words for "common life." Organized communities were governed by a spiritual leader called an **abbot** (from the Aramaic word for "father"). They usually followed a written rule and a routine of manual labor and public and private prayer. The rules and routines—along with the separation from society—were designed (in part) to help monks avoid sin. Basil of Caesarea, one of the Cappadocians, formulated a rule for cenobitic monasticism that stressed mutual service and works of charity. If you live alone, he asked, whose feet will you wash? (The reference is to Jesus's washing of his disciples' feet at the Last Supper in the Gospel of John.) Basil's rule has dominated monasticism in Orthodox Christianity.

The monk Evagrius (345–399) was Egyptian monasticism's most important teacher. From him stems the traditional list of the seven deadly sins, although his list actually included eight of them: gluttony, lust, love of money, sadness, anger, boredom, vanity, and pride. Monasticism also flourished in Syria, independent of developments in Egypt. Syrian monasticism was notable for its extreme forms of self-denial, such as that of the pillar saints.

Gradually, written and oral accounts, including Athanasius' *Life of Antony*, spread monastic theory and practice throughout the Christian world. Monasticism and ascetical ideals began to become popular in the West, starting in the late fourth century. In his *Confessions* (Book 8.6.14–15), Augustine, who had never heard of Christian monks, is amazed to learn of men who had been converted to an ascetical life by reading the *Life of Antony*. Books about the sayings and lives of the desert fathers and mothers (monasticism was open to women as well as men) became central texts in the spiritual literature of the Christian tradition, and monasticism would come to play a crucial role in the development of Christianity in the West.

Religious Life and Church Architecture

The newly won support of the Roman emperors and the rapid growth of the church affected the worship life of Christians. This is shown most visibly in the development of church architecture. For the first three centuries, Christians met for the weekly Eucharist and for other activities in private homes adapted for worship. Of these house churches, the best example is a mid-third century house church discovered in the Syrian town of Dura-Europas, on the Roman frontier with Persia. The town was abandoned by the Romans when the Persians attacked it in 256. As a result, it was not built over by later churches the way other house churches must have been. Only a short distance away, archaeologists found a Jewish synagogue. The house church consisted of an assembly hall, with a raised podium (presumably for the bishop), which had room for about sixty-five to seventy-five people. A smaller room had been altered into a baptistery (a place for Baptism), with a step-up basin covered by a canopy and arches. The baptistery's walls were decorated with frescoes (wall paintings) of subjects such as Adam and Eve, the Good Shepherd, the Samaritan Woman at the Well, David and Goliath, and Peter with Jesus, who was walking on the water.

Publicly identifiable Christian churches began to appear already even during the reign of the emperor Diocletian (284–305). One report indicates that there was a Christian church directly across the street from Diocletian's palace, an indication of the security the Christian community enjoyed prior to the unexpected trauma of the Great Persecution. After the rise of Constantine, church construction mushroomed, with the help of imperial subsidies, in order to accommodate the crowds of new converts and to celebrate the church's new status.

These new buildings were of three types. The most common is called a **basilica** (from the Greek word for "royal") because it was an adaptation of the standard rectangular layout of royal audience halls and public buildings in Roman cities. The Christian version of a basilica was an audience hall for Christ, the heavenly king. It consisted of a long rectangular building, often with two or even four side aisles along the central hall, which was called the nave. In larger churches a shorter cross-section called a transept was often built at the end or partway down the nave. A rounded extension called an apse was usually found at the east end of the nave, in the direction of Jerusalem. The bishop's chair, his cathedra (a

Figure 9–3 Church of Santa Sabina in Rome, early fifth century, showing the basilica plan.

bishop's church is therefore known as a **cathedral**), was on the back wall of the apse, where he sat with his priests in a semicircle around him. Sermons were given from this chair, the symbol of his teaching authority.

The basilica served the weekly liturgy of the Eucharist. The east end of the nave, where the apse was located, was called the sanctuary ("holy place") and was set off from the rest of the church by a screen or a rail, reflecting the distinction between the clergy and the laity. The altar, where the bread and wine of the Eucharist were consecrated, was a removable table placed in the nave. The only other furniture was a raised pulpit for reading the scriptures. There were no pews or kneelers; the congregation stood for the service. The interiors of large churches were richly decorated with hanging curtains, marble, lamps, gold inlay, and mosaics (pictures made of small fragments of colored glass) on the walls of the apse and sanctuary. Scholars have often noted the contrast between the plain exterior of the buildings, usually unadorned brick, and the rich ornamentation of the interior: Believers entered a place where the worship service, or liturgy (literally, "the people's work"), was a participation in the worship of the angels in the heavenly Jerusalem.

A quite different design from the long axis of the basilica was the centered structure of a type of church called a *memoria*, built to honor the tomb of a saint or martyr, or a holy site such as the cave in Bethlehem where Christ was believed to have been born. A *memoria* could be octagonal or cruciform in shape, or even circular, in which case it was called a rotunda. The lines of vision oriented the visitor to the middle of the building, where the shrine or tomb lay. The *memoriae* are important witnesses to the growing Christian devotion to the physical remains of the dead and to the belief in the spiritual power of the saints,

Figure 9–4 Sanctuary of the Church of Santa Sabina in Rome.

both in heaven and on earth. In the case of pilgrimage sites in Palestine, memorial churches testify to the growing desire to experience salvation in connection with the physical location of the saving events of Jesus's life.

A third type of Christian structure was the baptistery, where at Easter new Christians were initiated into the faith. A **baptistery**, like a *memoria*, had a centered design. Instead of a tomb, the focus was on the baptismal font into which the candidate stepped. The association with a tomb was intentional, since Christian Baptism was understood as an identification with Christ's death, burial, and resurrection. Baptisteries could be either freestanding or attached to churches.

The religious life of ordinary Christians was oriented around the sacraments of Baptism and the Eucharist. In the fourth century, Baptism for adults was still common, with many people intentionally deferring their Baptism until adulthood. Infant Baptism did not become the norm, apparently, until the fifth century. Most lay people received the Eucharist each week, unless they were **catechumens** (candidates for Baptism who were

Figure 9–5 Baptistery of the Orthodox in Ravenna, late fourth/fifth centuries.

undergoing instruction in the Christian religion) or **penitents** (people who were denied communion because of serious sin such as murder, adultery, or apostasy), both of whom had to leave the liturgy after the biblical readings and the sermon. Penitents for serious sin usually performed a lengthy public **penance** (a penalty) before they could be readmitted to communion. Postbaptismal forgiveness for serious sin was generally extended just once, after public confession to the bishop and his clergy. Otherwise, fasting, works of charity, and prayers, such as the Our Father (Matt 6:9–13), were recommended as the normal means of forgiveness for less serious sins.

The familiar year-long cycle of religious feasts began to take shape during the fourth century, anchored by Easter and its season of penitential preparation called **Lent**. Following Easter came the season of **Pentecost** (commemorating the day on which the Holy Spirit descended upon the apostles), a time of joy and also of further instruction for the newly baptized. Christ's birth (Christmas) was celebrated in the West on December 25, previously the pagan feast of the Unconquered Sun. The feast days of the martyrs' deaths were also becoming more prominent points in the calendar, and sometimes the occasion of riotous celebration—to the consternation of the bishops, who realized that some of the enthusiasm was a carryover of pagan habits of feasting at the graveside of deceased family members.

Key Terms

Constantine	Nestorius	abbot
Theodosius I	Council of Ephesus	basilica
ecumenical or general council	Council of Chalcedon	cathedral
	monophysites	*memoria*
Constantinople	patriarch	baptistery
dogma	pope	catechumen
Arius	papacy	penitent
Athanasius of Alexandria	asceticism	penance
Council of Nicaea	monasticism	Lent
Council of Constantinople	monk	Pentecost
Cappadocian Fathers	Antony of Egypt	
Apollinaris of Laodicaea	cenobitic monasticism	

Questions for Reading

1. In what ways did Constantine affect the development of the Christian tradition?

2. Part of Constantine's influence on the Christian tradition consisted of fostering a Christian devotion to the Roman Empire. Assess both the positive and the negative aspects of this identification with the state.

3. In rejecting Arius' teachings, the Council of Nicaea ruled that the Son was "one in being" with the Father. What did Arius teach, and why did Christians like Athanasius oppose his teaching?

4. How did the Cappadocians contribute towards the definition of the Trinity as this doctrine was declared at the Council of Constantinople? What were some other distinctive theological contributions that they made?

5. Contrast the different concerns and emphases in understanding the union of divine and human in the incarnation as we find them in the School of Antioch and the School of Alexandria.

6. What was the teaching of the Council of Chalcedon on the union of divine and human in the incarnation (answer using the terms *nature* and *person*), and why did many Eastern Christians refuse to accept the council's definition?

7. During the period of the fourth and fifth centuries, what was the status of the pope, the bishop of Rome, in the universal church? Describe this both from the Roman point of view, as seen in the writings of Pope Leo I, and from the point of view of Eastern bishops.

8. What was the historical circumstance in which monasticism arose? Although there are various parallels to Christian monasticism in the ancient world, what was its basic motive and its primary model?

9. How did the floor plan of the church design called the basilica reflect the distinction between laity and clergy in the church?

Works Consulted/Recommended Reading

Athanasius of Alexandria. *Life of Antony and the Letter to Marcellinus.* Translated by Robert C. Gregg. New York: Paulist, 1980.

Barnes, T. D. *Constantine and Eusebius.* Cambridge, MA: Harvard University, 1981.

Baynes, Norman H. "Eusebius and the Christian Empire." In Baynes, *Byzantine Studies and Other Essays,* 168–172.

———. *Byzantine Studies and Other Essays.* London: Athalone, 1955.

Brown, Peter. *Society and the Holy in Late Antiquity.* London: Faber & Faber, 1982.

Chitty, Derwas. *The Desert a City: An Introduction to the Study of Egyptian and Palestinian Monasticism under the Christian Empire.* Crestwood, NY: St. Vladimir's Seminary, 1966.

Clément, Olivier. *You Are Peter: An Orthodox Theologian's Reflection on the Exercise of Papal Primacy.* New York: New City, 2003.

Drake, H. A. *In Praise of Constantine: A Historical Study and New Translation of Eusebius' Tricennial Orations.* Berkeley, CA: University of California, 1976.

Eusebius of Caesarea. *Life of Constantine.* Translated by Averil Cameron and Stuart G. Hall. Oxford: Clarendon, 1999.

Hanson, R. P. C. *The Search for the Christian Doctrine of God: The Arian Controversy 318–381.* Edinburgh: T & T Clark, 1988.

Hardy, Edward R. *Christology of the Later Fathers.* Philadelphia: Westminster, 1954.

Jensen, Robin Margaret. *Understanding Early Christian Art.* London; New York: Routledge, 2000.

Kelly, J. N. D. *Early Christian Creeds.* 3rd ed. New York: Longman, 1972.

MacMullen, Ramsay. *Christianizing the Roman Empire (A.D. 100–400).* New Haven, CT: Yale University, 1984.

———. *Voting about God in Early Church Councils.* New Haven, CT: Yale University, 2006.

Mathews, Thomas. *The Clash of the Gods: A Reinterpretation of Early Christian Art.* Princeton, NJ: Princeton University, 1993.

McGuckin, John A. *St. Cyril of Alexandria: The Christological Controversy, Its History, Theology, and Texts.* New York: E. J. Brill, 1994.

Meer, F. van der, and Christine Mohrmann. *Atlas of the Early Christian World.* Translated by Mary F. Nelson and H. H. Rowley. London: Nelson, 1958.

Stevenson, J., ed. *Creeds, Councils, and Controversies: Documents Illustrative of the History of the Church 337–461.* Revised edition. London: SPCK, 1989.

Tsafrir, Yoram, ed. *Ancient Churches Revealed.* Washington, DC: Israel Exploration Society and Biblical Archaeological Society, 1993.

Weitzmann, Kurt, ed. *Age of Spirituality: Late Antique and Early Christian Art, Third to Seventh Century.* New York: Metropolitan Museum of Art, 1979.

Wilken, Robert L. *The Spirit of Early Christian Thought: Seeking the Face of God.* New Haven, CT: Yale University, 2003.

Chapter

AUGUSTINE OF HIPPO

TIMELINE

A.D. 311	Beginnings of the Donatist schism.
A.D. 354	Augustine is born in Thagaste in North Africa.
c. A.D. 374	Augustine joins the dualistic religion of the Manichees.
A.D. 384	Augustine arrives in Milan and meets Bishop Ambrose.
A.D. 387	Augustine is baptized by Ambrose.
A.D. 388	Pelagius comes to Rome to teach.
A.D. 391	Augustine is ordained a presbyter.
A.D. 396	Augustine becomes bishop of Hippo in North Africa.
A.D. 397–401?	Augustine writes the *Confessions*.
c. A.D. 410	Caelestius, one of Pelagius' disciples, begins to teach Pelagian doctrines in North Africa.
A.D. 410	Sack of Rome by the Visigoths; two years later Augustine begins to write *On the City of God* in response to the disaster.
A.D. 411	State-mandated conference in Carthage tries for definitive resolution of Donatist schism.
A.D. 418	The teachings of Pelagius are condemned by the bishop of Rome, and Pelagius and Caelestius are banished by the emperor.
A.D. 430	Augustine's death.

Among Western Christian thinkers in the early church, Augustine of Hippo was surely the greatest and the most influential. (Origen of Alexandria has that honor among Eastern Christian thinkers.) The extent of his work is staggering. Augustine wrote hundreds of treatises and sermons, ranging from philosophical discussions of the nature of good and evil to moral essays on marriage and celibacy, commentaries on the books of the Old and New Testaments, speculative theological treatises on the Trinity, and much more. Western Christian notions of original sin and grace received their distinctive character from Augustine's teaching. Catholic understandings of the sacraments and the nature of the church were also definitively shaped by his work. Augustine's thinking even affected Christian views on the relation between the church and the wider political and social world.

One of the remarkable things about Augustine in contrast to most ancient people is that we do actually know a lot about his life. Not only has he been blessed with gifted biographers (ancient and modern), but Augustine himself, in his *Confessions*, also narrated in some detail the course of his first thirty-three years. Although the *Confessions* is carefully constructed to convey Augustine's later theological understanding and interpretation of his life, nonetheless the basic accuracy of the events that he describes is not disputed.

HISTORICAL SITUATION

Augustine was born in the year 354 in the small backwater town of Thagaste in the Roman province of North Africa (modern day Algeria). Barely forty years had passed since the first Roman emperor had embraced the Christian faith, and it would take some time before Christianity became the official religion of the Roman Empire. The first fifty years of Augustine's life saw a dramatic change in the character of the church and society, which in many ways mirrored his own life and concerns.

The conversion of Constantine marked the end of nearly 300 years of intermittent persecution by the Roman authorities: The age of the martyrs had come to an end. The Christian church could now look forward to an unparalleled period of growth and development. Large numbers flocked to the Christian communities, encouraged by the imperial favor now bestowed on the Christian religion. Needless to say, these converts did not always reflect high standards of morality, and Christian preachers in the late fourth century A.D. often expressed their frustration at those who did not cease to be pagan when they entered the church doors. Some Christian teachers even looked back with nostalgia to the age of persecutions, when (so they claimed) the threat of death had produced more authentic Christians.

The question of how to be an authentic Christian troubled many Christians in the late fourth century, and it hovers persistently over Augustine's *Confessions*. The monastic movement, whose origins were discussed in the previous chapter, had posed the question in the starkest possible way: Is it necessary to abandon the city, to leave all that bound one to "the world" (sex, marriage, career, family) in order to follow Christ faithfully? The words of Jesus from Matthew's gospel were echoed again and again in the stories of the lives and deeds of the holy men and women who had given up the glamour and risks of secular society for monastic seclusion: "If you wish to be perfect, go, sell your possessions, and give the money to the poor . . . then come, follow me" (Matt 19:21, cited in Athanasius, *Life of Antony* 2).

The ascetic rejection of sex, marriage, property, and career became associated in the minds of many Christians with the path of perfection. The story of Augustine's own life, as he narrated it in the first nine books of his *Confessions*, presupposes this understanding of Christian holiness. Augustine's decision to accept the Christian faith and to be baptized at the age of thirty-three was intimately connected with his decision to renounce marriage and a successful career. Judging from his account in the *Confessions*, being a married Christian seemed like a pale approximation of authentic Christianity.

If Constantine's conversion and widespread optimism about the newly Christian Roman Empire characterized Christian hopes in the first half of Augustine's life, the opening decades of the fifth century brought profound disillusionment. In the year 410, the city of Rome was attacked and sacked by the Gothic chief Alaric (an Arian Christian). Twenty years later, as Augustine lay dying at Hippo, another northern people, the Vandals, were consolidating their control over Roman North Africa. The sack of Rome provoked Augustine to write *On the City of God*, his greatest book and the culmination of early Christian apologetics against paganism. Pagan critics blamed Christianity for Rome's decline. They said that when the empire ceased to worship the gods, the gods in turn had ceased to protect the empire. They also said that a perfectionist religion like Christianity was too other-worldly to be the religion of a great empire.

Augustine responded by saying that Rome had largely been built on the lust for power (*libido dominandi*) and that the gods had never kept Rome safe from disaster. God was not supposed to be worshiped merely for the sake of this-worldly advantage—God would use all empires and kingdoms, Christian and pagan alike, for his own purposes, which were often hidden from us. On this topic, Augustine was fond of quoting the words of Jesus from Matthew's gospel: "[Your Father in heaven] makes his sun rise on the evil and the good, and sends rain on the righteous and on the unrighteous" (Matt 5:45). The church, composed of saints and sinners alike, was the City of God on pilgrimage to the heavenly City of God. In the meantime Christians were obliged to contribute to the peace of the earthly city, even though that earthly city could never be confused with the kingdom of God.

Early Life and Conversion of Augustine

Augustine came from a family of modest means, not impoverished, but not excessively wealthy. His father does not seem to have had any serious religious affiliation until he became a Christian late in life. Augustine's mother, **Monica**, on the other hand, was a devout Christian who prayed eagerly for her son to embrace the faith and who, as time went on, exerted a great influence upon him. At a young age Augustine was enrolled as a catechumen (literally "a person undergoing instruction") in the church. But for someone of Augustine's depth and complexity, there was to be no easy entrance into the Christian religion.

Part of the difficulty stemmed from Augustine's own acute and restless intellect. He excelled in school, especially in the study of Latin rhetoric, or public speaking. After studying in his hometown of Thagaste, in nearby Madaurus, and later in the capital Carthage, Augustine became a teacher of Latin rhetoric. In an effort to escape horrendous teaching conditions and rowdy students, Augustine traveled from Carthage to Rome to Milan, where he received a distinguished post as professor of rhetoric.

But Augustine's love of ancient Latin literature drew him further and further from the Christianity of his mother. At the age of nineteen, Augustine read a philosophical work of Cicero, called the *Hortensius*, which included a review and critique of the various schools of

Figure 10–1 Benozzo Gozzoli. *Death of St. Monica*. 1464/65. Fresco, 220 × 230 cm. Apsidal Chapel of Sant' Agostino, San Gimignano, Italy.

ancient philosophy. The treatise filled him with a desire to "love and see and pursue and hold fast and strongly embrace wisdom itself, wherever found" (*Confessions* III.iv.8). When he dipped into the scriptures to see how they compared with the wisdom of Cicero, Augustine found them "unworthy in comparison," that is, inferior in literary style. More than ten years were to pass before Augustine could read the Bible again and take it seriously.

The other significant aspect of Augustine's life at this time was his discovery of the pleasures of sex. As he described it in the *Confessions*, the "bubbling impulses of puberty befogged and obscured my heart so that it could not see the difference between love's serenity and lust's darkness" (II.ii.2). After what may have been an initial period of promiscuity, Augustine settled down into a monogamous relationship, known to the Romans as "concubinage" (literally, "sleeping together"). Such liaisons were common, especially between upwardly mobile young men and women of servile or lower-class backgrounds. Augustine seems to always have regarded the relationship as a temporary one, a sexual convenience until it was time to contract a marriage with a woman of wealth and proper standing. Nonetheless, he loved the woman deeply and with her had a son, whom they named **Adeodatus**, literally, "gift of God." One of the most poignant passages in the *Confessions* is Augustine's description of the pain he felt when he and his partner finally separated after thirteen years together: "My heart, which was deeply attached, was cut and wounded and left a trail of blood. She had returned to Africa vowing that she would never go with another man" (VI.xv.25). Nowhere, however, in all his voluminous works, does Augustine ever tell us her name.

Around this time (c. 374), when Augustine was about twenty years old, he became involved with a new religion called **Manicheism**. It derives its name from its founder Mani, a prophet and visionary who lived in the third century A.D. in Mesopotamia. Mani was born into a baptizing religious sect that lived on the margins of Judaism and Christianity. As a result of his reading and visionary experiences, he believed he was inspired to found a new universal religion that would supersede all previously existing religions: Christianity, Judaism, Buddhism, and Zoroastrianism (the official religion of the Persian Empire, in which Mani was born). At the heart of Mani's teaching was the notion that from the beginning of time there have existed two fundamental realities: a principle or power of good (the kingdom of Light) and a power of evil (the kingdom of Darkness). The kingdom of Light basically consisted of spirit, and the kingdom of Darkness consisted of matter and the dark elements, such as smoke. These two powers, according to the Manichees, were coeternal and coequal.

Because of its inherent restlessness and desire for conquest, the kingdom of Darkness invaded the kingdom of Light and succeeded in swallowing up a large chunk of it. By generating an elaborate series of spiritual beings, the kingdom of Light defended itself and managed to produce a created world, though the material part of that world was considered to be evil. The aim of this creation was to liberate the elements of spiritual light that are still trapped in evil matter. The waxing and waning of the moon for the Manichees signaled special times when light was being returned to its source. One special place for the liberation of spirit from matter was the bodies of the Manichean leaders, the **Elect**. When these special persons, who were celibate and vegetarian, ate selected fruits and vegetables, their digestive organs were thought to facilitate the escape of the light from darkness. To engage in sex or to partake of meat, the Manichees believed, was to perpetuate the enslavement of spirit in matter. Although both of these activities were allowed to those on the fringes of the sect (the **Hearers**), they were forbidden to the Elect.

Augustine remained a Hearer in the Manichean sect for nine years. He was attracted by their clear answer to a question that would long exercise his mind: Where does evil come from? Since the Manichees believed (like some of the second-century gnostics) that the God of the Old Testament was a vicious demon, their criticisms of the Hebrew scriptures appealed to Augustine's sense that the Bible was a document unworthy of a philosopher. For example, the Manichees mocked the polygamy (multiple wives) of the patriarchs in Genesis as sexual degeneracy.

Most of all, Augustine was persuaded by the Manichees' dualistic conception of the human person. The Manichees could explain why it was that Augustine felt himself torn between his intellectual desire for truth and wisdom, on the one hand, and his craving for sexual delight and worldly success, on the other hand. Their answer was that Augustine's spirit belonged to the kingdom of Light, but his body belonged to the kingdom of Darkness. In other words, Manichean dualism helped explain Augustine to himself and, significantly, absolved him of responsibility for the actions of his "wicked" half. When Augustine finally does come to reject the views of the Manichees, an important aspect of his conversion away from Manicheism and toward orthodox Christianity came through a recognition that the human person is a unity and that this unity implies moral accountability.

During most of his twenties Augustine remained attached to the Manichees. However, as he tells the story in the *Confessions*, he was growing increasingly skeptical and critical of Manichean theology. In these years Augustine became interested in astrology and discovered the disconcerting fact that astrologers generally had more reliable scientific data (for example, for predicting eclipses of the sun and moon) than did the Manichees. This rational failure of the Manichees' science was troubling (see *Confessions* V.iii.6–v.9), and Augustine soon realized that even the most authoritative Manichean teachers were unable to answer his questions. Even more dissatisfying to someone as philosophically minded as Augustine was the Manichees' view of God (the kingdom of Light) as fundamentally weak and vulnerable to invasion by evil. Augustine came to see that even though the Manichees believed in a so-called "spiritual" world (light, goodness) in conflict with a "material" world (darkness, evil), their idea of God was really modeled on a kind of material substance. Such a God, Augustine came to hold, was not worth believing in (see *Confessions*, Book VII).

By the time that Augustine arrived in Milan, in the autumn of 384, he had virtually abandoned the Manichees but had not yet found a persuasive alternative. Augustine now encountered certain ideas and individuals who were to lead him back to the Christianity of his youth. He began to attend the sermons of **Ambrose of Milan**, a learned Christian bishop and former provincial governor. Ambrose was just the sort of eloquent, educated Christian that the young Augustine could admire. Furthermore, Ambrose was skilled in the allegorical method of biblical interpretation, which he had learned from Greek Christian writers, such as Origen of Alexandria. Ambrose taught Augustine that the embarrassing aspects of the Old Testament, which the Manichees had held up to ridicule, could be interpreted nonliterally, that is, as symbols of moral or spiritual truths.

Even more significant, at the urging of Simplicianus, a priest of Milan who had taken an interest in the young professor, Augustine began to read certain "books of the Platonists," namely the writings of the third-century A.D. philosopher Plotinus, as recorded by his disciple Porphyry. In these writings Augustine found a version of Plato's philosophy, now called Neoplatonism, which gave him a new way to think about God, the world, and evil that enabled him finally to break with the harsh dualism of the Manichees. Neoplatonism also was to serve as a sort of intellectual bridge that would lead Augustine ultimately to Christianity.

In the teaching of Plotinus, God was a reality that surpassed all human categories of knowing or describing. In fact, rather than use the name *God,* Plotinus preferred to speak of the supreme Being simply as "the One," to characterize its primary quality of pure simplicity or oneness. While the One could not be comprehended or grasped in its essence or entirety by the human mind (whose knowledge is always partial and fragmentary), nonetheless the Neoplatonists taught that this One produced a succession of other realities or substances from itself: Intellect, Soul, and, finally, Matter. Each level of being proceeds from the higher one and depends on the higher level for its life and order, just as in a human being one might say that the mind or soul serves to organize the physical functions of the body. Even Matter, Plotinus taught, was capable of being formed and directed towards the good, although left on its own it tended to disorder, corruption, and nonbeing. Only in this limited and non-moral sense could we speak of Matter as "evil."

Augustine found Neoplatonism a liberating alternative to the views of the Manichees. Here was a vision of God as truly supreme, the source of all being, goodness, and beauty; God was Being itself, the "I am who I am" of Exodus 3:14. If God and all that came from God was truly good, Augustine reasoned, then evil itself cannot be a substance in the sense that the Manichees taught. Evil (in the non-moral sense) is not a "thing," but merely the tendency in the lowest level of creation toward disorder, corruption, and nonbeing, and this is the very opposite of the order, life, and being that come from God. But Plotinus also taught that there is evil in the moral sense, when rational creatures freely choose to turn toward the lower goods rather than toward the One who is their source. As Augustine describes it in the *Confessions:* "I inquired what wickedness is; and I did not find a substance but a perversity of will twisted away from the highest substance, you O God, towards inferior things, rejecting its own inner life and swelling with external matter" (VII.xvi.22).

Neoplatonism, Augustine tells us, seemed to be profoundly compatible with what he knew of Christianity, especially as it was being preached by Bishop Ambrose. Its views of God, creation, and evil could easily be assimilated; the Christian elements that were missing from Neoplatonism (Augustine tells us in hindsight) were the doctrine of divine incarnation and the notion of divine grace (*Confessions* VII.ix, xviii–xxi). The *Confessions* says little about what led Augustine at this time to move toward an intellectual acceptance of Christian teachings, but we are well informed about the moral dimensions of his struggle to embrace Christianity fully. In the eighth book of the *Confessions,* Augustine describes in vivid detail the emotional turmoil he experienced as he tried to bring himself to the point of making a decision to be baptized.

The basic problem was that Augustine saw his conversion to Christianity as entailing a conversion to the monastic or ascetic way of life; to be a serious Christian meant that Augustine would have to abandon his career and his desire for sex, marriage, and family. After more than fifteen years of sexual activity, Augustine found himself subject to a habit that he no longer had the power to break: "I . . . was bound not by an iron imposed by anyone else but by the iron of my own choice. . . . The consequence of a distorted will is passion. By servitude to passion, habit is formed, and habit to which there is no resistance becomes necessity" (*Confessions* VIII.v.10). Augustine felt himself torn between two "wills," between two competing desires, neither of which was strong enough to overcome the other, and he found the internal division devastating.

In the famous garden scene in book eight of the *Confessions*, Augustine describes the moment when he finally decided to entrust himself into the hands of God. Looking back on his decision ten years later as he wrote the *Confessions*, Augustine saw the key to his conversion as his allowing God to produce in him the work of "continence" (that is, self-control in the face of tempting desires, which in this case meant abstention from sex), which he was unable to will on his own. As the figure of Lady Continence says in the paragraph preceding the garden scene: "Why are you relying on yourself, only to find yourself unreliable? Cast yourself upon him, do not be afraid. He will not withdraw himself so that you fall. Make the leap without anxiety; he will catch you and heal you" (VIII.xi.27). Only after experiencing himself as powerless and after reading the passage from Paul (Rom 13:14: " . . . put on the Lord Jesus Christ and make no provision for the flesh in its lusts") did Augustine find the division within himself healed: " . . . it was as if a light of relief from all anxiety flooded into my heart. All the shadows of doubt were dispelled" (VIII.xii.29).

Augustine's experience of his own conversion and his subsequent reflection on it were to prove foundational for the development of his theological vision. Central to this vision was Augustine's notion that human beings are impelled to their actions by their own deepest desires, by their "love." "A body by its weight tends to move towards its proper place . . . My weight is my love. Wherever I am carried, my love is carrying me." After the first sin of Adam and Eve, Augustine believed, all human beings are born with an inherent tendency to a pernicious form of self-love, a tendency to love the lower goods of the world rather than the God who is their source. Only the grace of God, the power of the Holy Spirit, can heal the damaged human will and transform it into a will that loves God and self properly: "By your gift we are set on fire and carried upwards: we grow red hot and ascend . . . Lit by your fire, your good fire, we grow red-hot and ascend, as we move upwards 'to the peace of Jerusalem'" (*Confessions* XIII.ix.10).

AUGUSTINE THE BISHOP

In the spring of 387 Augustine was baptized by Bishop Ambrose at the Easter vigil. He returned to Africa the following year, shortly after the death of his mother in Italy. Augustine had originally hoped to live quietly in a monastic community with some devoted friends, but a man of his talents was much needed in the North African church. By the year 391, he had been ordained presbyter (literally "elder" or priest) of the seaport town of Hippo Regius, and by 396 he had become bishop. Though he was now tossed into an active life, he remained supportive of the monastic movement and even formulated guidelines for the communal living of monks and nuns (*The Rule of St. Augustine*), which became very influential in the Middle Ages.

From this point onward, during the final three decades of his life, Augustine was to be preoccupied with preaching, pastoral concerns and the writing of numerous theological and polemical treatises against the pagans, the Manichees, and other Christian heretics. Among the controversies that absorbed his attention, the debates with the Donatists and the Pelagians were most bitter and the most consequential for later Christian theology.

The Donatist Schism

The North Africa to which Augustine returned in 388 was deeply divided in a schism that had already lasted for nearly a century. During the last persecution (c. 303) the emperor Diocletian had issued an edict directing Christian clergy to hand over all copies of the scriptures to be burned. Some bishops had cooperated with the authorities, and others had pretended to do so by handing over copies of heretical writings instead. In North Africa, where the spirit of the martyrs had long been strong, opposition to any collaboration with the persecutors was especially fierce. Those who handed over the scriptures were dubbed *traditores* ("traitors") and were judged guilty of apostasy (renunciation of one's religious faith); many Christians refused to acknowledge that these bishops or priests had any authority in the church.

In 311, when Caecilian, a new bishop of Carthage, was elected, great opposition arose. One of the bishops who had consecrated Caecilian, it was claimed, had been a *traditor*. Furthermore, Caecilian himself had had a dubious record during the recent persecution. A large number of bishops in North Africa refused to recognize the legitimacy of Caecilian and soon a rival bishop of Carthage was elected in his place. The opponents of Caecilian, soon to be called **Donatists** (from *Donatus,* the name of one of the early rival bishops of Carthage), appealed to the emperor Constantine. After consulting with the bishop of Rome and a Western council, the emperor decided against the Donatists. From this point onward, the Donatists regarded all non-Donatist Christians as illegitimate; in their view, Donatism represented the true Christian church, and outside of that church there was no salvation.

Throughout the fourth century, Donatism thrived in North Africa, especially in the countryside where hostility to Roman rule had always run high. In some places roving gangs armed with clubs—called "Circumcellions," a name based on a Latin phrase that reflected their association with rural shrines and altars—tried to enforce Donatism with violence. Some scholars have seen the movement as grounded in the social protest of the poor and disenfranchised against the power of wealthy landowners. But there was a serious theological side to Donatism as well. The Donatists saw themselves as the true continuation of the church of the martyrs. They emphasized that the church must be pure and holy and set apart from the world. As long as a bishop remained allied with the (false) church of Caecilian and his successors, the Donatists argued, he remained tainted by sin and unable to bestow the grace of God in any way. Donatists believed, therefore, that sacraments administered in the non-Donatist churches (for example, Baptism) were invalid because those churches did not possess the power of the Holy Spirit.

In the 390s when Augustine began his priesthood and episcopacy, Donatist Christians probably outnumbered Catholics in North Africa. Augustine immediately began to engage the Donatists in debate and to write polemical treatises against the sect. He challenged them on a variety of grounds. First he questioned whether their historical facts were correct. He cited the evidence of investigations showing not only that Caecilian and his consecrators had not been *traditores*, but also that certain Donatist bishops had been. But Augustine's most significant arguments were theological ones. Whatever holiness the Donatists might have possessed, he argued, was now destroyed by their schism. Unity is a primary characteristic of the church, and to violate that unity, Augustine taught, is to violate the essentials of Christian charity.

Furthermore, Augustine maintained, universality or catholicity was another distinguishing feature of the church. Both the promise made to Abraham (Gen 12:3), which St. Paul had recalled (Gal 3:8), and Jesus' own command to his disciples after the resurrection (Acts 1:8), were prophecies of the worldwide spread of Christianity. The Donatist claim to represent the faithful remnant, the only pure and holy church, was as arrogant as it was unfounded. The true church, Augustine argues, is the "catholic" church, that is, the church of Christians united throughout the world. The holiness of the church is the holiness of Christ, not the holiness of human beings. In this life good and bad persons are mixed together within the one body of the church. In fact, Augustine notes, in this life all people are stained by sin and that is why the church itself in all its members prays the words of the Lord's Prayer, "Forgive us our trespasses . . ."

In response to the Donatist notion that the sacraments administered by a sinful priest or bishop (that is, a *traditor*) were invalid, Augustine answered that Jesus Christ is the source of any grace conveyed in sacramental actions. Therefore, even when a minister is guilty of the gravest sins, the effectiveness of the sacraments themselves remains unchanged. A guilty priest brings greater guilt upon himself by his actions, Augustine argued, but the sacraments themselves remain effective. Augustine could even recognize the validity of the Baptisms conveyed by Donatist clergy, since they had been carried out in the proper form. Augustine's notion of the character of the sacraments, as well as his idea of the universality or catholicity of the church, were to become standard aspects of Catholic teaching from this point onward.

The Pelagian Controversy

It is ironic that Augustine's last and greatest opponents were to come from the very group that had so attracted him to orthodox Christianity: the monks and ascetics of Rome. Augustine's initial conversion to Christianity was very much a conversion to the life of ascetic renunciation and monastic seclusion. But in the decade or so after his conversion, leading up to his writing of the *Confessions* (c. 397), Augustine's thought had begun to turn in a fundamentally different direction than that of most of the leaders of the ascetic movement. By the time he wrote the *Confessions*, Augustine had developed two distinctive notions that deeply troubled many of his contemporaries. One is his view that sin, in particular the **original sin** of Adam and Eve, has thoroughly damaged human nature. Even the newborn baby is not innocent of the tendency toward greed and envy, which is the sign of a distorted will in the human person (*Confessions* I.vii.11). The other distinctively Augustinian idea is that God's grace, the gift of charity bestowed by the Holy Spirit, is absolutely necessary to change the orientation of the human will and to direct the human heart toward God.

Before the time of Augustine there had not been any extensive discussion among Christians about the effect of sin on the human will or the nature of the grace that saves humanity. If anything, in response to the fatalism and pessimism of gnostics and Manichees, most Christians, especially among the Greek fathers of the church, taught that human nature remained fundamentally sound. Original sin, however real and pernicious it may have been, did not deprive human beings of the two great gifts that represented the divine image in humans: freedom and reason. Especially in the monastic movement of the fourth century, we find Christian thinkers emphasizing that it is entirely within the power of human beings to free themselves from evil habits and to conform themselves to the precepts of Christ.

Pelagius was a monk from Britain who came to Rome probably about the same time as Augustine's last sojourn there (388). For more than twenty years, Pelagius taught and gave spiritual advice to Christians at Rome who were interested in pursuing the ascetic way of life. Like Augustine, Pelagius was a bitter opponent of the Manichees, and he attempted to undermine their influence among Christians. However, he was also a Christian reformer who sought to convince the wealthy and worldly Christians of Rome that they could be authentic Christians by turning away from sinful lives and living lives of simplicity and monastic rigor. In the process of developing this spiritual teaching, Pelagius also expressed views about sin, grace, and human nature that led to a serious conflict with Augustine.

The core of Pelagius' teaching, which he may have derived from Eastern Christian theologians, was that God has given human beings the power to know right from wrong (reason) and the ability to choose to do either (free will). To deny either of these, Pelagius reasoned, was to question the goodness of God's creation and to make nonsense of the Christian belief concerning the justice of rewards and punishments in the afterlife. God would be unjust to punish us for sins that we could not avoid. True, there is sin in the world, especially in the social customs of the non-Christian world, and sin can sometimes create habits that become almost second nature. Nevertheless, Pelagius argued, with sufficient effort and help from the grace of God (that is, the Jewish law, the teachings of Christ, and the forgiveness of sins), human beings are capable of overcoming the power of sin and living holy lives. The proof of the basic integrity of human nature, according to Pelagius, could be seen in the many examples of those who lived virtuously even before the coming of Christ.

Pelagius' teaching appears to have caused no complaints during the decades when he taught in Rome. However, in the wake of Alaric's sack of Rome in 410, Pelagius and some followers left the city and fled to North Africa and eventually to Jerusalem. While visiting Carthage, one of Pelagius' less-diplomatic disciples, Caelestius, began to teach Pelagian doctrines in an extreme form that shocked the North African bishops, Augustine among them. Caelestius denied that the sin of Adam and Eve caused harm to anyone but themselves. Newborn infants were born in exactly the same state in which Adam and Eve were originally created, that is, in innocence. The condemnation of Caelestius by a synod of African bishops in 411 marks the beginning of the Pelagian controversy. For the next twenty years, Augustine actively attacked traces of Pelagian views wherever he found them. Ultimately, the theology of Augustine and the North African bishops was to triumph, at least in the West. In the year 418 the teachings of Pelagius were condemned by the bishop of Rome, and Pelagius and Caelestius were banished by the emperor.

At stake in the Pelagian controversy, as Augustine saw it, was the very notion of Christian salvation. If, as Pelagius claimed, human nature had been left fundamentally undamaged by original sin, then there was no need for Christ's saving death or the action of God's grace. The test case was the Baptism of newborn children: If it is appropriate to baptize infants (both Pelagius and Augustine agreed on this point), then the infants must have inherited from their parents some sin that needed to be washed away in Baptism. Augustine found further justification for his understanding of inherited guilt in Paul's letter to the Romans 5:12–21; Augustine's text of Rom 5:12, in the Old Latin translation, read, "*in whom* [i.e. Adam] all have sinned," whereas the Greek original merely said, "*inasmuch as* all have sinned"—the Old Latin version more explicitly implicated all humans in responsibility for Adam's sin. Augustine's view of the damage done by original sin also led him to say that God's grace is necessary throughout human life in order to create in human beings the love that oriented them toward God. Whereas Pelagius had insisted on human freedom in order to urge people to take responsibility for their actions, Augustine saw this emphasis on human self-sufficiency as leading to pride. Human beings can take no credit for any good action, according to Augustine, since even the very will to do good has been created in them by the grace of God.

In the long run, Western Christian tradition was to side with the teaching of Augustine. Pelagianism was ultimately seen as too naive and optimistic a view of human nature after the Fall. On the other hand, there were also elements in Augustine's theology that the church did not embrace in their totality. One of these is the idea that God has decided beforehand that some people would be saved and others damned (**predestination**). In the course of the Pelagian controversy, Augustine eventually argued that, since salvation depends entirely on the will of God, God's grace must be completely effective and even irresistible; in other words, by not giving some people the grace to be saved, God was effectively choosing to condemn them.

Figure 10–2 Benozzo Gozzoli. *St. Augustine Reading the Epistle of St. Paul.* 1464/65. Fresco, 220 × 230. Apsidal Chapel of Sant' Agostino, San Gimignano, Italy.

Throughout the fifth century, especially in the monasteries of southern Gaul (modern-day France), some Christian monks and bishops questioned whether Augustine had gone too far in denying any role to the human will. While agreeing with Augustine on original sin and the absolute necessity of grace, these thinkers—who have come to be called, inaccurately, "semi-Pelagians"—argued that there must be cooperation between God and the person being saved, perhaps even a prior good disposition. If no human freedom was involved, they reasoned, there would be no point in preaching the gospel or offering correction to one's fellow monks. In a definition of faith issued at the Synod of Orange (529), the bishops of Gaul repeated the Augustinian teaching that God "first inspires in us both faith and love of himself, so that we will faithfully seek the sacrament of Baptism and then with his help be able to fulfill the things which please him after Baptism." Nonetheless, the bishops also emphasized that once grace has been received, the individual Christian must labor faithfully and cooperate with God's grace. There is no divine predestination to evil.

The questions raised in the Pelagian controversy were to be opened once again in the sixteenth century. When the Protestant reformers challenged the Roman Catholic practice of linking salvation with the performance of certain good works, they appealed to the authority of Augustine who had stressed the utter priority of God's grace before any human action. The Catholics responded by noting Augustine's teaching that God's grace creates in human beings a will transformed by love, which then desires to do good works. Both sides could appeal with some legitimacy to certain aspects of Augustine's teaching. Despite the divergences that developed between Protestant and Roman Catholic forms of Christianity, both sides still share Augustine's conviction that all human beings have lost their innocence in the sin of Adam and Eve and that the grace of the Holy Spirit must be given to move people toward God.

Key Terms

Augustine	Elect	original sin
Monica	Hearers	Pelagius
Adeodatus	Ambrose of Milan	predestination
Manicheism	Donatists	

Questions for Reading

1. How did the rise of the monastic movement affect Augustine's thinking about marriage in his *Confessions*?

2. What were the conditions that led Augustine to compose *On the City of God*?

3. What were some of the main ideas of the Manichees? What made these ideas attractive to the young Augustine?

4. What were the main ideas of the Neoplatonists? How did Neoplatonism help to free Augustine from the Manichees?

5. What was the problem of the "two wills" (or the "divided will") that Augustine experienced prior to becoming Christian? How did the advice of Lady Continence help to resolve this problem?

6. How did the Donatist schism begin? What were the Donatists' main theological ideas?

7. What were Augustine's primary theological arguments against the Donatists?

8. What were the main ideas of the monk Pelagius? What were Augustine's primary theological arguments against Pelagianism?

9. How did Augustine's ideas about sin and grace lead to the notion of predestination? How did the Synod of Orange respond to this view of Augustine?

Works Consulted/Recommended Reading

Bonner, Gerald. *Freedom and Necessity: St. Augustine's Teaching on Divine Power and Human Freedom.* Washington, DC: The Catholic University of America, 2007.

_____. *St Augustine of Hippo. Life and Controversies.* 3rd ed. Norwich: Canterbury, 2002.

Brown, Peter. *Augustine of Hippo: A Biography. A New Edition with an Epilogue.* Berkeley: University of California, 2000.

Chadwick, H. *Augustine.* Oxford: Oxford University, 1986.

Cooper, Stephen A. *Augustine for Armchair Theologians*. Louisville, KY: Westminster John Knox, 2002.

Dodaro, Robert. *Christ and the Just Society in the Thought of Augustine*. Cambridge, New York: Cambridge University, 2004.

Dodaro, Robert and George Lawless, eds. *Augustine and His Critics: Essays in Honour of Gerald Bonner*. London and New York: Routledge, 2000.

Harrison, Carol. *Augustine: Christian Truth and Fractured Humanity*. Oxford: Oxford University, 2000.

_____. *Rethinking Augustine's Early Theology: An Argument for Continuity*. Oxford: Oxford University, 2006.

Lancel, Serge. *St. Augustine*. London: SCM, 2002.

Markus, R. A. *Conversion and Disenchantment in Augustine's Spiritual Career*. Villanova, PA: Villanova University, 1989.

Meilaender, Gilbert. *The Way that Leads There: Augustinian Reflections on the Christian Life*. Grand Rapids, MI: Eerdmans, 2006.

O'Donnell, James J. *Augustine. Confessions*. 3 vols. Oxford: Clarendon, 1992.

_____. *Augustine: A New Biography*. New York: Ecco/HarperCollins, 2005.

Paffenroth, Kim, and Robert P. Kennedy. *A Reader's Companion to Augustine's Confessions*. Louisville: Westminster/John Knox, 2003.

Rombs, Ronnie. *Saint Augustine and the Fall of the Soul: Beyond O'Connell and His Critics*. Washington, DC: The Catholic University of America, 2006.

TeSelle, Eugene. *Augustine the Theologian*. New York: Herder, 1970.

_____. *Augustine*. Abingdon Pillars of Theology. Nashville, TN: Abingdon, 2006.

Wetzel, James. *Augustine and the Limits of Virtue*. Cambridge, UK: Cambridge University, 1992.

Chapter

11

EASTERN CHRISTIANITY

TIMELINE

A.D. 431	The Assyrian Church of the East rejects the decision of the Council of Ephesus to condemn Nestorianism and separates from the rest of the church.
A.D. 451	In the century after the Council of Chalcedon, dissent against the council leads to the creation of non-Chalcedonian Eastern Christian churches in Armenia, Syria, Egypt, Ethiopia, Eritrea, and India.
A.D. 527–565	Reign of Justinian, greatest Byzantine (Eastern Roman) emperor. Partial but temporary recovery of lost Western territory.
A.D. 538	Justinian rebuilds Hagia Sophia ("Church of Holy Wisdom").
A.D. 635	Chinese emperor authorizes Chinese translation of Bible, brought to China by Nestorian missionaries.
A.D. 787	Second Council of Nicaea decides in favor of the veneration of icons.
A.D. 867	Photius, patriarch of Constantinople, issues a letter condemning the Roman Church's use of the *filioque* clause in the Nicene Creed.
A.D. 1054	Traditional date for the definitive separation of Eastern and Western Christianity. Pope Leo IX and Michael Cerularius, patriarch of Constantinople, excommunicate each other.
A.D. 1204	Knights of the Fourth Crusade launch an attack against Constantinople.
A.D. 1296–1359	Life span of Gregory Palamas. He defends the hesychasts in his work known as *The Triads*.
A.D. 1439	Council of Florence attempts to heal the breach between Eastern and Western Christianity but is unsuccessful.
A.D. 1453	Ottoman Turks capture Constantinople; end of Byzantine Empire.

Many North Americans naively assume that the major forms in which Christianity has flourished are Catholic and Protestant, since these are the forms that have dominated the Western world, especially in Europe and the Americas. This chapter will provide a brief overview of another major branch of worldwide Christianity, namely Eastern Christianity. The sheer number and variety of Eastern Christian churches can be daunting to a beginning student. After a brief introduction on how Christianity came to be divided into East and West, we will consider four categories of Eastern Christian churches, determined by their acceptance or rejection of various ecumenical councils' teachings. We will first discuss the Eastern Orthodox churches, which accept the teachings of seven ecumenical councils. We will then sketch two other forms of Eastern Christianity: the non-Chalcedonian churches and the Assyrian Church of the East. We will conclude with a glance at the Eastern Catholic churches.

THE BYZANTINE CONTEXT

The development of Eastern churches, separate from their Western counterparts, was in part a consequence of the division of the Roman Empire into Eastern and Western halves. As noted in the previous chapter, the division was a gradual process. In the latter part of the third century, the emperor Diocletian (reigned 284–305) attempted to strengthen his empire, which had grown too large for a single person to govern, by dividing it between himself and a co-emperor, each with separate royal bureaucracies. When Diocletian went to live in the East, the balance of power and the empire's resources also shifted to the eastern part of the empire. Later, the emperor Constantine attempted to bring the empire back together again. In order to better position himself to lead the united Roman Empire, Constantine moved its capital from Rome in the western part of the empire to **Constantinople** (formerly known as Byzantium) in the East. After his death in 337, however, his three sons redivided the empire.

In the fifth century, foreign peoples, mostly Germanic tribes pushed west by invading Huns from central Asia, began settling in large numbers in the western half of the empire. A weakened imperial government gradually lost control, and in 476 the Roman Empire in the West came to an end. The emperor **Justinian** (reigned 527–565) later attempted to restore Roman rule in the West. His military expeditions into Italy and North Africa to reclaim Roman territory from the Germanic newcomers were generally successful, though the fighting left these lands economically destitute. Most of Italy was lost again to the Lombards immediately after his death, and North Africa succumbed to Islamic conquerors a century later.

From the reign of Justinian onward, historians are accustomed to call what was left of the Roman Empire the Byzantine Empire, from *Byzantium,* the former name for the city of Constantinople. Despite the name change, the Byzantine Empire is simply the direct continuation of the old Roman Empire. Though the language was Greek (Latin survived for a while as the language of the law), the empire considered itself authentically Roman, and the patriarchate of Constantinople always styled itself as the New Rome. The Byzantine Empire survived as a Christian bulwark in the Balkans, Asia Minor, and the eastern Mediterranean until its conquest in 1453 by the Ottoman Turks, who were Muslim.

Compared to the Byzantine Empire of the East, the Roman Empire of the West had a very different history in the early medieval period (see Chapter 13). Whereas the Eastern empire survived and the civilization of the ancient world continued without interruption into the fifteenth century, the Roman Empire of the West suffered under the strain of large migrations of people and struggles for power among competing forces. In fact, for all intents and purposes, it ceased to exist after the fifth century. Thus, as we shall see, Eastern (Greek) and Western (Latin) Christianity had very different histories and developed in different ways as a result.

THE EASTERN ORTHODOX CHRISTIAN CHURCHES

The primary form of Christianity that emerged in the eastern part of the Roman Empire is today known as Eastern Orthodoxy. The term **orthodox** is formed from two Greek words meaning "right praise" or "right opinion." Orthodox Christians consider themselves to be a single church in the sense that they share a single faith and the same Byzantine liturgical, canonical, and spiritual heritage. However, at the level of church government, Orthodoxy is a communion of churches. The bishops of these churches gather together at a council or regional synod to resolve theological questions or questions related to worship. Historically, these churches were led by the four ancient patriarchates of Constantinople, Alexandria, Antioch, and Jerusalem. The four functioned collegially, although all Orthodox Christians recognize the patriarch of Constantinople as "first among equals." From the ninth century onward, Byzantine missionaries established national churches among various ethnic groups outside the empire's borders. Their initiatives produced Orthodox churches of Russia, Romania, Greece, Serbia, Bulgaria, Georgia, Cyprus, Poland, Albania, and Slovakia, among others. Members of nearly all of these Orthodox churches currently reside in North America, although the greatest number are representatives of Russian and Greek Orthodoxy.

Since Orthodoxy comprises such diversity, we will consider here only a few aspects of this form of Christianity. First, we will look at its theory of church–state relations, that is, its understanding of the relationship between the emperor and the patriarch of the Orthodox Christian churches. Second, we will review the teachings of the first seven ecumenical councils in order to describe the distinctive doctrinal position of Orthodox Christian churches. Third, we will examine some characteristics of the worship and spirituality of this kind of Christianity: veneration of icons, Byzantine liturgy, and hesychast spirituality. Finally, we will examine some of the reasons for the permanent split between the Eastern churches and the Western Roman Catholic Church.

Church and State in Byzantine Theory

Bishop **Eusebius of Caesarea** (c. 260–339), the Christian scholar and apologist who celebrated Constantine's reign in several of his writings, formulated the fundamental principle of Byzantine imperial theory: "as in heaven, so on earth." According to this theory, the Byzantine emperor serves as God's lieutenant on earth, acting as the living representative of Christ. The emperor's rule on earth mirrors the rule of God in heaven. Byzantine social order, the harmonious activity of humankind in a Christian state under the emperor's absolute rule, parallels God's celestial order, the harmonious arrangement of all created things under divine sovereignty.

The fact that in the East (more so than in the West) the emperor played a major role in religious as well as political affairs can be illustrated by two actions of the emperor Justinian

Figure 11–1 Interior of Hagia Sophia in Constantinople. This great Christian church was converted into a mosque after the Muslim conquest of Constantinople in 1453.

(reigned 527–565). First, Justinian produced a monumental compilation of Roman law entitled the *Codex Juris Civilis* ("Code of Civil Law"), which combined the legal wisdom of Roman civilization, the moral principles of Christianity, and the heritage of Greek philosophy. Second, in 538 Justinian rebuilt the great **Hagia Sophia** ("Church of Holy Wisdom") in Constantinople as the image of the harmonious working together (*symphonia*) of empire and church for the common good. When the emperor entered the sanctuary of Hagia Sophia to offer to the patriarch and clergy the bread and wine to be transformed during the divine liturgy, he stood as representative of an empire under God.

Because church and empire were seen as one, the patriarch of Constantinople worked in concert with the emperor. However, the emperor had considerable power both in choosing the patriarch and in setting the agenda for meetings of church leadership. The difference between the power of the patriarch and the power of the emperor can be illustrated by the distinction between synods and councils. Working in close cooperation with the Holy Synod (a gathering of local bishops), the patriarch tried to resolve doctrinal and jurisdictional disputes so that the truth of the gospel might be maintained and the peace of the empire preserved. However, when issues of the highest importance were at stake, the emperor convened an ecumenical, or general, council of bishops who, in theory, represented the entire Christian world. The emperor was then responsible for proclaiming the council's decisions to the people as imperial law.

Western writers have sometimes termed this Byzantine political theory **Caesaropapism**, meaning that the civil ruler ("Caesar") also served as head of the church ("pope"). However, it would be more accurate to describe the emperor as the "supreme defender of the church" working in concert with the patriarch. The head of the Byzantine Church was always considered to be Christ, while the emperor was only his representative. This Eusebian theory of church–state relations recognized a sacred character in the state and contrasts with that worked out by Augustine in his *On the City of God*. Augustine denied that any "earthly city," in the sense of the state, could be the image of the "city of God" in heaven—insofar as the city of God existed on earth, it consisted of those inside (and those still outside) the church who were destined to be saved. Eusebius saw the emperor, ruler of the "earthly city," as also the representative of God's empire on earth.

Teachings of the First Seven Ecumenical Councils

In order to understand the distinctive character of Orthodox Christian churches, it is necessary to examine some of their teachings. Orthodox Christians recognize as dogma (a set of doctrines authoritatively proclaimed by a church) the teachings of the seven ecumenical councils, which were held between 325 and 787. Other Christian groups recognize fewer than these seven councils, while still others (for example, the Roman Catholic Church) recognize the teachings of these seven as well as the teachings of many other later councils. The topics treated by these seven councils that define the faith of Orthodox Christian churches fall into three categories: the nature of the Trinity, the proper understanding of Jesus, and the use of icons.

During the fourth century, the focus of attention was on the developing theology of the Trinity, articulated in central questions such as, "What is the relation of Christ to God the Father?" and "In what sense can God be Father, Son, and Holy Spirit and still be one?" The Council of Nicaea (A.D. 325) responded to these questions by teaching that Christ was "of the same substance" (*homoousios*) as God the Father, not a creature as Arius taught. The Council of Constantinople (381) clarified that the Holy Spirit was equal in divinity to the other two persons of the Trinity.

From 431 to 681 the focus of attention shifted to consider the proper understanding of Jesus, articulated in such questions as, "If Christ is true God, in what sense is he also authentically human?" and "If he is at the same time God and man at once, how can he be one reality?" The Council of Ephesus (431) taught that Mary, the mother of Jesus, should be venerated as *Theotokos* ("Mother of God"). This safeguarded the unity of the person of Jesus: Mary, as mother of the person of Jesus, could properly be called "Mother of God," since Jesus is one human–divine person. The Council of Chalcedon (451) further clarified that Christ "perfect in Godhead and perfect in humanity is made known to us in two natures . . . the difference of the natures is in no way destroyed because of the union, but rather the property of each nature is preserved, and both concur in one person and one hypostasis." Two additional councils were held in Constantinople, in 553 and 681 respectively, which further clarified the teaching of Chalcedon on the understanding of Christ as one person comprising two natures.

The third issue to receive attention during the era of the seven ecumenical councils was triggered by controversies over icons. An **icon** is a visual representation of Christ, Mary, angels, or saints. Icons are most commonly painted on wood but also appear as mosaics or frescoes affixed to church walls, as portraits in metal, or (rarely) as statues. Those who venerated icons (the **iconodules**) saw them not merely as a form of artistic decoration but also as fundamental to the authentic profession of Christian faith. Their opponents (the **iconoclasts**) considered the veneration of icons as superstitious at best and idolatrous at worst. The second ecumenical Council of Nicaea, held in 787, decided in favor of the iconodules. The bishops saw this controversy as a continuation of the earlier christological debates of the fifth through seventh centuries.

The teaching of the council was that since Christ did not simply "appear" on the earth but took a real human body enjoying a genuine human nature, it was not only possible but also necessary to portray him visually. The council's decree on icons stated:

> We declare that we defend free from any innovations all the written and unwritten ecclesiastical traditions that have been entrusted to us. One of these is the production of representational art . . . as it provides confirmation that the becoming man of the Word of God was real and not just imaginary, and as it brings us a similar benefit . . . The more frequently they [the

Figure 11–2 Andrei Rublev, "The Holy Trinity" (1411).

Figure 11–3 "Christ the Divine Wisdom," School of Salonica (fourteenth century).

images of Jesus Christ, Mary, the angels, and the saints] are seen in representational art, the more are those who see them drawn to remember and long for those who serve as models, and to pay these images the tribute of salutation and respectful veneration.

Distinguishing that veneration from the adoration due to God alone, the council went on to say:

> Certainly, this is not the full adoration in accordance with our faith, which is properly paid only to the divine nature, but it resembles that given to the figure of the honored and life-giving cross, and also to the holy books of the gospels and to other sacred cult objects. (Cited in Tanner 1990, 1:135–136)

Veneration of Icons

Icons play a central role in all Orthodox worship: Incense is burned before them, candles are lit to honor them, worshipers bear them in procession, prostrate before them, and/or kiss them. An important feature of Orthodox churches is the **iconostasis** ("icon screen"), a wall bearing icons arranged in a

Figure 11–4 "Virgin of Tenderness," School of Constantinople (fourteenth century).

prescribed order, which divides the sanctuary from the nave. Icons also adorn private homes and are even carried by faithful individuals as devotional aids, much as a Roman Catholic might wear a crucifix.

The Orthodox believe that icons confer grace, mediating between the divine and human realms. Therefore, as a means of communion between heaven and earth, icons play a sacramental role in Orthodoxy. By contemplating an icon, an Orthodox believer passes into sacred space and sacred time, effectively encountering the person or mystery depicted. Unlike many Western visual representations of biblical scenes or church legends, an icon does not attempt to provide a snapshot of a historical event or a psychological portrait of a historical person, but an encounter with a spiritual reality. This difference could easily be illustrated by the contrasting treatment of the light source in post-medieval Western religious painting and in Eastern iconography. In the Western pieces, the artist indicates "natural" light sources such as the sun, moon, candles, and the like, by carefully depicting shadows. But in an icon there are no shadows; the light sources lie "behind" or "within" the art piece, inviting the observer to enter into its radiant world. Icons also employ a fixed color scheme and method of depicting subjects. The one who produces an icon does not seek to express his or her individual artistic vision so much as to provide a means of encounter with the divine. Thus each step of producing an icon—from the preparation of the colors and brushes to the crafting of precious metal containers—is marked by prescribed prayer. In other words, producing an icon is not so much an artistic act as an act of worship.

Byzantine Liturgy

If icons represent the most characteristic visual artifacts of Orthodoxy, the Byzantine liturgy represents its most characteristic ceremonial creativity. Produced by a fusion of the monastic practices of Syria, Cappadocia, and Constantinople with the public worship of the imperial church, the Byzantine Eucharistic liturgy takes three characteristic forms: the Liturgy of St. John Chrysostom (the usual form), the Liturgy of St. Basil, and the Liturgy of the Presanctified Gifts. Only the Liturgy of St. John Chrysostom will be outlined here.

The Liturgy of John Chrysostom begins with the *Enarxis* ("Opening") consisting of prayers, hymns, and responses. The *Monogenes* ("Only-begotten") chant, a stirring and powerful expression of Orthodox faith in Christ as "one person in two natures," appears as part of the second hymn, sung by the assembled worshipers (or by the choir on their behalf):

> Only begotten Son and Word of God, although immortal You humbled Yourself for our salvation, taking flesh from the holy Theotokos and ever-virgin Mary and, without change, becoming man. Christ, our God, You were crucified but conquered death by death. You are one of the Holy Trinity, glorified with the Father and the Holy Spirit—save us.[1]

The liturgy continues with the part of the service devoted to readings from Scripture, beginning with the Little Entrance (a procession of clergy and ministers through the body of the church bearing a highly decorated book of scriptural readings) and the *Trisagion* hymn (another powerful expression of Orthodox Trinitarian faith sung by the assembly or the choir):

---

[1] All citations from the Liturgy of John Chrysostom are taken from the following Orthodox website: http://www.ocf.org/OrthodoxPage/liturgy/liturgy.html

> Holy God, Holy Mighty, Holy Immortal, have mercy on us (three times).
> Glory to the Father and to the Son and to the Holy Spirit, now and forever and to the ages of ages. Amen. Holy Immortal, have mercy on us.

This service of the Word continues with two readings: an epistle (usually taken from one of the New Testament letters) and a gospel. Preaching may follow at this point.

The ritual high point of the Orthodox liturgy then takes place: the Great Entrance. This is another procession of clergy and ministers through the body of the church, but this time they carry liturgical fans, incense, and the bread and wine, which will be consecrated later in the service. Popularly understood as a dramatic reenactment of either Jesus's triumphal entrance into Jerusalem or his funeral cortege, the congregation and/or choir accompanies the procession with the singing of the *Cherubic Hymn:*

> We, who mystically represent the Cherubim [an order of angels] and sing the thrice-holy hymn to the life-giving Trinity, let us set aside the cares of life that we may receive the King of all invisibly escorted by the Angelic Hosts. Alleluia!

After another prayer and the recitation of the Creed, the Eucharistic Prayer, or *Anaphora,* is prayed by the presiding priest with some sung interventions by the congregation and/or choir. The characteristic mode of Byzantine worship is wonderfully expressed in the opening of the *Anaphora* (the equivalent of the "Preface" in the Roman Catholic Mass). First, the priest and people exchange the dialogue: "The grace of our Lord Jesus Christ and the love of God the Father and the communion of the Holy Spirit be with you all"/"And with your spirit"/"Let us lift up our hearts"/"We lift them up to the Lord"/"Let us thank the Lord"/"It is proper and right." Then the priest rhapsodically exults in the mystery of God's interaction with humanity:

> It is proper and right to sing to You, bless You, praise You, thank You and worship You in all places of Your dominion; for You are God ineffable, beyond comprehension, invisible, beyond understanding, existing forever and always the same; You and Your only begotten Son and Your Holy Spirit. You brought us into being out of nothing, and when we fell, You raised us up again. You did not cease doing everything until You led us to heaven and granted us Your kingdom to come. For all these things we thank You and Your only begotten Son and Your Holy Spirit; for all things that we know and do not know, for blessings seen and unseen that have been bestowed upon us. We also thank You for this liturgy which You are pleased to accept from our hands, even though You are surrounded by thousands of Archangels and tens of thousands of Angels, by the Cherubim and Seraphim, six-winged, many-eyed, soaring with their wings, singing the victory hymn, proclaiming, crying out, and saying: [*here the people join in*] Holy, holy, holy, Lord Sabaoth, heaven and earth are filled with Your glory. Hosanna in the highest. Blessed is He who comes in the name of the Lord. Hosanna to God in the highest.

The consecration of the bread and wine is followed by another prayer and group recitation of the Lord's Prayer. After communion, the priest blesses the assembly with the remaining consecrated bread and wine while the congregation and/or choir sings:

> We have seen the true Light; we have received the heavenly Spirit; we have found the true faith, worshipping the undivided Trinity; for this has saved us.

Further prayers and blessings conclude the service. Then all who have attended, whether or not they have received sacramental communion, are invited to come forward to the priest before the iconostasis to receive a portion of the *antidoron*, blessed bread to be consumed for the journey back "into the world."

While this description of the liturgy and these few texts may suggest something of the other-worldly character of Orthodox worship, it cannot convey the complexity of the ceremony, its impact on all the senses, and its profoundly popular yet theologically sophisticated character.

Hesychast Spirituality

Another characteristic of Orthodox Christianity is its hesychast spirituality, especially associated with the fourteenth-century theologian Gregory Palamas. **Hesychia** means "inner stillness" or "silence of the heart." A hesychast is one who seeks *hesychia* through various spiritual disciplines, most notably the use of the **Jesus Prayer**. This is a very brief prayer (usually "Lord Jesus Christ, Son of the living God, have mercy on me, a sinner"), which the person repeats in rhythm, usually coordinated with his or her breathing and/or heartbeat. The goal of reciting the prayer in this manner is to have the prayer "descend from the mind into the heart," allowing the believer to enter into meditation, an experiential union with God. This Christian prayer technique might be compared to the mantras of certain non-Christian religions.

Barlaam the Calabrian, a South Italian monk and Neoplatonist philosopher living in Constantinople in the fourteenth century, attacked the hesychast movement as gross superstition. Did not scripture itself forbid "vain repetition" in prayer? Were not the physical techniques a form of self-hypnosis or an attempt to manipulate God through magic? Worst of all, was not the hesychasts' claim to experience God unmediated in the here-and-now a blasphemous denial of God's utter transcendence and unknowability? In response to Barlaam, **Gregory Palamas** (1296–1359), a monk of Mount Athos in Greece, defended the hesychasts' practice in his work commonly known as *The Triads*. Gregory here distinguished between God's essence, which remains unknowable to humans in the next life as well as in this, and God's energies, which are God-in-action encountering humanity. By means of the divine "energies," saints participate through grace in a union of love with the divine. Gregory's teaching on the energies of God was confirmed by three local councils held in Constantinople in 1341, 1347, and 1351: The hesychast movement was vindicated.

The Separation of Christian East and West

There were a number of issues that led to the division of Christianity into Eastern (Byzantine) and Western (Roman) churches. We have already noted differences in the ways that each understood the relationship between church and state. Political tensions were heightened in A.D. 800, when Pope Leo III crowned the Frankish king Charlemagne as emperor of a restored Roman Empire in the West (see Chapter 13). By this act, the papacy severed its historic political allegiance to the Roman Empire in the East and claimed the right to transfer the imperial title to the West. There were also considerable cultural differences between East and West, including language: The West was Latin speaking while the East was Greek speaking. Because of these cultural differences, Eastern Christianity developed a spirituality and worship style that was more mystical in orientation than Western churches.

While these differences are significant, they need not have led to the separation of Christianity into Eastern Orthodoxy and Roman Catholicism. In fact, it is difficult to name one particular event that brought about their separation. Instead, we will consider several situations that gradually, over an extended period of time, led to the separation of these two churches. One of the most decisive events was the Fourth Crusade in 1204. The crusades created considerable tension between East and West, as knights from the West marched through the Eastern empire, conquering lands that had been taken over by Muslims and then declining to return control of them to their original Byzantine rulers. More importantly, Orthodox Christians have never been able to forget how the knights of the Fourth Crusade, having become enmeshed in Byzantine court politics, besieged, conquered, and looted the city of Constantinople itself. Pope Innocent III, despite opposing the Western attack but eager to end a schism that had begun in 1054, acquiesced in the election of a Latin (Western) bishop as the new patriarch of Constantinople, and hoped (vainly, as it turned out) to bring the Greek church into line with Latin practices. Even today Orthodox Christians have not forgiven the Catholic Church for this disastrous chain of events, which weakened the Byzantine Empire in its defense against the Turkish military threat. In his 2001 visit to Athens, Pope John Paul II apologized to the Greek church for past and present Catholic sins against Orthodox Christians and expressed deep regret for the sack of Constantinople.

Another major issue that brought about the eventual separation of Eastern and Western Christians concerns the doctrine about the relationship of the Holy Spirit to the Father and the Son. Both Eastern and Western Christians believed that the Holy Spirit was personal, in the same way that the Father and Son are persons of the Trinity, and that the Spirit is fully divine. Orthodox Christians believed that the Father is the sole source of being in the Trinity. This belief was preserved in the original form of the Nicene–Constantinople Creed: "We believe in the Holy Spirit, who proceeds from the Father." However, as early as the sixth century some Christian churches in the West began adding the phrase "and the Son" to the creed, declaring that the Holy Spirit proceeded from the Father *and the Son*. In Latin the phrase is *filioque*. Orthodox Christians opposed this addition, because it denied to the Father what was distinctive to the person of the Father, namely, that he was the source of the other two persons of the Trinity.

The addition of the *filioque* to the creed was not formally accepted by the church at Rome until the eleventh century. When it was accepted, it was done without the consent of Eastern Christian leadership. Orthodox Christians consider the first seven ecumenical councils, from which the Nicene–Constantinople Creed originated, to be one of the highest expressions of God's continued presence in the church. Therefore, they argued that no one has the right to tamper with the contents of this creed. According to the decree on icons passed by the Second Council of Nicaea, the last of the early ecumenical councils (787), tradition was to be preserved intact: "We preserve without change or innovation all the ecclesiastical traditions that have been handed down to us, whether written or unwritten" (Cited above, p. 6). The *filioque* clause continues to be a major issue of separation between Eastern Orthodox and Roman Catholics today.

The *filioque* controversy is related to another issue that gradually separated Orthodox and Catholic Christians, namely, **papal primacy**. In Eastern Christianity church leadership is understood to be conciliar (working together in council), rather than monarchial (having a single ruler over all). Orthodox Christians honor the pope as the first and elder brother among the bishops of the churches throughout the world. However, they do not give him any special power or jurisdiction over the churches of the East nor do they attribute to him any spiritual gifts beyond those of other bishops. When it comes to speaking God's word to the world, neither the pope nor any other patriarch or bishop has highest authority. Rather, it is the ecumenical council where "the miracle of Pentecost is renewed; the Holy Spirit descends, the many become one in mind and heart, and the truth is revealed" (Ware 1992, 129).

Two situations in the history of the relationship between Eastern Orthodoxy and the Roman Catholic Church will help to illustrate the difficulties that arose over papal primacy. The first concerns Pope Nicholas I (reigned 858–867) and Photius, patriarch of Constantinople, in 861. Nicholas disagreed with Photius' appointment to the position of patriarch and reinstated his predecessor. Although the Eastern Orthodox churches simply ignored Nicholas' order, they resented his interference. Later, in 867, Photius issued a letter condemning the Roman Church's use of the *filioque* clause. In the same year, a council in Constantinople decided to excommunicate Pope Nicholas.

The second situation is sometimes called the *Great Schism of 1054*. The surface issues had to do with long-standing disciplinary and liturgical differences, which the Byzantines chose to complain about in 1053. Beneath the surface was ecclesiastical competition for control of territory where the pope's and the patriarch's jurisdictions confronted one another in southern Italy and in the Balkans. But the really fundamental disagreement had to do with different views of papal primacy, on which East and West had long differed (see Chapter 9). This was a particularly unfortunate time for the question of the pope's place in the universal church to become a hot issue, since both Michael Cerularius, the patriarch of Constantinople, and the papal delegate to Constantinople, Cardinal Humbert, were intolerant and overbearing. This was also a time when the papacy was gathering momentum in the great church renewal movement called the Gregorian Reform (see Chapter 13); Easterners were not prepared to listen to Pope Leo IX (reigned 1049–1054) when he proudly claimed in a letter, hand delivered by Humbert, that the Roman Church was "mother and head of all churches."

When the discussions between Cerularius and Cardinal Humbert got out of hand, the pope's delegate excommunicated the patriarch and his close associates. In response, a synod of Constantinople excommunicated Humbert, whom they accused of forging the pope's letter. No one at the time imagined that the controversy would harden into a definitive separation—prior ruptures had always been resolved—and the excommunications were personal, not applying to whole churches; furthermore, the pope and the Byzantine emperor remained on good terms and had a common political enemy in the aggressive Norman settlers in southern Italy. Nevertheless, under the influence of subsequent disasters like the Fourth Crusade, this separation hardened and became permanent. The excommunications were mutually withdrawn only recently, in 1965, but full communion between the churches has yet to be restored.

The churches of East and West differed in other ways, some more divisive than others. One such difference is clerical celibacy: Eastern Orthodox churches allow priests to marry, although their bishops must be unmarried and are therefore usually elected out of monasteries. However, precisely at the time of the 1054 schism, the papacy was trying to make old laws on celibacy apply universally to priests as well (see Chapter 13). Other differences included rules on fasting, the use of leavened or unleavened bread at Eucharist, circumstances in which divorce and remarriage might be permitted, teachings about purgatory, and the proper way to celebrate the sacrament of Confirmation. Whatever brought about the separation of Orthodox and Roman Catholic Christians, perhaps the overall problem was that, because of cultural and political circumstances, they had become strangers to each other (see Ware 1992, 147).

Today, as Orthodox and Roman Catholic Christians gather together in dialogue, perhaps reconciliation will eventually be possible. The late Pope John Paul II, the first pope from Eastern Europe, made such reconciliation a prime goal of his reign as pope, as may be seen in his encyclical letter *Ut Unum Sint* ("That They May Be One," 1995) and his apostolic letter, *Orientale Lumen* ("Eastern Light," 1995). But his hopes were disappointed, in spite of the changed political situation created by the fall of Communism. Some of the Orthodox resistance to his initiatives was due to long historical memories and to ancient disagreements and resentments. But a new problem since the fall of Communism has been Orthodox worries about the effect of rapid Westernization on their societies, newly open to Western economic, cultural, and religious influences. This is particularly true in Russia, where the Russian Orthodox Church, the largest in the Eastern Orthodox communion of churches, has been very cautious and even suspicious of Western efforts, Protestant as well as Catholic, to be part of Christianity's revival in Russia.

THE NON-CHALCEDONIAN EASTERN CHRISTIAN CHURCHES

Five ancient Eastern Christian churches originated in the fallout from the Council of Chalcedon (451): the Armenian Apostolic Church; the Coptic Orthodox Church in Egypt; the Ethiopian Orthodox Church, with a split-off church in the newly independent country of Eritrea; the Syriac Orthodox Church in Syria; and the Malankara Orthodox Syrian Church in India. Although they are completely independent of one another juridically, with different liturgical traditions and widely diverse histories, they share in common a rejection of Chalcedon's definition that Jesus Christ is "one person in two natures, undivided and unconfused." Because the members of these churches originally believed that such a definition compromised the unity of Christ's person by focusing too much on distinctions concerning his humanity and divinity, they preferred the formula proposed by Cyril of Alexandria, "one nature of the incarnate Son of God" (see Chapter 9). Although they clearly rejected the belief that the humanity of Christ had been absorbed into his single divine nature, these churches have often been erroneously called monophysite (from the Greek words for "of a single nature").

In the fifth century, these dissenters against Chalcedon represented a large segment of Eastern Christians in Armenia, Syria, Egypt, and Ethiopia. Today their numbers are greatly reduced due to conversions to Islam and to persecution under modern dictatorships. Nevertheless, even in their diminished state they represent a precious historical continuity with Christianity's ancient roots in the Middle East, and in the case of those with Syriac liturgical traditions, even with the Aramaic language of Jesus and his first followers. The contemporary resurgence of Islam, along with the heightened tensions with the West, has made them even more vulnerable by magnifying religious differences between them and their Muslim neighbors and fellow citizens. Those who can do so often choose to emigrate. As a result, in recent decades they have sought to improve relations with Catholic and Eastern Orthodox churches. Under Pope John Paul II, the Catholic Church has reached formal agreement with the Copts (in Egypt) and the Syrians, stating that the doctrinal differences that historically divided the Catholic Church from the non-Chalcedonian Eastern churches have more to do with the verbal formulations of the faith rather than with the substance of the faith itself.

THE ASSYRIAN CHURCH OF THE EAST

The proper name of the Assyrian Church of the East reflects its status as ancient Christianity's easternmost expansion, and its historic heartland in Assyria in the northern part of Mesopotamia (modern-day Iraq). Christianity spread into Mesopotamia no later than the mid-second century. By the early third century Christian communities had been founded in Persian territory, outside the Roman Empire altogether. Though never a majority of the Persian population, this Eastern church nonetheless grew to be quite large in the Middle Ages, spreading as far east as China and as far south as the southern tip of India. A celebrated monument to the Church of the East's evangelization of China is a ten-foot high, black marble block, inscribed in Chinese characters and Syriac script (Syriac is the church's liturgical language), dated to the year 781. It was discovered probably in 1625 and is now kept in Xi'an, in northern China. The Syriac inscription records the preaching of the Christian faith to the emperors of China, who are said to have authorized the translation of the Christian bible into Chinese in 635.

Inscription on the Xi'an Monument

The inscription on the Xi'an monument contains a summary of the Christian faith as it was preached to the emperors of China. It also includes the decree of the emperor T`ai-tsung (627–649), dated to the year 638, which shows the official imperial view of Christianity. An English translation of the decree follows:

> The Way [*religion*] had not, at all times and in all places, the selfsame name; the Sage [*the Divine*] had not, in all places, the selfsame human body. Heaven caused a suitable religion to be instituted for every religion and clime so that each one of the races of mankind might be saved. Bishop Alopên [*the original seventh century Assyrian missionary to China*] of the Kingdom of Ta-ch`in, bringing with him the Sûtras and Images, has come from afar and presented them at our Capital. Having carefully examined the scope of his teaching, we find it to be mysteriously spiritual, and of silent operation. Having observed its principal and most essential points, we reached the conclusion that they cover all that is most important in life. Their language is free from perplexing expressions; their principles are so simple that they would "remain as the fish would remain even after the net (of language) were forgotten." This Teaching is helpful to all creatures and beneficial to all men. So let it have free course throughout the Empire. (Cited in Saeki 1951, 54–58)

An interesting social institution of the Assyrian Church of the East was its hereditary patriarchate. From 1450 until the late twentieth century, the patriarchs of this church were all drawn from one family bloodline, usually passing the leadership from uncle to nephew. This practice produced some patriarchs who assumed the office at a very early age (for example, twelve) and whose older relatives governed for them as regents. This hereditary patriarchate came to an end in 1975 when Mar Shimoun XXIII was assassinated; his successor, Mar Dinkha IV, was freely elected from another bloodline.

The Assyrian Church of the East's numbers have decreased drastically in recent centuries because of conquests, massacres, and deportations. Today around 400,000 members of the church reside primarily in Iraq, Iran, Syria, and Lebanon. Like other Middle Eastern Christian peoples, they are under intense political pressure, and many, especially those in

Figure 11–5 Stone monument erected in 781 by Assyrian Christian missionaries to China. The monument is currently located at Xi'an, China.

Iraq, are trying to emigrate. The current patriarch of the Assyrian Church of the East, Mar Dinkha IV, now resides in the United States.

Doctrinally, the Assyrian Church of the East accepts only the first two ecumenical councils as authoritative, rejecting the formulations of the Council of Ephesus in 431. Instead, the Assyrian Church officially accepted the Christology promoted by Nestorius, who maintained that Jesus held two separate natures (one the perfect man without sin who is son of Mary in the flesh, the other the divine word of God, or *Logos*, settled within him). For this reason, the Assyrian Church had, in the past, been called **Nestorian**. However, contemporary scholars avoid the term since the members of the church consider it insulting. Many contemporary scholars suggest that this doctrine was embraced by the church more for political than for philosophical or theological reasons. The Christian faith as formulated at Ephesus was the official creed of the Roman Empire, with which the Persian Empire was often at war. The Assyrian Church of the East may have taken this doctrinal position to assert its independence from the Roman Empire and to prove its loyalty to the Persian Empire and its non-Christian fellow countrymen.

The Assyrian Church of the East recognizes seven sacraments, but their accounting varies. Universally accepted as sacraments are Baptism, Eucharist, Marriage, and Holy Orders. Other rituals or religious objects that have sacramental status in various accounts are the blessing of monks, the office for the dead, the oil of anointing, absolution, holy leaven, the sign of the Cross, and the consecration of a church or an altar. Baptism is usually performed in stages: At birth, a child is washed with water blessed by a priest, and on the occasion of a great feast the child is immersed in water three times facing east and totally anointed with holy oil during the course of an elaborate community service.

Another interesting social institution of the Assyrian Church is the marital status of its clergy. A fifth-century synod declared that celibacy should be obligatory for no one, including bishops and patriarchs, but from the sixth century on, the custom arose of only ordaining celibate monks as bishops. Those who take a monastic vow can return to secular life without disgrace or difficulty through a dispensation. Unlike other churches, the Assyrian Church of the East approves of the unlimited remarriage of priests when their wives die. A priest is usually selected by his future parishioners and then ordained by his bishop with the laying on of hands.

The Assyrian Church of the East has virtually no art comparable to that of the Greek Orthodox churches or even the West Syrian churches. They reject the use of icons and iconography, tolerating these holy images neither in their churches nor in their homes. They use simple crosses at the entrance to their churches and over the altar, but the crucifix (a cross upon which an artistic representation of the body of Jesus is placed) is banned from all parts of their religious buildings. The church buildings themselves are unostentatious and simple, recognizable only by the shape of a simple cross on the outer wall above the church entrance. The entrance is a narrow, low opening in the wall so that anyone entering has to stoop down to gain access.

Although the Assyrian Church of the East has traditionally had no official ties with other Christian churches, the present patriarch Mar Dinkha IV and the Roman Catholic

Pope John Paul II met in formal theological exchange in 1994. A "Common Christological Declaration" was formulated that removed the main doctrinal obstacle between the Catholic Church and the Assyrian Church of the East:

> The controversies of the past led to anathemas, bearing on persons and on formulas. The Lord's Spirit permits us to understand better today that the divisions brought about in this way were due in large part to misunderstandings. Whatever our christological divergences have been, we experience ourselves united in the confession of the same faith in the Son of God who became man so that we might become children of God by his grace. We wish from now on to witness together to this faith in the One who is the Way, the Truth and the Life, proclaiming it in appropriate ways to our contemporaries, so that the world may believe in the Gospel of salvation . . . Living by this faith and these sacraments, it follows as a consequence that the particular Catholic churches and the particular Assyrian churches can recognise each other as sister Churches. (John Paul II and Mar Dinkha IV 1994)

The churches also agreed to cooperate in such areas as education and priestly formation.

THE EASTERN CATHOLIC CHURCHES

The split between the Eastern and Western Christian churches, symbolized by the mutual excommunications of the bishops of Rome and Constantinople in 1054, became definitive in the minds of the common people of the East after the crusades and the sacking of Constantinople by Western Christians in 1204. Both the Second Council of Lyons (1274) and the Council of Florence (1439) attempted to heal the breach between Eastern and Western Christianity, but neither was successful. Over time, however, individual segments of the various Eastern churches have reestablished communion (formal ties) with Rome. The first to do so were the Maronite Christians of Lebanon, so-called from their ancient center in the monastery of St. Maroun in the mountains of Lebanon. At the time of the crusades, the Maronites re-entered into communion with Rome (1182), although they claim never to have actually been out of communion, just isolated from other Christian churches since the spread of Islam in the seventh century.

Today there are about twenty-one such Eastern Catholic churches, most of them rather small. Sometimes they are called "Eastern rite" churches because, as part of their reunion with Roman Catholicism and their acceptance of the pope's primacy, they were allowed to retain many of their traditional customs, such as their liturgies and elements of church law (most controversially, this usually included their custom of allowing priests to marry). These churches have also sometimes been called *uniates*, although this term is falling out of use today because Orthodox churches object to it.

Orthodox Christians generally reject these Eastern Catholic churches and view them as an obstacle to Catholic–Orthodox reunion. They feel that their very existence is a denial of the reality of the Orthodox churches, that these unions were efforts to split local Eastern Christian communities, and that Eastern Catholics are really Orthodox who were forcibly seized from their mother churches. Since the collapse of Communism in Eastern Europe, Orthodox resentment of these Eastern Catholic Churches has grown even stronger. This is particularly true of the tense situation in Ukraine, where the Ukrainian Catholic Church, the largest of the Eastern Catholic Churches, has come back to life after its brutal suppression under Communism in 1946. Ukrainian Catholics are trying to build bridges to the several groups of Orthodox Christians in Ukraine, but must work hard to defuse Orthodox anxieties that they are merely a Catholic vanguard to claim all of Ukraine for Catholicism.

The Decree on Eastern Catholic Churches, one of the documents of the Second Vatican Council (a gathering of Roman Catholic leaders held in the 1960s), presents present-day official Catholic teaching on these churches. It affirmed their equality with western Roman Catholics. It also called Eastern Catholics to a rediscovery of their own traditions and affirmed that they have a special vocation to foster ecumenical relations with non-Catholic Eastern Christians. Recent developments hold out hope that these and other ecumenical efforts may finally bear fruit and that at least some non-Catholic Eastern Christians may eventually be reunited with their Catholic brothers and sisters in the East and the West.

An outstanding example of recent ecumenical relations between the Assyrian Church of the East and the Catholic Church is the 2001 agreement to allow sharing of the Eucharist between Assyrian Christians and members of the Chaldean Catholic Church, which represents Assyrian Christians who have come back into communion with the Catholic Church. The agreement of these two churches to share Eucharist builds on the good faith created by the 1994 "Common Christological Declaration" mentioned above. It was inspired by the pastoral situation in war-torn Iraq and in the world-wide diaspora of Iraqi Christians, both Chaldean Catholics and Assyrians, who cannot always find a priest of their own church from whom to receive the Eucharist. In such situations it is now possible for them to receive the Eucharist from a priest of the other church.

Key Terms

Constantinople	icon	Gregory Palamas
Justinian	iconodules	*filioque*
orthodox	iconoclasts	papal primacy
Eusebius of Caesarea	iconostasis	Nestorian
Hagia Sophia	hesychia	
Caesaro-papism	Jesus Prayer	

Questions for Reading

1. Who governs the Eastern Orthodox churches? To what degree was the Byzantine emperor involved in the government of this church during the period in which the Byzantine Empire existed? What principle justified the emperor's involvement in the church?

2. Compare and contrast the various Eastern churches in terms of their acceptance or rejection of the teachings of the first seven ecumenical councils.

3. What is an icon? What arguments were made for and against the veneration of icons, and how was the dispute over icons finally resolved? What function do icons serve in the Eastern Orthodox Church? Do all Eastern churches accept the veneration of icons?

4. What is *hesychia*? How does one achieve it? What arguments were made for and against *hesychia*, and how was the dispute over it finally resolved?

5. What events or circumstances led to the separation of Eastern Orthodox and Roman Catholic Christians?

6. What are the distinctive elements in the beliefs and practices of the Non-Chalcedonian Eastern Christian churches and the Assyrian Church of the East?

Works Consulted/Recommended Reading

Atiya, Aziz. *A History of Eastern Christianity*. London: Methuem and Company, 1968.

Constantelos, Demetrios. *Understanding the Greek Orthodox Church: Its Faith, History and Practice*. New York: Seabury, 1982.

Ellis, Jane. *The Russian Orthodox Church: A Contemporary History*. London: Croom Helm, 1986.

Every, George. *Understanding Eastern Christianity*. Bangalore: Dharmaram Publications, 1978.

First Non-Official Consultation on Dialogue within the Syriac Tradition: Vienna, June 1994. Syriac Dialogue, 1. Vienna, Austria: Pro Oriente, 1994.

Hussey, Joan M. *The Orthodox Church in the Byzantine Empire*. Oxford: Clarendon, 1986.

John Paul II and Mar Dinkha IV, "Common Christological Declaration Between the Catholic Church and the Assyrian Church of the East," November 11, 1994. The Holy See–Vatican Web site; http://www.vatican.va/roman_curia/pontifical_councils/chrstuni/documents/rc_pc_chrstuni_doc_11111994_assyrian-church_en.html.

Liturgical Commission of the Greek Orthodox Archdiocese of North and South America. *The Orthodox Liturgy*. Port Townsend, WA: Graphic Arts, 1976.

Lossky, Vladimir. *The Mystical Theology of the Eastern Church*. Cambridge: James Clarke and Company, 1957.

Meyendorff, John. *Byzantine Theology: Historical Trends and Doctrinal Themes*. New York: Fordham University, 1974.

_____. *The Orthodox Church*. Crestwood, NY: St. Vladimir's Seminary, 1981.

Papadakis, Aristeides, and John Meyendorff. *The Christian East and the Rise of the Papacy: The Church 1071–1453 A.D.* Crestwood, NY: St. Vladimir's Seminary, 1994.

Pelikan, Jaroslav. *The Christian Tradition: A History of the Development of Doctrine*. Vol. 2: *The Spirit of Eastern Christendom (600–1700)*. Chicago: University of Chicago, 1974.

Podipara, Placid. J. *The Thomas Christians*. Bombay: St. Paul Publications, 1970.

Roberson, Roland G. *The Eastern Christian Churches: A Brief Survey*. 6th rev. ed. Rome: Pontifical Institute of Oriental Studies, 1999.

Saeki, P. Y. *The Nestorian Documents and Relics in China*, 2nd ed. Tokyo: Maruzen, 1951.

Schmemann, Alexander. *The Historical Road of Eastern Orthodoxy*. Crestwood, NY: St. Vladimir's Seminary, 1977.

Schulz, Hans-Joachim. *The Byzantine Liturgy: Symbolic Structure and Faith Expression*. New York: Pueblo, 1986.

Spidlik, Tomas. *The Spirituality of the Christian East: A Systematic Handbook*. Cistercian Studies, 79. Kalamazoo, MI: Cistercian Publications, 1986.

Tanner, Norman, ed. *Decrees of the Ecumenical Councils*. Vol. I. Washington, DC : Georgetown University, 1990.

Ware, Kallistos. "Eastern Christendom." In John McManners, ed. *The Oxford Illustrated History of Christianity*, pp. 123–162. Oxford: Oxford University, 1992.

——— *The Orthodox Church*. New York: Penguin Books, 1984.

——— *The Orthodox Way*. London: Mowbray and Company, 1979.

Chapter

ISLAM PAST AND PRESENT

TIMELINE

A.D. 570	Birth of Muhammad.
A.D. 610	Beginning of divine revelations to Muhammad, inaugurating his mission as Prophet.
A.D. 622	Flight of Muhammad and early followers to Medina, known as the *hijra*, marking year one of the Islamic calendar.
A.D. 632	Death of Muhammad and the appointment of Abu Bakr as the first caliph.
A.D. 661	Assassination of Ali and beginning of the Umayyad caliphate in Damascus.
A.D. 750	Umayyad caliphate overthrown, Abbasid caliphate established in Baghdad.
A.D. 868	Birth of Muhammad ibn Hasan, revered by Shi'a as the "hidden imam."
A.D. 1096–1291	Crusades are launched against the Muslims to recover the Holy Land.
A.D. 1258	Fall of the Abbasid caliphate and the sacking of Baghdad by Mongols.
A.D. 1453	Capture of Constantinople by Ottoman Turks, who continue to expand their rule across the Arab Middle East and the Balkans (southwestern Europe).
A.D. 1750s	Emergence of Salafi reform movement in the Arabian Peninsula.
A.D. 1798	Napoleon invades Egypt and then Syria, initiating modern European imperial expansion in the Islamic Middle East.
A.D. 1918	World War I ends leading to dismemberment of remaining territories of Ottoman Empire.
A.D. 1979	Islamic Revolution triumphs in Iran prompting new waves of Islamic activism.

As one of the world's great religious traditions, Islam has many dimensions and speaks in many voices. While all Muslims share a foundation of common beliefs and practices, a rich and varied history has followed from seventh century Arabia to the present, and continues to inspire a growing global community now totaling upwards of a billion adherents. Like Jews and Christians, Muslims trace the proper origins of their religion to Abraham, their father in faith, and beyond that to Adam and Eve, whom God called to submit in obedience to His divine commands. The literal meaning of the word **Islam** in Arabic is "submission."

Today many parts of the Muslim world are experiencing both internal tensions and external pressures, which have produced a variety of social and political movements broadly identified as Islamic. Unfortunately, because of the deeds of a few extremists, whom most Muslims themselves condemn, some of these Islamic movements are mistakenly seen as typical of Islam as a whole. When these negative impressions are added to past misunderstandings and rivalries between Islam and the Christian West, media presentations of Islam can sometimes be quite unflattering. However, this is far from a full and accurate picture of Islam and the Muslim way of life, which is rich and culturally diverse and deeply grounded in religious belief and practice.

The present chapter tries to give a brief but balanced portrait of Islam's origins, expansion, core religious beliefs and practices, and its engagement with modernity. Where appropriate, it also highlights some of the differences of theology and religious practice between Sunni and Shi'a, the two major divisions of Islam in the modern world. In addition, attention is paid to various ways in which the traditions of Islam and Christianity have interacted and how Islam regards Christianity. The chapter concludes with some recent statements of Christian churches regarding the need for religious dialogue with Islam.

THE PROPHET MUHAMMAD IN ARABIA

The central part of the Arabian peninsula, from the Fertile Crescent in the north to the fabled *Arabia Felix* of antiquity (roughly, today's Yemen) in the south, consists mainly of a broad arid plateau. A more populous mountainous region, called the Hijaz, runs along the Red Sea coast in the west, while deserts, with scattered oases, stretch out on other sides. At the time of the Prophet Muhammad's birth in 570, this remote land had begun to take on a new importance, bringing with it a growing prosperity, due largely to the way commercial traders successfully took advantage of its strategic location. As the native peoples of the peninsula asserted control over the caravan routes that crossed it, they were able to take advantage of an emerging power vacuum in the eastern Mediterranean and Middle East: The nearby superpowers of Persia and Rome were in the process of exhausting themselves in their long struggle for dominance.

The majority of the population who inhabited this large peninsula were Arabs, some of whom lived in settled communities, including a few sizable cities, while others were bedouins (nomadic desert people who provide for themselves by shepherding their flocks on the land). Their religion combined polytheism and animism (worship of the powers of nature), with cults centered in tribal sanctuaries where sacred objects were frequently venerated. Mecca was the home of the most famous of these sanctuaries known as the **Ka'ba,** which housed a sacred black stone. This sanctuary was part of a great shrine center, amounting to a sort of pantheon, where a large number of gods were honored by the local peoples.

Legends associated with the Ka'ba are rich and very old. Indeed, some traditions hold that the Ka'ba was originally built by Abraham and his son Ishmael, who were commanded to erect the shrine so that people could come to this place and worship the one true God, **Allah.** The word *Allah* is a contraction of the definite article and the Arabic noun, *al-ilah*, which shares parallels with an ancient Hebrew designation of God as *El.* Over time the site was corrupted by the worship of pagan deities, but the Prophet Muhammad would later destroy the idols that were housed there and restore the Ka'ba as a place for the worship of Allah.

In addition to the Arab populations who inhabited the peninsula, there were some Jewish tribes who called this place home and some Christians, who occupied an area known as Najran near modern-day Yemen. The prevailing religious consciousness was mainly expressed through values such as bravery, loyalty, hospitality, and revenge, together with a belief in an unchangeable fate. But evidence of a growing spiritual restlessness suggests that not everyone was satisfied with the available religious alternatives.

Muhammad was born into the Hashim clan of the Quraysh tribe, which dominated the wealthy city of Mecca, located on the eastern slopes of the Hijaz. He was orphaned while still a child and was raised by his uncle, Abu Talib. As a young man he worked in the caravan trade, which required him to make long journeys away from home. At the age of twenty-five, his life changed dramatically when his employer, a rich widow named Khadija, asked him to marry her. This marriage provided Muhammad with the means to devote himself more intently to meditation, as he was inclined to do. It was during one of these meditation periods that Muhammad first manifested his role as God's Prophet.

Sunnis and Shi'a differ on what they understand about when and how Muhammad first recognized that he was God's Prophet. There are Sunnis who accept the tradition that Muhammad was deep in meditation in a cave on the outskirts of Mecca in 610, when he experienced a profound religious encounter. Though initially frightened by the experience, he was encouraged by his wife Khadija, and he soon grasped that it had a heavenly origin and that it was entrusting to him a mission to proclaim God's message to others. However, Shi'a believe that Muhammad always knew that he was God's Messenger.

When Muhammad received the first of what would become a long series of divine revelations directed toward all humanity, it came to him in the form of a supernatural voice. It was the voice of the archangel Gabriel, and these are the words that Muhammad heard:

> Recite, in the name of your Lord who created,
> Created humankind from a blood clot.
> Recite, for your Lord is most beneficent
> Who taught by the pen,
> Taught mankind what they did not know. (Qur'an 97:1–5)

The first word of this initial revelation, *iqra* in Arabic, is a verb in the imperative form, which can be translated as "Recite!" or "Read!" The related noun is **Qur'an,** literally, "recitation," which subsequently became the name for the entire collection of divine revelations received by Muhammad intermittently until his death in 632.

While most of the early messages that Muhammad received had the character of short emphatic declarations, warning of God's judgment and denouncing those who refuse to believe and who oppress others, later revelations took other forms, including teachings, narratives, eschatology, laws, legal commentary, moral counsels, military directives, and spiritual exhortations. At the center of Muhammad's message was a condemnation of the polytheism which defined Mecca's religious establishment, as well as a forceful call for socioeconomic justice in a setting marked by stark inequities in status, wealth, and power.

Not surprisingly, while Muhammad's message appealed to many, especially among the poor and disenfranchised, he met with increasing opposition and eventual persecution from the ruling elite among the Quraysh tribe, to which he belonged. Tribal custom initially served to protect him from these hostile elements until the death of his uncle and patron Abu Talib in 619, which was also the year that his wife Khadija died. At that point, facing threats affecting both himself and his followers, he sought a new strategy and eventually succeeded in negotiating an agreement with leading representatives of Medina, another city in the Hijaz, to which he then fled. The tribal leaders of Medina who invited Muhammad had been engaged in a long series of bloody feuds, which they asked him to help them settle. The terms of their arrangement specified that they would recognize Muhammad as the Prophet of God and would defer to him in all matters of governance.

This relocation, known as the *hijra* or "emigration," took place in 622, which became Year One in the Muslim calendar. It marked a decisive new beginning for Muhammad and his followers, because it was in Medina that the Muslim community, or *umma,* took shape as an integrated religious and political society under Muhammad's direction. However, according to Sunni Muslims, this combination of sacred and secular authority in one divinely appointed individual could not be maintained in the same way after the death of the Prophet. Those who succeeded him as leaders could only claim the right to rule but could not assume his spiritual mandate. Shi'a Muslims, on the other hand, believe that this combination must endure until the Day of Judgment. Otherwise, the death of the Prophet would mean the death of Islam itself.

Regardless of these differences in point of view concerning Islam's religious and political society, the ideal of a unified Muslim polity (form of government) like the one established in Medina has persisted over the centuries and has given rise to numerous variations and controversies right up until the present day. Another reason the *hijra* was so important for the development of Islam is that Medina is where the original Muslim community began to develop many of the distinct institutions that would become the defining features of Islam. Here, for instance, the first mosque was established in the courtyard of the Prophet's house, which set a pattern for future places of prayer and assembly.

The security of the Muslim community in Medina was constantly at risk in the early years after Muhammad's arrival, because a virtual state of war existed between the Muslims and the nearby Meccan populations. The Meccans decided at one point to take possession of the emigrant Muslims' property, which they left behind in Mecca when they followed the Prophet to Medina. Those emigrant Muslims then beseeched Muhammad to allow them to raid a Meccan caravan, which was on its way back from the Levant, a region bounded by the Mediterranean Sea on the west, the Arabic Desert on the south, the Taurus Mountains on the north, and Mesopotamia on the east. This led to a series of larger violent confrontations that would eventually defeat those who were defending the old center of power in Mecca. The first of these, the Battle of Badr in 624, brought the Muslims victory even though they were greatly outnumbered. They regarded this triumph as proof of divine favor, and the Qur'an speaks of it as the work of God, who sent angels to assist Muhammad and the believers (Qur'an 8:9).

This show of strength bolstered the independence of Medina and drew a number of the surrounding bedouin tribes to align with the Prophet. The following year Meccan forces avenged their humiliation by defeating the Muslims at the Battle of Uhud, where the

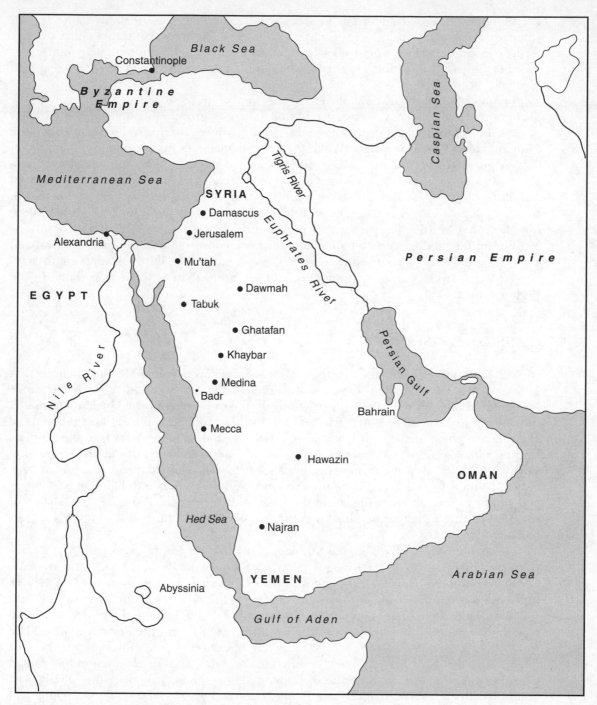

Figure 12–1 Map of Arabia in Muhammad's time.

Prophet himself was wounded. The final contest of arms, known as the Battle of the Trench (named for a trench which the Muslims dug as a defensive measure), was a failed attempt by the Meccans and their allies to besiege Medina in 627. In addition to these conflicts, the Prophet also confronted and expelled several Jewish tribes, which had become increasingly hostile to his mission.

Finally in 630 the leaders of Mecca negotiated a peaceful surrender. Resistance to Muhammad's ascendancy across the region faded as groups throughout the Arabian peninsula acknowledged the new order and pledged their loyalty by recognizing Muhammad as God's messenger. When the Prophet made his final trip to his native city in 632, he entered Mecca as supreme victor. Almost all its inhabitants had now declared themselves Muslims. Muhammad abolished all old blood feuds and granted amnesty to all but a few of his old foes. He also took charge of the Ka'ba in Mecca, having purged it of all the pagan idols and images and dedicated it to Allah alone. Thus it became identified as the direction that Muslims face when they pray and the place they would visit as pilgrims. In Muslim understanding, the Ka'ba had already been consecrated in the time of Abraham, who was said to have come to the site when God put him to the test by asking him to sacrifice his son. Muslims identify this son as Ishmael rather than as Isaac, as is stated in the Bible (Gen 22:1–19).

THE EXPANSION OF ISLAM

In 632 Muhammad died unexpectedly after a brief fever. Sunni Muslims believe that Muhammad's death left the community uncertain about how to choose a new leader, since Muhammad had left no specific instructions on the question and the Qur'an designated him as the "seal" or last of God's prophets (33:40). However, Shi'a Muslims believe that the Prophet was commanded by Allah to assign twelve **imams** to successively lead the Muslims starting with his cousin and son in law, Ali Ibn Abu Talib. Followers of the first school prevailed and came to rule the young Muslim nation, and they adopted the term **caliph** or "successor" as their formal title. They continued to govern in matters of religion as well as war and public affairs, and they did so on the basis of their interpretations of what Allah had revealed through the Prophet and what the Prophet had established through his sayings and actions.

The first caliph, Abu Bakr, was an older man, an early convert who had been a prosperous merchant in Mecca. His daughter A'isha was one of the Prophet's wives and, by many Sunni accounts, his favorite. Although Abu Bakr only reigned for two years (632–634), his influence was significant. He moved quickly to reestablish order by suppressing rivalries and rebellions at this critical moment. More importantly he launched a series of dramatic military campaigns into the territories of the Byzantine Empire and the Persian Empire. The rapid success of these invasions proved to be the start of one of the most sweeping periods of conquest the world has ever seen. Within a few decades, Muslim domination had spread north, east, and west, to incorporate the bulk of Mesopotamia, Syria, Palestine, Persia, and half of North Africa. Within a century, Islamic rule reached from the borders of China and India on one side of the globe to the Pyrenees Mountains, between Spain and France, on the other.

The formidable pace of this expansion brought radical changes to much of the landscape of what was then known as the civilized world. Conquered peoples were now part of what Muslim teaching calls "the Abode of Islam" (*dar al-Islam*), the world which acknowledges Allah and his Prophet, as opposed to the "Abode of War" (*dar al-harb*), which has yet to acknowledge God, and the "Abode of Treaty" (*dar al-ahd*), which includes those with whom Islam has established treaties. Contrary to what is often believed, however, forced conversion to Islam was quite uncommon, mainly limited to Arabia itself and to parts of North Africa. Jews and Christians, as "People of the Book" (Qur'an 5:15), were tolerated so long as they obeyed certain restrictions and paid a head tax (or a per capita tax) to the Muslim leadership. Eventually the Zoroastrians of Persia were given the same exemption. Muslim overlords, at first almost everywhere a minority, found it impractical to enforce conversion, which the Qur'an in one place at least actually forbade (Qur'an 2:256). Thus the overall Muslim record for tolerance, at least before the modern period, seems to have been decent—better, on the whole, than the pre-modern Christian tolerance of non-Christians. But the passage of time, the tax burden, relative isolation, and the discriminatory second-class status given to non-Muslim peoples ensured that subject populations tended, albeit slowly, to assimilate to the new faith.

Rapid expansion changed Islam as well. The new Muslim rulers had to devise innovative responses that would, in time, reconfigure basic features of the original community and affect virtually every aspect of its life. Further, following the death of Abu Bakr, disagreement over the choice of a leader intensified. Abu Bakr's next two successors as caliph, Umar (634–644) and Uthman (644–656), were both murdered. In 656, Ali was chosen as the fourth caliph but only over the objections of militant members of the Umayyad clan, to which the assassinated third caliph Uthman had belonged. Ali, the first male convert to Islam, was noted for his devotion and learning. He was also the Prophet's cousin (the son of Abu Talib) and his son-in-law, since he had married Fatima, the only child of the Prophet who survived into adulthood. Uthman's relatives and their supporters, led by Mu'awiyya, then governor of Syria, rebelled, because they believed that Ali was in some way implicated in the death of Uthman. They drew Ali and his forces into a decisive battle in 657, which ended with a truce when Ali, who had the upper hand in the fighting, agreed to accept arbitration.

Behind the dissension stood the competing claims of two major factions of Islam. One was led by members of the old Meccan elite, many of whom had only lately embraced Islam, but who had valuable experience in high administration. The other consisted mainly of believers who had fled with the Prophet to Medina or who had soon joined the cause in his adopted city. Those of the first camp generally favored a pragmatic leader who in their view would be an effective organizer and wielder of power. These became known as the **Sunni,** because they believed that the "right path" of leadership was to follow the Sunna (traditions and customary practices) of the Prophet and the teachings of his companions. Those of the other camp believed that since the message of Islam was in its entirety a divine revelation, the matter of succession must be decided by Allah alone, and that He chose Ali and eleven other disciples to be the successive imams of Islam until the last day. They supported the candidacy of Ali, against the protests of Mu'awijja and his supporters.

After the truce of 657, subsequent efforts to reach a settlement between these two factions collapsed amid accusations of deceit, betrayal, and bad faith. Mu'awiyya's position was strengthened as a number of Ali's followers were angered over what they felt to be his willingness to compromise regarding his sacred duty. One group of these dissenters, acting in the manner of puritans (people who live according to strict religious principles), broke entirely with the rest, receiving the name of *Kharijites* ("those who withdraw"), whereas the main body of Ali's followers became known to history as the **Shi'a** or "partisans" (of Ali).

When the Kharijites eventually succeeded in assassinating Ali in 661, Mu'awiyya seized the initiative, defeated his rivals, and was declared caliph. The establishment of Mu'awiyya's reign marked the end of a blessed formative era, which Sunni Muslims refer to as the period of the four "rightly guided" caliphs. In its place the Umayyad dynasty was founded, and the Muslims associated with this dynasty thereafter became known as the Sunnis. By moving the capital to Damascus, the Sunni leaders sought to distance themselves from the pious dissent that lingered in Mecca and Medina. They also drew heavily on existing Arab tribal loyalties and adopted many elements of late Roman administration and architecture. One lasting effect of this shift remains visible today in the Dome of the Rock and the Al-Aqsa Mosque, the Muslim holy sites that dominate the Temple Mount in Jerusalem. The Umayyads built the Dome of the Rock, in part as a public statement, symbolically placing Islam in the line of Abraham, surpassing both Jewish and Christian claims, and in the heart of Jerusalem. The Al-Aqsa Mosque got its name from a reference in the Qur'an to Muhammad's famous night journey, which was said to end at the "farthest mosque," traditionally understood to be the Temple precincts in Jerusalem (Qur'an 17:1). Along with Mecca and Medina, Jerusalem continues to be one of the three holiest cities for Islam.

Later, when Ali's younger son Hussein answered a call from Muslims in southern Iraq to lead them in an uprising against the Umayyads, a coalition of Shi'a marched against the forces of Mu'awiyya's son Yazid. This confrontation culminated in the celebrated battle at Karbala (680), on the lower Euphrates River, which ended with the defeat and death of Hussein. For Shi'a believers, however, the military outcome of this battle has long been overshadowed by its religious significance. For them, the death of Hussein, along with much of his family and his followers, is seen as a martyrdom: It represents the suffering which precedes the ultimate triumph that God assures to the righteous and the faithful, even as worldly injustice and cruelty seem to prevail.

Disputes over succession, pitting religious and political claims against one another, took a dramatic turn in the eighth century. Effective leadership from another branch of the Prophet's family emerged which managed to bring together numerous geographically dispersed opposition movements into a victorious force that finally overthrew the caliphs of Damascus. In 750 they established their own dynasty in Baghdad. This new caliphate of the Abbasids took its name from an uncle of the Prophet whose descendants alleged that the mantle of authority had been passed to them. The Abbasids did not, however, succeed in imposing their rule on all regions of the Islamic realm. In an area of Spain known by its Arabic name, *Andalus,* the Ummayads continued to rule for three more centuries, although they did not immediately assume the title of caliph. With its capital in Cordoba, Andalus became celebrated in the later Middle Ages for its openness and tolerance, which contributed to the flowering of an exceptionally rich intellectual and artistic culture involving Christians and Jews as well as Muslims.

The Abbasid dynasty survived for five hundred years, until it succumbed in 1258 to invading Mongol armies. This era is often regarded as the golden age of Islamic art, literature, and learning. At the dynasty's peak, Abbasid rulers presided over splendid courts as enlightened patrons of learning. In the advanced schools they sponsored, ancient texts of the Greeks, the Persians, and even some from India and China were studied, translated, and commented upon, creating a cultural ferment that produced remarkable advances in many scientific disciplines. There were also important developments in branches of study specific

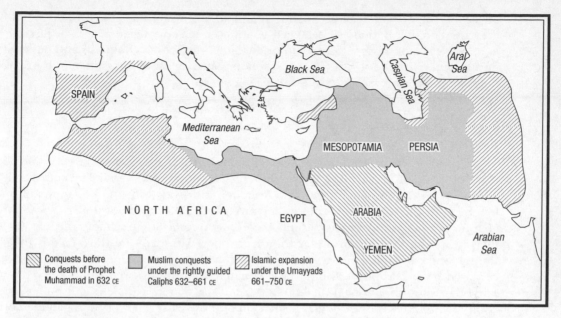

Figure 12–2 Islamic expansion after the death of Muhammad to A.D. 750.

to Islam, dealing with the interpretation of the Qur'an, the codification of law, and philosophical questions such as the relationship between faith and reason. Many technical terms and some familiar words in English associated with geography, mathematics, astronomy, or medicine derive from Arabic, such as algebra, alcohol, cipher, syrup, safari, and zenith.

The final collapse of the Abbasid Empire was preceded by a long decline marked by an increasing fragmentation of the political unity. Muslim rulers representing a variety of religious orientations, local circumstances, and ethnic groups, took control of different regions for long or short periods. In the east waves of Turkish tribes continued to migrate into the heartland of the Abbasid realm. The Turkish tribe known as the *Seljuks* effectively established themselves as the rulers of the eastern provinces by the middle of the eleventh century. Their leaders adopted the title of **sultan** or "holder of power," while leaving the caliph as a figurehead on the throne. Despite constant struggles among military elites, a rich cultural community was taking shape, concentrated in major urban centers, marked by a synthesis of Persian, Semitic, and Hellenistic traditions, and spread through the linguistic medium of Arabic.

But then came the crusades. The steady pressure from aggressive Turkish tribesmen encroaching upon the borders of the Byzantine Empire in Anatolia (modern-day central Turkey) was a major factor leading to the **crusades**, the long series of holy wars launched by Western Christians to recapture what Christians still regarded as the Holy Land (Chapter 14). The crusades created several small Christian states in Palestine and Syria that lasted from 1099 to 1291, though Jerusalem itself was reconquered by Saladdin in 1187.

The conduct of the crusaders included several notorious instances of destruction and brutality which today are difficult for us understand, much less justify. Though the immediate Muslim experience of crusader rule was not entirely negative, the long-term legacy has been bitter. For contemporary Muslims opposed to what they see as harmful Western influences on Islam, the crusades are an inviting template for Western aggression in general. When they are seen in full historical perspective, however, the crusades appear to be just one phase in a long cycle of warfare that began prior to the initial Arab conquests and has continued into the modern era of Western colonial dominance. History shows that both protagonists have had their turns as aggressors and as defenders.

THE QUR'AN AND THE SUNNA

The Qur'an is the sacred book of Islam. It consists of the revelations given to Muhammad from the time of his call until his death in 632, a period of 23 years. The entire collection, about four-fifths the size of the New Testament, is divided into 114 chapters of unequal length, with the longest ones at the beginning and the shortest at the end. An individual chapter of the Qur'an is called a **sura**. According to some Sunni schools, the text was assembled in its canonical form under the direction of Uthman, the third caliph (644–656), though Shi'a and many Sunni scholars agree that the Quran was completely assembled and reviewed by the Prophet during his last year, and that Ali reviewed and preserved it on the same day when the Prophet died. Otherwise, it was feared, parts of the Prophet's message could be lost after the deaths and dispersion of those early followers who had memorized it or written down bits of what they had heard from Muhammad. According to some traditions, the Prophet had ten scribes who wrote down the Qur'anic text per his instructions whenever a new verse was revealed. Thus, Shi'a Muslims believe that the Qur'an contains no errors in transcription.

The language of the Qur'an is Arabic. More precisely, it is a version of an ancient Semitic tongue that has since been codified by grammarians and established as the pure classical form of the Arabic language. Prior to the Qur'an, we know of only a few texts written or translated in Arabic. The sixth-century, non-canonical Arabic Gospel of the Infancy of the Savior is one example (available at www.newadvent.org/fathers/0806.htm). Thus among the benefits of preserving the written Qur'an was the way it stimulated improvements in the primitive writing system of the Arabic language, which later became the favored idiom for an immense scholarly and literary tradition.

Muslims understand the Qur'an to be the word of God in a different sense than most Christians and Jews view their own scriptures. Whereas Christians and Jews understand the written scriptures to be the word of God, most also recognize that its individual books were written by different authors at different times and in different places. By contrast, in Muslims' view, the Qur'an was "sent down" as divine speech (Qur'an 16:102). Salafi Muslims (see the following section on Salafism) believe that it is co-eternal with God, the creator. However, Shi'a and many Sunnis believe that the Qur'an was created and not co-eternal with God. The Qur'an itself describes its origin and purpose in these terms: "We have sent a Messenger from among you to convey our verses to you and to cleanse you and to teach you the Book and the wisdom and what you did not know" (Qur'an 2:151). The pronoun "we" refers to Allah, the almighty God.

Against those who would say that Muhammad or the compilers of the Qur'an borrowed from other religious literature of the time, Muslims contend that that the Prophet was illiterate and therefore uninformed about the contents of previous religious traditions. The revelations he related were not his but came directly from God, who also preserved him from error (Qur'an 4:113). When the Prophet was challenged to perform a miracle as proof of his sacred mission as God's messenger, the Qur'an responds that its verses are themselves miraculous (10:38), a theme that led later Muslims to formulate the doctrine of the literary and artistic "unsurpassability" of the Qur'an. In the same spirit, Muslims regard the Qur'an as a singularly moving and inspiring text whose real meaning, force, and beauty can only be appreciated in the original Arabic. All translations of this holy book are, therefore, considered to be mere interpretations. Only the Arabic recitation of the Qur'an is authentic.

The main themes of the Qur'an largely recapitulate many of the recognized moral teachings of the Jewish and Christian scriptures. For example, like the Bible's Ten Commandments, the Qur'an identifies humanity's greatest sin as idolatry, meaning worshiping anything else but God. The usual Qur'anic term for God is *Allah*, and Muslims recognize this as the same God worshipped by Jews and Christians. Frequently, indeed at the start of virtually every sura, the name of God is invoked, and God is described as merciful and compassionate. However, Muslims regard the scriptures of Christians and Jews, who are referred to in the Qur'an as "people of the book," as having been distorted and corrupted since the time when they were revealed, leaving the Qur'an alone as the pure, true, final, and definitive message from God to humanity (Qur'an 4:46 ff).

The Qur'an repeatedly calls upon believers to trust in God and to obey his commands. These injunctions are often accompanied by warnings of coming judgment, as well as positive examples of righteousness from the past, especially stories involving such figures as Abraham, Noah, Moses, Joseph, and Jesus. Muslims regard Jesus as a great prophet and a forerunner of Muhammad, but they firmly reject Christians' view that he is the son of God and deny such central Christian beliefs as the incarnation, the crucifixion, and the resurrection. Like Christians, they venerate Mary as the virgin mother of Jesus. In the Qur'an, the sura entitled "Maryam" describes the birth of John the Baptist, the annunciation of the angel Gabriel to Mary, and the nativity of Jesus as miraculous events. However, the Qur'anic version of some of these stories differs substantially from what is related in the gospels (Qur'an 19:1–36; cf. Matt 1:1–2:23, Luke 1:1–2:52).

In addition to the word of God that is the Qur'an, Muslims also revere the Prophet himself as a source of legislation but not revelation, with Shi'a believing that what he legislates is commanded by God. They regard his words and deeds as normative such that later generations should seek to know them and act accordingly. This exemplary character of Muhammad's life is explicitly affirmed by the Qur'an: "You have in the Messenger of God an excellent pattern of conduct for the one who places his hope in God and the Last Day and remembers God frequently" (Qur'an 33:21). The revelations that form the sacred book of the Qur'an came only at sporadic intervals, usually in response to a particular incident or question, but the things the Prophet said and did apart from these occasions also have inestimable value in the eyes of believers. Hence the accounts of his speech and behavior, known as the *Sunna* (meaning "tradition, customary practice"), were later collected, preserved, classified, and subjected to study.

The process of amassing these reports about the Prophet's words and deeds was a long and complicated task for the early Muslim community. At first, those in decision-making positions who had lived close to the Prophet tended to approach new problems with a certain freedom, based on their strong confidence that they were faithful to his teachings. As Islam spread, especially among non-Arabs, and as the founding generation disappeared, legal rulings that could be attributed to a prior teaching or practice of Muhammad naturally grew in prestige. As a result, the number of sayings and stories in circulation that were said to derive from Muhammad began to mount rapidly. Many of these were of questionable authenticity. Recognizing the threat this posed to the integrity of both the religion and the society, scholars tried to determine the relative validity of these reports. Eventually their labors produced several authoritative collections of what are called in Arabic the **hadith,** meaning individual accounts of the Prophet's remarks or behavior. But they also generated a refined methodology for interpreting this material, which even today requires specialized training.

During the late eighth and ninth centuries when the Sunna were being consolidated, the Muslim world was preoccupied with a number of other competing claims regarding revelation, doctrine, law, and the proper principles for their interpretation. Only toward the beginning of the tenth century did a relatively stable orthodoxy emerge as various formal schools of Muslim thought became more clearly defined. The spread of this consensus was followed by the increasing influence of the class of religious and legal scholars, collectively known as **ulama** ("those who are learned"), who were trained in the great mosque-colleges or **madrasas,** such as the renowned Nizamiyya in Baghdad, the Qarawiyyin of Fez, and the Azhar in Cairo.

For Sunnis, the growth of a comprehensive body of Muslim case law meant that the type of "free reasoning" or *ijtihad,* which earlier scholars had used to make legal decisions, was now considered illegitimate. This, in turn, led to what came to be known as the "closing of the door of *ijtihad,*" which meant that the range of opinions permitted to a jurist was now more severely limited. As a result, in the words of Fazlur Rahman, "throughout the medieval centuries, the law, definite and defined, was cast like a shell over the Community" (1979, 79), meaning that there was little room for interpretation of Muslim law. Only in the modern era, under mounting pressures from within and outside of Sunni Muslim communities, has this issue of fundamental legal reform again become a burning question at the center of Islamic self-scrutiny. By contrast, Shi'a Muslims never allowed the door of *ijtihad* to be closed, as Shi'a schools continued to produce *mujathids* (legal scholars) from the time of Imam Ali until today.

LAW, LIFE, AND SPIRITUALITY

Pious Muslims express their faith, that is, seek to submit to God, by obeying a code of law known as the **Shari'a**. This word, originally meaning "the path that leads to water," conveys the sense of an entire way of life that extends to every sphere of human endeavor, including the physical, social, political, mental, and ethical dimensions of one's life. Based ultimately on the Qur'an and the Sunna, the Shari'a consists of a vast body of ritual, moral, and legal materials considered to be applicable to all persons in all circumstances. Sunni Muslims consider the most basic obligations of Islam to be summarized in what are called the **five pillars,** although the implications of these principles extend much more broadly than their narrow literal expression.

The first pillar is the profession of faith, **shahada:** "There is no god but God, and Muhammad is the Prophet of God." In the classic understanding, the recitation of this phrase under proper conditions was considered sufficient to indicate conversion to this faith. Islam does not have a system of sacraments, like Baptism, in the manner understood by Christians, but it does recognize important life events from birth to death through the assumption of appropriate rights and duties ordained by God's law. For example, marriage is an important life event. Among Muslims it involves a solemn legal contract, but there is no further religious ceremony comparable to the Christian wedding celebration.

The second pillar, *salah,* "prayer," obliges Muslims to perform a series of ritual actions five times in each twenty-four hour period, namely at dawn, noon, afternoon, sunset, and nightfall. Muslims may do this practically anywhere, although a well-known *hadith* of the Prophet declares that it is much better to pray collectively than alone. For this reason, Muslims often gather in a mosque or somewhere else in order to pray together. Although the practicalities of schedule and convenience often play a large role in how and when observant Muslims follow this command, in most Muslim societies they have regular reminders in the voice of the *muezzin* (the person responsible for making the call to prayer), whether on broadcast media or from loudspeakers mounted on minarets (towers located on or near mosques). Of course, this formal obligatory daily prayer, which is preceded by a ritual washing and carried out in a precisely regulated fashion, is not the only form of prayer Muslims practice—they have an abundance of private devotions that also have a rich history.

Related to this second pillar is another duty incumbent particularly upon adult males: to attend, if possible, the Friday noon prayer service, which includes a sermon and is conducted in a mosque that is specifically designated for this purpose. In the Islamic tradition, the right to pronounce this Friday sermon belonged to the caliph and those whom he delegated to preach it in his place. Because the caliph's principal role was ruler, this speech from the mosque's pulpit (a raised platform that is used for preaching) gradually evolved into an occasion for political and social as well as religious commentary. Today the proper use of this forum has become a controversial topic in many places, leading many Muslim governments to implement measures that require preachers to obtain licenses or otherwise submit to restrictions on their speech before congregations. It might also be noted that although Friday is the "day of assembly" for Muslims, we should not think of it as a Sabbath or a day of rest. Nevertheless, in modern times most countries with large Muslim majorities tend to treat Friday as the "weekend" when official offices and schools are closed.

The third pillar, *sawm,* or fasting, requires Muslims who are of age and healthy to abstain from all food and drink from sunrise to sunset during the holy month of Ramadan. This kind of fasting, unlike parallel practices among Christians and Jews, does not represent an expression of penance or repentance. Rather, it is explained as a discipline that promotes meditation, self-control, and solidarity among believers. Many also argue that it has health benefits. Ramadan is typically a time of celebration, when life slows down, and family and friends gather after sunset to visit and to share elaborate holiday meals with treats for the children. Muslims believe that it was during Ramadan that Muhammad first received his call and thus they revere it as the time when the first verses of the Qur'an were revealed. This link between the Qur'an and Ramadan is also visible in the popular devotion associated with the "night of power" (Qur'an 97:1–5), which comes toward the end of the month. On this night Muslims are urged to pray with special fervor since God's blessings are said to be especially abundant.

The fourth pillar, almsgiving or *zakat,* obliges Muslims to give of their wealth, whether it be great or small, to sustain those in need, including the disadvantaged, the destitute, and those who must depend on the generosity of others. Questions about how much one should give and under what conditions have been addressed in many Muslim legal treatises over the centuries. In modern times some Muslim governments have sought to formalize charity by imposing a sort of charity tax, although many Muslims disapprove of this imposition as an intrusion upon their freedom to give as they feel called by God.

The fifth pillar, the obligation to perform the pilgrimage to Mecca, only applies to Muslims who have the means to do so, that is, who can afford the costs and whose health and personal circumstances allow it. The pilgrimage, or *haj,* is properly carried out in the twelfth and final month of the Islamic lunar calendar. At the start of this month, Muslims numbering in the hundreds of thousands converge on the Hijaz, the mountainous region that runs along the Red Sea coast in Saudi Arabia. When they arrive in Mecca, they are required to perform a series of prescribed rituals over a period of several days in and around the city. At the conclusion of the *haj*, on the tenth day of the month, Muslims throughout the world join in prayer with those at the sacred site to celebrate the Feast of the Sacrifice, which commemorates Abraham's willingness to sacrifice his son in obedience to God's command. This feast is known by various names, but Eid al-Adha or Adha Eid are common ones. It is one of the two great holy days in the Muslim year, the other one being Eid al-Fitr, which is celebrated at the end of Ramadan.

Shi'a Muslims share the same tenets of Islam, but they have a different method of categorizing them. Instead of talking about the pillars of Islam, they talk about the "Roots of Faith" and "Branches of Religion." The "Roots of Faith" include the *shahada,* or Oneness of God, Prophethood, The Day of Judgment, Imamate (the belief that an imam must exist at all times), and the Justice of God. The Branches of Religion include the same rituals practiced by Sunni Muslims, but Shi'a Muslims add *khums,* which is the payment of one-fifth of one's annual surplus income to specific causes, and a principle described as "ordering good and forbidding evil."

In addition to the pillars of Islam, which constitute the moral foundation of the Muslim community, a sixth obligation is sometimes added by the Salafi school of thought, namely **jihad,** meaning "exertion or struggle in the way of God." The Islamic tradition has surrounded this obligation with an extensive array of legal opinions that spell out the grounds for how, when, by whom, and against whom the legal enactment of this Qur'anic injunction may be invoked. Muslim doctrine on *jihad* is thus complex and varied: It was constantly evolving in response to changing conditions. It is also important to remember that the doctrine did not always reflect actual practice.

Jihad has been understood in more spiritual terms as the individual Muslim's inner struggle to resist temptation and practice virtue—"the greater *jihad,*" as it is traditionally called, in contrast to "the lesser *jihad*" of actual fighting. But some scholars argue that there is no distinction. The remarkable early conquests of Islam do not seem fully explainable unless we recognize that they were a form of missionary warfare: not the forcible conversion of the conquered to Islam, but the military extension of Islamic sovereignty, the expansion of the Abode of Islam (*dar al-Islam*). *Jihad* was also invoked for defensive warfare, as it was in the twelfth century in response to the Western crusades or in modern times in the face of what is perceived as hostile aggression by so-called unbelievers, such as carried out by the United States, Israel, or the Philippines. However, contemporary Muslims understandably emphasize the more spiritual and internal understandings of *jihad* over its historically more dominant interpretation as divinely ordained warfare.

The elaboration of the vast and diffuse legal system that makes up Shari'a, or Islamic law, stands as one of the most impressive intellectual achievements of medieval Islam. But that system operated for the most part in an isolated and refined context that has grown increasingly remote from ordinary believers in today's world. Shari'a retains many archaic features that leave it subject to widely variant interpretations without providing practical procedures for resolving them. Thus it functions more as a moral ideal than as a solid and practical basis for governing, like the civil and criminal codes that form the rule of law in modern liberal democracies. The one significant exception concerns disputes over personal status, that is, cases involving such matters as marriage, inheritance, the status and rights of women, and sexual morality—areas in which Western democracies have tended to differ most conspicuously from Shari'a governed societies. For these areas of behavior, many Muslim countries convene special religious courts to issue juridical rulings on the basis of tradition.

Against the legalism and sometimes sterile argumentation that characterized the expansion of Shari'a, Islam also saw the development of a spiritual and devotional movement known as **Sufism.** When the movement began in the late ninth and early tenth centuries, Sufis, including some women as well as men, tended to be ascetics (people who renounce worldly desires and pursuits) and holy wanderers, who placed an absolute trust in God at the center of their lives. In time, they developed a substantial body of teachings, which exalted detachment, voluntary poverty, purity of heart, and self-denial as the path to a loving relationship with God. Communities of these sacred seekers began to form and to grow, challenging the official learned establishment, as they called upon believers to prefer inner joy over conformity to external norms.

Sufis in time developed an extensive body of spiritual treatises and literary works of their own. This literature has enjoyed lasting popularity among Muslims of all social classes, although its appeal has been especially marked among the usually uneducated Masses. In many parts of the Islamic world, including West Africa, the Indian subcontinent, central Asia, and Indonesia, the spread of Sufism during the post-classical period (after the tenth century) occurred largely through the missionary activity and example of Sufis, who typically organized believers into mystical brotherhoods that often had political and economic as well as spiritual foundations. Some Islamic military movements have also incorporated mystical elements and organizational features resembling Sufi orders, such as occurred in the case of the so-called Mahdi Uprising of late 19th-century Sudan.

The tremendous scope and impact of these popular Sufi associations was due, in large measure, to the way they adapted the teachings of the Prophet to existing social structures and encouraged local cultures to give voice to Islamic values in their own native languages and idioms, not only in practical affairs, but in poetry, song, and dance. Thus Sufism produced some of Islam's most inspiring figures, including such giants as the poet Jalal ad-din Rumi, (1207–1273) sometimes called "the Persian Qur'an," whose followers founded the mystic religious order known as the "whirling dervishes," still centered in Konya, in present-day Turkey. Visionaries with roots in Sufism continue to have their impact in the contemporary world, as, for example, Muhammad Iqbal (1873–1938), the scholar and poet who is revered as the spiritual father of modern Pakistan.

"Vision of a New World" by Muhammad Iqbal
There is a world still lost in our hearts,
A world that still waits for the call of 'Rise?'
A world without distinctions of blood and colour,
Where evening shines brighter
Than morning in the West;
A world purged of sultan and slave,
Boundless as a believer's heart;
A glorious world, which had its seed cast
Into 'Umar's soul by a single holy look;
An eternal world, but one whose events are always new,
Ever new the fruit of its master principles;
Within, it is not afflicted with change,
But outward change is occurring every moment.

See, that world is inside you!
I will tell you what its master principles are . . .
     (J N 539–40 [655]; Mir 2000, 126)

Three short poems by Jalal ad-din Rumi
This moment this love comes to rest in me,
many beings into one being.
In one wheat grain a thousand sheaf stacks.
Inside the needle's eye a turning night of starts.
     (Barks 1995, 278)

I am so small I can barely be seen.
How can this great love be inside me?

Look at your eyes. They are small,
But they see enormous things.
     (Barks 1995, 279)

The sun is love. The lover,
a speck circling the sun.
A Spring wind moves to dance
any branch that isn't dead.
     (Barks 1995, 280)

Sufism has its appeal among both Sunni and Shi'a Muslims today. However, among the largest group of Shi'a, known as the Twelvers, certain aspects of this mystical tradition have taken on a new importance as a result of recent political developments, notably the triumph of the Iranian Ayatollah Khomeini and the establishment of the Islamic Republic of Iran in 1979. This branch of Shi'ism gets its name from their teaching concerning the twelve imams in the line of divinely sanctioned rulers, going back to the caliph Ali, cousin and son-in-law of Muhammad. Two principles form the foundation for their teaching about the necessity of an infallible guide who can only be assigned by God: (1) the message of Islam was entirely revealed by Allah to Muhammad; (2) justice is one of the essential attributes of God.

According to the Twelvers, God ordained that this infallible guide would serve as an example for humankind concerning their conduct so that they could become perfect examples of what it means to live God's message to its fullest extent. Otherwise, they believe, it would be unjust for God to expect fallible humans to fully understand and live God's message. Based on this teaching, Twelvers rejected the authority of the first three caliphs, since they were not assigned by God or named by Muhammad. As a result, the Twelvers developed unique interpretations of history, law, the Quran, and the Sunna of the Prophet. However, this also led to their continuous persecution by the Sunni majority until the advent of the Shi'a revolution in Iran.

ART AND ARCHITECTURE

As the art and architecture that are characteristic of Islam have tended to draw inspiration from older traditions already familiar to communities that were adopting the new religion, Muslim motifs have often brought forth fascinating adaptations and innovations. Given that

Figure 12–3 Photo of the Sankore Mosque in Timbuktu built in the fourteenth century.

Islamic public worship requires a large open space, facing the empty niche marking the direction of the Ka'ba, basic design tends to emphasize a bold simplicity augmented by a subtle and often exquisite décor. During its period of initial expansion, many Muslim conquerors converted churches, synagogues, and temples into mosques, absorbing existing aesthetic heritages into the artistic repertory of the new *umma* (Muslim community).

Two examples of former churches that were later transformed into mosques are the great Umayyad Mosque in Damascus and the Hagia Sophia in Istanbul (now a museum; see Figure 11–1 on page 197). Both of these monuments, in their own way, became prototypes for subsequent traditions of mosque design. Similarly, in Mughal India, which reached its peak in the early eighteenth century, mosques resonated with stylistic features echoing Hindu and Buddhist temples, while mosques in China were built with multi-tiered roofs reminiscent of a pagoda. Likewise, thick mud-brick walls and conical towers gave the contours to the great Sankore Mosque in Timbuktu (in modern-day Mali in West Africa).

Of course, mosques are not the only significant structures that drew upon the skills of Islamic builders and craftsmen. Palaces, schools, bazaars, and perhaps most imaginatively, tomb monuments have also brought forth masterpieces reflecting a particular religious sensibility. The Taj Mahal, begun in 1632 on the banks of the Jumna River in northern India, was constructed by Shah Jahan, then ruler of Hindustan, as a memorial for his deceased wife. Abounding in Qur'anic inscriptions, this complex is probably the best known example of an extensive tradition of mausoleums and stately cenotaphs (symbolic tombs without a body) spanning the vast reaches of the Muslim world. By its ingenious integration of a soaring lightness derived from solid stone with flowering gardens and crystalline pools, the Taj Mahal conjures up the splendors of *A Thousand and One Arabian Nights*, if not a vision of paradise as evoked by the Qur'an (18:31).

Today, supported by the new wealth of several oil-rich Gulf states and by the initiative of planners employing advanced building techniques, an impressive wave of contemporary mosque construction has begun which include striking examples in many Western cities. Recently, for instance, an Islamic Cultural Center, including the largest mosque in Europe, opened in Rome, which displays a number of striking features resulting from

Figure 12–4 Photo of the Taj Mahal.

Figure 12–5 Marble mosaic detail from courtyard wall of Umayyad mosque, Damascus, Syria, which was built and remodeled between seventh and fourteenth centuries. Photo by Carol Lahurd.

Figure 12–6 Calligraphic rendering of the Islamic statement of faith, in the shape of mosque towers, also called minarets.

the collaboration of Italian and Iraqi architects. It blends elegant cupolas (domes) with intersecting vaults and graceful arches into an angular four-sided structure that connotes the gesture of hands open in prayer.

Muslim art is known to avoid pictorial representation, especially of human forms, although this prohibition is not explicitly stated in the Qur'an and has not always been observed by all Muslim artists, notably among classical Persian and Mughal painters and manuscript illustrators. Nevertheless, the prevailing genius of Islamic decorative expression, which extends to household furnishings and fabrics, as well as ceremonial objects, has been most elaborated in ornate geometric patterns and especially calligraphy. The Arabic alphabet with its flowing forms and latitude for spatial variation is abundantly suited for this sort of visual embellishment. The related motif known as *arabesque* consists of extravagant, seemingly endless intertwining lines, often producing mirror effects and based on sophisticated mathematical rules. It has long been admired and often borrowed by graphic artists working in other traditions.

THE CHALLENGE OF THE MODERN WORLD

Most historians regard the sixteenth century as the critical period of transition for the Islamic world. It was at this time that the expanding Ottoman Empire reached its pinnacle and was about to begin its slow decline. Certain features of Ottoman governance, such as the tendency to allow local non-Turkish populations to manage their own internal affairs as long as they paid the required tribute and complied with policies imposed by the bureaucratic and military elites, set the stage for a steady deterioration in the cohesion of the empire. Also, a sense of unity based on loyalty to a religiously sanctioned political order grew weaker as pious Muslims increasingly perceived the Sultan and his court as paying little more than lip-service to Islam. Hence pressures for regional autonomy or national liberation movements began to gain momentum, especially after Napoleon's successful invasion of Egypt in 1798. It became increasingly difficult for the Ottomans to retain their hold over the territories they continued to reckon as their own.

Another important contributing factor in the decline of the Ottoman Empire, which at that time controlled the southern and eastern portions of the Mediterranean basin, was that it began to fall ever further behind the lands of the northern and western side of this sea in regard to exploration, wealth, technology, military power, and political prowess. The Renaissance, the Reformation, and Counter-Reformation; the new trade routes pioneered by Spanish and Portuguese sailors; the development of modern science; and finally Europe's industrial revolution, with its formidable demographic and military implications, led to a widening gap in power and influence between Muslim and non-Muslim territories. The Ottoman Empire became the "sick man of Europe," a term already in circulation in the 1850s.

Muslim reactions to the decline of the Ottoman Empire were varied but forceful. Some sought to secede and declare their independence from the Ottoman Empire. Others were intent on reforming and modernizing the empire's core institutions to make it more similar to and competitive with the advanced nations of Europe and thus resistant to further fragmentation. Such modernizers tended to be secular in their outlook. One movement, however, saw a radical religious revival as the only answer. It began in the 1740s in the remote eastern part of the land of the Prophet's birth, but would eventually spread to have an exceptionally dramatic impact. Muhammad ibn 'Abd al-Wahhab preached a puritanical form of Islam that sought to eliminate what he regarded as unorthodox "innovations" in the practice of religion due to centuries of corrupt legal learning and misguided piety.

Arguing for a return to the strict observation of Islam as lived by the Prophet and his first companions, this movement is sometimes called Wahhabism, from the name of its founder, but its adherents prefer the term **Salafism.** The term *Salafi* derives from an Arabic word that means "predecessors" or "early generations," after the fact that they look to the first three caliphs of Islam for their inspiration and guidance. Salafi Muslims eventually triumphed politically when its military wing, the Saudis, finally came to power in a newly independent Arabia in the 1920s. It saw the influence of its ideas spread ever further through the agenda of similarly inspired organizations including the Muslim Brotherhood of Egypt, the Jama'at e Islami in Pakistan and India, and the Taliban of Afghanistan. The goal of such groups has been to establish a new Islamic order by seizing political power and imposing their interpretation of Shari'a on the people.

After the First World War (1914–1920), the last remnants of the shrinking Ottoman Empire were carved up, reducing it finally to the modern state of Turkey. While much could be said about the crises facing Islam in this post-Ottoman period, a bare summary of three central issues will have to suffice. The first issue centers on the question of authority or, in political terms, legitimacy—How does a government establish legitimacy as judged by Muslim standards? Here Muslims were confronted with the challenge of rediscovering a consensus regarding the tensions between sacred and secular claims to power and privilege. Thus, controversies and even outright conflicts have arisen over the meaning of patriotism, the desirability of democracy, the possibility of equality, and the permissibility of implementing reforms or calling for revolutions that inevitably entail division and violence.

The second problem calls traditional gender relations into question. Historically speaking, most Muslim societies have long upheld various degrees of formal gender segregation between adult women and men who are not family members. But today many, most notably women, consider such practices as wholly unacceptable or in need of significant revision. Even so, others have argued for a return to the veil (*hijab*), claiming not only that it is a moral obligation but that it has certain social and political benefits as well, such as allowing women to publicly assert their religious identity or effectively protecting them from unwanted contact.

Many scholars who have labored over this issue have concluded that the classical justifications (especially if used to support the most drastic forms of female seclusion), including the Qur'anic texts that are frequently invoked in favor of women's segregation, have been wrongly interpreted and need to be corrected. For instance, while the Qur'an at one point famously allows men to take up to four wives, many who oppose polygamy point out that the same verse later adds that if a man cannot deal equally with all his wives, he should marry only one (Qur'an 4:3). They go on to note that the following admonition appears later in the same *sura:* "However you may try, you will never be able to treat your wives equally" (Qur'an 4:129). Given that both of these verses appear in the Qur'an, they argue, it is clear that God intended monogamy to be the only proper form of marriage. Of course not all Muslims would agree with this interpretation. However, on the basis of such arguments, a number of Muslim countries have introduced strict limits on certain traditional male prerogatives with respect to marriage and divorce or have prohibited polygamy altogether.

A third broad challenge facing today's Muslims are the consequences of globalization. Those who live outside of heavily Muslim countries struggle with countless complicated problems that have no clear solution in traditional Islamic sources and which prompt extensive disagreements. The economic practices of Western countries provide a good example. Islamic law has strict prohibitions against the collection or payment of interest, which extends to the use of most banking services, including loans and mortgages. Although some financial institutions have inaugurated a procedure known as "Islamic banking," which tries to work within Islamic law by setting up a commercial partnership for the transaction of money rather than a depository relationship, it has not satisfied the ethical concerns of observant Muslims or met the practical requirements of many who have no real choice but to function within the system of modern market-based capitalism.

Globalization is having an impact on many other aspects of traditional Muslim life, as well. For example, Western notions of personal freedom and individualism contrast sharply with Muslim understandings of communal and familial responsibility and the distinction between public and private activities. Likewise, many traditional Muslims struggle to reconcile Western ideals of tolerance with practices that they regard as categorically unacceptable, such as blasphemy, and with the degree of obligation owed to others who make claims in the name of race, nation, religion, sexual orientation, or political conviction. Such are the challenges of adapting some of the more archaic features of Shari'a law to the realities of the modern world.

CHRISTIAN–MUSLIM DIALOGUE

Today a responsible account of the Christian theological tradition cannot ignore Islam nor should it. Together with Jews and Christians, they are, to use the words of the Qur'an, one of the three great "peoples of the Book." The present chapter has provided a brief introduction to Muslim history, belief, and practice. Because of the mistrust and conflict that have so often marked Christian–Muslim interaction, the approach has tried to be as impartial as possible.

The effort to be impartial should not be misunderstood, however, as a false religious "neutrality," which would be a caricature of both Islam and Christianity. Rather, it reflects a necessary element of true religious dialogue—to respect the truth of the other as genuine and authentic in its own right. Admittedly, it was not always thus: In his *Divine Comedy*, Dante placed Muhammad in hell, as a heretic (*Inferno* XXVIII, 19–42), and medieval Christians generally treated Islam as a Christian heresy. However, the *Dogmatic Constitution on the Church* issued by the Second Vatican Council (1964) dramatically moderated this purely hostile estimate of Islam when it stated: "But the plan of salvation also embraces those who acknowledge the Creator, and among those the Muslims are first; they profess to hold the faith of Abraham and along with us they worship the one merciful God who will judge humanity on the last day" (§16, Tanner 1990, 2.861).

Since Vatican II, both popes John Paul II and Benedict XVI have stressed the importance of dialogue between Muslims and Christians. At his general audience of May 5, 1999, Pope John Paul II spoke these words: "We Christians joyfully recognize the religious values we have in common with Islam. Today, I would like to repeat what I said to young Muslims some years ago in Casablanca: 'We believe in the same God, the one God, the living God, the God who created the world and brings his creatures to their perfection'" (John Paul II, General Audience, 1999).

Some years earlier, John Paul II had said to the religious leaders in Jakarta, Indonesia,

> Respectful dialogue with others also enables us to be enriched by their insights, challenged by their questions and impelled to deepen our knowledge of the truth. Far from stifling dialogue or rendering it superfluous, a commitment to the truth of one's religious tradition by its very nature makes dialogue with others both necessary and fruitful. (John Paul II, Speeches, 1989)

Likewise, Pope Benedict XVI has stressed the urgency of dialogue with Islam. In his address to Muslim representatives in Cologne, Germany, on August 20, 2005, he said:

> Christians and Muslims, we must face together the many challenges of our time. There is no room for apathy and disengagement, and even less for partiality and sectarianism. We must not yield to fear and pessimism. Rather, we must cultivate optimism and hope. Interreligious and intercultural dialogues between Christians and Muslims cannot be reduced to an optional extra. It is in fact a vital necessity, on which in large measure our future depends. (Benedict XVI, Speeches, 2005)

The Vatican, the National Council of Bishops of the U.S.A., and many dioceses continue to sponsor dialogue between groups of Muslims and Christians, some of which have been going on for decades.

Of course, Catholic Christians are not the only ones who have been concerned with Muslim–Christian dialogue. For example, the World Council of Churches, in its 2002 Report on an International Consultation on "Christians and Muslims in Dialogue and Beyond," stressed the importance of informed dialogue as an avenue for peace, saying,

> As Muslims and Christians we welcome and affirm the fact of religious and cultural diversity as God's will. We particularly stress the role of education by and for our communities as a key arena in which to create the trust and mutual understanding which are essential to resist attempts to exploit religious differences for destructive ends. (World Council of Churches, 2002)

Likewise, in 2007, the Evangelical Lutheran Church in America issued an online primer on interreligious dialogue entitled *Windows for Understanding: Jewish–Muslim–Lutheran Relations*, which describes a number of topics concerning which Jews, Muslims, and Christians can learn from one another. Here is a brief commentary on the nature of the human person:

> Our Lutheran and biblical understanding of human nature is in tension with the "optimistic" perspective of both Judaism and Islam that God's law and guidance are sufficient to enable us to repent and be reconciled with God. Consequently, our Lutheran understanding counsels us against a "works righteousness" mindset. However, Lutherans can learn from their Jewish and Muslim partners to value more fully the role of God's guidance in the lives of Christians who have been justified by God's grace and to acknowledge that role in the lives of faithful religious others. (Evangelical Lutheran Church in America, 2007)

Finally, a recent statement by the Executive Committee of the World Methodist Council entitled, "Wesleyan/Methodist Witness in Christian and Islamic Cultures," outlines the commonalities and differences between Christianity and Islam and calls for the worldwide Methodist Church to witness to the gospel in the following four ways:

> First, to lovingly accept Muslim brothers and sisters as persons of faith; second, to stand firm against violence and hatred in all its forms; third, to stand with persons who are being persecuted and are suffering for their faith; and fourth, trusting in the power and guidance of the Holy Spirit, to share with all persons, including Muslims, the love and grace of our Lord Jesus Christ through our words, deeds and signs by the power of the Holy Spirit, and invite them into life-changing relationships with God through Christ. (Executive Committee of the World Methodist Council, 2002)

These are just a few examples of worldwide efforts to foster Muslim–Christian dialogue.

Certainly the war in Iraq has made dialogue between Muslims and Christians much more difficult in recent years, because of hateful stereotypes presented by the media on both sides of the conflict. All wars are polarizing, almost by definition. This war is no exception, and so extremists on both sides are increasing their harsh rhetoric against the other. Unfortunately, such behavior makes further war even more likely, but it also makes earnest and respectful dialogue between Muslim and Christian believers all the more urgent and necessary for the advancement of peace in our world today.

Key Terms

Islam	Shi'a	five pillars
Ka'ba	sultan	*shahada*
Allah	crusades	*salah*
Qu'ran	*sura*	*sawm*
hijra	Sunna	*zakat*
umma	*hadith*	*haj*
imam	*ulama*	*jihad*
caliph	*madrasa*	Sufism
Sunni	Shari'a	Salafism

Questions for Reading

1. Explain the meaning of the word *Islam*. Describe the social, political, and religious conditions that gave rise to Islam in seventh-century Arabia.

2. What were the contributions that Muhammad made to development of early Islam?

3. How and where did Islam spread during its period of expansion up to and including its "golden age" in the thirteenth century?

4. Jerusalem is a holy city for Jews and Christians. Why is it also a holy city for Muslims?

5. What is the Qur'an? What status does it have for Muslim believers? How does it compare with the Bible for Christians?

6. How would you compare the Muslim formation of an authoritative tradition beyond the Qur'an with what happened in Christianity in the second and third centuries (see Chapter 8)?

7. What are the five pillars of Islam, and how do they impact the way that Muslims live their everyday lives?

8. Describe some of the contributions that Islam has made to the arts, architecture, literature, mathematics, and medicine.

9. What are some of the social, political, and religious challenges that face Muslims today?

Works Consulted/Recommended Reading

Ahmed, Leila. *Women and Gender in Islam: Historical Roots of a Modern Debate*. New Haven, CT: Yale University, 1992.

Barks, Coleman. *The Essential Rumi*. Translated by John Moyne, A. J. Arberrry, and Reynold Nicholson. New York: HarperSanFrancisco, 1995.

Bayat, Asef. *Making Islam Democratic: Social Movements and the Post-Islamic Turn*. Stanford: Stanford University, 2007.

Benedict XVI. Meeting with Representatives of Some Muslim Communities, Cologne, Germany, August 20, 2005. www.vatican.va/holy_father/benedict_xvi/speeches/2005/august/documents/hf_ben-xvi_spe_20050820_meeting-muslims_en.html.

Bonner, Michael. *Jihad in Islamic History: Doctrines and Practices*. Princeton, NJ: Princeton University, 2006.

Cragg, Kenneth. *The Event of the Qur'an: Islam in its Scripture*. London: Allen and Unwin, 1971.

Crone, Patricia. *God's Rule: Government and Islam. Six Centuries of Medieval Islamic Political Thought*. New York: Columbia University, 2004.

Esposito, John. *Islam: The Straight Path*. 3rd ed. New York: Oxford University, 1998.

Evangelical Lutheran Church in America. "Windows for Understanding: Jewish–Muslim–Lutheran Relations," 2007. http://archive.elca.org/ecumenical/interreligious/images/primer_09.01.07_rev.pdf.

Executive Committee of the World Methodist Council. "Wesleyan/Methodist Witness in Christian and Islamic Cultures." September 18, 2004. www.worldmethodist.org/IslamStatement.htm.

Firestone, Reuven. *Jihad: The Origins of Holy War in Islam*. New York: Oxford University, 1999.

Gibb, H. A. R., et al., eds. *The Encyclopedia of Islam: New Edition*. 12 vols. Boston: Brill, 1986–2004.

Hammoudi, Abdellah. *A Season in Mecca: Narrative of a Pilgrimage*. New York: Farrar, Straus and Giroux, 2006.

Hodgson, Marshall G. S. *The Venture of Islam: Conscience and History in a World Civilization*. 3 vols. Chicago: University of Chicago, 1974.

Hourani, Albert. *A History of the Arab Peoples*. Cambridge, MA: Harvard University, 1991.

John Paul II. General Audience, May 5, 1999. *L'Osservatore Romano*, May 12, 1999, English edition.

_____. Meeting with the Leaders of the Major Religious Communities of Indonesia. Jakarta, Indonesia. October 10, 1989. www.vatican.va/holy_father/john_paul_ii/speeches/1989/october/documents/hf_jp-ii_spe_19891010_capi-religiosi_en.html.

Kelsay, John, and James Turner Johnson, eds. *Just War and Jihad: Historical and Theoretical Perspectives on War and Peace in Western and Islamic Traditions*. New York: Greenwood, 1991.

McAuliffe, Jane Dammen, ed. *Encyclopedia of the Qur'an*. 6 vols. Leiden: Brill, 2001–2006.

Mir, Mustansir, ed. and trans. *Tulip in the Desert: A Selection of the Poetry of Muhammad Iqbal*. Montreal: McGill-Queen's University, 2000.

Mottahedeh, Roy. *The Mantle of the Prophet: Religion and Politics in Iran*. New York: Simon and Schuster, 1985.

Rahman, Fuzlur. *Islam*. 2nd ed. Chicago: University of Chicago, 1979.

Renard, John, ed. *Windows on the House of Islam: Muslim Sources on Spirituality and Religious Life*. Berkeley: University of California, 1998.

Tanner, Norman P. *Decrees of the Ecumenical Councils*. Vol. 2. Washington, DC: Georgetown University, 1990.

Waardenburg, Jacques. *Islam: Historical, Social, and Political Perspectives*. Berlin: Walter de Gruyter, 2002.

World Council of Churches. "2002 Report on an International Consultation on Christians and Muslims in Dialogue and Beyond." Geneva, Switzerland, October 16–18, 2002. www.wcc-coe.org/wcc/what/interreligious/octconsul-rep.html.

Chapter

CHRISTIANITY IN THE EARLY MEDIEVAL PERIOD

TIMELINE

A.D. 330–379	Life span of Basil of Caesarea, the Father of Eastern Monasticism.
A.D. 360–435	Life span of John Cassian, the Father of Western Monasticism.
A.D. 480–547	Life span of Benedict of Nursia, the founder of Benedictine monasticism.
A.D. 590	Gregory I elected pope. He is the first to style the pope as "servant of the servants of God."
c. A.D. 785	The Roman Rite, the primary form of liturgy for the Roman Catholic Church, is established.
A.D. 800	Charlemagne is crowned Emperor of the Romans by Pope Leo III, thus restoring the imperial title in the West.
A.D. 910	Count William the Pious founds a new Benedictine monastery at Cluny. Beginning of the Cluniac reform movement.
A.D. 942–1022	Life span of Symeon the New Theologian, a noted monk, abbot, theologian, and mystic of Eastern Christianity.
A.D. 1033–1109	Life span of Anselm of Canterbury, a theologian known for his "debt-satisfaction" theory of the atonement and his ontological argument for the existence of God.
A.D. 1073	Pope Gregory VII is elected pope. The eleventh-century Gregorian Reform takes its name from him.
A.D. 1075	Gregory VII drafts his *Dictatus Papae* asserting the primacy of the pope.

Chapter 13 is the first of four chapters dealing with the Western Christian tradition during the Middle Ages, meaning the roughly one thousand years between the fall of the Roman Empire in the West (476) and the Renaissance and the Protestant Reformation of the sixteenth century. They are deemed "middle" according to a common division of history into three phases: ancient, medieval (from the Latin word for "middle age"), and modern, in which modernity was understood to begin with the Renaissance and the Reformation. Recognizing that all such divisions are somewhat subjective, this textbook has preferred to divide modernity itself into two phases, with the more crucial changes taking place *after* the Reformation, in the seventeenth and eighteenth centuries (see the introduction to Part III on p. 135).

This chapter will cover the early medieval period, the sixth through the eleventh centuries. In the popular imagination this era is frequently termed the Dark Ages because of the steep decline in the standard of living amidst waves of invasions and population movement in the centuries following the end of the Roman Empire in the West. The decline was long lasting and affected all areas of life: culture, population, economy, law, government, technology, and so on. But the decline also marked a beginning: the birth of Europe, a new cultural synthesis of classical antiquity, Christianity, and the cultures of the newly converted and civilized peoples, from Ireland to Russia, and from Scandinavia to Spain. Europe was "born," historians agree, during the great, though short-lived cultural revival known as the Carolingian Renaissance.

This chapter explores several features of early medieval Christianity: the fall of the Roman Empire in the West and its restoration by the popes as the Holy Roman Empire; the development of monasticism; and the evolution of the papacy, specifically the pope's authority. We will also explore some of the cultural contributions of this period and some of its major theological figures.

THE HOLY ROMAN EMPIRE

The end of the ancient Roman Empire in the West was marked by great movements of peoples. Historians term these movements as migrations or invasions, depending on whether they are considered circumstantial accompaniments to the fall of the empire or its cause. After the last resident Western emperor, Romulus Augustulus, was deposed in 476, a Frankish warrior chieftain named Clovis, who converted to Christianity and was baptized in 498, collaborated with the remaining Romans to establish a Christian dynasty north of the Alps, in ancient Gaul (modern-day France). Clovis' dynasty is identified as the Merovingian kingdom, named after his grandfather Merowig. The Frankish peoples controlled considerable territory in Europe at this time, but their organizational structure was mostly tribal, with local chieftains governing smaller autonomous regions. Although the Merovingian kings attempted to create a centralized government, they were never successful in doing so. Severely weakened during the seventh century in a series of internal power struggles, the Merovingian kings finally ceded power to a leader of the major landowners in the region, Charles Martel.

Charles Martel gave his name to the Merovingians' successor dynasty, the Carolingians. He is best known for his military victory in 732–733 over the Arabs of 'Abd ar-Rahman who were approaching Tours (in modern France) on a looting raid of the wealthy shrine of St. Martin there—a battle that marked the westernmost advance of Muslim armies. Charles also led a series of campaigns in Burgundy and Aquitaine, extending Frankish dominion beyond northern Gaul. A significant feature of the Carolingian dynasty was its relationship with the

Catholic Church. With the approval of Pope Zachary (reigned 741–752), Charles Martel's son, Pippin III, forced the last of the Merovingian kings into a monastery, and in 751 was acclaimed king by the Frankish nobility and anointed by St. Boniface (see the following section), acting as the pope's legate or representative.

The papacy's role in the deposing of the Merovingians implicitly acknowledged its right to arbitrate in political struggles. The anointing of the king with oil also implied the king's quasipriestly character and connoted divine approval of his coronation. Later, at the request of Zachary's successor, Pope Stephen II (reigned 752–757), the Carolingian kings became the political protectors of the papacy as replacements for the ineffective Byzantine governor in Ravenna (northeast Italy). Pippin made good on this agreement in 754 and again in 756, when he invaded Italy to restrain the Lombards from menacing the pope. On the second trip he donated conquered Lombard land in central and northeastern Italy to St. Peter (Peter was thoroughly identified with his tomb as though he were still alive, and the pope was regarded as his vicar or spokesman); this Donation of Pippin was the beginning of the Papal State, the territory which the popes governed as their own state up until the final unification of Italy as a single nation state in 1870. (Since signing a Treaty with the Italian state in 1929, the popes have received the one square mile area in Rome called Vatican City as their sovereign territory.)

It was Pippin's son, Karolus, who became the most famous of the Carolingian rulers, known by the name Charlemagne ("Karolus the Great"). During his long reign (768–814), he had significant impact on the development of Christian worship by imposing the liturgical practices of Rome throughout his empire. He also made important contributions to the development of culture by establishing a scholarly brain trust at his court and raising the educational standards of his clerics and courtiers. The so-called Carolingian Renaissance produced a group of scholars whose work in poetry, history, textual criticism, theology, and philosophy represented the major creative achievement of the early medieval period, and whose preservation projects transmitted much of the classical Greco-Roman heritage to the later Middle Ages.

On Christmas Day 800, Pope Leo III crowned Charlemagne, who already styled himself as king of the Franks and of the Lombards, as emperor of the Romans, thereby restoring the Roman imperial title in the West (despite the strong disapproval of the Byzantines). By the time of his death in 814, Charlemagne had created a Christian empire stretching from the Spanish March (near the border between modern-day Spain and France) to the edge of Germany, and from northern Italy to the straits of Dover (between modern-day England and France). His empire would come to be known as the *Holy* Roman Empire, because of its close association with the church. During its turbulent thousand-year history until its dissolution by Napoleon in 1806 (it was the original thousand-year Reich), the Holy Roman Empire would be the primary political carrier of the medieval Catholic ideal of a single universal Christian state.

Charlemagne's son and heir, Louis the Pious, sponsored continued church reform, most notably imposing the Rule of Benedict (see the following section) as the sole organizational document for all monks and nuns in the empire. However, from the late 820s through Louis' death in 840, he was in continual conflict with one or more of his sons and a bitter civil war broke out at Louis' death. By the Treaty of Verdun in 843, the Carolingian Empire was split into several different parts. It remained divided and weakened through the latter part of the ninth century and into the early part of the tenth century.

The Holy Roman Empire experienced a revival under the leadership of Henry I (919–936) and Otto I (936–973), the founders of the Ottonian dynasty, whose power lay in what is now Germany. Otto I proved himself a strong supporter of the church, appointing clerics to positions of responsibility, sponsoring missionary encounters in Eastern Europe,

Figure 13–1 The Carolingian empire at the Treaty of Verdun, 843. At his death, Louis the Pious' empire was divided among his three children: Charles the Bald, Lothar, and Louis the German. Lothar retained the title "Holy Roman Emperor."

and even responding to a papal request for military assistance. In gratitude for Otto's services, Pope John XII anointed and crowned him emperor, a title and position conferred in turn on Otto's son and grandsons. The yoking of papal and imperial power in the Ottonian dynasty eventually led to numerous conflicts over control of the church. These conflicts would reach their climax in the eleventh century in a dramatic confrontation between Pope Gregory VII and Emperor Henry IV (see the section on Gregory IV).

THE DEVELOPMENT OF MONASTICISM

The term *monasticism* comes from the Greek word *monos*, meaning "one," "solitary," or "alone." Early forms of monasticism were primarily lay movements. While deacons, priests, and bishops might associate themselves with monastic ideals and practices, most monks and nuns were lay people passionately concerned with their own salvation and convinced that they needed to separate themselves from mainstream society in order to achieve salvation. In Eastern Christianity, the monastic movement had its roots in the third and fourth centuries A.D. Some monks lived as hermits in the desert. The most famous of these early hermits was Antony of Egypt (251–356). Some, like Antony's contemporary Pachomius (290–346), lived an organized communal life in monasteries located in the wilderness far from society. Still others, under the direction of **Basil of Caesarea** (330–379), developed a kind of monasticism that might be described as urban monasticism. Basil saw hospitality for society's marginalized as a special mark of the monastic vocation, and so his monks lived in buildings close to cities and villages where the monastic community could provide various forms of social service: caring for the sick, raising orphans, providing food and clothing for the poor, offering employment for the destitute. Basil's influence on the development of monasticism was so great that he is known as the Father of Eastern Monasticism.

The Father of Western Monasticism was **John Cassian** (360–435). After ascetic training in both Bethlehem and Egypt, John organized monasteries for monks and nuns near Marseilles and in the region of Provence (southeastern France). John wrote two famous works, which took the ideals of Eastern monasticism and applied them to Western situations. His purpose was to establish a standardized form of monasticism for Christianity in the West. In *The Conferences*, he outlined the progressive stages of the spiritual life as he had come to understand them from personal experience and from conversation with famous Eastern spiritual guides. In *The Institutes,* he described the pattern of living that was characteristic of a genuine monastic community and prescribed practical methods of overcoming spiritual failings.

Although John Cassian founded no monastic communities in the British Isles, his ideals were highly influential on the forms of monastic life that developed there. Celtic monasticism originated sometime toward the end of the fifth century or the beginning of the sixth century. Its two emphases were to have strong impact on the rebirth of civilization in the early Middle Ages. The first was the love of scholarship. Although other monastic communities gave rudimentary education to their members, Irish monks developed more highly specialized monastic schools, placing high priority on literacy, preservation and transmission of knowledge, and on the production of manuscripts. The second legacy of Celtic monasticism was the penitential practice of self-imposed exile from the monastery. This Irish monastic practice sent monk-missionaries throughout vast stretches of northern Europe to preach the gospel message. The combination of scholarship and missionary activity made Irish monks important sources of social and cultural transformation in northern Europe.

The standardized form of Western monasticism so desired by John Cassian finally appeared in the *Rule for Monasteries* of **Benedict of Nursia** (480–547). Little is known of Benedict's life other than his Roman ancestry, his life as a hermit in a cave, and his establishment of a monastic community at Monte Cassino. Monks who followed Benedict's *Rule* took vows of poverty, chastity, obedience, and stability (permanent commitment to a particular community of monks). They gathered eight times a day for community prayer. Lauds (Morning Prayer at dawn), Vespers (Evening Prayer at sunset) and Matins (a lengthy vigil prayed in the dead of night) were the hinges of the *Opus Dei* ("work of God"). Shorter prayers interrupted the workday (Tierce, Sext, and None). Other prayers were prescribed for the dormitory at rising (Prime) or before sleep (Compline). Each monk had particular work responsibilities assigned him by his monastic superiors. They ate their meals together in silence or accompanied by spiritual readings. Although the ascetic practices outlined in Benedict's *Rule* were quite moderate and balanced by comparison to other monastic rules, the monks still fasted for a significant proportion of the year. Thus, the essence of Benedict's *Rule* can be summed up in a Latin motto: *Ora et labora* ("Pray and work").

Benedictine monasticism eventually became the primary style of monastic life in the West. Its dominance was so complete that historians have sometimes called the sixth through eleventh centuries the Benedictine centuries. The self-sufficiency of Benedict's communities made them well suited for the reduced conditions in the West after the fall of the Empire. As urban life disappeared along with the institutions associated with cities (schools, learning, government, trade, health care, etc.), monasteries slowly took on many of these functions by default. And as they were endowed with lands by the wealthy classes who wanted monks and nuns to pray for their souls after death, monasteries became significant economic institutions. By the ninth and tenth centuries, the Benedictine monasteries, far from being the withdrawn communities that Benedict had envisioned, were essential pillars of the early medieval world.

This degree of worldly involvement created problems. Secular rulers and wealthy nobility naturally wanted to exploit the resources of prosperous monasteries and did everything they could to increase their control over them. In some ways this was beneficial for monasteries, because they depended upon powerful benefactors to be their protectors and financial supporters in time of need. In other ways, monasteries suffered under this influence. When wealthy landlords deeded the monks land to build their monasteries, the monastery became, for all practical purposes, part of the **feudal system**. Their abbot was now a vassal of the lord, owing the lord certain services like military assistance against his enemies, and the monastery now needed serfs or peasants to help farm the land. The monastery, in turn, was responsible to provide the serfs with basic necessities of life.

Monasteries lost even more independence through **lay investiture**. According to this practice, the emperor and secular leaders took upon themselves the right to appoint bishops, abbots, and other church officials. Their appointees were not necessarily holy men, nor were they necessarily trained in spiritual matters. Rather, they were given appointments because of their family connections. Sometimes they obtained their appointments through **simony** (the buying and selling of spiritual things, including church leadership positions). All of these factors contributed to the gradual decline of the spiritual focus of the monastery.

The decline of monasticism began to change when William the Pious founded a new Benedictine monastery at Cluny in A.D. 910. This monastery committed itself to a reform of monasticism by demanding the strictest observance of Benedict's *Rule of Monasteries* and renewed dedication to the liturgical (worship) practices of monastic life. The Cluniac reform movement, under the direction of the monasteries' abbots, was determined to maintain the spiritual character of the church. The abbots spoke out against secular leaders who attempted to wield control over bishops and other clergy. Cluny's great innovation was to sponsor the creation of new monastic communities without allowing them to have their own abbots; instead, the new daughter communities were enrolled as affiliates of Cluny in a kind of federation (before this time Benedictine communities had been essentially free-standing operations), which increased their political leverage. They taught that the pope in Rome

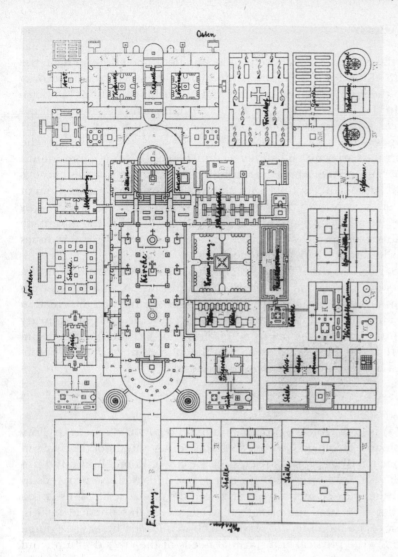

Figure 13–2 Floor plan of an ideal medieval monastery, based on the floor plan of the Monastery of St. Gall.

was the only one who ought to have authority over the clergy, and they put the whole Cluniac federation under the pope's special protection.

The monastic reformers also spoke out against **concubinage**. Although celibacy was required of monks, it was not universally required of "secular" clergy, that is, what today would be called parish priests: clergy who did not belong to a monastery and who lived in the cities and villages, ministering to the people there. As a result some of these "secular" clergy maintained concubines in a relationship something like marriage. The Cluny reformers denounced this practice, arguing that the clergy ought to be celibate so that the church might be their spouse and so that the Eucharist might be offered by pure hands unsullied by sexual contact. The position of the reformers eventually won the day, and Roman Catholicism has continued to require celibacy of its bishops and priests to the present day.

THE EVOLUTION OF THE PAPACY

The relationship between the emperor and church leadership developed differently in the Eastern and Western halves of the Roman Empire. In the East the emperor had authority over the patriarchs even to the point of calling councils and prescribing solutions to doctrinal issues in the church. In the West the pope and other bishops maintained their independence a little more successfully, though strong rulers like Emperor Justinian I (527–565) were able to bend even popes to their will.

The pope's prestige in the early church had been connected with Rome's importance as the site of the tombs of Saints Peter and Paul, and also as the capital of the empire. Though the city's political importance waned with the decline of the Western Roman Empire in the fifth and sixth centuries, its significance as a pilgrimage center only increased. In addition, the decline of civil authorities in the West worked to the advantage of the popes, who, by default as much as by design, began to take on purely secular duties as the *de facto* rulers of the city and the surrounding territory.

The early medieval period saw three further highly significant developments in the history of the papacy: the conversion of the peoples of northern Europe, which the popes actively supported; the eighth-century alliance with the kings of the Franks and the creation of the popes' own state; and the papal supremacy promoted by the eleventh-century "Gregorian Reform." The histories of two popes from this era, Pope Gregory I at the beginning and Pope Gregory VII at the end, demonstrate the first and third of these developments in action; the second has already been discussed previously.

Pope Gregory I

Pope **Gregory I** (c. 540–604) is so notable a figure that tradition recognizes him as Gregory the Great. The son of a Roman nobleman, Gregory spent his young adulthood in civic service so that eventually he occupied the office of prefect of the city of Rome. By around 574 Gregory retired from public life, sold his inherited possessions, and used the proceeds to care for the poor. He established several monasteries and lived the monastic life himself, following the *Rule* of Benedict with such intensity that he damaged his physical health. Eventually he was called out of the monastery to serve as a church leader, first as a regional deacon, charged with care for the physical and spiritual needs of the city's destitute, and later as an ambassador to Constantinople. After another interlude in the monastic life, Gregory was elected pope in 590.

The fourteen years that Gregory served as pope were notable for his missionary outreach. Gregory himself sought to evangelize the Lombards on the Italian continent. His most important accomplishment was to direct Augustine of Canterbury to undertake a missionary tour to the British Isles to preach the Christian message to the pagan Anglo-Saxons, who had migrated there from northern Germany. Later popes imitated Gregory's initiative by sponsoring similar missionary efforts, such as Pope Gregory II's support for the Anglo-Saxon monk St. Boniface (c. 672–754), celebrated as the Apostle of Germany, who brought Christianity to the peoples living beyond the old northern border of the former Roman Empire. Sponsoring such missions helped to promote a strong sense of loyalty between these newly converted peoples and the papacy in Rome.

Gregory the Great accomplished his missionary outreach while maintaining cordial relations with the Byzantine emperors, keeping up communication with the Christian communities in the surviving urban areas of the West, and overseeing the day-to-day functioning of the city of Rome. More than 850 of Gregory's letters are preserved, addressed to emperors, patriarchs, bishops, subdeacons, and notables, revealing a man of prodigious energy, convinced that the future of Christianity lay with the Germanic peoples north of the Alps and not simply in the Christian East. He was the first to style the pope as *servus servorum Dei* ("servant of the servants of God").

Pope Gregory VII

Gregory VII (c.1020–1085) was elected pope nearly 500 years after Gregory I's pontificate (reign as pope). The reign of Pope Gregory VII demonstrates how the institution of the papacy developed into a European political power in addition to its role as a religious center. His given name was Hildebrand, and he had committed himself at an early age to the life of a monk. For over twenty years he had served as secretary to five popes and was firmly convinced of the need for a strong church independent of lay political control if its spiritual life was to be reformed. Hildebrand was a person of passionate moral uprightness—a friend once described him as a holy Satan. He is so closely associated with the reform movement that historians have named it the Gregorian Reform, even though it was well underway before he became its leader.

From the time of his election in 1073, Gregory VII vigorously attacked three issues: simony, clerical concubinage, and lay investiture. Why were these so important to him? The ultimate goal of the reform movement was "the freedom of the church" (*libertas ecclesiae* became almost a political slogan), meaning the liberation of the priestly structure of the church from control by powerful lay people, in order to make the church the effective spiritual conscience and controller of a Christian society. In the process he differentiated lay from clerical more radically than had any before him; from this time on *the church* without qualification meant essentially the ordained clergy (i.e., bishops, priests, deacons).

The clergy themselves were to take on the style of a new type of worldly monk, an activist monasticism as it were. Celibacy was thought to be necessary for two distinct reasons. An unmarried priesthood was bound more tightly to the clerical structure of the church: Because clerical dynasties were (in theory) now impossible, it was harder for powerful local families to get control of the church's property and to keep it in the family. A second reason for requiring clerical celibacy was a widespread belief that sexual intercourse was intrinsically impure and therefore inappropriate for someone who offered the sacrifice of the Mass. The same desire to hold priests to a higher standard was behind the Gregorian reformers' demand that the clergy not carry weapons and shed blood. And rooting out simony meant returning control of the church to its rightful owners, the monks and clergy, who should be able freely to elect their abbots and bishops. It would also rid the church of the further worldly taint of money.

All of this would have been explosive enough on its own terms. But Gregory incorporated one further ambition that made his reforms downright revolutionary: the elimination of lay investiture, so-called because of the practice in which a nobleman or king would "invest" a prospective abbot or bishop with the spiritual symbols of his office, as part of the ceremony in which the candidate in return made feudal homage to his temporal lord as his vassal. In 1075, the Holy Roman Emperor Henry IV touched off a controversy over lay investiture, when he appointed three bishops to sees, a bishop's official seat or center of authority, in Italy, all of which were under the pope's ecclesiastical jurisdiction but in imperial territory. Gregory VII responded by excommunicating Henry and calling on Henry's subjects to force him to recant.

In 1077 Henry did public penance, standing for three days in the snow outside of Gregory's castle retreat at Canossa and was temporarily reconciled with the pope. But in 1080 the breach reopened. Gregory again excommunicated Henry, and, in response, Henry appointed and installed his own anti-pope Clement III. The stakes were heightened by Gregory's unprecedented claim that an excommunicated ruler was also deposed from his office and his subjects absolved of their oath of obedience to him. That was the most radical claim of all, and it remained the papacy's political trump card throughout the Middle Ages, until it was used for the last time (in vain) by Pope St. Pius V in 1570 against the Protestant queen of England, Elizabeth I.

The investiture conflict, as it is called, was not just an institutional struggle but a battle for public opinion. It was not settled until 1122, long after Henry and Gregory were dead, with the compromise known as the Concordat (Treaty) of Worms. The emperor renounced his claim to appoint bishops, who would now be elected freely by the clergy. But he retained the right to be present at such elections and to receive feudal homage (the ceremony in which a vassal pledged himself to his lord) for whatever lands the new bishop received as a vassal of the emperor—both of which concessions gave him ways to influence the choice of candidates.

The long-term significance of Gregory's reform program lay in his twin effort to detach the clerical order from lay and local control and to incorporate it in an international hierarchy with the papacy at the top. The effect was to radically distinguish what we now call church and state in an unprecedented way. While there was still a single Christian society (see discussion of Christendom in the next chapter), more clearly than ever there were now two heads. Another Constantine, another Justinian, or even another Charlemagne (who had regarded the pope as a sort of court chaplain), was unlikely. The ruler would no longer be considered sacred in the same way; royal anointing would continue as a ceremony, but its religious significance was greatly weakened—even though centuries later Shakespeare's Richard II would protest, "Not all the water in the rough rude sea can wash the balm from an anointed king" (*Richard II*, Act III, Scene 2). Nonetheless, the first, very tentative steps, towards the secularization of the state had been taken.

Gregory's program is famously expressed in a short set of 27 theses called the *Dictatus Papae* ("Statements of the Pope") probably written in 1075, perhaps as the table of contents for a collection of church laws in support of his program. They proclaim that the pope, as supreme judge under God alone, holds supreme power over all Christian souls; all bishops and abbots are subject to him, and he alone holds absolute powers of absolution (the power to forgive sins) and excommunication (the power to exclude someone from membership in the church). It also proclaims the pope's right to depose princes (§22; cited in Tierney 1983, 143). The history of the papacy in the High Middle Ages will witness the practical working out of these claims.

CULTURAL CONTRIBUTIONS OF THE EARLY MEDIEVAL PERIOD

A number of remarkable and significant cultural developments took place in the Western Roman Empire during the early medieval period, especially during the so-called Carolingian Renaissance. We will consider three expressions of this cultural creativity: the forging of the Romano–Frankish liturgy (the Roman Rite), the creation of Romano–Frankish (Gregorian) chant, and the development of Romanesque architecture.

Figure 13–3 "Christ in Majesty." Illumination from a tenth-century French manuscript (Bibliotheque Sainte-Geneieve; Ms. 9657, fol. lv), an example of the artistic contributions of the Carolingian period.

Before the Carolingian period, Christian worship in the West was conducted in Latin, but otherwise there was no standardized form of service. Prestigious cities such as Milan, Braga, Lyons, and Paris developed texts and ceremonies as well as calendars of feasts and occasions that were particular to their own location. In an attempt to unify his empire, Charlemagne directed that the Christian worship practices of the city of Rome should become the norm throughout his territories. To this end Charlemagne sent one of his scholar–courtiers to ask Pope Hadrian I for a "pure Gregorian" **sacramentary** (a book of the prayers needed by a priest to celebrate the Eucharist) popularly believed to have been composed by Pope Gregory I. Around 784–785, Hadrian sent such a book to the imperial court at Aachen, where it was deposited in the palace library to serve as the exemplar for all copies of sacramentaries to be used in Charlemagne's empire. However, the book was incomplete, and as a result it was supplemented with texts and ceremonies familiar to Frankish worshipers. This fusion of sober, classical Roman prayer with the dramatic, exuberant Frankish prayer forms the core of the **Roman Rite,** the primary form of liturgy for the Roman Catholic Church.

This attempt to standardize worship throughout the Carolingian Empire encouraged much artistic activity. The prayer texts themselves had to be copied into volumes intended for liturgical use. These manuscripts were often decorated with intricate designs or devotional pictures. The ceremonial clothing worn by the clergy during public worship demanded the skills of weavers, dyers, and embroiderers. Workers in precious metals and stones produced covers for the liturgical books and vessels for housing saints' relics, burning incense, and serving holy communion.

In conformity with his unification policy, Charlemagne's *General Admonition of 780* mandated, among other reforms, the use of Roman music at worship services throughout the empire. The **Gregorian chant** that was created for Roman Rite worship seems to be a fusion of chants used in the city of Rome together with the native chants of the Frankish churches. These chants were sung in unison, and they varied in complexity from simple recitation tones, which allowed biblical texts to be heard by worshiping assemblies prior to the invention of microphones, to melismatic melodies in which fifty or more notes might decorate a single syllable. This chant repertoire is one of the richest expressions of the Christian spirituality in the early medieval period.

By the ninth century, some worship centers (bishops' churches and major monasteries) developed liturgical music in which more than one melody was sounded. Music of such complexity demanded the development of notational systems, which were developed in the ninth century. By the eleventh century, notation had become so accurate that one could learn a new chant directly from a written page without the guidance of a singer who already knew the piece. The development of notation in turn led to further advances in musical art.

Figure 13–4 Charlemagne's palace chapel at Aix-la-Chapelle, exterior.

Another important cultural development of this period was Romanesque architecture. Strictly speaking, **Romanesque architecture** refers to the style of buildings constructed in Western Europe between the end of the eleventh century and the rise of the Gothic style in the middle part of the twelfth century, but we will use it to refer to the buildings developed during the Carolingian and Ottonian dynasties. Romanesque was an adaptation of ancient Roman architectural practices to the changed circumstances of the early Middle Ages. The outstanding achievement of Romanesque architects was the development of stone vaulted buildings that would replace the highly flammable wooden roofs of pre-Romanesque buildings. Introducing vaulting (especially in "barrel" or "tunnel" form) led to the erection of heavy walls and piers in place of the light walls and columns that had been used to support wooden roofs. These thick-walled buildings usually had only small openings for light, creating a fortresslike impression. Churches built in this style probably symbolized safety and security in the turbulent society of the tenth and eleventh centuries. A fascinating example of the transition into Romanesque architecture is Charlemagne's palace chapel at Aachen built between 792 and 805. On the one hand, its polygonal, domed shape is reminiscent of Byzantine architecture; on the other, its massive walls, narrow windows, and vaulting all look forward to later developments.

Churches in the early medieval period underwent a number of artistic and architectural changes. Carolingian architects created what was termed westworks, a multistoried facade usually flanked by bell towers before the entrance of the church building. Monastic communities developed churches with multiple chapels and altars for the devotional practices of individuals or groups, thus transforming the earlier patristic principle of "one people gathered around one altar in one church building." Churches at major shrines developed special walkways called ambulatories that allowed visitors access to the saints' relics even when services were being held in the main body of the church. Facades, doors, and windows of Romanesque churches were often decorated with carvings and sculptures that served to teach people the Bible stories and other elements of their faith through the medium of art.

MAJOR THEOLOGICAL FIGURES IN THE EARLY MEDIEVAL PERIOD

The scholars of the early medieval period suggest that this era provided us with rather few great popes or theologians. While this may be generally correct, particular theologians of eminence still grace this epoch, indicating that critical reflection upon the reality of God

Figure 13–5 Charlemagne's palace chapel at Aix-la-Chapelle. The interior shows Charlemagne's throne in the seating area set aside for the king.

and the beliefs and practices of the Christian religion did, in fact, take place in the early medieval period. We will consider two representatives each from the Eastern and Western theological tradition.

Probably the most important early medieval Eastern theologian is **Pseudo-Dionysius the Areopagite.** The real identity of this author remains unknown. In some of his writings the author claims to be a young man who heard Paul the Apostle preach in Athens and was thus converted to the Christian faith (Acts 17:34). Because of this claim, many medieval theologians, Thomas Aquinas among them, considered his writings to have considerable authority, second only to sacred scripture itself. In fact, the author was probably a Syrian monk writing in the early sixth century, since the texts reveal a strongly Neoplatonic philosophical foundation typical of that time. Pseudo-Dionysius is perhaps most famous for his so-called *via negativa* ("negative approach") in which all affirmations concerning God must be denied since the divine reality so supersedes any earthly quality that might be used to describe it. Pseudo-Dionysius' characteristic theological method appears in this passage from *The Mystical Theology*:

> The Cause of all is above all and is not inexistent, lifeless, speechless, mindless. It is not a material body, and hence has neither shape nor form, quality, quantity, or weight. It is not in any place and can neither be seen nor be touched. It is neither perceived nor is it perceptible. It suffers neither disorder nor disturbance and is overwhelmed by no earthly passion. It is not

powerless and subject to the disturbances caused by sense perception. It endures no deprivation of light. It passes through no change, decay, division, loss, no ebb and flow, nothing of which the senses may be aware. None of all this can either be identified with it nor attributed to it. (Pseudo-Dionysius 1987, 140–141)

Another Eastern theologian who is representative of the early medieval period is **Symeon the New Theologian** (942–1022). Born into the Byzantine Empire, Symeon was a monk, abbot, theologian, and poet—one of the most Spirit-centered of all Christian writers. Anticipating the claims of twentieth-century charismatic Christians, Symeon asserted that it was possible for every baptized Christian to attain direct, conscious experience of the Holy Spirit even in this life. The spiritual experience in which a person achieves direct communion with the divine is called **mysticism.** His *Hymn 25* communicates both mystical insight and theological precision in a rapturous outpouring of language:

—But, Oh, what intoxication of light, Oh, what movements of fire!
Oh, what swirlings of the flame in me, miserable one that I am,
coming from You and Your glory!
The glory I know it and I say it is Your Holy Spirit,
who has the same nature with You and the same honor, O Word;
He is of the same race, of the same glory,
of the same essence, He alone with Your Father
and with You, O Christ, O God of the universe!
I fall down in adoration before You.
I thank You that You have made me worthy to know, however little it may be,
the power of Your divinity.
I thank You that You, even when I was sitting in darkness,
revealed Yourself to me, You enlightened me,
You granted me to see the light of Your countenance
that is unbearable to all.
I remained seated in the middle of the darkness, I know,
but, while I was there surrounded by darkness,
You appeared as light, illuminating me completely from Your total light.
And I became light in the night, I who was found in the midst of darkness.
Neither the darkness extinguished Your light completely,
nor did the light dissipate the visible darkness,
but they were together, yet completely separate,
without confusion, far from each other, surely not at all mixed,
except in the same spot where they filled everything.
So I am in the light, yet I am found in the middle of the darkness.
So I am in the darkness, yet still I am in the middle of the light.
—How can darkness receive within itself a light and, without being dissipated by the light,
it still remains in the middle of the light?
O awesome wonder which I see doubly,
with my two sets of eyes, of the body and of the soul!
            (Symeon the New Theologian 1980, 24–25)

The first representative of Western early medieval theology has already appeared in our discussion on the evolution of the papacy. Pope Gregory I was not only a statesman and an important church leader, he was also a noted pastoral theologian. His *Homilies on Ezechiel* and his *Homilies on the Gospels* are filled with exegetical insights applied to the life situation of his hearers. His *Dialogues* is a delightful collection of anecdotes about the saintly ascetics and wonder-workers of Italy. More importantly, in his *Pastoral Rule* and *Moral Teachings from Job*, Gregory created the earliest manuals of moral and ascetic theology. In the following passage from the *Moral Teachings from Job*, Gregory discusses a core issue of soteriology (doctrine about salvation): why Jesus had to be sacrificed for humanity.

> [T]he Devil himself, tripping us up radically in our first parents, held man bound in his captivity in a seemingly just way,—man, who, created with a free choice, consented, under his persuasion, to what was unjust. For man, created unto life in the freedom of his own will, was, of his own accord, made the debtor of death. This fault, therefore, had to be taken away; but it could not be taken away except through sacrifice. A sacrifice, then, was to be sought; but what kind of a sacrifice would be discovered that would suffice for the absolving of men? It would not be just that victims from among brute animals should be slain on behalf of rational man. . . . If the victim was to be rational, a man would have to be offered; and if it was to cleanse men of sin, the victim must be a man without sin. But how should a man be without sin, if he were the offspring of a sinful heritage? That is why the Son of God came, for man's sake, into the womb of the Virgin, where, on our behalf, He was made Man. From mankind He took its nature, but not its fault. He made a sacrifice on our behalf. For the sake of the sinner He delivered up His body as a Victim without sin, a Victim who would be able both to die in respect to His humanity and to cleanse us in respect to justice. (Cited in Jurgens 1979, 316)

Another Western theologian who is representative of the early medieval period is **Anselm of Canterbury** (1033–1109), who could equally well be considered a figure transitional to the High Middle Ages. Anselm was a Benedictine monk who eventually rose to the position of Archbishop of Canterbury. Anselm made several great contributions to the Christian understanding of God, two of which will be described here. First, in his *Cur Deus Homo* ("Why Did God Become Man?"), Anselm constructed a "debt-satisfaction" theory of the atonement, arguing that the sin of Adam could only be forgiven if sufficient satisfaction for that sin were offered to the Father. But only a divine person could adequately resolve the debt incurred by human sin. Therefore, God had to become human if humanity was to be restored to God's friendship. However, Anselm's greatest theological contribution appears in his so-called ontological argument for the existence of God. In his *Proslogion*, Anselm argued that God, understood as "a being than which nothing greater can be thought," must necessarily exist, since if that being existed only in thought, one could conceive of that being also existing in reality, which would be greater.

To conclude this section, three things can be said about the theological developments of the early medieval period. First, in an era of great social and political turmoil, theologians took great pains to preserve the heritage of patristic thought (that is, the thought of the early church fathers). They did this by means of compilations of early Christian literature: collections of ancient Christian sermons, extracts from patristic writings, "chains" of patristic commentary on the Bible, systematized lists of citations on a particular topic, and canonical collections (in which patristic teaching on Christian living and church discipline appeared). Second, monasteries were primarily responsible for developing a theology aimed at helping Christians attain sanctification. The writers of these texts consciously employed images and symbols in an attempt to evoke an experience of God for their readers. These images and symbols dealt with archetypal human experiences of fear, anxiety, humiliation, sickness, hope, joy, confidence, and friendship. Thus theology was never simply intellectual speculation but a response of the whole person to the divine mystery (for example, Symeon the New Theologian's *Hymn 25*). Third, toward the end of the period, theologians evinced an ever-more confident trust in human reason and developed new forms of systematic inquiry (for example, Anselm of Canterbury's *Proslogion*) that would bear fruit in the high medieval scholastic period.

Key Terms

Basil of Caesarea
John Cassian
Benedict of Nursia
feudal system
lay investiture
simony
concubinage

Gregory I
Gregory VII
sacramentary
Roman Rite
Gregorian chant
Romanesque
  architecture

Pseudo-Dionysius the
  Areopagite
Symeon the New
  Theologian
mysticism
Anselm of Canterbury

Questions for Reading

1. Why is John Cassian known as the Father of Western Monasticism? What contribution did he make to its development?

2. What were the two major contributions of Celtic monasticism to the development of the early medieval Western Roman Empire?

3. What was the Cluniac Reform Movement? Where did it originate? What abuses was it addressing?

4. Who was Gregory I? What were his major accomplishments?

5. Who was Gregory VII? Describe the investiture controversy in which he was involved. What was the outcome of the controversy?

6. Identify and briefly describe the roles of the three dynasties involved in the formulation of the Holy Roman Empire during the early medieval period.

7. Describe one major theological contribution of two Eastern theologians of the early medieval period, Pseudo-Dionysius the Areopagite and Symeon the New Theologian.

8. Describe one major theological contribution of two Western theologians of the early medieval period, Pope Gregory I and Anselm of Canterbury.

Works Consulted/Recommended Reading

Bede. *Ecclesiastical History of the English People,* Rev. ed. Translated by Leo Sherley-Price. R.E. Latham. London and New York, NY: Penguin, 1990.

Cowdrey, Herbert Edward John. *The Cluniacs and the Gregorian Reform.* Oxford: Clarendon, 1970.

Fichtenau, Heinrich. *The Carolingian Empire.* Translated by Peter Munz. New York: Harper and Row, 1963/1965.

Hillgarth, J. N. *Christianity and Paganism, 350–750: The Conversion of Western Europe,* Rev. ed. Philadelphia: University of Pennsylvania, 1986.

Hunter Blair, Peter. *The World of Bede.* New York: St. Martin's, 1971.

Jurgens, W. A. *The Faith of the Early Fathers*, Vol. 3. Collegeville, MN: Liturgical Press, 1979.

Kantorowicz, Ernst Hartwig. *The King's Two Bodies: A Study in Mediaeval Political Theology*. Princeton, NJ: Princeton University, 1957.

Lawrence, Clifford Hugh. *Medieval Monasticism: Forms of Religious Life in Western Europe in the Middle Ages*. 2nd ed. London: Longman, 1989.

Leyser, Karl J. *Rule and Conflict in an Early Medieval Society: Ottonian Saxony*. Bloomington: Indiana University, 1979.

McKitterick, Rosamund. *The Frankish Church and the Carolingian Reform 789–895*. London: Longman, 1977.

Noble, Thomas F. X. *The Republic of Saint Peter: The Birth of the Papal State, 680–825*. Philadelphia: University of Pennsylvania, 1984.

Pseudo-Dionysius. *The Complete Works*. Translated by Colm Luibhead. Classics of Western Spirituality. New York: Paulist, 1987.

Riché, Pierre. *Education and Culture in the Barbarian West, Sixth Through Eighth Centuries*. Translated by John J. Contreni. Columbia: University of South Carolina, 1976.

Southern, Richard William. *Saint Anselm: A Portrait in a Landscape*. Cambridge: Cambridge University, 1990.

Symeon the New Theologian. *The Discourses*. Translated by C. J. DeCatanzaro. Classics of Western Spirituality. New York: Paulist, 1980.

Tellenbach, Gerd. *The Church in Western Europe from the Tenth to the Early Twelfth Century*. Translated by Timothy Reuter. Cambridge Medieval Textbooks. Cambridge: Cambridge University, 1993.

Tierney, Brian, ed. *The Middle Ages*. Vol. I, *Sources of Medieval History*. 4th ed. New York: Alfred A. Knopf, 1983.

Ullmann, Walter. *A Short History of the Papacy in the Middle Ages*. London: Methuen, 1972.

Wallace-Hadrill, John Michael. *The Frankish Church*. Oxford: Clarendon-Oxford University, 1983.

Chapter

CHRISTIANITY
IN THE HIGH MIDDLE AGES

TIMELINE

A.D. 1096–1291	Crusades are launched against the Muslims to recover the Holy Land.
A.D. 1098	The Cistercian order is founded to restore Benedictine life to its original form.
A.D. 1184	The Council of Verona condemns the Waldensians as heretics.
A.D. 1198–1216	Reign of Pope Innocent III.
A.D. 1209	Francis of Assisi founds the mendicant order known as the Franciscans.
A.D. 1215	Fourth Lateran Council institutes some reforms of the clergy and defines the dogma of transubstantiation.
A.D. 1220–1221	Dominic Guzman founds the mendicant order known as the Dominicans.
A.D. 1232	Emperor Frederick II issues an edict permitting the hunting of heretics. The period of the inquisitions formally begins.
A.D. 1294–1303	Reign of Pope Boniface VIII.
A.D. 1302	Pope Boniface VIII issues bull *Unam Sanctam*, an extreme statement of church authority over temporal power.

The twelfth and thirteenth centuries are often called the High Middle Ages in order to distinguish them from the prior period (approximately 500 to 1050, when Western Europe reorganized itself after the fall of the Roman Empire in the West) and from the one that followed (Chapter 16), which led up to the Protestant Reformation. The twelfth and thirteenth centuries are also "high" in the sense that they mark numerous peak developments and events of lasting importance in the Christian tradition. During this period of tremendous ferment, Christianity became thoroughly identified with European culture and society. The medieval church ran schools, licensed universities, owned and farmed land, tried to control fighting and violence and bring stability and discipline to economic life, rebuked kings and emperors, engaged in its own diplomacy and politics, cared for the poor and the sick, and exercised legal control over issues relating to marriage, family, and inheritance. Modern historians have given the name of **Christendom** to this unprecedented merging of Christianity and culture.

This chapter describes trends in the practices, doctrines, and institutions of Catholic Christianity during the High Middle Ages. The following topics are examined: the spirit of creativity and innovation found in religious reform movements, both within and outside of the institutional church; the papacy and its emerging role as spiritual head of Christendom; devotional practice and religious life in the medieval period; the spread of the Gothic style in church architecture; and Christendom's relations with non-Christians. Theology and the medieval universities will be treated in the next chapter.

THE FOREIGN POLICY OF CHRISTENDOM: PAGANS, JEWS, AND MUSLIMS

The Latin word *Christianitas*, not meaning "Christianity" as a religion but "Christendom" in the sense of a closed and totally Christian society and territory, became widespread around the time of the First Crusade (1095). From this time, European Christians began to think of their society as defined by its religious identity, in conscious opposition to groups that did not share that identity: pagans, Jews, and Muslims.

Paganism in Retreat

By the end of the eleventh century almost all of Europe had become Christian. Scandinavia, central Europe, and part of Eastern Europe, especially the Poles and Hungarians, had accepted Latin Christianity (the Christianity of Western Europe which had identified itself with the pope in Rome). The Slavic peoples living in what is now Russia, Belarus, and Ukraine, and most of the peoples of the Balkans, were in the cultural and political orbit of the Byzantine Empire and therefore became Orthodox.

The last large concentration of pagan peoples lay along the Baltic seacoast in northeastern Europe. Their incorporation into Christendom occurred in the twelfth century after two and a half centuries of warfare and colonization. Prior to this time, when people converted to Christianity, it was usually because their king or noble elite became Christian and brought the people along with them. There were exceptions, of course: for example, Charlemagne's forced conversion of the Saxons in 772 to 804. However, beginning in 1147, with a new type of religious warfare called the *crusade* (see the following section on medieval Christianity and Islam), Christianity began to see many more conversions by conquest. The Wendish crusade is an example. German and Danish leaders wanted to

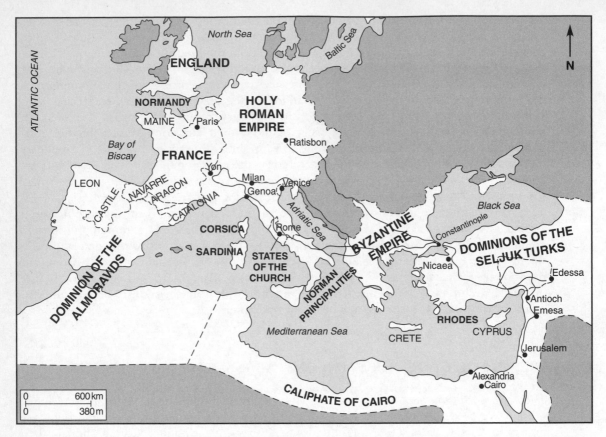

Figure 14–1 Boundaries between Christianity and Islam at the time of the First Crusade.

expand into the territory of a Slavic people, called the Wends, in central and eastern Germany, and they used the crusade as religious justification. When St. Bernard of Clairvaux (see the following section on monastic renewal) predicted that the Wends would have only two choices—Baptism or death—he was not trying to justify forced conversion of individuals but stating the blunt fact that the survival of the historic identity of pagan peoples depended on their conversion. Nevertheless, his call to arm the faithful "with the Holy Cross of Christ against the enemies of the Cross of Christ" (cited in Tyerman 2006, 679) helped to sanction what amounted to glorified land grabbing.

Although official church teaching opposed the use of armed force to baptize large numbers of people, involuntary Baptism became part of a pattern of militarized expansion. Thus in 1209 Pope Innocent III urged the Danish king Valdemar II to pursue "the war of the Lord . . . to drag the barbarians into the net of orthodoxy" (cited in Tyerman 2006, 683). The brutal culmination of this policy was the hundred years and more during which the military crusading order of the Teutonic Knights (see the following section on medieval Christianity and Islam) fought to conquer, convert, and govern Prussia and Livonia (modern-day Latvia). The Teutonic Knights also would have annexed Lithuania, home of the last pagan holdouts, had not the crusading impetus petered out after the Lithuanians made a diplomatic conversion to Christianity in 1386.

Jews in Christian Society

In Christendom the Jews were the only "outsiders" who remained. Medieval Jews suffered from numerous injustices. They were restricted to their own quarter of the city (the original *ghetto*) and made to wear identifying signs on their clothing. They could not appear in public at Eastertime. They were prohibited from owning Christian slaves, exercising dominance over Christians (which kept them out of local government), and acquiring land. In addition, they were occasionally subjected to violent and bloody persecutions, and their goods were liable to seizure. Sometimes they were forced by law to attend Christian services, where attempts were made to convert them. Eventually they were expelled altogether from the western parts of Europe: England (1290), France (1306), and, at the very end of the medieval period, from the newly unified kingdom of Spain (1492) and from Portugal (1497).

Why were Jews singled out for such treatment? There appear to have been two major sources of medieval anti-Judaism: popular prejudice and bigotry against Jews and traditional Christian religious teachings about Judaism. Some of the popular prejudice was based on economic resentment. Jews first prospered as artisans and traders of goods. Since church law forbade Christians to loan money at interest to other Christians, civil authorities allowed Jews to move into money lending and perform the banking services that were so important to the economic wellbeing of medieval Europe. This is the context in which the traditional hostile stereotypes of Jews as grasping and greedy originated. The Jews were also vulnerable targets for Mass resentment in turbulent or troubling times. Rumors about Jews killing Christians and using their blood to make bread for their festivals began to spread in the twelfth century, as did stories about Jews desecrating the consecrated bread of the Eucharist. During the fourteenth-century plague known as the Black Death, Jews were accused of causing the disease by poisoning wells. Pogroms (massacres) of Jews also frequently broke out in the wake of the crusading movement.

Another source of medieval anti-Judaism was the traditional Christian teaching that the Christian church was the true Israel and the belief that the Jews inherited a collective punishment for the murder of Jesus ("His blood be on us and on our children," Matt 27:25). Such teaching was not the primary cause of medieval anti-Judaism, but it certainly contributed to people's fears and prejudices once these began to appear. To their credit, the popes regularly condemned persecutions and forced Baptisms of Jews, and tried to discourage popular prejudices about ritual murder and well poisoning. However, they also firmly supported the legalized subordination of Jews to Christians and, from the thirteenth century onward, increased efforts to convert Jews.

The prejudice and persecution experienced by medieval Jews is not the whole story, for Jewish and Christian interaction in the medieval period was rich and many sided. Jewish and Christian scholars and theologians, for example, made constructive contacts over the study of the Bible. The great Jewish scholar Rashi wrote biblical commentaries that were also used by Christian scholars. At St. Victor's Abbey in Paris, the twelfth-century theologians known as the Victorines learned Hebrew from Jewish biblical experts and consulted them in their study of the sacred scriptures. In general, Christian scholars gradually recognized that they had much to learn from Jewish biblical interpretation, especially where the original Hebrew text was concerned.

Medieval Christianity and Islam: Holy Wars

One cannot talk about medieval Christianity and Islam without talking about the crusades, which were Christian military expeditions launched against unbelievers, especially Muslims and heretics. Prior to the crusades the church had made serious efforts to curb the violence that was ingrained in feudal society. In church-sponsored movements such as the Peace of God and the Truce of God, for instance, bishops had tried to limit both the extent of knightly violence—they could not attack certain noncombatants like women, children, peasants, and the clergy—and the times and seasons in which war could be conducted. With the rise of crusading, some of that pent-up violence got exported outside Christendom.

Given the fact that the earliest Christians were opposed to shedding blood, one might wonder how the crusades came to play such a significant role in late eleventh- and twelfth-century Christendom. As the Roman Empire converted to Christianity in the fourth century, Christianity began to qualify its initial opposition to shedding blood by the gradual adoption of the concept of a just war (Chapter 9). The crusades represented a further stage in the Christianizing of military service—and the militarizing of Christianity—by adopting the biblical concept of a *holy war,* a war willed by God himself.

The chief promoters of holy war and the inventors of the crusading movement were the popes of the Gregorian Reform (see Chapter 13). Because the reformers forbade the clergy to shed blood themselves, they delegated this division of social labor to the laity. Here is the somewhat condescending way in which a monastic writer described the layman's new vocation in his history of the First Crusade (1096–1099):

> God has instituted in our time holy wars, so that the order of knights and the crowd running in their wake, who following the example of ancient pagans have been engaged in slaughtering one another, might find a new way of gaining salvation. And so they are not forced to abandon secular affairs completely by choosing the monastic life or any religious profession, as used to be the custom, but can attain in some measure God's grace while pursuing their own careers, with the liberty and in the dress to which they are accustomed. (Guibert of Nogent, *The Deeds of God through the Franks,* cited in Riley-Smith 1987, 9)

The church had long encouraged the faithful to fight for Christendom and had even promised eternal life to those who died in battle defending it against unbelievers. In 1095, when Pope Urban II delivered the speech that launched what later came to be known as the First Crusade, he promised a plenary indulgence (a kind of "blanket pardon" where punishment for all of an individual's sins was canceled) to all who took the crusading oath to aid Eastern Christians and free the holy places of Jerusalem from their oppressors. Normally Christians on pilgrimage to sacred sites were forbidden to carry arms, but these new-style pilgrims were "an army of God." In the past, soldiers who had killed even in a just war had to do penance for the bloodshed; now killing itself was conceived as an act of penance. What made crusading distinctive was its character as an armed penitential pilgrimage.

The response to Urban's appeal was overwhelming. Within four years Western armies had reconquered Jerusalem and established a network of Latin states in Syria and Palestine that lasted for almost two centuries. These Christian invaders were no doubt motivated in part by greed for land and booty, but crusading was too risky and expensive to have been driven by economic motives alone. Idealistic and spiritual motives were at work as well. Doing penance for one's sins was a powerful spiritual factor. Another was the old Germanic warrior ideal of loyalty to the lord of one's war-band: Just as the oath of allegiance required one to avenge wrongs that were done to one's lord, so crusading could be seen as avenging wrongs done to Christ. An especially powerful motive was the religious aura of Jerusalem, which for centuries had been a popular pilgrimage site for Christians. Jerusalem exercised a profound fascination on the religious imagination of medieval Christians, particularly as Christians became interested in imitation of the earthly life of Jesus during the High Middle Ages. The church guaranteed the crusader the same traditional privileges as the pilgrim, such as the protection of his land and family in his absence. He made a vow when he "took the cross," which he wore as his symbol, and his slogan was "God wills it."

The ultimate expression of warfare in the service of the gospel was the rise of the hybrid institution of the military order. These were originally religious orders of knights who took monastic vows to defend pilgrims and the holy places. The most famous military orders were the Teutonic Knights, who from 1245 had a papally granted right to perpetual crusade in their own state along the Baltic coast; the Knights Templar, so called from their headquarters in Jerusalem; and the Knights of St. John or Hospitallers, so called because their original work was the maintenance of the Hospital of St. John in Jerusalem. The military orders were always controversial. Some critics were scandalized by the union of the sword and monastic vows and the orders' often brutal activities, but others were simply jealous of their power and independence.

The effects of the crusades are hard to assess. Although the First Crusade did succeed in recapturing Jerusalem in 1099, within less than a hundred years Jerusalem—a holy city for Muslims as well—was again in Muslim hands. The last crusader state in the Middle East fell in 1291. During the two centuries of Western settlement in "Outremer" ("The Land beyond the Sea"), as medieval French writers called it, Christians and Muslims practiced an uneasy co-existence. Intermarriage was not common. Western interaction was with local non-Catholic Christians more than with Muslims, while Arabic-speaking Middle Eastern Christians played a role as go-betweens. Muslims received roughly the same measure of disdainful tolerance they had extended to conquered Christian populations.

Europe continued to enjoy some benefits of Christian holy war movements into the seventeenth and eighteenth centuries. Crusading was at least partially responsible for the recovery of Sicily and Spain from Islam, the former in the mid-thirteenth century and the latter in the late fifteenth century. In the early modern period, when Turkish expansion again threatened Christendom with Muslim invasion, reaching as far as Vienna in central Europe by 1683, the Holy Leagues, which were essentially papally inspired defensive crusades, stopped their advance. The military crusading order called the Hospitallers exercised control of Malta, an island nation south of Sicily in the Mediterranean Sea, until Napoleon's arrival in 1798. However, by the eighteenth century the concept of holy war gradually fell out of favor among most Christians, and growing secularization forced Christianity to think in less territorial terms than it did in the medieval period. Today Christian moral reflection on war tends to move between the poles of just-war theory and updated versions of early Christian pacifism.

Finally, it would be misleading to characterize medieval Christianity's relations with Islam exclusively in terms of warfare. In areas like Spain and Sicily, where Christians and Muslims lived close to one another, commercial, cultural, and intellectual relations were rich and varied. By the twelfth century the Qur'an had been translated into Latin, so that Western Christians could read it. Occasionally, peaceful if ineffective efforts were made to convert Muslims to Christianity. The new religious orders of the Franciscans and Dominicans (see the following section on the mendicant orders) saw it as part of their mission to preach the gospel to unbelievers, chiefly Muslims. A famous episode in the life of St. Francis of Assisi was his audience before the sultan of Egypt in 1219 during the Fifth Crusade, which had gone to Egypt rather than to Palestine or Syria. Francis risked his life by walking unprotected into the Muslim camp in order to preach to the sultan and his court. The sultan, Malik al-Kamil (1180–1238), resisted advice to have Francis executed immediately and allowed him to preach. Although he failed to convert al-Kamil, Francis made a powerful impression with his courage and integrity.

THE PRIMACY OF THE PAPACY

In the early medieval period, Pope Gregory VII had envisioned the pope as the spiritual head of a single Christian society. His successors came close enough to realizing this vision that the High Middle Ages are sometimes called the period of the papal monarchy. This does not mean that popes tried to replace kings and emperors as rulers of nations, but that kings and emperors were now subjected to the moral and religious scrutiny of the popes in ways that previous kings had not experienced.

The increasing power of the papacy was accompanied by a growing church bureaucracy in Rome. The twelfth century saw the rise of the papal court, or **curia,** staffed by the college of cardinals. The term *cardinal* originally was an honorary title for certain ordained clergy who assisted the pope in his liturgical and administrative tasks in the city of Rome. In 1059 a papal decree granted these cardinal clergy the exclusive right to elect the pope. The popes then began to extend the title to important churchmen outside of Rome. The college of cardinals thus came to assist the pope in governing the universal church, particularly through their management of the curia, which handled official correspondence, finances, record keeping, and legal business. Training in canon law became a virtual requirement for the papal office, as the papacy became a popular court of appeal for litigants from all over Europe. At the same time, friendly critics pleaded with the popes not to let their spiritual mission get swallowed up in bureaucratic routine. Pope Innocent III and Pope Boniface VIII are two popes of the High Middle Ages whose reigns coincide with the height of papal power and the beginning of its decline.

Pope Innocent III and the Zenith of Papal Power

Innocent III (reigned 1198–1216) became pope at the age of thirty-seven, the youngest person ever to hold the office. He is perhaps best known for his political involvements. Besides being ruler of the Papal States, the popes' own realm in central Italy, Pope Innocent also had special feudal rights over Poland, Hungary, Aragon (in Spain), and Sicily. He believed he could intervene in political affairs when moral or religious issues were involved. The church could and did claim competence in affairs and transactions that might seem personal but were inevitably public and political as well. One example is the centrality of personal oaths in feudal political relations. Another is marriage and reproduction: The church's power to determine marital legitimacy could affect dynastic successions and diplomacy, which was often based on marital alliances.

Oath of Peter II, King of Aragon, made to Pope Innocent III

"I will defend the catholic faith; I will persecute heresy; I will respect the liberties and immunities of the churches and protect their rights. Throughout all of the territory submitted to my power I will strive to maintain peace and justice." (Cited in Morris 1989, 427)

An example of Innocent III's power over kings is his disciplining of the king of England in a dispute over who would be appointed archbishop of Canterbury. When the king objected to the canonically elected archbishop, Innocent III excommunicated the king and put all of England under interdict for five years. An **interdict** is a kind of strike in which the church shuts down the sacramental system (Eucharist, Baptism, Penance, etc.). Most English clergy seem to have honored the interdict. Eventually, the king of England surrendered and even gave England to the papacy as a feudal holding, meaning that the king presented himself as the pope's vassal, though this was more a symbolic relationship than a legal one.

Innocent always denied that he was taking over the legitimate rights of kings. His decrees and letters say plainly that he recognized the distinction between the two public authorities, civil and ecclesiastical, of the one Christian society. However, he was capable of speaking in very bold terms about the pope's unique authority:

> To me is said in the person of the prophet [Jeremiah], 'I have set thee over nations and over kingdoms, to root up and to pull down, and to waste and destroy, and to build and to plant' (Jer 1:10) . . . thus the others were called to a part of the care but Peter alone assumed the plenitude [fullness] of power. You see then who is this servant set over the household, truly the vicar [substitute] of Jesus Christ, successor of Peter, anointed of the Lord, a god of Pharaoh, set between God and man, lower than God but higher than man, who judges all, and is judged by no one . . . (Cited in Tierney 1964, 131–132)

Some of Innocent's policies failed badly. The crusade that he called against the Albigensian or Cathar heretics in southern France (see the following discussion of Catharism) backfired when nobility and clergy from northern France used the war as an opportunity for conquest and exploitation. Twenty years of war (1209–1229) that began as a crusade to eliminate heresy had as its main result the French monarchy's political annexation of a large part of what is now southern France. The Fourth Crusade, which he first proclaimed in 1198, never even got to the Holy Land. Instead, the crusaders, desperately short of money, were forced to hire out their services, first to Venetian merchant-princes and then to a discontented Byzantine prince who hired them to put him and his deposed father back on the imperial throne in Constantinople. When they didn't get the money they were promised, the crusaders sacked the city in 1204 and elected one of their own leaders to become emperor. They also made a Western priest the patriarch of Constantinople. This Latin empire and Latin patriarchate lasted until 1261. The experience embittered Orthodox Christians so much that reunion under any terms became unthinkable, even when the Muslim Turks finally destroyed the Byzantine Empire in 1453. Disillusioned Orthodox Christians are reported to have said, "Better the turban of the sultan than the tiara [crown] of the pope."

Innocent's most fateful political decision may have been his sponsorship of the youthful Frederick II (reigned 1212–1250), heir of the Hohenstaufen dynasty of the Holy Roman Empire, as the rightful claimant to the imperial throne. In return for his support, Innocent made Frederick promise not to unite the empire, which controlled the north of Italy, with the kingdom of Sicily in the south. The medieval popes' greatest security fear was that the same ruler would control both the northern and southern borders of the Papal States. Unfortunately, Frederick reneged on the agreement after Innocent died. The papacy eventually triumphed in a long and ferocious war against Frederick, but the struggle sapped its financial strength and its spiritual prestige. The war was an important turning point in the later medieval papacy's declining sense of spiritual mission.

The climax of Innocent's reign was the **Fourth Lateran Council** (1215). The council pressured the clergy to fulfill their pastoral duties of preaching, saying Mass, and hearing confession. (Clergy, especially at higher levels, were often "absentee" because governments

Figure 14–2 "The Dream of Pope Innocent," in which Francis shores up a collapsing church building, which happens to be the Basilica of St. John Lateran, the home church of the pope as bishop of Rome.

siphoned off church salaries and personnel for government service; universities were another drain on clerical talent and resources.) To keep lay people in contact with the sacramental system (see the following section on the seven sacraments), the council instituted the "Easter duty" (still in force among Catholics), which required all Christians to go to confession and to receive communion at least once a year. It also defined the dogma of **transubstantiation,** concerning the manner in which Christ's real presence in the Eucharist was to be understood. According to this teaching, when a properly ordained priest consecrates the Eucharistic bread and wine, the substance of the bread and wine becomes the body and blood of Jesus Christ, even though they retain the appearance of ordinary bread and wine.

Innocent's greatest service to the church may have been his endorsement of St. Francis of Assisi and his order of friars. Innocent prevented Francis' movement from suffering the fate of similar movements like the Waldensians (see the following section on dissent and heresy) by approving its rule and keeping it within the institutional system of religious orders, despite its unique character. Perhaps he recognized that it could provide the institutional church with desperately needed religious vitality and inspiration.

Pope Boniface VIII: The Papacy and National Kingdoms

The pontificate of **Boniface VIII** (reigned 1294–1303) demonstrates the real-world limits of papal power in the High Middle Ages. Emerging national dynasties like those in England and France were growing in power. By the beginning of the fourteenth century, the old ideal of an international Christian empire was all but dead: It suffered a mortal wound with the papally inspired execution in 1254 of the last of the Hohenstaufen rulers of the Holy Roman Empire. During the Late Middle Ages, the church would find itself steadily subjected to the political demands of national kingdoms. Boniface VIII twice collided with the powerful French king Philip IV, and twice he lost. The first conflict involved the right of kings to tax the clergy of their realm, and the second the pope's jurisdiction over the French bishops. In the latter struggle he failed to win the obedience of the French clergy, more than half of whom supported their king over their pope—a forecast of the future trend toward the nationalization of Christianity.

In retaliation, Boniface issued the bull *Unam Sanctam* (1302), probably the most famous medieval statement on church and state. Its teachings have often been cited as reasons for seeing Catholicism and the papacy as a threat to the stability of the political order. Boniface and the papacy paid a price for his boldness. Several months after *Unam Sanctam* appeared, Philip's agents arrested him. He died soon afterwards, perhaps of injuries suffered from his brutal treatment. Within two years a French pope, Clement V (1305–1314), moved the papacy from Rome to Avignon in southern France, where it remained for much of the fourteenth century.

Pope Boniface VIII in *Unam Sanctam*

We are taught by the words of the gospel that in this church and in her power are two swords, a spiritual and a temporal one. . . . But the one is exercised for the church, the other by the church, the one by the hand of the priest, the other by the hand of kings and soldiers, though at the will and sufferance of the priest. . . . If the earthly power errs it shall be judged by the spiritual power. . . . Therefore we declare, state, define, and pronounce that it is altogether necessary for salvation for every human creature to be subject to the Roman pontiff. (Cited in Tierney 1964, 188–189)

REFORM WITHIN THE SYSTEM: NEW RELIGIOUS ORDERS

After the eleventh century the institutional church struggled to keep control of the religious zeal and creative energies unleashed by the Gregorian Reform. At first enthusiasm for reform stayed mainly within the bounds of the institutional church and produced a variety of new religious movements.

Monastic Renewal: The Cistercians

The *Rule* of St. Benedict inspired several new monastic orders. The most successful of these new orders was the **Cistercians,** whose name is taken from their first house at Cîteaux in France. The Cistercians sought to restore the original simplicity of Benedictine monasticism by emphasizing a highly austere way of life, which included manual labor and economic self-support. They departed from the *Rule* in not accepting children into the monastery, in developing a strong governmental system that united all the houses of the order under a centralized authority (in contrast to the Benedictines' decentralized model), and in sponsoring a second order of lay brothers, the *conversi* (literally, "converts"), who took care of most of the day-to-day activities involved in running a monastery.

The Cistercians built their monasteries in marginal and unsettled areas, significantly expanding the amount of European land under cultivation. Their numbers grew rapidly, partly because of the prestige brought to the order by **Bernard of Clairvaux** (1090–1153), whose writing, preaching, and fiery temperament made him the dominant religious figure in the twelfth century. Ironically, their success eventually led to some of the same temptations of wealth and comfort that had plagued the Benedictine communities from which the Cistercians had split.

The Mendicant Orders: Franciscans and Dominicans

The most innovative orders were those of the **mendicants** (from a Latin word for "begging") or **friars** (from Latin *frater,* "brother"). The mendicants grew out of a widespread popular religious movement called the *vita apostolica*, which sought to restore the "apostolic life" of Christ and his first followers, above all by imitating Christ's poverty. At first the mendicants avoided priestly ordination. Their founders located their communities in towns and cities rather than in monastic isolation in the countryside. The cities were home both to the uprooted poor and the newly prosperous middle class. Bringing the ideals of Christ and his apostles home to these people meant leaving the monastic cloister for the city street. The two most important founders of mendicant orders in the High Middle Ages were St. Francis of Assisi and St. Dominic.

Francis of Assisi (c. 1182–1226) was born into a merchant family in Assisi in central Italy. As a young man he chose, rather like Antony of Egypt, to heed the gospel by abandoning his wealth and adopting a life of poverty. Unlike Antony, Francis gathered followers around him and commissioned them to preach the gospel and to witness to it in action. His new community became known as the Order of Friars Minor ("the lesser brothers") or **Franciscans.** Francis taught the renunciation of the goods of this world for the sake of the gospel, but also the affirmation of the world's goodness. He sang nature's praises in poetry and popularized the use of the Christmas crêche (the stable setting of Jesus' birth) to show how God humbled himself for our sake by being born into the world. Francis sought to bring back to life the radicalism of Jesus' preaching in the Sermon on the Mount. For him that meant avoiding anything resembling an institutionalized religious life (income, property, books, houses, etc.). At the same time, he required his movement to be totally loyal to the church's clerical leadership.

The Franciscan movement became enormously popular. However, its popularity proved the undoing of its founder's vision. The institutional church, hungry for dedicated preachers and confessors, and for talented teachers in the new universities, tried to shape the order along more conventional lines. Eventually a conflict broke out between a radical minority party called the Spirituals, who were fanatically faithful to Francis' ideal of absolute poverty, and a majority party called the Conventuals, who were willing to make compromises for the sake of a broader mission. The Spirituals wanted to withdraw for the sake of preserving Francis' vision in all its purity. However, Francis' vision had also included the obligation to obey the church. When the church took the Conventuals' side by endorsing compromises in the observance of poverty, the Spirituals were forced to choose. At the Council of Vienne (1311–1312), Pope Clement V rejected both the Spirituals' insistence on real, practical poverty and their petition to secede from the order. Many of the Spirituals chose to reject the pope and the council, and thus became heretics in the eyes of the church.

Dominic Guzman (d. 1221) was a Spanish contemporary of Francis of Assisi who founded an order of a similar character, marked by a commitment to a life of communal poverty and public preaching. The mendicant orientation may have come from contact with Francis' movement. Unlike the Franciscans, the **Dominicans** at least allowed the acceptance of money. They also developed a strong organizational structure, again, quite unlike the Franciscans, based on the principle of representative government. The Dominicans were further distinguished by the emphasis on preaching against heresy, which led them more quickly to the new universities and to a mission more directly identified with study. For this reason they are called the Order of Preachers. St. Thomas Aquinas (1225–1274), who is featured in the next chapter, belonged to the Dominicans and became their most accomplished theologian.

The Beguines: Independent Lay Communities for Women

This period saw a rise in communities of sisters or nuns who were sponsored by orders of friars and monks and who adopted their rules. For example, the Franciscans sponsored the Poor Clares, who lived by a rule that Francis had given to Clare of Assisi. The enthusiasm for preaching and living the apostolic life (imitating the life of the early church communities) also led to the formation of independent communities of laywomen known as **Beguines.** These groups had no rule or permanent religious vows but shared some form of common life and were either engaged in contemplative prayer or in ministries of caring for the sick and the poor. They were not obliged to renounce property, though many did, nor were they bound to a lifetime commitment to the community. There was no centralized structure beyond the local community. Because of the flexibility and openness of these new religious movements, whether they were communities of men or women, they became vital sources of renewal and devotion, but also of dissent and heresy.

DISSENT AND HERESY

With rare exceptions, medieval heresy did not involve questions about beliefs and doctrines as much as debate over practical issues of worship, discipleship, and ministry. Lay reform movements that failed to gain acceptance by the institutional church often became intensely anticlerical (critical of the church's clergy). The clergy left themselves open to criticism when they failed to live up to the high standards and expectations set for them by the Gregorian reform of the eleventh century (Chapter 13). Anticlericalism also led to criticism of the sacraments of the church, because it was the clergy's duty to administer the sacramental system. People who held anti-sacramental views rejected the church's control of the forgiveness of sin, the doctrine of the real presence of Christ in the Eucharist, and the practice of praying for the dead. They opposed praying for the dead because clerics made considerable income by saying private Masses for the dead.

The Poor Men of Lyons or **Waldensians,** named for their founder Valdes, are the best example of an apostolic movement that was forced into dissent and subsequently took up anticlerical and anti-sacramental heresy. Valdes studied the Bible and preached and practiced voluntary poverty, but he and his movement were denied official permission to preach, principally because they were using unapproved translations of the Bible. When they persisted, they were condemned at the Council of Verona in 1184. The condemnation hardened his group's resistance and turned them into an underground alternative church.

The **Cathars** (from the Greek word for "the pure ones"), who appeared in the mid-twelfth century, were rooted in the same soil of popular disenchantment with the clergy and the sacramental system. However, their critique was far more radical, for the Cathars taught an absolute dualism of a good god and an evil god (note similarities to the Manichean dualism that originally attracted Augustine; see Chapter 10). The world and the flesh were the work of the evil god. Marriage and reproduction were therefore rejected, as was eating any food that originated in animal intercourse, such as meat and dairy products. All forms of killing and violence were also rejected. Catharism's organization mimicked the structure of the Catholic Church, with an ordained male clergy of bishops and deacons. It had a spiritual elite called the "Perfect," who blended priestly and ascetical functions and could be male or female. It also had a rank and file of laity who were known simply as "believers."

Only the Perfects were required to adopt the full ascetical discipline of the Cathars, and only they could administer the Cathar sacrament of the *consolamentum,* a "laying on of hands" that prepared the recipient on his deathbed for birth into eternal life. Catharism was appealing to lay Christians in part because of the spiritual superiority of the Perfects as compared to many of the Catholic clergy. Catharism was most widespread in southern France, where the town of Albi gave rise to the name by which they were also known, the **Albigensians.**

To deal with heretical movements like the Waldensians and the Albigensians, the medieval church developed a two-pronged strategy: It promoted the good example and preaching of the mendicants, and it instituted the machinery of religious repression known as the **Inquisition.** In 1184 bishops were authorized to conduct investigations, or inquisitions, into accusations of heresy. At first the accused had the traditional protections of Roman law, which required accusations to be made in the form of sworn testimony. The accused were examined and if found guilty given a chance to repent. The unrepentant were excommunicated and imprisoned by the secular authorities. After 1231 the papacy began to license teams of investigators who traveled around and collected testimony wherever they could find it. It became customary to rely on anonymous accusations and to deny the accused the right to call witnesses on their behalf. After 1252, torture was used to get confessions, but only in rare cases were unrepentant heretics executed. One scholarly study of the penalties imposed in mid-thirteenth century investigations of Catharism in southern France estimated death sentences at one percent and imprisonment at ten to eleven percent, with the rest being given lesser penances such as the compulsory wearing of a cross (Tyerman 2006). The worst abuses occurred in the fourteenth and fifteenth centuries, when secular governments used the inquisition as an instrument of political control.

MEDIEVAL RELIGIOUS PIETY: THE MEDIATION OF GRACE

Religious piety in the High Middle Ages was characterized by increased attention to the sacraments, devotions to Mary and the saints, and a variety of religious practices that appealed to ordinary lay Christians whose experience of Christianity had become increasingly different from that of the clerics and nobility.

The Seven Sacraments

For the first thousand years of its history, Christianity did not have a rigidly defined list of the rituals called sacraments. For example, the early medieval ritual for anointing a king at his coronation was often considered a sacrament. In the twelfth century, however, the number of the sacraments was fixed definitively at seven. Each **sacrament** had a symbolic ritual consisting of words and visible gestures or material substances (bread, wine, water, oil, etc.). When properly performed for a recipient who was open to its action, the sacrament became the visible means of transmitting the invisible reality called grace, God's gift of his own presence. The sacrament caused God's grace in the soul *ex opere operato*, "by the very performance of the action," so that the effectiveness of the sacrament was not dependent on the worthiness of the one who administered it, a principle established long ago by Augustine in his controversy with the Donatists (Chapter 10).

The seven sacraments embraced all the significant moments of a Christian's life from birth to death. Baptism brought the newborn Christian into the new life of grace. Extreme Unction (from the Latin words for "last anointing"), the sacrament today called the Anointing of the Sick, was given at life's end. Confirmation, the sealing in the Holy Spirit, was originally part of Baptism, as it still is in the Orthodox churches. But in the Latin West, Confirmation became a rite distinct from Baptism because it required the presence of a bishop, who would not have been available every time Baptisms were performed. Matrimony (Christian marriage) developed as a means of sanctifying the life of the laity. Its distinctive marks were its permanence and its foundation in the consent of the married couple. Holy Orders, the rite of priestly ordination, set a man apart from the laity and enrolled him in the international priestly class that governed the church. The Gregorian program of priestly celibacy was intended to detach the clergy from their local connections to family and property and to bind them to a higher calling as the ritually pure gatekeepers of the sacramental system.

The Eucharist—at which Christians ate bread and drank wine that had been transformed into the body and blood of Jesus—was the fundamental sacrament. The bread was eaten in the form of a white wafer called a host, made with unleavened bread in memory of Jesus' Last Supper—which the synoptic gospels describe as a Passover meal—when Jesus instituted the Eucharist. The reality of the presence of Christ's body and blood in the bread and wine was taken with the utmost seriousness, to the point that tales were told about hosts that bled or visions of the child Jesus in the hands of the priest. Mention has already been made of the formal definition of transubstantiation as the way in which the change in the bread and wine was to be understood. Respect for the Eucharist was so powerful that people frequently avoided receiving it, out of fear of receiving it unworthily. By this time lay people were no longer allowed the Eucharistic wine at all, which was reserved to the clergy.

Though the frequency of reception of the Eucharist declined during the High Middle Ages, Eucharistic devotion actually intensified. At the consecration of the Mass, bells were rung as the host and cup were raised for viewing. During the ceremony known as benediction and in public processions, the host was shown for veneration in ornate display cases called monstrances. In the churches, a lit candle signaled the presence of the host in the tabernacle, or storage chamber, on the altar, toward which respect was shown by genuflection (bending the knee, as would a vassal before his lord). The Eucharist even received its own day in the calendar, the feast of Corpus Christi ("Body of Christ"), established by the pope in 1264 in response to popular demand, especially from Beguine communities. Corpus Christi was observed at the end of May or in June and became a hugely popular feast day, marked by public processions, dramatic performances, and fairs.

The sacrament of Penance also held a predominant place in the life of the Christian. Its three elements were defined as sorrow for sin, confession, and penance. The term *penance* comes from Latin *poena*, "penalty" or "punishment," and reflects the practice of the early church, when sinners who had been expelled from the community for their sins had to perform penitential works of "satisfaction" before being readmitted. The period of penitential rehabilitation could last for years. In the early Middle Ages it became customary to accept substitutes, such as reciting prayers, giving alms, or going on pilgrimage in lieu of the long periods of penance. At the same time, it also became normal to grant absolution (forgiveness) for sin before the penance was completed. On special occasions the church granted cancellations called **indulgences** for penance not yet performed. A plenary indulgence (a kind of "blanket pardon," where punishment for all of an individual's sins was canceled) was first granted by the pope to those who pledged to go on the First Crusade (1095).

Applying such cancellations to those who had already died represented a significant extension of indulgences. The extension was justified on the basis of the traditional practice of praying for the dead, and of the doctrines of **vicarious satisfaction** (the possibility that someone could pay the debt of another person's sin) and of the **communion of saints** (the belief that deceased holy ones share a relationship with the living members of the church). Just as Christians could pray to the saints for intercession, so could they perform works of satisfaction on behalf of all the faithful departed, not merely those recognized as saints.

Integral to this change was the development of the doctrine of **purgatory.** Early Christianity had held various notions of a transitional state of the soul after the body's death, as the *Martyrdom of Perpetua* showed already at the beginning of the third century. In the medieval period, these notions crystallized around the doctrine of purgatory as a place or temporary state in which the soul was purified before its admission to heaven. This temporary stage of purification was only open to those who had not died in **mortal sin** (sin that is committed willfully and deliberately and with the understanding that it is serious wrongdoing). The feast of All Souls Day (November 2) was instituted in 998 specifically to pray for those who had died with unperformed penances. By the fourteenth century the church took the further step of applying indulgences (as well as works of satisfaction like prayers and alms) to benefit the souls of the dead who might still be in purgatory. Eventually the bishops and the papacy, pressed for revenue, began to license traveling preachers in effect to sell such indulgences. Although these preachers were not supposed to claim that they could release the souls of the dead from purgatory, many did so anyway. That was the system in place in 1517, when it would arouse the ire of Martin Luther and lead ultimately to the Protestant Reformation (see Chapters 18 and 19).

Human Mediators: Christ, Mary, and the Saints

From the beginning, Christianity had seen Jesus Christ as "the judge of the living and the dead." In the Book of Revelation, he is the King of Kings who will sit on the throne of judgment at the end of the world. Christians of the Middle Ages were fascinated with this picture of Christ as king and judge. However, a powerful new devotion to Christ's suffering humanity also came into being during this period. Earlier representations of Christ on the cross showed him in a stiff, heroic, victorious pose. By the end of the medieval period, the crucified Christ was rendered so graphically as to border on the fantastic. Bernard of Clairvaux and other mystics fostered this devotion to Christ's human suffering.

This shift in focus to the suffering Christ was due in part to medieval Christians' enthusiasm for the "apostolic life," based on a desire to imitate Jesus's earthly life as fully as possible. The Stations of the Cross (a fourteen-step pattern of prayer in remembrance of the events of Christ's passion and death) became a popular devotion, as did the veneration of the Five Wounds of Christ on the cross. No one preached and lived the imitation of Christ more convincingly than St. Francis. In an apparently miraculous occurrence, he became the first person to manifest the mystical phenomenon of the *stigmata* (bleeding wounds in hands, feet, and side).

Mary also received enormous devotion from medieval Christians. Her popularity as Mother of God and as the Blessed Virgin goes back to the early church, but the new attention to the humanity of Christ gave devotion to Mary a further boost. Traditionally she had been represented as seated with the child in her lap. In the medieval period, these representations of mother

Figure 14–3 Bronze crucifix from the Church of St. Francis in Assisi.

Figure 14–4 Mary Seated with Child, tympanum of west right-hand door of Chartres cathedral. This pose became known as the *Sedes Sapientiae*, "Seat of Wisdom," because the Divine Wisdom of the Logos became incarnate in Mary. To symbolize the medieval conviction that classical and Christian learning could be harmonized because they came from the same divine source, the seven liberal arts and seven Greek and Roman masters are sculpted in the archivolts (the semicircular archway).

and son evolved toward more realistic poses in the same way that images of the crucifixion changed. Eventually these led to a set of standard artistic representations of mother and son, such as the laughing child, the child playing with an apple or ball, the caressing child, and the nursing child. Pictures of Mary without the child also became popular, especially representations of her enthroned in heaven. Toward the end of the medieval period, she appears frequently as the *mater dolorosa* ("the mother of sorrows"), holding the body of Christ after it was taken down from the cross, and as mother of mercy and pity.

The Cistercians, the Franciscans, and the Beguines were especially devoted to Mary. All Cistercian monasteries were under her protection, and it was the Cistercians who popularized the use of the prayer called the *Ave Maria* ("Hail Mary"). The rosary (the recitation of fifty "Hail Marys" along with other prayers, usually using a set of beads to help count the prayers) also came into use at this time. A number of feasts that commemorated events in her life were added to the year's cycle of worship. From the twelfth century, literary collections with titles like *Miracles of the Virgin* were made, which celebrated the favors she had granted to those who honored her. These stories typically show her as the dispenser of undeserved mercies that soften or even subvert the normal workings of justice.

An Excerpt from *Miracles of the Virgin*

A certain thief called Ebbo was devoted to the Virgin, and was in the habit of saluting her even on his marauding expeditions. He was caught and hanged, but the Virgin held him up for two days, and when his executioners tried to fix the rope more tightly, she put her hands on his throat and prevented them. Finally, he was released. (Cited in Southern 1953, 247)

Medieval Christians greatly desired human mediators in their relationship with God, in part because they viewed God as utterly transcendent. As mother of Christ, Mary had access to God, but as a human mother, Christian believers could have access to Mary and thus have access to God.

Another expression of the medieval desire for human mediators with God was the veneration of saints, a practice still observed in Catholic and Orthodox churches. It originated in the early church's belief concerning the communion of saints: The worship of the church on earth was a participation in the heavenly liturgy of the angels and the souls of the righteous. Since Christian martyrs were guaranteed a place in this company, it became customary to pray to them to intercede with God and to recommend them as role models for believers attempting to live the Christian life. These two functions of intercession and imitation became the foundation of the veneration of the saints. Neither intercession nor imitation were seen as a devaluing of Christ's status as mediator or as example. Rather, the saints were thought of as "grafted on" to Christ in a corporate identity in which all Christians were called to participate.

The medieval veneration of saints yielded a rich harvest of religious devotion, along with more than a little commercialism, legend, and sometimes outright fraud. Devotion to the saints ranged from the sublime case of St. Francis to the cult of St. Cunefort, venerated as a healer of children, who was originally a dog that died while rescuing a child (as the very name reveals: "brave dog"). In earlier centuries, the process of declaring someone a saint tended to focus on local church communities. By the twelfth century, when responsibility for approval of saints was placed in the hands of the papacy, **canonization** (the process of nomination and approval for sainthood) became more centralized and more bureaucratic. Though fewer saints were recognized officially, popular piety continued to nominate them at the local level.

The Religion of Lay People

The nobility practiced their religion with the help of priests who lived on their estates, or through monasteries that they founded and supported financially. Elaborately illustrated prayer books, called "books of hours" (so called because they adapted the monastic routine of daily prayer for lay use), helped their devotional life. Ordinary lay people depended on the parish system that had spread almost everywhere by now as a kind of "branch office" of the bishop's cathedral. Lay people could not understand the Latin Mass, but they heard the scriptures read in translation and were taught the commandments and basic prayers like the Our Father, the Creed, and the Hail Mary. Pictures, statues, and religious plays were also used for instruction. Preaching was more the work of the friars than of parish priests, who often lacked education and sometimes could not themselves understand Latin, since seminaries (special schools for the education of the clergy) were not established until the sixteenth century.

Germanic and Slavic paganism left its mark on the religious practice of lay people. Folkloric religion merged with Christianity so thoroughly that the two are sometimes hard to distinguish, for example, the rural belief in holy wells and woodlands and the widespread practice of blessing animals, crops, houses, or weapons. Blessed objects called **sacramentals** (a term coined by medieval theologians, who distinguished sacramentals from sacraments by saying that the former dealt with sanctifying *things* while the latter sanctified *people*) became and have remained popular features of Catholic life. Holy water is an excellent example. The blessed water used in Baptism was kept near the church door, and people dipped their fingers and made the sign of the cross over themselves when entering the church. They might also take some home to protect their houses and families.

Expressions of religious life among lay people could be found in a variety of places. Groups called confraternities or guilds offered lay people an opportunity for fellowship and support, because they were based on common interests such as a profession or trade. A prime religious function of such groups was to pay for prayers and private Masses for their deceased members. Pilgrimages to shrines near and far were another expression of lay piety. The most popular sites were Jerusalem and Rome, followed by Compostela in Spain, where St. James was believed to be buried. Compostela was so popular that medieval art always represents James in the traveling garb of a pilgrim. Other major destinations were the Church of Mary Magdalene at Vézelay in France and the tomb of Thomas Becket in the Cathedral of Canterbury in England.

Christian shrines were another major attraction, principally because of their relics (physical remains, articles of clothing, or possessions thought to have come from Christ, Mary, or the saints). Relics were prized for protection and healing, but they were also a major source of revenue. Churches, towns, and monasteries sought them eagerly because of their spiritual power and because they attracted travelers and donations. Their profit potential was so ironclad that they were used as collateral in loans. Theft of relics was common and expeditions were even mounted to seize them by force. In 1087 seafaring residents of Bari in southern Italy stopped in Myra in Asia Minor (modern Turkey) and liberated the relics of a fourth-century bishop, St. Nicholas of Myra, thus inaugurating his long and gradual transformation into the secular cult of Santa Claus. However, the greatest seizure of relics came when the Fourth Crusade sacked Constantinople in 1204 and took home great quantities of Byzantine relics.

CHURCH ARCHITECTURE: THE GOTHIC STYLE

To a modern observer, the most dramatic testimony to the spirit of Christianity in the High Middle Ages is the Gothic cathedral, "the mind of the Middle Ages made visible," as a modern scholar has said of the cathedral of Chartres. From its homeland in central and northern France, Gothic architecture spread to neighboring countries and gradually displaced the previously dominant Romanesque style. The chief technical advance that led to the new style was the perfection of the groined or ribbed vault, in place of the older barrel or dome vaulting, and the replacement of the rounded arch by the pointed arch. These developments made it possible to raise the height of the building while reducing the amount of stone needed to bear the load. Buttresses were added outside the building to further distribute the weight. Walls became less massive and ponderous, allowing the extensive use of stained glass windows and greatly increasing the amount of light that shone into the nave of the church. As a result, the visual lines of a Gothic cathedral were strikingly vertical, the whole building seeming to soar and to direct the eye upward. The use of light and material decorations was meant to raise the minds of worshipers to the incorporeal light of God and to Christ, the true Light of the World. The careful geometrical calculations and balanced ratios that underlie Gothic architecture have led people to compare it with the grand design and careful structure of medieval theology.

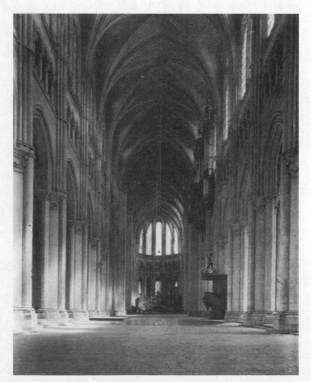

Figure 14-5 The interior of Chartres cathedral, illustrating both the verticality of the design and the abundant light of the Gothic style of architecture.

Gothic cathedrals served many purposes besides spiritual inspiration and aesthetic beauty. With their stained glass windows and abundant statuary—Chartres is said to contain as many as 6,000 painted or sculpted personages—they became instruments of instruction for those who could not read. They were also powerful expressions of the social fabric of medieval Europe: Contemporary sources tell of entire populations, from the nobility to the peasantry, working voluntarily to build them. Financing such massive projects came from voluntary donations, from conquest, and from the profits of saints' shrines in the church precincts. Adjacent to the great churches, a host of related businesses flourished.

The massive size of the great cathedrals was not meant so much to accommodate large congregations at Mass, but to allow space for public processions and crowds of pilgrims coming to see the collections of relics and to pray at shrines. The shift of focus from communal celebration of the Eucharist to private devotional practices is reflected in the displacement of the bishop's seat from its old central position in the apse, looking out to the congregation, to a side wing in the crossing, in order to make room for shrines containing relics. Walkways called ambulatories were added behind the apse to ease the traffic flow. Side altars were built along the ambulatories for the saying of private Masses. Thus, the building was actually more of a cluster of buildings, segmented for several distinct functions. The separation between clergy and laity, which became more pronounced at this time, was symbolically represented by the wall or screen, called a rood screen (from a Saxon word for "cross," because an image of the crucified Christ was always placed at the top of the screen), which separated the congregation of lay people in the nave from the clergy who celebrated Mass in the sanctuary.

Key Terms

Christendom	mendicant	Inquisition
curia	friar	sacrament
Innocent III	Francis of Assisi	indulgences
interdict	Franciscans	vicarious satisfaction
Fourth Lateran	Dominic Guzman	communion of saints
Council	Dominicans	purgatory
transubstantiation	Beguines	mortal sin
Boniface VIII	Waldensians	canonization
Cistercians	Cathars	sacramentals
Bernard of Clairvaux	Albigensians	

Questions for Reading

1. Describe the relationship between Christians and Jews during the High Middle Ages. What were the conditions that brought about discrimination against the Jews and occasional persecution in this period?

2. What various motives inspired the military campaigns called the crusades? Who started the movement? Against whom were they directed?

3. On what basis did medieval popes like Innocent III claim to intervene in secular affairs? Why was Pope Boniface VIII less successful than Innocent III had been in his efforts to deal with Christian rulers?

4. How did the new mendicant religious orders of the High Middle Ages differ from the already established monastic orders? Explain the main issue in the struggle that broke out within the Franciscan order over the meaning of Francis' vision. Which party eventually triumphed, and why?

5. What was anticlericalism, and why was it often a factor in medieval heresy?

6. How did the medieval church officially define the real presence of Christ in the Eucharist? Describe some of the beliefs and practices that illustrate the centrality of the Eucharist in medieval Christian life.

7. What is the relationship between the medieval form of the sacrament of Penance and the developing doctrine of purgatory? (Include an account of indulgences in your answer.)

8. What basic shifts occur in artistic representations of both Jesus and Mary during the High Middle Ages?

9. Describe how the Gothic style of church architecture differed from the previously dominant Romanesque style. How does this shift relate to Christians' understanding of God and God's relationship to humanity?

Works Consulted/Recommended Reading

Bredero, Adrian H. *Christendom and Christianity in the Middle Ages*. Translated by Reinder Bruynsma. Grand Rapids, MI: Eerdmans, 1994.

Brooke, Christopher N. L. *The Medieval Idea of Marriage*. New York: Oxford University, 1989.

Chazan, Robert. *The Jews of Medieval Western Christendom, 1000–1500*. Cambridge: Cambridge University, 2006.

Duffy, Eamon. *The Stripping of the Altars*. New Haven, CT: Yale University, 1992.

Katzenellenbogen, Adolf. *The Sculptural Programs of Chartres Cathedral*. Baltimore, MD: Johns Hopkins, 1959.

Knowles, David, and Dimitri Obolensky. *The Middle Ages*. The Christian Centuries, Vol. 2. New York: Paulist, 1969.

Lambert, Malcolm. *Medieval Heresy: Popular Movements from the Gregorian Reform to the Reformation*. Malden, MA: Blackwell, 2002.

Le Goff, Jacques. *The Birth of Purgatory*. Translated by Arthur Goldhammer. Chicago: University of Chicago, 1981.

McGinn, Bernard. *Visions of the End: Apocalyptic Traditions in the Middle Ages*. New York: Columbia University, 1979.

Morris, Colin. *The Papal Monarchy: The Western Church from 1050 to 1250*. Oxford: Clarendon, 1989.

Riley-Smith, Jonathan. *The Crusades: A Short History*. New Haven, CT: Yale University, 1987.

Rubin, Miri. *Corpus Christi: The Eucharist in Late Medieval Culture*. Cambridge, England: Cambridge University, 1991.

Schimmelpfennig, Bernhard. *The Papacy*. Translated by James Sievert. New York: Columbia University, 1992.

Simson, Otto von. *The Gothic Cathedral: Origins of Gothic Architecture and the Medieval Concept of Order*. 2nd ed., rev. Bollingen Series 48. Princeton, NJ: Princeton University, 1962.

Smalley, Beryl. *The Study of the Bible in the Middle Ages*. Notre Dame, IN: University of Notre Dame, 1964.

Southern, R. W. *The Making of the Middle Ages*. New Haven, CT: Yale University, 1953.

———. *Western Society and the Church in the Middle Ages*. Pelican History of the Church, Vol. 2. Baltimore, MD: Penguin, 1970.

Stow, Kenneth. *Popes, Church, and Jews in the Middle Ages: Confrontation and Response*. Burlington, VT: Ashgate, 2007.

Stow, Kenneth. "The Church and the Jews: St. Paul to Pius IX." In Stow, *Popes, Church, and Jews in the Middle Ages: Confrontation and Response*, 1–70.

Tierney, Brian, ed. *The Crisis of Church and State, 1050–1300*. Upper Saddle River, NJ: Prentice Hall, 1964.

Tyerman, Christopher. *God's War: A New History of the Crusades*. Cambridge, MA: Harvard University, 2006.

Voragine, Jacobus de. *The Golden Legend: Readings on the Saints*. 2 vols. Translated by William Granger Ryan. Princeton, NJ: Princeton University, 1993.

15

THOMAS AQUINAS

TIMELINE

c.A.D. 1224	Thomas Aquinas is born in Roccasecca in southern Italy.
A.D. 1244	Thomas joins the Dominican order and resides at Paris under the instruction of Albertus Magnus.
A.D. 1266	Thomas begins to teach after a brief stay at the Dominican *studium generale* in Cologne.
A.D. 1272	Thomas moves to Naples to set up a Dominican school. There he begins work on his *Summa Theologiae*.
A.D. 1273	Thomas has a profound spiritual experience of which he writes "All that I have written seems to me like so much straw compared to what I have seen and what has been revealed to me."
A.D. 1274	Thomas dies, leaving his *Summa Theologiae* unfinished.
A.D. 1323	Thomas is canonized as a saint.
A.D. 1567	Thomas Aquinas is declared Doctor of the Church.

The most famous and influential of the theologians of the medieval period was St. Thomas Aquinas, a thirteenth-century Dominican friar and university professor who wrote dozens of works of theology and philosophy. The thinking embodied in these writings would revolutionize Christianity in the same way that the writings of Augustine had in the fifth century. Thus, beginning in the thirteenth century, a gradual but decisive shift took place in the general theological orientation of Western Christianity from an "Augustinian" perspective to a "Thomistic" one.

THE THIRTEENTH CENTURY

The writings of **Thomas Aquinas** can be very difficult for a modern person to read and understand. Part of the reason for this is that Aquinas was very much a man of his time. His writings were profoundly influenced by the cultural and intellectual climate of the thirteenth century. Therefore, in order to understand Aquinas, one must understand the history and culture of the thirteenth-century world.

The Christian World

In the time that had passed between Augustine and Thomas Aquinas, the borders of the Western Christian world had shifted dramatically. In Augustine's time, Christianity was the dominant religion throughout the Roman Empire, which included all the regions that bordered on the Mediterranean Sea: southern Europe, Asia Minor, the Middle East, and North Africa. However, the reach of Christianity had not yet fully extended to northern and eastern Europe, which were still largely controlled by non-Christian barbarians. By Aquinas' time, many of the Christian territories that had been part of the Roman Empire had been lost to the Muslims—for example, the Middle East, North Africa, and even part of Spain. Asia Minor was controlled by the Byzantine Empire, the home of the Eastern Orthodox Church, which was no longer allied with the Western Roman Catholic Church. The sphere of influence of Western Christianity was now confined almost exclusively to Europe. However, during that time the church had sought to Christianize the barbarians of Europe and had been largely successful in that process. By Aquinas' time, northern and central Europe were firmly established as Christian regions, and they combined with southern Europe to define the reach of Western Christendom.

Intellectual Climate

The thirteenth century saw a fortunate combination of factors favoring the intellectual growth of

Figure 15–1 Portrait of Thomas Aquinas.

Europe. It was an unprecedented time of economic prosperity. This was the only time between the fall of Rome in the fifth century and the Enlightenment of the eighteenth century that Europe saw almost two centuries of good harvests without major wars or plague. By contrast, beginning in the fourteenth century, Europe would be ravaged by the Black Death, which killed about one-third of the population in some areas of Europe. The thirteenth century was also a time of outward curiosity and fascination. Those who returned from the crusades flooded Europe with news of far away, exotic lands. Contact with Eastern Christians and Muslims brought classical texts such as the philosophical works of Aristotle to the attention of European scholars, who began to translate these texts into Latin. It was a time in which higher education was able to flourish. It also marked the emergence of the university.

As a result of these circumstances, a flood of new learning poured into Europe. This new learning can be divided into four streams: Greek patristic (Eastern Christian), classical (pagan) Greek, Muslim, and Jewish.

The *Greek patristic stream*—that is, the Greek writings of the early church fathers—came by way of contact with Eastern Orthodox Christianity, which had been renewed through the crusades and through expanding trade. The resulting interchange brought the writings of the early Greek church fathers to the attention of Western European theologians. Much of this literature was being translated and studied by the Dominicans, the order to which Thomas Aquinas belonged. The biblical interpretations of the church fathers John Chrysostom and Origen were especially important to Aquinas.

The *classical (pagan) Greek stream* was represented especially by **Aristotle.** His writings were translated both directly from Greek manuscripts and secondhand from Arabic copies that included Muslim commentary. Aristotle's ideas were a great challenge to Jews, Christians, and Muslims alike, because scholars found themselves confronted by a non-Christian, non-Jewish, and non-Muslim account of reality that seemed more complete, more sophisticated, and more coherent than their own.

The *Muslim stream* was represented especially by **Avicenna** (980–1037) and **Averroes** (1126–1198). Avicenna was noted for writing medical commentaries on the classical Greek physician–scholars Galen and Hippocrates, mathematical commentaries on the classical Greek mathematician Euclid, and philosophical commentaries on Aristotle. A century later, Averroes' commentaries on Aristotle were so esteemed in the West that he was called simply "the Commentator," as Aristotle was called simply "the Philosopher."

The *Jewish stream* was represented especially by **Moses Maimonides** (1135–1204), writing from Morocco where he had fled from Christian persecution in Spain. In his famous book *Guide of the Perplexed,* he synthesized rabbinic Judaism and the Muslim form of Aristotelian philosophy. He also wrote very influential works on medicine and Jewish law.

While European scholars actively sought out this new learning, it created for them a considerable problem. However, the problem was not what one might have expected. They were not so much worried about how to answer their challenges as how to *integrate* those positions into Christian thinking—how to bring in the truths they expressed without being absorbed by them.

SCHOLASTICISM AND THE RISE OF THE UNIVERSITY

Under the impact of these new ideas, both the setting and the method of Christian theology changed. The effect of these changes was to turn theology into something it had never been before: an academic subject, taught and written about by professors for students in school and aimed at a deeper understanding of the truths of faith.

The Setting

In the early Christian church, theology was mainly the work of bishops and their advisors. Its goal was to defend and preserve the faith and apply it to the various circumstances in which congregations found themselves. By contrast, theology in the early medieval period had mainly been the work of monks in monasteries. There, the Bible and the writings of the church fathers were read, studied, and preserved, often in excerpts and condensed versions. An important outcome of monastic theology was to preserve the heritage of early Christianity. Monasteries became important centers for storing and copying manuscripts (literally, "handwritten books") in the early medieval period. They also conducted schools for young monks and sometimes for children of the nobility.

In contrast with monastic schools, schools organized by bishops were called cathedral schools because they were connected to the bishop's church. The subjects taught at monastic and cathedral schools were the traditional seven liberal arts: grammar, rhetoric, logic, arithmetic, geometry, astronomy, and music. At some point new subjects were added to these arts: canon law (church law), civil law (based on rediscovered Roman legal codes), medicine, and theology. Some of the masters (named from the Latin word *magister*, "teacher") at these schools became famous enough to attract students from abroad. Masters such as Hugh, Richard, and Andrew, known collectively as the Victorines, gave the School of St. Victor its illustrious reputation.

By the thirteenth century, scholars had responded to the new challenges by transforming the cathedral schools at Paris, Oxford, and Bologna into the first **universities.** Medieval society often formed associations, or guilds as they were called, of tradesmen or craftsmen. The term *university* originally meant the guild of teachers and students united in the "craft" of teaching and learning. However, these new universities developed permanent faculties, regular course offerings, examinations for formal degrees, a student body, and charters from the papacy or from royal authorities that gave them some degree of self-government. Students flocked to the university because of the opportunities that a degree made possible. The basic degree was the *baccalaureate* (from which we get our phrase *bachelor's degree*) in arts, that is, the liberal arts just listed. After studying the arts, a student might go on to specialize in canon law, civil law, medicine, or theology. Students became teachers themselves when they passed the master's exams and became doctors (from another Latin word, which means "teacher"). Schools were often known for their academic specialization: Bologna for civil and canon law, Montpellier for medicine, and Paris for theology. Thus, the institution of the university was to become one of the medieval world's lasting legacies.

The Method

Medieval theology began as commentary on authoritative texts such as the Bible, written primarily by monks to aid them in their spiritual life. In the eleventh and twelfth centuries, theology began to give more attention to focused studies called questions. With access to these new sources of knowledge, scholars contrasted and compared traditional authorities, as they became aware of contradictions in their sources. A more rigorous attention to logic, or dialectic as it was then called, also became evident.

In the thirteenth century, another innovation was the integration of Christian faith with a naturalistic view of the world, that is, with an understanding of the world as a purely natural system that can be understood by human reason without the aid of revelation. As more of Aristotle's works were translated into Latin, theologians found themselves confronted by a complete and rational worldview that seemed to have no need of divine revelation or any place for a personal God who created the world. Masters on the "arts" faculty—what today would be called the humanities and the sciences—studied Aristotle's works most eagerly. Some of these masters held the radical view that Christian faith was incompatible with the new Aristotelian view of the world. Others, including Thomas Aquinas, believed that it was possible to integrate this new knowledge into the faith.

The theology that was written and studied in these new schools and universities has been given the name **scholasticism,** from the Latin word for "school." In general, scholastic theology, the theology of the "Schoolmen," sought to harmonize faith with reason. Scholasticism took the truths uncovered by philosophers like Aristotle and tried to show how they were compatible with Christianity. It did this not by denying or revising elements of Christian faith, which depended on divine revelation, but by showing how reason could deepen one's understanding of what one believed because of God's revelation. This was how they interpreted the traditional definition of theology as "faith seeking understanding."

In the fourteenth century, many theologians would lose confidence that this harmonization was really possible. However, in the late nineteenth century, Pope Leo XIII revived scholasticism so that it again dominated Catholic theology until after the Second Vatican Council (1962–1965). The lasting influence of scholasticism, and that of its leading representative, Thomas Aquinas, is reflected in the fact that so many Catholic colleges and universities are named after Aquinas, and many colleges and universities of all kinds include his works in their coursework.

MEDIEVAL TEACHING AND LEARNING

To understand the writing that these new medieval scholars produced, one needs to recall that thirteenth-century scholars and students taught and learned very differently from the way twentieth-century scholars and students do. One needs to understand how they learned before one can begin to understand why they wrote the way they did. Scholastic professors used two basic strategies for learning and teaching: They commented on texts, and they disputed questions.

Texts

It was primarily through rediscovered texts that new learning was coming into Europe. The task of the scholar was to read the texts, understand them, and then try to figure out what to do with the new ideas contained in them. One strategy for teaching and learning was the *lectura,* the Latin source of our modern word *lecture,* in which a scholar publicly read a key text, such as a book of the Bible or the famous theological book, the *Sentences* of Peter Lombard, interspersing the reading with commentary. This strategy was only the beginning of the process, however. There remained the task of relating these ideas with other ideas into a larger whole, especially when there seemed to be conflicts between the various ideas.

Disputes

The process of relating the ideas found in texts from disparate worldviews into a new, larger whole was carried on in public disputes, which were something like a trial run for writing a book. As modern scholars write articles for journals to test out new ideas, medieval scholars held disputes for the same purpose. Anyone could show up at these public disputes.

A disputed question would be posed by the master, usually in the form "whether . . . or not," for example, "Whether God exists or not." The question was posed in an open way without presupposing which answer was correct. The audience began the discussion by proposing arguments for or against the question. One of the master's graduate students would try to respond to the arguments. In some cases the debate would become quite heated. It was not unusual to have noisy arguments and verbal fights on the floor of the meeting room.

The master listened carefully to what was said and then had time to prepare an answer. In his reply, the master first would restate as clearly and effectively as possible every argument that had been offered; then, in the light of that discussion, he would give his answer to the question he had proposed. Finally, he would clarify any of the arguments that agreed with his position but may have been inexact and answer all the objections on the other side. Effective masters tried to reconcile as many of the seemingly conflicting points as possible.

Quodlibetal Debates

Sometimes professors held quodlibetal debates (loosely translated as "whatever you would like to debate") in which they did not announce a question beforehand. Rather they offered to respond to any question at all that anyone cared to ask. Only very good or very self-confident professors dared to hold one of these debates. From the standpoint of their colleagues, these provided an excellent opportunity to attack or embarrass the master. If a master argued poorly in the presence of his peers and attending students, he could lose his students, which could be financially and professionally disastrous. In medieval universities, professors did not have classrooms full of students delivered to them—students contracted individually with professors. Naturally, no student would want to contract with a professor who had been publicly humiliated or whose lack of intelligence had been demonstrated for all to see.

THOMAS AQUINAS

Into this European university culture of the thirteenth century came a powerful new thinker—the Italian Thomas Aquinas, member of a new order of beggar preachers known as the Dominicans. Aquinas was born in 1224 or 1225, the son of a nobleman at Roccasecca in southern Italy. At a young age, Thomas was sent to the most famous Benedictine monastery of the day, Monte Cassino, for his schooling. His father hoped that some day Thomas might become the abbot of that prestigious monastery. Thomas did choose a religious life, but he did not choose to become a Benedictine.

Thomas was attracted to the new Order of Preachers (the Dominicans), an order that emphasized learning and poverty. Dominic, who died four years before Thomas was born, had founded his order to preach by word, deed, and a life of holiness. The Dominicans also practiced radical gospel poverty. Thus they were not allowed to own any possessions of their own but instead relied on the charity of others, often by begging in the streets. When members of the order traveled from country to country, they walked. Dominicans were not allowed to ride. In addition to their vow of poverty, Dominicans vowed chastity and obedience. Unlike the older monastic orders, which usually set up their monasteries in rural areas, the Dominicans lived in the midst of the medieval city, where their twin vocations of preaching and hearing confessions would be most useful. The Dominicans were also devoted to scholarship. They set up their own schools and programs of lifelong study to train their members. In addition, many Dominicans studied and taught in the most prestigious scholarly institutions of the day, the universities of Paris, Naples, and Oxford.

Thomas' family strongly disapproved of his decision to join the Dominicans. This new order was not nearly as prestigious as the older Benedictine order and the idea of Thomas joining an order of "beggars" probably did not appeal to his affluent family. When Thomas refused to yield to his family's wishes, his older brothers captured him and locked him up in a tower of the family castle while they attempted to change his mind. His brothers tried to expand his horizons and redirect his interests by bringing him a prostitute, but Thomas seized a poker from the fireplace and convinced her to leave.

Despite his family's desire to have Thomas choose another way of life, he was an exemplary prisoner in a situation of friendly house arrest. He was allowed visits by Dominicans, who brought him books to read. Eventually, after he had spent more than a year in the tower, he escaped. His family decided that they were not likely to change his mind, so they let him carry out his strange dream to live as a "beggar friar."

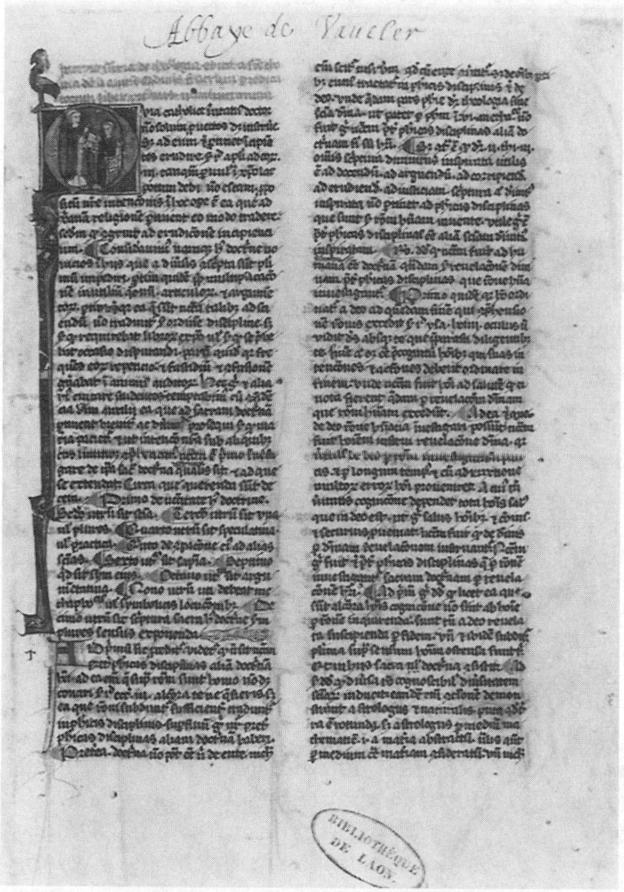

Now free, Thomas began his education as a Dominican. Thomas did not seem impressive to his fellow classmates, at least at first. Thomas was large and unusually quiet. He came from southern Italy, which was not considered the center of scholarship. His brother Dominicans called him the "dumb [silent] ox" because he seldom spoke in class. However, during the course of his education, Thomas impressed one of his teachers, Albert the Great (*Albertus Magnus* in Latin), the greatest scholar in the Dominican order in his day. Albert recognized and appreciated the promise of his young scholar. He commented to Thomas' classmates one day: "Gentlemen, you call Thomas the 'dumb ox.' But some day that ox will let out such a bellow that his noise will fill the earth."

Thomas began his teaching career at the University of Paris, the leading university of the day. He also taught in several Dominican schools in Italy. It was during these periods of teaching that Thomas wrote most of his theological works, of which there were a great many. His greatest work, the **Summa Theologiae** (literally a "summary or

Figure 15–2 An illuminated manuscript page from St. Thomas on the *Metaphysics* of Aristotle.

Figure 15–3 An excerpt of a manuscript page containing Thomas' own handwriting.

compendium of theology"), runs from 3,000 to 4,000 pages in most editions. Thomas also wrote two other *Summas*, commentaries on all the writings of Aristotle, commentaries on most of the New Testament and parts of the Old Testament, collections of disputed questions, and small treatises on various other topics.

The incredible body of work produced by Aquinas in a relatively short amount of time can be attributed to his sheer genius and his extraordinary powers of concentration. He was accustomed to writing three or even four different books simultaneously. He would dictate part of the first book to one secretary (or scribe), and while the scribe was writing, he would dictate part of the second book to another scribe, and so on. As far as we can tell, Thomas worked out his most famous book, the *Summa Theologiae*, in his head before he put anything down on paper: There are no rough drafts of the book. In those cases where we do have work in Thomas' own handwriting, he wrote so rapidly and with so many abbreviations that only a few modern specialists are able to read it.

MAJOR THEMES OF THE THEOLOGY OF THOMAS AQUINAS

Thomas' theology greatly influenced Western theology since his time. Here are some of his major themes:

1. There is a natural order accessible to humans through their physical senses and through human reason. This order of reality is called nature. Beyond this, there is another order of reality not accessible to humans through their own powers. This order of reality is called "the supernatural" or "the transcendent." The idea of an invisible, transcendent order of reality would later come under sharp critique by many thinkers of the Enlightenment, an eighteenth-century intellectual movement.

2. Human beings would never be able to understand the supernatural order or even know about most of it, if God had not revealed to us both its existence and its meaning. We would not be able to respond to it unless God freely gave us the power to do so. Theologians call this freely given power grace.

3. Although the supernatural order essentially transcends the natural order, the two orders are in harmony because the one God created both of them. The supernatural order is known by faith, and the natural order is known by reason. One cannot come to understand the supernatural order by reasoning from the natural order. Nonetheless, faith properly understood cannot contradict reason properly understood, and the power of grace perfects human nature and reason without destroying or replacing them. This insight is central to the idea of a Catholic university and justifies the role of theology in relation to secular disciplines. This part of Thomas' theology was rejected by the later medieval movement called nominalism (see Chapter 16), a movement that was very influential in the time of Martin Luther.

4. Although reason can demonstrate a few facts about the invisible order, such as the existence of God, most truths of revelation, such as the Trinity, can be neither proved nor disproved by human reason.

5. God is the primary cause of everything in the universe; nevertheless, humans act freely because God always moves things according to their natures and it is the nature of humans to act freely. Because God moves humans to act freely, humans are the secondary cause of their own acts. If a human does anything meritorious, it is because God gave the grace to act that way. If a human does anything evil, it is the human's own fault.

6. Humans, exercising their freedom, have in fact sinned, breaking their relationship with God. This sin dates from the very beginning of human history. Because it goes back to the very beginning and because all humans are affected by this reality of sin from the beginning of their lives, theologians speak of original sin. God became human to rescue humans from the results of original sin. Thomas taught that if the first human had not sinned, God would not have become human. Other theologians of his day, especially Franciscan theologians, disagreed with this last point. They claimed that, while it was fitting for God to rescue humans from original sin by becoming human, nevertheless God would still have become human even if humans had never sinned.

7. In the sacraments we come into contact with the passion and death of Jesus. The sacraments are the instruments God uses to cause grace in humans. Because it is Jesus who acts in the sacraments, they are effective whether the human minister is "worthy" or

not. This was the principle Augustine used to combat the Donatist claim that Catholic bishops, whom they saw as "traitors," could not give valid sacraments.

8. It is the vision of God face-to-face in heaven that gives humans their highest happiness. To see God in this way, the human mind must be transformed and elevated by God's grace.

THE *SUMMA THEOLOGIAE*

The best known and most influential of Thomas' writings is the *Summa Theologiae*. A *summa* is a summary or a comprehensive treatise on a particular subject. The *Summa Theologiae* is a "summary of theology." One of Thomas' greatest accomplishments is that he integrated Aristotle's philosophy into Christian theology, but Thomas would never have called himself a philosopher. Thus, although there are quotations and insights drawn from philosophers in the *Summa,* it is a theological work. Unlike the philosophers of Thomas' time, who would argue that they work from reason alone, without using any knowledge that is "revealed" by God, Thomas accepts revelation from God as a valid source of knowledge. Thus, Thomas quotes from the Bible and assumes that biblical teachings are true without needing to defend them.

The preceding point shows that Thomas' goal in the *Summa* was not to prove the articles of the Catholic faith. Thomas knew that no one could provide arguments for the truths of the faith based on reason alone. However, he did feel that one could offer arguments for theological positions about those articles of faith or arguments that draw out their implications. For example, human reason cannot prove that God is a Trinity, but human reason can explain the implications of understanding God as a Trinity. Human reason cannot prove that God became incarnate in Jesus of Nazareth, but it can explain how it was "fitting" for God to do so. Thomas used reason to connect the various truths of revelation to each other and to explain their meanings and implications in a world of ideas that seemed in constant danger of falling apart.

Thomas indicated in the prologue to the *Summa* that he was writing for beginners. However, this statement can be misleading. The beginners that Thomas spoke of were those who were beginning their study as theologians. This means that they already would have earned a baccalaureate degree and hence would have completed six years of philosophical studies. In addition, they probably had already memorized one of the gospels, and they likely knew most of the major characters and stories of the Bible.

The Form of the *Summa*

As already mentioned, Dominic founded his order to preach by word, deed, and a life of holiness. Pope Honorius III added a second mission to the order: to hear confessions. To help Dominicans carry out these two tasks, the order produced numerous guides for preachers and confessors. These guides were essentially practical treatises on the virtues (moral excellences, such as justice, charity, or fortitude) and vices (moral faults, such as hatred, gluttony, or pride).

This context helps explain why the largest part of Thomas' *Summa Theologiae* is the second part—a treatise on the virtues and vices. But the *Summa* differs from (most) other Dominican treatises because Thomas puts this section into a larger theological context: (1) where humans come from (God, whose image they are); (2) where they are going (to God) and how (by practicing virtues and avoiding vices); and (3) who and what gives them the capacity to go there—the power to practice virtue and avoid vice (Jesus Christ through the sacraments). These three topics form the three parts of the *Summa Theologiae*. The second part, the longest, is itself subdivided into two. Thomas wrote all of parts one and two, and a bit over half of part three; the rest of part three (called the supplement) was completed by his assistant. Each part is divided into questions, each question into articles.

The Form of an Article

The fundamental building block of the *Summa,* the **article,** is based loosely on the disputed questions that had become a basic part of university life. Following the pattern of the disputed question, a written article contains (1) a question and arguments, both (2) against and (3) for the proposition. Then (4) the master/author gives his own view and (5) responds to the arguments with which he disagrees. The articles in the *Summa* differ from disputed questions in that they do not record oral disputations that took place in Thomas' teaching career. Rather, they were written in the study.

Each article in the *Summa Theologiae* takes a standard five-part form, as follows:

1. Statement of the question, framed to expect the answer yes or no. For example,

   "Whether God exists?"

   The question is always an open question; the form of the question itself does not suggest what its answer should be.

2. Arguments on one side of the issue. Thomas almost always begins by outlining the arguments that are opposite to the position that he will eventually take. For example,

   "It seems that God does not exist . . ."

   Thomas will then outline the arguments, with their supporting reasons, in defense of this side of the issue. In this case the arguments will support the claim that God does not exist. Usually these arguments are numbered in some way. Thomas will later raise objections to these arguments but not until he reaches the part of the article that is devoted to such objections. Articles in the *Summa* tend to have a relatively small number of arguments in comparison with the number of arguments that might arise in disputed questions. In other words, Thomas does not include every possible argument on each side of the issue in an article.

3. An argument from an authority on the other side of the issue. Usually this involves a quotation from the Bible or from an early church father (usually a bishop) or theologian. The statement does not generally argue for its position, except insofar as the quotation from an authority itself qualifies as an argument. This part of the article is called the *Sed contra,* and it indicates the position that Thomas will eventually take as his own. However, Thomas has not yet indicated (for certain) his own position or his reasons for holding it. The *Sed contra* usually appears in the following form:

   "But against this . . ." or *"On the contrary . . ."*

4. The body of the article, or response. In this part of the article Thomas gives his own view of the issue in question and his reasons for holding that view. Often Thomas will

"divide the question," making distinctions to show that the proposal is true in one respect but false in another, or true in certain circumstances but false in others. This part of the article begins,

"I answer that . . ." or "Response: . . ."

5. Thomas concludes by giving replies to each of the arguments with which he expressed disagreement, usually the arguments with which the article began. This part begins,

"To the first argument . . ." or "Reply to the first objection: . . ."

Thomas now applies the insights of his response to the first objection, agreeing with as much of it as he can while explaining why it is not true as it stands.

The Article Form: An Example
Question 2, Article 3

Whether God exists?

It seems that God does not exist.

1. First argument against God's existence.
2. Second argument against God's existence.

But against this [a quotation from the Bible supporting God's existence].

I answer that [Thomas' own position and his reasons for holding it].

Replies to arguments with which Thomas disagrees.

> To the first argument: [a reply to the first argument against God's existence].

> To the second argument: [a reply to the second argument against God's existence].

BIBLICAL COMMENTARIES

The twelfth and thirteenth centuries were times of vigorous study of the Bible, and Thomas Aquinas was an outstanding participant in this study. It was during this period that the Bible was divided into chapters, and a start was made toward further subdivision into verses. Copies of the Bible were compared with ancient manuscripts to correct mistakes that had been introduced in the transmission of the biblical text. Lists of such mistakes, with their corrections, were published during this time. In addition, the concordance, which lists all the passages containing a particular word or idea, was developed to help scholars find particular passages in the Latin Bible and in the church fathers. New dictionaries and other study aids were also produced.

Thomas was committed to the primacy of the literal meaning of the Bible. At the very beginning of the *Summa Theologiae* (Pt. I, q. 1, art. 10), he explained that the literal meaning of the biblical text is simply the things that the words signified or what the author intended. Thus, the literal meaning also included what we call metaphorical meaning. For example, biblical references to "the arm of the Lord" were references to God's active power, not to the belief that God had a body. Theological argument could be based only on the literal sense of the Bible. However, biblical texts could also be interpreted spiritually. In Thomas' words, "The interpretation wherein things signified by words stand for other things is called the spiritual interpretation, which is based on the literal and presupposes it." (Fairweather 1954, 48). Following a conventional interpretation, he distinguished three different kinds of spiritual interpretation: one that sees the text as an anticipation of a future development in God's plan; one that sees the text referring to something in the life to come (what we would call *eschatological*); and one that sees the text as referring to some aspect of Christian morality or practice. He calls these three modes of spiritual interpretation the *allegorical*, the *anagogical*, and the *moral*, respectively. In his *Commentary on Galatians*, he gives an example of all four categories, the literal as well as the spiritual:

> When I say "Let there be light" and speak of corporeal light, it pertains to the literal sense. If "Let there be light" is understood as "let Christ be born in the church," it pertains to the allegorical sense. If it is understood as "let us be introduced into [eternal] glory through Christ," it pertains to the anagogical sense. If it is understood as "let us be illumined in our intellects and inflamed in our affections," it pertains to the moral sense. (*In Gal.* c.v, lect. 7, cited in Montague 1997, 58–59)

For Thomas, the existence of spiritual interpretations did not threaten the integrity of the literal meaning, "since nothing essential to the faith is contained in the spiritual sense of one passage which is not clearly expressed in the literal sense of another" (from *Summa Theologiae* Pt. I, q. 1, art. 10 in Fairweather 1954, 49).

POETRY AND MYSTICISM

Modern students, confronted with Thomas' relentlessly logical and systematic theology, may be surprised to learn that Thomas also wrote poetry: the hymns for Corpus Christi, the feast day in honor of the Eucharist, which was instituted during his lifetime. The translation of Thomas' hymn *Pange lingua gloriosi* demonstrates a wonderful union of theological insight and devotional yearning for God. Here are stanzas one, three, and five:

> Hail our Savior's glorious Body,
> Which his Virgin Mother bore;
> Hail the Blood which, shed for sinners,
> Did a broken world restore;
> Hail the sacrament most holy,
> Flesh and Blood of Christ adore!
>
> On that paschal evening see him
> With the chosen twelve recline,
> To the old law still obedient
> In its feast of love divine;
> Love divine, the new law giving,
> Gives himself as Bread and Wine!

> Come, adore this wondrous presence;
> Bow to Christ, the source of grace!
> Here is kept the ancient promise
> Of God's earthly dwelling-place!
> Sight is blind before God's glory,
> Faith alone may see his face!
>   (Quinn 1994, 59)

Thomas' poetry and his theology were nourished by a deep and continuing experience of prayer. There is even evidence that he had periodic mystical experiences of conversations with certain saints over one or another aspect of his writing. This aspect of Thomas' scholarship reflects the Catholic teaching about the communion of saints. Part of this teaching involves the idea that the dividing lines between this life and the next are not absolute and that those on each side continue to care about their brothers and sisters on the other.

In one particular vision, as Thomas finished one section of what is today the "Third Part" of the *Summa*—specifically the part about Jesus Christ—an icon (painting) of Christ spoke to Thomas and said, "You have written well of me, Thomas. What would you like in return?" Thomas answered, "*Non aliam nisi Te*" (nothing but you). Near the end of his life Thomas had a vision of God so powerful that he quit writing altogether, even as his assistants urged him to complete the *Summa*. Thomas responded to their request, "After what I have seen, all that I have written seems to me like so much straw."

Shortly after his final vision, Thomas Aquinas died. He was canonized as a saint in 1323, and in 1567 he was proclaimed a **Doctor of the Church,** an honor reserved for those whose teaching and scholarship have reflected Catholic Christian beliefs and have been important in the lives and faith of others. The church, by declaring him a saint, expresses its conviction that he received from God what he had seen in vision: He received that reality that made all his writing seem in comparison like "so much straw," the "nothing but you" that he had asked for earlier and had briefly glimpsed in his final vision.

Key Terms

Thomas Aquinas	Moses Maimonides	article
Aristotle	university	Doctor of the Church
Avicenna	scholasticism	
Averroes	*Summa Theologiae*	

Questions for Reading

1. What factors contributed to the rise of scholarship in the thirteenth century? What four streams of new ideas influenced medieval European scholarship? What challenge faced European scholars in the presence of this new knowledge, and what did they try to do in the face of the challenge?

2. Describe the emergence of the university in medieval Europe.

3. Give an overview of the main features and major events in the life of Thomas Aquinas.

4. List and explain some of the main points of Thomas' theology. In particular:

   a. Explain the natural and supernatural orders. How can we come to understand and respond to the supernatural order?

   b. How do the natural and supernatural orders relate to each other? Can faith and reason contradict each other?

5. What two main tasks were undertaken by the Dominican order, of which Thomas was a member? How do those tasks relate to the *Summa Theologiae*?

6. Explain the structure of an article in the *Summa Theologiae*. Why did Thomas divide the *Summa* into three parts?

7. What does Thomas mean by the literal sense of a biblical passage? By the spiritual sense? Which can be used as a starting point for arguing to a theological conclusion?

Works Consulted/Recommended Reading

Chenu, M. D. *Toward Understanding St. Thomas*. Translated by A. M. Landry and D. Hughes. Chicago: Regnery, 1964.

Davies, Brian. *The Thought of Thomas Aquinas*. Oxford: Oxford University, 1992.

Fairweather, A. M, ed., trans. *Nature and Grace: Selections from the* Summa Theologiae *of Thomas Aquinas*. The Library of Christian Classics, Vol. XI. Philadelphia: Westminster, 1954.

McGonigle, Thomas D., and James F. Quigley. *A History of the Christian Tradition: From Its Jewish Origins to the Reformation*. New York: Paulist Press, 1988.

Montague, George. *Understanding the Bible*. New York: Paulist Press, 1997.

Pegis, Anton C., ed. *Introduction to St. Thomas Aquinas*. New York: Modern Library, 1948.

Quinn, James. *Praise for All Seasons*. Kingston, NY: Selah, 1994.

Weisheipl, James A. *Friar Thomas d'Aquino: His Life, Thought and Works*. 2nd ed. Washington, DC: Catholic University of America, 1983.

Chapter

16

CHRISTIANITY IN THE LATE MEDIEVAL PERIOD

TIMELINE

c. A.D. 1285–1347	Life span of William of Ockham, famous for the nominalist principle known as Ockham's Razor.
A.D. 1309–1377	The period of the Avignon Papacy, when the pope moves the papal residence to Avignon, France.
c. A.D. 1342–1413	Life span of Julian of Norwich, an English mystic who records her visions in *Showings*.
A.D. 1347–1351	The bubonic plague, also known as the Black Death, strikes Europe, with enormous loss of life.
c. A.D. 1347–1380	Life span of Catherine of Siena, religious mystic and prominent writer.
c. A.D. 1375	John Wycliffe begins spreading his teachings of reform within the church.
A.D. 1381	The Peasants' Revolt.
A.D. 1378–1417	The Great Schism in the papacy: The church had first two, then three popes at the same time.
A.D. 1415	John Hus is put to death as a heretic.
A.D. 1414–1418	The Council of Constance asserts the authority of conciliarism to end the Great Schism and condemns the teachings of John Wycliffe.
c. A.D. 1551	Catherine of Genoa's book *Purgation and Purgatory* is published posthumously.

The late medieval period (roughly 1300–1500) is often seen as a time of decline, disintegration, conflict, and upheaval. Weather conditions in Europe were appalling, causing widespread drought and starvation. The bubonic plague, or Black Death, was ravaging Europe, destroying nearly one-third of its population in some areas (1348–1350). The European economy was in shambles, and its social institutions were crumbling as well. The church hierarchy, which people had come to depend on as a source of safety and security, had become a source of scandal. And France and England were engaged in an extended conflict that would come to be known as the Hundred Years' War (1337–1453). In spite of all these difficulties, this was also a time of great creativity that paved the way for later accomplishments in the Renaissance period.

The disintegration and the creativity of this period resulted in a number of very real challenges and opportunities for Christian faith and life. First, shifts in the intellectual climate of the late medieval period gave rise to nominalism, a development within scholasticism that would have a radical impact on theological inquiry. Second, there was the scandal of the Avignon papacy, the Great Schism, and the responses of reformers who sought to bring the church back to holiness. Third, the Black Death had a profound impact on the Christian imagination, specifically its art and literature. Finally, the late medieval period saw the rise of mysticism, a spiritual phenomenon that provided people with direct experiences of humanity's deeply personal and intimate relationship with God.

SCHOLASTICISM AND NOMINALISM

In the High Middle Ages, education was greatly influenced by the scholastic method. Its assumption was that truth was already available to the learner, whether in the writings of ancient authorities, in scripture, or in church teachings. One only needed to organize it properly, explain it clearly, and defend it appropriately. As a result, logic became an important part of the educational endeavor. The primary emphasis of scholasticism was not empirical investigation. Instead, scholars debated important texts in their field and speculated about what conclusions they might draw from the texts. In the area of theology, the "Schoolmen" tried to take the truths uncovered by the philosophers and show how they were compatible with elements of Christian faith, which depended on divine revelation. They tried to show how reason could deepen one's understanding of what one believed on God's authority.

The impact of scholasticism on theology was profound, as we can see from Thomas Aquinas' *Summa Theologiae*. However, in the late medieval period, there was a development within scholasticism called **nominalism**. The person most often associated with nominalism is William of Ockham (c. 1285–1347). He argued that only individual things exist. Universal natures or essences, such as human nature, existed only as general concepts in the mind; they did not exist outside of the mind or in God. Universal or general terms like *human nature* were merely linguistic constructions necessary for communication. A consequence of this view was that one could not know anything about God by reason. Aquinas had argued that we could understand something about God's goodness and wisdom by using the analogy of human goodness and wisdom: Divine goodness and wisdom were like human goodness and wisdom but freed from every limitation and hence infinitely more perfect. For Ockham, on the other hand, wisdom and goodness were only concepts, not universal natures or qualities. Hence, according to Ockham, we can only know about God through revelation, accepted in faith, not through reason. Faith, not reason, is the basis for our relationship with God.

Some scholars suggest that nominalism was a particularly appropriate philosophy for this period because of its focus on the individual and its pessimism about one's ability to reason about God. It was an important movement because it would set the stage for several later developments. In particular, William of Ockham's nominalism, with its conviction that God could be known only through revelation, accepted by faith, would prepare the way for sixteenth-century Reformation theology and its emphasis on justification by faith. Likewise, nominalism's concern about acquiring knowledge through the experience of particular occurrences would lay the foundation for the development of the natural sciences in the later eighteenth-century Age of Enlightenment.

THE AVIGNON PAPACY AND THE GREAT SCHISM

Throughout most of the Middle Ages, the Roman church was a dominant force for the preservation and development of the Western world. In the late medieval period, however, the church, or more accurately, the papacy, became a source of disunity and scandal. Once seen as the spiritual center of Europe, the activities taking place in Rome became increasingly confusing to the average Christian. Likewise, the pope, once seen as a bulwark of authority in both the religious and political spheres of influence, became little more than a pawn of the emerging national kingdoms. Two related incidents that characterize the extent of the crisis facing the church of the fourteenth century are the Avignon Papacy and the Great Schism.

The Avignon Papacy

In 1309, the newly elected French Pope Clement V moved the papal court from Rome to Avignon in southeastern France. There were many circumstances that contributed to this move to Avignon. Rome had become a rather dangerous place to live because of some disturbing political and religious fighting going on there—the consequence of a nasty fight between Clement's predecessor, Pope Boniface VIII (1294–1303), and the French king Philip IV. Philip may even have pressured Clement into the move, since he had just recently been elected pope under Philip's influence. Some have suggested that the move was made because the climate was more conducive to the health of the pope and his court. In fact, Clement himself, as pope, had the right to move the seat of the papacy anywhere he wished. However, the move, which appeared at first to be temporary, lasted well past Clement's lifetime, through six more popes, until 1377. The period of the **Avignon Papacy** would later be referred to derisively as "the Babylonian Captivity," taking its name from the original captivity of Jews in Babylon in the sixth century B.C.

The Avignon Papacy was compared to the Babylonian Captivity with good reason. While the papacy was centered in Rome it had a particular status, because of the authority of tradition which associated St. Peter and the apostolic succession with Rome. By contrast, the papacy at Avignon was obviously under French influence, if not under France's complete control. This disturbed both the allies and enemies of France. Both feared that, with the "captivity" of the pope, the French could control all of European affairs from Avignon.

To make matters worse, the pope lived richly in Avignon, and the luxuries of the papal court were paid for in part by practices that many considered contrary to Christian faith and church law. These practices included the selling of church offices (simony), the selling of indulgences (a pardon for punishment due as a result of a person's sin) to support the financial obligations of the Avignon papacy, and **nepotism** (making exceptions to church laws for the advancement of one's relatives).

The problems of the Avignon Papacy were made worse by the emergence of national kingdoms. While the Late Middle Ages still had a feudal social structure, national identities and interests were beginning to develop, supported by developments in particular languages, a rising merchant class, and the acceleration of trade. The pope was supposed to represent the universality of the church and the Christian faith. Instead, during the Avignon Papacy, the people had a pope seemingly under the control of one nation and one king. This would inevitably lead to a weakening of the authority and power of the papacy. Questions about the pope's role as a temporal and spiritual leader also eventually poisoned Christian thinking about the meaning and importance of the notion of a universal church.

The Great Schism

By the middle of the fourteenth century, there was growing pressure from different circles for the pope to return to Rome. However, the Avignon controversy would not be settled quickly or easily. Pope Gregory XI moved the papal court back to Rome in 1377, only to die the following year. When the new pope Urban VI announced that he planned a reform of the curia (college of cardinals), a large faction of cardinals, most of them French, protested by calling for a return of the papacy to Avignon. Claiming that they had been pressured into a hasty election, they withdrew their vote and elected a substitute, who took the name of Clement VII. Urban VI stayed in Rome, while Clement VII returned to Avignon. Thus began the era in papal history known as the **Great Schism**. For almost forty years the church would have two, and ultimately three, popes at the same time. This period is not to be confused with the separation of Eastern and Western Christianity (1054), which is also known as the Great Schism.

During the Great Schism (1378–1417) of the papacy, the problem of identifying the legitimate pope was, in the end, a contest between the emerging nations and city-states of Europe for control of the papacy and the power thought to go with it. France and its allies (Scotland, Navarre, Castile, and Naples) sided with the pope in Avignon, calling the pope in Rome the antipope. England and its allies (Scandinavia, northern Italy, Ireland, and Portugal) declared for the pope in Rome, calling the pope in Avignon the antipope. While some were motivated by purely political goals, many declared for one pope or the other because they authentically believed, on theological grounds, that the pope they supported was the proper successor of St. Peter.

After scandalizing the Christian world and being condemned by holy persons and saints, the schism was finally healed by a series of councils held in the early fifteenth century. The Council of Pisa (1409) elected a new pope, presumably to replace the two currently reigning popes, but they refused to abdicate. Now there were actually three popes competing for support. Five years later a renewed effort was made to solve the schism at the Council of Constance (1414–1418). The participants at Constance defended the legitimacy of their meeting, which had only shaky papal support, by appealing to the principles of **conciliarism**, a theory of the church which had become popular among some theologians.

The decree known as *Haec Sancta*, adopted by the Council of Constance on April 6, 1415, reads: "First, it [the Council] declares that, legitimately assembled in the holy Spirit, constituting a general council, and representing the catholic church militant, it has power immediately from Christ" (Tanner 1990, 409); therefore, everyone, including the pope, must be obedient to its authority. On this basis the council deposed all *three* popes and elected Martin V (reigned 1417–1431) to replace them. Because Martin's legitimacy was eventually recognized, Constance could be said to have successfully ended the schism, though the Catholic Church has only accepted the decrees of the council from the time of Martin's election (1417).

Later, the Council of Basel (1431–1449) also appealed to the principles of conciliarism in discussing the reform of the church. When Basel invoked Constance's doctrine that a council was superior to a pope, Pope Eugene IV in 1437 withdrew his support from the Basel meeting and moved the council to Ferrara in Italy. In 1460 Pope Pius II condemned conciliarism insofar as it taught that a council was superior to a pope. In that sense the papacy survived the crisis of the fourteenth and fifteenth centuries. But grave damage had already been done to papal prestige and authority. It was more and more difficult to see the church, under papal leadership, as a universal reality that could overcome the boundaries of class and nation, of feudal obligation and responsibility. The movement toward national and territorial churches would not be stopped.

THE BLACK DEATH AND THE CHRISTIAN IMAGINATION

Because of the Black Death, it must have seemed to the population of Europe that the world was about to come to an end in 1347 to 1351. Traveling from the Middle East, ships returning to Europe carried rats and fleas, which spread two virulent forms of bubonic plague: one spread by contact with the blood of its victims, the other by respiration as a form of pneumonia. We must bear in mind as the story unfolds that the ancient and medieval worlds were accustomed to periodic ravages by famine, plague, and illness. However, they had never experienced anything quite like this plague. It caused widespread panic and a belief that perhaps the biblical plagues of the book of Revelation had finally come upon them.

Bubonic plague, which still exists in small pockets today, was especially devastating to late medieval Europe for a variety of reasons. One was the speed with which it killed. While the first form of this plague could take up to five days for the victim to die, the second spread so quickly that the healthy could become ill and die in a night. Another was the horror of the disease itself. It was familiarly known as the Black Death, because black growths and pustules appeared on the victim's body. These would burst, and gradually the entire body would swell, discolor, and decay. Yet another reason for its devastation was the mystery of its transmission. Although doctors of the time did not know much about how diseases were transmitted, they usually learned by process of elimination how to protect others from their spread. The fact that the plague was spread in two forms by two hosts made it virtually impossible to understand how it was being transmitted, and, since both fleas and rats were a fact of life in the medieval world, they were not suspected. This pestilence, or "the pest" as it was called, knew and respected none of the trappings of wealth, influence, or status. It seemed to strike at random, killing rich and poor, in cities and in the countryside, sinners and holy people. It simply did not discriminate.

Figure 16–1 The Crucifixion, from the Isenheim Altarpiece by Matthais Grüenwald (1510–1515).

Perhaps the greatest effects of the plague were on the Christian imagination. Panic increased as the disease spread and as others abandoned the suffering victims. Many could not receive the last rites (the sacrament of anointing of the sick), because a priest was not available or because he would not come out of fear of contamination. Special dispensations were given for lay persons to hear the last confessions of the dying to reassure them that God would not forget them but forgive them at the end. A new kind of religious piety (devotional practice) also began to emerge, as some Christians chose to identify with the suffering of victims and families by increasingly meditating on the sufferings of the crucified Christ. Processions of flagellants (people who beat themselves as an act of penance) began to appear in the streets, praying for God's intervention in ending the plague. Tragically, some Christians made the Jews the scapegoats for the plague, and in some cities pogroms (organized massacres) erupted against them.

The Black Death produced several indelible artistic images that reflect the sentiments of the times. The first is a gruesome representation of death as a grinning skeleton holding the traditional scythe (a tool for gathering in the harvest), hovering over the dead and decaying, and showing the healthy and prosperous where their futures lie. The second is the bloody portrayal of Christ on the cross, with discolored flesh and weeping wounds. These artistic representations of Christ's crucifixion were meant to warn people that this world was passing away. However, they also gave hope to Christians, because they believed that, by Christ's redemptive death on the cross, better things awaited those who experienced great suffering as Christ had suffered. The third artistic representation typical of this time was the figure of the **pietà**, in which Mary mourns over her crucified son. It encouraged Christians to identify their suffering and death with that of Christ and to wonder at the amazing love of God present even in life's most difficult moments.

While many Christians fled from the infected (contemporaries observed that "charity was dead"), others helped the ill and dying, ministering to them despite great risk to themselves. Many were clergy and religious; others were devout lay persons. Among them were two saints named Catherine: Catherine of Siena, who will be discussed in a later section of this chapter, and Catherine of Genoa.

Figure 16–2 A pietà from Germany c. 1300. The crucified Christ in the arms of his mother.

Catherine of Genoa (1447–1510) chose to live amid the plague victims and people suffering from other diseases, establishing a hospital for all the needy. Her husband later joined her, and together they pledged their lives to chastity and to the service of the poor. Her most lyrical and important work is the *Purgation and Purgatory*, which speaks of the cleansing given to us by God, a cleansing that will leave us shining brightly, as gold is refined in the fire. Her attitude is characteristic of many devout Christians of the late medieval period who decided that, in solidarity with those who suffer, they wanted to be like Christ in the world, working and caring for others through God's strengthening spirit.

In this selection from her works, Catherine describes the process of God loving and cleansing the souls here and in purgatory:

> Not that those souls dwell on their suffering;
> they dwell rather on the resistance they feel in themselves
> against the will of God,
> against His intense and pure love bent on nothing
> but drawing them up to him.
> And I see rays of lightning
> darting from that divine love to the creature,
> so intense and fiery as to annihilate not the body alone,
> but, were it possible, the soul.
> These rays purify and then annihilate.
> The soul becomes like gold that becomes purer as it is fired,
> all dross being cast out.
> (Catherina of Genoa 1979, 79)

The importance of the Black Death cannot be underestimated. Its toll was devastating not only in the depletion of Europe's population, but also in the loss of a sense of certainty about life, in the breakdown of social organization, and in radical changes in Christian attitudes and lifestyle. In addition, the enormous number of clergy and religious who died during the great pestilence left a vacuum that needed desperately to be filled. Priests were ordained as quickly as possible so as to have the sacraments available once more to the populace, but many were uneducated and unlettered. Some were probably not morally suited to priesthood either. Abuses were on the rise, whether from ignorance, misinformation, or deliberate callousness. Thus, preachers arose who rallied the people against the abuses of a corrupt church, suggesting that these abuses were the cause of God's wrath upon the people. We now turn to these figures and the religious and social unrest caused in large part by the plague.

REVOLTS AGAINST CHURCH AND STATE

As the legitimacy of the Avignon Papacy weakened, the monarchies of France, England, and Germany attempted to put controls on the church's leadership and on its ability to raise taxes to support its projects. Opposition was not limited to the political arena, however. Lay religious movements were beginning to emerge as critics of church corruption and religious superstition. Two reformers of the late medieval period, John Wycliffe and Jan Hus, are often mentioned together and seen as forerunners of the Protestant Reformation. In reality, Wycliffe and Hus lived in different places at different times and left legacies that are distinct from one another.

John Wycliffe

John Wycliffe (c. 1330–1384) was a highly controversial figure in the Late Middle Ages, a man of quick temper and incisive thought. He was well educated and an ordained priest. Indeed, Wycliffe even had a patron who supported his work financially and a steady church post in England. In the early phase of his preaching, Wycliffe appealed not only to Christians scandalized by the Avignon Papacy, but also to advocates of English nationalism. He believed that the clergy ought to live a life of poverty, without ownership of property, somewhat like the mendicant orders, and therefore he began to preach against the wealth and power of the clergy and the Avignon Papacy. He also believed that the English kings ought to have the right to appoint candidates to key church positions and to collect taxes in their own land. Both practices currently belonged to the authority of the pope, but Wycliffe saw them as sources of corruption in the church.

Wycliffe also challenged or denied several widely held church doctrines. For example, he held that it was not the "visible" church represented by the church of Rome that counted, but the "invisible" church of the saved. The trappings of the external church and its claims to be the source of salvation for Christians were both wrong and dangerous. Those whom God had predestined for salvation were chosen by God alone. He also taught that personal holiness ought to be the basis of religious authority in the church, not one's ecclesiastical rank or ordination. Wycliffe also attacked the doctrine of transubstantiation and the notion of the real presence of Christ in the Eucharist. If the bread and wine became in substance Christ's body and blood, then bread and wine must be destroyed in order to become Christ's body and blood. This destruction seemed to Wycliffe to have no place in the image of the loving God who had created universal realities in the first place. He called his doctrine one of "remaining." Christ was present in the Eucharist in a spiritual way, but the bread remained bread.

Wycliffe advocated a translation of the Bible into English. In fact, two translations were begun under his commission between 1380 and 1381, although neither was completed. He also wanted to found a group of poor followers who would preach as he did and represent a contrast to the corrupt clergy and religious orders. His ideal of a community of the poor eventually materialized in a group known as the Lollards, who implemented his ideas in a more radical way than Wycliffe probably intended. They were preachers but were much more active politically than Wycliffe was. They advocated clerical poverty and confiscation of church property. They also distributed vernacular translations (in the language of the people) of the Bible and preached a return to the simple, scripture-based Christianity of the early church. Whether or not Wycliffe was actually involved in the founding of the Lollard movement in England is a matter of dispute. However, they certainly spread his ideas and kept his legacy alive. They were active in several social uprisings, and as a result many were put to death.

Jan Hus

Jan Hus (c. 1372–1415) was born in Bohemia (in the modern-day Czech Republic) shortly before the death of John Wycliffe. Like Wycliffe, he was well educated and an ordained priest. The figure of Wycliffe was to be a powerful one in his life, because they shared a number of common concerns about church reform. In fact, many of his teachings were taken directly from the writings of Wycliffe. For example, Hus accepted Wycliffe's teaching about the authority of scripture as the source of doctrine. However, he did not accept Wycliffe's doctrine of "remaining" in the Eucharist. What prompted him to begin preaching reform was the Great Schism. Appalled by the Schism, yet part of it (since Bohemia supported one of the antipopes), he refused to support any of the various popes' actions. He was completely scandalized by the intention of one of the antipopes to send a crusading force against Christians in Naples. He railed against this move and against the corrupt practice of selling indulgences. This put him in jeopardy with the king of Bohemia, who profited from these practices. He preached widely in Czech and wrote on the Ten Commandments and the Lord's Prayer. His most important work was *De ecclesia* ("On the Church"). In it, he described the church as "the body of Christ," with Christ as its only head.

Hus was finally ordered by the pope to appear at the Council of Constance (1414–1418). The king of Bohemia, who had been protecting Hus against his opponents, released him under safe conduct to attend. Although Hus denied the allegations brought against him, especially concerning the Eucharist, the council did not believe him. They claimed that, like Wycliffe, Hus taught the doctrine of "remaining." When asked to recant (take back his radical beliefs), he protested that he could not take back what he never had believed in the first place. In the end, the council decided that Hus was a dangerous heretic, spreading the ideas of Wycliffe. He was stripped of his priesthood, condemned, and turned over to the secular authorities to be put to death. His execution served to increase the devotion of his followers who considered him a martyr. In Bohemia and among its close neighbors, his death resulted in the establishment of a Czech national church known as the Hussites in 1420, a century before the Reformation.

The Peasants' Revolt

Although the Peasants' Revolt of 1381 was confined to England, it is a powerful symbol of the social and political unrest engendered by the plague. In large part, the revolt was caused by the farm labor shortage resulting from the plague. The shortage was made even worse by the fact that peasants who had been farmers were leaving the farms for more interesting jobs as artisans. The large landowners were not pleased about their loss of income and the higher wages they had to pay the workers who remained in farming. In order to recoup their losses and stop the flow of peasants off the land, the landowners shifted to wool production and other more profitable, less labor-intensive crops. They also managed to get extremely repressive legislation passed to keep peasants on their farms. They froze farm wages at very low levels and exacted very high taxes from the peasants.

The Peasants' Revolt came about because of the mistreatment and overworking and overtaxing of the peasantry. The preaching of the Lollards also inflamed an increasingly discontented populace. While the unrest in England proved serious, it did not threaten the social fabric for long. Within a year the revolt was extinguished with deadly force. Yet, this revolt and others like it would mark the beginning of the end of a workable feudal economy.

MYSTICISM IN THE LATE MIDDLE AGES

Although mysticism had been part of Christianity from its beginnings, it burst forth again with particular force in the fourteenth century. **Mysticism** is a particular spiritual phenomenon that expresses itself in direct, intense experiences of union and oneness with God. The mystical journey at its simplest consisted of three phases: purgation (cleansing from sin), illumination (an attraction to all the things of God, especially scripture and the divine office, the official prayer of the church), and finally union (the state of oneness with God). The experience of union might have been momentary, but it had lasting effects on the mystic, leaving him or her with an assurance of God's constant presence. Perhaps the reason that mysticism flourished in the fourteenth century was that the passionate and prophetic character of the mystic was sorely needed in a time when the church and the Christian people were wondering if they had indeed been abandoned by God, or if they were victims of God's wrath. In these troubled times, when the world seemed to be falling to pieces, people needed the guidance of the mystics.

Although mystics throughout the ages share certain characteristics in common, they also differ from one another. Some mystics were primarily visionaries, whose union with God produced visions which taught them about faith and often called them to prophecy or to service. Others were so overcome by the presence of God that they would experience ecstasies (from *ek-stasis,* "standing outside"). While in ecstasy, they experienced supernatural phenomena of various sorts: raptures, trances, various types of transformation (levitation, changes in appearance, miraculous events). Still others did not see visions or have raptures but felt drawn closer to God in an experience of the "divine darkness" where they realized the full extent of how little God can be understood or perceived. Yet, whatever the differences in their experiences of God, mystics maintained that the most important quality of their extraordinary gifts was the love and union with God that these experiences brought about.

The church in general has always been somewhat suspicious of mysticism for a variety of reasons. Some persons claimed to have revelations from God but did not. These people simply used the claim for their own purposes (for example, status, recognition, or special favors). Another factor that influenced the church's reluctance to endorse mystical experiences was the number of women who had such experiences. Their claims of authority from God were a threat to the medieval understanding of woman's traditional role. In fact, mystics came from all social classes and levels of education, from many walks of life (they were not always clergy or religious), and from the ranks of both men and women. Some, whether their mystical experiences were genuine or not, held strange or possibly heretical ideas about God, Christ, or salvation. Mystics were usually judged during and after their lifetimes by their fidelity to the doctrines of the church, their accurate expression of Christian faith, their service to others, and their conformity to some known pattern of mystical growth.

In looking at Catherine of Siena and Julian of Norwich, two important mystics of the fourteenth century, and in referring back to Catherine of Genoa, we can see the similarities and the differences of mystical experience in its immediacy, and in the way it inspired those who experienced God in this way to participate in the world and to act on its behalf.

Catherine of Siena

Born Caterina Benincasa, **Catherine of Siena** (c. 1347–1380) was the daughter of a large family of lower rank in Siena. From an early age, she saw herself as dedicated to Christ alone. Her opposition to marriage infuriated her parents, who confined her to their home where she decided to serve them lovingly. Her parents reluctantly accepted her choice when Catherine began having powerful prayer experiences, visions, and raptures. She continued to live at home, devoted to contemplation. Catherine's prayer life had led her into a vision of mystical marriage to Christ. Her visions were often of the nourishing and cleansing blood of the sacrifice of Christ on the cross. Her emphasis on the blood of Christ may be due both to her Eucharistic devotion and to the suffering caused by the presence of plague among the populace. Yet, she was destined for more than contemplation in her short lifetime. In 1363, she became a Dominican tertiary (member of the lay third order) dedicated to serving and especially to feeding the poor. She would give up her own meals to feed others, convinced that she could live on the substance of the Eucharist alone. Many sought Catherine's help, advice, or counsel because of her closeness to God and her saintly reputation. Before long, she became a local celebrity of sorts.

Living during the time of the Avignon controversy, Catherine criticized and implored the church to heal itself of scandal and abuse. She wrote letters to influential church figures all over Europe, including the popes, calling them back to the ways of God and God's church. Her greatest desire was to see an end to the captivity of the papacy in Avignon, and she lived long enough to help bring it about, only to see it fall into the situation of the Great Schism. Catherine also wrote of her experiences of God, not as autobiography, but as a way to inspire other Christians to be faithful to the church despite its abuses. Her most famous work is *The Dialogue*. God is speaking in this excerpt:

> So the memory, all imperfect past, is filled at this breast
> because it has remembered and held
> without itself my blessings. Understanding receives the light.
> Gazing into the memory,
> it comes to know the truth and shedding the blindness of selfish
> love, it remains in the
> sunlight of Christ crucified in whom it knows both God and
> humanity. Beyond this knowledge,
> because of the union [with me] that she has realized, the soul
> rises to a light
> acquired not by nature nor by her own practice of virtue but by
> the grace of my gentle Truth
> who does not scorn any eager longing or labors offered to me.
> (Catherine of Siena 1980, 178–179)

Because of her deep spirituality, her thoughtful theology, and her devotion to the church, Catherine was declared a saint in 1461. Later, in the twentieth century, she was proclaimed a Doctor of the Church, an honor reserved for those whose teaching and scholarship have reflected Catholic Christian beliefs and those who have been important in the lives and faith of others.

Julian of Norwich

We know very little about **Julian of Norwich** (c. 1342–after 1417), except from her own writings and those of Margery Kempe, a contemporary of Julian's. Like Catherine, Julian had mystical experiences. Unlike Catherine, her mystical experiences were limited to one overwhelming set of visions during a brief period of illness. She spent the remainder of her life contemplating and interpreting these visions (which are called "shewings" or "showings"), in order to achieve a greater theological understanding of their meaning. Her mystical experiences are recorded in both a short text and a long text. One hypothesis, generally accepted, is that the short text was written immediately after her mystical experience, and the long text provides the reflection, thought, prayer, and theological explanation of the original visions.

We do not know whether or not Julian had already chosen her vocation at the time of her "showings," but we do know that before, or shortly after, she chose to live the life of an **anchoress** (a recluse who lived in solitude). Anchorites, male or female, were common in this period. They pledged to spend their entire lives in prayer and contemplation, and when they entered the anchorhold (their private rooms attached to a church) they were enclosed as if they were being buried. The symbolism was that of dying to the world outside and devoting one's life to God in silence and prayer. When enclosed, they took on the name of the church to which they were related. Thus, we do not know Julian's birth name or history. Julian was the anchoress of the church of St. Julian at Norwich, England. Julian would have had one or two rooms in which to live, she would have had a single servant who took care of tasks in the outside world such as shopping for food, and she would have been permitted a pet for company. She would also have had two windows in her enclosure: One looked into the church, so that she could hear the Mass and participate in the Eucharist; the other looked out to a small room where those seeking her wisdom and advice could come during certain hours of the day. These hours were limited so as not to disturb prayer but were considered essential as a way of being of service to God's people. In many ways, anchorites acted as the spiritual counselors of their time.

Although not entirely unique to her, Julian speaks in her showings of the Motherhood of God and the Motherhood of Christ. Her use of gender references is fluid, moving easily from masculine to feminine and back, when speaking of God. In this way, she both incorporates and transcends gender limitations when imaging God. Also in her visions, she is especially

Figure 16–3 The anchorage at the Church of St. Julian in Norwich, England.
Photo by Gary Hart.

aware of the suffering Christ who redeems all. Her reflections on that mystical experience show that she spent her life dealing with the tumult of plague and disorder in Norwich. She speculates on the meaning of sin and struggles with the question of why God allows sin and evil to exist. Thus, her assertion, "All will be well," is not empty optimism, but thoughtful and prayerful conviction.

CONCLUDING REMARKS

The combination of the problems of the papacy and the occurrence of the Black Death was devastating to people's beliefs about divine order in Christendom. Each alone would have produced major shifts in Christian thought and practice, and together they changed the landscape of the Christian imagination. This unrest led people to pay attention to charismatic figures who seemed to have answers to the difficult problems of life, whether heretical preachers, orthodox mystics, or teachers and educators of the nominalist school. Later in the fifteenth century, the fall of Constantinople, the invention of the printing press, and the Spanish Reconquest, which drove the Muslims and Jews out of Spain, would lead to other new and dramatic changes. In the next chapter, we look at some of those dramatic changes in the movement that would come to be called the Renaissance.

Key Terms

nominalism	conciliarism	mysticism
Avignon Papacy	pietà	Catherine of Siena
nepotism	John Wycliffe	Julian of Norwich
Great Schism	Jan Hus	anchorite/anchoress

Questions for Reading

1. Why do we speak of the fourteenth century as one of change and crisis?

2. What is nominalism? How does it differ from the scholasticism of the Middle Ages?

3. To what situation does the Avignon Papacy refer? Why is it sometimes called the "Babylonian Captivity"? How does the Avignon Papacy relate to the Great Schism, and what was the effect of these two situations on the church of the time?

4. What was the Black Death, and how did this plague get its name? What was the impact of the Black Death on religious art and literature? On the social structure of Europe at the time?

5. Who were John Wycliffe and Jan Hus? What were their concerns? What were the religious teachings that brought them into conflict with the authorities?

6. What exactly is mysticism, and why was it considered an essential part of the spirituality of the Late Middle Ages? What are the stages of mystical experience?

7. How does Julian of Norwich resemble Catherine of Siena in her mystical experience? How is she different?

Works Consulted/Recommended Reading

Bynum, Caroline Walker. *Jesus as Mother: Studies in the Spirituality of the High Middle Ages.* Berkeley: University of California, 1982.

Catherine of Genoa. *Purgation and Purgatory and The Spiritual Dialogue.* Translated by S. Hughes. New York: Paulist, 1979.

Catherine of Siena. *The Dialogue.* Translated by S. Noffke. New York: Paulist, 1980.

Chadwick, Owen. *The Reformation.* Baltimore, MD: Penguin, 1964.

Copelston, Frederick. *History of Philosophy*, Vol. 3. New York: Doubleday, 1963.

Egan, Harvey. *Christian Mysticism.* Collegeville, MN: Liturgical, 1992.

Huizinga, Johan. *The Waning of the Middle Ages.* New York: St. Martin's, 1985.

Jantzen, Grace. *Julian of Norwich, Mystic and Theologian.* New York: Paulist, 1988.

Julian of Norwich. *Showings.* Edited by. Edmund Colledge and James Walsh. New York: Paulist, 1978.

Pelphrey, Brant. *Julian of Norwich: Christ Our Mother.* Collegeville, MN: Liturgical, 1989.

Tanner, Norman P., ed. *Decrees of the Ecumenical Councils.* 2 vols. Washington, D.C.: Georgetown University, 1990.

Tuchman, Barbara. *A Distant Mirror: The Calamitous 14th Century.* New York: Ballantine, 1978.

Ullman, Walter. *The Short History of the Papacy in the Middle Ages.* London: Methuen, 1972.

Zeigler, Philip. *The Black Death.* New York: A. Knopf, 1969.

THE MODERN PERIOD

Western history has traditionally been divided into three periods: ancient, medieval, and modern. But there are problems with such a scheme. When, exactly, does the modern period begin? What are its characteristics? What makes it different from the medieval period? There is no universally accepted answer to these questions. In fact dividing history into periods is an artificial construct of historians. History itself, like an individual life, flows along from year to year without sharp breaks. Still, periodization is a useful device to organize the huge Mass of historical information. In the same way, we find it convenient to divide an individual life into childhood, adolescence, maturity, and old age, though we know there are no sharp breaks between these episodes.

The modern period follows the medieval and is in many respects its opposite. Let us consider, first, the characteristics of the medieval period, then of the modern.

THE MEDIEVAL PERIOD

Medieval social structure was strongly hierarchical. The French notion of the three estates of society was typical of late medieval social structure: The third or lower estate was made up of peasants, merchants, and tradesmen; the second estate was the clergy; the first estate was the nobility, made up of counts, dukes, princes, and headed by the king. This notion of hierarchy survived in France until the king and aristocracy were overthrown by the French revolution in 1789. In the medieval period, one's loyalties were not pledged to a state or nation, but to one's immediate feudal superior: A peasant was bound to his lord, that lord to a higher vassal, and that vassal to a higher lord or the king. The church was also structured hierarchically, with laity subordinate to priests, priests subordinate to bishops, and bishops subordinate to the pope. Likewise, individual religious orders had their own hierarchical chain, with each person subject to an immediate superior. Needless to say, women were subordinate to men in almost all cases.

The aim of this hierarchy was social unity. The idea was that if each person observed his or her place in the hierarchy, social order would be maintained. The medieval period was the last age in Western history that attempted to achieve a universal social unity, and this unity was built on the Christian religion. The goal was to produce a Christian society (identified by the term *Christendom*), which was understood as an organic whole and which included all members of society (except Jews, Muslims, and heretics), governed by the emperor and the pope.

Just as medieval people saw society as hierarchically structured, so they also saw the cosmos and its inhabitants structured according to a great chain of being, stretching from simple, inanimate beings like rocks, through plants, animals, human beings, angels, and finally to God. Beings higher in the hierarchy were thought to have more life, consciousness, and freedom than lower beings. Humans were capable of sinking to the level of animals or rising almost to the level of angels, depending on their participation in God's grace. Medieval people pictured the universe or cosmos with the earth at the center or lowest point, hell at the center of the earth, and the moon, planets, and stars circulating around the earth. Above the moon was the region of the planets, above that the region of the stars, each governed by its own angel, and above that the Empyrean, the region of God and heaven, where the Risen Christ and the blessed dwelt. Fellowship with God was seen as the end or goal of humanity and the angels. Generally, medieval thinkers like Aquinas were more interested in the place of creatures in this hierarchical scheme, and how creatures are directed to and return to God, than in individual creatures as such.

The most typical artistic expression of the medieval period was probably the cathedral. Cathedrals were vast towering buildings whose spires reached for the sky, symbolizing the medieval thrust toward the transcendent. Probably the greatest medieval theological work was Aquinas' *Summa Theologiae*, which analyzed the procession of all creatures from God and explained how they returned to God. The greatest work of medieval literature was Dante's *Divine Comedy*, an imaginative vision of Dante's descent into hell, ascent through purgatory and through paradise, to the vision of beatitude (blessedness). In sum, the overriding medieval interest, as expressed in art, philosophy, and theology, was in the relation to and the return of creatures to God.

The Modern Period

The modern period contrasts sharply with the medieval period because of its overriding interest in exploring the secular world, human beings, and nature, as they exist in themselves, rather than in their relation to God. Thus the modern attitude may be characterized as secular (nonreligious), whereas the medieval attitude was more religious and transcendent. Six major movements characterize the modern period: globalization, pluralism, nationalism, individualism, democracy, and interest in nature. The latter led to the development of modern natural science, the dominant intellectual force of modernity. Let us consider these six in order.

Globalization and Pluralism.   Medieval society was unaware of the enormous expanse of territory and the variety of races, languages, and religions that exist on the earth. Their principal experience of foreigners was of the Jews and the Muslims. But in 1492 Columbus discovered America, and in 1498 Vasco da Gama discovered a sea route around Africa to India. Within decades the West Indies and Americas were being colonized and missionaries were traveling to Asia. Suddenly, the medieval church was confronted with whole new continents and races that had never heard of Christianity. This immense broadening of horizons is what scholars mean by globalization—the consciousness of living in a global world rather than just in one's immediate neighborhood, town, region, or country. Pluralism is the encounter with a diversity of non-Christian and foreign peoples, including civilizations like India and China, which are much older than Western Christianity.

Nationalism.   Characteristic of the early modern period was the development of national consciousness, national languages, and nation states. Although nationalism was beginning to emerge in the Middle Ages, it was subdued because the universal language of scholars and politics was Latin, and Christendom was (theoretically) united under one pope and one emperor. However, during the fifteenth and sixteenth centuries, modern nations began to develop. In 1492 Ferdinand and Isabella joined their kingdoms to create modern Spain. In the early part of the sixteenth century, Henry VII and Henry VIII unified England into a national entity. Francis I and later kings did the same for France. During the sixteenth and seventeenth centuries, national languages began to replace Latin in religion (at least among Protestants), scholarship, and politics. Thus, in 1521 Luther translated the New Testament into German and thereby shaped the emerging German language. Shakespeare's plays and the King James translation of the Bible (1611) shaped the development of English. By the mid-sixteenth century, it was clear that the medieval ideal of one universal Christian empire sharing one language and consciousness was defunct.

Individualism.   Medieval life was corporate. People thought of themselves not as individuals but as members of a social group, and the organic unity of society was strongly emphasized. But both the Renaissance and the Reformation stressed the importance of the individual. Renaissance art glorified individuals, usually noblemen; the individual portrait is virtually a creation of the Renaissance. The Reformation emphasized that persons are saved by their individual faith in Jesus Christ, more than by being members of the church. Before this time, medieval Catholics typically trusted in God's salvation because of their participation in the sacraments and their membership in the church. Reformation Lutherans were confident of salvation because of their individual faith in Jesus as savior. Where medieval piety emphasized corporate and communal salvation, Reformation piety emphasized individual salvation.

Democracy.   The Reformation and Renaissance emphasis on individualism led to more representative and democratic forms of government, in contrast to medieval hierarchical and monarchial models. Representative government began to develop in the free cities of Renaissance Italy and in other free European cities. Likewise, Reformation and Radical Reformation churches were organized in ways that were less hierarchical and more congregationally structured—individual congregations could elect their own ministers. This was the pattern of the Puritan churches of colonial New England, whose church government patterns influenced the development of American democracy. In most countries, governments have become steadily less aristocratic and more democratic all through the modern period.

Nature and Science.   The new interest in individual things led to an interest in nature for its own sake. In the Renaissance, there was much interest in observing and drawing nature— landscape paintings appear for the first time since antiquity. Leonardo da Vinci and others dissected human corpses to study human anatomy. By the seventeenth century, this new interest in individual beings and in nature led to the development of modern science, the intellectual movement that has most shaped modern consciousness.

Each of these movements has continued to develop throughout the modern period, and each of them is more pronounced in this century than in any previous century. Most of them have their roots, however, in the Renaissance and the Reformation. The Renaissance and the Reformation are the subjects of Chapters 17 through 21. In turn, the Renaissance and the Reformation provide the context for the Enlightenment and its aftermath, more properly called the modern period. The issues and movements connected with the modern period will be treated in Chapters 22 through 25.

17

THE RENAISSANCE

TIMELINE

c. A.D. 1350	Beginnings of the Renaissance movement.
c. A.D. 1450	The invention of movable type makes modern printing possible.
A.D. 1453	Constantinople falls to the Muslim Turks.
A.D. 1461–1559	Feudal territories of France are consolidated into a single kingdom.
c. A.D. 1466–1536	Life span of Desiderius Erasmus. Erasmus' New Testament became the basis for many subsequent translations of the Bible into the vernacular.
A.D. 1469	Ferdinand and Isabella unite their Spanish kingdoms in alliance.
A.D. 1478	Ferdinand and Isabella persuade Pope Sixtus IV to set up an inquisition to investigate and punish heretics in Spain.
A.D. 1485–1547	The Tudor kings, Henry VII and Henry VIII, strengthen and consolidate English monarchial powers.
A.D. 1492	The Christian reconquest (*reconquista*) of Spain from the Moors. Columbus sets sail for the Americas. Jews are exiled from Spain.

As the previous chapter indicated, the late medieval period was a time of chaos and suffering, affecting almost every aspect of people's lives. However, it was also an unprecedented time of growth and creativity. It was during this time that many of the characteristics that we associate with modernity began to appear. There was an expansion of trade, banking, and craft manufacturing, organized by a wealthy merchant class who patronized art and architecture. Under the rule of powerful kings and queens, the modern nation-states of France, Spain, and England gradually emerged. The invention of the printing press led to an enormous increase in the number of books available to people and an expansion of education. Navigators explored the coast of Africa, opened sea routes to India and the East, and discovered the Americas.

During the late medieval period and into the early modern period, roughly 1350 to 1600, there was also a renewed interest in the Latin and Greek classics, in the natural world, in the individual person, and in history and literature, and an astonishing burst of creativity in art and architecture. This cultural movement, this "rebirth" of learning and art, is called the **Renaissance**, which means "rebirth." The movement began in Italy and subsequently spread to other European countries. Gradually it transformed the Christian European worldview from a medieval outlook, which emphasized community more than the individual and the next life more than this life, to a more modern outlook, which emphasized the individual, the natural world, and the opportunities available to the human person in this life.

THE BEGINNINGS OF THE RENAISSANCE MOVEMENT

Along with the rapid surge in population after the devastation of the bubonic plague, there are a number of factors that set the stage for the cultural movement known as the Renaissance. These included the development of a new commerce that had its source in trade, the emergence of nation-states, and the invention of printing.

The New Commerce

From 900 to 1100 Europe's economy had been largely agricultural, and its social structure was based on the principles of feudalism. Peasants worked on large estates owned by wealthy landlords, producing food and clothing for themselves and their lords. Trade was conducted largely by barter (exchange of goods using no money). Gradually during the twelfth through sixteenth centuries, trade, towns, and a money economy began to increase. The merchants of Venice, Genoa, and Pisa in Italy made fortunes shipping spices from the East to places like Flanders and England and carrying back wool, cloth, and metal. In the fifteenth century, the Medici family of Florence, Italy, controlled an international banking system with outlets in eight European cities; their banks also sold wool, silk, and other merchandise. Some of their profits were paid to Florentine artists who beautified their city with buildings, sculptures, frescoes, and paintings. Over time, a wealthy urban business class emerged, a class that would eventually displace the landed aristocracy as the dominant class in society.

The Nation-States

In theory, Christendom of the late medieval period was unified by the spiritual authority of the Catholic Church and the political authority of the Holy Roman Emperor. In practice,

Plate 1 *The Crucifixion*, c. 1420-25, by Hubert and/or Jan van Eyck. The Metropolitan Museum of Art, Fletcher Fund, 1933.

This famous painting in the Metropolitan Museum of Art (New York City) depicts a traditional theme: the crucifixion of Jesus. This crucifixion scene is part of a pair of panels in the Ghent Altarpiece; the second panel depicts the last judgment (Matt 25:31-46). The artist(s) achieved a sense of perspective by gradually decreasing the intensity of colors and clarity of objects from the foreground to the background. The mountains and the city of Jerusalem are barely distinguishable as the background seems to fade in the distance.

Plate 2 *The Adoration of the Shepherds*, 1476, by Hugo van der Goes. Center panel of the Portinari Altar piece. Uffizi, Florence, Italy.

This painting shows Mary, angels, and the shepherds adoring the infant Jesus (Luke 2:9-20). The flowers in the foreground symbolize Mary's purity. Realistic treatment of rustic scenes and people, made possible by oil paint, was to become characteristic of Northern European painting.

Plate 3 *St. Francis in the Desert*, c. 1485, by Giovanni Bellini. The Frick Collection, New York.

Here the Renaissance rediscovery of the beauty of landscape and nature is evident. The beauty of God, experienced by St. Francis, in mystical ecstasy, is mirrored in the landscape, radiant in its purity. The saint's sandals are in the hermitage behind him, and he stands barefoot before the holiness of God, as did Moses before the burning bush (Exod 3:5).

Plate 4 *Christ Delivering the Keys to Saint Peter,* 1482, by Pietro Perugino. Sistine Chapel, Vatican Palace, Vatican State.

This illustrates Matthew 16:19, in which Jesus says to Peter, "I will give you the keys of the kingdom of heaven." Popes had argued that this scriptural passage meant that Jesus has passed supreme apostolic authority to Peter, who had then passed the authority to the bishops of Rome. The scene is set in a Renaissance public square (piazza), and shows striking use of perspective; the tile lines converge to a central vanishing point.

Plate 5 *Annunciation,* c. 1490–95, by Lorenzo di Credi, Uffizi, Florence, Italy.

A beautiful rendering of a traditional theme: the angel announces to Mary that she will bear a son who will be called "son of God" (Luke 1:26-38). The scenes below the central painting are from Genesis, showing Eve being born from Adam's side, the temptation by the serpent, and the expulsion from Eden. Mary is here seen as the new Eve, who by her own obedience to God (see Luke 1:38) brings about reconciliation between God and humanity, even as Eve's disobedience brought about a divorce between God and humanity. Note the Renaissance architecture, the use of perspective, and the window opening out to nature—a favorite theme.

Plate 6 *The Last Supper,* c. 1495–98, by Leonardo da Vinci. Sta. Maria delle Grazie, Milan, Italy.

This badly damaged fresco in Milan shows Jesus at the last supper with his disciples. Note the use of perspective: the lines of the architecture converge on a vanishing point directly behind Jesus' head, while the light from the window functions as a natural halo. This fresco has become the archetype for thousands of pious imitations of the Last Supper scene, right down to our own time.

Plate 7 *Pieta,* c. 1500, by Michelangelo Buonarroti. St. Peter's Basilica, Vatican State.

This is one of the world's masterpieces of sculpture, completed by Michelangelo at age 24. Mary here holds the dead Jesus, resigned in her acceptance of God's will. Her face, too young for her age at this time of Jesus' death, was said by Michelangelo to express her purity. This is a very large sculpture (5'8" high), carved from one block of marble. It combines a medieval theme (Mary holding the dead Jesus), with a classical realistic treatment of the human body. In the judgment of Michelangelo's contemporary, the art historian Georgio Vasari, this sculpture, in its beauty and technical perfection, set a standard that would never be surpassed.

Plate 8 *David*, c. 1501–4, by Michelangelo Buonarroti. Frontal view. Accademia, Florence, Italy.

David is shown here in the style of Greek and Roman sculpture; one of the first free-standing nude sculptures done since ancient times. Note the classical emphasis on the beauty of the human body, and on balance, proportion, and restraint. This gigantic statue (13' 8" high) was placed by the Florentines in their central piazza to symbolize their city's independence and resistance to tyranny. It is a portrait in marble on the Renaissance ideal: the self-sufficient man of action. Typical of the Renaissance, it combines a classical treatment with a biblical theme.

Plate 9 *Desiderius Erasmus,* c. 1523, by Hans Holbein the Younger. The Metropolitan Museum of Art, Robert Lehman Collection, 1975.

An example of Renaissance portraiture, expressing their interest in the individual, by a master famous for the psychological sensitivity of his portraits.

Plate 10 *Saint Peter's Basilica and Piazza,* 1748, by Giovanni Battista Piranesi. The Metropolitan Museum of Art, Harris Brisbane Dick Fund, 1937.

This is a drawing of St. Peter's basilica (largely designed by Michelangelo) showing the huge dome, piazza, and colonnade (designed by Bernini, 1656). St. Peter's basilica was until recently the largest church in the world; most churches would easily fit inside it. It was erected on the sight of old St. Peter's (a basilica built by Constantine 324–25) which in turn had been built over the tomb of St. Peter, the apostle. St. Peter's is the principal church used by popes; from its front balcony the pope addresses crowds assembled in the piazza. The obelisk in the center had been brought from Egypt by the Roman emperor Caligula in 41 AD.

Europe was a patchwork quilt of small kingdoms, principalities (territories ruled by princes), and duchies (territories ruled by dukes), with little centralized power. During the Renaissance, however, powerful kings and queens began to control larger regions, notably Spain, France, and England. The feudal territories of France, originally governed by independent nobles, were consolidated into a single kingdom during the period from 1461 to 1559. Likewise, English monarchial power was strengthened and consolidated by the Tudor kings, Henry VII (1485–1509) and Henry VIII (1509–1547). The result of these consolidations was the emergence of national monarchies that were often at odds with the church. In 1534, Henry VIII declared himself head of the church in England and thereby separated the Church of England from the Roman Catholic Church.

The situation in Spain was somewhat different from that of France and England. When Ferdinand of Castile and Isabella of Aragon married in 1469, they brought together two kingdoms in an alliance with considerable political and economic power. Both Ferdinand and Isabella were Catholic, and together they set out to strengthen their borders and Christianize their domain. In 1492, after centuries of war between Spanish Christians and Muslims (Moors), Spain succeeded in capturing the last independent Muslim Spanish city, Granada, in southern Spain, thus completing the 700-year reconquest (*reconquista*) of Spain from the Moors. Finally, in 1502 Muslims who refused to convert to Christianity were forced to leave Granada altogether.

Ferdinand and Isabella held firm control over the Spanish church, and in that way helped to ensure the unity of Spain. In 1478, Ferdinand and Isabella persuaded Pope Sixtus IV to set up in Spain a legal body, called the Inquisition, to investigate and punish heretics. This legal system, though nominally controlled by the church, was actually under the control of the Spanish crown. The Inquisition was used to persecute and even kill those thought to be enemies of the state or the church—especially Spanish Jews who had converted to Christianity (usually under threat of force) and who were suspected of secretly practicing Judaism. In 1492 Spanish Jews were forced into exile. On the very day that Columbus set sail from Seville, shiploads of dispossessed Sephardic Jews (that is, Jews of Spanish descent) were leaving for ports in Egypt and Turkey.

Printing

The invention of movable type and hence of modern printing was perfected in Mainz, Germany, in about 1450. Before this time, books (known as manuscripts) were copied by hand. This was a very slow process. According to a contemporary observer, the invention of movable type made it possible for one person to print as much in one day as many could copy in a year.

Printing led to two major changes. One was an enormous expansion in learning. Previously books were so expensive that they were owned mostly by institutions such as universities or monasteries, or by noble families. Printing allowed the emerging middle class also to own books. It is estimated that 6,000,000 books were printed between 1450 and 1500, more than had been produced in the previous thousand years. Of course, this had consequences for theological history. Between 1517 and 1520 about 300,000 copies of books and tracts by Martin Luther, who began the Protestant Reformation, were printed. This made the Reformation a Mass movement, something that would have been impossible a century before.

A second change was that scholars could all work on identical printed texts, so that learning became a cooperative and cumulative endeavor, rather than an individual enterprise.

Before printing, books that were copied by scribes each contained different errors and pagination, so that scholars could never be sure if they were working with an accurate text or if they were working with the same text that other scholars were using. Errors accumulated over the years, as they were passed on in successive copyings, so that by 1450 texts of the Bible (and other texts) contained many copyists' errors. Printing allowed scholars to begin to establish uniform, accurate texts, especially uniform texts of the Bible, which became more accurate with successive editions.

RENAISSANCE HUMANISM

Renaissance **humanism** was an intellectual movement that sought to revive and teach Latin and Greek classics. It began in the cities of northern Italy, especially Florence, Rome, and Venice. Humanists sought out forgotten Latin texts in the libraries of old monasteries, studied Latin authors such as Cicero, and assimilated their values. The humanists also greatly expanded the study of Greek in the West. The interest in studying Greek was partly the result of an influx of Greek scholars from the Byzantine Empire, who were fleeing from the advancing Muslim armies of the Ottoman Turks. In 1397 a Greek scholar named Manuel Chrysoloras came to Florence from Constantinople and began teaching Greek at the University in Florence. Later, after the fall of Constantinople to the Muslim Turks in 1453, many more Greek scholars fled to the West.

Greek studies were important especially because they allowed biblical scholars to study the New Testament in its original Greek language and hence to come closer to certain aspects of its original meaning. However, the enthusiasm for Greek studies was not restricted to study of the Bible. It also led to the rediscovery of other elements of classical Greek knowledge and learning. When Plato's dialogues were translated into Latin in 1469, they became the basis for a recovery of a Christian Neoplatonic philosophy. Greek philosophy was widely influential during the Renaissance, but people were also interested in the recovery of Greek mathematics (especially Archimedes). The latter became crucial for the emergence of the scientific revolution in the seventeenth century.

It is hard today to imagine the excitement generated by Latin and Greek studies in the Renaissance. In 1488, when a visiting Italian humanist lectured on the second satire of Juvenal, a Roman poet, at the University of Salamanca in Spain, the throng of students was so thick that after two and one-half hours the lecturer had to be passed bodily over the heads of the audience in order to leave. A famous letter by the Florentine statesman Niccolo Machiavelli expresses a similar enchantment with the classics. Machiavelli had been exiled from Florence and had been living at a country farm. His only companions during the day were uneducated country people, but in the evening he would read classics and imagine himself conversing with the great writers of antiquity:

> At the door I take off my muddy everyday clothes. I dress myself as though I were about to appear before a royal court as a Florentine envoy. Then decently attired I enter the antique courts of the great men of antiquity. They receive me with friendship; from them I derive the nourishment . . . for which I was born . . . I talk with them and ask them the causes for their actions; and their humanity is so great they answer me. For four long and happy hours I lose myself in them. I forget all my troubles; I am not afraid of poverty or death. I transform myself entirely in their likeness. (Cited in Rice 1970, 66)

Renaissance humanists were not the first ones to read classical authors. Works such as Virgil's epic poem *The Aeneid* had been preserved in monasteries and read throughout the Middle Ages. However, the Renaissance brought to this reading a difference in interpretation and understanding. The earlier medievals read *The Aeneid* as though it were a Christian parable, with little sense of the difference between medieval and Roman culture. Similarly, the medieval morality plays of Jesus's passion and death typically showed Jesus and his contemporaries as medieval people, not as ancient Jews. Renaissance humanists, on the other hand, were able to enter into the world of ancient Roman and Greek authors, recognize it as different, and absorb its values. In reappropriating ancient values while remaining Christian, they created a very different Christian culture from that of the Middle Ages. In particular, they forged a very different view of humanity and the world.

The Renaissance View of Humanity

Because the medieval world had been mostly rural and agricultural, people were very much aware of the communal nature of humanity. They were not much concerned about individuality or worldly accomplishment. As a result, we know the names of few medieval artists or architects. Medieval people tended to see life in this world as directed to eternity, therefore placing their hopes in the next life, rather than this life. It would make sense, then, that the medieval period's most characteristic work of art was the cathedral, whose soaring spires and light-filled heights expressed the human desire for heaven and God. By contrast, the Renaissance strongly valued the individuality of the human person and emphasized individual accomplishment, fame, and glory (values that were Roman, but not medieval). Renaissance artists decorated their city squares with the statues of great men. Renaissance persons, as entrepreneurs, artists, soldiers, and explorers, stressed human opportunities in this world. This attitude was summed up by the architect Leon Battista Alberti, who proclaimed "Men can do anything with themselves if they will" (Cited in National Geographic Society 1970, 19).

Humanists unashamedly placed humanity at the center of their world and declared, following the ancient Greeks' view that "man was the measure of all things." Thus, the typical work of Renaissance art was the individual portrait (a painting that seeks to create a realistic likeness of the person being portrayed), an art virtually unknown in the ancient world. The outlook of Renaissance writers, artists, and explorers was **anthropocentric**, or human centered, whereas that of the medieval period had largely been **theocentric**, or God centered. If the medieval ideal was the bishop, priest, pilgrim, or monk, the Renaissance ideal was the educated civic leader, soldier, nobleman, artist, or man of affairs, who could speak and reason eloquently and serve the public good. Wealthy Renaissance merchants typically donated a large portion of their profits for artwork to beautify the city.

The emphasis on the dignity of man, however, so characteristic of Renaissance thinking, did not translate into equal roles for women. Women above the shopkeeper class were largely confined to the care of household and family, even more so than they had been in the medieval period. Juan Luis Vives' *The Education of the Christian Woman*, published in Latin in 1529 and translated into six languages, "emphasized that a woman's role should be restricted to the home and not overlap with that of men" (Hale, 1994, 270). Because of the availability of printed books, some women, such as Thomas More's daughters, were educated at home, but few played prominent parts in public life, which was thought of as the province of men. There were exceptions, however: Elisabetta Gonzaga and Isabella d'Este founded famous literary salons, and Caterina Sforza personally led her armies against Cesare Borgia. Ironically, the latter part of this period witnessed the rise of several female rulers: Mary I and Elizabeth I of England and Mary, Queen of Scots.

In sum, the Renaissance ideal of humanity was more secular (nonreligious), individualistic, and modern than the medieval ideal. To reconcile this more secular view of humanity with Christianity, Renaissance thinkers appealed to Genesis 1:26 ("And God said, 'Let us make humankind in our image, according to our likeness'") and Genesis 1:28 ("Have dominion over the fish of the sea and over the birds of the air and over every living thing that moves upon the earth"), thinking that God gave humanity a godlike status and authority over the earth (Trinkaus 1983, 344). As the image and likeness of God, persons were thought to be free and endowed with an almost divine creativity. They believed that the possibilities of human persons were unlimited: They could sink to the level of the beasts or become like an angel or a son of God, so great was their freedom.

THE RENAISSANCE VIEW OF THE WORLD

The Renaissance was also marked by a new interest in and discovery of the natural world through art and the sciences. In art, the discovery of perspective (about 1420) brought about a revolutionary realism to painting, especially paintings of architecture. This realism also extended to paintings of the human body. The artist Leonardo da Vinci dissected over thirty cadavers in order to discover from his own experience the structure of human anatomy. Landscape painting appeared shortly thereafter, a type of art that had disappeared during the Middle Ages. From the early 1500s, there developed an enthusiasm for cartography (mapmaking) all over Europe. In earlier medieval maps theology tended to dominate actual geography. For example, lands were shown radiating out from the center of the world at Jerusalem, the Holy City. In contrast, Renaissance maps were far more accurate and reflected more realistically the world as it actually was. Thus, geography became an independent science not subordinated to theology (Hale, 1994, 15–20).

Finally, the Renaissance coincided with the great age of exploration. The Renaissance movement's interest in and discovery of the natural world involved travel to distant lands. Portuguese sailors explored the coast of Africa in the 1400s, and by 1498 they had sailed around the Cape of Good Hope to reach India. Columbus' discovery of the Americas opened up vast colonizing, commercial, and missionary possibilities. In earlier medieval times, although pilgrimages to holy places were common, there had been relatively little interest in exploration for its own sake. For those people, the primary journey was vertical: the journey of the soul to God. However, the Renaissance, while still Christian, was far more interested in horizontal expansion and in discovering the beauty, structure, and commercial opportunities of this world.

HUMANIST EDUCATION AND HISTORICAL CRITICISM

The humanist ideal carried with it a new educational program as well, which spread gradually over all of Europe. Humanists exalted human freedom and potential and saw education as the way to develop that potential. In particular, they stressed knowledge of literature and history and the development of civic virtue, character, discipline, and eloquence. Their studies were centered on the ***studia humanitatis*** (humane studies) or liberal arts: Latin and Greek literature, history, and ethics. In studying Latin, students learned to read, write, reason, and speak well. These skills were especially necessary for civic leaders and scholars. The study of ethics taught the student duties to God, country, family, and oneself. The study of history taught ethics by example: In history one saw the concrete results of a life of virtue, or a life of vice, and learned noble examples on which one could pattern one's life. According to the Renaissance concept, these studies were liberal (from Latin, *libertas*, "liberty") because they freed persons to develop their full human potential. The Renaissance educator Pietro Vergerio (1370–1444) wrote:

> We call those studies liberal which are worthy of a free man, those studies by which we attain and practice virtue and wisdom. That education which calls forth, trains, and develops those higher gifts of body and mind which ennoble men, and which are rightly judged to rank next in dignity to virtue alone. (Cited in Spitz 1971, 157)

This education was mainly for nobility, but also for socially ambitious laymen (such as the sons of merchants), and, occasionally, for women. Isabella d'Este, a daughter of the ruling family of Ferrara (Italy), mastered Latin and some Greek, performed well on the lute, embroidered faultlessly, and could converse on equal terms with ambassadors (Plumb 1987). Proficiency in Latin was essential to the Renaissance experience, since it was the language of the church, diplomacy, scholarship, law, and medicine. However, a humanist education also stressed training in virtue, physical excellence, and Christian religion. This notion of education remained the standard in Europe and America until the present, where it is gradually being displaced by an emphasis on vocational and scientific training. Nonetheless, the ideal of a liberal education as necessary for the full development of human potential is still carried on in liberal arts schools, a legacy of the Renaissance.

The humanists, with their love of history and with more accurate printed texts, developed **historical criticism**, that is, the use of historical knowledge to evaluate existing traditions and institutions. An example of this is Lorenzo Valla's (1407–1457) efforts to expose the "Donation of Constantine" as a forgery. This document was allegedly a deed written by the emperor Constantine (c. 330), which granted the pope title to many of the imperial lands in Italy. These lands had since become the basis for the Papal States. Valla, with his extensive knowledge of classical Latin, was able to show that the "Donation of Constantine" could not have been written in the fourth century, as claimed, because it used Latin words (such as the word used for the papal crown) that were not in use in the fourth century. Rather, he argued, it must have been written in the eighth century and was therefore a forgery. This undercut the pope's claim to political authority in the Papal States (though these states were not dissolved until the unification of Italy in 1870). This use of historical scholarship to criticize traditions, especially claims of the papacy and the church, was to become a major factor in the Reformation. Luther acknowledged Valla and John Wycliffe (1328–1384), author of the first English Bible, as important authorities in the area of historical criticism (Spitz 1971).

SOUTHERN AND NORTHERN RENAISSANCE

A distinction can be drawn between the southern Renaissance, centered in Italy, and the northern Renaissance, centered in northern Europe. The southern Renaissance was primarily concerned with the recovery of Latin and Greek literature, art, and sculpture. In contrast, humanists of the northern Renaissance used their knowledge of Greek and Latin to study the Bible and the church fathers in their original languages and to urge a reform of the church based on the ideals of the Bible and the writers of the early church. The greatest of the northern humanists was **Desiderius Erasmus** (c. 1466–1536), a scholar learned in the literature of both the Latin and Greek early church writers and the most famous writer of his age. In his *Handbook of the Christian Soldier*, Erasmus argued that true piety depends on the inner virtue of the Spirit, rather than on conformity to external rites of the church. His popular satire *In Praise of Folly* lampooned the worldliness and vices of society and the church of his time. In 1516 he published a new edition of the Bible in Greek (the first since ancient times), accompanied by his own Latin translation. To arrive at the most accurate version, he had to compare many ancient Greek manuscripts of the New Testament. Erasmus' New Testament became the basis for many subsequent translations into the **vernacular** (language of the common people), including Luther's translation of the New Testament into German. Though he was later accused of undermining the institutional church by his satire and criticisms, Erasmus did not follow Luther in separating from the Roman church but remained a devout yet critically minded Catholic.

THE RENAISSANCE POPES

The popes of the Renaissance were humanists, patrons of art, and builders. Pope Nicholas V (1447–1455) collected over 5,000 books to begin the Vatican library (one of the great libraries of the world). Julius II (1503–1513) commissioned art works from Michelangelo and Raphael, excavated the ruins of Rome to recover ancient statues, and began the rebuilding of St. Peter's Basilica (which was continued under successive popes). The Renaissance popes rebuilt Rome, making it the center of the Italian Renaissance and making the Vatican Museum one of the great art museums in the West. Unfortunately, they were less concerned about the spiritual reform of the universal church. For a century or more, earnest Catholics had been attempting to reform many abuses in the church: simony, clerical worldliness and corruption, uneducated clergy and laity, absentee bishops, abuses of celibacy, the misuse of indulgences, and laxity in the practice of the faith. Instead of helping to address these concerns, the Renaissance popes were occupied with Italian affairs and behaved more like Italian princes than shepherds of the universal church. For example, Julius II, the "warrior pope," donned armor and rode at the head of the papal troops in attacks on the Italian cities of Modena and Mirandola. As a result, though some individual churches and religious orders were reformed, the church as a whole was not. When substantial reform did come, beginning in 1517 with Luther, it was met with papal opposition, not cooperation. This reform effort ended by fragmenting the Western church, a tragedy whose legacy is still with us today.

RENAISSANCE ART

The Renaissance was one of the greatest periods of Christian and Western art. The discovery of perspective, of oil paints (by Flemish painters in the early 1400s), the rediscovery of portrait and landscape painting after almost a thousand years, and the return to classical and human-centered models of art and sculpture, all made Renaissance painting and sculpture brilliantly lifelike and realistic. Most Renaissance artists were Christians and there-fore emphasized Christian themes in their art. However, unlike medieval artists, they also celebrated secular and pagan subjects, such as portraits of wealthy nobles or paintings of Greek or Roman gods. For more information, see Creighton Gilbert's *History of Renaissance Art* or the Metropolitan Museum of Art's *The Renaissance in the North*.

The color plates provide a glimpse of the magnificence of Renaissance art.

Key Terms

Renaissance	theocentric	Desiderius Erasmus
humanism	*studia humanitatis*	vernacular
anthropocentric	historical criticism	

Questions for Reading

1. Discuss the factors that contributed to the birth of the Renaissance movement.
2. What was Renaissance humanism, and why was it important?
3. Contrast the medieval and Renaissance view of humanity.
4. Contrast the medieval and Renaissance view of the world.
5. Explain the goal and practice of humanist education.
6. Why was the development of historical criticism important?
7. What were the strengths and weaknesses of the Renaissance popes?
8. What were the main characteristics of Renaissance art? Illustrate each of these by refer-ring to one of the plates described in this chapter.

Works Consulted/Recommended Reading

Bridenthal, R., C. Koonz, and S. Stuard, eds. *Becoming Visible: Women in European History*. 2nd ed. Boston: Houghton Mifflin, 1987.

Gilbert, Creighton. *History of Renaissance Art*. Upper Saddle River, NJ: Prentice Hall, 1973.

Hale, John. *The Civilization of Europe in the Renaissance*. New York: Atheneum, 1994.

Kelly-Gadol, Joan. "Did Women Have a Renaissance?" In Bridenthal, Koonz, and Stuard, *Becoming Visible: Women in European History*, 137–164.

National Geographic Society. *The Renaissance, Maker of Modern Man*. 1970.

Plumb, John H. *The Italian Renaissance*. Boston: Houghton Mifflin, 1961.

Rice, Eugene F., Jr. *The Foundations of Early Modern Europe, 1460–1559*. New York: Norton, 1970.

Spitz, Lewis W. *The Renaissance and Reformation Movements*. Vol. 1. Chicago: Rand McNally, 1971.

Trinkaus, Charles. *The Scope of Renaissance Humanism*. Ann Arbor: University of Michigan, 1983.

Chapter

18
MARTIN LUTHER

TIMELINE

A.D. 1483	Martin Luther is born in Eisleben, Germany.
A.D. 1504–1505	Luther enters a monastery and is ordained a priest.
A.D. 1512	Luther begins his career as professor of biblical studies at the University of Wittenberg.
A.D. 1517	Luther posts his *Ninety-Five Theses* on the door of the Wittenberg Castle church calling for a debate on the issue of indulgences.
A.D. 1519	Luther and John Eck debate at Leipzig and Luther publicly denies the authority of the pope.
A.D. 1520	Luther writes several documents, including *On the Babylonian Captivity of the Church* and *Christian Liberty*, which summarize his theology and describe his call to reform.
A.D. 1521	Luther is formally excommunicated by the pope.
A.D. 1521	The Holy Roman Emperor Charles V issues the Edict of Worms, declaring Luther an outlaw.
A.D. 1524–1525	The Peasants' Revolt.
A.D. 1525	Luther marries Katherine von Bora.
A.D. 1529	Six Lutheran princes protest the agreements made at the Second Diet of Speyer and thereby acquire the name *Protestant*.
A.D. 1530	The *Augsburg Confession* is signed.
A.D. 1546	Luther dies in Eisleben, the place of his birth.

Why are some Christians today known as Catholics and others identified as Protestants? To answer this question we need to look at the life of Martin Luther, a sixteenth-century monk and university professor. Luther's life was shaped by his struggle with a central question: How are humans saved? He believed he found the answer to that question in his reading and study of the Bible. However, the answer to this question became explosive when it led him to criticize the theology and practices of the church.

The call for reform has been—and continues to be—a constant element in the history of the church. We have already seen the spirit of reform working in the medieval monastic communities and the friar movement. In the sixteenth century, however, efforts at reform led to the fragmentation of Catholic Christianity and the establishment of the Lutheran Church (among others). This was a consequence Luther himself had neither intended nor foreseen. Although Luther called for change and reform, he did not see himself as a religious innovator, introducing new ideas and practices into the Christian tradition. He understood his criticisms as an attempt to "re-form" the church in accordance with the beliefs and practices of the early church.

Who was this person? Why did he have such a powerful effect on the church and society at large? This chapter will focus on Martin Luther. The following chapters will examine other reform movements, both Catholic and Protestant, which occurred during and immediately following Luther's life.

LUTHER'S EARLY LIFE

Luther was born on November 10, 1483, in the town of Eisleben, today located in northeastern Germany. At the time Luther was born, Germany did not yet exist and Eisleben was in Saxony, one of the many territorial states that formed the Holy Roman Empire. Luther's father, Hans, was from a family of peasants, but he turned to the mining business and eventually owned his own mine shafts and copper smelters. Hans had high hopes for his son and was very pleased when Martin received his master's degree from the University of Erfurt. Hans assumed his son would now prepare for a career in law. However, Martin's plans suddenly and unexpectedly changed. Luther was returning to the University of Erfurt after a visit with his parents when he was caught in a violent thunderstorm. A bolt of lightning threw him to the ground, and Luther cried out to the patron saint of miners: "Help me, St. Anne! I will become a monk!" A few weeks later, at the age of twenty-one, Luther entered an order of the Observant Augustinians.

This decision may not have been as sudden and unexpected as it appears. When Luther was caught in the thunderstorm, he was returning to the university from a leave of absence, taken just one month after beginning his law studies. He vowed to become a monk, a holy vocation that he believed would most nearly assure his salvation, at a significant crossroads in his life. When his father reacted with fury at his decision, Luther reminded him that he could do much more for his family with his prayers as a monk than he could ever do with his wealth and position as a lawyer. As with many others in his day and time, Luther had chosen the holiest life one could lead in order to secure salvation for himself and others.

Luther took his vow seriously and appears to have been a very conscientious and dedicated monk. Only one year after entering the monastery Luther was ordained as a priest. Shortly thereafter the leader of his order, John von Staupitz, selected him for further education and a teaching career. Many years later, Luther declared, "If anyone could have gained heaven as a monk, then I would indeed have been among them" (WA 38,143). However, Luther's dedication to the holy life of a monk did not bring him the assurance of salvation he was seeking.

Some of Luther's doubts and questions can be traced to the nominalist theology he learned at the University of Erfurt. Nominalist theology saw salvation in terms of a contract between humans and God. If humans fulfilled their part of the contract by doing their best, then God would fulfill God's part by giving them grace. This was summed up in the phrase, "God will not refuse grace to those who do what is within them." Humans could not achieve salvation on their own, but if they did their best, God would graciously grant them the grace they needed to be saved. This understanding of salvation caused Luther incredible anguish and despair. He constantly wondered whether he had done his best. He saw himself as a poor, miserable sinner and God as a holy and righteous God. How could he ever do enough to earn the grace he needed to be saved?

The church offered grace and hope to sinners in the sacrament of Penance. As a monk, Luther confessed his sins daily, but this did not bring him peace. Grace was offered in the sacrament, but had he done his best? Had he confessed all his sins? Was he truly sorry for his sins? Tormented by these questions, Luther came dangerously close to the unforgivable sin of despair. His confessor was finally driven to say, "God is not angry with you, but you are angry with God" (LW 54:15; WATr 1,47).

JUSTIFICATION BY GRACE THROUGH FAITH

Luther finally found peace with God through his study of the Bible. In 1512 Luther began his career as professor of biblical studies at the University of Wittenberg, a new school with only a few hundred students. His lectures during the next few years (on the Psalms, Romans, Galatians, and Hebrews) indicate that Luther experienced a gradual change in his understanding of God and God's relationship to humanity. This new view can be summed up in the phrase *justification by grace through faith*. It may be helpful to look at each element of this phrase in detail.

Justification means "to be put right with God." This was Luther's central question: How can miserable, sinful humans "be put right with" a holy, righteous God? Years later, he said that he found the answer to that question through a new understanding of the righteousness of God. The righteousness of God originally terrified him because he understood it to refer to the holiness and perfection of God, and he hated this righteous God who punishes unrighteous sinners. As he studied Paul's letter to the Romans, however, he came across the phrase, "The one who is righteous will live by faith" (Rom 1:17). Luther said that righteousness here does not refer to a quality that God possesses in order to judge people but to a gift God gives in order to save people. Luther later referred to this as **passive** or **alien righteousness** because it is *God's* righteousness (and not their own) that justifies people before God. Salvation does not depend on their own goodness or righteousness, but on God's righteousness, freely and lovingly given to sinners (LW 34:336–7; WA 54,185–6).

Justification is therefore *by grace;* it is a free gift from God. As sinners, humans do not deserve it, and they can do absolutely nothing to earn it. Luther rejected nominalist theology with its call to "do what is within you," and he responded that justification is by grace *alone*. Humans do nothing to justify themselves before God. How, then, does God justify sinners? Through faith in Christ. Humans are saved by what God has done for them in Christ, not by what they do themselves. If people continue to bring their works before God, seeking to be saved by them, then they really do not have faith in what God has done for them in Christ. They need to depend completely and entirely on Christ, not on what they do.

Luther argued that even faith in Christ is not something people do. In other words, faith does not come because people try as hard as they can to believe. Luther described faith as a response to the Word of God, and that response is a gift from God. Luther understood the Word of God as preeminently Christ himself (John 1:1), but he also used this phrase to refer to preaching about Christ or to the Bible as a written testimony to Christ. However, Luther did not understand faith in Christ as assent to certain ideas or propositions about Jesus. It is much more than that. Thus, faith might better be translated as trust, the willingness to risk anything and everything for Christ. For Luther, the central question was no longer, "Have I done what is within me?" Luther now asks: "Where do I place my ultimate faith and trust? In myself? Or in Christ?"

THE INDULGENCE CONTROVERSY

Luther may have found the answer to his religious dilemma, but this does not explain how this brilliant but relatively obscure professor became a man known to popes and princes in his own day and acknowledged for his influence today, five hundred years later. His fame stems from his attack on the sale of indulgences, a practice associated with the sacrament of Penance. Penance was composed of several elements: **contrition** (sorrow for sin), confession of sin to a priest, **absolution** (forgiveness for the guilt associated with sin), and **works of satisfaction** (to remove the penalties or consequences of sin). These works might involve special prayers, fasting, pilgrimages, or giving alms (money) to the poor. They were called works of satisfaction because they were intended to provide satisfaction or compensation for sin. If these penalties were not paid in this life, then they would be in the next—in purgatory. Purgatory is a place or state following death in which sinners destined for heaven undergo the punishment still remaining for forgiven sins and thereby are purged in order to be made ready for heaven.

According to the theology of the church, indulgences were only applied to the last stage in Penance, works of satisfaction. This meant that the sinner should still feel sorrow for sin, confess the sin, and receive forgiveness for the guilt associated with the sin. Indulgences released people from the penalties or works of satisfaction they still owed by drawing on the surplus good works of the saints and of Christ. These good works formed a **treasury of merit** under the control of the pope. When an indulgence was granted, the pope transferred these excess merits to the repentant sinner. Thus, for example, a sinner might receive an indulgence to offer prayers and alms instead of a pilgrimage as her work of satisfaction, and the merits of Christ and the saints would make up the deficiency.

Unfortunately, this practice of granting indulgences became vulnerable to abuse, especially as a means of raising funds. In 1517 Pope Leo X authorized Archbishop Albrecht of Mainz to sell a special indulgence throughout much of northern Germany. The proceeds for this indulgence were to be used to build St. Peter's Basilica in Rome and to pay the debts Albrecht had accumulated in acquiring the office of archbishop. In his instructions to the indulgence sellers, Albrecht claimed that the indulgences would remove guilt as well as punishment, persons already in purgatory could be released, and those who contributed money on their behalf need not be contrite or confessed.

The *Ninety-Five Theses*

Luther became involved in the issue of indulgences because a Dominican friar named Johann Tetzel was selling this special indulgence just across the border of Saxony, and some of Luther's own parishioners were purchasing it. As a professor and priest, Luther decided to address this issue by calling for a discussion of indulgences in a public university debate. On October 31, 1517, Luther followed the usual practice for announcing public debates and posted his *Ninety-Five Theses* on the door of the Wittenberg Castle church. These theses were written in Latin, the language of the educated class, and were intended for an academic audience. The academic character of this debate changed when Luther's *Ninety-Five Theses* were translated into German, the vernacular, and were rapidly disseminated by means of the printing press. Soon his *Ninety-Five Theses* were being discussed and debated by people throughout the Holy Roman Empire and beyond.

Why did the *Ninety-Five Theses* have such an impact? Luther clearly and powerfully expressed the reservations and questions that many others had regarding indulgences. He attacked the practice of selling indulgences on both theological and moral grounds, as indicated by the following examples:

> Thesis 36: Any truly repentant Christian has a right to full remission of penalty and guilt, even without indulgence letters.
>
> Thesis 43: Christians are to be taught that the one who gives to the poor or lends to the needy does a better deed than the one who buys indulgences.
>
> Thesis 82: Why does not the pope empty purgatory for the sake of holy love and the dire need of the souls that are there if he redeems an infinite number of souls for the sake of miserable money with which to build a church?
>
> Thesis 86: Why does not the pope, whose wealth is today greater than the wealth of the richest king, build this one basilica of St. Peter with his own money rather than with the money of poor believers? (LW 31:25–33 [some changes in translation]; WA 1:233–238)

Luther identified the last two questions as questions that were being asked by ordinary lay people. They would certainly have received hearty approval from those Germans who felt resentment and anger because the pope was taking money from them to build a church in Rome. Whereas strong central governments had developed in England, France, and Spain, the Holy Roman Empire was an empire in name only. It was actually a loose union of many independent states, unable to resist the financial demands of the Renaissance popes who needed to raise money for their building projects and art collections. However, Luther's criticisms about the church went deeper than German complaints about the pope's financial demands. He began by raising theological and moral questions about the current practice of selling indulgences, but soon he would raise more challenging questions about the authority of the pope himself.

The Leipzig Debate

In the summer of 1519, Luther was engaged in a heated debate with John Eck, a fellow professor and theologian. Representatives of the church had already challenged Luther's criticism of indulgences by appealing to the authority of the pope. Luther therefore prepared for this debate by studying the decrees establishing the authority of the papacy. This research led him to question the preeminence and infallibility of the pope. In the course of the debate, Eck confronted Luther with the traditional arguments for the authority of the pope and then declared that anyone who denied this authority agreed with Jan Hus, the reformer who had been burned at the stake for heresy by the Council of Constance in 1415.

Luther initially denied that he was a Hussite, but during a break in the proceedings he read Hus' statements on the church and was surprised to discover that he agreed with him. Luther returned to state that many of Hus' declarations were not heretical and that he should not have been condemned by the Council of Constance. Eck thus succeeded in having Luther publicly deny not only the authority of the pope but also the authority of the councils of the church. Thus the controversy over indulgences, a specific practice of the church, had become a controversy over church authority.

Luther's Excommunication

John Eck traveled to Rome with notes on the Leipzig Debate and condemnations of Luther by the universities of Cologne and Louvain. In June 1520 a **papal bull**, a formal document issued by the pope, was published in Rome. This bull gave Luther sixty days to recant (formally deny his statements) or be excommunicated along with his followers. The bull, according to custom, called for the burning of Luther's books. Students and faculty at the University of Wittenberg responded by burning books of church law and scholastic theology. In an act of defiance, Luther also threw the papal bull that had condemned him into the flames. In January of 1521, Luther was formally excommunicated by the pope.

Writings of 1520

Throughout these events Luther continued to write, composing three very significant works in the year 1520. In his *Address to the Christian Nobility of the German Nation*, he called on the German princes and rulers to enact the reforms that church officials refused to undertake. He defended their right to do so by outlining his doctrine of the priesthood of all believers. In this doctrine Luther said that all Christians are made priests by Baptism, faith, and the gospel, but not all are called to exercise that office in the church. If church officials fail to reform the church, however, then Christian princes have the right to do so by virtue of their Baptism.

In his next treatise, *On the Babylonian Captivity of the Church*, Luther argued that the sacraments, especially the Eucharist, were being held "captive" by the church. Luther accepted the teaching about the real presence of Christ in the Eucharist (as opposed to a spiritual or figurative presence) because Jesus referred to the bread and wine as his body and blood. Luther, however, denied **transubstantiation**, the transformation of the bread and wine into the body and blood of Christ. This doctrine used concepts from the philosophy of Aristotle to describe how the bread and wine can continue to look, taste, and feel the same even after this change has occurred. According to the doctrine of transubstantiation, the substance (underlying reality) of the bread and wine changes into the substance of the body and blood of Christ, while the accidents (outer appearance) remain the same. Luther rejected this on the grounds that it is not biblical and that it relies on scholastic philosophy. Luther concluded that one should simply accept Jesus's words in faith and not attempt to use philosophy to describe or explain them. This agreed with Luther's general understanding of the sacraments in terms of the Word and faith; a Word of promise is offered in the sacrament and accepted by faith.

Figures 18–1 and 18–2 Title pages of Luther's Reformation writing: *To the Christian Nobility of the German Nation Concerning the Reform of the Christian Estate* (August 1520); *The Freedom of a Christian* (November 1520). Woodcuts.

At first glance, Luther's understanding of sacraments appears to conflict with the practice of infant Baptism. How can an infant hear and accept the Word in faith? If faith is so important, would it not make more sense to baptize believing adults? Luther rejected this argument, in part because the church had been baptizing infants for centuries. He was a conservative reformer who believed that the tradition of the church should be preserved unless it was contradicted by the Bible. In Luther's view, infant Baptism not only did not contradict the Bible, but it also proclaimed the central message of justification by grace through faith. The infant is given faith by God, completely apart from its own efforts and abilities. Faith is a gift, and nowhere is this seen more clearly than in the Baptism of an infant.

Many of Luther's contemporaries, including Erasmus, saw *On the Babylonian Captivity* as his most radical work to date, for in it Luther criticized the very heart of the church, its theology and practice of the sacraments. Of the seven sacraments of the church, Luther retained only two: Baptism and the Eucharist. At the beginning of his treatise, Luther still referred to Penance as a sacrament (because it was instituted by Christ and carries a Word of promise), but by the end of the treatise he concluded that it is not a sacrament because it lacks a "visible sign" (like the water of Baptism or the bread and wine of the Eucharist). He continued, however, to regard private confession as a useful practice in the life of the Christian.

In Luther's third treatise, *Christian Liberty*, he described his theology of justification by grace through faith and outlined its consequences for living a Christian life. He posed the question this way: If justification is by faith alone, are Christians then free to live immoral lives? Luther answered this question by defining Christian freedom and describing the proper relationship between faith and works in the life of a Christian.

Diet of Worms

While Luther continued to write, his immediate political superior, Frederick the Wise of Saxony, was trying to negotiate a hearing for Luther before the princes and rulers of the Holy Roman Empire. Frederick had supported the election of the current emperor and persuaded him to promise that Luther would not be condemned without a hearing. Emperor Charles V therefore invited Luther to attend the next formal meeting, or **diet**, of the Holy Roman Empire of the German Nation. The emperor soon withdrew his invitation, however, when the pope's representative pointed out that Luther had already been condemned by the church and should not be granted a hearing by the laity. The tide changed yet again when the diet convened at Worms in 1521, and the rulers of various states and cities called on the emperor to bring Luther before them. They claimed that Luther's teaching had become so influential that condemnation without a hearing might lead to rebellion. The emperor once again invited Luther to attend the diet.

This political maneuvering would become commonplace in the years to come and was a significant factor in the success of the Lutheran Reformation. Although Charles V had inherited the right to rule over a substantial portion of Western Europe (Spain, Austria–Hungary, parts of Italy, and the Netherlands), he was strongly opposed by the other European powers, especially the popes and the king of France. The Ottoman Turks also presented a significant military threat as they pressed up the Danube and into Charles' Austrian lands. Faced with the daunting task of ruling an extensive empire, without the benefit of modern communication or transportation, Charles was forced to compromise with the German princes again and again. His preoccupation with other threats meant that Charles could never fully devote himself to the religious and political divisions developing within the Holy Roman Empire.

These divisions would soon become apparent when Luther arrived at the Diet of Worms. Luther was hoping for an opportunity to present and defend his views, but those hopes were quickly dashed. As he stood before the assembly, a representative of the archbishop of Trier pointed to a pile of books and asked Luther two questions: Had he written these books? Was there a part of them he would now choose to recant? Momentarily taken aback, Luther asked for some time to consider his answer. He appeared before the imperial diet on the following day and this time his answer was clear and unequivocal:

> Unless I am convinced by the testimony of the Scriptures or by clear reason (for I do not trust either in the pope or in councils alone, since it is well known that they have often erred and contradicted themselves), I am bound by the Scriptures I have quoted and my conscience is captive to the Word of God. I cannot and will not retract anything, since it is neither safe nor right to go against conscience. May God help me! Amen. (LW 32:112–3; WA 7,838)

Luther's declaration that he would not recant was followed by several days of unsuccessful meetings and negotiations. He finally left the city, and soon after the emperor issued the **Edict of Worms**, declaring Luther an outlaw and subject to capital punishment. Luther the monk and professor was now a heretic and outlaw. At the Leipzig Debate, Eck had compared Luther to Jan Hus, the reformer condemned and killed by the Council of Constance. How would Luther avoid meeting the same fate?

EXILE AND RETURN

On his way home from the Diet of Worms, Luther's wagon traveled down an empty road in the woods. Suddenly armed horsemen attacked the wagon, his companions fled, and he was dragged away by his assailants. As word of his capture spread, many thought that they had heard the last of Luther. However, Luther's "kidnapping" had been arranged by his ally and ruler, Frederick the Wise of Saxony. To prevent discovery, Luther grew a beard, exchanged his monk's habit for the attire of a knight, and adopted the name Junker Jörg (Sir George). The protection Luther received from some of the German princes, especially Frederick of Saxony, ensured his continued survival. He would spend the next ten months hidden at Elector Frederick's castle, the Wartburg.

Wartburg Castle

Luther struggled with ill health and depression during his exile at Wartburg Castle and yet these were some of the most productive months of his life. In addition to publishing over a dozen books, Luther translated Erasmus' Greek text of the New Testament into German. This translation was so influential and widely read that it helped to create the modern German language. Luther translated the New Testament into German because he believed that scripture was the sole authority in matters of faith and that all Christians should be able to read it in their own tongue.

In his preface to the New Testament Luther offered guidance on the proper way to read and interpret scripture. He admonished Christians to properly distinguish between the law (the commandments of God) and the gospel (the promises of God). The law (which is found throughout the Bible, including the New Testament) condemns people, shows them their sin, and prepares them to receive the good news of the gospel. Keeping in mind that distinction between law and gospel, Luther emphasized once again that people are not saved by doing the works of the law but by trusting the promises of the gospel.

Return from Exile

As Luther continued to write and translate at Wartburg Castle, he heard disturbing reports of violence and upheaval at Wittenberg. Some of his friends and colleagues, in particular a fellow professor and priest named Carlstadt, had begun implementing Luther's reforms, creating considerable unrest in the process. On Christmas Day 1521, Carlstadt celebrated the Mass without wearing the traditional robes and vestments, delivered parts of the liturgy in German instead of Latin, and distributed both bread and wine to the assembled worshipers, instead of bread alone. Luther agreed with these reforms, at least in principle, but he was disturbed by the coercive manner in which they were carried out. He was especially troubled by episodes of **iconoclasm**, or image-breaking, in which statues, stained glass, and paintings were forcibly destroyed or removed from churches. He was also concerned that others were implementing reforms without consulting him and without regard for proper order and authority.

The town council of Wittenberg, seeking leadership and guidance, invited Luther to return. When he informed Frederick the Wise of the council's request, Frederick responded that he could not protect Luther if he came out of hiding. Luther returned to Wittenberg despite the warning and preached a series of sermons declaring that reform should be accomplished by persuasion and love, not by violence and force. He argued that faith must come freely, without compulsion, and that reform inevitably will follow when the word of God is preached and believed. His call for moderation and patience was heeded, and order was restored in Wittenberg.

The Peasants' Revolt

A few years later, another group tried to push Luther's call for reform in a more radical direction. In 1524 and 1525 a group of peasants in southern Germany appealed to Luther's ideas in their call for economic and social justice. The princes had consolidated their power by imposing greater taxes and services on the peasants and displacing local law codes, which guaranteed common land, in favor of Roman law, which acknowledged only private property. In one of the most widely circulated lists of peasant demands, *The Twelve Articles*, the authors used Luther's language and ideas to prove the justice of their cause.

Luther responded with his own tract entitled *An Admonition to Peace*. In this tract, Luther condemned the princes and lords for their unjust treatment of the peasants and declared that they were bringing revolt on themselves. Luther then addressed the peasants, and although he acknowledged the justice of many of their demands, he rejected their call for rebellion and violence. Luther stated that even unjust and cruel rulers are ordained by God and Christians are required to obey them. Christians may only disobey the proper authorities when the gospel is in jeopardy. Luther did not believe that was the case here, and so he objected to the peasants' appeal to the gospel and Christian freedom to support their social and economic demands. He concluded that there was nothing specifically Christian at stake in this revolt and called on the princes and peasants to negotiate a peaceful resolution.

Luther traveled about the countryside, admonishing the peasants to maintain the peace, but he was met with jeers and threats. Luther responded to the peasants' continued rebellion with his infamous treatise *Against the Robbing and Murdering Hordes of Peasants*. In this work, he called on the princes to give the peasants one last chance to negotiate. If the peasants did not lay down their arms, Luther proposed the following measures:

> Therefore let everyone who can, smite, slay, and stab, secretly or openly, remembering that nothing can be more poisonous, hurtful, or devilish than a rebel. It is just as when one must kill a mad dog; if you do not strike him, he will strike you, and a whole land with you. (LW 46:50; WA 18,358)

This tract was published just as the princes were killing the peasants by the thousands, even those who had surrendered or been taken prisoner. Luther was criticized for this treatise in his own day, but he maintained his position against rebels, especially those who claim the word of God to justify their rebellion. Luther's response to the Peasants' Revolt clearly demonstrated that he did not equate social, political, or economic reform with his call for religious renewal.

LUTHER'S MARRIAGE

In 1525, at the peak of the Peasants' Revolt, Luther took the sudden and unexpected step of marrying a former nun. Although Luther had taught for several years that celibacy and monastic asceticism were contrary to the Bible and that priests, monks, and nuns should be free to marry, he had not indicated any desire to do so himself. His change of heart was precipitated by the plight of Katherine von Bora, one of several nuns he had helped smuggle out of a Cistercian convent two years earlier. By 1525 Luther had found homes or husbands for all of the women but Katherine. At the age of twenty-six Katherine's chances for marriage were slim, and after several potential suitors proved unacceptable, she offered to marry Luther himself. Luther accepted her offer in order to provide his father with grandchildren, to spite the pope who forbade clerical marriage, and to witness to his convictions before his martyrdom.

Luther's anticipated martyrdom never occurred, and the marriage he entered into at the age of forty-two would last until his death two decades later. Although Luther declared that he felt neither "passionate love" nor the "burning" of desire when he married, genuine affection and love developed between husband and wife (LW 49:117; WABr 3,541). Luther and Katherine had six children, four of whom survived into adulthood. Katherine

Figure 18–3 Portrait of Martin Luther.

Figure 18–4 Portrait of Katharine von Bora.

managed the household, which included several relatives, student boarders, and frequent guests. Money was a constant concern, especially given Luther's reckless generosity. Katherine took charge of the family's finances and proved to be a shrewd businesswoman who supplemented the family's income by farming, brewing beer, breeding pigs, and taking in lodgers.

THE PROTESTANTS

In the years following Luther's marriage the division between those who accepted his reforms and those who did not continued to widen. In 1526 the First Diet of Speyer decided that until a council could be held to discuss recent religious developments, each German prince was free to act as he saw fit before God and the emperor. Some princes supported Luther while others remained loyal to the Roman Church. This compromise was challenged three years later when the majority of princes at the Second Diet of Speyer declared that Lutheranism would be tolerated only in those areas where it could not be suppressed without violence. The diet further decided that religious liberty must be extended to Catholics in Lutheran lands, but the same liberty would not be given to Lutherans in Catholic lands. Six Lutheran princes protested this arrangement and thereby acquired the name **Protestant**. This attempt to reestablish Catholic faith and practice throughout Germany failed and Germany was divided into two camps, Catholic and Protestant.

Emperor Charles V came to Germany the following year (1530) to preside over the Diet of Augsburg, a meeting of German rulers summoned for the purpose of resolving the religious question. Luther was not permitted to attend this meeting since the Edict of Worms was in effect, and he was still considered an outlaw. His friend and colleague Philip Melanchthon represented the Lutheran position and drafted a statement of faith known as the *Augsburg Confession*. Melanchthon hoped for a reconciliation between Catholics and Protestants, and thus he stressed their common ground. The differences between the two parties were too deep to be resolved in this way, however, and the *Augsburg Confession* was rejected not only by Catholics but also by certain Protestants. The Protestants of Switzerland and the south German cities submitted their own statements of faith, while the Lutherans signed the *Augsburg Confession*. To this day the *Augsburg Confession* remains an important statement of Lutheran doctrine.

At the conclusion of the diet, Charles V ordered all Protestant territories to return to traditional religious practices by the following year or prepare for war. He was not able to act on his threat when the year ended, but eventually he did engage the Protestant princes in battle. Neither side achieved a decisive victory, and finally they were forced to reach a compromise.

In 1555, after twenty-five years of conflict, the Peace of Augsburg established the principle that each prince was free to choose either the Roman Catholic or the Lutheran tradition. This was not religious freedom in the modern sense, however, for all the subjects of the prince were expected to follow the religion of their ruler. Those who did not share the religion of their prince were permitted, after selling their property, to migrate to another territory. As a result of this agreement, most of southern Germany remained Catholic while northern Germany adopted Lutheranism. The Lutheran faith eventually spread beyond Germany to Scandinavia, where it displaced Catholicism as the established church.

THE LUTHERAN CHURCH

Although the most dramatic events of his life were behind him after 1525, Luther spent the next twenty years working with his supporters to form the Lutheran Church. What structure or organization should this new church have? Luther was inclined to locate power in local, independent congregations, but he concluded that they did not have the resources to deal with the problems facing the reform movement. He was unable to maintain the traditional episcopal structure in which bishops exercise authority, in part because the bishops had generally remained loyal to the Roman Church. In addition, he was persuaded that the term *bishop* in the New Testament did not refer to a distinct office but to every pastor. Luther finally called on the princes to function as "emergency bishops" and assume responsibility for the work of reorganizing the church. However, Luther did not live to see the Peace of Augsburg and the establishment of the Lutheran Church in Germany and Scandinavia.

Luther was primarily concerned with the preaching and worship life of the new church, not its structure. He believed the true church was found where the Word of God was truly preached and the sacraments rightly administered. He did not think he was establishing this church for the first time or even reestablishing it after years of neglect. On the contrary, he believed that the true Christian church had existed without interruption from the time of the apostles to his own day. Thus, despite his criticisms of the Roman Church, Luther held that God had preserved the true church—through the preaching of the Word and the administration of the sacraments—even under a church structure that had erred in many ways. Luther did not identify the church with a particular structure or organization but with a community of believers called by God. Those who responded to the Word in faith were the true but hidden church.

Luther believed, however, that the true preaching of the gospel and the proper administration of the sacraments were being obscured by the current practices and structures of the Roman Church. He concluded that the Lutheran Church required a good translation of the Bible, a catechism to instruct the young, a reformed liturgy to correct abuses in worship, and a hymnbook to inspire and instruct the people. Luther himself would fulfill each of these requirements (Bainton 1983).

The Bible

Luther translated the New Testament into German during his exile at Wartburg Castle and started his translation of the Old Testament after his return to Wittenberg. A translation of the entire Bible was not printed until 1534 and he continued to revise this translation until his death. Luther believed the church must be founded on the Word of God and this Word should be accessible to all believers in their own language.

The Catechisms of 1529

Luther thought that Christians also required instruction in the doctrines and practices of the church. To determine the current state of Christian belief and practice, Luther asked his new prince, Elector John of Saxony, to organize a formal visitation of churches in his territory. Appalled by the results of the visitations, especially the lack of religious knowledge among the common people, Luther composed two **catechisms** (manuals of Christian doctrine) to instruct believers. Luther was following an ancient tradition in doing so, for catechisms can be traced to the earliest days of the Christian church. Luther organized his catechisms around five elements: the Ten Commandments, the Apostles' Creed, the Lord's Prayer, Baptism, and the Eucharist. Luther wrote a *Large Catechism* for adults but his *Small Catechism*, written for children, had the greatest influence. Many Lutheran churches encouraged the practice of committing the *Small Catechism* to memory, a practice that still continues today.

Liturgy

Luther was a conservative reformer, inclined to maintain the status quo except where he felt it contradicted the gospel. This is evident in his reform of the liturgy. In the Mass, the priest on behalf of the people offers the body and blood of Christ as a sacrifice to God. Luther objected to this on the grounds that it makes the Mass into a good work that humans perform for God. To emphasize the word of promise that God offers in the sacrament, he changed the traditional Eucharistic prayer (with its reference to sacrifice) to a simple reading of the account of the Last Supper. However, since the prayers of the Mass were still in Latin, Luther feared that most worshipers would not understand the significance of the change. As a consequence, he translated the liturgy of the Mass into German. Luther maintained many of the traditional elements of the liturgy, but he emphasized proclamation of the Word and religious instruction through the sermon.

Hymnbook

One of the most significant changes Luther made in the service was the active involvement of the congregation in the singing of hymns. The first German hymnal was published in 1524, containing four hymns written by Luther himself. Luther continued to write the words and occasionally the music for many other hymns, drawing on portions of scriptures (especially the Psalms) and Latin liturgical chants for inspiration. In his most famous hymn, "A Mighty Fortress Is Our God," Luther adapted Psalm 46 to express his faith in the midst of struggle:

> God's Word forever shall abide,
> No thanks to foes, who fear it;
> For God himself fights by our side
> With weapons of the Spirit.
> Were they to take our house,
> Goods, honor, child, or spouse,
> Though life be wrenched away,
> They cannot win the day.
> The Kingdom's ours forever.
> (*Lutheran Book of Worship*, Hymn 229)

LUTHER'S DEATH

In 1546, Luther traveled to Eisleben, the place of his birth, to settle a feud between the local rulers. Luther was sixty-two years old and had struggled with ill health throughout his life. He fell ill during this visit to his hometown and died of heart failure on February 18. A slip of paper found in his pocket summed up his central conviction that people are saved by grace alone: "We are beggars. That is true" (LW 54:476; WATr 5,318). Luther's influence is still felt today in his theological and biblical writings, his hymns, and the catechism he wrote to instruct children. His ideas and convictions have left their mark on the church that bears his name. His call for reform was one of many, however, and the impetus for reform did not end with his death. Other reform movements—both Catholic and Protestant—continued to address questions of authority, human nature, and salvation.

Key Terms

passive or alien righteousness	treasury of merit	iconoclasm
contrition	papal bull	Protestant
absolution	transubstantiation	*Augsburg Confession*
works of satisfaction	diet	catechism
	Edict of Worms	

Questions for Reading

1. Why did nominalist theology cause problems for Luther?

2. What did Luther mean by *justification by faith*? How did he come to this idea?

3. What were indulgences, and how were they related to the sacrament of Penance? Why and how did Luther become involved in the indulgence controversy?

4. How did Luther's *Ninety-Five Theses* relate to the controversy over indulgences? How did this controversy become a controversy over church authority?

5. What was Luther's general understanding of a sacrament? How did this affect his views on Eucharist and Baptism?

6. Why did Luther refuse to recant at the Diet of Worms?

7. What did Luther do during his exile at Wartburg Castle? Why did he return to Wittenberg?

8. Why did Luther oppose the Peasants' Revolt? What does this tell you about his understanding of reform?

9. What is the origin of the word *Protestant*?

10. How did Luther define the true church? When and where does it exist?

11. What innovations did Luther make with respect to the Bible, the catechism, the liturgy, and the hymn book? Why did he consider these changes necessary?

Works Consulted/Recommended Reading

Atkinson, James. *Martin Luther and the Birth of Protestantism.* Atlanta: John Knox, 1968.

Bainton, Roland H. *Here I Stand: A Life of Martin Luther.* Nashville, TN: Abingdon, 1983.

Brecht, Martin. *Martin Luther: Shaping and Defining the Reformation, 1521–1532.* Translated by James L. Schaaf. Minneapolis, MN: Fortress, 1990.

Edwards, Mark, and George Tavard. *Luther: A Reformer for the Churches.* Philadelphia: Fortress, 1983.

Inter-Lutheran Commission on Worship. *Lutheran Book of Worship.* Minneapolis, MN: Augsburg, 1978.

Kittelson, James M. *Luther the Reformer: The Story of the Man and His Career.* Minneapolis, MN: Augsburg, 1986.

Loewenich, Walther von. *Martin Luther: The Man and His Work.* Minneapolis, MN: Augsburg, 1982.

Luther, Martin. *D. Martin Luthers Werke: Kritische Gesamtausgabe.* 73 vols. 1883. Reprint, Weimar: H. Böhlaus Nachfolger, 2000–2007.

Luther, Martin. *D. Martin Luthers Werke: Kritische Gesamtausgabe. Briefwechsel.* 18 vols. Reprint, Weimar: H. Böhlaus Nachfolger, 2002.

Luther, Martin. *D. Martin Luthers Werke: Kritische Gesamtausgabe. Tischreden.* 6 vols. 1912. Reprint, Weimar: H. Böhlaus Nachfolger, 2000.

Luther, Martin. *Luther's Works,* eds. Jaroslav Pelikan and Helmut T. Lehmann. 56 vols. Philadelphia: Fortress; St. Louis: Concordia Publishing House, 1955–1986.

Metzger, Bruce, and Roland Murphy, eds. *The New Oxford Annotated Bible with Apocrypha, New Revised Standard Version.* New York: Oxford University, 1991.

Nestingen, James Arne. *Martin Luther: His Life and Teachings.* Philadelphia: Fortress, 1982.

Oberman, Heiko A. *Luther: Man between God and the Devil.* Translated by Eileen Walliser-Schwarzbart. New Haven, CT: Yale University, 1989.

Ozment, Steven. *The Age of Reform 1250–1550: An Intellectual and Religious History of Late Medieval and Reformation Europe.* New Haven, CT: Yale University, 1980.

Spitz, Lewis W. *The Protestant Reformation, 1517–1559.* New York: Harper and Row, 1985.

Chapter

OTHER PROTESTANT REFORMERS

TIMELINE

A.D. 1484	Ulrich Zwingli is born in the Swiss canton of St. Gall.
A.D. 1509	John Calvin is born in Pont-l'Evêque, France.
A.D. 1519	After successful preaching in several small parishes, Zwingli comes to preach at a major church in Zurich. This marks the beginning of his reform preaching.
A.D. 1525	Former followers of Zwingli defy the Zurich city council by baptizing one another as adult believers, marking the emergence of the Radical Reformation or Anabaptist movement.
A.D. 1527	William Tyndale publishes a translation of large portions of the Bible in English.
A.D. 1529	Zwingli and Luther debate their differences regarding theology and church reform at Marburg.
A.D. 1531	Zwingli dies at the battle of Kappel, a conflict that broke out when an incident of iconoclasm got out of hand.
A.D. 1533–1553	Thomas Cranmer, archbishop of Canterbury, provides a stabilizing force for the English reform movement.
A.D. 1534	King Henry VIII declares himself head of the church in England.
c. A.D. 1535	Calvin begins his involvement in the Reformation and moves to Geneva.
c. A.D. 1539	Calvin writes his famous *Reply to Sadoleto* in which he defended the principles of the Reformation.
A.D. 1553	Queen Mary attempts to reverse England's reform movement and return the church to its pre-Reformation state.
A.D. 1558	Queen Elizabeth I resumes the course of English reform and establishes the Church of England as it is known today.
A.D. 1564	Death of John Calvin.

The last chapter began with the question, Why are some Christians today known as Catholics and others identified as Protestants? It then went on to tell the story of Martin Luther and how his efforts to reform the church resulted in some new interpretations of traditional theological claims. At the end, the chapter described how the efforts of Luther and his followers led to the formation of the Lutheran Church.

Of course there are other Christians besides Lutherans and Roman Catholics. There are Methodists, Episcopalians, Presbyterians, and Baptists; there are members of the United Church of Christ, the Disciples of Christ, and the Assemblies of God. Indeed there are dozens of major Christian churches, and many more subdivisions of those churches. Do the members of one of these denominations have very different beliefs from the members of another group? Why and how did Christians split into so many different groups?

The answers to these questions require an investigation of events in the sixteenth century—specifically, of reform movements that took place at the same time as, or immediately after, the work of Martin Luther and his followers. These movements will help explain the differing interpretations of the Christian message that characterize the various Christian denominations today. This chapter will examine a small but representative sample of four of these reform movements—two that center on a particular individual and two others that draw on the contributions of a variety of thinkers.

THE SWISS REFORMATION

The country that we English-speakers know as Switzerland has an official Latin name: *Confederatio Helvetica*, or the Helvetic Confederation. Like the United States, Switzerland actually comprises a number of smaller states, called cantons. In the sixteenth century, these

cantons were largely independent from one another, though they sometimes entered into federations as a means of maintaining their distance from the emperors of the Holy Roman Empire who sometimes sought to control them. A religious leader who could form an alliance with the government of a canton would receive the same kind of military protection that Luther received from Elector Frederick of Saxony. This is precisely what happened in the case of a bright and ambitious young priest by the name of **Ulrich Zwingli**.

Zwingli was born in 1484, making him just a few months younger than Martin Luther. His family members were farmers, but because he showed some early intellectual gifts and an ear for music, more attention was given to his schooling. He attended university in Vienna (in modern-day Austria) and Basel (now on the French–Swiss border).

Another Erasmus

Basel was a city that had absorbed the "new learning" of the Renaissance with great enthusiasm. It had an active university, busy printing presses, and much scholarly discussion of

Figure 19–1 Portrait of Ulrich Zwingli in his elder years.

the work of humanists such as Erasmus. Zwingli's education was a classical one, with a focus in philosophy. By 1506 he had finished the master of arts degree and was ready to pursue theology. At about the same time, a position came open for a parish priest in the town of Glarus, near his own hometown; as a well-educated local, he was the natural choice for the job. He became a priest and served the town for the next ten years. He continued to read and study the Greek and Latin classics, as well as the Bible and the writings of theologians such as Augustine and John Chrysostom.

In 1516 he also took on the responsibilities of priest at the nearby parish of Einsiedeln. There he became concerned about the same thing that had worried Luther: the tendency for Christians to forget that their salvation comes solely from God. Zwingli saw this occurring not only in the sale of indulgences (as had Luther) but also in the popular devotion to images. Zwingli's new parish had a shrine—a statue of the Virgin Mary—to which some people had attributed magical healing powers. Zwingli saw many people who visited the shrine and worried that many of them had decided to worship a statue rather than God. His preaching at this popular shrine became well known, and at the beginning of 1519 he came to Zurich—the biggest city in the region—to be the main preacher at the largest church in town.

In Zurich, Zwingli's extensive learning served him well; he read the Bible to large audiences in this powerful city. Practically no one owned a copy of the Bible, and the few who did would likely have been unable to read it. Zwingli's straightforward explanations of biblical stories must have shaken the people of Zurich out of their slumber. They started to ask questions, to think seriously about certain controversial questions (such as the morality of indulgences), and to ask themselves about the meaning of their beliefs. In short, they started to be interested in theology.

Agreements with Luther

Like Luther, Zwingli argued that the Bible alone should be the focal point for Christians. Human interpretations—no matter how authoritatively issued (for example, by the pope)—were not as reliable as the biblical text itself. Zwingli argued that if a traditional religious practice (such as fasting during Lent, the forty-day period leading up to Easter) was not required by scripture, it should be considered optional. His view was not far from that expressed in Luther's treatise *Christian Liberty*. Zwingli's position obviously put him into conflict with his immediate superior, the bishop of Konstanz, who sent a deputy to give an address on the importance of adhering to the traditional teachings. However, Zurich was a sovereign canton, and the local council backed Zwingli; he was not punished for his dissenting views.

Zwingli reached similar conclusions to those of Luther on a number of other issues: Faith was the first Christian virtue, without which no one could be saved; individual bishops, and even church councils, could make mistakes; and clergy should be allowed to marry (Zwingli himself secretly married Anna Reinhart in 1522). However, also like Luther, he continued to uphold many of the traditional beliefs of the church—including beliefs that some later Protestant Christians would deny or deem irrelevant, such as the perpetual virginity of Mary and the importance of regular participation in communion. Nevertheless, on matters of difference, he was willing to take on the bishops and learned doctors in debate and discussion. His great learning and thorough knowledge of the original biblical languages made Zwingli an easy winner in these disputes.

Differences with Luther

Zwingli also went farther than Luther on some issues. He spoke loudly against image worship, which, he emphasized, is prohibited by the second commandment ("You shall not make for yourself an idol"). Drawing on his experiences at the shrine in his old parish at Einsiedeln, Zwingli concluded that if the people are surrounded by images, they will too easily forget that the image is meant simply to remind them to worship God alone and will thus slip into the worship of the image instead. He thus argued that images should be removed from churches. This position, often known as iconoclasm, became one of the hallmarks of the Swiss Reformation. The removal of images was not always very peaceful and orderly. Rather than simply taking the statues from churches and placing them in museums, iconoclasts sometimes smashed windows and toppled statues. Within the city of Zurich itself, however, things were usually kept calm.

Zwingli also went farther than Luther on the question of the sacraments. Like Luther, he accepted only two sacraments, Baptism and the Eucharist. Concerning the Eucharist, he too rejected the idea of transubstantiation and argued that there is no "sacrifice" in the Mass (Christ having already been offered, once and for all, as the only necessary sacrifice). The distinctive element in Zwingli's doctrine of the Eucharist, however, was that he offered a purely spiritual interpretation of the description of Christ's body and blood. He based his claim on a quotation from the Gospel of John: "The spirit gives life; the flesh is useless" (John 6:63). Whatever value comes to believers during the Eucharist must come spiritually, not in any physical form. Thus Zwingli rejected the traditional doctrine of the "real presence" of Christ in the Eucharist, because Christ's risen body was present with the Father in heaven. Thus, for Zwingli, the Eucharistic service merely concentrates the mind and allows believers to remember the actions of Jesus in giving himself for their sake. The service is best understood as a "remembrance."

Zwingli's differences with Luther came to a head when they met at the city of Marburg in 1529 to debate their issues of disagreement. Both of them were stubborn, holding fast to their own interpretations. Neither one flinched, and both went away convinced that the other was simply wrong. Thus, on the one hand, the **Marburg Colloquy**, as it became known, was a failure: It showed that nothing could be settled merely by appealing to the Bible as "the final authority," since people would continue to disagree about the best interpretation of a biblical text. On the other hand, Zwingli helped Luther see just how far his own position was from that of the Roman Catholic Church and just how difficult any kind of reconciliation between them would be.

Coming to a Bad End

The success of the Reformation in Zurich and other major Swiss cities led to considerable nervousness in those Swiss cantons that continued to accept all the teachings of the Roman Catholic Church. Zwingli was strongly opposed to any compulsion of religious belief, but many political leaders on both sides saw that differences in religious belief could provide an opportunity to gain new territory and additional income. To oppose the power of Zurich, five of the Catholic cantons formed a "defense league," allied to both the pope and the Holy Roman Empire. There were further outbreaks of dramatic and excessive iconoclasm, which had been easier to keep peaceable inside Zurich than in the general countryside. Eventually, full-scale war broke out, and Zwingli himself died in 1531 at the battle of Kappel, fighting on the side of Zurich—the city he had led through the Reformation.

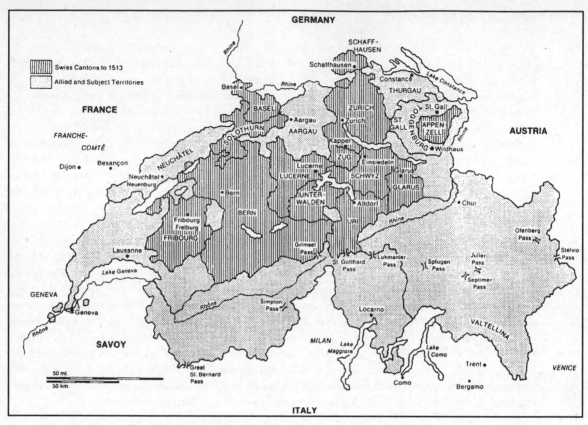

Figure 19–2 Map of the Swiss Confederation at the time of Ulrich Zwingli.

Zwingli's influence is still strongly felt among many Protestants—especially those who are not Lutheran. His understanding of the Eucharist and his disapproval of images in worship have influenced many Protestant denominations in Switzerland, the Netherlands, England, and eventually, the United States. This influence is most clear in denominations that organize themselves around the "congregational" model (in which there are no bishops or regional synods, but in which the individual congregation makes most decisions). These denominations include the Christian Church (Disciples of Christ), United Church of Christ, and many Baptist churches.

THE GENEVAN REFORMATION

The city of Geneva (also in present-day Switzerland) was, at first glance, in much the same situation as Zurich. Fiercely independent, the city was situated on a border—with the Swiss cantons on one side and a major political power (in this case, France) on the other. The Genevan people relished their resistance to foreign powers, whether political or religious. In addition to the similarities of these two cities, the two men who led them through the Reformation had certain similarities as well.

The Lawyer-Theologian

John Calvin was born in 1509 in Pont-l'Evêque, a city in northwestern France. His family was well connected, and he and his brothers were prepared for the priesthood from an early age. He had many advantages and showed himself to be something of a prodigy. He quickly mastered Latin and the whole range of classical texts and learned the medieval method of disputation. By 1525, Calvin had received the master of arts degree and was fully prepared for a course of theological study. Suddenly, though, his father withdrew him from the University of Paris and sent him instead to Orléans to begin a degree in law. Some historians have speculated that this change of mind may have been due to the outbreak of the Reformation and its increasing impact on the whole church after 1520. Perhaps Calvin's father wanted to keep his son out of the debates and division that seemed to be breaking out everywhere in the church. If so, he was ultimately unsuccessful; in 1531 Calvin abandoned his life as a lawyer and returned to theology.

By the mid-1530s, many of the ideas of the Reformation were beginning to reach France, and they caught Calvin's attention. He had made his views sufficiently well known that when a series of anti-Catholic posters appeared overnight in Paris, Calvin was numbered among the suspects. He and a friend escaped to Basel, a free city that was thoroughly on the side of reform, where a number of the chief architects of the Reformation lived. Through conversations with them and through his own diligence, Calvin began to produce the work for which he is most famous, and which he would continue to revise throughout his life. His *Institutes of the Christian Religion* is an attempt to provide a systematic statement of the beliefs of the Christian faith, written for the French rulers and others in France who wanted to learn about the new vision of Christianity that was being developed in the Reformation.

Figure 19–3 Portrait of John Calvin.

Calvin's Thought

Theology, Calvin says, is about our knowledge of God and our knowledge of ourselves. God has revealed to us what we should think and do by giving us the Law; but because it is impossible to obey this Law in its entirety, we are forced to confess our weaknesses and ask for God's mercy. Calvin, then, is very much of the same mind as Luther in his emphasis on the inability of human beings to save themselves by fulfilling the Law. They must rely on their faith alone, for only God can bring about their redemption.

One of Calvin's teachings concerns the doctrine of **election**—the idea that God chooses certain people with whom to enter into a special relationship, or covenant. Given our present-day emphasis on equal treatment for everyone, God's decision to "elect" certain persons may seem odd to us. Yet the Old Testament repeatedly describes God as calling out certain people and entering into a special relationship with them. Abraham and Sarah are chosen to be the founders of a new nation. The nation of Israel is chosen by God and is bound to God by the covenant between them. The prophets, too, are appointed, or chosen, by God. In the New Testament, God intervenes decisively by sending Jesus, who in turn chooses or calls particular followers. Later, the church is said to be composed of those who are "called out" of their everyday lives in society and enter into a special relationship with God.

Calvin saw two reasons for God's election. First, the doctrine of election emphasizes God's sovereignty. God, being God, can make choices that we cannot comprehend. Second, election is meant to motivate and inspire those who are elected. It is not an act of favoritism, nor is it a reward for those who have done good deeds. In fact, being elected by God is something of a burden. It might even be dangerous: Prophets were often exiled or killed, as were many of the early members of the church. Election is thus a forward-thinking idea; people are chosen not because they *are* already holy, but as a statement of God's plan to *make* them holy—to set them apart for a special task.

Calvin therefore argued for a logical extension of this idea: God has already chosen some for salvation and others for damnation. This concept is often called the doctrine of **double predestination**. Calvin reasoned that, if God is truly sovereign (supremely powerful and free from external control), the decision to save someone must be God's alone—it cannot depend on the decisions that human beings make during their lifetimes. Thus, we cannot know for certain, by looking at people's lives, whether or not they are among the "chosen," since predestination (like election) is not a reward for good deeds. On the other hand, however, the way we act can be a probable sign of the destiny that God has chosen for us.

At first glance, this view would appear to take away any motivation to do good. One might assume "God has already decided my fate; nothing that I do will make any difference." But Calvin believed that double predestination was a *freeing* doctrine: It meant that people did not need to be anxious about the destiny of their souls, since that had already been determined. They could thus get on with the business of doing God's work in the world. Moreover, Calvin argued, God continues to act in the lives of the chosen, regenerating and sanctifying them. So people should not be fatalistic about their election but should allow God to use them to do good. Apparently, Calvin's views had precisely this effect on a great many people, given the enormous energy for social activism in those denominations that owe their beginnings to Calvin and his associates.

Calvin's understanding of the sacraments has many similarities to that of Luther and Zwingli. He too accepted only two sacraments—Baptism and the Eucharist. He understood Baptism as a symbol of forgiveness, an act of grace that welcomes people into the Christian faith and unites them with Christ. He believed that infants should be baptized, since all human beings are born in sin and are therefore in need of forgiveness. He also valued the Eucharist very highly, seeing it as the way in which God nourishes us (he often uses the phrase "The Lord's Supper" to refer to the act of communion). Like Luther and Zwingli, Calvin denied that Christ is "sacrificed" in the Mass, and he was dubious about the language of transubstantiation. However, he attempted to transcend the question about the "real presence" (which divided Luther and Zwingli), arguing that we should dwell not so much on how the body of Christ is present in the *Eucharist*, but rather, how the body of Christ becomes present in *us*. In other words, how is it that, through the Eucharist, Christians become more perfectly united to Christ? He had three answers. First, it reenacts Jesus' willingness to give himself to us, to sacrifice himself for our sake. Second, it is a thanksgiving and therefore a declaration of our faith, in which we accept what Christ has done for us. Finally, it is a communion, in which many Christians are united because they all partake of one body.

Calvin in Geneva

Calvin was passing through Geneva in 1536, shortly after the city had voted to become Protestant. One of the city's preachers pressed him into service to help educate the city about the Reformation. Thus began John Calvin's long and stormy relationship with this turbulent city.

In Geneva, Calvin was forced to face what had become, for the churches of the Reformation, their greatest problem: church authority. Under the Roman Catholic Church, the lines of authority had sometimes been abused, but at least they had been clear: Everyone knew who had to be obeyed and who could be ignored. But such clear lines of authority were not available in Protestantism, given its claims about Christian liberty, the priesthood of all believers, and sole authority of the Bible (despite the different ways it was interpreted). One of Calvin's unique contributions is his attempt to supply an understanding of authority for the Reformation.

Calvin argued that, according to the Protestant understanding, the church and its leaders still have authority, but this authority is based only on their willingness to preach the word of God. In other words, the ministers have authority only as long as they express the will of Christ. How could this be assured? Calvin was worried that things would not go well if the task of exercising authority were entrusted *only* to government leaders or *only* to church leaders. He therefore established in Geneva a **consistory**, something like a city council, which had twelve members: four from the government, four from the church leadership ("pastors"), and four church members who were not pastors ("elders"). Calvin also established other councils and committees to aid in the governance of the church and the city. The idea was to create a balance of power so that discipline would always be exercised in the spirit of Christ, and not for the interests of a particular person or group.

The idea of balancing power in this way is a noble one, but it does not always work. There were external pressures from powerful cities such as Bern and Zurich, concerning (for example) precisely what should be done at church services. There were conflicts within the consistory itself, and there were disagreements with the government. Calvin, being a Frenchman, was at various times suspected of trying to undermine the Genevan government (which he was certainly not trying to do).

In the end, the delicate balance broke down, and Calvin and his colleagues were run out of town. They were replaced with weak, ineffective ministers, which led to such disorder that the Roman Catholic Church thought the city might be persuaded to return to the fold. The pope asked Cardinal Sadoleto to draft an appeal to the Genevan people, encouraging them to return to the traditions of Rome. The Genevans were unpersuaded, but they did want to write an effective reply to this well-constructed appeal. After asking several people and receiving several rejections, they turned reluctantly to Calvin.

He wrote a famous tract, now usually known as the *Reply to Sadoleto*, in which he turned the arguments of Cardinal Sadoleto back against the Roman Catholic Church. He argued that it was not the *Protestants* who had drifted away from the traditions of the church, but rather the *Catholics* who had done so—by not giving sufficient attention to the Bible. The following passage provides a taste of the polemical edge of Calvin's reply to Sadoleto:

> You teach that all that has been approved for fifteen hundred years or more by the uniform consent of the faithful is, by our rashness, torn up and destroyed. . . . [But] our agreement with antiquity is far closer than yours; all we have attempted has been to renew the ancient form of

the Church which, at first distorted and stained by illiterate men of indifferent character, was afterwards criminally mangled and almost destroyed by the Roman pontiff and his faction. (Cited in Reid 1992, 231)

Elsewhere in his reply, Calvin commented on his continuing paternal affection for the Genevan church. This comment was seen as an opening by some of the leaders of that city, who invited him to return; after considerable hesitation, he accepted.

Back in Geneva, Calvin helped the ministers draw up ordinances for the proper operation of religious services. He preached and taught, and in general he helped to shape the whole of the Protestant Reformation by making the city of Geneva into a grand religious experiment. Of course, Calvin's strong personality placed him in more or less constant conflict with some of the rulers of the city. Some of the religious laws of the city were quite strict by today's standards (for example, they forbade dancing, restricted public free speech rather severely, and regulated the names that could be used for newborn children). Some people chafed under these restrictions. Even so, the pious and serious Calvin probably did not expect to find the following unsigned note left in his pulpit one day:

> Big pot-belly, you and your fellows would do better to shut up. . . . We've had enough of blaming people. Why the devil have you renegade priests come here to ruin us? Those who have had enough take their revenge. . . . We don't want all these masters. Beware of what I say. (Cited in Parker 1975, 128)

The investigations of this apparent death threat turned up deeper levels of opposition in the city—not only religious, but political too (some government officials were accused of subversive discussions with France). Slowly, those who opposed Calvin's views gained power, but many also realized that his tough discipline and strong views had some value. He remained in the service of the Genevan church until the end of his life. He died in 1564 following a long illness, and was buried—as was his wish—in a common cemetery, without a tombstone.

Calvin's theological legacy is best exemplified today in the Christian Reformed Church, which continues to adhere fairly closely to his interpretation of the Bible. It has also followed Calvin in questioning and criticizing the (often anti-Christian) political and philosophical assumptions of the modern age. Calvin is also an important founding figure for the Presbyterian Church, even if it does not always place as much stress on the specifics of his theology. Following Calvin, the Presbyterian Church stresses the importance of learning biblical languages and of studying the Bible with care. In addition, Calvin's system of church government led to what is now called the presbyterian system, which uses a number of presbyteries and synods, small representative bodies composed of lay people, rather than bishops to govern the churches. In addition to providing a blueprint for the structure of the modern-day Presbyterian Church, this system has influenced a number of other denominations to develop a more representative system of church government. It also had a political influence, affecting the development of representative democracy in the United States and elsewhere.

THE RADICAL REFORMATION

While the Reformation is dominated by the figures of Luther, Calvin, and Zwingli, it would not have had such significance and scope were it not for the hundreds of smaller, grass-roots movements that spread like wildfire through sixteenth-century Europe. Because these groups were many and various, we should use caution when grouping them all under the single heading of "the Radical Reformation." The differences among them could be very great. There were evangelical radicals who usually objected to any form of violence and hoped to invite others to join them through their example of a quiet witness. There were revolutionary radicals, who believed that Christ was due to return to earth at any minute and that the ungodly were to be converted as soon as possible—and by force if necessary. There were also spiritual radicals, who emphasized the mystical elements of the faith and minimized the importance of church services and political action. Given this diversity, this discussion will require a good deal of overgeneralization.

The Radical Reformers are so called because they sought to radicalize the thought of the better-known Protestant Reformers. The word *radicalize* attempts to suggest that these thinkers pushed certain Reformation claims to their logical conclusions; they went "one up" on reformers such as Luther, Zwingli, and Calvin by taking one of their principles and emphasizing it more strongly. For example, some groups went further than Luther in their sole reliance on the Bible. Others went further than Zwingli in their rejection of traditional claims about the Eucharist and other sacraments. Still others went further than Calvin in their claims about divine election and the need for a strict code of conduct. Whatever the specifics of each group's position, each sought to out-reform Luther, Calvin, and Zwingli, moving yet farther away from the practices that had dominated Christianity throughout the medieval period.

Four Distinctive Elements

What holds these diverse Radicals together? Four factors unite *most* (though not all) of these groups. First and foremost was their agreement about the **voluntarist principle**—that is, that becoming a Christian (and a member of a church) always requires an active decision. It never occurs simply because of where people live or because of their parents' beliefs. For the Radical Reformers, the church was always a "gathered" church, in which members actively sought out other like-minded individuals. It thus stood in opposition to the parish system (common in Roman Catholic, Lutheran, and some Reformed denominations), in which a person simply attended the church of one's own town or region.

This voluntarist understanding of church membership had a special effect on the Radical Reformers' views about Baptism. Almost all of them had doubts about the appropriateness of infant Baptism, and some were explicitly hostile toward it. They agreed that Baptism was a cleansing from sin and a dying and rising with Christ. However, they wondered in what sense Baptism brought the believer into a relationship with the community. While the Christian tradition generally claimed that it was certainly a welcoming of a person into the community, the Radical Reformers described it as an entry into a covenant with God. As such, it required a positive, active belief on the part of the person who would be baptized. Thus, they argued, only adults who were old enough to make such a decision could be baptized. This is usually referred to as **believer's Baptism**. Because many of the first generation of Radical Reformers had been baptized as infants, their critics sometimes called them Anabaptists, which means "rebaptizers." Although they argued that only their adult baptism counted, the name stuck, and today the term applies to a number of churches including the Amish, Hutterites, Mennonites, and Church of the Brethren. However, believer's Baptism continues to be practiced today in churches that are not called Anabaptist, for example, certain Baptist denominations and the Christian Church (Disciples of Christ).

Secondly, the Radical Reformers were not interested in making minor modifications in the church; instead, they advocated **restorationism**. They wanted a reconstitution of Christ's original church. Some groups thought this could be gained by returning to the church as described in the biblical book of the Acts of the Apostles; others looked forward to a future return of Christ that would restore the church with power. In either case, most groups were highly committed to basing their beliefs and actions upon a literal interpretation of the scripture. Some—the Hutterites, for example—argued against the ownership of private property, noting that the earliest Christians would "sell their possessions and goods and distribute the proceeds to all, as any had need" (Acts 2:45, 4:32–35). Others turned to the teachings of the Sermon on the Mount, in which they were urged to strive toward perfection (Matt 5:48).

Many Protestant denominations espouse some degree of restorationism, but very few are wholly committed to the idea. The culture of the ancient world was very different from ours today, and few are willing to adopt, without question, the attitudes toward (for example) women, slaves, and nonbelievers that seem to be promoted in the Bible. Nonetheless, some denominations practice restorationism by focusing on specific concerns that are present (or absent) in the Bible. For example, "noninstrumentalist" denominations refuse to use or play any musical instrument that is not specifically mentioned in the Bible. This is a form of restorationism, in that it seeks to restore the precise structures of the earliest Christian communities as they are described in the Bible (see Chapter 23 on restorationism in American Protestantism). Due to their emphasis on restorationism, some of the groups that trace their roots to the Radicals—the Mennonites, the Amish, and the Moravian Brethren, for example—are often held up by society at large as communities that have come the closest to living out the teachings of Jesus.

Thirdly, the Radicals saw themselves as a chosen few, a righteous remnant to whom salvation had been granted. Their movement spread mostly through missionary work, but there was little interest in half-hearted believers. The Radical Reformers recognized that people cannot be coerced into true belief and opted instead for a small but very devoted community. Most groups enforced fairly strict moral codes, but they rarely had the troubles that Calvin experienced in Geneva, because they did not typically believe that the civil authorities should be charged with enforcing religious rules. Instead, the religious community itself exercised authority, censuring or expelling those members who violated the codes of conduct. Closely related to this was their rejection of the idea of an invisible church, where only God knows which persons are saved and which are damned. Salvation came through a conscious, free act of the believer; those who made this choice and stuck with it were the elect. One finds this emphasis today in a number of Protestant denominations, especially those that tend to see their own gathered community as distinct in some significant ways from the normal way of life in the outside world.

Finally, the Radical Reformers were very pessimistic about the rest of the world, that is, about those who stayed outside their own community. Violently persecuted, they often had no choice but to live in separation from the rest of the society, sometimes in wholly isolated communities. Most would not hold public office or fight in wars. Their views were based on the Sermon on the Mount (Matt 5–7), in which Jesus prohibits his followers from doing things that the civil government (or the culture) often encourages or requires—such as suing people, taking oaths, protecting one's property, judging others, and hating one's enemies. The Radical Reformers believed that the laws of the government should be obeyed, but only as long as they did not conflict with religious laws such as these.

While Radical Reformers were not expected to serve the government, they were expected to serve the Christian community. Congregations managed their own affairs, enforced their own rules of conduct, and chose their own pastors. This required much more commitment to the Christian community than is commonly practiced today. Nevertheless, it can still be seen in some Amish communities, where longstanding Christian traditions take precedence over the changing practices of society. For example, the Old Order Amish refuse to use electricity in their homes or travel in automobiles, using a horse and buggy instead, in order to maintain their principle of separation from the world (2 Cor 6:14, 17; Rom 12:2). Other groups retain at least some aspects of this separation from society but allow the use of electricity and cars. Many Radical Reformers are pacifists, refusing to take part in war or in violence of any kind: for example, the Amish, some Mennonite groups, and the Society of Friends, also known as the Quakers.

Isolation and Persecution

The distinctive practices of the Radical Reformers often put them at odds with more powerful forces in society. They were persecuted from all directions—not only by Catholics, but also by the mainstream Reformers. Luther was so distraught by many of their practices that he considered reincorporating many Catholic elements into his theology. Zwingli described the advocates of believer's Baptism as heretics and had them drowned. The Radicals were also persecuted by secular society, since many of their practices put them outside the mainstream of culture and sometimes even outside the civil law.

The unremitting persecution, which they experienced from all sides, created in the Radicals something of a siege mentality, and their own rhetoric sometimes became very fiery and dramatic—not an uncommon occurrence when a person or group feels cornered or surrounded. Here, for example, are the words of Melchior Hoffman, written in 1530:

> Infant Baptism is absolutely not from God but rather is practiced, out of willfulness, by Antichrists and the satanic crowd, in opposition to God and all his commandments, will, and desire. Verily, it is an eternal abomination to him. Woe, woe to all such blind leaders who willfully publish lies for the truth; their inheritance and portion is eternal damnation. (Cited in Williams and Mergal, 1957, 192)

These lines, worthy of the most fiery late-night television preacher, are the sort of thing that can inspire fanaticism. Overall, sixteenth-century religious debates were highly polemical and all sides used harsh language at times, though many of the Radical Reformers were quietly confident in the rightness of their cause and the injustice of their persecution. Consider these words by a Dutch woman who advocated believer's Baptism, written just before her execution and addressed to her infant daughter:

> There are many in this world who are enemies of the cross [of Christ], who seek to be free from it among the world, and to escape it. But, my dear child, if we could with Christ seek and inherit salvation, we must also help bear His cross; and this is the cross which He would have us bear: to follow His footsteps, and to help bear his reproach. . . . He himself went before us in this way of reproach, and left us an example, that we should follow His steps; for, for His sake, all must be forsaken, father, mother, sister, brother, husband, child, yea, one's own life. (Cited in Hillerbrand, 1968, 148)

These two passages provide enough contrast to remind us that, even though we are here describing the Radical Reformers as one group, they also varied greatly from one another. But they were certainly united in the persecution they suffered.

Many Christian groups of the Radical Reformation eventually settled in the American colonies, primarily in an attempt to escape religious persecution in Europe. Ironically, their conviction that they should be able to worship without fear of persecution and their principle of separation from society may have contributed to the development of the notion of the separation of church and state found in the U.S. Constitution (see Chapter 23).

THE ENGLISH REFORMATION

In England, we witness the Reformation of an entire country, carried out by the will of its government. In this sense it is unlike the stories of those reformers who were working with either one particular city government (Zwingli in Zurich or Calvin in Geneva) or in direct opposition to all civil government (most of the Radical Reformers). The English Reformation was officially begun, driven, and completed at the behest of the English crown. Yet it was also the product of more than two centuries of serious theological reflection.

A Variety of Causes

The story behind the English Reformation, as it is usually told, is a rather ugly one. The decision by **King Henry VIII** of England to break with the Roman Catholic Church was not due to any dispute over its teaching or doctrine. In fact, when the Reformation broke out, Henry remained on the Catholic side. Henry had even authored (or, at least, had signed his name to) a document upholding the validity of the seven traditional sacraments, thus receiving from the pope the title of Defender of the Faith. Rather, it appears that Henry's first marriage (an arranged royal marriage to the daughter of the king of Spain, Katherine of Aragon) was the precipitating factor. Katherine was the widow of Henry's brother, so the marriage had required a papal dispensation in the first place. While they did have several male children, all died in infancy, leaving only one female child, Mary, to survive to adulthood. Later, Henry wanted the marriage annulled, but his request was refused, and he was unable to change the pope's mind on the issue. Whether related to this matter or not, Henry was persuaded by some scholars around him that the monarch rightfully had power over the church, much as the Byzantine emperors had exercised power over the patriarchs of the Eastern church.

Figure 19–4 Portrait of Henry VIII, king of England.

Already at this time, there had been a gradual but consistent rise in the power of the English royalty throughout this era. These monarchs enjoyed increasing freedom in their dealings with the church, and especially with the pope. Another factor was the fourteenth-century reforms of John Wycliffe who focused on the Bible as the source of doctrine and believed that it should be available to the people. He rejected transubstantiation and argued that the body and blood of Christ were present in the Eucharist not corporally, but "sacramentally, spiritually, and efficaciously." He also doubted the supremacy of the pope, advocated married clergy, and believed that temporal rulers should work to reform the church.

The early sixteenth century also witnessed a flourishing intellectual rebirth in England. The great medieval universities of Oxford and Cambridge had been breeding grounds for all sorts of critical challenges to the traditional interpretations of the faith. Erasmus was professor of Greek at Cambridge for a while; a strong humanist tradition flourished. Thinkers such as Thomas More and John Colet were attracted by the rediscovery of ancient languages and classical modes of study, and this stimulated a fresh study of the scriptures. In 1527, an admirer of Luther named **William Tyndale** published a translation of significant parts of the Bible into English for the first time—a move that made it available to the common people and thereby threatened the monopoly that the church had enjoyed over its interpretation. In fact, Tyndale came under vicious attack from traditionalists in England, and he had to live in exile to continue his translation project.

We will never know precisely what motives eventually led King Henry VIII to side with the forces of reform. He may have been acting primarily due to his divorce case or perhaps because of his general suspicion of Catholic countries such as Italy and Spain. He may have had some appreciation for the new humanism that flourished in this period, or he may have just had a shrewd political instinct for recognizing which way the wind was blowing. In any case, he did three things in the early 1530s that changed the English Reformation from an intellectual and religious undercurrent into the official policy of the nation. First, he formally broke with the pope. Second, he placed the church under the control of the crown through Parliament. Finally, he dissolved the English monasteries and took control of their property holdings, thus creating a national church that was both politically and financially secure (and providing himself with considerable spoils with which he could win friends and influence people). However, in terms of doctrine and religious practice, Henry did not embrace the kinds of reform movements that were found on the continent. In fact, some have described Henry's brand of reform as Catholicism without the pope.

Opposition and Consolidation

The English Reformation met with considerable opposition in some cases. For one thing, many families of the aristocracy had profited greatly from the systems of power and privilege that had accompanied their support of the traditional church structures. The translation of the Bible into English and the reduction in the power and influence of the clergy had made life more difficult for some of these families. Neither was the peasant class fully supportive of the reform. Popular piety was strong, and there was clearly considerable resentment at the official effort to remove those elements of the faith upon which people had depended for centuries—including prayer for the dead, the belief in purgatory, and other elements of late medieval religion. England also saw its fair share of iconoclasm; most churches lost their images (including stained glass, sculpture, and other decoration). In Switzerland, the removal of images had enjoyed popular support, but in England it was often regarded as an excessive governmental intervention into the personal lives of believers.

When Henry died in 1547, he was succeeded by his only son by a later marriage, Edward VI (reigned 1547–1553). Because he was only nine years old at the time, the country went through a stormy period of political intrigue. These struggles were mostly won by advocates of reform; thus, during Edward's short reign, the country took a great leap away from traditional Catholicism toward Calvinist and Zwinglian reform. The strong-willed Protestant leaders who were part of Edward's court swept away any traces of the former king's caution about the reform. All restrictions on reading, teaching, or preaching the scriptures were removed. Private chapels were closed. They repealed the treason and heresy laws and clergy were being allowed to marry, as was the practice in the Protestant Reformation. They also argued against the doctrine of the real presence in Eucharist.

In the face of this upheaval, one of the stabilizing forces of the English Reformation was the archbishop of Canterbury, **Thomas Cranmer**, who held that office throughout the entire period (1533–1553). He was politically astute and wanted the English Reformation to proceed slowly and in stages. In a first stage of reform, he argued successfully for the wider distribution of the Bible and for further reductions in the social and financial privileges of priests. He helped to carve out the basic beliefs of the English Reformation, which were finalized after his death in a document called the *Thirty-Nine Articles.* This document sets out the specific similarities and differences between the Church of England and the Roman Catholic Church. He also wrote much of the language of the *Book of Common Prayer*—the first major liturgical document written in the English language. The *Book of Common Prayer* set a standard for the language of worship in the English-speaking world that continues to the present day.

The last powerbroker during Edward's reign, the duke of Northumberland, was so extreme in carrying out measures of reform that he probably did more damage to the cause of the English Reformation than all of its Catholic opponents together. By enforcing all kinds of highly restrictive laws against the practice of traditional Christian piety, he offended just about everyone. King Edward's health failed in 1553, and the rightful heir to the throne was Mary, the elder daughter of Henry VIII. Mary had remained a devout Roman Catholic throughout the English Reformation, and everyone expected that she would reverse the reform if she became queen. At one point, the duke of Northumberland attempted to remove her from the line of succession, an act that outraged the people because she had broad popular support.

Figure 19–5 Portrait of Thomas Cranmer.

Mary became queen in July 1553 and began to reverse many of the reforms that had been enacted in the previous decades, though with substantial opposition from some circles. The English Parliament opposed attempts to reestablish the papacy. Monasteries had to be newly endowed. In 1554, after a plot to overthrow her failed, Queen Mary quickly began to deal with her opponents more sternly. In 1555 the heresy laws were reinstated and a number of heresy trials began. A significant number of the advocates of reform—bishops, clergy, teachers, and common people—were burned at the stake, including Thomas Cranmer himself. During this same time, Mary presided over a disastrous war with France and a severe outbreak of disease in England. When Queen Mary died in 1558, all of England was ready for a reign more moderate than either hers or that of the duke of Northumberland.

The Elizabethan Settlement

All of this helps to explain the significance of Elizabeth I, whose long reign established the Church of England as we know it today. She resumed the course of the reform, reversing much of the return to Catholicism that her sister had advocated during her short but dramatic reign. Elizabeth was successful because she avoided the excesses of earlier Protestant advocates, allowing for some degree of religious toleration and providing for the practice of popular piety. During her reign, England experienced an enormous flowering of intellectual and cultural life, for which it had had little leisure during the stormy first half of the sixteenth century.

Although Thomas Cranmer had already been dead for three years when Elizabeth ascended the throne, her reforms were very closely modeled on the first-stage reforms he had worked to establish. Cranmer's hope was to move toward further reform, though slowly and at a pace that people could tolerate. Elizabeth's approach was to try to create a broad umbrella for the church, bringing together the best of both the Catholic traditionalists and the Protestant reformers. A good example of Elizabeth's approach to reform can be found in the understanding of the Eucharist that developed in the Church of England. Cranmer did not accept the doctrine of transubstantiation but understood the bread and wine as a memorial of Christ's death (as Zwingli had taught). This was the view of Eucharist that was represented by the 1552 *Book of Common*

Figure 19–6 Portrait of Elizabeth I.

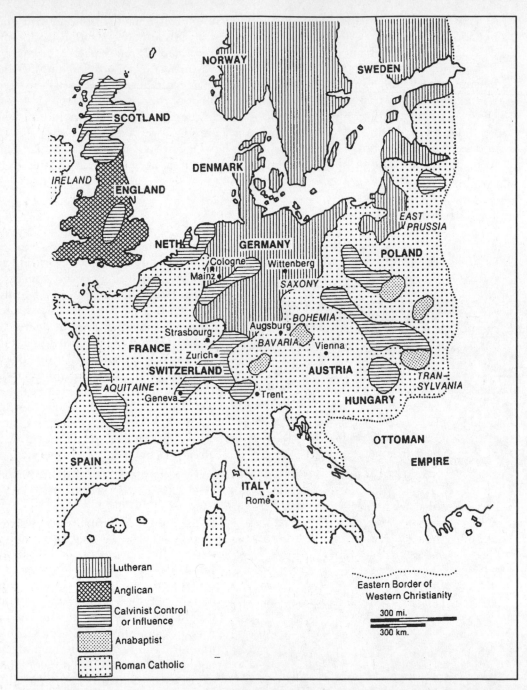

Figure 19–7 Map of the division of Christendom by the Reformation (mid-sixteenth century).

Prayer. In the 1559 *Book of Common Prayer*, Elizabeth was persuaded to keep the wording of the Communion rite from the 1552 prayer book, but arranged to blend that with the wording of the 1548 Communion rite, which suggested the real presence of Christ in the Eucharist, so that in the end both views were represented there. Thus, Catholic and Protestant understandings of Eucharist were fused together—a phenomenon that has become the hallmark of the English church.

Later Influence

At various times in its history, the Church of England (today also known as the Anglican Church) has swung in a more Protestant or a more Catholic direction. In the eighteenth century, for example, a certain degree of routine and apathy in the church led **John Wesley** to advocate a much more lively form of religion, with considerably more attention to personal spirituality, Bible study, and evangelistic preaching. Although he wanted his movement to stay within the Church of England, it eventually became more and more independent and is today known as the **Methodist Church**.

In the nineteenth century, a group of teachers in Oxford rallied against England's interference in the workings of the Irish church, and the **Oxford Movement** was born. This group was concerned about what appeared to be a decline in church life and advocated for a return to some of the devotional and liturgical practices that had been part of its heritage in the seventeenth century. Their sermons, tracts, and books led to a considerable revival of the Catholic elements of English Christianity. When they were opposed by liberals at the university and by some of the bishops of the Church of England, some members of the Oxford Movement gradually shifted their allegiance to Rome. One of the leaders of the movement, **John Henry Newman**, converted to Roman Catholicism and was eventually named a cardinal.

With the expansion of the British colonial empire throughout the centuries following the English Reformation, the Church of England has had a considerable impact on Christianity throughout the world. In many countries, a slightly altered version of the Church of England has taken root—for example, the Church of Australia, the Church of Ireland, and (in the United States) the **Episcopal Church**.

This chapter has provided a small sampling of the reform movements of the sixteenth century. While it has certainly not covered them all, it may help provide some sense of the origins of some of the Protestant denominations that are found in North America and Europe, among other places. It also gives us a better understanding of the different directions in which Christian theology developed during this period—especially in its understanding of authority, ministry, and the sacraments.

Key Terms

Ulrich Zwingli	voluntarist principle	John Wesley
Marburg Colloquoy	believer's Baptism	Methodist Church
John Calvin	restorationism	Oxford Movement
election	King Henry VIII	John Henry Newman
double predestination	William Tyndale	Episcopal Church
consistory	Thomas Cranmer	

Questions for Reading

1. List at least two similarities and two differences between the teachings of Zwingli and Luther. Why was Zwingli so adamantly opposed to the use of images in worship?

2. Briefly describe Calvin's doctrine of election. Include a description of "double predestination."

3. How does Calvin's understanding of the Eucharist differ from that of Luther and that of Zwingli?

4. How did Calvin address questions about church authority? Include at least one specific example from his experience in Geneva.

5. Summarize the basic argument of Calvin's *Reply to Sadoleto*.

6. Why are the Radical Reformers called "radical"? List and briefly describe the four distinctive elements that characterize most of the Radical Reformers.

7. Why were the Radical Reformers especially subject to persecution?

8. List at least three events or movements that led to the English Reformation.

9. In what ways did the English Reformation meet resistance? Name at least two distinct sources of this resistance.

10. List the three monarchs who followed Henry VIII and summarize the religious policy of each.

11. List the chief contributions of Thomas Cranmer and William Tyndale to the English Reformation.

12. List at least two movements or denominations that developed within the Church of England after the Reformation era.

13. Name at least one Christian denomination that has been significantly influenced by each of the four reformers or movements described in this chapter (Zwingli, Calvin, the Radical Reformation, and the English Reformation).

Works Consulted/Recommended Reading

Calvin, John. *John Calvin: Theological Treatises*. Translated by J. K. S. Reid. Philadelphia: Westminster, 1954.

Dickens, A. G. *The English Reformation*. Glasgow: William Collins and Sons, Fontana, 1967.

Dickens, A.G., and Dorothy Carr, eds. *The Reformation in England to the Accession of Elizabeth I*. Documents of Modern History. London: Edward Arnold, 1967.

Duffy, Eamon. *The Stripping of the Altars: Traditional Religion in England, 1400–1580*. New Haven, CT: Yale University, 1992.

Hillerbrand, Hans J., ed. *The Protestant Reformation*. New York: Harper, 1968.

Metzger, Bruce, and Roland Murphy, eds. *The New Oxford Annotated Bible with Apocrypha, New Revised Standard Version*. New York: Oxford University, 1991.

Parker, T. H. L. *John Calvin*. Icknield Way, England: Lion, 1975.

Potter, G. R. *Zwingli*. Cambridge: Cambridge University, 1976.

_____. ed. *Huldrych Zwingli*. Documents of Modern History. London: Edward Arnold, 1978.

Potter, G. R., and M. Greengrass, eds. *John Calvin*. Documents of Modern History. London: Edward Arnold, 1983.

Williams, George H. *The Radical Reformation*. 3d ed. Kirksville, MO: Sixteenth Century Journal, 1992.

Williams, George H., and Angel M. Mergal, eds. *Spiritual and Anabaptist Writers*. Library of Christian Classics, Vol. 25. Philadelphia: Westminster, 1957.

Chapter

THE CATHOLIC REFORMATION

20

TIMELINE

A.D. 1495–1517	Cardinal Ximenes leads Catholic reform activities in Spain.
A.D. 1517	The Oratory of Divine Love is founded in Rome.
A.D. 1529	The Capuchins, a reform branch of the Franciscans, is officially recognized by the pope.
A.D. 1540	Ignatius of Loyola founds the Society of Jesus, also known as the Jesuits.
A.D. 1534–1549	Pope Paul III institutes a limited number of reforms prior to the Council of Trent.
A.D. 1545–1547	First session of the Council of Trent.
A.D. 1551–1552	Second session of the Council of Trent.
A.D. 1562	Teresa of Avila founds her first house of reformed Carmelites.
A.D. 1562–1563	Third session of the Council of Trent.
A.D. 1580	Discalced Carmelites given legal status and receive their own province.
A.D. 1593	Discalced Carmelites make final break with Carmelites, forming their own order.

The Roman Catholic Church responded to the Protestant Reformation with two overlapping yet distinct movements. One is called the **Counter-Reformation** and the other is called the **Catholic Reformation**. The Counter-Reformation, as its name implies, refers to the efforts of those who were loyal to the pope and supportive of the customary practices of the Roman Catholic Church to counter (go against) the teachings and practices of the Protestant reformers. Because it was a movement designed to aggressively stop Protestant teachings, ideas, and practices, it was polemical and negative in its form. In contrast, the Catholic Reformation refers to the efforts of those who wanted to bring about the internal rebirth of Catholic sensibility—in theology, spirituality, religious piety, and morality.

Although the Catholic Reformation is often studied in relationship to the Protestant Reformation, it is not a movement that simply reacted to the Protestant Reformation. In fact, it began before the initial crises of the Protestant Reformation and continued even after the Reformation had resulted in the establishment of distinctive Protestant churches. Many of the figures belonging to the Catholic Reformation were as critical of the corrupt practices of the church as any of the Protestant reformers were. Rather than leaving the church, these Catholic reformers saw the abuses as an opportunity to call the church back to godly ways by reclaiming the traditions it had ignored or forgotten.

This chapter will focus on the Catholic reform movements prior to, during, and immediately following the Council of Trent (1545–1563). The Council of Trent is an important event in Catholic reform because one of its functions was to respond to the Protestant Reformation. Another function was to initiate an internal reform and spiritual reawakening based upon a reevaluation of doctrinal issues that impacted the lives of sixteenth-century Catholics. This chapter will look at the major movements of the Catholic Reformation, including the Council of Trent, the standardization of Catholic doctrine and practice, and the new spiritual awakening in Catholicism expressed both in the founding of religious orders and in the art of the period.

PRE-TRIDENTINE REFORM

Even before the Protestant reformers entered the scene, there were several early indications that Catholics were indeed ready for widespread reform and revival. The Catholic reform movements that took place immediately before the Council of Trent are sometimes called pre-Tridentine reforms. Foremost among these was the reform that took place in Spain under Cardinal Ximenes (1495–1517). After the Spanish *reconquista* ("reconquest"), Spain became an ardently Christian country. Monks and friars were required to make reforms consistent with their vow of poverty. Religious houses that did not comply with approved standards of behavior were dissolved, their revenues going to the education of children, hospitals, and the poor.

Cardinal Ximenes also created a university at Alcala that encouraged the study of Hebrew and Greek for the training of scholastic theologians and the encouragement of scholarly thought. A group of scholars under the cardinal's direction produced a critical edition of the Bible in Hebrew, Greek, and Latin, with commentaries. The Spanish Inquisition would later destroy many of these **"polyglot" Bibles** (containing several languages) along with the scriptures and numerous spiritual writings that had been translated into the vernacular (common speech) of the country. This was, in part, a Counter-Reformation movement directed against Protestant reformers who encouraged the common people to read the Bible and who spread their reform ideas through literature written in the vernacular. These Bibles appear also to have encouraged the Council of Trent's decision to declare that only one particular Latin translation of the Bible, the Vulgate, was the authoritative Bible of the Catholic Church.

During this time, many new religious orders were founded to revitalize the church, some coming out of this early Spanish reform. One of the most interesting developments of the pre-Tridentine period was a number of groups called **oratories**. These oratories were groups of clergy who banded together for the purpose of prayer, meditation, and mutual support as they participated in discussions about how they might reform the church. The most famous of these was the Oratory of Divine Love, which was founded in Rome circa 1517. Likewise, a new religious order known as the Theatines was founded in 1524 by two members of the Oratory of Divine Love for the purpose of combating the abuses and scandals that corrupted the church at that time by training reform-minded clergy for positions of leadership in the church.

Other religious orders dedicated to reform include the Congregation of the Mission founded by St. Vincent de Paul in 1625 and the Ursulines founded in 1535. The Congregation of the Mission (also known as the Lazarists or the Vincentians) contributed to the Catholic Reformation by preaching missions (renewal retreats for lay people) and by preparing young men for ordination to the priesthood. One of the reasons the Catholic Church suffered so much abuse and corruption was that many of its priests had little education and were poorly trained for the priesthood. The Ursulines were the first religious order of women to dedicate themselves to teaching. These new orders represent what we call the "active" life. They did not withdraw from the world, as monks and nuns had done for centuries before. Rather, their entire mission was directed outward in ministry to those in need. They lived an ascetic lifestyle and devoted themselves to serving others in hospitals, orphanages, and schools for children. They also placed great emphasis on living a life of charity, a life lived for others that was socially responsible and Christian in its inspiration.

Perhaps the most influential of these new orders was the **Society of Jesus** or the Jesuits, founded by **Ignatius of Loyola** in 1540. The small band that joined together with Ignatius was first called "the Company of Jesus." Like the mendicant orders, they lived a simple lifestyle, relying on alms for their livelihood. Ignatius intended for the Society to minister to the poor and to unbelievers, in particular, and to work with children and those who could not read or write. His interest in converting unbelievers would anticipate one of the results of the Catholic Reformation, namely, a trend of missionary expansion into newly discovered lands. He was also committed to the reform of the church and to the education of its members. Thus the order became renowned for its achievements in education, especially higher education, including the education of members of the upper classes and the training of clergy. Their establishment as professors in the university system enabled the Jesuits to use their study of theology not only to serve the pastoral needs of the church, but also in disputes with the Protestant scholars of their times. The Jesuits viewed the Protestant reformers as disobedient to the church, whereas the Jesuits themselves took a vow of absolute obedience to the pope. They vowed to go without question and without delay wherever the pope might order them for the salvation of souls and the spreading of the true faith.

Ignatius of Loyola, the founder of the Jesuits, could not have seemed a more unlikely candidate for the religious life and sainthood. He was a Spaniard trained as a knight, shaped by a military background and way of thinking. His life before his conversion was not an exemplary one. He was even arrested once and accused of crimes in Pamplona, Spain, although we do not know the nature of the charges brought against him. His conversion came during a long convalescence after he was gravely injured during a battle. He had been reading devotional books, including a life of Christ and lives of the saints—the only books that were available to him. Inspired by these stories, he decided that he would become a soldier for Christ. Shortly afterward he went to a monastery and dedicated himself to prayer and meditation. He discovered—as did Luther—that he was tortured by his sins and by scruples. He was finally commanded by a confessor to stop punishing himself through excessive penance. He obeyed, and it is in this story of his life that we can see the great importance he would place on obedience in his new order.

During his stay in the village of Manresa, Ignatius also drafted the first sketch of his **Spiritual Exercises**, which would become the tool of spiritual formation for those who joined him in his quest. It is a month-long examination and participation of the individual in the drama of sin and salvation, leading to a turning over of everything, especially the will, to obedience to one's religious superior and to the teachings of the church and its traditions. With his band of followers, Ignatius set off to offer himself to the pope for whatever service the church might need. Despite the papacy's resistance to the establishment of new religious orders, the Jesuits were officially recognized in 1540. Their motto sums up the Ignatian approach nicely: *Ad majorem Dei gloriam* ("To the greater glory of God").

In addition to these new religious orders, significant reforms resulted in new branches of already existing orders. These include the **Capuchins**, a reform branch of the Franciscan movement, and the Discalced ("without shoes") Carmelites, a reform branch of the Carmelite order. Both of these reforms met with great success but were at times in great peril. The Capuchins, whose influence and preaching would be vital to the Catholic reform movement, were almost condemned when their superior (and popular preacher) Bernardino Ochino converted to the Protestant cause. This scandal, plus the unwavering opposition of the Observant Franciscans to this new branch of the order, almost led to their suppression. They weathered the crisis, however, and the Capuchins were recognized by the pope in 1529, getting their name from the unique four-pointed hood, which they wore with their brown habit. They were perhaps the most successful of the movements to reconstruct the spirit of an older order, and much of the credit for this goes to their founder Matteo da Bascio.

There were papal reforms, as well. Pope Paul III (reigned 1534–1549) was elected pope upon the recommendation of the previous pope who had attempted reform but was unable to carry it out. Although he was very much a Renaissance pope—enjoying the comforts of wealth and the power of his office—he was also intent on internal reform of the church. He appointed a number of reformers to the **College of Cardinals** (advisors to the pope and second in line of authority after the pope), all former members of the Oratory of Divine Love. He also appointed a reform commission to recommend changes in the way the church was run. Their report revealed some very serious problems: The papal office had become too secular; the cardinals needed to be less infatuated with the power and wealth of the world and more concerned about spiritual matters; abuses such as the selling of church offices and indulgences needed to be stopped. Pope Paul III instituted a few reforms immediately as the result of this commission, but many others would have to wait for the Council of Trent.

THE COUNCIL OF TRENT AND CATHOLIC REFORM

It is difficult to neatly untangle the threads of the Catholic Reformation into those reforms that occurred before the important **Council of Trent** and those that took place afterwards. In general, Catholics agreed on the need for an official council to either reconcile with the reformers, especially Luther, or to refute them and inaugurate reform from within the church itself. Already in 1535, Pope Paul III had announced his intention to call a council, but the council did not actually take place until 1545. There were a number of factors that led to this delay.

First, there was a problem about its location. The cardinals insisted it be in Rome, and the Holy Roman Emperor, Charles V, insisted it be in Germany. Second, Charles V was pressuring Pope Paul III to call the council, but the emperor wanted the council to deal with the Lutherans who were causing political havoc in his territories. More specifically, he wanted some quick practical religious compromises to defuse the tension. The pope and the bishops, however, wanted to hold a doctrinal council rather than a practical one. They wanted to come to grips with the basic teachings of the church and then initiate an internal reform that would flow from this doctrinal clarification. Third, some church leaders wanted to avoid a council altogether. Those with pure motives doubted whether it was possible to convene a general (ecumenical) council that would include all Christendom. Some opposed the council because of political motives. The French king was often at war with Germany, and a council held in Germany would offend French church leaders. Others opposed it out of fear. They were not certain that the pope would be able to maintain control of the council and its proceedings.

When the Council of Trent was finally convened in 1545, its location was somewhat of a compromise. The city of Trent, located in the Italian Alps and situated between southern German and northern Italian regions, was barely inside Charles' domain, yet it offered easy access to Italy. The council was made up of three separate sessions, which spanned eighteen years and the reigns of four different popes. The first session (1545–1547) was largely controlled by representatives of the pope and so dealt with doctrinal definitions. The second session (1551–1552) dealt with a mixture of doctrinal and practical matters. The third and final session (1562–1563) concentrated mainly on disciplinary correction and means of regulating church activities in the future. Some meetings were poorly attended, the first session having only twenty-eight delegates. A number of Protestants were present at the second session, but discussions between the two sides broke down without coming to any mutual understandings. Italian church leaders attended in the greatest numbers; French church leaders were noticeably absent. Some sessions had huge delegations from Spain and Portugal. Others did not. Yet, despite all its difficulties, the Council of Trent was successful in initiating reform within the Catholic Church.

The council addressed a number of doctrinal issues that had relevance for the Protestant Reformation. In response to the Protestant reformers who said that a person was justified by faith alone, the delegates of the council essentially made a distinction between justification and salvation, asserting that a person is justified by faith, that faith is a gift, and that faith is the first stage of human salvation. When a person is justified, they are infused with faith, hope, and charity, all of which are necessary for the person to be united to Christ. Further, they affirmed that a person can increase in justness through faith united to good works. By contrast, the Protestant reformers had said that humans were incapable of any good work apart from grace. The fathers of the council said that nothing could be done without God's grace, but that humans were capable of assent to and cooperation with God's grace. In developing these arguments about justification, they referred frequently to the letters of Paul. The council also said that faith, which is a grace from God, could not be lost. However, it could be denied, as in the sin of apostasy. With the Protestant reformers, they acknowledged that human nature remains disordered after Baptism. However, against Luther and other reformers, the fathers of the council denied that our nature had been severely damaged by the Fall and had been made incapable, apart from grace, of any good during this life.

Confronted by the Protestant reformers' appeal to the Bible as the sole authority, the council stated that unwritten tradition of the church must also be received with reverence, since it too contains the word of God, having its origins in the teaching of the apostles. The sacraments were reasserted as essential to the Christian life. The number of sacraments was fixed at seven: Baptism, Confirmation, Eucharist, Matrimony, Holy Orders, Penance, and Extreme Unction (Anointing of the Sick). They also developed the notion of *sacramentals*, those religious objects or devotions that convey spiritual benefits, though they do not have the full efficacy and centrality of the seven official sacraments. Holy water, as it is traditionally called, is an example of such a sacramental.

Luther and other reformers had attacked the traditional idea that the Mass (the Eucharist) was a reenactment of Christ's sacrifice (see Chapter 18). The Council of Trent recognized that Christ died once and for all for sin, but said that the Mass was a re-presentation of that one sacrifice. The council also defined the order and shape of the liturgy in a more uniform way than before. This ended many local variations and created the fixed form of the Mass as Catholics were to know it until the Second Vatican Council (see Chapter 24). The **Vulgate** (a Latin translation of the Bible widely in use in the West at least from the sixth century and containing the books of the Apocrypha) was declared to be the only authoritative translation of the Bible. At the time of the Council of Trent, Latin was still the recognized, official language of the universities and the educated. However, it had already begun to fall into disuse among the common people. In response to this cultural change, Protestant reformers had been commissioning vernacular translations of the Bible. However, because of certain doctrinal issues that were of concern to the reformers, they had been using versions of the Bible that did not contain the apocryphal books for their vernacular translations. Thus, Catholics and Protestants emerged from the Reformation with two different canons of scripture.

Although the Council of Trent had addressed a number of doctrinal issues, it was also a pastoral council dedicated to eliminating abuses and inspiring holiness among the church's clergy. To correct abuses, the fathers abolished the office of seller of indulgences. Bishops were given the power of supervision in their dioceses. Simony and nepotism were abolished; penalties were imposed for blasphemy and violation of celibacy. Luxurious dress and affluent lifestyles were discouraged among all Christians. Clerics who had previously worn the ordinary clothes of the time now had to wear special clerical garb. The **breviary** (prayer book containing the liturgy of the hours, the official prayer of priests and monks) was reformed to make it clearer and simpler to use and included more prayers and readings from scripture.

The Council of Trent also exhorted the clergy to be devout shepherds of souls, and to that end, it called for reforms that included education of clergy. Bishops were instructed to send their candidates for ordination to the university, or if there were no universities in the diocese, they should establish a **seminary** for their training. The Jesuit order was especially influential in implementing this aspect of the reforms. It greatly improved the clergy's ability to preach the Word, one of the principal reasons that many of the people had abandoned the Catholic Church for the preachers of the Protestant reformation. Bishops and clergy were now to be preachers and teachers of their flock. Therefore, after the council was concluded, a short summary of what had been upheld by Trent was put together to provide clergy with uniform instruction on doctrine and religious practice. This document was called the Roman Catechism, though it was not a catechism in the usual sense of the word, because it was intended for the instruction of clergy.

As had been the case in the Protestant Reformation, the Catholic Reformation produced a large number of catechisms for the instruction of lay people. These catechisms usually contained summary teaching on the Apostles Creed, the Lord's Prayer and the Hail Mary, the Ten Commandments, the commandments of the church, the sacraments, and the virtues and vices. Perhaps the most respected and widely read Catholic catechism was *Summa Doctrinae Christianae* (1554) written by Peter Canisius, a Jesuit. This catechism was admired by many, even by Protestant preachers, for its clarity and persuasiveness. Another important figure in Catholic religious education was Charles Borromeo, who established the Confraternity of Christian Doctrine (1566) for the instruction of children.

THE REVIVAL OF MYSTICISM IN SPAIN

Although many new religious orders were founded and older orders were reformed in the period immediately preceding the Council of Trent, others were being established or reformed during and immediately following the council. Some of these were vital to the conciliar process and its implementation; all of them were important because of the spiritual fervor with which they led the people to a greater understanding of church doctrine and practice. In particular, Spain was experiencing a reform of the Carmelite order and the revival of mysticism in the persons of Teresa of Avila and John of the Cross.

Teresa of Avila had spent much of her life in a struggle between worldly comforts and the interior life of prayer. At the age of forty she experienced such a profound conversion, accompanied by ecstasies and visions, that she felt called to return to the simpler, harsher rule of the Carmelite founders. Thus Teresa and her protégé and follower, **John of the Cross**, established the Discalced Carmelites. The term *discalced* means "unshod," referring to the spiritual practice of going barefoot in order to fulfill Jesus's mandate to provide oneself with nothing for the journey, not even sandals (Matt 10:9–10). Teresa's primary calling was to poverty and prayer. The "barefoot" Carmelites were to rely only on charity and the providence of God to support them. Teresa's first foundation was made in Avila in secret, for she knew the opposition her reforms would face. She ultimately made seventeen separate foundations during her lifetime, traveling widely throughout Spain to do so. These foundations were made up of sisters who followed her example and teaching. However, there was no official recognition of these foundations or the Carmelite reform movement until 1580, when permission finally was granted for them to form a separate province within the Carmelite order. Later, in 1598, the order of **Discalced Carmelites** received its own superior and became a separate order. Teresa's combination of common sense, political acumen, and profound spirituality enabled her to establish her foundations against opposition from other Carmelite branches and in spite of the suspicions of the Spanish Inquisition.

We have many of Teresa's writings because the priests who served as her confidantes and advisors insisted that she write down her life and her method of prayer as a means of convincing the inquisitors that she was not a heretic. The most famous of these are her *Life*, an autobiographical account, and the *Interior Castle*, a description of her method of prayer. We also have a number of the writings of John of the Cross, including his exquisitely written poems in the *Ascent of Mount Carmel* and his *Dark Night of the Soul.* Teresa and John's contemplation of God and their life lived from the center of that contemplation was one of the great contributions of the Carmelite reform movement. The simple beauty of their prayer of the heart and their focus on the love of God can be seen in these brief excerpts from their writings.

> The important thing is not to think much but to love much;
> and so do that which best stirs you to love.
> > (Teresa of Avila 1979, 70)

> To come to the knowledge of all desire,
> the knowledge of nothing . . .
> To come to the knowledge you have not
> you must go by a way you know not.
> > (John of the Cross 1987, 137)

> Let nothing upset you,
> Let nothing startle you,
> All things pass;
> God does not change.
> Patience wins all it seeks.
> Whoever has God lacks nothing;
> God alone is enough.
> > (*Prayer of St. Teresa*, written on the inside of her prayer book;
> > Teresa of Avila 1996, 33)

> How gently and lovingly
> You awake in my heart,
> Where in secret You dwell alone;
> And in your sweet breathing,
> Filled with good and glory,
> How tenderly You swell my heart with love.
> > (John of the Cross, "The Living Flame of Love," in Adels 1987, 203)

Both John of the Cross and Teresa of Avila are saints and Doctors of the Church. Teresa is one of only two women to have been awarded this title.

ART AS A REFLECTION OF THE REFORMATION PERIOD

The art of the Reformation period, both Catholic and Protestant, reflects a number of theological issues. When Protestant Reformation communities, particularly those associated with the later reformers, built new churches, they built them with a simplicity and austerity that did not exist in churches dating from the Middle Ages or before. Most often, however, older churches were merely taken over and the ornamentation removed. The walls were whitewashed to cover paintings and elaborate decorations on the walls and to bring a greater sensation of light and simplicity into the worship space. They stripped churches of their statues and ornamentation in order to concentrate on the centrality of the Word. On occasion these churches would even be stripped of their furniture so that only a pulpit (preaching stand) remained in a central place in the church. This stripping of ornamentation was consistent with their ban on the use of images. Lutheran churches, which tended to be more moderate in their reforms, often retained the ornamentation of pre-Reformation churches.

The art of the Renaissance movement is recognizable for its realism. Among artists of the Protestant Reformation this realism was especially evident in their subject matter. Although some depicted actual scenes from the Bible, others focused on everyday life situations that could be used as visual metaphors for preaching and teaching about the moral life. In particular, the Dutch artists of the late sixteenth and early seventeenth centuries sought to depict in portraits, landscapes, and other types of art a variety of ordinary circumstances of life illustrating the beauty of creation, the positive and negative sides of human nature, the vanity of striving for power, and the human need for salvation. Germany did not produce any famous Protestant artists during the Reformation. However, it did create new kinds of music designed for the participation of large congregations of lay people. The hymns were sung in the vernacular (rather than Latin). Some of our most well-known Christian hymns, including several new arrangements by Johann Sebastian Bach, date back to the time of the Reformation.

In contrast with their Protestant counterparts, Catholics not only preserved the architecture of the medieval churches whenever possible but also commissioned new ornamentation and art which would dramatically illustrate the truths of Catholic orthodoxy. The style begun in this period is termed the **Baroque**. While it had been influenced by the realism of the Renaissance, Baroque art and architecture added the dimension of light and darkness, suggesting that the division between this world and the heavenly realm is penetrable, at least through the mediation of the Virgin Mary and the saints. In Figure 20–1, we have a scene in which Paul experiences his conversion on the road to Damascus. What is uniquely different is the perspective of the scene: The artist is clearly trying to personally involve the observer, who looks up at the horse and sky as if he or she is lying on the ground with St. Paul. The artists attempted to involve the worshipers, appealing to their feelings and engaging them in the movement of faith. Observers, as believers, were invited to put themselves into the story, to see the conversion as St. Paul experienced it. Note also the use of light to express the drama of the event.

Baroque art also sought to impress its viewers with awesome displays of riches and to evoke in the viewer a sense of awe. Baroque churches were filled

Figure 20–1 This famous painting of Paul's conversion on the way to Damascus is by Caravaggio, c. 1601, and typifies Baroque art. Cerasi Chapel, Santa Maria del Popolo, Rome.

Figure 20–2 *St. Teresa in Ecstasy* by Bernini, 1646. Santa Maria della Vittoria, Rome. Photo by Thomas King-Lenzmeier. This statue portrays the piercing of the heart that Teresa reports in *Life*, 29:13–14.

with rich and ornate illustrations of the great events of the Bible and church history. It would overwhelm the visitor with dramatic representations of the avenues of salvation available to the believer: Mary, the saints and relics, the crucified Christ, and symbols of the Eucharist.

In Figure 20–2, the observer looks up at Bernini's famous statue *St. Teresa in Ecstasy*. This statue conveys to the observer complex devotional and erotic overtones as it portrays the saint caught up into the divine realm as her heart is pierced. The church is small and dark; the statue is a glance into the realms of heavenly light in which the human and the divine meet and are joined in bliss.

Figure 20–3 sums up many of the themes of this chapter and draws together the many strands of the Catholic Reformation. It shows a processional float, honoring a saint by bringing the presence of the art and ornamentation out of the church itself and into the everyday settings and lives of the people. As an art form, it was the intention of the Baroque to bring immediacy of experience, to appeal to the feelings and the emotional side of faith, to illustrate doctrine in a way that made pastoral sense and yet was compelling religiously and artistically.

Figure 20–3 A typical processional reflecting the Baroque Catholic sense of bringing the sacred out of the church and to the people. Photo by Susan Webster.

CONCLUDING REFLECTIONS

The Reformation period was a turbulent time for both Catholics and Protestants. Yet from this age of turmoil emerged a clearer understanding of Christianity. Despite the scandal of disunity, Christians were now more apt to know what they believed and why. They were more informed participants in worship, and they had more powerful and inspiring preaching available to them. For Catholics, there was the additional result of the new spiritual awareness of the traditions of the church, their valuing of the sacraments, the desire to express their faith through charity and actions for the salvation of souls. Forced by crisis to define itself at the Council of Trent, Catholicism began to express in new ways what it held to be true. Through the council, the catechism, the new and reformed religious orders, and the artistic and popular revivals of spiritual devotions, the Catholic Church found its way both to an inner reform and to a new place in the world.

Key Terms

Counter-Reformation   Spiritual Exercises   seminary
Catholic Reformation   Capuchins   Teresa of Avila
polyglot Bible   College of Cardinals   John of the Cross
oratories   Council of Trent   Discalced Carmelites
Society of Jesus   Vulgate   Baroque
Ignatius of Loyola   breviary

Questions for Reading

1. What is the difference between the Counter-Reformation and the Catholic Reformation? How are they related to one another?

2. What signs of reform were present in the Catholic Church even before the challenge of Luther and other Protestant reformers?

3. Who was Ignatius of Loyola, and how did he shape the movement he founded? Why did this movement become so important to the effort of Catholic reform?

4. For what purpose was the Council of Trent called? What difficulties did it encounter?

5. What were the doctrinal issues addressed by the Council of Trent, and what is their importance?

6. What were the disciplinary or practical reforms made by the Council of Trent?

7. What are the seven "official" sacraments? What is a sacramental?

8. Name three of the new orders founded during the Catholic Reformation. How are they different from previous religious orders?

9. Contrast the worship styles and decoration of churches in the Protestant and Catholic traditions during the Reformation period. What is the Baroque style of art, and how is it representative of the Catholic Reformation?

Works Consulted/Recommended Reading

Adels, Jill Haak, ed. *The Wisdom of the Saints: An Anthology.* New York: Oxford University, 1987.

Chadwick, Owen. *The Reformation.* Baltimore, MD: Penguin, 1965.

Dupre, Louis, and James Wiseman, eds. *Light from Light: An Anthology of Christian Mysticism.* New York: Paulist, 1988.

Egan, Harvey. *An Anthology of Christian Mysticism.* Collegeville, MN: Liturgical, 1991.

———. *Ignatius of Loyola the Mystic.* Collegeville, MN: Liturgical, 1991.

Hempel, Eberhard. *Baroque Art and Architecture in Central Europe.* Baltimore, MD: Penguin, 1965.

John of the Cross. *Ascent of Mount Carmel and The Dark Night of the Soul.* Translated by Kiernan Kavanaugh. New York: Paulist, 1987.

———. *Collected Works.* Translated by Kieran Kavanaugh and Otilio Rodriguez. Washington, DC: ICS, 1976.

———. *Selected Writings: John of the Cross.* Translated by Kieran Kavanaugh and Otilio Rodriguez. New York: Paulist, 1987.

McNally, Robert. *The Council of Trent, the Spiritual Exercises, and the Catholic Reform.* New York: Fortress, 1970.

Olin, John. *The Catholic Reform: From Cardinal Ximenes to the Council of Trent, 1495–1563.* New York: Fordham University, 1990.

Sheldrake, Philip. *Spirituality and History.* New York: Crossroad, 1992.

Short, William S. *The Franciscans.* Collegeville, MN: Liturgical/Michael Glazier, 1989.

Teresa of Avila. *Collected Works*, Vol. I. Translated by Kieran Kavanaugh and Otilio Rodriguez. Washington, DC: ICS, 1976.

———. *The Complete Poetry of St. Teresa of Avila: A Bilingual Edition.* Edited and translated by Eric W. Vogt. New Orleans: University Press of the South, 1996.

———. *The Interior Castle.* Translated by Kieran Kavanaugh and Otilio Rodriguez. New York: Paulist, 1979.

Wisch, Barbara, and Susan Scott Munshower, eds. *"All the World's a Stage—": Art and Pageantry in the Renaissance and Baroque.* University Park: Penn State University, 1990.

Chapter

GLOBAL EXPANSION AND THE COLONIAL CHURCHES

TIMELINE

A.D. 1271	Marco Polo travels to the Orient.
A.D. 1349	The Arab scholar Ibn Batuta travels to parts of Africa and the Orient.
A.D. 1415	Henry the Navigator sends Portuguese ships south to explore the coast of Africa.
A.D. 1482	Catholic missionary activity begins in the Congo with the conversion of King Afonso the Good and his family.
A.D. 1492	Christopher Columbus sails west under the patronage of the Spanish government in order to find a new route to the Indies.
A.D. 1493	Pope Alexander VI issues a series of bulls establishing a line of demarcation whereby newly discovered lands east of the line belong to Portugal and lands west of the line belong to Spain.
A.D. 1498	The Portuguese explorer Vasco da Gama sails around the Cape of Good Hope.
A.D. 1502	The Dominican friar Bartolomé de Las Casas is ordained a priest. He would later fight against the abuses of the *encomienda-doctrina* system in Spanish mission territories.
A.D. 1542–1552	The Jesuit Francis Xavier is involved in missionary activity in India and Japan.
A.D. 1582–1610	The Jesuit Matteo Ricci is involved in missionary activity in China.
A.D. 1622	Pope Gregory XV establishes the Sacred Congregation for the Propagation of the Faith.
A.D. 1633	French Catholic missionaries begin to arrive in the Americas.

One of the direct consequences of the Catholic Reformation was the expansion of Christianity into the New World. However, this expansion was only one more stage in the gradual and persistent growth of Christianity in the Western world. The first three stages involved (1) the establishment of Christianity in the Roman Empire in the first to fourth centuries; (2) the Christianization of barbarian Europe in the fifth to ninth centuries; and (3) Christian missionary efforts in the Islamic world in the eleventh to fifteenth centuries. In order to appreciate better the distinctive character of the fourth stage of the missionary effort, we will review briefly the circumstances of the three earlier missions. We will end this chapter with a description of the fifth stage of missionary effort, which brings us to the contemporary experience.

In the first stage, the most influential and firmly established early Christian communities were still to be found primarily along the Mediterranean coast. Palestine was still the heart of Christian territory. It was the place where the apostles who had been witnesses to Jesus's life began their preaching. Asia Minor, where Paul had established a number of churches, was its backbone. By the end of the fourth century the Roman Empire as a whole had become Christian territory, despite the large pagan populations remaining within it. Already by the second century Christianity had spread to Mesopotamia (Iraq), beyond the empire's eastern border, and to Persia (Iran) by the third century. During the fourth century, missionaries brought Christianity to Gothic tribes north of the empire and to Ethiopia south of it. By the end of the fifth century, St. Patrick is credited with bringing Christianity from Roman-occupied Britain to Ireland.

In the second stage of the expansion of Christianity, the Roman Empire's locus of power had shifted to Byzantium in the East. The Byzantine Empire encouraged conversion partly as a way of pacifying warlike peoples on its northern and eastern borders. The greatest fruit of this policy was the conversion in 988 of Vladimir, prince of Kiev (capital of modern-day Ukraine), which ensured Russia's historic identity as an Orthodox Christian nation. The Western part of the Roman Empire was weaker and eventually collapsed (Chapter 13), leaving the Christian church as the dominant institution. At first there was little in the way of a planned "mission" program: Evangelization was mostly the work of wandering Benedictine and Celtic monks. Beginning with Pope Gregory the Great's sponsorship of the mission to the Anglo-Saxons in England (594), the early medieval popes increasingly became patrons of such efforts. Regardless of the patron or the missionary, the standard pattern for conversion was of whole peoples, not just individual persons. These Mass conversions had more to do with loyalty to one's local chief (ensuring political security and satisfying material needs) than to deep spiritual convictions. As a result, although Christianity might become a unifying cultural force, one could not assume that those who were baptized fully embraced the Christian faith.

These first two stages of expansion were significant because they began to set the standard for future mission policy. In the feudal economy of the Early Middle Ages, monasteries and dioceses were given lands and sovereign powers over all conquered peoples on that land. They also were able to institute the feudal principle of **sanctuary**, which states that all who take refuge from civil authority in a church or on church land cannot be removed without the permission of the abbot or bishop. Thus, the autonomy of ecclesiastical lands was established. Secondly, during these early stages of expansion, the church at Rome had managed to establish itself as the central authority whereby people would be commissioned to go out and introduce the Christian faith into new areas. They were allowed a certain freedom in accommodating the teachings of Christianity to these "tribal" peoples, but the church at Rome retained its place as the symbol of catholicity (universality). Finally, the principle of **indigenization** (that the native people of the country take charge of the church in that country) was set forth as a basic ecclesiastical mission policy during these early stages. Thus the most promising young men among these new Christian communities were selected for training as priests and future bishops.

For the most part, the third stage of the mission effort of the church of Rome (eleventh to fifteenth centuries) was initiated because of the failure of the crusades against the Muslims. The new mendicant orders of friars were largely responsible for the missionary effort among the Muslims, and they brought to the church's mission endeavors a different theology. Persuasion, not conquering force, was their approach. Their emphasis was on the lived example of Christianity, and so they sought to show the world of Islam the moral and intellectual strengths of Christianity. The friars were also responsible for spreading Islamic language and culture to the Western Christian world. Educated Europeans were well aware of the scientific, medical, and philosophical knowledge that the Islamic communities had shared with their Mediterranean neighbors. As a result, the friars established "mission preparation" schools that taught Arabic and Islamic culture in order to prepare future missionaries for dialogue with the Muslims. It was during this time that the missionary effort of Christianity began to take on a more formal structure.

This third stage of the expansion of Christianity corresponded with the beginnings of European exploration of new lands. Already in the 1290s, people living along the Mediterranean coast of Europe were beginning to hear fantastic tales of the Orient. An Italian named **Marco Polo** (1254–1324) had visited these strange lands to the east and had found places of great wealth (spices, drugs, perfumes, and cloth) and great rulers. His memoirs became the core of the European knowledge of the people and places of these unseen lands of the east. Italians were not the only Europeans aware of places and peoples beyond their view. Portugal and Spain were also interested in exploring these new lands of which they had heard. **Ibn Batuta** (1304–1368), the Arab scholar who in 1349 traveled through parts of Africa and the Orient and recounted in his memoirs the splendor of other cultures, thereby confirming the tales of Marco Polo. He noted the extensive trading system that had developed across the Sahara and in the cities along the east coast of Africa. He also noted that these kingdoms of the interior of Africa based their trade on gold. Europeans were hungry for gold; it provided wealth and independence from the feudal system, and it assured them a place in the international trading system. Finally, in 1487, following a route similar to that of Ibn Batuta, some traders from Portugal reached the Mali capital of Timbuktu, reputed to be the wealthiest city in the interior of Africa. By 1500, the Spanish were visiting it as well.

Both the church leaders and the secular rulers of Europe wanted to control the wealth they saw in Africa, but they used separate avenues to accomplish their goals. The church of Rome made ecclesiastical overtures to those areas that it hoped to control. One such area was Ethiopia, which had had a Christian king and government since the conversion of King Ezana of Aksum in the fourth century. At this point in history, Ethiopia was under the jurisdiction of the Coptic Orthodox patriarch of Alexandria (in schism from both Rome and Constantinople since the Council of Chalcedon in 451), but the pope invited the rulers of Ethiopia to enter into alliance with Rome instead. Similarly, the rulers of Spain and Portugal offered invitations designed to establish friendly relations with areas with which they hoped to trade, but independent of church leadership. Although the efforts of the Roman church failed in Ethiopia, the rulers of Spain and Portugal had more success. The third stage of

Christian expansion resulted in a widening of Europe's geographical and cultural horizons, but church and state were not yet working together in the missionary effort. In the fourth stage, finally, church and state would be engaged in joint efforts of exploration and missionary work.

THE PORTUGUESE MISSION TO AFRICA

The fourth stage of the expansion of Christianity, roughly fifteenth to sixteenth centuries, represents the first unified church/state effort in encountering new peoples. Portugal's prince **Henry the Navigator** (1394–1460) was primarily responsible for early efforts to expand the borders and the influence of both the European culture and the Christian faith. After his conquest of Ceuta, Morocco, in 1415, Henry sent ships south to explore the coast of Africa. A number of islands along the coast were later colonized by Portugal. By Henry's death in 1460, his trading ships had reached 600 miles down the coast to Sierra Leone. The chain of islands known as Cape Verde became Portugal's permanent base for trade with the nearby Guinea coast (the western coast of Africa from modern-day Sierra Leone and Liberia to Nigeria). In every colonizing effort, Henry, a grand master of the Order of Christ (an order of Christian knights), saw to the spread of the Christian message. Thus under Henry the Navigator, church and state were now working together.

Perhaps the best example of an early attempt at church/state cooperation in the Portuguese expansion was Portugal's attempt to gain control of the Congo in Africa. In 1482, Portuguese ships under the command of Diogo Cao reached the mouth of the Congo River (Angola), some 500 miles south of the equator. Here they encountered **Afonso the Good** (c. 1482–1543), the eldest son of Nzinga of Nkouwou, king of the Congo. Nzinga, together with his household, readily accepted the Catholic faith. In turn the Portuguese readily allied themselves with him. Given the superficiality of Mass conversions, some, like Afonso, remained Catholic, while his brother and others maintained their traditional religion. A struggle ensued between the Christian and non-Christian factions at the time Afonso was to ascend to power. Afonso won his throne with the help of his Portuguese allies. He ruled from A.D. 1506 to 1543. As king, Afonso's major concern was maintaining a balance between acquiring European technology and holding back Portuguese greed. He wanted his people to convert to Catholicism. He also wanted to acquire the benefits of Portuguese technology for his people, but he clearly saw the need to control the Portuguese's insatiable appetite for riches and slaves.

From the beginning, Portugal's missionary effort in the Congo was badly mismanaged. Relations between Afonso and both Manuel I (A.D. 1495–1521) and Joao III (1521–1557), kings of Portugal, were friendly, and mutually beneficial relations were within the realm of possibility. The church, however, did not flourish in Africa, and the Africans hardly benefited from their encounter with Europeans. In large part, this failure was due to the poor example set by those who professed to be Christian. Manuel I sent Augustinian canons (priests who lived a semi-monastic lifestyle, in this case, under the rule of Augustine) from Lisbon to the Congo. Within a short time, the canons gave up their common life, took native women as their concubines, and began trafficking in slaves. The same was true of the masons and artisans sent by Manuel to teach the Africans their trades. Their behavior did not set an example of good Christian living for the native African Christians. Later, Afonso tried to acquire European technology for his people by sending a group of his Congolese people to Portugal to learn Portuguese trades. Instead, a number of them were enslaved upon arrival.

Despite the misbehavior of the missionaries in Africa and the mistreatment of Africans by Portuguese both in Africa and in Portugal, the Congolese king continued to labor to bring his society into the mainstream of church life. Afonso sent his eldest son, Henrique, to study for the priesthood. Ordained a priest by the age of twenty-three, he was later ordained a bishop at the request of the Portuguese king Manuel I and served as the auxiliary bishop of the Portuguese church of Funchal in the Madeira Islands. Eventually, he returned home and worked in the Congo until his unexpected early death in 1531. With his death, Afonso's hope for a church with an indigenous clergy directly connected to Rome also died, since no other native clergy arose to take his place.

Likewise, Afonso's hope for technological development also perished, this time because of the explosive growth of the slave trade. In fact, slavery became the major issue in the Congo encounter. Portuguese slavers kidnapped Afonso's own subjects. Though Afonso protested in letters to Manuel I and Joao III, it was to no avail, because both government officials and clergy were absorbed in greed, striving for financial independence and the acquisition of a higher social rank. After Afonso's death, his brother, with the full support of the people, disbanded the church and began the fight against the Portuguese.

THE MISSIONS IN THE NEW WORLD

Portugal and Spain continued to explore new worlds. The Italian Christopher Columbus sailed West under the patronage of the Spanish government in order to find a new route to the Indies in 1492. The world he encountered became known as the West Indies, and later, the Americas. In 1498, the Portuguese explorer, Vasco da Gama, sailed three ships around the Cape of Good Hope (on the southern tip of Africa) and into the Indian Ocean. Opero Cabal's voyage took him to Brazil, also on behalf of the Portuguese. Within twenty years of Columbus' voyage, Magellan had sailed through the straits on the southern tip of South America to reach the Pacific Ocean from the Atlantic. Eventually, Magellan would circle the globe, providing the westward route to India. The explorers claimed territories in the name of Christianity and the kings who sponsored them. Unfortunately, many of these explorations were made in a spirit of conquest rather than good will.

The initial explorations launched by Portugal in the 1400s set off a chain of events on the European scene. First, Spain sought to create its own group of explorers in competition with the Portuguese, and it succeeded admirably. This competition created a great deal of tension between Spain and Portugal, which led the church in Rome (the arbitrator of all disputes between Christian countries at that time) to "divide up" the New World between Spain and Portugal. In 1493, Pope Alexander VI issued a series of five bulls (the most solemn and weighty form of papal letters) that set the stage for mission and exploration policy for the next century. All peoples and lands encountered while going west of a line drawn through the Atlantic belonged to Spain. New lands discovered east of the line belonged to the Portuguese. The pope's decision created a new cooperative system between church and state in which the two kings not only became responsible for colonization of these new lands, but also for the ecclesiastical organizations within their jurisdictions.

In the mission territories of both Spain and Portugal, the church was administered by the state in a system called royal patronage. The term refers to the sum total of privileges

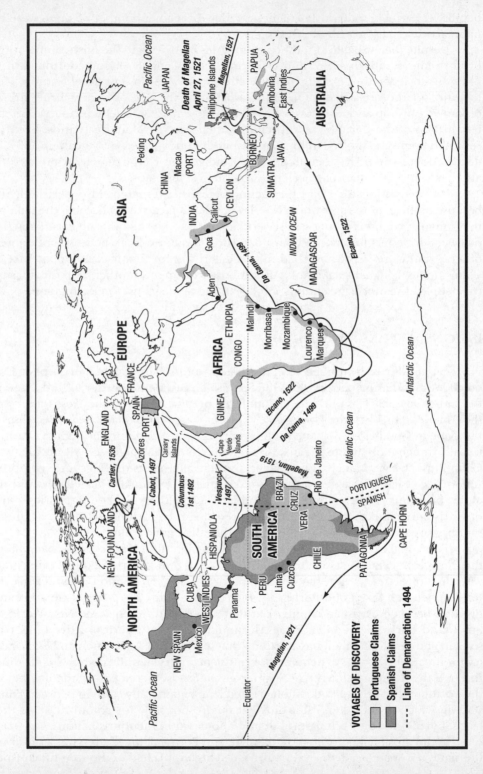

Figure 21–1 Map illustrating European voyages of discovery during the fifteenth and sixteenth centuries and the colonial claims of Spain and Portugal.

that the church conceded, along with certain burdens, to Catholic founders of a church or to those who acquire the right of patronage from the founders. These patrons were given the right to create dioceses in their newly colonized lands, to name bishops, abbots, and priests in those dioceses, and, in general, to control the direction of missionary efforts in their colonies. Since patronage not only provided benefits but also made demands on the kings, it was an acceptable arrangement for the church. The crown was financially responsible for the missions and their personnel, but, at the same time, the missions were a financial resource for the crown. Rome knew well that this would encourage Portugal and Spain to carry the Christian faith overseas. Over the years the popes added an extensive list of indulgences and privileges to this overseas royal patronage.

ROYAL PATRONAGE AND THE MISSIONARY EFFORT

The concept of royal patronage gave the kings of Spain and Portugal exclusive rights and responsibilities for the missionary evangelizing work of the entire world. Neither the pope nor anyone else in Rome could interfere. Thus, the fourth stage of the church's expansion marked the greatest and fastest growth of Christianity in its history. Because of the problems that arose with this type of Christianizing effort, the effects of which are still felt today, it also forced the Catholic Church to reexamine the way in which it had carried out its missionary work.

Efforts to evangelize new peoples under the royal patronage system were subject to all of the evils of conquest, greed, colonization, and political manipulation. The kings were primarily interested in trade and gold. Thus, colonization was primarily a process of military conquest. The native peoples who managed to survive, in particular those who lived in the areas near the colony's base settlements, were totally subjugated. Agricultural production and mining for gold were the main concerns. The missionary effort was secondary. Anyone who wished to complain about this could not appeal directly to Rome, because all communication with Rome had to be sent via the crown. Thus, patronage was protected.

In the Spanish territories of the Western hemisphere, the conquistadors set up an organized system of *pueblos* called the **encomienda-doctrina system**. The system was a cooperative effort between the *encomendero* (*conquistador* or his descendant) and the *doctrinero* (usually a mendicant friar) to build a sound economic and spiritual base in the new territories. The system was set up to integrate the Native Americans into the social and economic life of Spain but also to establish Western Christian culture among the native peoples. Thus, the Native Americans living in the pueblo learned Spanish economics. In the village workshop, skilled artisans wove cloth, made pots, and worked leather in order to build their churches and to pay the taxes demanded by their *encomendero*. Additional costs of the pueblo were defrayed partially by the crown and the *encomendero*. There were schools to teach the children Christian doctrine, Spanish literacy, arithmetic, and music. Christian education for the community at large was usually provided in weekly group lessons. Emphasis was placed on the basics: prayers, the creed, the commandments, and the sacraments. At first, the friars were the teachers in the pueblo, but later educated natives did the teaching.

The greatest boost to the growth of Catholicism in the Spanish new world came as a result of the event that took place on December 9, 1531. On that day the Virgin Mary is said to have appeared to an elderly native man at Tepeyac, on a hill northwest of Mexico City. His name was Juan Diego. In the vision he was instructed to tell the bishop to build a church on the site at Tepeyac. In a second appearance three days later, the Virgin instructed Juan Diego to pick flowers and take them to the bishop. As he opened his cloak to present the flowers, a miraculous event took place. A type of Spanish rose not grown in Mexico fell out of his cloak, and on the cloak was imprinted a painted image of Mary, now known as **Our Lady of Guadalupe**. Because of this apparition, devotion to Mary became the central devotion of Spanish-American Catholicism. Even today, many people associate Spanish-American Catholic spirituality with the image of Our Lady of Guadalupe.

Perhaps the best known of the friars in the New World was **Bartolomé de las Casas** (1474–1566). As a young cleric he moved to the West Indies (modern-day Haiti and the Dominican Republic). In 1502, he was the first to be ordained a priest in the New World. Once a landowner, now a Dominican friar, de las Casas began to question the morality of the enslavement of the Native Americans. He recognized that the *encomienda* system was destroying the native peoples, and he was determined that the system was immoral. He began to preach the cause of the Native Americans in the colony and traveled back and forth to Spain to have his voice heard before the council responsible for the governing of the Indies. In his enthusiasm, in 1516 he suggested to the crown that the colonies be permitted to import slaves from Africa, rather than forcing the indigenous peoples into slavery—a proposal he later regretted.

Figure 21–2 The Virgin Mary is said to have appeared to Juan Diego in 1531 at Tepeyac, near Mexico City. The image he saw in his vision has come to be known as Our Lady of Guadalupe. Devotion to Mary under this title continues to be an important part of Spanish-American Catholicism.

While de las Casas was concerned about the morality of slavery, his was primarily an ecclesiastical concern; because they were Christians, Native Americans living in the pueblos should not be enslaved. He was not addressing the larger question of the morality of slavery itself or of a commercial enterprise that required the use of slaves. However, in defense of de las Casas, it should be noted that he did not initiate the idea of importing Africans as slaves. Portugal already had begun an African slave trade in 1442. The Spanish crown did not give permission for this practice until 1511. Even then it did so on the basis of its belief that enslaving prisoners of war was legitimate. Spain had been at war with the Muslims for years. Since sub-Saharan Africans also lived in Muslim territory (according to Spain's geography), the Spanish felt justified in making slaves of them as well.

The church's law (called canon law) on slavery had been adapted from Roman law and the writings of Aristotle. According to this law, one could legally enslave or have another person under captivity for several reasons. For example, captives of war could be enslaved, although this law was later modified so that only non-Christian captives could be made slaves. Likewise, criminals were often punished with slavery. In this case, slavery was seen as a substitute for capital punishment. Sometimes those who could not repay their debts were enslaved. Since failure to pay one's debts was also a criminal offense, the debt was "paid" with a period of servitude. In some cases, children were sold by their (usually impoverished) parents into slavery. Likewise, adults sometimes sold themselves into slavery. Those who were destitute and hopeless could at least gain shelter and subsistence in this way. Finally, many people were slaves because they had been born to a slave mother. Slavery therefore became part of the caste system, a station in life that was passed from generation to generation.

Bartolomé de las Casas challenged the morality of the laws governing the *encomienda* system and appealed to Rome on behalf of the Native Americans living in the pueblos. As a result, in 1537 Pope Paul III, in the bull *Sublimis Deus*, set forth the rights of the Native Americans and challenged their enslavement. However, the pope did not address the morality of slavery itself, but only the more technical legal aspects of title, or right of ownership. Slavery was understood to be a question of property rights and not human rights. Thus, although the pope supported de las Casas, the core issue of the immorality of slavery remained unresolved. Nonetheless, de las Casas continued to fight.

In 1544 Bartolomé de las Casas became the bishop of Chiapas in southern Mexico. He quickly instructed his priests not to absolve the slaveholders of their sins until they promised to free their Native American slaves. The bishop's order had significant consequences. Because the slaveholders refused to release their slaves, they were not allowed to participate in the sacrament of Penance, and as a result they could not receive communion when they went to Mass. By Easter of 1545, the Spaniards rioted because they could not fulfill their Easter duty (the requirement that every Catholic receive the Eucharist at least once a year during the Easter season). Threats became public and de las Casas, faced with a violent uprising, returned to Spain and resigned his see in 1547. While he did not change the slave trade in the *encomienda* system, he was able to bring to public debate the issue of the morality of slavery and challenge the attitudes of the explorers as they encountered peoples in different parts of the world. Bartolomé de las Casas challenged Aristotle's principles on slavery, thus helping to lay the foundation for today's understanding of human rights.

By 1575 some 9,000 *encomienda* system campuses could be found in Latin America. At its peak, the population of the pueblos was well into the millions. However, their numbers steadily declined after 1575 because the evangelizing effort in many regions still included slavery. The Spanish themselves could not distinguish between the Christian message and their Spanish culture, which was the bearer of the message. Their efforts to impose Spanish culture on the indigenous peoples resulted in disaster. Fortunately, the failure of the *encomienda* system would give rise to a new Spanish missionary effort known as the mission, the fifth stage in Christian missionary expansion. Before this could happen, however, there were other lessons to be learned in missionary ventures in the Orient.

THE MISSION TO THE ORIENT

The Roman Catholic Church had learned many lessons over the years concerning the ways in which missionary expansion ought to be conducted. Principal among these was that the system of royal patronage, which appeared to be so effective in the early decades of the sixteenth century, was no longer concerned with the missionary task of teaching the Christian message. Patronage had become, quite simply, an instrument of colonial and imperial policies. Gradually the church realized that relying on the new religious orders of the Catholic Reformation to spread Christianity would be more effective and less harmful to the local populations than relying on state governments like those of Portugal and Spain, which had been given all such rights as part of the system of royal patronage.

Foremost among the new religious orders of the Catholic Reformation were the Jesuits, founded by St. Ignatius Loyola (1491–1556) and the Capuchins, founded by Matthew of Bascio (d. 1552). Almost immediately, the Jesuit order became the backbone of the mission effort. One of the first Jesuit missionaries to the East was St. **Francis Xavier** (1506–1552), a companion of Ignatius Loyola. In 1542, Francis Xavier began his missionary preaching in Goa, the Portuguese seaport in India. Skilled at language and flexible in lifestyle, he attracted many of the lower caste to the faith both in India and Ceylon, but he was not able to convert the upper classes. By 1545, the Jesuits had sent additional missionaries to Goa so that Xavier himself was able to move on to Malacca on the Malay peninsula while sending Jesuits to other Portuguese seaports in the Orient. However, it was not until he reached Japan that he realized that something was wrong with his mission policy. Xavier noticed that, unlike his experience in India, apostolic poverty did not impress the Japanese. He adopted a better quality of dress like the local leaders, and within two years he had over 2,000 converts. Thus the practice of missionaries adapting to the cultural norms of the indigenous peoples gradually became a standard part of mission policy.

Due to the exceptional growth of the Catholic Church in the East, the Jesuits appointed Xavier to be the superior of the new Jesuit province of India in 1551. He had already established a mission center for learning the languages and customs of the many peoples of the East. However, Xavier's final interest was China. He studied the language and set out for the coast near Canton in 1552. While trying to finalize his plans to move to the interior, he fell sick with a fever. Francis Xavier died on the morning of December 3, 1552. Though he was originally buried in China, the Jesuits exhumed his body and returned it to Goa, where it is enshrined today. Despite the fact that he never got to preach the Christian message in China, Xavier's dreams were not lost; he had set the pattern for how missionary work would be done in the East, and others would soon follow.

An Italian Jesuit, **Matteo Ricci** (1552–1610), followed Xavier's missionary example with a special emphasis on conversion through learning. He sought to confront the learned elite of China in their own language and by following their customs. He also used his superior talent to impress them with Christianity. Ricci adopted the garb of a Buddhist monk and by 1585 he and his companion had dedicated a church and residence in Chaoking. His vision of winning the Confucian masters, whom he believed the Masses would then follow into the Christian faith, was in process. He robed himself in the square hat and silks of a scholar and gradually gained a reputation as the "Doctor for the Great West Ocean." Thus Christianity was granted the respect and privileges due to members of the Mandarin bureaucracy. Finally, in 1598, Ricci made his first move toward Beijing. Initially

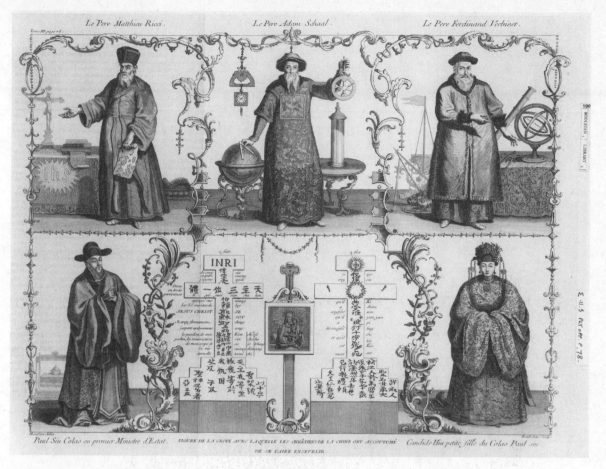

Figure 21–3 The upper level of this print depicts Fr. Matteo Ricci (1552–1610) and two other missionaries, along with symbols of the sciences for which the Jesuits in China became famous. The lower level depicts two Chinese converts to Christianity making their profession of faith.

he was unsuccessful, but in 1601 he presented gifts to the throne and was granted residence and a subsidy for his reflections in mathematics and astronomy. Known throughout the realm as "Li Madou," Matteo Ricci remains the most celebrated foreign figure in Chinese literature.

The Jesuits would continue to be successful in their missionary work in India and China, primarily because they had chosen to become a part of the culture in which they had come to live. They took the dress and lifestyle of the holy men of those cultures and even participated in the native religious ceremonies. They learned the languages and traditions of the native peoples and only gradually introduced elements of Christian doctrine and practice, as the culture would allow. Not everyone was happy with this blending of Christianity with native culture and religious practice. Throughout the seventeenth century Catholic authorities in Rome hesitated about where to set appropriate boundaries. In China the controversy over "the Chinese rites," as they were called, focused on such things as the proper name for God (the Jesuits had adopted the Chinese character meaning "Heaven" as a substitute for "God," because "Lord of Heaven" was more familiar to Chinese as a reference to divinity), the Mandarin ceremonies in honor of Confucius, and ancestor worship. Ricci and his Jesuit successors argued that the ceremonies were civil and not religious. Their critics thought they constituted idolatrous practices in which Christians could not participate. By the eighteenth century a strong anti-Jesuit backlash in Europe, the resentment of missionary competitors among other Catholic religious orders, and the papacy's desire to gain closer control of missionary work everywhere, all came together to spell the end of such experiments in accommodation. In 1715 Pope Clement XI issued a decree condemning Catholic participation in ancestor worship and the cult of Confucius. That judgment and a subsequent papal condemnation in 1742 led to persecution by the Chinese government and are sometimes blamed for Catholic Christianity's failure to develop further in China.

However, before this would happen, the Catholic Church would move into its fifth stage of mission expansion: the mission.

THE CONGREGATION FOR THE PROPAGATION OF THE FAITH

The decisive step in the fifth stage of missionary expansion occurred in 1622, when Pope Gregory XV created a new congregation (i.e., an office or department) in the Curia (papal government) to deal with missionary activity in non-Christian lands. It was given the official title the "Sacred Congregation for the Propagation of the Faith." Within five years (by 1627), Pope Urban VIII had provided this formal body with a central missionary training seminary, the *Collegium Urbanum* (Urban College), which became the first center for mission training in Europe.

Francesco Cardinal Ingoli (d. 1649), the first secretary of the Congregation for the Propagation of the Faith, established the basic principles of the Catholic missionary process: independence from control by the colonial countries and development of an indigenous clergy in the mission churches. In 1659, ten years after the death of Cardinal Ingoli, the Congregation for the Propagation of the Faith issued another statement that would set the future direction of missionary activity:

> Do not regard it as your task, and do not bring any pressure to bear on the peoples, to change their manners, customs, and uses, unless they are evidently contrary to religion and sound morals. What could be more absurd than to transport France, Spain, Italy, or some other European country to China? Do not introduce all that to them, but only the faith, which does not despise or destroy the manners and customs of any people, always supposing that they are not evil, but rather wishes to see them preserved unharmed. (Cited in Neill 1984, 174)

This respect for the unique cultures of the newly encountered communities did not materialize immediately. In actuality, the imperial political powers (Spain and Portugal) maintained control of their colonies for a long time afterwards—well into the twentieth century, when the first group of indigenous bishops was ordained in 1939. Yet gradually the passage of time would bring new players and new attitudes into the colonizing effort.

FRENCH MISSIONS IN THE NEW WORLD

The year 1588 marked a major change in European history and world colonization efforts. The Spanish Armada was defeated by the British, thus ending the growth of the Spanish empire. At the same time, other powers in Europe were beginning to explore the New World. France was a major participant in this adventure. By 1630, France had become a leading colonial power, partly due to the political leadership of Cardinal Richelieu (1585–1642). He had entrusted the missionary efforts of France to his Capuchin secretary and confessor, Père Joseph Leclerc du Tremblay (d. 1538). It was Fr. Joseph who sent the Capuchins to most of the colonies of France. Eventually, Fr. Joseph du Tremblay was made the first "prefect apostolic" (religious superior) of what is today called New England.

The Capuchin friars were the primary French missionaries in the New World. By 1633 they had established stations in the Antilles (St. Kitts), La Heve, and Port Royal (Maine). Within five years they had expanded to the islands of St. Vincent, Martinique, Dominica, Marie Galante, and Guadeloupe in the Caribbean. Guadeloupe became the main station for their missionary activity. By 1647, the church in Rome had approved a proposal to establish a college on the island of Les Saints, much like the one in Goa, for the training of friars in the languages and customs of the people of the area. At the same time, friars were being called to do missionary work in Africa. They were assigned to missions in the Ivory Coast (1634), the Congo (1645), and the Cameroons (1650). In the early eighteenth century, they would turn their attention to North America as the center of French mission activity. Their mission policy was similar to what the Jesuits had done in the Orient: They became part of the culture they were coming to evangelize and they taught about Christianity by example. Because these missionary efforts were under the direct control of the church in Rome, they were able to prevent the newer colonizing countries (like France) from developing a social and economic system similar to the royal patronage system found in the Spanish and Portuguese colonies.

INCULTURATION

Recently there has been a renewed awareness that the message of Christianity ought not to be bound to any one cultural form, but should be able to reach all peoples within their own cultural context. This awareness is expressed by the term **inculturation**. It is an extension and adaptation of the sociological term **enculturation**. Culture is "a society's design for living" (Luzvetak 1988, 156). Thus enculturation refers to the process by which *an individual* learns to live and act within a particular culture in such a way that the culture's particular pattern of actions and thought becomes second nature. One normally enculturates to one's home society as one grows up. Inculturation refers to the process by which *a religion* "learns" to live and act within a culture different from the one in which it began. The inculturated religion, like an enculturated individual, may challenge the culture, but it does so in terms the culture can understand, because it has learned to act naturally within that culture's pattern of actions and thought.

The first Christian inculturation took place within the first few centuries of its existence, when a religious movement that began in a Palestinian Jewish culture learned to live and act within a Greco-Roman culture. It accomplished the task so well that today many people think of Christianity as a Western religion. If the church is to successfully inculturate itself into a new society, it does so through the two primary agents in mission, namely, the Holy Spirit and the local church (local leaders and lay Christians who belong to the society where the mission is working). Neither the missionaries nor the leaders of the worldwide church can determine for the local church exactly what it means to be Christian in that cultural context. Rather, the local leaders who truly experienced the deep realities at the core of the religion are often the best people to express these realities and to shape appropriate ways to live them out in the language, art, music, architecture, and cultural patterns of their own society. This process of inculturation, the church believes, is guided by the Holy Spirit and is therefore trustworthy. Diversity of cultures allows the Christian message to be interpreted in new and more meaningful ways for all peoples. At the same time, the Christian message can bring enlightenment and growth to individual cultures. The result is an experience of mutual enrichment.

Key Terms

sanctuary	Afonso the Good	Matteo Ricci
indigenization	*encomienda-doctrina* system	inculturation
Marco Polo	Our Lady of Guadalupe	enculturation
Ibn Batuta	Bartolomé de las Casas	
Henry the Navigator	Francis Xavier	

Questions for Reading

1. Review the five stages of the missionary expansion of Christianity. When did each stage occur, and what areas were covered in it? Who led the missions, and how were conversions brought about?

2. Discuss the relationship between exploration and mission in the third and fourth stages of missionary expansion. What motives did the missionaries and the explorers have in common?

3. Review the main events of the Portuguese mission to Africa and explain why this mission was largely a failure.

4. Explain how Spain and Portugal came to dominate the missions in the New World and evaluate their performance in this area.

5. Who was Bartolomé de las Casas? How and why did he try to reform the missions in the New World? What impact did his efforts have?

6. How were the missions conducted by the Jesuits and Capuchins in the fifth stage of missionary expansion *different* from those conducted under the direction of the Spanish and Portuguese? Who were the main leaders of the missions conducted by the Jesuits and Capuchins? What were their major accomplishments?

Works Consulted/Recommended Reading

Arias, David. *Spanish Roots of America.* Huntington, IN: Our Sunday Visitor, 1992.

Blaut, J. M. *1492: The Debate on Colonialism, Eurocentrism, and History.* Trenton, NJ: Africa World Press, 1992.

Brockey, Liam Matthew. *Journey to the East: The Jesuit Mission to China, 1579–1724*. Cambridge, MA: Harvard University, 2007.

Casas, Bartolomé de las. *The Devastation of the Indies: A Brief Account*. Translated by Herma Briffault. Baltimore, MD: Johns Hopkins University, 1992.

Davis, Kortright. "'Sunshine Christopher': Bearer of Christ in Caribbean History." *Journal of Religious Thought* 49 (1992–1993): 7–24.

Holder, John. "The Issue of Race: A Search for a Biblical/Theological Perspective." *Journal of Religious Thought* 49 (1992–1993): 44–59.

Hopkins, Dwight N. "Columbus, the Church, and Slave Religion." *Journal of Religious Thought* 49 (1992–1993): 25–35.

Luzvetak, Louis J. *The Church and Cultures: New Perspectives in Missiological Anthropology*. Maryknoll, NY: Orbis Books, 1988.

Neill, Stephen. *A History of Christian Missions*. New York: Penguin, 1984.

Poole, Stafford. *Our Lady of Guadalupe: The Origins and Sources of a Mexican National Symbol, 1531–1797*. Tuscon: University of Arizona, 1995.

Riga, Peter J. "Columbus, the Church and the Indians: A Reflection." *Journal of Religious Thought* 49 (1992–1993): 36–43.

Shorter, Aylward. *Toward a Theology of Inculturation*. Maryknoll, NY: Orbis, 1988.

Spence, Jonathan D. *The Memory Palace of Matteo Ricci*. New York: Penguin, 1985.

Williams, Eric. *From Columbus to Castro: The History of the Caribbean, 1942–1969*. New York: Vintage, 1970.

MODERN CHALLENGES TO CHRISTIANITY

22

TIMELINE

A.D. 1543	Nicholas Copernicus proposes his theory that the earth and other planets revolve around the sun.
A.D. 1610	Galileo Galilei discovers evidence in support of Copernicus' theory.
A.D. 1687	Isaac Newton publishes his *Principia* in which he shows that the laws by which the planets move are the same laws that govern the motion of bodies on earth.
c. A.D. 1700	Beginning of the movement known as the Enlightenment.
A.D. 1776–1781	The American Revolution
A.D. 1789–1799	The French Revolution
A.D. 1848	Karl Marx publishes the *Communist Manifesto*.
A.D. 1859	Charles Darwin publishes *The Origin of Species* describing his theory of evolution, thereby raising significant questions about the authority of the Bible.

Christianity has faced intellectual, social, and political challenges in each period of its history, from its birth under the Roman Empire onwards. This is certainly true of Christianity's experience of modernity. The present chapter treats the "modern" period as beginning around 1600. It focuses mainly on challenges that developed prior to 1900, which included the scientific revolution, the emergence of the modern nation-state, the cultural and intellectual movement known as the Enlightenment, and nineteenth-century social and economic changes (the free market economic system, urbanization, industrialization, the labor movement, the movements for women's emancipation, etc.). There were other marked changes as well, such as intellectual developments in biology and historical study, political upheaval, especially the French and American Revolutions, in whose wake came modern liberal democracy, and the Russian Revolution of 1917, which inaugurated the twentieth century's disastrous experience with communism.

At the core of these diverse developments, it is possible to see the emergence of the supreme value put on freedom and self-determination. The demand for autonomy, which literally means "one's self as law," is a hallmark of modernity. During this time human beings have put more and more importance on their right to determine their own destiny. Technological advances, political change, and social transformation have all strengthened humanity's confidence in its ability to shape both human beings and the world in which they live. This confidence has not always been justified in practice, as the history of the modern world has too often shown. Some of the unhappy fruits of the desire for autonomy have been colonialism, brutal totalitarian regimes, economic exploitation of the poor, consumerism, sexual license, family breakdown, and environmental degradation. In practice the modern desire to see human beings as ends in themselves has often entailed turning *other* human beings into mere instruments for those ends.

For Christianity, and indeed for any religion which depends on a historical tradition for its lifeblood, the modern valuation of freedom raises a fundamental theological question which can be put two different ways: Is modern freedom really a revolt against God and against the very idea that the order of the world is in some sense a "given" that we are not free to refashion as we wish? Or, on the other hand, may we see modern autonomy as a divinely willed fulfillment of human destiny and a true consequence of the biblical doctrine that all human beings are made in the image and likeness of God? The answer, most modern Christians would agree, must surely be a measure of "both–and": modernity *both* as revolt *and* as divinely willed maturity. Trying to find out just where one ends and the other begins, however, is anything but clear. In reading this and succeeding chapters, pay attention to how the Christian tradition has tried to read what the Second Vatican Council called "the signs of the times." Also note how the deepest disagreements *within* modern Christianity really seem to be disagreements about where to strike the balance between seeing modernity as revolt vs. seeing it as the adulthood of the human race.

The present chapter will give special attention to intellectual challenges to Christianity, particularly those posed by scientific discovery. In the modern period, science has been so successful at explaining its subject matter—whether it is human beings or the world—that the scientific way of looking at the world has become deeply ingrained in the modern human consciousness. For many modern people, it is simply taken for granted that the only way of understanding reality properly is the scientific way. Thus the Christian worldview that was shared almost universally in the West in medieval times has been replaced by a scientific worldview, and Christianity has struggled to maintain its place in a world dominated by science.

THE NEW COSMOLOGY

Although there was occasional speculation in both antiquity and the Middle Ages that the sun was the center of the universe, it was the geocentric (earth-centered) universe of Aristotle and Claudius Ptolemy (Greek astronomer, c. A.D. 140), which was the standard until the seventeenth century. Aristotle pictured the earth at the center of the universe, orbited by the moon, Mercury, Venus, the sun, Mars, Jupiter, and Saturn, in that order.

This **cosmology** (picture of the cosmos or universe) was accepted by medieval Christian thinkers, such as Aquinas and Dante. But beyond the sphere of the fixed stars Christian thinkers placed the "empyrean," meaning the highest heaven where God and the angels dwelt. Thus medieval Christians would have assumed that Jesus after his resurrection ascended into the empyrean, above the realm of the stars.

In 1543 a Polish Catholic astronomer, **Nicholas Copernicus**, published *On the Revolutions of the Heavenly Spheres,* which proposed that the earth and other planets revolved around the sun. This proposal did not immediately cause controversy; it was only an interesting hypothesis. But in 1610 **Galileo Galilei** focused his new telescope on Jupiter and discovered that the planet had four moons revolving around it. This showed that, contrary to Aristotelian theory, not all heavenly bodies revolved around the earth. Because of this discovery (and other related discoveries), Galileo championed Copernicus' theory (Langford 1971, 39–41).

This new cosmology was a challenge to traditional Christianity partly because it appeared to contradict the Bible, which was thought to teach that the sun revolved around the earth and that the earth was the center of the universe. For example, Joshua 10:12–13 states that Joshua prayed that the sun would stand still, and the sun did stand still. In addition, Psalm 93:1 states "He [God] has established the world firm; it shall never be moved." Galileo was told that he could teach Copernicus' theory as a hypothesis, but he insisted on teaching it as fact (though he did not actually have sufficient evidence to prove it to be fact). Eventually, in 1616, the Holy Office, the church body that protected the integrity of Christian doctrine, condemned the Copernican theory as heresy and forbade Galileo to teach it.

As Pope John Paul II admitted several years ago, this was a disastrous mistake. It had long been held in Catholic tradition that the Bible is not meant to teach scientific fact—Augustine had already pointed out the harm that could be done to the credibility of religious authority when revealed religious truth was confused with scientific truth (see *Confessions* V.v.8–9). Rather, the Bible teaches those truths about God and humanity that are necessary for human salvation. As Cardinal Baronius said at the time of Galileo: "The Holy Ghost intended to teach us [in scripture] how to go to heaven, not how the heavens go." But the condemnation of Galileo permanently damaged the authority of the Catholic Church, especially among scientists, many of whom to this day see the church as opposed to science. The lesson to be learned from this is that various disciplines have to respect the boundaries proper to their own discipline

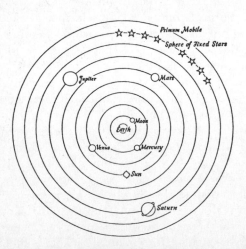

Figure 22–1 The Aristotelian universe.

and not intrude on the territory of other disciplines (John Paul II 1992, 369–373). Theology cannot teach matters falling within the domain of science (such as whether the sun revolves around the earth). Conversely, science should not presume to teach in areas that cannot be investigated by its material and mathematical methods (such as whether God exists, whether humans have a soul, and whether there is life after death). Rather, John Paul II teaches that science and theology, reason and revelation are complementary: *Both* are necessary for a complete understanding of reality, since reality is both material and spiritual.

THE NEW SCIENCE

Modern physical science was inaugurated in the seventeenth century through the work of Galileo Galilei, Francis Bacon, René Descartes, Isaac Newton, and others. What the new science displaced was the older Aristotelian belief that nature functioned like a living organism and that natural entities such as plants and animals were animated by "substantial forms"—approximately what we would call souls—and that each organism had an intrinsic purpose, to actualize the goal or end of its form. For example, the goal of the acorn is to become an oak tree and to reproduce. The new science, however, eliminated substantial forms and purposes from its explanations. Instead, it attempted to explain events in nature—such as the motion of falling bodies or the planets—by laws which could be (1) formulated mathematically and (2) tested by experiment. This was the core of the new scientific method and was exemplified in Galileo's explanation of the law of falling bodies. This law could be captured in a mathematical formula and tested experimentally.

Aristotelian physics was gradually discarded. In its place, a new physics grew up, based on the idea that matter was made up of tiny particles—atoms, which followed mathematical and mechanical laws. Everything, it was thought, could be explained as a combination of atoms; there was no need to bring in substantial forms or purposes (what Aristotle called "final causes"), which could not be measured or tested empirically. For the new science, the only kind of cause that mattered was mechanical cause and effect, which Aristotle had called "efficient cause." As a result, the new science came to view nature as a vast machine, like a watch or clock, governed not by souls but by mechanical principles alone.

The culmination of the new science was expressed in the synthesis of **Isaac Newton**, published in Latin in 1687. Usually known as the *Principia*, its English title is *Mathematical Principles of Natural Philosophy*. Newton showed that the laws by which the planets moved were the same laws that governed the motion of bodies on earth. The motion of the planets was due to their inertial momentum (inertia being the tendency of a body to remain at rest or in motion in the same straight line unless acted upon by another body) and the force of gravity. Thus the explanation of the cosmos according to mechanical principles—matter, external force, and inertia—was largely complete.

The new understanding of the world as a machine was to have far-reaching implications. Effectively it removed God from the world. According to this view, the world ran on its own—without God's help—like a perfectly designed clock or watch. The new mechanical philosophy, which in time came to influence the method of one science after another, would eventually lead to a worldview in which neither God, nor spirits, nor souls had any real place in nature. Nature could be explained by the simple operation of mechanical laws, which made God's presence superfluous and which also eliminated purposes from nature. This view came to prominence in the eighteenth century in the writings of men such as

Baron d'Holbach, who succeeded thereby in making atheism intellectually respectable. A similar view continues to be argued today by some prominent scientists and philosophers, who believe that the universe and life can be explained by the chance interactions of atoms, governed by mechanistic laws and the probabilistic laws of quantum mechanics.

THE CHALLENGE TO TRADITION

Modern science was founded in a spirit of skepticism and antitraditionalism. Scientific method demanded that knowledge be verified by experiment, not simply accepted on faith from tradition. Indeed, much of Aristotle's physics, which had been accepted for centuries, proved to be incorrect. Thus, seventeenth-century scientists had good reason to be skeptical of tradition. This skepticism was embodied in the philosophy of **René Descartes**. Descartes began his philosophical method by systematically doubting everything he had been taught—all tradition—in order to arrive at what was absolutely certain. By process of elimination, the one thing he was unable to doubt was his own thinking consciousness—hence the famous line, "Cogito, ergo sum" ("I think, therefore I am")—which became the basis on which certain knowledge could be reconstructed.

Although Descartes himself lived and died a devout Catholic, his method of systematic doubt was extended by his philosophical successors to include most aspects of Christian revelation and tradition, and even the idea of tradition itself. Systematic doubt of what has been revealed by long-dead religious teachers, like Moses and Jesus, and handed on in tradition obviously poses a severe challenge to Christianity. Christianity, after all, rests largely on the teachings of Jesus, which were passed on to the apostles, handed on in tradition, and believed by subsequent generations on faith.

Deism

The new mechanical philosophy, which understood the world as an exquisitely designed machine, produced a religious phenomenon called **Deism** (from Latin *Deus,* meaning "God"). Deists believed in a God who designed the world-machine and started it going—as a clockmaker might make a watch and wind it up. But thereafter God did not intervene in the workings of the universe, which ran on its own like a watch. The idea that God had to intervene occasionally to adjust the motion of the planets was scornfully dismissed by the Deists, because it implied that God was an imperfect creator. A perfect creator would make a perfect creation: a world machine that needed no interventions to keep it going.

A rejection of the possibility of divine intervention entailed a rejection of much of Christian belief. Deists generally rejected prophecy, miracles, special providence, the incarnation, and the resurrection. They minimized special revelation and argued instead that God had given people all the revelation they needed in nature itself. The magnificent design of nature pointed to a perfect creator. What Deists espoused, essentially, was a religion based on nature and reason alone. Thus, an early English Deist, Lord Herbert of Cherbury (1583–1648) maintained that there were only five religious truths: (1) God exists; (2) it is our duty to worship him; (3) virtue and piety are important parts of worship; (4) people ought to repent of their sins; and (5) rewards or punishments will follow death. Notice that this creed says nothing about the divinity of Jesus, the Trinity, the possibility of God's providential action in history, miracles, or supernatural revelation. Typically, Deists argued that revelation was not necessary and that it merely duplicated what could be known about God by reason.

Deism in England lasted about a century, but it did have important influences, particularly in France and America. Indeed, the most important idea of the Deists—that God created the world but is extrinsic to it and does not intervene in it, so that the world runs by its own autonomous laws—is a very common idea today. Hindu children, when asked where God is, point to their hearts. Christian children, asked the same question, point to the sky: God is "outside" the world (see Griffith 1983, 24).

THE ENLIGHTENMENT

The developments of seventeenth-century science, the emphasis on reason, and Deism all converged in the eighteenth-century intellectual movement known as the Enlightenment, a cultural spin-off of the scientific revolution, which emphasized reason, science, the goodness and rights of humanity, religious toleration, progress, and human freedom. The Enlightenment was an international phenomenon, with representatives from all over Europe and even in colonial America: The "apostles" of the Enlightenment included writers and philosophers such as David Hume and Joseph Priestley in England, Voltaire, Jean-Jacques Rousseau, and Denis Diderot in France, Immanuel Kant in Germany, and Thomas Jefferson, Benjamin Franklin, and Tom Paine in America.

Enlightenment Rationalism

Because of its great confidence in the power of reason to grasp reality, the Enlightenment has been called the Age of Reason. This confidence was rooted in the scientific success of Isaac Newton and his generation in appearing to reduce reality to a simple and beautifully explanatory system. The Enlightenment's celebration of reason often went so far as to deny that there was any other route to reality and truth *besides* reason, an intellectual thesis which is known as **rationalism**. Rationalism sees no need to resort to supernatural revelation to understand the world, humanity, or the moral law. Nature, it was thought, was governed by a few simple laws, and knowledge of these laws and of the laws of human society would create a good life in this world. According to Ernst Cassirer,

> The basic idea underlying all the tendencies of the Enlightenment was the conviction that all human understanding is capable, by its own power and without any recourse to super-natural assistance, of comprehending the system of the world and that this new way of understanding the world will lead to a new way of mastering it. (Cited in Hallowell 1967, 8:702)

What stood in the way of the progress envisioned by rationalists were superstition, ignorance, and feudal or clerical hierarchical authority. The enemy was tyranny and "priestcraft," as Enlightenment thinkers put it. For them, superstition, ignorance, and repressive authority were summed up in Christianity. Like the Deists, Enlightenment philosophers (at least those who were not atheists) promoted a religion that was simple, rational, virtuous, and nonsupernatural, in which Jesus was a great moral teacher but not the incarnate Son of God. Thomas Jefferson himself gave us a memorable example of this view of Jesus in his little book *The Life and Morals of Jesus of Nazareth*, Jefferson's version of Jesus's *real* teaching, minus the supposed distortions and misunderstandings of Jesus's disciples. He described his approach to the teachings of Jesus in a letter written to a Unitarian minister in 1820:

> Among the sayings and discourses attributed to Him by His biographers, I find many passages of fine imagination, correct morality, and of the most lovely benevolence; and others, again, of so much ignorance, so much absurdity, so much untruth, charlatanism and imposture, as to pronounce it impossible that such contradictions should have proceeded from the same Being. I separate, therefore, the gold from the dross; restore to Him the former, and leave the latter to the stupidity of some, and roguery of others of His disciples. (Cited in Church 1989, 28)

Similarly, the great German philosopher Immanuel Kant argued that where Jesus endorsed what is reasonable, he should be respected, but where he went against reason, his teaching should be rejected. For Kant "enlightenment" meant that persons should be free to use their own reason. His 1784 essay "Answering the Question, 'What is Enlightenment?'" became a classic expression of the Enlightenment's self-understanding:

> Enlightenment is humanity's release from his self-incurred tutelage. Tutelage is man's inability to make use of his understanding without direction from another. Self-incurred is this tutelage when its cause lies not in lack of reason but in lack of resolution and courage to use it without direction from another. *Sapere aude!* "Have courage to use your own reason!"—that is the motto of enlightenment. (Kant 1990, 83)

The two things that filled him with awe and wonder, wrote Kant in *The Critique of Practical Reason*, were "the starry sky above me and the moral law within me" (meaning the natural world and conscience), words which were engraved on his tombstone (Cited in Schönfeld 2007).

Many Enlightenment figures were Deists. Voltaire, for example, believed in a Creator God, whose grandeur was expressed in nature (though his confidence in this Deist God was badly shaken by the disastrous Lisbon earthquake of 1755). But he was fiercely opposed to Christianity and rejected the Christian beliefs in the incarnation, the resurrection, providence, miracles, and sacraments as irrational. Especially in the last years of his life, he poured scorn on the notion of supernatural revelation; the doctrines of the Trinity, the virgin birth of Jesus, and the presence of Christ in the Eucharist; and religious authority in general. His *Dictionnaire Philosophique* was burned by authorities in Geneva, the Netherlands, France, and Rome. Voltaire's attitude toward Christianity (and democracy) is summed up in his words to Frederick the Great, King of Prussia: "Your majesty will do the human race an eternal service in extirpating this infamous superstition [Christianity], I do not say among the rabble, who are not worthy of being enlightened and who are apt for every yoke; I say among the well bred, among those who wish to think" (Cited in Cragg 1974, 241). The French Enlightenment, led by men like Voltaire, Rousseau, and Diderot, was thus much more anti-Christian and anti-clerical than the English, American, or German Enlightenments. Much of the Enlightenment's **anticlericalism** (antagonism toward priests and clergy) survives in France to this day, where it has become virtually a tradition in its own right.

The Enlightenment's skepticism of anything supernatural was particularly evident in its critique of miracles. The Scottish philosopher David Hume argued that the laws of nature are so firmly established by universal common experience, that any testimony of a violation of those laws (that is, a miracle) would be unconvincing (Hume 2007, 100–101).

Similarly, Diderot stated that even if the whole population of Paris assured him that a man had risen from the dead, he would not believe it. Such skepticism—much of which persists to this day—has made it more difficult for Christianity to defend the doctrine of Jesus's divinity on the basis of his miracles and his resurrection. Few thinkers before the Enlightenment had doubted that miracles occurred, or that Jesus had been a great miracle worker. Jesus's miracles and resurrection were among the "proofs" offered for Jesus's divinity, for who but God could perform miracles such as this? But after the rationalist critique of miracles (especially Hume's), many intellectuals assumed that miracles had been shown to be superstitions or absurdities. This led to skepticism about Jesus's divinity as well.

Human Nature and Progress

A major disagreement between traditional Christianity and the Enlightenment philosophers centered on the nature of humanity. Both Catholic and Protestant Christians, following Augustine, had taught that human beings were born with original sin. This did not mean that people were by nature evil—after all, everything created by God is good. But it did mean that human beings were born with a natural tendency toward selfishness and sin. Enlightenment thinkers denied this, asserting that humanity had no inherent propensity to sin but was naturally inclined to good. The evils in human society were due to ignorance, superstition, and entrenched political and religious authority. These could be overcome with proper education and freedom from superstition, dogmatic religion, and political tyranny. The most radical assertions were made by Jean-Jacques Rousseau, who argued that humans in a state of nature were naturally free and equal. His influential book *The Social Contract* (1764) begins with the ringing words, "Man was/is born free, and everywhere he is in chains" (Rousseau 1994, 131). It was the establishment of organized society itself, with its institution of private property, which was responsible for the inequality between persons: "The first person who, having fenced off a plot of ground, took it into his head to say *this is mine* and found people simple enough to believe him, was the true founder of civil society" (Rousseau 1992, 43).

This belief in the inherent goodness of humanity, in the power of reason, and in the advances of natural science led to an optimistic belief in progress. In Europe the greatest exponent of progress was the Marquis de Condorcet. He argued that the history of the past showed that the human race is moving to an ultimate perfection. The future would bring (1) equality among nations, (2) equality of freedom and rights among individuals, and (3) the indefinite perfectibility of human nature itself, intellectually, morally, and physically. Condorcet was hostile to all religion, to monarchy, and especially to Christianity. His optimism was based on his belief that the true system of the universe had been discovered by Newton and the true understanding of human nature by John Locke. Such progress in understanding, Condorcet thought, would continue and be spread by public education so as to elevate the whole race of humanity.

Not all thinkers were as optimistic as Condorcet was. Benjamin Franklin combined a faith in scientific progress with skepticism about moral progress:

The rapid progress true science now makes occasions my regretting sometimes that I was born too soon. It is impossible to imagine the height to which may be carried, in a thousand years, the power of man over matter. We may perhaps learn to deprive large masses of their gravity, and give them absolute levity, for the sake of easy transport. Agriculture may diminish its labor and double its produce; all diseases may by sure means be prevented or cured. . . . O that moral science were in as fair a way of improvement, that men would cease to be wolves to one another, and that human beings would at length learn what they now improperly call humanity!" (Cited in Mapp 2005, 36)

Freedom and Religious Toleration

Enlightenment thinkers were passionate advocates of liberty, by which they meant freedom from political and religious authoritarianism. It must be remembered that before the French Revolution (1789) France was still governed by kings and freedom of religious belief was largely unknown. The medieval idea, going back to Constantine, had been that religious unity was essential to the unity of a people and a country. Before the Enlightenment, this was accepted by both Catholics and Protestants, with the exception of a few groups, notably the Anabaptists (literally "rebaptizers," part of the Radical Reformation—see Chapter 19), and the Society of Friends, or Quakers. In France, Louis XIV in 1685 revoked the Edict of Nantes, which had granted religious liberty to Protestants. Thereafter, Protestants, atheists, and dissenters from Catholicism, the official religion imposed by the French king, could be punished by civil law. Even in England, dissenters from the "established," or national church, the Church of England (Anglican), were subject to various penalties until well into the nineteenth century. For example, they could not hold civil office or go to the universities. Nor was religious liberty universal in the United States until after the American Revolution and the signing of the U.S. Constitution, which were themselves the products of Enlightenment thought—see Chapter 23.

Enlightenment notions of political liberty derived largely from the seventeenth-century English thinker John Locke, who had maintained that governments derived their legitimacy from the consent of the governed. Rousseau, in France, also argued this. Although the Enlightenment philosophers were generally not proponents of democracy (recall Voltaire's views of the masses, previously stated), they did argue for republican forms of government, in which people govern themselves through elected representatives.

Ideas of religious freedom followed from the Enlightenment notion that the "natural religion" of humanity was a simple belief in God the creator, virtue, and the goodness and freedom of humanity. From this perspective wars over religious differences were scandalous and irrational and were essentially the result of religious authorities trying to force assent upon everyone. Enlightenment philosophers looked back on the religious wars of past centuries (for example, the French wars of religion, 1562 to 1598; the Thirty Years War in Germany, 1618 to 1648; and the English civil war, 1640 to 1660) as abominations. They argued that the kind of coercion practiced by most religious authorities destroyed free choice, which was the essence of religious commitment. As Diderot wrote,

> The mind can only acquiesce in what it accepts as true. The heart can only love what seems good to it. Violence will turn a man into a hypocrite if he is weak, and into a martyr if he is strong. . . . Teaching, persuasion, and prayer, these are the only legitimate means of spreading the faith. (Cited in Bokenkotter 1979, 270)

The Enlightenment quest for religious freedom achieved its fullest triumph in America, when freedom of religion was written into the Bill of Rights (see Chapter 23). Since the eighteenth century, freedom of religion has become generally accepted worldwide. The Second Vatican Council (1962–1965) issued a document declaring that all persons ought to enjoy freedom of religion (see Chapter 24).

CRITICISM OF THE ENLIGHTENMENT AND ITS AFTERMATH

The aftermath of the Enlightenment in France was the French Revolution (1789–1799), in which the ideas of Voltaire, Rousseau, and others were carried to extremes by radicals. The radicals instituted a reign of terror to enforce their demands, executing the king and queen of France and thousands of others by the guillotine. They also attempted to displace Christianity with a "religion of reason" and went so far as to enthrone a goddess of reason (played by an actress) on the high altar of Notre Dame Cathedral in Paris. In light of the French Revolution, the confidence of the Enlightenment in the goodness of humanity, progress, and the power of reason received understandable criticism. In England, the conservative reaction was voiced by Edmund Burke, who argued that the rationalism and skepticism of the Enlightenment thinkers had led to the wholesale destruction of social tradition and values.

Tradition, in Burke's analysis, was not just a result of political and religious repression; it was the repository of the wisdom of the race. Through tradition, what had worked well in the past was handed on to the future. This was particularly true of social values, which should not be lightly overthrown for untested, idealistic, and rationalist social schemes. The Catholic defense of tradition was similar. Religious tradition, while it might be deformed in some instances, is basically an accumulation of the insights and wisdom of the race in spiritual matters, and it ought to be received with respect, not rejected because it is "unscientific." The Romantic reaction, which dominated the nineteenth century, asserted that the excessive Enlightenment emphasis on reason had ignored the importance of mystery, wonder, beauty, and intuition in life. This reaction resulted in powerful Romantic movements in music, painting, and literature.

Again, the assumption of Enlightenment thinkers that reason alone could explain all of reality has been criticized as too exclusive. Are there not other types of knowledge, for example knowledge of another person, or mystical knowledge, or intuition of spiritual things, which go beyond reason, and know dimensions of reality that reason cannot explore? As the great French mathematician, scientist, and philosopher Blaise Pascal put it, "The heart has its reasons, which reason does not know" (*Pensées*, Section IV §277). Moreover, in the light of the savage dictatorships and wars of the twentieth century, sometimes called the bloodiest century in human history, many people have lost faith in the natural goodness of humanity and in the notion of unlimited progress.

Nonetheless, many of the Enlightenment ideas have become permanent fixtures of the modern world. Most persons today accept that religious choice ought not to be coerced and that diversity of religions should be tolerated. Most parties accept the basic Enlightenment idea that governments ought to rest on the consent of the governed and that humans have certain inalienable human rights. Even the skepticism engendered toward myth, miracles, the resurrection, and the supernatural has become a permanent part of modern life. The Enlightenment was also the first period in Western history when a large number of intellectuals became atheists and when atheism became intellectually respectable. This legacy is still with us.

The Enlightenment, then, marked the end of the centuries when the Christian church had uncontested moral and intellectual authority and when the church, allied with the state, could ensure (often by force) uniformity of religious belief in a given region or country. After the Enlightenment, Christianity has had to survive in an environment of denominational and religious diversity and in an atmosphere of increasing intellectual secularism and skepticism.

THE NINETEENTH CENTURY

In the vast and crowded canvas of the nineteenth century, we will focus on three significant movements: the challenge posed by liberalism, the problems created for Christianity by the theory of evolution, and the rise of scientific historical and biblical criticism.

Liberalism

Liberalism in the nineteenth century carried forward the Enlightenment ideas that humans were naturally good and free and that the source of their corruption was decadent social institutions. Therefore, liberals thought, the best atmosphere for human development was freedom: political freedom from kings, tyrants, a ruling class, and a national church, and economic freedom from government restrictions such as tariffs, price controls, and so on. Nineteenth-century liberals, especially in Europe, tended to be anti-Christian and anticlerical. Their goal was a complete separation of church and state and the foundation of autonomous secular nation-states, governed by representative democracies.

In Italy liberalism and nationalism inspired the *Risorgimento*, the movement to unite Italy as a secular state. A primary obstacle to unification was the Papal States, the large territory in central and northern Italy that the popes had governed directly since the eighth century. Fifty years of revolutions and wars culminated in 1870 in the capture and dissolution of the Papal States and the unification of Italy under King Victor Emmanuel II. In protest Pope Pius IX (reigned 1846–1878) went into seclusion as "the prisoner of the Vatican" and refused to recognize the new Italian state. The standoff lasted until 1929, when the Vatican signed the Lateran Treaties with Mussolini's Fascist government. All that would remain of the pope's temporal power is the Vatican City, a one-square-mile sovereign enclave in Rome governed by the pope and the curia (the administrative structure of the Catholic Church). Nineteenth-century popes resisted the loss of their state and in the process opposed all that liberalism stood for. This opposition was voiced forcefully by Pius IX in his 1864 encyclical *Quanta Cura* and its appendix, known as the *Syllabus of Errors*, which condemned fundamental liberal doctrines, such as the separation of church and state and religious freedom. The Catholic Church did not substantially change this position until the *Declaration on Religious Freedom* was proclaimed at Vatican II in 1965.

Economic liberalism, or the doctrine of *laissez faire* (a French phrase meaning roughly "let people act alone"), is the doctrine that there should be no interference by the state in the free market. Economic liberalism rested on the assumption that there are certain natural laws of economic production and distribution (precisely analogous to the physical laws which govern the universe) that, if not interfered with, will naturally produce wealth, reward the industrious, and punish the indolent. The doctrine of economic liberalism was set out in Adam Smith's classic *Wealth of Nations*. There Smith argued that individuals, in pursuing their own self-interest, are led by the action of an "invisible hand" to also promote the public or common good.

In practice, pure *laissez-faire* capitalism led to horrendous injustices: child labor in factories and mines, sixteen-hour workdays, dangerous working conditions, no provision for sickness, accidents, or retirement—in short, extreme exploitation of workers by owners, as well as environmental degradation. One response to this was the socialism developed by Karl Marx and others. Another response, more common in the West, has been the development of labor unions, as well as laws that regulate child labor, demand worker compensation for job-related injuries, limit the length of workdays and workweeks, impose work safety standards, and limit environmental damage. The only examples of unregulated economies now are in Third World countries, where worker exploitation and environmental damage continues.

The Catholic Church opposed and continues to oppose unrestricted economic liberalism. Popes from Leo XIII (reigned 1878–1903) to John Paul II (reigned 1978– 2005) have written extensively on this question. While the church insists on the right of individuals to own private property, so as to support families, it also insists on the limitation of the free market by provisions for the common good. As John Paul II puts it, there is a "social mortgage" on private property. The rights of property owners are not absolute but are to be balanced by the rights of the larger community, including the rights of workers, such as the right to earn a living wage. The exact nature of this balance continues to be a matter of extensive debate. John Paul II in particular produced a large body of commentary on questions of economic and social justice; see especially his encyclical letters *Laborem Exercens* ("On Human Work," 1981), *Sollicitudo Rei Socialis* ("On Social Concern," 1988), *Centesimus Annus* ("On the Hundredth Anniversary," 1991), and *Evangelium Vitae* ("The Gospel of Life," 1995).

The Theory of Evolution

Although many of the church fathers (for example, Augustine) were open to a symbolic interpretation of the stories in Genesis 1–11, by early modern times it was held by both Catholics and Protestants that Genesis 1–11 was a historically accurate account of the creation of the world and humanity. In the seventeenth century Anglican Bishop James Ussher, using only biblical data (such as the ages of Adam and his descendants), put the creation of the earth at 4004 B.C. Following Genesis, all species were thought to have been created directly by God in their present form, during the first six days of creation.

During the eighteenth and nineteenth centuries, however, the science of geology gradually developed. By the early 1800s geologists realized that the major features of the earth (mountains, valleys, etc.) had been shaped, not suddenly by catastrophes like Noah's flood, but by very gradual processes, such as creation of sedimentary rocks by deposit of sediment in ancient oceans, the uplifting of rocks to form mountains, and erosion. Since the rate of change brought about by these processes is extremely slow, geologists reasoned that the earth had to be much older than the Genesis account indicates.

In 1859 **Charles Darwin** published his epochal book *On the Origin of Species by Means of Natural Selection*. Here, Darwin brought together an enormous mass of evidence and offered a simple, plausible explanation for the emergence of species by natural processes alone, rather than by the miraculous creation of God. This explanation is known as the theory of **evolution**. All living species, he argued, are made up of members that have individual

Figure 22–2 The cover of *Punch's Almanak for 1882* is a satirical cartoon criticizing Darwin's theory of evolution and raising the question about what it means to be made "in the image of God."

variations. Also, all species overpopulate, so that only some—those individuals whose physical traits are best adapted to the environment—survive. Since only the survivors leave progeny, the offspring will carry the physical traits of their parents, while the traits of those who do not survive will die out. Thus, over many generations, traits that are advantageous in a particular environment will develop in the species, while disadvantageous traits will be eliminated from the population.

Gradually, this transformation of the character of individuals in a species will lead to the development of new species. Thus, for example, in a population of horselike animals, some individuals in each generation are born with longer than average necks: These individuals can eat leaves on trees that short-necked individuals cannot reach. Therefore they will tend to survive in the struggle for existence and leave more progeny. This process, repeated over thousands of generations, would lead to a long-necked species of horse—the giraffe, which eats leaves from acacia trees that shorter-necked animals cannot reach. It should be noted that animal breeders have practiced these same principles for centuries.

Darwin did not invent the notion of evolution; what he did was provide a simple explanation of its mechanism. There were three elements to this explanation: (1) random variation among individuals, (2) a struggle for existence, so that only some survive, and (3) **natural selection**, that is, the principle that over generations, certain traits are "selected" for survival, while other traits perish (this has been called the "survival of the fittest"). In addition, he accumulated a huge amount of evidence in favor of the theory.

On the Origin of Species made an immediate, powerful, and lasting impact: The first edition of 1,250 copies sold out in one day. Although met with vigorous opposition from scientists as well as churchmen, Darwin's ideas eventually triumphed; the theory of the emergence of species by gradual evolution has become accepted as fact in almost all intellectual circles. Probably no single idea so decisively separates modern from premodern times as the idea of evolution.

In 1871, Darwin published *The Descent of Man*, in which he argued that human beings, like other animals, emerged from animal ancestors and were not miraculously created by God. This was taken as attacking the Christian belief that humans are made in God's image, that they have a spiritual soul, intellect, and free will, and that humans therefore differ from animals in *kind*, not just in *degree*. Rather, one could argue from Darwin that humans are made in the image of their animal ancestor and therefore differ from animals only in degree: Humans are like apes, only with a larger brain and the ability to use language. Thus, with Darwin, the modern scientific attempt to explain all phenomena by natural causes alone was extended to the creation of humanity also. Darwin himself, once an Anglican Christian, lost his faith as a result of his own theory.

Darwin's ideas are incompatible with a literal reading of Genesis 1–3. Thus, a battle emerged between those who defended Darwin and those who argued that Genesis, being the revealed word of God, had to be right and Darwin had to be wrong. From about 1895 to 1920, evangelical Protestant churches (for example, Baptists and Presbyterians) split between those who accepted evolution and those who rejected it. Those who rejected it—called Fundamentalists, because they thought of themselves as upholding the fundamentals of Christianity—in many cases separated from their parent denominations. Many evangelical Christian denominations, such as the Southern Baptists, today reject the teaching of evolution. In some cases, evolution is not being taught in public schools because of pressure from antievolutionist groups. This pressure exists even to the present day.

A qualified Catholic acceptance of the theory of evolution came in 1950, when Pope Pius XII, in his encyclical *Humani Generis* ("On the Human Race"), cautiously acknowledged that the process by which the human body may have emerged "from pre-existent and living matter" was a fit subject of scientific investigation. The human soul, on the other hand, must be recognized as having been created directly by God (1950, §36). In 1996, Pope John Paul II repeated this view and went on to describe evolution as "more than an hypothesis":

> Today, more than a half-century after the appearance of that encyclical [*Humani Generis*], some new findings lead us toward the recognition of evolution as more than an hypothesis. In fact it is remarkable that this theory has had progressively greater influence on the spirit of researchers, following a series of discoveries in different scholarly disciplines. The convergence in the results of these independent studies—which was neither planned nor sought—constitutes in itself a significant argument in favor of the theory. (John Paul II 1996, 352)

Catholic theologians thus agree that Genesis 1–11 contains spiritual and theological truth about God and humanity but recognize that it was not intended to be a scientific account of human origins.

Many apologists for modern evolutionary theory argue that evolutionary theory is sufficient to explain the whole process of creation by natural causes alone and that no God or transcendent causes exist. This view is contrary to Catholic teaching about creation. Most Catholic theologians maintain that God creates the world and humanity through the process of evolution, an idea known as "theistic evolution." Whereas Genesis tells us *who* created the world, the theory of evolution tells us *how* it was created. Theistic evolution is also strongly defended by some prominent biologists, for example Kenneth Miller (see his book *Finding Darwin's God)* and Francis Collins, the Director of the Human Genome Project (see his book *The Language of God).*

Scientific History

Though an analytical approach to historical texts had already developed during the Renaissance, in the nineteenth century the notion of a truly scientific history emerged, "scientific" insofar as it aimed to be as objective as the natural sciences, on which it was modeled. Premodern historians told their historical stories with a view to teaching moral lessons. For example, the Roman historian Sallust describes the decline of the Roman Republic and the rise of the Roman Empire (in which the people were ruled by dictators) as due to a loss of public virtue and morality, and the rise of corruption due to the love of wealth and power. Ancient historians also depicted historical events as controlled by supernatural as well as natural causes. The biblical book of the Acts of the Apostles, for example, sees the expansion of the early Christian church as due to the power of the Holy Spirit, which inspires the apostles, works miracles through them, and converts their hearers. Finally, ancient historians tended to repeat the words of other historians without checking their veracity.

Scientific history, which emerged first in Germany, changed many of the practices of premodern history. First, scientific history sought to eliminate the biases and values judgments of the author from the telling of history. These modern historians wished to describe history "as it actually was." Second, it became axiomatic for them (as for all modern scientists) to assume that past events were controlled by the same forces that control present-day events and that these forces were natural, not supernatural. Thus, modern historians, even if Christian, would probably not describe the expansion of the early church as due to the Holy Spirit. Instead they would focus on natural causes, such as the state of society, economics, the power of Christian enthusiasm and the example of Christian witness in the face of death, and the superiority of Christian morality and social welfare systems. Finally, scientific historians did not accept the work of earlier historians uncritically (as the ancients often did); they sought to verify the data by returning to primary sources, such as archival records, contemporary accounts, and letters and to inform the reader of these sources by footnote citations and bibliography.

This scientific view of history was modeled on the natural sciences, especially Darwin's theory of evolution, which explained the past in terms of natural causes only. This in turn has had an incalculable influence on our modern view of the world. In both scholarly and popular writing events are typically explained by social, economic, political, psychological, or other causes. There is usually no reference to God's action or providence, because the scientific mindset is skeptical of ascribing the cause of events to supernatural activity. The scientific view of history has therefore been a major shaper of the modern secular and antisupernatural view of the world.

Scientific Biblical Criticism

The scientific view of history in turn led to a scientific and historical approach to interpreting the Bible. Biblical scholars of the nineteenth and twentieth centuries increasingly treated the Bible like any other book, subjecting it to scientific scrutiny and asking if the events it records can be verified historically the same way that other historical facts are verified. In addition, the developing science of archaeology was unearthing the records of ancient cultures contemporary with biblical cultures, and these records affected the interpretation of biblical stories.

In the centuries since the death of Christ, both the Old and New Testaments had been understood as inspired by God. The primary author of the texts was thought to be the Holy Spirit. This view was and is shared by both Christians and Jews. However, the notion of how inspiration took place was somewhat naive: The Holy Spirit was thought to have dictated the words of scripture to the ancient author. If that were the case, the Bible should be factually accurate in all respects. This view came to be substantially modified by the new biblical criticism, as the following example suggests.

In the late nineteenth century, the developing science of archeology began unearthing texts of great relevance to the Bible. The British excavations of the great library of Assurbanipal in Nineveh, the capital of ancient Assyria, were particularly important. Archeologists discovered cuneiform texts that told the Babylonian myth of creation—the *Enuma Elish*—which had apparently served as a model for the authors of Genesis, and an ancient flood story (the *Epic of Gilgamesh*) with a hero like Noah, which again seemed to have been a model for the biblical story of Noah and the flood. The fact that the creation and flood stories in Genesis seem to have been influenced by earlier Babylonian accounts conflicts with the idea that the only influence on the biblical authors was the voice of the Holy Spirit.

Other excavations in Palestine itself, in Egypt, and in other Near Eastern lands have greatly increased our knowledge of the cultures and peoples contemporary with the biblical authors. As a result, it is now possible to read the biblical stories with a much better knowledge of the contexts in which they were written. This improved knowledge of the original context is now seen as the first condition for recovering the original and intended meaning of a biblical text, insofar as that is possible at all. Along with the rise of modern natural science, this has led to a different understanding of the ancient texts, and hence of the meaning of inspiration. Genesis 1–11, for example, is read as a mythical account of origins, similar to the creation myths of Israel's ancient neighbors, such as the Babylonians and Egyptians. It is not scientifically or historically accurate but nevertheless conveys permanent spiritual truths about God and humanity through symbolic stories, such as the stories of the creation, the Fall, and the flood.

But this view of inspiration has been fiercely resisted by many groups of Christians. As mentioned above, fundamentalist Christians insist that the biblical accounts are *literally inerrant*. The fundamentalist view is that every part of the Bible is historically and scientifically accurate, including the parts about the origin of the world and human beings (note that this would seem to entail that the sun goes around the earth, as Galileo's opponents thought). These groups reject evolution, but they also reject modern biblical criticism, because they believe that it undermines Christian revelation. Fundamentalist approaches to the bible are discussed in more detail in Chapter 23.

KARL MARX AND MARXISM

Karl Marx, the founder of Marxian socialism, lived from 1818 to 1883, but the influence of Marxism was felt mainly in the twentieth century. Marx's core idea was that economic conditions determine history, and that history was marked by perpetual class conflict. In any age, what Marx called the economic "mode of production" determines the ruling class, and the ruling class in turn determines the dominant ideas of the age. So, for example, in a feudal mode of production, the ruling class was the aristocratic landlords, who stressed the ruling ideas such as social hierarchy and fealty (fidelity to one's lord). In a capitalist mode of production, the ruling class are those who control the capital, and the ruling ideas concerned freedom of enterprise (i.e., economic liberalism; see the previous section on liberalism). Marx thought that the capitalist mode of production would give way, by means of violent revolution, to another mode of production, namely socialism, in which workers owned the capital. This would be a classless society, in which workers would wrest control from the capitalist overlords and the means of production would be communally rather than privately owned. Marx first laid out these ideas in his 1848 pamphlet *The Communist Manifesto*, which ends with the words, "Workingmen of all countries, unite!" These ideas are also addressed in his great work on economics entitled *Capital*, the first volume of which appeared in 1867 and was finished after his death by his collaborators.

Marx's ideas, which form the core of modern communism, presented a grave threat to Christianity, although they also opened the door to some needed self-criticism. He assumed that history is governed by simple economic forces, in the same way that nineteenth-century scientists thought matter was governed by simple forces like gravity. Marx did not think there was any divine or spiritual influence in history. Though religion could sometimes appear to be, in his words, "the heart of a heartless world," in reality it was only the "opium of the people," a drug which kept the lower classes passive and resigned in their economic oppression. When that oppression was removed, he theorized, religion would wither away, because people would be fulfilled and would no longer need the false consolations of religion. Modern Christianity has had to develop many types of response to this powerful criticism; some of these responses have been more adequate than others (see Chapters 24 and 25). Most importantly, Marxism has forced Christians to show how Christianity *contributes* to human emancipation and autonomy, rather than *subverting* it. Christians have had to show that Christianity was not a religion that encouraged the poor to resign themselves passively to their fate.

Marx's vision of a workers' paradise proved to be powerfully attractive in countries like Russia and China, which traditionally had been controlled by an elite class, resulting in oppression of the workers and peasants. Even today, one can see the extravagant luxury enjoyed by the Russian aristocracy in their palaces, especially Peterhof, the enormous palace of the tsar (the Russian word for "king", derived from Latin *Caesar*) in St. Petersburg. During the Russian revolution (1917–1921), Marxian communists gained control of Russia. They immediately set about creating a communist society in which most private property, including farmland, was taken over by the state, churches were seized, and religion was controlled or driven underground. Unfortunately for Russia, communism had no system of checks and balances on power, and from the time of Lenin political authority was wielded by a series of brutal dictatorships. Though Christianity was not officially outlawed, the Russian Orthodox Church and other Christians were ruthlessly persecuted and Russian students were taught a system of Marxist materialism that ridiculed Christian belief. Despite occasional periods of toleration, such as the national crisis provoked by the German invasion in World War II, this oppression lasted until the collapse of the Union of Soviet Socialist Republics in 1989. Though deeply infiltrated during the Soviet period, the Orthodox Church survived, and Christianity is returning to life in Russia. Nevertheless, decades of official atheism have left their mark on Russian society and will not disappear soon.

Other countries also became communist during the twentieth century, notably China, Eastern Europe, North Korea, North Vietnam, and Cuba. Recently, however, China, while remaining nominally communist, has prospered under a capitalist economic system and become a powerful force in the global economy. And Christianity is growing rapidly in China, though the Chinese government keeps strict control of Christian churches, persecuting those that are not approved by the communist party. The officially tolerated version of Catholicism, called the Chinese Patriotic Catholic Association, is not at present in communion with the Roman Catholic Church. The strongest remaining bastions of Communist ideology today are North Korea and Cuba.

Ironically enough, though Marx emphasized that economic conditions determine history, Marxism itself dramatically illustrates the power of ideas to shape history. Marxism triumphed in Russia and China not because the economic mode of production had progressed through capitalism to socialism, but because of the great appeal of its utopian vision of a classless workers paradise, in which there would be no inequality. This was summed up in the slogan: "From each according to his abilities, to each according to his need." This ideal was similar to that of the early church (see the Acts of the Apostles 2:44–45 and 4:32–37) in which property was shared in common. Many scholars have noted that Marxism seems to be a kind of inverted and materialistic substitute for Christianity. Like Christianity it visualized a paradisal state at the end of history. Unlike Christianity, it did not rely on God but attempted to bring about this state through economic and political force. Instead of the triumph of divine justice in a transcendent world beyond death, Marxism expected the triumph of justice *within* the historical process. Instead of a divine–human Messiah dying a vicarious atoning death and rising from the dead, Marxism expected that a collective human messiah, the workers, would triumph in a successful and irreversible revolution. Critics of Marxist Leninism, the version of communism that came to power in Russia and elsewhere, have often noted how it functioned as a substitute for religion, as a kind of *political* religion, with its own heresies, schisms, founding scriptures, prophets, hierarchical authorities, shrines, relics, holy days, and cult of the dead.

CONCLUSION

The modern challenge to Christianity has largely been driven by modern science, whose methods have been adopted by one field after another. The goal of the scientific method is to explain events and phenomena in nature (including human beings) by causes that can be experimentally tested and measured. Supernatural causes, such as God, are not part of scientific explanations. Scientific method does not rule out the possibility of supernatural realities, but because its method focuses on what can be tested and measured, such realities fall outside its scope. However, because of the great success of the scientific method in explaining nature, some people assume that there are no supernatural realities, given that scientific knowledge about them is impossible. Such critics take for granted that science has demonstrated that the natural order is all that exists. As astronomer Carl Sagan once put it: "The universe is all that is, all there ever was, and all that ever will be" (1980, 4). This assumption is called philosophical materialism or philosophical naturalism; it assumes that only matter and nature are real, and that therefore there is no God, no angels, no souls, and no afterlife. But this assumption is not genuinely scientific—it cannot itself be demonstrated by scientific experiments. It is actually a *philosophical* assertion, and proving it or disproving it entails *philosophical* arguments about what human reason can actually know (what philosophers call epistemology) and what is the basis of reality (what philosophers call metaphysics). Such arguments are outside the domain of scientific method in the proper sense of the word. When philosophical materialism dresses up as science rather than philosophy, it would be more accurate to call it **scientism**, meaning that it functions more like an ideology than like real science.

Fundamental to Christianity (and all other religions) is the belief that reality is comprised of both material (physical) and spiritual dimensions. There need be no conflict between science and Christianity if it is recognized that scientific methods are valid for investigation of material reality, while revelation, faith, and theology are valid means of discovering truths about spiritual reality. Certainly there are many areas of overlap. An example is investigation of the human person, in whom there are physical aspects, explored by disciplines such as biochemistry, but also spiritual aspects (such as free will, the soul, and grace), explored by philosophy and theology. In such areas a full understanding can be had only by recourse to many disciplines, scientific, philosophical, and theological.

Problems arise when either theology (as in the Galileo case) or science oversteps its legitimate boundaries and claims to have answers that pertain to another discipline. Fortunately, in recent decades an exciting and fruitful dialogue has developed between science and theology. Some scientists are writing books on theology, and many theologians are incorporating science into their theology. In many ways, theology and science are closer now than at any time since Darwin. Like any other challenge, the challenge of science to Christianity has been difficult but also offers great opportunity.

Key Terms

cosmology	Deism	natural selection
Nicholas Copernicus	rationalism	Karl Marx
Galileo Galilei	anticlericalism	scientism
Isaac Newton	Charles Darwin	
René Descartes	evolution	

Questions for Reading

1. What seems to be the most basic value recognized by human beings in the modern period? What are two possible interpretations that modern Christianity has given of this fundamental value?

2. What was "new" about the scientific method of the scientific revolution, how did it change the way human beings thought about the natural world, and why was this a challenge to traditional Christianity?

3. What was Deism, and did it differ from Christianity?

4. Explain what is meant by the Enlightenment and by the rationalism of the Enlightenment. Why was it such a challenge to traditional Christianity?

5. Explain the disagreement between Enlightenment philosophers such as Condorcet and traditional Christianity on the subject of human nature and progress. Which side do you think was right? Why?

6. Why did Enlightenment thinkers insist so strongly on freedom of religion? What did they see as opposed to religious freedom?

7. Describe the aftermath of the Enlightenment. What criticisms have been leveled against Enlightenment thought? What facets of Enlightenment thought have become widely accepted?

8. Explain the beliefs of (a) liberalism and (b) economic liberalism. How did Pope John Paul II criticize economic liberalism?

9. Why was the theory of evolution seen as a challenge to traditional Christian belief? How do Catholic theologians deal with this challenge? Explain the idea of theistic evolution.

10. How does scientific history differ from older forms of history? In what way has it been a major shaper of a secular view of the world?

11. Explain scientific biblical criticism. How has it changed the Catholic and many Protestant views of Genesis 1–11?

12. What kinds of criticism does Marxism make of religion? What is the most significant way in which Marxism has offered a *constructive* criticism to Christianity? Finally, in what ways could Marxian communism, as it developed in Russia for instance, be described as a pseudo-religion or a political religion?

Works Consulted/Recommended Reading

Barbour, Ian. *Religion and Science: Historical and Contemporary Issues*. San Francisco: Harper and Row, 1997.

Bokenkotter, Thomas. *A Concise History of the Catholic Church*. Rev. ed. New York: Doubleday, Image, 1979.

Church, F. Forrester, ed., *The Jefferson Bible*. Boston: Beacon, 1989.

Collins, Francis. *The Language of God*. New York: Free Press, 2006.

Cragg, Gerald. *The Church and the Age of Reason*. Rev. ed. Harmondsworth, England: Penguin, 1974.

Gaustad, Edwin S. *Faith of Our Fathers*. San Francisco: Harper and Row, 1987.

Gay, Peter. *The Enlightenment: An Interpretation*. New York: Random House, 1966.

Griffith, Bede. *The Cosmic Revelation: The Hindu Way to God*. Springfield, IL: Templegate, 1983.

Hallowell, J. H. "Liberalism." In *New Catholic Encyclopedia*, 8 (1967) 701–706.

Hume, David. *An Enquiry Concerning Human Understanding and Other Writings*. Cambridge Texts in the History of Philosophy. Edited by Stephen Buckle. New York: Cambridge University, 2007.

John Paul II. "Lessons of the Galileo Case." *Origins* 22 (1992) 369–373.

_____. "Message to Pontifical Academy of Sciences on Evolution." *Origins* 26 (1996) 350–352.

Kant, Immanuel. *Foundations of the Metaphysics of Morals and What Is Enlightenment?* Translated by Lewis White Beck. New York: Macmillan, 1990.

Langford, Jerome J. *Galileo, Science, and the Church*. Rev. ed. Ann Arbor: University of Michigan, 1971.

Mapp, Alf J. Jr. *The Faiths of Our Fathers: What America's Founders Really Believed*. Oxford, England: Rowman and Littlefield, 2005.

Miller, Kenneth. *Finding Darwin's God*. New York: HarperCollins, 1999.

New Catholic Encyclopedia. New York: McGraw-Hill, 1967.

Pascal, Blaise. *The Provincial Letters, Pensées, Scientific Treatises*. Great Books of the Western World, Vol. 33. Chicago: Encyclopaedia Britannica, 1952.

Pius XII. *Humani Generis. Encyclical Letter of Pope Pius XII, Concerning Some False Opinions Which Threaten to Undermine the Foundations of Catholic Doctrine*. Washington, DC: National Catholic Welfare Conference, 1950.

Polkinghorne, John. *Belief in God in the Age of Science.* New Haven, CT: Yale University, 1998.

Rousseau, Jean-Jacques. *Social Contract, Discourse on the Virtue Most Necessary For a Hero, Political Fragments, and Geneva Manuscript.* Collected Writings of Rousseau, Vol. 4. Edited by Roger D. Masters and Christopher Kelly; translated by Judith R. Bush, et al Vol. 4. Hanover, NH: University Press of New England, 1994.

_____. *Discourse on the Origins of Inequality (Second Discourse), Polemics, and Political Economy.* Collected Writings of Rousseau, Vol. 4. Edited by Roger D. Masters and Christopher Kelly; translated by Judith R. Bush, et al Vol. 4. Hanover, NH: University Press of New England, 1992.

Sagan, Carl. *Cosmos.* New York: Random House, 1980.

Schönfeld, Martin. "Kant's Philosophical Development." In Zalta, Edward N., ed. *Stanford Encyclopedia of Philosophy,* January 2007 edition. http//plato.stanford.edu/entires/kant-development.

Chapter

23

CHRISTIANITY IN AMERICA

TIMELINE

A.D. 1607	The Jamestown settlement in the colony of Virginia is established.
A.D. 1620	The Puritans, including both Presbyterians and Congregationalists, arrive on the Mayflower and establish a colony at Plymouth in Massachusetts.
c. A.D. 1650	Lutherans from Germany, Austria, and the Netherlands begin to migrate to America.
A.D. 1682	William Penn founds the Pennsylvania colony as a haven for the Religious Society of Friends, also known as the Quakers.
A.D. 1718	The French Catholic settlement of New Orleans is established.
c. A.D. 1740	The Great Awakening spreads throughout New England and the other British colonies. The beginning of the rise of denominationalism in the United States.
A.D. 1784	The Methodist Episcopal Church is established in the Americas.
A.D. 1787	Richard Allen leads a protest of Negro Methodists in Philadelphia, which eventually led to the establishment of the African Methodist-Episcopal (A.M.E.) Church.
A.D. 1789	John Carroll is chosen to be the first American Catholic bishop.
A.D. 1830	Joseph Smith establishes the Church of Jesus Christ of Latter-Day Saints, also known as the Mormons.
c. A.D. 1860	William Miller establishes the Seventh-Day Adventist church in the United States.
c. A.D. 1872	Charles Taze Russell establishes the International Bible Students Association, later known as the Jehovah's Witnesses.
c. A.D. 1906	Pentecostal churches begin to emerge out of a variety of interdenominational revivalist churches in America.

Christianity has left a deep imprint on America's laws, its politics, its moral values, its educational system, its social relations, its wars, and its foreign policy. That is true of the past and, despite increasing secularization and religious diversity, it remains true today. More than three-fourths of adult Americans still claim Christianity as their religion (Kosmin, Mayer, and Keysar 2001). But the United States is also the first state in the Christian tradition to have effected a legal separation from Christianity, indeed, from any official national religion. This separation is epitomized in the First Amendment to the Constitution of the United States.

CHURCH AND STATE ACCORDING TO THE FIRST AMENDMENT

The First Amendment to the Constitution was ratified in 1791, and it reads as follows: "Congress shall make no law respecting an establishment of religion, or prohibiting the free exercise thereof." Neither the Supreme Court nor legions of commentators have managed to agree on how those words should be understood. One school of thought, sometimes called **strict separationism**, holds that the First Amendment erected "a wall of separation between church and state" (even though this phrase originated not in the Constitution but in a letter of Thomas Jefferson's). People who hold this view argue that government should make no acknowledgement of religion, which must be kept out of the public square as much as possible and confined to a totally private and voluntary sphere. The Constitution never mentions God, they note, and its only reference to religion is the stipulation in Article VI that "no religious test for office" shall be required of holders of office in the national government.

Others, however, argue that strict separationism actually establishes **secularism** ("the religion of no religion at all," they would say) as the public religion and that the founders never intended such a thoroughgoing secularization of public life. People who hold this view point to historical documents such as the Constitutional Convention's Northwest Ordinance of 1787, Article 3 of which states: "Religion, morality, and knowledge, being necessary to good government and the happiness of mankind, schools and the means of education shall forever be encouraged." They also note that the First Amendment originally applied only to the national government; it was not applied to the states for another century and a half. Therefore, they believe, government is free within certain limits to *accommodate* religious belief and practice, so long as one religion is not privileged over another. As Justice William O. Douglas wrote in a 1952 Supreme Court opinion defending the constitutionality of "released time" (releasing children from public school to receive religious education at a religiously affiliated institution), "We are a religious people whose institutions presuppose a Supreme Being . . . ."

Regardless of which of these two interpretations of the First Amendment is more correct, both of them recognize that the United States had embarked on something decisively new, what Thomas Jefferson called a "fair experiment:"

> We have solved by fair experiment, the great and interesting question whether freedom of religion is compatible with order in government, and obedience to the laws. And we have experienced the quiet as well as the comfort which results from leaving everyone to profess freely and openly those principles of religion which are the inductions of his own reason, and the serious convictions of his own inquiries. (Cited in Mead 1963, 59)

The new nation was in fact reversing what had been two nearly universal assumptions going back to the fourth century, when Constantine converted to Christianity and the Roman emperor struck an alliance with the Christian church: on the one hand, that the stability and well-being of a state required religious uniformity among its people; on the other hand, that Christianity required and was best served by legal establishment.

This chapter consists of three parts: first, an overview of the development of Protestantism in America, noting the diversity of new churches which have come into being here and the emergence of what has been called a "two-party system" among American Protestants; second, an account of how Catholicism, mainly a European transplant, has adapted itself to American conditions; and third, a description of how America itself has been understood in religious terms, and the implications that this understanding has had for Christianity.

PROTESTANTISM IN AMERICA

The United States is not only Christian, it is a mainly *Protestant* Christian nation. More than half of all adults, according to the 2001 CUNY survey cited previously, identify themselves with Protestant Christianity. That is how this nation began and how it still is, despite the great increase of religious pluralism since Protestant hegemony was first challenged by Catholic immigration in the nineteenth-century. For about the first half of the nation's history, Protestants maintained a broad consensus about America, which they envisioned as a virtual "evangelical empire"—separation of church and state notwithstanding. Since about 1900, however, Protestants have split into two camps over how they see their faith in relation to America as a whole.

The word *evangelical* can mean several things. In the broadest sense, it means, "having to do with the gospel or the Bible." It has also been used as a synonym for *Protestant*, which is what the word meant for most of American history and how it is used in the phrase *evangelical empire.* However, since the fundamentalist–modernist controversy of the early twentieth century (see the following section entitled "Fundamentalism and Christian Protest Against Modernity"), it has come to mean more traditional forms of Protestant Christianity, which stand in contrast to churches that are accused of having gone too far in accommodating modernity. The slogan of the National Association of Evangelicals, "Cooperation without Compromise," expresses that spirit of resistance. Finally, it often refers specifically to born-again Christianity in the revivalist sense. Care should be taken to distinguish the term *evangelical* from *fundamentalist.* The two terms overlap but are by no means synonymous.

Birthright Churches from the Colonial Period

In the colonial period, the original English colonies were dominated by churches from Great Britain. In New England were the Congregationalists (commonly called Puritans), whose Holy Commonwealths, as they styled them, were to be the model for reforming the Church of England back home. From Virginia Southwards was the established Church of England, or Anglicans (they renamed themselves Episcopalians after American independence made loyalty to King George III impossible), to whose control Maryland and New York later fell.

The middle colonies claimed a variety of churches, notably William Penn's original experiment in religious liberty in his Quaker colony of Pennsylvania, where Baptists, Lutherans, Mennonites, Catholics and Jews were also free to settle. Presbyterians (ecclesiastical cousins of the Congregationalists; see Chapter 19) were scattered from New York

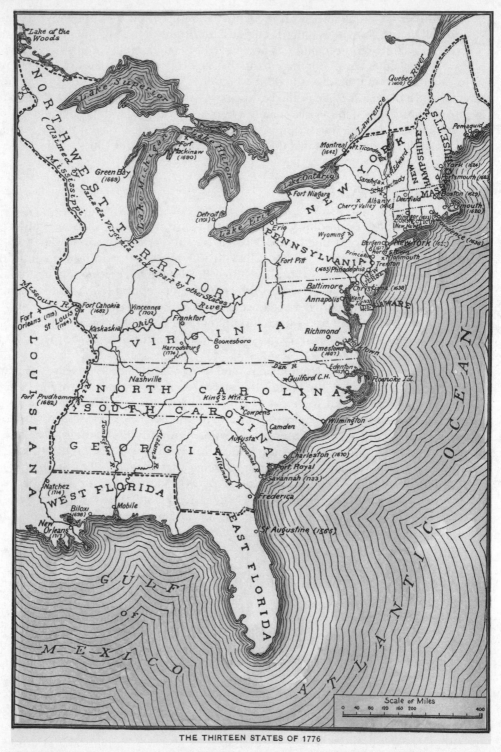

THE THIRTEEN STATES OF 1776

Figure 23–1 The thirteen English colonies and the French explorations and settlements to the west.

through the Shenandoah Valley of Virginia and into the south. Baptists also settled in Roger Williams' enclave of dissenters in tiny Rhode Island. Reformed (Calvinist) Christians in New York were reminders of that colony's Dutch origin as New Amsterdam. And once John Wesley's reforming movement withdrew from the Church of England in 1784, the Methodists, too, joined the spectrum as a distinct church.

Because the previously named churches were already introduced in our treatment of the Protestant Reformation (see Chapters 18–19), the present discussion will focus on new developments in America. It is enough to say that, for all their diversity, the British transplants to the colonies share a common birthright or sense of entitlement where America's spiritual identity and welfare are concerned. These churches and their numerous American offspring have always shown a special sense of responsibility for American life as a whole, because, from their point of view, they were there at the conception and birthing of the new nation. They did not see this birthright as contradicting the First Amendment, because for them religious disestablishment did not entail total public secularization. America was still substantially a Christian, indeed Protestant nation.

Throughout the nineteenth-century, churches shared a moral duty or obligation, a form of public service, and a basic consensus about how to make America into a "righteous empire," a beacon to the world. They were the original WASPs (White Anglo-Saxon Protestants), though many were actually Scottish, Irish, or Welsh. Today, however, American Protestants are bitterly divided over how to exercise their historic custodial responsibility, and a kind of two-party system has emerged—the modernists and the fundamentalists, as explained in the following sections.

The Denominational System: Democracy, Revivalism, and New Churches

The number of different Christian churches made it a foregone conclusion that the new United States of America would not have a national church, since no church could make a credible claim of majority support. There was also a widespread feeling that religion prospered more in conditions of religious freedom than of state establishment. As a result, even churches that were accustomed to state support gradually learned to survive without it. With the passage of the United States' Bill of Rights, the federal government got out of the religion business. It "deregulated" religion, so to speak. The result, naturally, was new churches in an endless proliferation that shows no sign of stopping.

Religious entrepreneurship was made all the more explosive by the democratic ethos that spread throughout America in the decades after the Revolution. Christianity itself became democratized as never before, once ordinary people were told that every individual person should be "considered as possessing in himself or herself an original right to believe and speak as their own conscience, between themselves and God, may determine" (the words of a preacher in 1806, as cited in Wood 1997 194–195, 1997). In short, every man (and eventually every woman) is his own interpreter of scripture.

The new religious configuration that resulted from this momentous change is called **denominationalism**. One definition of *denomination* is "a voluntary association of like-minded and like-hearted individuals, who are united on the basis of common beliefs for the purpose of accomplishing tangible and defined objectives" (Mead 1963, 104). In a denominational system, the various churches accept the separation of church and state and the right of religious freedom. They also agree to live and let live. The denominations are understood simply to be different—and, some would argue, equally valid—ways of being

Christian and of naming Christian communities. In return for religious freedom, they agree to support democratic government and the basic goodness of the American way of life.

Defenders of denominationalism say it broadens personal choice and has ensured the vitality and adaptability of churches in the United States, where church attendance and involvement are much higher than in European countries with histories of religious establishment. Critics of denominationalism (and the democratic, voluntary principles underlying it) say it treats believers like consumers and the faith like a product, muzzles true religious debate, and turns churches into conformist look-alikes. Churches and movements that do not endorse denominationalism or that resist giving their support to mainstream American values tend to become marginalized, and sometimes condemned, as sects.

A further ingredient in the new denominational system was the spread of **revivalism**, or born-again Christianity, which is based on the experience of a personal conversion to Jesus Christ as one's Lord and savior. American Protestants who today identify themselves as evangelical are likely to have had a born-again experience. In the nineteenth-century, revivalism became almost generic in American Protestantism. However, its ultimate origins are in the seventeenth-century European religious movement called **pietism**. European Pietists had sought to renew the Protestant Reformation by turning passive conformity or indifference into a lively, effective, and heartfelt faith. They tried to promote a warm and personal relationship to Jesus through Bible study, prayer, works of charity, and supportive membership in small Christian communities.

Though usually very conservative in their beliefs, Pietists avoided divisive discussions about religious doctrine. They preferred to work within existing churches rather than create new ones. And yet they have left a permanent mark on Christianity. Anyone who has ever been part of a prayer or bible study group stands in a historical chain that goes back to pietism.

Methodism and Its Revivalist Offspring

In England, pietism had its greatest impact on the reforming movement of John Wesley, the Anglican priest whose own conversion had occurred in 1738, while visiting a Pietist group called the Moravian Brethren. The experience led him to form a network of prayer fellowships to promote similar conversions—the beginning of what would come to be known as **methodism**. Wesley sought to move Christians beyond justification to what he called "entire sanctification," meaning the restoration of original righteousness such as existed before the Fall. Christian perfection was therefore attainable in this life. Such a doctrine set Wesley's ideas apart from Lutheran and Reformed (Calvinist) theology. Despite Wesley's resistance to the formation of a separate church, Methodists in America finally withdrew from the Anglican Church in 1784 and organized the Methodist Episcopal Church.

In America, the Pietist impact was mediated through the **Great Awakening**, a religious revival movement that swept through the colonies in the 1740s. The Great Awakening created the template for all future revivalism in America. In the view of some historians, it may also have paved the way for the American Revolution. Gifted and tireless preachers like George Whitefield (1714–1770) traveled the length and breadth of the colonies to stir up religious zeal in a population that had gotten relaxed and comfortable amidst the economic opportunities of the New World. Large outdoor meetings provided a festive atmosphere removed from daily life, in which preachers discovered they could evoke spectacular emotional responses in their listeners. The great Puritan theologian Jonathan Edwards (1703–1758) provided a theological account and rationale for the movement.

Figure 23–2 This painting depicts a revival camp meeting, which included preaching and the singing of hymns. In the foreground you can see the emotional responses people had to the preacher's call to conversion.

Revivalism has had a mixed legacy. Today its association with television evangelists, faith healing, and crusades against evolution can make it seem anti-intellectual and backward, at least in the eyes of its critics. But this was by no means true before the advent of fundamentalism. In the nineteenth-century, revivalist Christians were in the forefront of reform movements of every kind: anti-slavery and abolitionism, temperance (the fight against alcohol and the social ills that accompanied it), prison reform, charitable work, and education. A large number of private colleges and universities owe their origin to educational energies unleashed by revivalism. Revivalism can thus claim much credit for the ongoing vitality and adaptibility of American Protestantism, which is well suited for a society in which religious commitment is voluntary.

Today the Protestant denominations that are growing fastest are those in which born-again Christianity dominates. Revivalism has also stimulated wave after wave of new church formations. In the early nineteenth-century, a Second Great Awakening, this one on the western frontier at Cane Ridge, Kentucky, produced the Restoration movement of Alexander Campbell and Barton Stone. Restorationism claimed to end church division and return to a "pre-denominational" state by appealing to Scripture alone. To symbolize the goal of restoring a lost original unity, the movement called itself simply "the Christian Church" and also the "Disciples of Christ." Despite its intentions toward reunification, the perhaps inevitable result was to create still more denominations. The Restoration movement eventually split three ways over the use of musical instruments in church services and issues related to its growing organizational structure.

Out of nineteenth-century methodism came the **Holiness movement**. It began with worries among Methodists that Wesley's doctrine of Christian perfection was in danger of being ignored. Some religious communities became impatient with human progress in responding to the call of the revivalist. They sought perfection in this world with an emphasis on sinlessness and love. These Christians believed that holiness was an attainable and necessary objective and that Christians should be free of outward sin. Christians concerned with "full sanctification" held annual camp meetings, sponsored Bible conferences, founded urban missions, published newspapers, and, inevitably, became separate churches. Thus the Holiness churches (such as the Free Methodist Church, Holiness Christian Church, Church of the Nazarene, and the Church of God) separated from the Methodist tradition to develop a lifestyle of personal holiness that reflected a stricter code of behavior than that held by their parent churches. As a response to what they called "the second grace of God" (the conversion made available to the Christian through the revivals), they developed an asceticism that rejected worldliness.

The Holiness movement in turn produced the intensely charismatic type of Christianity known as **Pentecostalism**. It takes its name from the Pentecost miracle recounted in the Acts of the Apostles 2:1–21, when the Holy Spirit was poured out on Jesus's followers and gave them the gift of "speaking in tongues" (sometimes called by its Greek name of **glossolalia**), a type of ecstatic group prayer mentioned in some of Paul's letters (e.g., 1 Cor 12:10). Pentecostalism's founder was Charles Parham (1873–1929), a Holiness preacher whose Sunday school students experienced "Spirit Baptism" and the gift of tongues in 1901. A related event was the famed Azusa Street Revival in Los Angeles (1906–1909), led by African-American preacher William Seymour (1870–1922).

Worldwide Pentecostalism is growing faster than any other type of Christianity. Pentecostal churches now number in the hundreds, including large denominations like the Assemblies of God (to which prominent televangelist Oral Roberts once belonged), the United Pentecostal Church International (UPCI), and the Church of God in Christ, the fastest growing African-American Pentecostal church. Some, such as the UPCI, are non-Trinitarian and practice Baptism in the name of Jesus only. Common to all is the belief that "Spirit Baptism" must be manifested as speaking in tongues, though other spiritual gifts such as faith healing and prophecy are also expected fruits of the Spirit. Pentecostal Christianity is marked by highly emotional prayer services, traditional codes of morality, biblical literalism, missionary zeal, and millennial expectations (the imminent second coming of Jesus). Despite their contemporary association with conservative political causes, Pentecostal churches have sometimes shown greater racial diversity and openness to women's leadership than more established churches. For example, the International Church of the Four Square gospel was started and led by Aimee Semple McPherson (1890–1944), whose flamboyant career made her a media celebrity.

Millennialism and the Coming of Christ's Kingdom

Pentecostalism's millennial fervor represents yet another pervasive feature of revivalism: the hope for Christ's imminent return and earthly reign. Fresh outbursts of revivalist enthusiasm always rekindled hope that the great end-time drama described in the Bible—above all, the promise of the millennial kingdom in the Book of Revelation—was not far off. According to Revelation 20:1–10, at the second coming of Jesus Christ, the bodies of the saints will be raised and the saints will reign with Christ for a thousand years in an earthly kingdom.

Christians have long debated whether these promises should be understood literally or symbolically. The dominant view, represented by St. Augustine in early Christianity, is that the thousand years should be seen as a symbolic number (see Augustine's *On the City of God* 20.7–9). For Augustine and many others, the promised reign of Christ on earth was already fulfilled in the life of the church, the city of God, on pilgrimage in this world.

Among American Protestants this interpretation came to be known as **postmillennialism**, because Christ's second coming would take place *after* the symbolic millennium, when the gospel had been preached to the whole world and human history was fully developed and ready for his return. Postmillennialism reflects an optimistic opinion of the progress of Christianity and of human development. Up to the end of the nineteenth-century it was the dominant viewpoint among American Protestants, no doubt reflecting their sense of confidence about their own preeminence in American culture and their beliefs about the place of America (and the gospel) in the world.

Other Protestants, however, held onto a more literal understanding of the millennial kingdom. For them it was more natural to think that Christ's return would happen *before* the millennium promised in Revelation. This viewpoint is therefore called **premillennialism**. Combined with a method of biblical interpretation called dispensationalism, premillennialism would become a powerful force in modern fundamentalist Christianity (see the following section on fundamentalism). Already in the nineteenth-century, several very distinctive new churches came into being as a result of longings for the establishment of Christ's millennial kingdom: the Seventh Day Adventists, the Jehovah's Witnesses, and, most spectacularly, the Mormons.

The **Seventh-Day Adventists** originated with the prophecies of William Miller (1782–1849) concerning the end of the world, which he mistakenly predicted in 1843 and again in 1844. His movement survived the disappointment thanks to the leadership of James and Ellen White. Reorganized in 1860 as the Seventh-Day Adventists (the name indicating their adoption of Saturday as the biblically ordained day of rest), they abandoned their expectation of an imminent second coming and today are known for their missionary zeal, their medical work, and their dedication to a healthy and simple way of life. Adventists give prophetic authority to the voluminous writings of Ellen White, which grew out of the visionary experiences she enjoyed throughout her life.

The **Jehovah's Witnesses**, as they have been known since 1931, were founded by Charles Taze Russell (1852–1916). He prophesied that Christ would return secretly in 1874 and would begin his public reign in 1914. The Witnesses appear to deny the full divinity of Jesus Christ, although they have no systematic and fixed body of teaching. They have continued to be intensely focused on eschatology and on Christ's return. Their refusal to shed blood has led to their rejection of military service and of blood transfusions. Their allegiance to a theocratic kingdom (a kingdom ruled by God alone) prevents them from recognizing the legitimacy of any state or church. Their aggressive preaching of their faith has made them known far beyond their numbers.

The **Church of Jesus Christ of Latter-Day Saints** (LDS) was founded in 1830 in upstate New York. The Mormons, as they are commonly called, take their name from the Book of Mormon, which their founder Joseph Smith (1805–1844) claimed to have translated from golden plates revealed to him in 1827 by an angel named Moroni. Along with the Christian Bible and certain documents of the Mormon Church, the Book of Mormon is a basic component in the church's canon of inspired writings. The LDS church considers Joseph Smith, who was known to be disturbed by the variety and divisions among Christian denominations, to be a revealer and a prophet of the last days and the church itself to be Christ's kingdom once again established on the earth, preparatory to Christ's second coming. Mormonism thus fits into a familiar nineteenth-century American restorationist and millennialist pattern. But its basic belief structure certainly takes it beyond what was conventional in American Christianity then or now.

Joseph Smith's movement led a complex and turbulent history from its New York origins to its eventual destination in Utah, under the leadership of Brigham Young (1801–1877), who succeeded Smith after he was murdered by a mob in Illinois. The early Mormons inspired suspicion and fear, in part because of Smith's endorsement of plural marriage (polygamy), a practice that the church repudiated in 1890 when Utah was trying to gain admission to the Union as a state. From its base in Salt Lake City, home of the Mormon Temple, the religion has spread worldwide and continues to grow rapidly. The public face of Mormonism now looks typically denominational in its emphatic identification with the American way of life. Mormon teaching even regards the Constitution as an inspired document. It is doubtful, however, whether the church's doctrine is compatible with orthodox Christianity.

Apart from specific theological questions, the Mormon claim to possess a new, canonical revelation (supplemented by further revelations to the prophet Joseph Smith and his successors) would seem to set Mormonism apart as a new religion altogether, despite its profession of faith in Jesus Christ. Further, its Book of Mormon purports to be the work of multiple, long-dead authors, part of a migration of ancient peoples from biblical Israel around 600 B.C. who came to America long before Columbus. Mormonism thus seems to stand roughly in relation to Christianity as Christianity itself does in relation to Judaism.

Regardless of whether it is new or merely a creative restatement of Christianity, Mormonism has proven to be very adept at fitting into its American environment, as shown by its strong patriotism, its exuberant optimism about human potential, its emphasis on a strong family structure, and its high valuation of material prosperity. The tenth article of Joseph Smith's "Articles of Faith" proclaims: "We believe in the literal gathering of Israel and in the restoration of the Ten Tribes; that Zion (the New Jerusalem) will be built upon the American continent; that Christ will reign personally upon the earth; and, that the earth will be renewed and receive its paradisiacal glory." The expected millennial kingdom may not have arrived in its fullness, but Mormonism itself seems as at home in Zion as any other comfortably American church.

The Church as a Community Called Out From the World

Quite different from the millennialist movements, though sharing their dissent from American denominationalism, is a small group of Christian churches sometimes called collectively the **peace churches**. Primarily they include the Mennonites, Amish, Hutterites, and Church of the Brethren. The Quakers—or to call them by their proper name, the Society of Friends—are often grouped with the peace churches, but they have a very different history and character, owing to their origin as a "birthright" church.

The peace churches in the narrower sense, are descended from the Anabaptists ("re-baptizers") of the Radical Reformation (see Chapter 19). They practice believer's Baptism (meaning adult Baptism, usually by full immersion) and live a simple way of life intended to set them apart from the larger secular society. Traditionally this often meant distinctive dress, separate schooling, and life in closed rural communities. The most controversial form of their dissent has been refusing to fight in wars, which is based on their reading of Jesus's call to discipleship in the Sermon on the Mount (Matthew 5–7). Although many of them are now somewhat modernized (for example, by dress and participation in mainstream education), they still maintain their pacifist tradition. Their conscientious refusal to fight, along with that of the Quakers and also of the Jehovah's Witnesses, contributed to the American government's recognition of a right to a religiously based conscientious objection to military service (expanded in 1971 to include a right to non-religiously based conscientious objection).

By far the most numerous Protestant grouping consists of the **Baptist churches**, the biggest of which is the Southern Baptist Convention (SBC). Two large African American Baptist denominations are the American Baptist Churches USA and the National Baptist Convention USA, Inc., which is second in size only to the SBC. Baptists' respect for congregational freedom has produced tremendous doctrinal and denominational diversity. Most Baptists, however, hold conservative views on the authority and inspiration of the Bible, and many are fundamentalists. As explained in Chapter 19, the original Baptists were English Puritans who wished to reform themselves independently and without waiting for the approval of the English government. While in exile in the Netherlands, some of them adopted believer's Baptism from Dutch Mennonites because they concluded that adult Baptism was the logical corollary of separating from a state establishment.

All American Baptists have maintained this original commitment to religious liberty and church independence. Nevertheless, unlike the peace church descendants of the Anabaptists, they show their Puritan roots by their sense of birthright responsibility for the whole social order: They tend to be strongly patriotic and want to shape American law, government, and culture according to Christian standards. Baptists were prime movers in the resurgence of conservative Christian political activism that began in the late 1970s, when the Rev. Jerry Falwell (1933–2007) founded the Moral Majority (1978), which became the inspiration for numerous later conservative Christian political organizations.

Fundamentalism and Christian Protest Against Modernity

For a generation now, the re-emergence of conservative Christian activism has been a potent force on the political landscape. But it is only the latest phase in a long cultural war within American Protestantism that began over a century ago and ended up destroying the broad Protestant consensus about a Christian America that had prevailed since the nation's founding. Since the destruction of that consensus, Protestants have been divided by conflicting opinions of how Christians should relate their faith to the modern world. The bitter struggle that historians today know as the controversy between fundamentalists and modernists broke out over how Christians should respond to a whole range of developments: the intellectual challenges provoked by modern science, Darwinian evolution above all, and modern historical study of the Bible; the social changes produced by immigration and urbanization; and the cultural challenge provoked by the spread of a Mass consumer culture.

The **fundamentalist movement** began as a militant and defensive reaction to the threats posed by these new developments, which conservative Protestants feared were eating away the supernatural basis of traditional Christian faith and corrupting American culture. The movement took its name from a series of pamphlets called "The Fundamentals," published between 1910 and 1915 by conservative Protestants, which stressed that there were certain fundamental Christian beliefs that could not be changed or watered down. A list of these basic beliefs drafted by the northern Presbyterian Church in 1910 contains five

doctrines: biblical inerrancy, the deity and Virgin Birth of Christ, his substitutionary atonement (death on behalf of others), his bodily resurrection, and his miracles. In 1919 William
B. Riley (1861–1947), a prominent Minnesota fundamentalist, anti-evolution crusader, and
founder of the World's Christian Fundamentals Association, added the second coming of
Christ to the list. Fundamentalism, then, in the narrow sense of the word refers to the
inerrancy of scripture and, in a broader sense, to a militant Christian opposition to particular aspects of modernity.

Fundamentalism allied itself with a new way of understanding the Bible called
dispensationalism. This method of biblical interpretation divided the scriptural narrative of
God's dealings with humanity into seven stages called dispensations. Each stage moved
God's plan for humanity forward toward its completion. The idea itself is found already in
the theology of the second-century bishop Irenaeus of Lyons (see Chapter 8). Modern dispensationalism is new, however, in the way it uses the stages as the key to unlock the Bible's
prophetic message about the end of time, especially the setting up of Christ's millennial
kingdom. Dispensational premillennialism, as this system of prophetic interpretation is
known, holds that certain biblical prophecies, especially in Daniel and Revelation, must be
literally fulfilled before Christ begins his earthly reign. These prophecies include God's
promises to Israel. The restoration of Israel therefore plays a central role in this scheme.
Dispensational premillennialists are strong supporters of the modern state of Israel because
they see the return of the Jews to their homeland as an outstanding clue that the prophetic
end-time clock has begun ticking.

Another distinctive feature of this interpretive system is the doctrine of the Rapture,
meaning the snatching up of true Christians (see 1 Thess 4:17) to save them from the tribu-
lations of the End. The contemporary series of apocalyptic novels called *Left Behind* is based
on dispensationalist doctrines about the Rapture. Dispensational premillennialists are usually pessimistic about the moral and spiritual condition of America. They also tend to see
mainstream Christian churches, both Protestant and Catholic, as apostate (fallen away)
churches that have abandoned real faith in Christ. They are therefore often hostile to ecumenical movements for Christian reunion and even to dialogue with other churches.
Dispensational premillennialism was popularized by the hugely successful study bible called
the *Scofield Reference Bible*, first published in 1909 and still in print. Dispensational premillennialism remains a highly influential form of eschatology (end-time teaching) among fundamentalist Christians.

African American Christianity: From Slavery to Segregation to Civil Rights

Attention has already been drawn to several African American denominations. The history
of black Christianity in the United States is inextricably linked with the history of slavery and
racial segregation. Both free and enslaved blacks were evangelized by Protestant churches,
but when full participation was denied to them, separate black churches were organized as
soon as America became independent. In 1787, Richard Allen (1760–1831) led a protest of
Negro Methodists in Philadelphia against practices that excluded African Americans from
full participation in the Methodist church. This protest community eventually became the
African Methodist-Episcopal (A.M.E.) Church. In 1796 African Americans in New York who
encountered similar resistance organized a similarly named A.M.E. church, which later
added *Zion* to its name. Among A.M.E. Zion's members were prominent black abolitionists
such as Frederick Douglass, Sojourner Truth, and Harriet Tubman. After emancipation,

everywhere that African Americans settled, churches became one of their most vital social institutions and seedbeds of the Civil Rights movement of the 1950s and 1960s (see the section on Dr. Martin Luther King).

CATHOLICISM IN AMERICA

America has a Catholic past as well, with roots that go even deeper than those of the British Protestant "birthright" churches of the east coast, though in much of the United States visible evidence of the Catholic past may be confined to familiar but very un-English place names like Los Angeles—shortened from *El Pueblo de Nuestra Señora la Reina de los Angeles de Porciúncula*, "The Town of Our Lady Queen of Angels of the Portiuncula." The name itself encapsulates a great deal of Catholic history. The town took its name from its river, so named by the Spanish Franciscans who discovered it on August 2, 1769, that being the day on which the Franciscan order celebrated the church in Italy where St. Francis of Assisi was buried. Benedictine monks had given Francis an abandoned chapel dedicated to Our Lady Queen of Angels. The site of the chapel was referred to simply as "the Portiuncula," from an Italian word for the "little portion" of land on which it was located. Likewise, in 1678, the French explorer Louis Joliet named St. Louis for King Louis XIV of France. He also claimed the whole Mississippi valley for France under the name of Louisiana.

We will survey American Catholic history in four broad phases, beginning with the French and Spanish colonization of America, in the seventeenth and eighteenth centuries, and the British colonial and American Revolutionary movements of roughly the same period, extending through the era of the immigrant church in the early-nineteenth and mid-twentieth centuries and into the present period of the Catholic Church's assimilation into American culture.

French and Spanish Exploration and Colonization

French and Spanish exploration of the New World took place in earnest in the seventeenth and eighteenth centuries. Of the two, the Spanish experience in America left the more lasting imprint, because the French made fewer permanent settlements south of Quebec, New Orleans being their most prominent settlement. In a great arc from Florida through Texas and the Southwest to San Francisco Bay, the Spanish established a chain of missions, military garrisons, and towns whose Catholic character survived American conquest and annexation in the nineteenth-century. Thanks to that history and to surging immigration from Mexico, California and the Southwest today are home to one-third of America's Catholic population.

With colonization went conversion, as heroic French and Spanish missionaries risked their lives to bring Christianity to Native American peoples. Their efforts met with mixed success. Today there is debate about the mission enterprise and its overall effect on Native American culture. In California the legacy of Fr. Junipero Serra (1713–1784), Franciscan friar and so-called Apostle of California, has become something of a battlefield in the culture wars over America's religious identity, especially since Pope John Paul II in 1985 promoted him to beatification, the last stage before his full canonization as a saint of the Catholic Church. Fr. Serra's many admirers praise his saintly character, the mission system he built, his evangelization of California's indigenous peoples, and the economic progress in which he pioneered. His detractors condemn what they call his use of coercive measures with the Native Americans, his role in the destruction of California's native cultures, and the disastrous demographic decline that accompanied Spanish settlement.

British Colonial and American Revolutionary Era

On the east coast of what would later be known as the United States, Catholics were a tiny minority in an overwhelmingly Protestant land. In Maryland, founded in 1634 as a proprietary colony by the Catholic family of the Calverts, Catholics for a time enjoyed political toleration. In general, however, Catholics in the British colonies suffered from traditional English Protestant hatred and suspicion of their church. As a result Catholics did not get their own American bishop until after the Revolution, when, in 1789, John Carroll was elected by his priests and named by Pope Pius VI to be the first bishop of the New World.

Era of the Immigrant Church

In the early nineteenth-century through the mid-twentieth century, wave after wave of immigration, mainly from Europe, kept the Catholic Church busy constantly absorbing new arrivals. The major challenge was adjusting European habits and assumptions to American conditions, and the major question facing Catholics was "How do we fit in?" Catholic immigrants were resented by many Americans who saw them as religiously alien and potentially disloyal because of their allegiance to the pope. They were often scorned as socially and educationally backwards and declared unfit for democracy because so many came from countries that were still monarchies.

Partially to compensate for such suspicions, Catholics tried hard to prove their patriotism and loyalty to their new country, for example by serving in America's wars in numbers well beyond their percentage of the population. To ease the transition to America, the Catholic Church developed its own subculture, complete with schools, professional associations, labor unions, religious societies, clubs, magazines, and newspapers. This was the era of "brick and mortar Catholicism," so called from the great churches that still dominate urban landscapes all over the Northeast, the Midwest, and the Great Lakes region, and the sprawling parish complexes of rectory, convent, parochial school, and gymnasium. It was also an era of exceptional clerical dominance over the laity, whose energies were spent on establishing themselves and their families in a challenging new world. Historians of immigration have noted that the new immigrants often became *more* religious than they had been in the old country, as the churches played a vital supporting role in their adjustment to America. This deepened religious practice, in turn, was to bottom out somewhat in the fourth stage.

Era of Assimilation

In the post-World War II period (c. 1950), many of the earlier obstacles to the advancement of Catholics in American culture withered away. John Kennedy's election as the first Catholic president in 1960 expressed a widespread sense that Catholics had finally "arrived." At the same time, however, what it *meant* to be Catholic became less certain throughout this period. Catholic identity was harder to take for granted once the dense ethnic solidarity of the big Eastern and Great Lakes cities and Midwestern rural communities, where most Catholics lived, started to dissolve and the post-war exodus to the suburbs began. Increased education and greater prosperity had a similar diluting effect on religious identity. Another factor at work after the 1960s was the question of where America itself was heading in an age marked by the civil rights movement, violent racial conflict, the Vietnam War, the cultural upheavals of the sixties, and the women's liberation movement.

To many Christians, a series of Supreme Court cases from the late 1940s to the landmark 1973 *Roe v. Wade* decision, which struck down state anti-abortion laws as unconstitutional, seemed bent on erasing every trace of America's Christian heritage from public life and law. The very definition of America seemed up for grabs. As a result, debates within the church about Catholic identity often reflected how Catholics felt about what was going on in the wider culture *outside* their church. Positions taken by Catholics in an emerging culture war in society at large tended to coincide with the positions they were also taking in the hostile and polarized climate that developed in the church after the Second Vatican Council (see Chapter 24).

The most important theological voice produced by American Catholicism was the Jesuit theologian John Courtney Murray (1904–1967). Murray's great achievement was his development of a Catholic understanding of the American system of religious freedom and non-establishment. For most of its history the Catholic Church had enjoyed legal benefits and privileges from Christian states, privileges that it claimed by right as the true church of Jesus Christ. This traditional Catholic expectation of state sponsorship was reemphasized by papal teaching after the French Revolution. In America, Catholics enjoyed the benefits of religious freedom and had no desire to make their church an established church. But they lacked any way to convince their fellow citizens of this, since nineteenth-century Catholic doctrine was so critical of religious freedom and indeed of liberal democracy in general.

Thus, Murray tried to demonstrate that religious freedom and the separation of church and state were positive goods, not just circumstances that Catholics had to tolerate because they were powerless to change them. America's historical experience appeared to prove that religious freedom could ensure both stable government and religious flourishing: On the one hand, religious uniformity was not necessary for sound government, so long as the social order outside of the state—what Murray called "civil society"—possessed a healthy capacity for moral judgment; and on the other hand, American democracy permitted a great deal of practical freedom to all religions. Murray held that Catholicism had always recognized a certain dualism and independence of function in church and state. He saw American liberal democracy as a legitimate heir, in modern conditions, of the church–state dualism of the Catholic Middle Ages, except that the American version of liberalism had not exerted the kind of state control over the church that was typical of European liberal regimes.

Such ideas were more controversial than one may think. Church authorities suspected that religious freedom implied that one religious choice as good as another—in other words, relativism, or what Nineteenth-century popes called indifferentism. The endorsement of religious freedom also appeared to be a change from past papal teaching. For several years in the 1950s Murray was prohibited from publishing his work. Nevertheless, his ideas, as popularized in his book *We Hold These Truths: Catholic Reflections on the American Proposition*, eventually received a practical vindication when Kennedy was elected president. The book played a role in reducing public anxiety about the possibility of a Catholic president in the White House, as *Time* magazine recognized by putting Murray on its cover the month after the election. In 1963 he received a belated vindication within the Catholic Church as well when Cardinal Francis Spellman, archbishop of New York City, asked him to serve as his theological advisor at the Second Vatican Council, where he contributed to the drafting of Vatican II's *Declaration on Religious Liberty* (see Chapter 24).

The various crises of the 1960s and 1970s, above all the war in Vietnam, led some Catholics to subject Murray's ideas to a different kind of criticism. Because Murray had made a clear distinction between the secular and the religious spheres, with each having its appropriate degree of freedom, there was a danger that Catholics might defer too easily to the demands of the state. They feared that Catholics who became unquestioning supporters of everything that America did had failed to form their consciences first. Did religious freedom bring with it a risk of self-imposed moral handcuffs? Catholic critics who worried that it did pointed to such things as America's dependence on a massive nuclear deterrent during the tense years of the Cold War against the Soviet Union. It was not easy to reconcile the use of atomic weapons of Mass destruction with the traditional criteria for fighting a just war, which forbid the targeting of non-combatants. Thus, during the Reagan administration, the American Catholic bishops published a pastoral letter entitled *The Challenge of Peace* (1983), in which they expressed their concerns about America's reliance on nuclear weapons and advised Catholics on how to form their consciences on questions of war and peace.

Figure 23–3 Photo of Jesuit theologian John Courtney Murray (1904–1967).

A more conservative critique of Murray's reconciliation of American ideals and Catholicism has focused on his assumption that, under democratic conditions, civil society had matured sufficiently that "the people" could make responsible moral judgments about the common good. Critics of Murray observe that his claim has been severely tested by *Roe v. Wade* and by subsequent judicial decisions, legislative actions, and popular referenda on controversial issues such as the legalization of same-sex unions, physician-assisted suicide, and stem cell research. If such developments do end up being supported by a majority of the American people, then it is clear that Murray overestimated the moral capacity of civil society and gave it too much credit.

To use abortion as an example, Catholic teaching forbids the practice on the grounds that human life begins at conception and that all human beings have an inalienable right to life; therefore Catholic officeholders who defend legal access to abortion understand it as a religious issue. They justify themselves by saying that they must keep their personal religious beliefs separate from their duties as the elected representatives of

Figure 23–4 Photo of Dorothy Day, founder of the Catholic Worker Movement.

constituents who may disagree radically with Catholic teaching. In a similar way, Catholics who vote for pro-choice candidates may argue that criminalizing abortion in all circumstances would be bad law because it lacks popular support and may be unenforceable. As a result, Catholic office holders have sometimes been accused of sacrificing their moral integrity in order to stay in office. Such accusations have become more widespread in recent years. Some bishops appointed under Pope John Paul II have been less willing than their predecessors to tolerate what they see as equivocation and disobedience on the part of Catholic candidates and officeholders—and even Catholic voters.

One of the most radical critics of Catholic compromises over issues of American culture was Dorothy Day (1897–1980), a journalist and social activist who converted from atheism to Catholicism in the 1920s. The Catholic Worker Movement, which she and Peter Maurin founded in 1933, continues to espouse her ideals of pacifism, anarchism, and direct service to the poor and outcast. In 2000 Pope John Paul II authorized the beginning of a process for her canonization.

AMERICA: NATIONAL DESTINY AND RELIGIOUS REFLECTION

"Consider that we shall be as a city upon a hill, the eyes of all nations will be upon us . . ." So spoke John Winthrop on board the Puritans' flagship the *Arbella*, as he and his co-religionists sailed to New England in 1630. Winthrop was alluding to the words of Jesus in the Sermon on the Mount: "You are the light of the world. A city built on a hill cannot be hid. No one after lighting a lamp puts it under the bushel basket, but on the lampstand, and it gives light to all in the house. In the same way, let your light shine before others, so that they may see your good works . . ." (Matt 5:14–16).

God's New Israel: American Exceptionalism

The biblical image of the new community as a beacon that illuminates the world and that "all nations" look to as an inspiring example has exerted a powerful influence on America's self-understanding. Presidents have often exploited it in ceremonial speeches, such as Ronald Reagan's farewell address:

> I've spoken of the shining city all my political life, but I don't know if I ever quite communicated what I saw when I said it. But in my mind it was a tall proud city built on rocks stronger than oceans, wind swept, God blessed, and teeming with people of all kinds living in harmony and peace, a city with free ports that hummed with commerce and creativity, and if there had to be city walls, the walls had doors and the doors were open to anyone with the will and the heart to get here. That's how I saw it and see it still. (Reagan 1989)

Students are most likely to have encountered this national self-image in its secularized form as *manifest destiny,* a phrase that first emerged in connection with American expansion at the time of the Mexican War (1846–1848). But the religiously framed version has been just as potent. Calling America "a city on a hill" says that America's experiment in democratic government is uniquely important to the rest of the world. Abraham Lincoln went so far as to call that experiment "the last, best hope of mankind."

Though never baptized or a member of any church, Lincoln could fairly be called our greatest public theologian for his profound meditations on the meaning of the Civil War, above all in his Second Inaugural Address. He spoke of Americans as "this almost chosen people," a phrase that suggests a providential national calling or destiny like the one possessed by Israel in the Bible. The trope (figurative expression) of America as "God's new Israel" originated with the Puritans. But it was equally popular with founders like Jefferson and Franklin, who otherwise were religious rationalists (see Chapter 22). For example, for the Great Seal of the United States, Franklin proposed the defeat of Pharaoh and his army as recounted in the Book of Exodus, and Jefferson suggested the people of Israel in the wilderness, led by the pillar of cloud and the pillar of fire.

Since its creation, then, and even more strongly since its emergence as a world power in the twentieth century, the United States has acted as though it has an exceptional status and role among the nations of the world. "American exceptionalism," as this sense of national mission has been called, can obviously be a double-edged sword. On the one hand, it can mean that the nation is a law unto itself and need not answer to any standards but its own. Critics of American foreign policy ever since Woodrow Wilson's administration (1912–1920) argue that it has sometimes led to a self-righteous blindness that prevents America from seeing itself the way the rest of the world does. On the other hand, American exceptionalism can also express a set of ideals by which the nation is willing to be judged and an awareness that its many blessings are given in a form of stewardship, for which an account is owed.

This self-critical capacity too can be traced to America's origins, for it is rooted in the biblical idea of the covenant, according to which Israel was obliged to fulfill certain terms in its special relationship with God. To quote John Winthrop's shipboard sermon again:

> Thus stands the cause between God and us. We are entered into Covenant with him for this work, we have taken out a Commission, the Lord hath given us leave to draw our own Articles . . . Now if the Lord shall please to hear us, and bring us in peace to the place we desire, then hath he ratified this Covenant and sealed our Commission [and] will expect a strict performance of the Articles contained in it. . . . (Cited in Cherry 1998, 40)

A Nation with the Soul of a Church: The Civil Religion Question

As the biblical allusions mentioned in the previous section demonstrate, America's sense of itself as a nation has often been expressed in religious terms. This has not ceased to be true in spite of the First Amendment. In a famous essay published in 1967, the sociologist Robert Bellah proposed that, despite the free exercise and no establishment clauses, America still has something that looks very much like a national religion. Because it is distinctly political in its expression and cannot be identified with any existing church—or for that matter, with any existing religion—Bellah called it a civil religion. In his view it was nevertheless a genuine religion, as shown by its possession of belief in a deity ("the nation under God"), sacred texts (the Constitution and the Declaration of Independence), founders, martyrs (e.g., Lincoln and Martin Luther King), myths of creation and redemption (the Revolution and the Civil War), sacred shrines and sites, sacred times and commemorations, and sacred hymns and symbols (e.g., the flag). Its tenets and practices were specific enough to constitute a religion but broad enough to include most Christians and Jews. It was also broad enough to minimize the offense to those who professed no religion at all. Today the concept of "Abrahamic faiths" has enabled the inclusion of Islam into what had been a Judeo-Christian partnership in America.

The function of this civil religion was to express and reinforce the basic values that unified Americans as a distinct nation. It was the mechanism that helped turn the slogan on our coins into a reality—*E pluribus unum* ("Out of many, one"). While recognizing that America's civil religion could easily become idolatrous, Bellah argued that it had a powerful positive potential as well. He admired the way it could energize and inspire Americans to live up to the high ideals formulated in the nation's foundational documents. He saw the greatest example of this in the Civil Rights movement, in which religious symbols and motivations served legal and political goals.

No one perfected this religious and political synthesis more powerfully than Dr. Martin Luther King, Jr., a Baptist minister and the son of a Baptist minister. King's vision of racial justice drew both on core biblical sources and ideals and on distinctively American values and traditions: From the Bible came the Exodus story of liberation from slavery, the prophets' demands for social justice, and the Sermon on the Mount's teaching on non-violence; from America's founding came the democratic and egalitarian values of the Declaration of Independence. Dr. King's "Letter from a Birmingham Jail" (1963) and his "I Have a Dream" speech, delivered in 1963 from the steps of the Lincoln Memorial at the Civil Rights movement's greatest rally, have become canonical documents in America's civil religion. The speech, which was ranked in a 1999 poll of scholars as the greatest American speech of the twentieth century, burns with the fiery rhetoric of a revivalist sermon. But the "call"—an integral feature of a revivalist sermon is the altar call, when those ready to declare themselves for Christ come down in front of the congregation—is a summons to legal equality and human brotherhood and dignity.

Not everyone has agreed with Bellah's thesis. Some deny that we have a civil religion at all, preferring instead to see our unifying national "myths" as technology, capitalism, or freedom, shorn of any religious halo or sanction. Others think that an American civil religion does exist, but they condemn it—either because they are secularists who oppose any connection between government and religion, or because they are believers who see it as a political distortion of genuine religion. Even if Bellah overstated the internal coherence and the pervasiveness of this unifying national symbol system, it does seem to be true that in the United States the nation itself has taken on sacred dimensions. It is the *nation* that dwarfs any Christian church as a powerful locus of group identity and membership. In the words of G. K. Chesterton, a British Catholic observer of the American scene, the United States is "a nation with the soul of a church" (Chesterton 1990, 41–45).

Christianity and America

This notion of an American civil religion presents actual Christian churches in America with a grave problem. Insofar as they stress what is unique and essential to them as individual churches, they risk looking like intolerant and small-minded sects. But if they choose to emphasize what they can contribute in common to the larger national welfare, they may become nothing more than interchangeable training schools for democratic participation and good citizenship. The downside of religious toleration, it turns out, may be religious irrelevance!

This dilemma confronts all churches, regardless of whether they are liberal or conservative in their religious doctrine or in their political involvement. The emergence of the modern nation-state and the ideology of nationalism (see Chapter 22) have made this a problem everywhere, of course, including countries where Christianity still enjoys some degree of religious establishment. But the dilemma is especially acute in the United States, where the political and religious conditions referred to in the previous section entitled "Protestantism in America" have created a fragmented denominational mosaic. The result is to make the nation look all the bigger and the churches all the smaller.

Given the immense global power of the United States today, Christianity pays a big price if American churches allow themselves and the gospel to be nationalized. Christianity must not identify itself exclusively with any particular political or economic system. Chapter 10 in this textbook referred to St. Augustine's great apologetic work *On the City of God*, in which he had reminded Christians that the sack of Rome in 410 showed that God could use empires, even Christian empires, as he wished, and could discard them when they had served his purposes. According to the New Testament's Letter to the Hebrews, "we have here no lasting city, but we seek one which is to come" (Heb 13:14). In America, Christians have sometimes imagined they are already living in the heavenly Jerusalem (cf. Heb 12:22) and have forgotten that they are only pilgrims en route to it.

Since the end of the cold war with communism, and especially since the terrorist attacks of September 11, 2001, America's belief in its exceptional role in the world has inspired an aggressively interventionist foreign policy, especially in the Middle East, where the current war in Iraq is being justified both as self-defense and as a campaign to spread freedom and democracy. Christians who are skeptical of policies that claim to restore "national greatness" suspect that what is really afoot is the construction of an American empire and a *Pax Americana* like the *Pax Romana*, the Rome-dominated peace of the ancient world.

Other Christians, it must be said, conscientiously support the war because they see America arrayed against radically politicized Islam in a global "clash of civilizations" in which Christians have no right to pretend they are neutral. Those who hold such views run the risk of equating God's will with American policy. No one was more aware of this danger than Reinhold Niebuhr (1892–1971), American Protestantism's greatest social ethicist. Niebuhr was an ardent defender of a special American role in the world, because he believed America had an obligation to use its economic and military power to good ends. But he also shared Augustine's awareness of human fallibility and the danger of the sin of pride, as he showed in his many books and articles, notably in *Moral Man and Immoral Society* (1932) and *The Nature and Destiny of Man* (1941 and 1943). In an essay written during World War II, Niebuhr had this to say about America's special mission, and about the temptation to self-righteousness that went with it:

> If we know that we have been chosen beyond our deserts, we must also begin to realize that we have not been chosen for our particular task in order that our own life may be aggrandized. We ought not to derive either special security or special advantage from our high historical mission. The real fact is that we are placed in a precarious moral and historical position by our special mission. It can be justified only if it results in good for the whole community of mankind. Woe unto us if we fail. For our failure will bring judgment upon us and the world. That is the meaning of the prophetic word, "Therefore will I visit you with your iniquities." This word must be translated by the church today into meanings relevant to our own history. If this is not done, we are bound to fail. For the natural pride of great nations is such that any special historical success quickly aggravates it until it becomes the source of moral and political confusion. (Reprinted in Cherry 1998, 299)

Key Terms

strict separationism
secularism
evangelical
denominationalism
revivalism
pietism
methodism
Great Awakening

Holiness movement
Pentecostalism
glossolalia
postmillennialism
premillennialism
Seventh-Day
   Adventists
Jehovah's Witnesses

Church of Jesus Christ
   of Latter-Day Saints
peace churches
Baptist churches
fundamentalist movement
dispensationalism

Questions for Reading

1. Cite the exact wording of the First Amendment's religion clauses. Describe two broadly different ways in which the religion clauses have been interpreted.

2. What is the special role in American society that the churches of the original English colonies claimed as their responsibility?

3. Explain the main factors that contributed to the denominational system that came into being in the United States after independence. What are some of the pros and cons of that system?

4. Describe the various ways in which pietism has contributed to the shaping of Christianity in America.

5. Millennialism is a prominent theme in American Protestant history. What are the two millennial expectations, and how have they influenced the creation of new churches in America? Distinguish between the different ways in which the two millennial expectations view the direction of history.

6. List the core fundamentalist principles, and describe the central motivations of the fundamentalist movement. How has dispensational premillennialism shaped fundamentalist ways of understanding biblical prophecy?

7. What primarily distinguishes the third from the fourth phase of Catholic history in America? Answer in terms of how Catholics see themselves in relation to America.

8. How did John Courtney Murray defend, on Catholic grounds, the theological acceptability of religious freedom and democracy? What sorts of criticisms have his ideas received since Murray's death in 1967?

9. What are the religious sources of American exceptionalism, the sense that the nation has a special mission or destiny? How is it possible for that "exceptional" sense of mission to function in a *critical* way?

10. Explain what is meant by the term *civil religion*, illustrating its possible relevance to understanding America's sense of itself as a nation. What are the challenges that an American civil religion would pose to actual Christian churches?

Works Consulted/Recommended Reading

Ahlstrom, Sydney E. *A Religious History of the American People.* Garden City, NY: Doubleday, 1975.

Albanese, Catherine L. *America: Religion and Religions.* 2nd ed. Belmont, CA: Wadsworth, 1992.

Allitt, Patrick. *Religion in America Since 1945: A History.* New York: Columbia University, 2003.

Bacevich, Andrew J. *American Empire: The Realities and the Consequences of U.S. Diplomacy.* Cambridge, MA: Harvard University, 2002.

Bellah, Robert. "Civil Religion in America." *Daedalus 96* (1967): 1–21.

Buhle, Mari Jo, Paul Puhle, and Dan Georgakas, eds. *Encyclopedia of the American Left.* New York: Garland, 1990.

Cherry, Conrad, ed. *God's New Israel: Religious Interpretations of American History,* Rev. ed. Chapel Hill: University of North Carolina, 1998.

Cuddihy, John Murray. *No Offense: Civil Religion and Protestant Taste.* New York: Seabury, 1978.

Curry, Thomas J. *The First Freedoms: Church and State in America to the Passage of the First Amendment.* New York: Oxford University, 1986.

Doyle, David Noel, and Owen Dudley Edwards, eds. *America and Ireland, 1776–1976.* Westport, CT: Greenwood, 1980.

Gaustad, Edwin S. *Faith of Our Fathers: Religion and the New Nation.* Grand Rapids, MI: Eerdmans, 1993.

Guelzo, Allen C. "God's Designs: The Literature of the Colonial Revivals of Religion, 1735–1760." In Stout and Hart, eds., *New Directions in American Religious History,* 141–172.

Hackel, Steven W. "The Competing Legacies of Junipero Serra: Pioneer, Saint, Villain." *Common-place* 5:2, http://www.common-place.org/vol-05/no-02/hackel/index.shtml.

Hatch, Nathan, and Mark A. Noll, eds. *The Bible in America: Essays in Cultural History.* New York: Oxford University, 1982.

Hatch, Nathan O. *The Democratization of American Christianity.* New Haven: Yale University, 1989.

Hennesey, James. *American Catholics: A History of the Roman Catholic Community in the United States.* New York: Oxford University, 1983.

Kosmin, Barry A., Egon Mayer, and Ariela Keysar. *American Religious Identification Survey 2001,* Graduate Center of the City University of New York. http://www.gc.cuny.edu/faculty/research_studies/aris.pdf.

Lipset, Seymour Martin. *American Exceptionalism: A Double-Edged Sword.* New York: W. W. Norton, 1996.

MacIntyre, Alasdair. "America as an Idea." In Doyle and Edwards, eds., *America and Ireland, 1776–1976,* 57–68.

Marsden, George. *Fundamentalism and American Culture 1875–1925.* 2nd ed. New York: Oxford University, 2006.

Martin E. Marty. *Righteous Empire: The Protestant Experience in America.* New York: The Dial Press, 1970.

McGreevy, John T. *Catholics and American Freedom: A History.* New York: W.W. Norton, 2003.

Mead, Sidney E. *The Lively Experiment: The Shaping of Christianity in America.* New York: Harper and Row, 1963.

Murray, John Courtney. *We Hold These Truths: Catholic Reflections on the American Proposition.* New York: Sheed and Ward, 1960.

National Conference of Catholic Bishops. *The Challenge of Peace: God's Promise and Our Response.* Washington, DC: National Conference of Catholic Bishops, 1983.

Niebuhr, Reinhold. "Anglo-Saxon Destiny and Responsibility." In Cherry, ed., *God's New Israel: Religious Interpretations of American Destiny,* 296–300.

Noll, Mark A. *America's God: From Jonathan Edwards to Abraham Lincoln.* New York: Oxford University, 2002.
_____. *The Civil War as a Theological Crisis.* Chapel Hill, NC: University of North Carolina, 2006.

Noonan, John T. *The Lustre of Our People: The American Experience of Religious Freedom.* Los Angeles: University of California, 1998.

Peterson, Merrill D., and Robert C. Vaughan, eds. *The Virginia Statute for Religious Freedom: Its Evolution and Consequences in American History.* New York: University of Cambridge, 1988.

Raboteau, Albert J. *Slave Religion: The "Invisible Institution" in the Antebellum South.* Updated edition. New York: Oxford University, 2004.

Reagan, Ronald. Farewell address to the nation, Washington, DC, January 11, 1989. http://www.reaganfoundation.org/reagan/speeches/farewell.asp.

Reid, Daniel G., et al., eds. *Dictionary of Christianity in America.* Downers Grove, IL: InterVarsity, 1990.

Sandos, James A. "Junipero Serra's Canonization and the Historical Record." *American Historical Review* 93 (1988): 1253–1269.

Shipps, Jan. *Mormonism: The Story of a New Religious Tradition.* Urbana, IL: University of Illinois, 1985.

Stout, Harry S., and D. G. Hart, eds. *New Directions in American Religious History.* New York: Oxford University, 1997.

Weber, Timothy P. *Living in the Shadow of the Second Coming: American Premillennialism, 1875–1982.* Chicago: University of Chicago, 1987.

_____. *On the Road to Armageddon: How American Evangelicals Became Israel's Best Friend.* Grand Rapids: Baker Academic, 2004.

Wilentz, Sean. "American Exceptionalism." In Buhle, Puhle, and Georgakas, eds., *Encyclopedia of the American Left,* 20–22.

Witte, John. *Religion and the American Constitutional Experiment: Essential Rights and Liberties.* Boulder: Westview, 2000.

Wood, Gordon S. "Religion and the American Revolution." In Stout and Hart, eds., *New Directions in American Religious History,* 173–205.

Chapter

THE SECOND VATICAN COUNCIL IN CONTEXT

The final three chapters of this book describe some of Christianity's responses to the challenging conditions of the modern world that were described in Chapter 22. The present chapter covers nineteenth- and twentieth-century developments in the Catholic Church, for which the Second Vatican Council (1962–1965) was the central defining event. Chapter 25 will consider contemporary Christianity after the council, in a cultural situation that some now characterize as *post*-modern. Chapter 26 will consider how the globalization of modern Christianity has forced it to rethink the relationship between non-Christian religions and the Christian tradition. In these final chapters the focus will once again be on Catholicism, with briefer reference to non-Catholic developments.

CATHOLICISM AFTER THE FRENCH REVOLUTION

Following the French Revolution (1789–1799), the Catholic Church went into a reactionary mode that lasted for over a century. The Revolution had been a traumatic experience for the church, first by nationalizing the French hierarchy as an arm of the state, then by executing the king, and finally by the radical effort to de-Christianize France altogether. The Revolution was followed by Napoleon's dictatorship and his humiliating treatment of the popes and the Papal States. As a result, nineteenth-century popes were hostile to "the principles of 1789" ("Liberty, Equality, Fraternity") and generally thought the church's interests lay with an "alliance of throne and altar" as protection against the anti-clericalism and atheism which the popes saw as the natural fruit of democratic systems, whether liberal or socialist.

In the years after the Papal States were returned to the pope by the Congress of Vienna (1814–1815), the papacy and Catholicism as a whole experienced a powerful rejuvenation. Intellectuals and artists who had misgivings about aspects of the Enlightenment or about modernity in general sometimes found Catholicism and its medieval heritage (architecture, art, music, social theories, etc.) an attractive alternative. New religious orders grew up to meet practical needs in education, health care, and missionary work, especially missions in parts of Africa that European states were just beginning to colonize. Traditional devotion to Mary as the Blessed Virgin and the Mother of God grew even stronger, nourished by numerous occurrences in which Mary was said to have appeared to believers. In 1854 Pope Pius IX proclaimed the dogma of the Immaculate Conception, which holds that Mary was conceived in the womb of her mother without inheriting original sin. Because this teaching is not attested in the Bible, the pope consulted with bishops around the world before declaring that it was a truth revealed in tradition even if it wasn't clearly stated in scripture. This belief in Mary's immaculate conception—not to be confused with the virginal conception of Jesus in Mary's womb—is not accepted by other Christian churches.

Four years later in the southern French town of Lourdes, a peasant girl named Bernadette Soubirous claimed that Mary had appeared to her and declared, "I am the Immaculate Conception." Lourdes became an immensely popular pilgrimage center and also the site of healing miracles. Other sites of modern Marian apparitions also became particularly popular pilgrimage destinations: Knock in Ireland in 1879; Fatima in Portugal in 1917, where Mary was said to advocate devotion to the rosary; and Medjugorje in 1981 in Bosnia. The most recent of these, the Medjugorje apparitions, have yet to receive official recognition from church authorities.

During this period, the pope's place in the Catholic Church became even more firmly established at the top of the clerical hierarchy. Several factors promoted a trend toward centralization that has continued up to the present day, with the exception of the period of the Second Vatican Council. One such factor was heightened popular devotion to the popes themselves. Devotion to the person of the pope, as distinct from the status conferred by his office, was something relatively new. It originated in sympathy for the difficulties which Pope Pius VII (reigned 1800–1823) endured at the hands of Napoleon, who had captured the pope and put him under virtual house arrest in France. It was enriched by affection for the person of Pius IX (reigned 1846–1878), in whose pontificate papal infallibility was defined as a revealed dogma.

In the twentieth century this "personalization" of the papacy has increased steadily, augmented by the austere persona of Pius XII (reigned 1939–1958) and by the moral and intellectual stature and powerful charisma of the late Pope John Paul II (reigned 1978–2005). Loyalty to the pope was fostered by improved travel and communications, which made it easier for Catholics around the world to visit Rome and to keep informed about the pope. The advent of photography made it possible for everyone to see just what the pope looked like: His picture hangs in schools, rectories, convents, and homes. At the same time the curia, the governing structure of the church, used such technical advances to make the universal governing authority of the papacy more effective all over the globe.

Another factor was the anticlerical policies of governments of many countries in which Catholics lived. Where it still enjoyed or had in the past enjoyed state establishment, the church resisted giving up control over spheres such as education, marriage, or censorship. These were areas which the church had always regarded as its social responsibility but which modern states were now seeking to control. Many of the church–state conflicts of the nineteenth and twentieth centuries, for example, focused on efforts to make marriage a civil contract and to legalize divorce. State control of ecclesiastical affairs was also an issue, such as clerical appointments, church property and funds, and church communications. Bishops who might once have valued distance from Rome came to appreciate papal authority when they needed external help against hostile governments. An example of such hostile state pressure in the 1870s was the *Kulturkampf* ("culture war"), the term used to describe the German Chancellor Otto von Bismarck's campaign to subordinate the Catholic Church to the newly formed German Empire.

Many nineteenth-century Catholics were also eager to strengthen the pope's authority because his teaching office was seen as the last bastion against the intellectual challenges to Christianity, which were surveyed in Chapter 22. Some Catholics saw the modern world in apocalyptic terms as a place crippled by doubt, uncertainty, and loss of faith. They believed that the church needed to present itself to human beings as the ultimate authority that could end argument and debate by delivering a final and irreversible judgment against the dangers of the modern world. For people who shared this pessimistic outlook, maximizing papal authority answered a need somewhat similar to the role which scriptural inerrancy played for fundamentalist Protestants (see Chapter 23).

FIRST VATICAN COUNCIL (1869–1870)

The nineteenth-century tendency to exalt the authority of the papacy is called **ultramontanism**, "beyond the mountains," referring to Rome's location south of the Alps. Ultramontanism reached its high-water mark at the **First Vatican Council** (1869–1870). An overture to that council was the **Syllabus of Errors** issued by Pope Pius IX in 1864. It consisted of eighty condemned propositions, some of which concerned basic religious liberties, such as no. 15 on freedom of religion and no. 55 on the separation of church and state, and several others concerned with the temporal power of the pope. The defiant spirit of the Syllabus is captured in its eightieth and final condemned proposition: "The Roman Pontiff can, and ought to, reconcile himself, and come to terms with, progress, liberalism and modern civilization."

The First Vatican Council, which was the first Catholic ecumenical council to be convened since the Council of Trent three hundred years earlier, was intended in part to rally the Catholic world around the pope. Pope Pius IX convened it at a time when the Papal States, the papacy's temporal domain in Italy, were gravely threatened by the movement to unify the Italian peninsula into a single nation-state. By 1860, years of terrorism and civil war had put the nationalist movement at the gates of Rome, and Pius IX was desperate not to lose what remained of papal territory. An urgent need was felt to establish beyond all doubt the unique governing and teaching authority of the pope.

This council produced a document called *Pastor Aeternus* ("Eternal Pastor"), which declared that the pope had a primacy of jurisdiction (legal governing authority) over the whole church that was universal, ordinary, and immediate (*Pastor Aeternus* §3), meaning that the pope was a bishop of the universal church, with a direct governing authority over all churches. However, it was not explained at this First Vatican Council how the pope's authority could be reconciled with the authority of individual bishops in their dioceses. Because the seizure of Rome by Italian troops in August 1870 forced an abrupt end to Vatican I, this question was never resolved and was not broached again until the Second Vatican Council a century later. The council also declared that under certain circumstances the pope's teaching authority possessed a divinely granted protection against error:

> We teach and define that it is a dogma divinely revealed that when the Roman pontiff speaks *ex cathedra*, that is when in the exercise of his office as shepherd and teacher of all Christians, in

virtue of his supreme apostolic authority, he defines a doctrine regarding faith or morals to be held by the whole church, he possesses, by the divine assistance promised to him in blessed Peter, that infallibility which the divine Redeemer willed his church to enjoy in defining doctrine concerning faith or morals. Therefore, such definitions of the Roman pontiff are of themselves, and not by the consent of the church, irreformable. (*Pastor Aeternus* §4; Tanner, *Decrees of the Ecumenical Councils*, 2: 816)

The definition carefully hedged the doctrine of papal infallibility with important conditions. The pope's infallibility was not his personal prerogative but the church's; it extended to subjects involving "faith and morals", not to any subject whatsoever; and it applied only when it was explicitly invoked. Infallibility also did not mean the capacity to produce new revelation—Catholic teaching has always held that public revelation ended with the death of the apostles. Apart from the dogma of the Immaculate Conception, which was proclaimed in 1854, the only occasion when a pope appealed to papal infallibility was Pope Pius XII's declaration in 1950 of the dogma of the Assumption of Mary into heaven.

Perhaps the fundamental significance of the dogma of infallibility is that such definitions were "irreformable of themselves and not by the consent of the church," meaning that there was no higher court of appeal. It was intended chiefly to answer the long-standing problem the papacy had faced of national hierarchies of bishops that chose to obey their governments rather than Rome. This was an old issue with the French bishops, for example, who, following the theory of church structure known as Gallicanism, held the view that, on issues pertaining to the state, they were answerable to their king first of all, rather than to the pope. This becomes an even more pressing issue with powerful modern governments that might be hostile to Christianity, such as the current standoff between the Vatican and the Peoples Republic of China (see Chapter 22).

TRENDS IN THEOLOGY BETWEEN VATICAN I AND VATICAN II

In the century between the two Vatican councils, what was theology, and who studied it? The latter question is easily answered: Catholic theology was almost exclusively the work of priests, and generally priests who were members of the leading religious orders: the Jesuits first of all, followed by the Dominicans, Franciscans, Benedictines, and others. The major centers of theological study were in Europe, especially in Germany, France, and Belgium. Roman schools generally could not match the academic quality of institutions north of the Alps. In the United States the first graduate programs in theology were opened at the Catholic University of America in Washington, DC. Other Catholic universities did not really commit themselves to such programs until the middle of the twentieth century and later.

Most American theological education took place at houses of study run by religious orders primarily for their own members. A distinctive American development was the trend of women religious (meaning nuns or sisters, women who live in their own religious communities) seeking advanced theological degrees. This developed only slowly, but once it began to happen, women theologians could count on finding teaching positions in the women's colleges run by their religious orders. With rare exceptions, laypeople, both men and women, did not begin to study theology until after the Second Vatican Council.

Because theology was a clerical enterprise, it was subject to the close supervision of church authorities. The chief authority was the pope himself, but the curial office in Rome that had immediate responsibility for overseeing doctrine was the Sacred Congregation of the Holy Office, known up until 1908 as the Holy Office of the Universal Inquisition, and since 1965 as the Congregation for the Doctrine of the Faith (CDF). The current pope, Benedict XVI, born Joseph Ratzinger, was a distinguished academic theologian in Germany before becoming prefect (head) of the CDF, a post he held for a quarter of a century prior to his election as pope in 2005. Between Vatican I and Vatican II, there were two episodes in which especially stern disciplining occurred—the modernist controversy at the beginning of the twentieth century and the 1950s attack on "the new theology."

Modernism is a loose label for trends in Catholic theology that sought to express Catholic teaching in ways that were more consistent with modern intellectual methods, especially in history and philosophy (much less so in the natural sciences). Adopting historical methods meant recognizing ways in which doctrine changed and developed, and acknowledging human limitations in the writers of the Bible. Likewise, trends in philosophy that emphasized action and vital experience (as opposed to abstract speculation) inclined some Catholic theologians to treat the truth value of Catholic doctrines in terms of their practical implications and their origin in subjective religious experience. Such developments alarmed Pope Pius X (reigned 1903–1910). In 1907 he published the decree *Lamentabili*, which condemned modernism as "the synthesis of all heresies." A fierce campaign followed to eliminate any trace of modernism. In 1910 an oath against modernism was imposed on all clergy and seminary professors, an obligation that continued in force until 1967. However mistaken some of the efforts of the modernists were, the anti-modernist reaction discouraged theological research for the next generation.

The Thomist Revival

During the century between Vatican I and Vatican II, Catholicism's theological renewal took numerous forms. The form most favored by the papacy was an appeal to the medieval harmonization of faith and reason, especially as expressed by Thomas Aquinas (see Chapter 15). That was stated officially by Pope Leo XIII (reigned 1878–1903) in 1879 in his encyclical letter *Aeterni Patris* ("Of the Eternal Father"), in which the pope recommended Aquinas' philosophy and theology as the outstanding instrument with which Catholic theologians should engage the modern world. Endorsing Aquinas meant endorsing scholasticism, the method of argument practiced in the medieval schools, and also the philosophy of Aristotle, which had been Aquinas' and scholasticism's chief philosophical resource. The pope envisioned that theological students would first master scholastic philosophy before going on to study theology.

Because of the way in which Thomas' philosophy was taught—depending especially on later sixteenth- and seventeenth-century commentators on Thomas—it is customary to call this revival of scholastic philosophy **neo-scholasticism**. Neo-scholasticism was an attractive preparation for theological study for several reasons:

- the clarity of its concepts and definitions, and its logical rigor;
- its conception of truth as constant and unchanging;
- the objectivity of its truth claims (meaning that it claimed to produce knowledge about an objective reality that transcended the consciousness and experience of the individual knower);
- and its rationality, which did not depend on revelation.

Partly as a consequence of the reaction against modernism, theology students up to Vatican II were required to take several years of neo-scholastic philosophy, framed around twenty-four theses or propositions that were thought to express the essence of Thomas' philosophy.

The Thomist revival produced impressive results in the first half of the twentieth century, in both the areas which Pope Leo had identified: first, in the historical recovery and interpretation of Thomas' writings; second, in the creative development of his ideas. Étienne Gilson (1884–1978) was perhaps the most eminent thinker in the first category, and Jacques Maritain (1882–1973) in the second. Gilson was both a historian of medieval philosophy and a philosopher in his own right. His approach to Thomas Aquinas argued that Thomas was the Christian philosopher par excellence, because his approach to the most fundamental question in philosophy, the question of being ("what does it mean to be?"), has never been surpassed. Of Gilson's many books, perhaps those that achieved the widest popularity were two that originated in lectures series given in the English-speaking world, *The Spirit of Medieval Philosophy* (English trans., 1940) and *The Unity of Philosophical Experience* (1937).

Jacques Maritain, who along with his wife Raïssa (the daughter of Russian Jewish immigrants to France) converted to Catholicism in 1906, was no doubt the most influential advocate of **neo-Thomism** (the application of Thomas' thought to distinctively modern conditions and problems). In an astonishing outpouring of writings over the course of a long life, Maritain produced original works on philosophy, politics, art, literature, education, spirituality, and much else. *The Degrees of Knowledge* (1932; English trans., 1959) presented a hierarchy of scientific ways of knowing that sought to restore metaphysics (the study of being as such) as a genuine science, along with and above physics and mathematics. *Man and the State* (1951) applied the concept of natural law to the modern state and affirmed the goodness of freedom and democracy, values that had not been popular with the nineteenth-century papacy. One of the chief testimonies to his commitment to human rights was his contribution to the United Nations Declaration of Human Rights (1948). *Integral Humanism* (1936; English trans., 1968) praised what Maritain found good and admirable in modern culture, such as the greater awareness of cultural diversity and the deepened sense of the importance of the free and conscious development of the human person—values that would be recognized at Vatican II.

The Turn to the Subject

Not everyone thought that neo-scholasticism was the best philosophical foundation for modern theology. The condemnation of modernism in 1907 did not succeed in permanently halting efforts to enrich theology with insights from modern philosophical sources. One such effort was launched by Catholic thinkers inspired by the Thomist revival but who were also sympathetic to the "critical philosophy" of Immanuel Kant (1724–1804), so-called because it had introduced a powerful critique of the human mind's ability to know objective reality. Kant had stressed the creative role which the mind plays in grasping the intelligibility of the world around it. This development in Catholic theology has been called "the turn to the subject" because of its attention to the more personal aspects of human knowing.

Some of the leading Catholic theologians prior to Vatican II come out of this development. These include figures such as the German Jesuit Karl Rahner (1904–1984), perhaps the dominant Catholic theologian of the twentieth century. His concept of revelation is discussed in Chapter 26. The Canadian Jesuit Bernard Lonergan (1904–1984) concentrated on questions of method in theology. Lonergan was an exceptionally original thinker.

His book *Insight* (1957) led the reader through a set of intellectual exercises designed to let the reader discover for himself or herself the character and implications of what Lonergan called "the unrestricted desire to know." *Insight* breathed an optimism about human knowing that saw intelligence as the complement to faith, not its enemy. The book laid the basis for his later work *Method in Theology* (1973), an ambitious proposal for the complete reorganization of Catholic theology that sought to integrate the many academic specializations into which theological research had become divided, in particular by making more room for historical study and religious experience.

Among the Catholic theologians of this period, there were some who never fit into the neo-scholastic mode at all. Two figures who should be mentioned here are the English convert John Henry Newman (1800–1890) and the Swiss theologian Hans Urs von Balthasar (1905–1988). Balthasar, whose influence is particularly strong today, was keenly interested in literature and the arts, in theological reflection on beauty, and in mystical experience. Newman was an Anglican convert to Catholicism who became perhaps the most original Catholic thinker of the nineteenth century. Before his conversion, he was a prominent figure in the Oxford Movement in the Church of England (see Chapter 19), but his historical studies convinced him that Roman Catholicism preserved more of the historic core of patristic Christianity than had Anglicanism. His *Essay on the Development of Christian Doctrine* (original edition in 1845 while Newman was still an Anglican, reissued in 1878 after his conversion) defended elements in Roman Catholicism that appeared to depart from biblical precedent by arguing that later doctrines could be legitimate developments of earlier ones. This was a novel theory at a time when Catholics (and many other Christians, as well) believed that orthodox doctrine had never changed.

Some of the theologians who were suspected of modernism regarded Newman as an inspiration. This slowed the appreciation of his ideas in the minds of some Catholics, but Newman was a prolific writer of considerable influence. *An Essay in Aid of a Grammar of Assent* presented a subtle account of how an individual person came to adopt and hold religious convictions. His *Apologia Pro Vita Sua* ("Defense of His Life") is an intellectual and religious autobiography that became a literary classic. *On Consulting the Faithful in Matters of Doctrine* offered a theological assessment of the place of the laity in the church that anticipated some of the ideas of the Second Vatican Council. An articulate defender of religious authority, which he saw threatened by individualistic liberalism, Newman nevertheless wrote a classic defense of the rights of individual conscience in the church, if that conscience was rightly formed. His *Letter to the Duke of Norfolk*, written in 1872, right after Vatican I, defended English Catholics against the charge of political disloyalty to Queen Victoria.

As an Englishman and a convert, Newman was a bit of a theological oddity in the Catholic world. He did not depend on the kind of logical argumentation and metaphysical categories that were basic to neo-scholasticism. His thinking and writing drew more from history and literature, and from profound reflection on his own personal experience.

The "Return to the Sources"

There are several theological renewal movements that, for all their differences, shared a common desire to rejuvenate theology by recovering older sources in scripture and tradition—*ressourcement*, "going back to the origin," as it was called in France—to which neo-scholasticism was thought to have done scant justice. In all of these cases there was a practical and pastoral incentive at work, a wish to reinvigorate the actual life of the church as a whole, not just in the classroom. In this sense they were all direct forerunners of the Second Vatican Council.

During the 1940s in France, a generation of theologians born around the turn of the last century became disenchanted with the neo-scholasticism they had learned as students. They included names such as the Jesuits Henri de Lubac (1896–1991) and Jean Daniélou (1905–1974), and the Dominicans M. D. Chenu (1895–1990) and Yves Congar (1904–1995). Several of them had a significant hand in the drafting of the documents that were adopted at the Second Vatican Council. Indeed, in his obituary for Yves Congar, the American theologian Cardinal Avery Dulles said, "Vatican II could almost be called Congar's Council," so fundamentally did its key texts reflect his ideas (Kerr 2007, 34). By one estimate, he was involved in drafting half of its documents. As far back as the 1930s, long before it was acceptable, Congar had committed himself to promoting the cause of the reunion of the separated Christian churches. He wrote ground-breaking works on the concept of reform—again, at a time when nervous Catholic Church authorities would only associate the word with the Protestant Reformation—on the nature of tradition, and on the place of the laity in the church. His Dominican colleague M. D. Chenu specialized in the study of Thomas Aquinas. Chenu was not as involved at Vatican II as Congar, but is credited with having urged the council to take a positive stance towards the modern world (see the following discussion of Vatican II's document *Gaudium et Spes*).

De Lubac and Daniélou devoted themselves to intensive reading in Christian literature that had been written prior to the flourishing of scholasticism in the medieval universities, particularly in patristic literature, the writings of the early Christian fathers (see Chapters 8, 9, and 10). They believed that these earlier writers were more in touch with the biblical sources of the Christian tradition, more attuned to the actual living of the Christian life in the churches, and more sensitive to the symbolic and spiritual meanings of the Bible than their later medieval successors. They co-founded a massive publication project called *Sources chrétiennes*, almost five hundred volumes long by now, which printed ancient and early medieval writings in the original Greek or Latin (and even a few in Syriac, a dialect of Aramaic), plus French translations, with extensive notes and introductions.

Besides a book on the great patristic theologian Origen of Alexandria (d. 253), and a very long study of the tradition of the spiritual interpretation of scripture, De Lubac published several of the most important works of twentieth-century Catholic theology. His book *Catholicism: A Study of the Corporate Destiny of Mankind* stressed the social dimensions of Catholicism, as a way of answering the criticism that Catholics were taught to care only about individual salvation in heaven and not about their role in affecting the destiny of the human race in this world. The criticism came especially from defenders of collectivist political movements who emphasized that human fulfillment could not be a merely individual matter. De Lubac argued that the chief effect of sin was precisely to destroy human unity and solidarity, and that the church was called to be the instrument of the restoration of unity: ". . . redemption being a work of restoration will appear to us by that very fact the recovery of lost unity—the recovery of supernatural unity of man with God, but equally of the unity of men among themselves" (de Lubac 1950, 22).

De Lubac's most controversial book, published in 1950, was entitled *Surnaturel* ("Supernatural"). In this book, de Lubac used the theological concepts of nature and grace to reunite an understanding of the "natural" and "supernatural" orders that he claimed neo-scholasticism had separated. He accused neo-scholasticism of teaching that human beings had two distinct ends or destinies, one natural and the other supernatural. To counter this view, he argued that the constant teaching of early and medieval Christian writers (including Thomas Aquinas) had been that human beings, as actually created in the image of God, had only one single supernatural end, the gift of God's grace as promised in the New Testament. The theologian Fergus Kerr presents de Lubac's thesis in this way: "According to traditional Catholicism, human beings by *nature* were destined to enjoy by divine *grace* everlasting bliss with God" (Kerr 2007, 76). Furthermore, de Lubac argued that Catholic theologians invented the distinction of *two* ends in the sixteenth and seventeenth centuries, with the unhappy result that modern Catholics seem to live with a split between their private, individual pursuit of their supernatural end, eternal life with God, and the rest of their secular life in this world. *Surnaturel* thus complemented the argument of *Catholicism*, with its emphasis on the social dimension of the faith.

It was *Surnaturel*, in particular, that is sometimes seen as the trigger for Pope Pius XII's 1950 encyclical *Humani Generis* ("Of the Human Race"), which among other things criticizied—without naming names—a certain "new theology" that seemed to make the supernatural order gratuitous and unnecessary (see Kerr 2007, 72–77; and McCool 1989, 200–233, esp. 202–212). The encyclical launched almost a decade of repression, during which several of the theologians reviewed in this chapter suffered from disapproval by church officials, only to experience a measure of redemption a decade later when Pope John XXIII convened the Second Vatican Council.

The Liturgical Movement

The liturgical movement came into being in order to revitalize Catholics' experience of the Mass. Its roots go back to the nineteenth century, when French Benedictines sought to recover medieval musical traditions as part of the monastic revival after the French Revolution. In the early twentieth century the movement was centered in Benedictine monasteries in Germany, from where it was exported to the United States, especially to St. John's Abbey in Minnesota.

The liturgical movement envisioned reforming the worship experience not just for monks but for ordinary laypeople as well. Its promoters were most concerned about the Mass, which they thought was no longer at the center of Catholics' spiritual lives. It seemed to have become the exclusive business of the priest, who "said" the Mass in Latin, a language which people could no longer understand. Over the course of the centuries, additional prayers and ceremonies had obscured the inherently collective and communal meaning the Mass had once possessed when the liturgy was more truly "the work of the people," which is what "liturgy" literally means in Greek. If the overlays were peeled away—rather like restoring a painting to its original brilliant colors—perhaps a simplified and more understandable liturgy would remind Catholics that they were not just random individuals who happened to be in church to fulfill their individual Sunday obligation, but an actual community and the very body of Christ: Christ's body was not only the consecrated Eucharistic bread but the community constituted by their reception of the Eucharist.

Then, or so the reformers hoped, this sense of belonging to a community that was Christ's body in the world might carry over to daily life outside the church, in a world that was becoming more secular by the day. Liturgical reform was therefore not just about worship but about the way in which what was believed and expressed in worship was lived out as well. With these larger goals in mind, liturgical scholars labored over ancient and medieval texts in an effort to recover and return to what they thought were older and more authentic forms of worship than what had marked Catholic life in more recent centuries.

Biblical Studies

Biblical studies was another area where scholarship helped to make Vatican II possible. Catholic biblical scholarship gradually recovered from the damage inflicted by the modernist controversy. In 1890, Marie-Joseph Lagrange, O. P., a true godfather of modern Catholic biblical studies, had founded the École Biblique in Jerusalem as a center for scientific study of the Bible in the setting in which it originated. Lagrange escaped being condemned during the anti-modernist repression, and his institute is now in its second century of existence as a research center open to members of all faiths.

In 1943 Pope Pius XII's encyclical *Divino Afflante Spiritu* ("Inspired by the Divine Spirit") gave a cautious endorsement to the full use of all means available (linguistic, archaeological, literary, historical) to uncover the intended meaning of the canonical texts. This included, significantly, the necessity of recognizing the literary genre or "forms of expression" (Pius XII 1943, §36) used by the inspired writers. This cautious endorsement was ratified in Vatican II's statement on divine revelation (*Dei Verbum* §12; see the following section on the theology of revelation). Today Catholic biblical scholars utilize the same historical scientific methods used by scholars of other ancient texts. It is true, of course, that such methods are in themselves insufficient for a full grasp of the divinely intended meaning of scripture. This is why the Pontifical Biblical Commission argued in its 1993 document, "The Interpretation of the Bible in the Church," that Catholic biblical scholars ought to "approach the biblical text with a pre-understanding which holds closely together modern scientific culture and . . . a dynamic pattern of interpretation that is found within the Bible itself and continues in the life of the church" (§III introduction).

As a reaction against some of the limitations of historical scientific approaches to the Bible, which seem to filter God and deeper religious meanings from interpretation, some Catholics are calling for a return to premodern forms of interpretation, which, they argue, depend on faith and nurture faith rather than ignore it. Their concerns are understandable and are reflected in the statement from the 1993 Pontifical Biblical Commission quoted above. But efforts to rehabilitate premodern forms of interpretation cannot be allowed to cancel the irreversible gains made by historical scientific biblical criticism (see Chapter 22). To cite a crucial example, it is thanks in part to historical methods that Catholic theology now has a much clearer grasp of Christianity's roots in Judaism and of the Jewishness of Jesus.

SECOND VATICAN COUNCIL

The **Second Vatican Council**, or Vatican II as it is often called, met in the Basilica of St. Peter's in Rome, from October 1962 to December 1965. In Catholic reckoning, Vatican II is the twenty-first in the list of general or "ecumenical" (universal) councils that began with Nicaea. In attendance with voting rights were over two thousand Catholic bishops and abbots from around the world, along with their theological advisors. Protestant and Eastern Orthodox representatives were also on hand as invited observers, though they could not participate in the public deliberations or cast a vote. Nevertheless, they made their presence felt indirectly by their contact with Catholic bishops and theologians outside of the formal sessions of the council. In recognition of the importance of their presence, the first English language edition of the council's official documents contained responses and reactions by selected Protestant and Eastern Orthodox commentators (Abbott 1966). With the passage of time

Figure 24–1 Photo of Pope John XXIII, 1963.

since the council ended in 1965, it has become clear that Vatican II was one of the major events of the twentieth century, with an impact on the world outside the Catholic Church as well as within it.

The Second Vatican Council was the idea of Pope John XXIII (reigned 1958–1963). Nearly eighty years old at the time of his election, John was widely regarded as a "caretaker" pope, an uncontroversial man who could provide a breather of sorts after Pius XII's long and eventful pontificate. Three months after his election, however, he surprised everyone by declaring his intention to call a general council, an idea he credited to the inspiration of the Holy Spirit. Many assumed the council would simply reaffirm the teachings of the councils of Trent and Vatican I, and perhaps provide further definition to existing doctrines. But John declared that his council was going to be *pastoral* in its purpose, by which he meant that it was supposed to focus on the lives of believers and their experience of living the faith in the world as it is today.

In his opening address to the council on October 11, 1962, Pope John XXIII emphasized that while the church was committed to handing on the sacred doctrine of past councils, it was also important to present this doctrine in a way suitable to the present: "The substance of the ancient doctrine of the deposit of faith is one thing, and the way it is presented is another" (Abbott 1966, 715). The two words that summarized Pope John's hopes for the council were *dialogue* with those outside the church, instead of the too often negative and hostile posture the church had adopted in the modern period; and *aggiornamento*, an Italian word that means roughly "a bringing up to date."

The following sections summarize five areas in which Vatican II made notable contributions: the reform of the liturgy; the self-understanding of the church as "the people of God"; relations with other Christian churches and with non-Christian religions; the church's relationship to the modern world; and the Catholic understanding of revelation.

Reform of the Liturgy

Most obvious to the average Catholic were the changes in the liturgy. As noted above, prior to the council all Catholic Masses were said in Latin, and the priest celebrated the Mass with his back to the people, except when he had finished reading the Epistle and gospel in Latin and would turn toward the people to reread the two scripture readings in translation. The sanctuary where the priest celebrated the liturgy was separated from the nave (body) of the church by a low railing called the communion rail, where people knelt to receive the Eucharist. Lay people were not allowed in the sanctuary. This separation expressed a strong distinction between the supernatural and the natural, the sacred and the profane, the clerical and the lay. The divine presence in the sanctuary itself was concentrated in the Eucharist, which the priest consecrated on the altar during the Mass. Consecrated hosts were kept in the tabernacle, the locked box typically located on the altar itself, so that even apart from the Mass people could pray to the perpetual presence of Christ on the altar. On certain occasions during the year, the Eucharistic host was brought forward by the priest for public procession and worship in the ceremony known as Benediction. A major symbolic effect of all of this was to emphasize the separation between the clergy and the laity, and, whether it was intended or not, to reduce the laity's role to passive observation.

The first document issued by the council, the *Constitution on the Sacred Liturgy*, introduced sweeping reforms, many of them advocated by the liturgical movement described above. The Mass could now be celebrated in the vernacular (the language of the people), as well as in Latin. The altar was turned around, so that the priest faced the people. This made the Mass more of a dialogue with the congregation rather than a monologue prayer said by the priest on behalf of the people. More popular and contemporary forms of music were allowed, and new music was composed that tried to reflect the spirit of participation and dialogue for which the council called. Eventually, the readers and lay ministers (to help distribute the Eucharist) were allowed to take an active role in the Mass. It was a refreshing change to see women readers and lay ministers in the sanctuary. Private devotions during the Mass (for example, saying the rosary) were discouraged, since there was a desire to restore a sense of the Mass as a communal celebration.

One of the consequences of the shift toward more active participation in the Mass was a change in church architecture. From the time of Constantine until the Second Vatican Council, Catholic Church buildings were usually built in the shape of a Latin cross, with the clergy and sanctuary separated from the laity. After Vatican II, new churches were often built in circular or semicircular form so that the congregation surrounded the altar, and even older churches were rearranged inside so that the congregation sat on three sides of the altar. This new architecture emphasized the active participation of the whole congregation in the liturgy.

From the vantage point of several decades later, it is clear that not everything that reformers hoped for has come to pass. Much of what was valuable and familiar in traditional devotional practices was thrown out with scant respect and no explanation; Because ritual depends in part on familiar and habitual responses, the changes left some people confused and resentful. Critics of contemporary liturgical music complained that it was too often bland, vulgar, or badly performed, and the lyrics not always adequate expressions of the faith. Others were concerned that the reformed liturgy too easily "flattened out" the experience of worship, so that the worshiping congregation seemed more focused on itself than on God. The new structure of the celebration, with the priest facing the people, subtly changed the character of the Mass from an encounter with the transcendent God, present in the sanctuary, to a conversation between priest and people.

It is ironic that the priest's about-face has put the spotlight squarely on him more than on the congregation, and thus put unprecedented emphasis on the priest's personal style and appearance (the law of unintended consequences at work?). The sense of community

Figure 24–2 Aerial view of the interior of the Liverpool Cathedral. Note the circular seating arrangement and the central placement of the altar. Photo by David S. Cunningham.

may have been heightened, but for many Catholics the sense of the sacred, almost palpable in pre-Vatican II churches, has been subtly diminished. There was also a decline in prayers such as the rosary, personal devotion to the saints, and the adoration of the Eucharist, especially among young Catholics, many of whom today are unfamiliar with prayers and practices which had nourished their ancestors' faith for generations. At the same time, the liturgical reforms of Vatican II have enhanced laypeople's understanding of what happens in the liturgy and have given them opportunities to be active participants in the worship of the church, not merely passive observers.

The Church as People of God

A second major area of development resulting from the council concerned its understanding of the church, which was expounded in the conciliar document known as *The Dogmatic Constitution on the Church* or *Lumen Gentium* ("Light of Nations"). Prior to the Second Vatican Council, the church had often simply been equated with the hierarchy, as in the phrase "The church teaches." This conception of the church could be diagrammed like a pyramid: The pope was the leader at the top, and he alone was called the "vicar [representative] of Christ." Under him were the bishops, seen as deputies of the pope, then the priests, then members of religious orders (monks and nuns), then the laity at the bottom. Authority and power flowed from the top down but not from the bottom up. Catholic laity tended to look to the clergy and pope for answers. This was very much the model endorsed by the First Vatican Council, which addressed the pope's primacy of universal jurisdiction and his infallible teaching authority, but which had had to suspend its work before it could consider the corresponding status of the bishops.

By contrast, Vatican II's *Lumen Gentium* uses a variety of images for the church. The first chapter (§§1–8) presents the church as a "mystery," in the sense that its reality cannot be fully expressed in human language and categories. By virtue of her connection with Christ, who is the Light of Nations, the church is said to be "a kind of sacrament or sign of intimate union with God, and of the unity of all mankind" (§1; Abbott 1966, 15). The second chapter (§§9–17) described the church as the "Holy People of God." Not until chapter three (§§18–29) does *Lumen Gentium* consider the hierarchical structure of the church. The hierarchy of ordained clergy has the special function of administering the sacraments, preserving the teaching of the apostles, and maintaining church discipline. Here the document repeats Vatican I's assertion of the pope's primacy in the church (see especially §25). But it also asserts the essential place of the bishops, who are not simply deputies or delegates of the pope. They too are successors of the apostles and constitute a "college" (a group of clergy with certain rights and responsibilities), with the pope as their head: "Together with its head, the Roman Pontiff, and never without this head, the episcopal order is the subject of supreme and full power over the universal Church" (§22; Abbott 1966, 43).

Returning to the topic of the second chapter of *Lumen Gentium*, the notion of the church as "the whole people of God" is thoroughly ancient, being rooted in both the Bible and tradition. In the Old Testament, Israel is the people of God by virtue of the covenant, and the New Testament extends that status to the new people of God, the church (§9). Before "laity" came to mean those who were not ordained clergy or in religious life, the Greek word from which it derives, *laos*, embraced all the baptized. The *whole* church constitutes the people of God, not merely the hierarchy. Thus, in embracing the notion of church as "People of God," Vatican II was actually returning to a more ancient conception of the church and correcting a tendency which came about because of exaggerated interpretations of Vatican I—that the Holy Spirit speaks to the church only through the pope, who then tells the rest of the church what to believe. In fact, the Holy Spirit speaks through all the members of the church.

The subject of the fourth chapter of *Lumen Gentium* (§§30–38) is the laity (understood in the narrower sense of those who are not ordained), which it recognizes in a special way as the church's presence in the world: "A secular quality is proper and special to laypeople . . . they can work for the sanctification of the world from within, in the manner of leaven" (§31; Abbott 1966, 57). The document also asserts that, among laity and clergy, there is "no inequality" and "an equal privilege of faith" in the church, even though there are manifestly different roles and responsibilities (§32; Abbott 1960, 58).

The best example of Vatican II's doctrine of the church as the People of God is the Second Vatican Council itself. Its teachings were not simply the thoughts of the pope, accepted without question by the bishops. In fact, Popes John XXIII and Paul VI intervened only rarely in the council's proceedings. Instead, the proclamations of Vatican II were the result of a long collective discernment process in which theological experts spoke and bishops debated until consensus was reached. Thus they represent, to a great degree, the mind of the whole church, the People of God.

A practical result of the revised conception of the church as the whole "People of God" is the creation of parish councils. Previously, priests usually had the sole authority in a parish. After Vatican II, the priest and bishop still retained legal rights to make decisions for the local parish, but most parishes instituted parish councils, made up of laypersons, to advise and assist the priest in parish administration. Another result was the development of national conferences of bishops, such as the U.S. Conference of Catholic Bishops. The bishops of a given nation meet together periodically (usually once a year) to discuss issues facing their churches. Since the Second Vatican Council, the U.S. Conference of Catholic Bishops has issued notable teaching statements on war and peace, the U.S. economy, the environmental crisis, and other matters. Again, this reflects the Second Vatican Council's notion that the bishops are not just deputies of the pope, but, as successors to the apostles, are teaching authorities in their own right.

A third result of the council is the emergence of lay theologians. As stated above, prior to Vatican II, religion classes in Catholic schools and colleges were taught by priests or nuns. After the council, Catholic university departments of theology opened their facilities to lay students of theology, so that lay persons could earn graduate degrees in theology and teach theology in colleges and universities. Now most theology teachers in Catholic colleges are laypersons.

The Ecumenical Movement and Interreligious Dialogue

A third major area of development flowing from the Second Vatican Council involves the relationship of Catholic Christians to non-Catholic Christians and non-Christian religions. Before Vatican II, Protestants were viewed as heretics or schismatics who were therefore not a part of the church (Pius XII *Mystici Corporis*, 23; cited in Carlen 1981, 41). In contrast, the documents of Vatican II address Protestants as "separated brethren," not as heretics. The *Decree on Ecumenism* states that a chief concern of the council was to restore unity among Christians. It further states that all baptized Christians are in real, though imperfect, communion with the Catholic Church (§§1, 3; Abbott 1966, 341–366).

A result of these discussions at the council is greatly improved relations between Catholics and Christians of other denominations. It is now frequent to have marriages between Catholics and Protestants, whereas before Vatican II, these kinds of marriages were discouraged. Catholic theologians regularly use Protestant texts in their research, writing, and teaching. In Minnesota, the Lutheran and Catholic bishops have committed themselves to a covenant or agreement on major points of the Christian faith, the first time this has happened anywhere in the world. In 1999, the Lutheran World Federation and the Catholic Church produced a *Joint Declaration on Justification*. It said that there was a "consensus in basic truths" in their respective teachings on justification, that such differences as continued were nevertheless "acceptable," and that the condemnations produced by both Lutherans and Catholics in the sixteenth century did not in fact apply to what Lutherans and Catholics were now understood to teach (see especially sections 40–41).

In addition to the *Decree on Ecumenism*, the Second Vatican Council issued a short *Declaration on the Relationship of the Church to Non-Christian Religions*, also known by its Latin title as *Nostra Aetate* ("in our time"), which affirms that the Catholic Church respects all that is true and holy in any religion (see *Nostra Aetate* §2). It notes that Jews, Muslims, and Christians all worship the same God, and it condemns any form of discrimination based on race or religion (§5). The council continued to uphold the traditional teaching that the fullness of revelation is found only in Jesus the Christ, but it also said that other religions "often reflect a ray of that Truth which enlightens all men" (§2; Abbott 1966, 662). Although the precise meaning of this statement is disputed, at the minimum it asserts some degree of compatibility and overlap between the Christian revelation and non-Christian religions. In its most significant and controversial passage, the *Declaration* states that Jews are not to be regarded as having inherited guilt for the death of Jesus, nor are they to be regarded as accursed or rejected by God, "as if such views followed from the holy Scriptures" (§4; Abbott

1966, 666). The rejection of the doctrine that Jews bore a curse for the death of Jesus thus corrected a widespread and ancient Christian teaching that had justified centuries of Christian hostility to Jews and Judaism. "Anti-Semitism, directed against the Jews at any time and from any source" (§4; Abbott 1966, 667), was firmly rejected.

Since Vatican II, extensive dialogue between Catholics and Jews, Muslims, Buddhists, and Hindus has developed. Such inter-religious dialogue is discussed at length in Chapter 26 of this book.

Dialogue with the Secular World

As explained in Chapter 22, the intellectual, political, cultural, social, and economic changes that characterized the modern world had a profound impact on Christianity. Among cultures most affected by these changes, human life and the experience of the world have tended to seem less religious and more secular in character. People may be less likely to belong to religious institutions (measured by such things as church attendance or financial support), to invoke religious values in defense of their actions, to adopt religious practices and symbols, to accept religious authority, and to believe religious explanations of the meaning of human life and the natural world.

For the monotheistic religions (Christianity, Judaism, and Islam), of course, the world does not cease to be God's world, even though humans do not acknowledge God. Nevertheless, each religion has had to come to terms with secularization and explain what place it has in God's plan. For Catholic Christianity, secularization is a particular challenge because of Catholicism's strong belief that the church and the gospel are supposed to pervade and shape the social order. As noted above, Vatican II taught that the church is the "sacrament . . . of the unity of the human race" (*Lumen Gentium* §1; Abbott 1966, 15). This means that Catholicism is obliged to be an active presence and voice in the modern world. The church seeks to identify those elements in modern life that seem most compatible with the gospel and therefore as evidence of God's continuing involvement in human affairs, not just in the church, but outside it as well.

Vatican II addressed this issue most directly in the *Pastoral Constitution on the Church in the Modern World*, known also by its Latin title, *Gaudium et Spes*, from its opening words, "The joys and the hopes, the griefs and the anxieties of the men of this age, especially those who are poor or in any way afflicted, these too are the joys and the hopes, the griefs and the anxieties of the followers of Christ" (*Gaudium et Spes* §1; Abbott 1966, 199–200). In this document, the church sought to speak to the whole human family (§2). Christians were told they must continually examine the "signs of the times" (§§4, 11). Modern cultural and scientific advances should not be seen in a merely negative light but should be acknowledged as having important positive meanings as well. Religion, for example, could be purified from a more magical view of the world and advance to a more mature understanding (§7). Modern men and women were increasingly "conscious that they themselves are the artisans and the authors of the culture of their community" (§55; Abbott 1966, 260–261). They possessed a growing sense that they were personal agents in their own right and not just the passive objects of the actions of others—what Pope John Paul II would call "acting persons," a development that the council described as "of paramount importance for the spiritual and moral maturity of the human race" (§55; Abbott 1966, 261). Modern atheism was not always and everywhere a revolt against God; sometimes it contained powerful elements of moral protest (§§19–20). Sometimes believers themselves were responsible for modern unbelief (§21).

Further, *Gaudium et Spes* noted that, despite modern movements towards human autonomy, religion was still essential as the answer to our deepest questions and to conflicts that seemed forever to escape our solving (§§9–10). It also taught that the ultimate basis of human dignity and therefore of authentic humanism is humanity's creation in the image of God—our final defense against reducing ourselves or others to mere objects of use or consumption (§12). The definitive model for human development was Jesus Christ, "the desire of the nations," "the Alpha and the Omega" of human history, who was destined to recapitulate in His risen self the whole of human history at its endpoint (§§10, 22, 45). The church is called to work alongside men and women of good will, even if they do not share Christian assumptions, if their work seeks to serve the same ends of social justice and the common good to which Christians too were committed (§21 et passim). Christian involvement has to respect the legitimate autonomy of the secular spheres in which Christians work and live (§36), but it is the special duty of laymen and laywomen to be the transforming Christian presence in the secular world (§43).

Such was Vatican II's effort to understand theologically the world in modernity. In the generation since the council, Catholics have found themselves in deep disagreement about how best to implement the council's exhortations to engage in a new dialogue with the secular world. The disagreements are generally not about the wisdom and necessity of engaging the world, but about the way in which the "signs of the times" should be read. Precisely *which* movements and developments should be endorsed and supported? The postconciliar divisions in the church often stem from disagreement about what will actually promote moral progress and what will lead to moral decline.

The Theology of Revelation

A fifth area which saw significant development because of Vatican II concerns the theology of revelation. The *Dogmatic Constitution on Divine Revelation*, known by its Latin title as *Dei Verbum* ("The Word of God"), built on the results of biblical and historical studies prior to the council in order to advance the understanding of revelation in several respects. The first had to do with the understanding of how God's revelation is transmitted. In reaction to the "scripture alone" doctrine of the Protestant Reformation, the Council of Trent had simply asserted the traditional teaching that there were two channels of revelation, one written and the other oral. Today we identify these two channels as scripture and tradition. *Dei Verbum* sought to show how the two were intrinsically and mutually related, so that they could not be completely separated from one another: "For both of them, flowing from the same divine wellspring, in a certain way merge into a unity and tend toward the same end" (*Dei Verbum* §9; Abbott 1966, 117; in general see §§7–10).

Second, *Dei Verbum* recognized that even though the one revelation had not changed, the *understanding* of that revelation had indeed undergone deepening and change over the course of time: "The tradition which comes from the apostles develops in the Church with the help of the Holy Spirit. For there is a growth in the understanding of the realities and the words which have been handed down . . . as the centuries succeed one another, the Church constantly moves forward toward the fullness of divine truth until the words of God reach their complete fulfillment in her" (*Dei Verbum* §8; Abbott 1966, 116). Third, *Dei Verbum* recognized the role of human authorship in the biblical books. Although the authors were divinely inspired, the books they wrote needed to be studied according to ancient literary forms if their meanings were to be rightly understood (§12).

Fourth, *Dei Verbum* asserted that the teaching authority of the church has the exclusive task of authentically interpreting scripture and tradition, which constitute "the one deposit of faith." Even so, the constitution recognizes that the teaching office "is not above the word of God, but serves it, teaching only what has been handed on . . ." (§10; Abbott 1966, 118). Fifth and last, *Dei Verbum* strongly recommends greater attention to the Bible in every aspect of the church's life: on the part of all the faithful (§22); on the part of those who preach and preside in the liturgy (§§23, 25); and in the study of theology itself (§24).

Key Terms

ultramontanism
First Vatican Council
Syllabus of Errors

neo-scholasticism
neo-Thomism
ressourcement

Second Vatican Council
aggiornamento

Questions for Reading

1. Describe some of the main features of Catholicism as it was practiced after the French Revolution and before the First Vatican Council.

2. When was the First Vatican Council called, and what was its purpose? What was its most important teaching, and how was this teaching intended to be understood?

3. What is neo-scholasticism, and what contributions did it make to Catholic theology in the period between the First and Second Vatican councils?

4. What is *ressourcement,* and what contributions did this movement make to Catholic theology in the period between the First and Second Vatican councils?

5. What were some of the goals of the Catholic liturgical movement in the period between the First and Second Vatican councils? How did it anticipate some of the reforms of the Second Vatican Council?

6. What were some of the developments in Catholic biblical studies during the period between the First and Second Vatican councils? How did these developments anticipate the Second Vatican Council's teaching on revelation?

7. When was the Second Vatican Council called, and what was its purpose? Why did some persons consider it to be an ecumenical council, while others did not?

8. Describe the major contributions of the Second Vatican Council in the following areas:

   a. Reform of the liturgy
   b. Church as "People of God"
   c. The ecumenical movement
   d. Dialogue with the secular world
   e. The theology of revelation

Works Consulted/Recommended Reading

Abbott, Walter M., S. J., ed. *The Documents of Vatican II.* New York: Herder and Herder, Association Press, 1966.

Bokenkotter, Thomas. *A Concise History of the Catholic Church,* Rev. ed. New York: Doubleday, 1979.

Brezik, Victor B., ed. *One Hundred Years of Thomism.* Aeterni Patris *and Afterwards.* Houston: Center for Thomistic Studies, 1981.

Carlen, Claudia, ed. *The Papal Encyclicals, 1939–1958.* Wilmington, NC: McGrath, 1981.

de. Lubac, Henri *Catholicism: A Study of the Corporate Destiny of Mankind.* London: Burns, Oates, and Washbourne, 1950.

———. *Surnaturel; Etudes Historiques.* Paris: Aubier, 1946.

Flannery, Austin P., ed. *Vatican Council II: The Conciliar and Post Conciliar Documents.* Collegeville, MN: Liturgical Press, 1975.

Kerr, Fergus. *After Aquinas: Versions of Thomism.* Oxford: Blackwell, 2002.

———. *Twentieth-Century Catholic Theologians: From Neoscholasticism to Nuptial Mysticism.* Oxford: Blackwell, 2007.

McCool, Gerald. *From Unity to Pluralism: The Internal Evolution of Thomism.* New York: Fordham University, 1989.

———. *Nineteenth-Century Scholasticism: The Search for a Unitary Method.* New York: Fordham University, 1989.

National Conference of Catholic Bishops. *The Challenge of Peace: God's Promise and Our Response.* Washington, DC: National Conference of Catholic Bishops, 1983.

———. *Economic Justice for All: Pastoral Letter on Catholic Social Teaching and the U.S. Economy.* Washington, DC: National Conference of Catholic Bishops, 1986.

Official Dialogue Commission of the Lutheran World Federation and the Vatican. "Joint Declaration on the Doctrine of Justification." *Origins* 28 (1998): 120–127. Also available at http://www.vatican.va/roman_curia/pontifical_councils/chrstuni/documents/rc_pc_chrstuni_doc_31101999_cath-luth-joint-declaration_en.html.

Pius XII. *Divino Afflante Spiritu. Encyclical of Pope Pius XII on Promoting Biblical Studies, Commemorating the Fiftieth Anniversary of Providentissimus Deus.* 1943. http://www.vatican.va/holy_father/pius_xii/encyclicals/documents/hf_p-xii_enc_30091943_divino-afflante-spiritu_en.html.

Pontifical Biblical Commission, "Interpretation of the Bible in the Church." *Origins* 23 (1994): 497–524. Also available at http://www.vatican.va/roman_curia/congregations/cfaith/pcb_index.htm.

Sullivan, Francis, S. J. *Salvation Outside the Church? Tracing the History of the Catholic Response.* Mahwah, NJ: Paulist, 1992.

Tanner, Norman P., ed. *Decrees of the Ecumenical Councils.* 2 vols. Washington, DC: Georgetown University, 1990.

Chapter

CHRISTIANITY AND THE CONTEMPORARY SITUATION

In every period of history, Christianity, like any other religion, has had to deal with changing cultural realities. When cultural changes are moderate and gradual, the ways in which religion both adapts to culture and impacts the development of culture can be subtle and even indiscernible, except with the passage of time. However, this is not always the case. In some periods, Christianity has exercised an active, perhaps even dominant role in shaping the development of culture. The most obvious example is that of European society in the High Middle Ages, which came to be known as Christendom (see Chapter 14). At other times, Christianity has struggled to adapt to cultural changes that impinge upon it from the outside—for example, in the Age of Enlightenment and its aftermath (see Chapter 22).

For the Roman Catholic Church, the challenge to respond to changing cultural realities ushered in by the Age of Enlightenment was made even more difficult by the fact that the church had changed very little from the time of the Council of Trent (1545–1563). The only ecumenical council called between the Council of Trent and the mid-twentieth century was Vatican Council I (1869–1870). This council, under the direction of Pope Pius IX, made important statements about the infallibility of the pope and about the harmony of reason and faith, but its work was cut short by the Franco-Prussian war. Its discussion of the nature of the church would not be finished until Vatican Council II (1962–1965). Change came quickly after Vatican Council II and without much explanation, at least where the laity was concerned. Thus the period immediately after the council was exciting for some but fraught with anxiety and frustration for others. Even today, more than forty years later, Catholic bishops, theologians, and communities of faith are still trying to discern the proper interpretation of the council's documents for the future of the church (see Chapter 24).

The topic of this chapter is Christianity and the contemporary situation—generally speaking, the latter half of the twentieth century to the present. This period is most closely identified with postmodernity and the development of postmodernism. Therefore, we will begin with a brief survey of some of the early manifestations of postmodernism in art, architecture, and

441

philosophy and some comments about the impact of postmodernism on the way that people think about religious questions. Second, we will look at some examples of the range of contemporary Christian theologies that have developed as a response to postmodernist worldviews. Finally, we will explore two emerging church movements that show how Christian churches are attempting to adapt themselves to diverse cultural experiences and rapidly changing circumstances today.

POSTMODERNISM

If you are a student of art or literature, music or film, or even architecture or philosophy, you may have heard the term *postmodernism*. But to what does it refer, and what does it mean? First, we should note that scholars in these various academic disciplines do not agree on a definition of postmodernism. This is due in part to the different disciplines themselves. Postmodernist architecture, for example, brings together traditional and modern styles in a way that is intended to surprise, amuse, or entertain. The University of Minnesota's Weisman Art Museum and the Guggenheim Museum in Bilbao, Spain, both designed by Frank Gehry, are examples. Against modernist architecture, which was stark and utilitarian, the postmodernists reintroduced ornamentation to capture a sense of whimsy and an aura of transcendence or otherworldliness.

Similarly, whereas modern art tends toward geometric abstraction, stripping images down to their simplest forms, postmodern art seeks to reintroduce classical painting and the realistic representations of earlier times. However, postmodern art does more than simply offer a corrective to the extremes of modern art. It goes beyond the boundaries of modern art, overturning traditional notions of what makes art "art." For example, postmodern art might involve mixing found objects with various artistic media to create enormous collages of contradictory and dissonant images or multimedia presentations of music, images, and performance art, which engage all of the viewer's senses. Postmodern art works from the assumption that art is created by the viewers as

Figure 25–1 Photo of exterior of Weisman Art Museum at the University of Minnesota.

Figure 25–2 Christo and Jean-Claude, "Gates," Central Park Project, February, 2005. New York City. An example of postmodern conceptual art.

they view the experience, and it seeks to challenge common understandings of beauty by offering its viewers objects that confront and offend rather than please the senses. As a consequence, the artistic event does not have a single definitive meaning. In fact, it can have as many interpretations as it has viewers.

Hopefully these two examples from art and architecture provide some idea of the scope and direction of the postmodernist movement. But what is **postmodernism**? It is a cultural and intellectual movement that emerged out of modernism and therefore has some continuity with it. Some would go so far as to say that it is impossible to talk about postmodernism outside of modernism. Because postmodernism follows upon modernism, this term also carries connotations of building upon or providing a corrective to modernism. For example, if modernism is characterized by reliance on reason and scientific methodology as the measure of human progress and as the manner in which knowledge is acquired, postmodernism calls attention to the limits of reason and offers a critique on the assumption that scientific methodology can produce certitude or that reason, by itself, can uncover truth. Whereas the Age of Enlightenment promised freedom from the tyranny of superstitions and ignorance, postmodernism seeks to reveal that this so-called freedom was actually slavery to intellectual theories and rationalist worldviews that left no place for chance or creativity (see Chapter 22 and Chapter 24 for more on the Age of Enlightenment and modernism). The postmodernist period is generally understood to have been well underway by the middle of the twentieth century.

Before we can talk about postmodern trends in theology, there are at least two philosophers whom we ought to mention, because their writings radically changed the way that postmodernist theologians do their work. They are Friedrich Nietzsche (1844–1900) and Jacques Derrida (1930–2004). In the history of philosophy, Friedrich Nietzsche is usually considered in the modernist period, because of the time in which he lived. However, already in 1872 and 1873, his writings demonstrate a clear dissatisfaction with the ideals of modernism—especially, rationalism and the idea that there exist certain universal constants—in favor of themes that are often characterized as postmodernist. Although Nietzsche wrote on a wide range of topics, he is perhaps most famous for his assertion, "God is dead." His parable of the madman, contained in his book, *The Gay Science*, sometimes translated *The Joyful Science*, provides some context:

> The madman.—Have you not heard of that madman who lit a lantern in the bright morning hours, ran to the market place and cried incessantly: "I seek God! I seek God!"—As many of those who did not believe in God were standing around just then, he provoked much laughter... The madman jumped into their midst and pierced them with his eyes. "Whither is God?" he cried. "I will tell you. We have killed him—you and I! All of us are his murderers! But how did we do this? How could we drink up the sea? Who gave us the sponge to wipe away the entire horizon? What were we doing when we unchained this earth from its sun? Whither is it moving now? Whither are we moving? Away from all suns? Are we not plunging continually? Backward, sideward, forward, in all directions? Is there still any up or down? Are we not straying as through an infinite nothing? Do we not feel the breath of empty space? Has it not become colder? Is not night continually closing in on us? Do we not hear nothing as yet of the noise of the gravediggers who are burying God? Do we smell nothing as yet of the divine decomposition?—Gods, too, decompose! God is dead! God remains dead! And we have killed him! How shall we comfort ourselves, the murderers of all murders? (Nietzsche 1974, Book 3, aphorism 25)

Nietzsche's madman represents people who have come to realize that God and godly things are an illusion. Sensing the disillusionment of modernity, he saw that humans were spiritually hungry, but unable to believe in a cosmic order that presupposes the existence of God. Hence, the madman's cry: "I seek God!" Further, he recognized that humanity needs the myths of God, the "good and the beautiful," to maintain stability and protect itself from the truth that humanity and creation itself is dark and meaningless. The madman's confrontative inquiry—"Whither is God?"—and his response represent a shattering of that false sense of stability, realizing finally the death of God. The rhetorical questions that follow the madman's declaration highlight the **nihilism** (the belief that there is no objective basis for truth and that human values are worthless) that, according to Nietzsche, accompanies humanity's recognition that God is dead. If God is dead, humanity cannot talk with certainty about anything. Everything dissolves into darkness. If God is dead, civilization's moorings are severed, so to speak, and humanity is now drifting into an infinite sea of nothingness. The pessimistic and brooding tone of the parable of the madman suggests that this realization was the source of considerable grief for Nietzsche.

Nietzsche blamed Christianity, or at least the Christian hierarchy, for the plight of humanity, because it advocated what he called "slave morality" for the Masses—meekness, obedience, self-sacrifice, submissiveness—at the same time that it practiced "master morality" for its own benefit—pride, courage, strength, health. In place of traditional moral values, he called for a transvaluation of values, which he understood would result in the recovery of human freedom and creativity, where people could learn to create themselves anew, without the baggage of the past. For Nietzsche, Christianity was baggage of the past:

> Christianity as antiquity.—When we hear the ancient bells growling on a Sunday morning we ask ourselves: Is it really possible! This, for a Jew, crucified two thousand years ago, who said he was God's son? The proof of such a claim is lacking. Certainly the Christian religion is an antiquity

projected into our times from remote prehistory; and the fact that the claim is believed—whereas one is otherwise so strict in examining pretensions—is perhaps the most ancient piece of this heritage. A god who begets children with a mortal woman; a sage who bids men to work no more, have no more courts, but look for the signs of the impending end of the world; a justice that accepts the innocent as a vicarious sacrifice; someone who orders his disciples to drink his blood; prayers for miraculous interventions; sins perpetrated against a god, atoned for by a god; fear of a beyond to which death is the portal; the form of the cross as a symbol in a time that no longer knows the function and ignominy of the cross—how ghoulishly all this touches us, as if from the tomb of a primeval past! Can one believe that such things are still believed? (Nietzsche 1996, sect. 405)

In sum, Nietzsche viewed Christianity as something that was accepted principally because of its antiquity but whose tenets could not verified in the age of modernity. Consequently, it was a mystery to him that Christianity would have been believed at all in his day.

After Nietzsche came a number of philosophers like Michel Foucault, Richard Rorty, and Jacques Derrida who were influenced by his thinking and who likewise questioned the extent to which humanity could know certain things. Among these, Derrida is important for the development of a postmodern approach to reading and interpreting texts called **deconstruction**. Applied first to philosophical texts and later to other literature, including religious writings, deconstructionist approaches to reading reveal how the text might not mean what it appears to mean and ultimately how its central message will always elude the reader.

One of the strategies of deconstruction is to look at language and communication in terms of traditional dualities (oppositions) and then overturn their commonly accepted hierarchical order to see how they affect the process of reading. For example, in Western cultures, at least, the spoken word is considered more valuable than the written word. Similarly, light is traditionally favored over darkness, the mind over the body, rationality over foolishness, and wealth over poverty. Concerning our attachment to these traditional dualities, Derrida wrote:

If one is always bound by one's perspectives, one can at least deliberately reverse perspectives as often as possible, in the process undoing opposed perspectives, showing that the two terms of an opposition are merely accomplices of each other. (Derrida 1976, xxviii)

Drawing upon Derrida's insight that these dualities are accomplices and not opponents of one another, deconstructionists give priority to the subordinate, rather than the dominant, element of these dualistic pairs in order to break open the meaning of the text under investigation. By paying careful attention to aspects of the text that are seldom noticed, they uncover places where the meaning of the text seems to fracture and become unstable. Then they probe and prod at these fracture points until the meaning of the entire text begins to unravel. Thus, deconstructionist strategies do not provide us with a single definitive interpretation of a text, nor do they offer a range of reliable interpretations. Instead, they produce a multitude of questions that expose the text to new possibilities. Needless to say, for those who accept its presuppositions, deconstruction is playful study, but for those who do not deconstruction is the epitome of frustration and a challenge to the nature of meaning itself.

But deconstruction is more than a playful and sometimes seemingly irreverent manipulation of authoritative texts. Jacques Derrida was a philosopher of language, a subdiscipline of philosophy that is concerned with the nature and use of language, the meaning of meaning and its relationship to language, and the relationship of language to truth and reality. In *Of Grammatology*, Derrida overturns the assumed oppositional relationship of speech and writing. He observed that philosophers and great thinkers of the West, in particular, tend to favor speech over writing because they see speech as a system of signs that represents a mental experience of communicating meaning. By contrast, they see writing as simply a system of signs that represent speech. Against this view, Derrida argues that all signs—even the signs involved in speech—are derivative. That is, all signs refer to other signs, and you can never get to the sign that refers to meaning itself. Furthermore, speech is as much of a "sign of a sign" as is the written word.

Of course, Derrida is talking about so much more than the mechanics of writing—putting words on paper. Rather, he is referring to two core attributes of the writing experience. The first is the recognition that there is an enduring gap between what the writer intended to communicate and what is actually communicated now and in the future. The second involves the written word itself and the recognition that the full meaning of the text will always escape us. This brief quotation from *Of Grammatology* demonstrates:

> The "formal essence" of the sign can only be determined in terms of presence. One cannot get around that response, except by challenging the very form of the question and beginning to think that the sign is that ill-named thing, the only one, that escapes the instituting question of philosophy: 'what is…' (Derrida 1976, 18–19)

Derrida's phrase *formal essence* describes the thing to which a sign ultimately refers, its essential meaning. Notice the *X* superimposed on the words *is* and *thing*. These "cross-outs" are used to alert the reader to the fact that, although we need these very familiar words even to be able to read the text, we can never know fully what they signify. Derrida's point then is this: However long we pursue the meaning of a sign, whether speech or writing, we will never arrive at the *thing* and its presence, its "isness" (*is* is a form of the verb *to be*) or its beingness. This is the philosophy that grounds deconstructionist approaches to interpreting traditional religious and philosophical texts.

In concluding this brief overview of postmodernism, we should note that not everyone thinks there is such a thing as postmodernism. Rather, some would describe what is happening in the Western world today as simply a continuation of the modern period. However, for those who do see postmodernism as a distinctive movement, they understand it to be characterized by a critique of the narrow constraints of rationalist thinking and by a plurality of voices asking new kinds of questions that would have been incomprehensible in earlier periods. They see postmodernism as focused on the particular rather than the universal, giving preference to individuals' experience in specific sociological contexts. They reject the notion that there exists a single value system (something roughly equivalent to Western culture) to which everyone should aspire in favor of multiple value systems and increased awareness of other cultures that were previously neglected or discounted. Efforts to produce conformity of thinking are replaced by the desire to establish ways of coming to better understand the other. Finally, they recognize that postmodernism is a transitional state of mind or worldview. What will follow has yet to be revealed.

THE SHAPE OF POSTMODERN CHRISTIAN THEOLOGY

Needless to say, postmodernism has profoundly impacted the way that contemporary Christian theology is done. Against the modernist value of secularism (the belief that religion or religious principles have no place in the public realm), postmodernism evokes a return to the sacred. However, even as people are turning more and more to religious matters, they no longer feel obligated to pursue their spiritual longings within a single religious system, instead picking bits and pieces of different religious traditions without regard for how the various pieces cohere. Therefore, one of the tasks of postmodern theology is to articulate a clear and coherent system of thinking about God and humanity's relationship to God, which takes into account people's contemporary experience of the divine. Likewise, under the influence of postmodernism, theology's work has expanded beyond the search for objective truths to include an increased appreciation for the view that theology does not stand apart from human history but that it is fittingly conducted within particular historical and cultural settings.

Postmodern theology differs from that of previous eras in other ways as well. Although scripture and tradition continue to be important sources of theology today, postmodern theologians focus more attention on particular human experiences and the needs of the community as a starting point for theology. As a result, contemporary theology is closely tied to ethics. Some would say that postmodern theology is driven by ethics, whereas in earlier periods theology came first and ethics was derived from it. Moreover, the globalization of contemporary cultures means that theology has had to incorporate many diverse worldviews, from African to Hispanic to Asian. Thus one of the dominant features of contemporary theology, both Catholic and Protestant, is its marked pluralism. Finally, in the postmodern period, which encourages interdisciplinary activities, theology likewise participates in interdisciplinary conversations with science, art, politics, economics, and other academic disciplines.

All this means that it is difficult to bring together the various movements of contemporary theology under a unified set of categories. Our goal in this next section simply is to sample some of its major movements. These include new approaches to biblical studies and Historical Jesus research as well as the interdisciplinary study of science and theology and Catholic social teaching. We will also provide brief overviews of liberation theology, feminist theology, and black theology, each of which has as its starting point the experience of those whom the dominant powers of society consider to be of lesser value.

NEW APPROACHES TO BIBLICAL STUDIES

During the modernist period, biblical scholars developed certain approaches to studying the Bible that are generally described as historical scientific methodologies. They used these methods to reconstruct, when necessary, the original wording of ancient manuscripts, identify sources employed by their historical authors, and uncover the layers of editing that went into creating the final form of biblical books. They also used what they learned from archeology, literature that is contemporaneous with the Bible, and social history to better understand the intent of the biblical author. But postmodernism challenged the validity of these historical scientific methodologies by questioning whether it is possible to discover what the historical author intended to say when he wrote his biblical book and whether that information is relevant for understanding how the text makes meaning today.

Thus influenced by the intellectual and cultural movements of the postmodernist period, biblical scholars are developing new methodologies that are marked by "the practice of resisting and recentering the assumptions and norms of modern biblical criticism" (Adam 2004, 173). They answer questions like, "How does language work as a 'sign system' to give the biblical text meaning?" or "What is the deep structure of particular types of biblical narrative that drives the plot forward and makes them effective?" and "What are the fault lines in a biblical text that make its meaning unravel or implode?" Other methods focus on literary analysis of biblical narratives, addressing questions like, "What kind of narrator does the story have, what can we know about its characters, and how does the rhetoric of the story contribute to its meaning?" Still other methods help biblical scholars inquire about how the reader makes meaning of the story in the process of reading.

Postmodern approaches to the Bible also include various cultural and gender-based readings of biblical texts. Generally speaking, their starting point is the conviction that minority voices and non-Western cultures must be recognized as making important contributions to the interpretation of the Bible. For example, Afrocentric biblical interpretation reminds its readers that the Bible contains many references to African countries like Egypt and Ethiopia and that the civilizations of both countries were important in shaping the world of the Bible. It also asserts that the racism we experience today did not exist in the same way in the ancient world and that the people of the Bible were, for the most part, Afro-Asiatic, that is, people from the land Mass to the east of the Mediterranean Sea, extending from Egypt and Ethiopia through Canaan (later known as Palestine and Israel) and into the Fertile Cresent all the way to ancient Mesopotamia between the Tigris and Euphrates Rivers (now Iran and Iraq). It calls attention to biblical characters like Moses' wife, who is described as a Cushite or Ethiopian (Num 12:1), and the Queen of Sheba, who was a black African (1 Kings 10:1–13). Finally, it relates Afro-Asiatic folk tales and cultural practices that shed light on the meaning of biblical texts, most of which originated in the same part of the world.

Likewise, Asian and Hispanic biblical interpretations presuppose that their interpreters approach the Bible from within their own cultural contexts and with reference to their traditional religions. For example, some Asian biblical interpreters draw parallels between biblical texts and Confucianist sayings or Buddhist and Hindu religious literature, while others use the social history of Asian peoples as a lens through which they interpret biblical texts. Likewise, scholars who engage in Hispanic biblical interpretation draw upon stories and images of traditional religions and upon their social and cultural contexts, which are very different from American and European cultural contexts. Many Asian and Hispanic biblical scholars also employ liberation and feminist perspectives in the interpretation of the Bible, perhaps because they can easily relate their own peoples' economic and political struggles to the biblical stories of liberation and because women often suffer most in situations of oppression.

Archie C. C. Lee on the David and Bathsheba Story

Dr. Lee is a biblical scholar who has done substantial research and writing on Old Testament texts, which speak to the historical experiences of the Chinese people, and for which he has comparable texts or traditions from China's ancient past. This brief excerpt from his essay entitled, "The David-Bathsheba Story and the Parable of Nathan," includes an interpretation of the biblical story of the death of David and Bathsheba's son (2 Sam 12:13–25), which draws upon wisdom literature from the Bible and a traditional Chinese story:

David's reaction to the death of his child ushers in his new understanding of the reality of death and hence the meaning of life. He realizes that there is a mystery in life which man as creature can never grasp. Life has limitations in the face of great possibilities. The author expresses his profound faith in God through David's words: "While the child was still alive, I fasted and wept; for I said, 'Who knows whether the Lord will be gracious to me, that the child may live?' But now he is dead; why should I fast? Can I bring him back again? I shall go to him, but he will not return to me." (2 Sam 12.22–3)

This trust in the creator, accepting the givenness of life and acknowledging the mystery of reality, are the basic elements of Wisdom Literature.

> A man's mind plans his way, but the Lord directs his steps (Prov 16.9).

> A man's steps are ordered by the Lord; how then can man understand his way? (Prov 20.24).

> The horse is made ready for the day of battle, but the victory belongs to the Lord. (Prov 21.31)

These quotations from Proverbs explain the proper way of looking at life's possibilities and limitations, hopes and frustrations. There is always the presence of an element of mystery, the recognition of which can also be found in a popular Chinese folktale, *Sai Weng Shih Ma,* "A Skilled Horse-rider of the Frontier Losing His Horse":

> Once there lived in the frontier an old skilled horse-rider whose favorite horse ran away and disappeared. The old man's friends felt sorry for him, but he shrugged it off and said: "Well, maybe this will bring me good luck later."
>
> In a few days, the horse found its way back, not alone, but with another noble horse. Friends heard of it and came to congratulate him. The old man was not overjoyed at this good fortune and said: "Yes, I have one more noble horse in my stable, but it might also bring me bad luck. Who knows?"
>
> The man's son loved the new horse, and rode it often. One day, he fell off the horse and broke one of his legs. Friends came to console the old man for his son's mishap.
>
> "Well," said the old man this time, "My son's leg will eventually heal. The accident may be a blessing in disguise."
>
> Soon afterwards, war broke out between the two bordering countries. All the able bodied men were drafted into the army, and most of them died at the front. But the old man's son, owing to disability, was exempted from military service.

The skilled horseman was wise enough to perceive the inevitability of happenings in life and he was able to face all these happenings without losing his serenity. (Lee 1991, 201–202)

Not all contemporary biblical scholars accept the methods and presuppositions of literary and postmodern biblical interpretation, preferring instead historical scientific methods or other approaches. The many who do accept these new methods often use a variety of approaches (including historical scientific methods) to break open the biblical text and give it meaning for today's readers. In most cases, these different methodologies are seen as complementary and not contradictory, each contributing to a better appreciation of the sacred text. This multifaceted approach to biblical studies is a good example of how modernist views do not simply disappear as postmodernist approaches take hold. Rather, they exist together in a creative interchange, and hopefully each is better for it.

The Quest for the Historical Jesus

Exactly who was this Jesus of Nazareth whom Christians call the Christ? Prior to the Age of Enlightenment and the development of modern scientific methods, Christians thought they knew the answer to this question. They knew the gospel stories about Jesus, the teacher and miracle worker. They also knew the creeds that acclaimed his status as God's son and savior of humanity. In addition, there were the statements of church councils concerning his full humanity and divinity and other doctrinal formulations, together with centuries of Christian art depicting Jesus as the beloved child of the Virgin Mary, the one who could heal diseases and raise the dead, the crucified and resurrected Christ, and the judge of humanity in the end time.

But in the post-Age of Enlightenment period, modern scientific and historical research challenged many of the truth claims about Jesus that had been taken for granted for centuries. How can we reconcile the biblical notion of Jesus' virgin birth with modern scientific discoveries about how conception and birth take place? Shouldn't we dismiss faith claims about Jesus's miracle working as mythic or legendary embellishment of the gospel story, because science cannot validate such deviations from the laws of nature? And what about Christians' claims concerning the resurrection of Christ? Scientists argued that such a proposition simply could not be supported. Likewise, modern historical research and literary analysis challenged the view that the gospels were some sort of chronological narrative of the life of Jesus. Using scientific and literary methods of analysis, biblical scholars were discovering instead that these biblical texts were comprised of many smaller units of tradition, which had been adapted and knit together into longer narratives in order to address the questions and concerns of their historical authors and original intended audiences. In sum, modern scientific and historical methods challenged the very truth of the gospels and the Christian doctrines that relied upon the gospel story.

These modernist challenges to the truth of the gospels gave rise to a new area of scholarly research called the **Quest for the Historical Jesus**. The term *Historical Jesus* refers to the actual historical person named Jesus of Nazareth, whose story has been stripped of exaggeration and theological interpretation and reconstructed based upon verifiable historical and scientific evidence. This quest proceeded in several stages. What is now known as the First Quest began in the late eighteenth century and continued into the late nineteenth century. The scholars involved in this quest used historical scientific methods to analyze the gospels and separate out the details that could be attributed to the Historical Jesus from those that characterized the preaching of the apostles. They also used literary analysis to determine which of the canonical gospels was the earliest, thinking that it would also be the most historical (and least theologically interpreted) gospel. From this effort came the Two-Source Hypothesis (see Chapter 6) and the recognition that Jesus' teachings should be understood within the context of the Jewish religion.

By the beginning of the twentieth century the Quest for the Historical Jesus started to hit some major roadblocks. Using newer and more refined historical scientific and literary methods, biblical scholars discovered that earlier portraits of the Historical Jesus were flawed and that Mark's gospel, which is considered to be the earliest, is every bit as theological as the other gospels. In addition, historical scientific research on the synoptic gospels revealed that their stories about the words and deeds of Jesus were not necessarily arranged chronologically, calling into question the validity of scholars' attempts to construct a portrait of the Historical Jesus by tracing Jesus' personality development from the beginning to the end of the gospel. Biblical scholars who were engaged in the Quest during this period gradually concluded that it was impossible to separate the Historical Jesus from the Jesus of the gospels. As a result, they shifted their focus to the Christ of Faith, that is, to an articulation of the faith of early Christians, who preached the risen Christ, messiah and Son of God. This is why some historians of the Quest for the Historical Jesus call this the period of No Quest.

The period known as the New Quest for the Historical Jesus began in the 1940s and extended into the early 1970s. It was made possible by the development of some new historical scientific approaches to the gospels, which involved uncovering the oral traditions (e.g., sayings of Jesus, parables, miracle stories) that had been incorporated into the written gospels and then mapping out a theory about how the gospel writer adapted and edited these oral traditions, together with written sources, to construct the final written gospel. Using these new methods, scholars of the New Quest focused on finding points of similarity between the gospels (the preaching of the early church) and the words and deeds of the Historical Jesus. Their goal was to discover what parts of the preaching of the early church were already present in the teaching of Jesus. Contrast this approach with that of the First Quest, which sought to develop a portrait of the Historical Jesus that was completely separate from the teaching of the early church. A major contribution of this period was the recognition that Jesus was a Jew and that Christianity began with the Easter proclamation (the announcement of Jesus' resurrection from the dead by his apostles and disciples).

The present stage of Historical Jesus research began in the 1970s and is called the Third Quest. It is similar to the earlier two quests in the sense that it still relies on historical scientific methods. However, it differs in several important ways. First, the historical scientific methods that biblical scholars use today have been refined to the point that they give us much more reliable data concerning the Historical Jesus than was ever available to scholars of the first and second quests. Second, the Third Quest employs a wider variety of methods that include archeology, sociology, philology (the study of ancient languages and texts), and cultural anthropology. This interdisciplinary approach, together with important discoveries of ancient Jewish and Christian religious texts such as the Dead Sea Scrolls at Qumran and the Nag Hammadi Library in Egypt, have made it possible for scholars of the Third Quest to construct a fuller picture of the historical, political, cultural, and religious contexts in which Jesus lived. Third, whereas the earlier quests were mostly the work of German Protestant biblical scholars, the Third Quest is both ecumenical and interreligious. Thus, today, scholars who are involved in Historical Jesus research represent the full spectrum of Christian denominations as well as Judaism. All three of these differences make it possible for scholars of the Third Quest to engage questions of Historical Jesus research more deeply and with greater reliability than in preceding decades.

One of the more controversial projects of the Third Quest was the Jesus Seminar. It was first convened in 1985 by a group of biblical scholars who held public debates on the authenticity of the gospel sayings of Jesus. Their task was to determine how many of the words attributed to Jesus in the gospels were actually spoken by the Historical Jesus. The group closed their debate on each gospel saying with a vote on its authenticity. They used colored beads to signify their judgments concerning the saying's level of authenticity, and after the vote they calculated weighted averages as follows:

COLOR	SIGNIFICANCE	WEIGHT
Red	Jesus actually spoke these words, or he said something very close to these words.	3.0
Pink	Jesus probably said something like these words.	2.0
Grey	Jesus did not say these words, but the ideas contained in this saying may be similar to what Jesus said.	1.0
Black	Jesus did not say these words; these ideas come from the teaching of the early church.	0.0

The Jesus Seminar participants announced their results in books and in other venues that were accessible to non-specialists—weekly news magazines, newspapers, and television—because of their conviction that everyone had a right to know what biblical scholars were learning about the Historical Jesus. The response they received was mixed at best. Many who were not biblical scholars were startled at the news that fewer than 20% of the sayings they had investigated were judged to be the actual words of Jesus (red bead) or something like what Jesus might have said (pink bead). A number of biblical scholars were also concerned, but for other reasons. They observed that the Jesus Seminar's portrait of the Historical Jesus looked more like a portrait of the scholars of the Jesus Seminar than that of a first-century Jew, prompting them to question whether the methods used by the Jesus Seminar were appropriate and properly executed.

The scholars of the Third Quest continue to explore new approaches to the question of the identity of the Historical Jesus. For example, biblical scholar Markus Borg describes him as a charismatic, compassionate sage (a wise teacher) who had mystical experiences (visions of God and the divine realm). By comparison, E. P. Sanders portrays him as a charismatic Jewish prophet of the end of the world, whose miracles pointed to a time when "pain, suffering, and death would be overcome" (Sanders 1993, 168) and who "regarded himself as having full authority to speak and act on behalf of God" (238). Richard Horsley describes Jesus as a social revolutionary who stood against the abusive powers of the elite. Elizabeth Schüssler Fiorenza examines the wisdom traditions and proposes that the Historical Jesus was a wisdom teacher who considered himself a prophet and child of Sophia (personified wisdom). Finally, John P. Meier portrays Jesus as a "marginal Jew"—meaning that he was both fully a part of the mainstream of Judaism and that he stood in opposition to some of its beliefs and practices—who was influenced by John the Baptist and whose ministry was characterized by miracle-working and prophecy concerning the end time.

Meier's portrait of the Historical Jesus points to one of the most important contributions of the Third Quest, namely, the recognition not only that Jesus was a Jew but that his teaching and his activities must be understood from within his Jewish context. In some respects, this may sound like a return to the First Quest. However, thanks to continued improvements in historical scientific methods and new insights from archeology, philology, and the social sciences, today's biblical scholars have a much better understanding of first-century Judaism than ever before. In fact, this is another important contribution of the Third Quest. Biblical scholars now have a more historically accurate picture of early Judaism, with its diversity of practices and beliefs, which they can use as a social, religious, and cultural context for investigating questions about the Historical Jesus.

Science and Theology

Christian theologians today are involved in a wide range of interdisciplinary studies. The interdisciplinary study of theology and science is just one example. However, this was not always the case. One of the characteristics of modernism was the view that science has no relationship with theology and that religious truth claims have no standing because they cannot be verified by empirical evidence. In recent decades, however, there has been greatly renewed interest in the relationship between theology and science, both on the part of scientists, especially physicists, and on the part of theologians. In 1995, the American Association for the Advancement of Science inaugurated sessions on religion and science for the first time in its history. The John Templeton Foundation is sponsoring courses on religion and medicine in leading medical schools. In colleges and graduate schools interdisciplinary courses in theology and science are proliferating. Two spectacular developments in astronomical physics have contributed to this renewed interest in the relationship of science and theology: the Big Bang theory and new evidence concerning the design of the universe.

Up until the mid-twentieth century, most scientists believed that the universe had no beginning (that is, it was eternal). However, modern discoveries have suggested that all the galaxies are moving apart from each other, leading to the theory that the universe began in a colossal explosion. According to the Big Bang theory of the origins of the universe, all the matter/energy in the universe exploded outward from a tiny point at the beginning of time. One cannot speak of either space or time "before" the Big Bang; rather, time, space, and matter all apparently emerged in a single instant. This raises the obvious question, "What caused the Big Bang?" Some scientists hold that there was a succession of universes before this one, each created by a process of expansion, collapse, and re-expansion. However, the physical evidence currently available does not support this oscillating universe model. Others are content to say that the question has no answer. Many Christians would say that God created the universe from nothing. The Big Bang theory is consistent with that belief: If there was a creation from nothing, this is how it might look.

In the same way that the Big Bang theory forced people to reexamine the question of the source of creation both from a scientific and a theological perspective, so too new evidence for design in the universe raised a similar set of questions. Until modern times, the argument from design had appeared to be an irrefutable argument for the existence of God. How could the universe be so perfectly and beautifully designed, so the argument went, unless it had a designer? William Paley, an English theologian, had argued that if one found a watch in a barren desert, one would assume it had been designed and made by an artificer (a craftsperson), not that it somehow had come into being by accidental processes. So it is with nature. The human eye, for instance, is so intricately designed and so perfectly adapted to its surroundings, that it could not have been created by chance but must have been created by a designer-artificer, namely, God, who designed and created all of nature.

However, Charles Darwin's explanation about different species emerging due to evolutionary processes in which small variations were filtered by natural selection seemed to have destroyed arguments like the one advanced by Paley. A Darwinian would have argued that some primitive creatures by random mutation were born with light-sensitive cells that gave them a survival advantage in their environment. Consequently, they left more progeny, some of which had more highly developed light-sensitive cells. They in turn left more progeny whose light-sensitive cells were beginning to develop into primitive eyes, and so on. As a consequence, since the introduction of Darwin's theory of the evolution of the species, theologians did not rely much on the argument from design to prove the existence of God.

Now more recent cosmology has shown an incredible degree of balance in the laws and physical constants of the universe. The strength of gravity, for example, has to balance exactly the initial rate of expansion of the universe in the first moments of the Big Bang. If the universe had expanded slightly faster (or if the gravitational force had been slightly less), the matter in the universe would have kept on expanding so fast that it would never have condensed into stars and galaxies, and life could never have appeared. On the other hand, if the rate of expansion had been slightly slower (or the gravitational attraction slightly stronger), matter would have condensed into stars too rapidly, and the heavy elements necessary for life could not have been created in the interior of the stars. The gravitational force, then, had to be exactly balanced by the rate at which the emerging universe expanded just after the initial explosion. Physicists have discovered a whole series of such amazing accidents.

John Polkinghorne, an English particle physicist and an ordained Anglican priest has given what is probably the best explanation of the relation between theology and science. Science, he says, in its explorations of physical reality, eventually raises questions it cannot answer. For example, "Why are the physical laws so precisely balanced?" Theology does have an answer for these questions: God created the universe; therefore it shows traces of God's design. Science and theology, then, are complementary, not in conflict. Each supplements the other, and together they give a complete explanation for why the universe is the way it is. This is a modern restatement of the position of Thomas Aquinas in the thirteenth century, who argued that reason leads to and supports faith, and faith completes reason.

John Polkinghorne on the Relationship Between Science and Religion

I have spent most of my working life as a theoretical physicist and all of my consciously remembered life as part of the worshiping and believing community of the church. I want to take absolutely seriously the possibility of religious belief in a scientific age. I believe that science and religion are friends and not foes.

To see that, we must recognize two things:

1. We must take account of what science has to tell us about the pattern and history of the physical world. Of course, science itself can no more dictate to religion what it is to believe than religion can prescribe for science what the outcome of its inquiry is to be. The two disciplines are concerned with the exploration of different aspects of human experience: in the one case, our impersonal encounter with a physical world that we transcend; in the other, our personal encounter with the One who transcends us. They use different methods: in the one case, the experimental procedure of putting matters to the test; in the other, the commitment of trust which must underlie all personal encounter, whether among ourselves or with the reality of God. They ask different questions: in the one case, how things happen, by what process? In the other: why things happen, to what purpose?

Though these are two different questions, the ways we answer them must bear some consonant relationship to each other. The fact that we now know that the universe did not spring into being ready made a few thousand years ago but that it has evolved over a period of 15 billion years from its fiery origin in the Big Bang, does not abolish Christian talk of the world as God's creation, but it certainly modifies certain aspects of that discourse.

2. We must understand that religious belief, just like scientific belief, is *motivated* understanding of the ways things are. Of course, a religious stance involves faith, just as a scientific investigation starts by commitment to the interrogation of the physical world from a chosen point of view. But faith is not a question of shutting one's eyes, gritting one's teeth, and believing the impossible. It involves a leap, but a leap into the light rather than the dark. It is open to the possibility of correction, as God's ways and will become more clearly known . . .

My Christian belief in this age of science has to be motivated belief, based on evidence that I can point to. The center of my faith lies in my encounter with the figure of Jesus Christ, as I meet him in the gospels, in the witness of the church, and in the sacraments. That is the heart of my Christian faith and hope. Yet, at a subsidiary but supportive level, there are also hints of God's presence which arise from our scientific knowledge. The actual way we answer the question "How?" points on to the question "Why?" so that science by itself is found not to be sufficiently intellectually satisfying. (Polkinghorne 1996, 11)

CATHOLIC SOCIAL TEACHING: OPPORTUNITIES FOR DIALOG

Beginning with Pope Leo XIII's encyclical *Rerum Novarum* in 1891 there has been a steady stream of writings by popes, conferences of bishops, the Second Vatican Council, and individuals trying to deal with the new social issues raised by the developments of the modern and postmodern periods. These include the Industrial Revolution, capitalism, socialism, communism, the Great Depression of the 1930s, nuclear weapons, the morality of war, and biomedical and environmental ethics. Here are some of the key themes that Catholic social teaching has emphasized in dealing with these issues, particularly as they relate to human dignity and the common good.

Human Dignity and the Common Good.   The core principles of Catholic social teaching are human dignity and the common good. The church teaches that all humans have worth, regardless of who they are or what they can do, because they are created in the image and likeness of God. The church's teaching about the common good flows directly out of its teaching on the human dignity of all persons. The term *common good* refers to the physical, social, and economic conditions that benefit everyone and make it possible for all people to live in dignity. The church teaches that politicians, church officials, and business leaders have a responsibility to manage government and the economy in a way that will benefit *all* people, not just a small elite. All humans should recognize their common standing, and live in solidarity with each other.

Ownership of Private Property.   The Catholic Church teaches that the right to own private property is one of the rights afforded to all humans by virtue of the fact that they are created in the image of God. On a practical level, private ownership is important for the common good because people care for property better when they own it. They have more incentive to work well, and they have the security of being able to pass something on to their children. However, there is a social mortgage on private property: The right to private property is secondary to the principle that God created the earth and its goods for the common good of all humans. No one has the right to own and manage large areas of productive land or a monopoly corporation if, as a result, they are allowed to hoard wealth, while other humans starve. Likewise, it is morally permissible to confiscate property that is used for evil purposes and reappropriate it for the common good.

The Right to a Living Wage.   A long-standing and often repeated theme of Catholic social teaching is that workers ought to be paid a living wage, earning enough to support themselves, a spouse, and a family in decent conditions. The two core principles of Catholic social teaching are again at work here: human dignity and the common good. Workers have a right to provide themselves and their families with nourishing food, adequate clothing, decent housing, education, and health care. They also have a right to safe working conditions and the ability to organize in unions to protect their common interests. No one has the right to pay laborers less than a living wage, even if "market demands" force them to accept lower wages.

The Value of Human Labor.   Whether someone is an assembly line welder or a chief executive officer, a computer analyst or a restaurant worker, all human beings have a right to meaningful and beneficial labor. According to Catholic social teaching, humans ought to be able to accomplish three things in their work: They should be able to express themselves in a creative way, support their families, and make a contribution to the larger society. If their work does not allow them to accomplish all three things, Catholic social teaching would indicate that there is something wrong with the way their work has been organized. But how does labor relate to capital? Capital includes the money or material resources (for example, factories, machines, books, and accumulated files of information) that people use to do their labor, as well as the assets that result from work. But humans made the things that people on all levels of the economic spectrum use to do their work and to generate wealth. Therefore, labor always has priority over capital.

Subsidiarity.   According to the principle of subsidiarity, decision making and community initiatives should be done at the lowest possible level of authority. Power and control should not be centralized beyond what is necessary for the well-being of all. Underlying this principle is the recognition that human beings are social creatures and they have a right to organize themselves to address common needs. However, there are certain social needs, which individuals and small groups cannot provide for themselves but which are their right as persons of dignity. In those cases, higher levels of authority are obligated to provide whatever aid the lower levels may need to carry out their responsibilities. For example, decisions about child care are best handled on the family and local level. They should not be taken over by state levels of government, except to insure the rights of children to quality care.

Stewardship of the Earth.   The U.S. Catholic bishops, in their 1991 pastoral statement entitled "Renewing the Earth: An Invitation to Reflection and Action on Environment in Light of Catholic Social Teaching," say that the notion of a universal common good can and should form the basis for a global environmental ethic that recognizes the interdependence of humanity and the whole created universe. Further, this environmental ethic requires, on our part, solidarity with developing nations and with the world's poor who disproportionately experience the brunt of today's ecological problems. They also note that respect for human life and respect for nature are closely intertwined. Together humans and the rest of creation give glory to God and reflect God's goodness. Therefore, one cannot be exploited without causing damage to the other.

War and Peace.   Catholic social teaching has also addressed issues of modern war and the possibility of nuclear war, in particular. The Second Vatican Council said, "Any act of war aimed indiscriminately at the destruction of entire cities or of extensive areas along with their population is a crime against God and man himself. It merits unequivocal and unhesitating condemnation" (*Pastoral Constitution on the Church in the Modern World*, §80; Abbott 1966, 294). The U.S. Conference of Catholic Bishops further specified that Christians must refuse to legitimate the idea of a nuclear war that kills people indiscriminately.

> Under no circumstances may nuclear weapons or other instruments of Mass slaughter be used for the purpose of destroying population centers or other predominantly civilian targets... We do not perceive any situation in which the deliberate initiation of nuclear warfare, on however restricted a scale, can be morally justified. (*The Challenge of Peace*, §147, 150)

The U.S. Conference of Catholic Bishops has spoken on other issues of modern warfare, too, like just cause (meaning that the aggressor's actions against a group or nation are "lasting, grave, and certain" (*Catechism of the Catholic Church*, §2309, cited in "Statement on Iraq," November 14, 2002) and proportionalism (meaning that the war does not cause greater harm than the circumstances that precipitated it). Related topics include proper conduct in war and the use of legitimate authorities (e.g., Congress or the United Nations) in declaring war. The U.S. bishops have also made it clear that war should always be considered an avenue of last resort, when other avenues to the peace and well-being of the victims of aggression have been exhausted.

Opportunities for Dialogue

As this brief review suggests, Catholic social teaching embraces a wide range of issues including a theology of work, the justice of capitalism, the morality of war, and the ethics of environmental activism. Because these are issues of common concern to all peoples today, Catholic social teaching is opening up many new opportunities for dialogue among Christian churches and between Christianity and other faith traditions. This is fitting and proper because the Second Vatican Council and the popes and bishops' groups who have written on Catholic social teaching view themselves as prophets, working through the power of God, to address issues of justice and well-being that pertain to all God's people not just Catholic Christians. Broadly understood, Catholic social teaching also provides a framework for talking about several other movements that emerge within Christian churches of our time—namely, the impact of feminism on Christian theology, as well as the emergence of black theology and liberation theology. All three movements address in some fashion issues of human dignity, solidarity, and social justice.

LIBERATION THEOLOGY

Over the centuries since the first Spanish and Portuguese conquests, Catholic Church leaders in Latin America have usually supported political and economic leaders who oppressed their people. Theological arguments have often been used to support that oppression. For example, the poor were told that it was their obligation to be obedient to the authorities. They were told that they ought to be glad to suffer as Christ had suffered and that they would receive their reward in heaven if they accepted suffering on earth. As a result of Catholic social teaching and the Second Vatican Council, some church leaders in Latin America (clergy and laity) began to support the poor against their nations' leaders and to challenge those leaders to take responsibility for their nation's poverty. This shift in emphasis was called *the preferential option for the poor*. In reaction, some of the elite felt that the church, or at least certain elements in the church, had abandoned them.

The Peruvian Catholic theologian Gustavo Gutierrez is usually identified as the founder of Latin American liberation theology, which launched in 1971 with the Portuguese edition of his book, later translated into English as *A Theology of Liberation*. At approximately the same time, Rubem Alves, a Presbyterian theologian from Brazil and José Míguez Bonino, a Lutheran theologian from Argentina, began writing on the same subject. Likewise, in 1970, James Cone, an African-American theologian, published his *A Black Theology of Liberation* in 1970. Liberation theologians argue that the dominant reality of our world is oppression and that Christians who take the Bible and the message of Jesus seriously ought to have something to say to it. Christianity cannot preach the kingdom of God as good news to people who are living desperate lives.

Liberation theology often appeals to the biblical imagery of the Israelites in slavery in Egypt to explain God's activity on behalf of the poor. God confronted Pharaoh and rescued the Israelites from their human slavery. It also argues that oppressors are harmed even more by their injustice than the oppressed are: Oppressors lose their humanity, their relationship with God, and their eternal destiny in heaven. Thus, liberation theology aims to liberate both oppressors and the oppressed.

Base Christian Communities

In the parishes of Latin America, where the poor and their needs had often been ignored because there are few priests and much poverty, small groups formed called **base Christian communities**. These communities provide a place for discussion, mutual support, and common action. More traditional clergy were sometimes alarmed by this development, both because they feared a transfer of power from clergy to laity and because these small local groups often raised embarrassing political questions, even about the church itself, and engaged in activities that threatened the status quo from which the elite were benefiting.

Laity, empowered by small-scale local action, began to form larger associations and networks and to hold regional and national meetings. In Brazil, the bishops quickly approved of the base Christian communities, providing yearly discussion guides and protecting them from hostile political pressures. Some of the church leadership in other countries have been less encouraging or even directly hostile to the base communities. The integrated discussion and action of these base Christian communities came to be called **praxis**. Praxis is activity that is reflected upon and consciously chosen to produce a particular effect, namely, a comprehensive transformation of society. The base Christian community's activity and reflection go together and influence each other.

Structural Violence

A key insight of liberation theology is the concept of structural violence. If the laws and the way they are carried out result in half of the children in a country dying before age five, as is true in many Latin countries, then those people who develop, support, defend, or fail to

Figure 25–3 Nossa Senhora Aparecida, one of two thousand *favelas* (slums) in Sao Paolo, Brazil, which all together house approximately 2 million people. This *favela* has piped water and sewers, but the sewers are so clogged that most sewage runs on the surface in open ditches. A base Christian community was organized here in about 1968.
Photo by David Smith, 1988.

confront those laws and practices are guilty of violence against the poor. One can share guilt for the death of children by supporting laws and practices that prevent adequate nutrition, even if one never physically attacks the children directly.

The base Christian community movement and liberation theology have come under attack in some circles because of the criticism that they accept violent revolution as a valid response to injustice. Some are accused of being communists. The Vatican Congregation for the Doctrine of the Faith has published two documents on liberation theology endorsing its "preferential option for the poor" and also expressing cautions about its use of Marxist methods of analysis. A passage from the first document illustrates that, despite its concerns about liberation theology, the Congregation does not intend to support oppression by unjust governments:

> In certain parts of Latin America, the seizure of the vast majority of the wealth by an oligarchy of owners bereft of social consciousness, the practical absence or the shortcomings of a rule of law, military dictators making a mockery of elementary human rights, the corruption of certain powerful officials, the savage practices of some foreign capital interests constitute factors which nourish a passion for revolt among those who thus consider themselves the powerless victims of a new colonialism in the technological, financial, monetary or economic order. The recognition of injustice is accompanied by a pathos which borrows its language from Marxism, wrongly presented as though it were scientific language. (Congregation for the Doctrine of the Faith 1984, VII. 12)

From its beginnings in the Latin American situation, liberation theology has inspired or encouraged those in situations of oppression or marginalization to make sociological analyses of their situation and to use theological reflection to come to a just and meaningful response. Some examples of related movements are feminist theology, which analyzes the oppression of women, black theology, which analyzes the effects of slavery and segregation, and Oriental liberation theologies, which analyze interfaith relations with non-Christian religions and the injustices caused by Western colonialism. We will examine in greater detail two of these related movements, namely, feminist theology and black theology.

Gustavo Gutierrez on the Nature of Social Sin

In our relationship with God and with others there is an inescapable personal dimension: to reject a fellow human—a possibility implicit in our freedom—is to reject God as well. Conversion implies that we recognize the presence of sin in our lives and our world. In other words, we see and admit what is vitiating our relationship with God and our solidarity with others—what, in consequence, is also hindering the creation of a just and human society. The situation of tragic poverty in which Latin America is living only intensifies this awareness on our part.

To sin is to deny love, to resist welcoming the kingdom of God. Many of those who are committed to the poor freely admit the difficulties they have, as human beings and believers, in loving God and neighbor and therefore their need of repentance and a break with deviant practices. A Christian community in Lima writes "There are defects in our lives. Sin is among us too, and we are not always faithful. We do not always live up to our commitments; there are little betrayals, acts of cowardice, falls, selfish and underhanded actions." Unless we see our personal connivances with elements that are keeping an inhuman and unjust situation in existence, we run the risk of pharisaism: of seeing the speck in our neighbor's eye but not the beam in our own.

One type of connivance, which is clearer today now that we have a better knowledge of our social reality, takes the form of sins of omission: "We regard ourselves as guilty for keeping silence in the face of the events agitating our country. In the face of repression, detentions, the economic crisis, the loss of jobs by so many workers, murders and tortures, we have kept silent as though we did not belong to that world."[1] The cowardice that keeps silent in the face of the sufferings of the poor and that offers any number of adroit justifications represents an especially serious failure of Latin American Christians. However, it is not always easy to be lucid in this regard. (Gutierrez 1984, 97)

---

[1]Pastoral ministers, priests, religious women, and pastors of Bolivia, Jan. 20, 1973, in *Praxis del martirio ayer y hoy* (Bogotá: CEPLA, 1977), 125–126. Or again: "In view of the fact that we ought to be engaged in struggle and in view of the suffering of our people, individualism, fearfulness, and cowardice are sins" (from the Fourth Meeting of the Christians of Puno [Peru], 1980; text published in RIMAC, the documentation service of the Instituto Bartolomé de las Casas).

FEMINIST THEOLOGY

Like most postmodern theologies that arise out of a particular need of society, feminist theology developed out of an awareness that gender stereotypes and various cultural and political pressures, over time, have affected women's status in the churches and even how we think about God and humanity's relationship to God. Among the many tasks they have undertaken, feminist theologians seek to reconstruct women's place in the history of religious traditions, offer new and more gender inclusive interpretations of scripture, and introduce women's perspectives into questions of theology and ethics.

Although feminist theologians examine many of the traditional themes of theology, they do so from the point of view of women's experience and with attention to how gender categories impact our understanding of theology. Typically, the feminine perspective emphasizes wholeness, ecological interconnectedness, and human relatedness. Some would argue that it is a counterbalance to the masculine perspective on theology, which emphasizes distinctness, domination, and power. In fact, feminist theology cannot easily be compartmentalized or stereotyped because women's experiences are so diverse.

Among the traditional themes of theology, feminist theology concerns itself with how we image God. Sally McFague, for example, argues that, although feminine images of God as mother, lover, and friend can be found both in the Bible and in Christian tradition, the images of God as father, king, and judge have dominated our language about God. She reminds her readers that all our images of God are metaphorical or analogical, and she argues that male images of God must be balanced with female images of God, because humans are both female and male and we relate to God through our human experience. Similarly, she argues that images that stress the imminence (nearness) of God should be used to balance images that stress God's transcendence (otherness). Thus, feminist theologies of God help us to understand the God of Judeo-Christianity as a personal God, but they also remind us that we cannot identify God with any one particular set of characteristics and that God is so much more than what human language and experience can capture.

Sally McFague on God as Mother-Creator

What, then, about the model of God as mother? Is that not stereotyping by suggesting as a major model for God one activity of females and the one most closely identified as stereotypically feminine, namely, giving birth to and raising children? My answer is twofold. First, although this particular essay will focus on God as mother in order to balance and provide a new context for interpreting God as father, other divine activities will also be imaged in female form, especially those concerned with creation and justice. Second, although mothering is a female activity, it is not feminine; that is, to give birth to and to feed the young is simply what females do—some may do it in a so-called feminine fashion, and others may not. What is more important for our purposes is that the symbolic material from the birthing and feeding process is very rich and for the most part has been neglected in establishment Christianity . . .

God as mother-judge condemns those who selfishly refuse to share. When judgment is connected to the mother-creator, it is different from when it is connected to the king-redeemer. In the picture of the king-redeemer, individuals are condemned who rebel against the power and the glory of the monarch, assigning to themselves the status that only the king deserves. The king judges the guilty and metes out punishment, or as the Christian story happily concludes, takes the punishment upon himself and thus absolves those condemned. In the picture of the mother-creator, however, the goal is neither the condemnation nor the rescue of the guilty but the just ordering of the cosmic household in a fashion beneficial to all. God as mother-creator is primarily involved not in the negative business of judging wayward individuals but in the positive business of creating with our help a just ecological economy for the well-being of all her creatures. (McFague 1987, 101, 117)

On the topic of church and the nature of the Christian community, feminist theologians generally stress relationships of mutuality and partnership over relationships of hierarchy and dominance. Some feminists argue that the traditional hierarchical structure of the church is a product of a culture of male dominance and should be replaced altogether with a more egalitarian ecclesial structure. Other more moderate feminist theologians suggest that more wholistic and relationally oriented models of church can exist in tandem with more hierarchical models for the well-being and healing of the whole church community. Two models of church that are often embraced by feminist theologians are the church as a prophetic voice in the world, speaking the truth against injustice, and the church as a sign of the kingdom of God.

Feminist theologies, like other postmodern theologies, have a strong ethical component. They focus on theological questions of human dignity and solidarity. Since women have been excluded from leadership in most religions, one finds feminist theology in a variety of religious traditions (Judaism, Islam, Buddhism, etc.). Overall, feminist theologians are very concerned with justice for women and other marginalized groups. Consequently, they focus on theological questions of human dignity and solidarity. Feminist theologians have also been concerned about ecological issues. Authors such as Sally McFague and Rosemary Radford Reuther argue that Western attitudes that condone the exploitation of nature have led to considerable destruction of the environment and threat to its inhabitants. These attitudes, they argue, stem from a patriarchal point of view that values dominance over interrelatedness. Thus, ecofeminist theologies tend to focus on creation and humanity's relatedness to the earth.

Equality of Women in the Churches

In Western Christianity, women make up the majority of persons who attend church services and participate in the churches' ministries of service to others. This seems especially true in the Latin American and Mediterranean Catholic countries. In contrast, throughout most of Christian history the leaders of the churches have been exclusively male. This pattern gradually started to change in the twentieth century as women gained more equal status with men in other areas of society. Many Protestant denominations (e.g., the Evangelical Lutheran Church in America, Presbyterian, Methodist, Episcopal, United Church of Christ) now ordain women pastors. At the same time, there are other denominations that do not (e.g., Southern Baptist, and Wisconsin/Missouri Synod Lutherans). Likewise, in non-Protestant traditions, Eastern Orthodox Christians and Roman Catholics do not ordain women.

At the heart of the problem of the equality of women in the churches is the issue of ordination. A number of arguments have been advanced both for and against women's ordination. Those who argue against women's ordination do so on the basis of tradition. In ancient Israel, there were female prophets and judges (for example, Miriam and Deborah), but the priests who offered sacrifices to God for the people were male. Likewise, the gospels include women among Jesus's followers, but the prominent apostles, those who assumed leadership positions in the early church, were male. Further, modern churches that claim to follow Jesus's teachings and practices say that they do not have the authority to ordain women, because Jesus did not commission women to be apostles. Another argument heard mainly in Roman Catholic circles is that the priest represents Christ before the congregation and therefore should bear a natural (that is, physical) resemblance to Christ.

Against these arguments, Christians who support ordination for women argue that the Bible, as well as Christian doctrine and religious practices, have been reinterpreted over time to adapt to the changing needs of people and to account for cultural differences. Modern churches ought not to prohibit women's ordination, simply because first-century, Middle Eastern patriarchal culture would have made it unlikely for women to be included among Jesus's twelve apostles. By comparison, modern churches do not condone slavery, even though the New Testament indicates that slavery was a reality of life, even in early Christian communities, and that neither Jesus nor Paul condemned it. Furthermore, they argue, Paul does indicate the presence of women apostles in the early church (see Rom 16:7). Another argument advanced by supporters of women's ordination is the possibility that the early church *did* ordain women, but that records of such ordinations were expurgated by the male writers who handed on the tradition. A third argument involves the notion that the priest represents Christ. Supporters of women's ordination argue that a woman can represent Christ in the celebration of the liturgy in the same way that a man does. If the priest must bear a natural (that is, physical) resemblance to Christ, why should gender be the deciding factor? Should we not also demand that the priest be Jewish, as Jesus was? They would argue, instead, that spiritual similarity to Jesus (that is, similarity in love) is what really matters.

Although women's ordination is rather widely accepted in some Christian traditions, it remains a deeply divisive issue for others and one that will not be easily resolved, especially among those whose practice is deeply rooted in theological principles and in traditional readings of scripture. Likewise, when it comes to arguments based on tradition, the case for or against women's ordination is made extremely difficult by insufficient historical information concerning the organization and structure of the early church. Even from the perspectives of sociology and culture, resolving the question of women's ordination is complicated by ongoing tensions around women's roles in society and by human resistance to change.

BLACK THEOLOGY

Christianity has had an ambiguous relationship with the institution of slavery in the United States. On the one hand, slaveholders were quick to point to the many biblical texts that seem to accept slavery. On the other hand, abolitionists argued that the whole message of Christianity was primarily one of human dignity and liberation from oppression. Similarly, for the slaves themselves, Christianity was a "knife that cuts both ways." They were often forced to convert to Christianity and to attend church services; many slaveholders seemed to think that this would create a more docile slave population.

Yet, because of the liberating message of Christianity, many slaves heard the gospel as a call for their release. So, for example, in one of the most important musical traditions of the slaves—the spirituals—a Christian story was often used as a coded message of escape and liberation. No slaveholder could reprimand a slave for singing about one of the most memorable stories in the Bible:

> Go down, Moses,
> Way down to Egypt land.
> Tell old Pharaoh,
> "Let my people go!"

But of course this song also applied to the slaves' own situation. Many slaves understood it as a plea for *their* release from captivity—just as the Israelites had been freed from Egypt.

The ambiguous relationship between Christianity and slavery came to the fore once again in the 1960s Civil Rights movement. Black leaders argued among themselves about the appropriateness of Christianity for blacks. After all, it was the religion of the oppressor that was forced on the black slaves and used for centuries to justify slavery. On the other side of the argument, black leaders would say that Jesus himself proclaimed "release to the captives" and worked "to let the oppressed go free" (Luke 4:18). They would also appeal to the writings of Paul, saying that he prepared the way for the abolitionists by claiming that in Christ "there is no longer . . . slave or free" (Gal 3:28).

Perhaps the best-known advocates of the two sides of this argument were Martin Luther King, Jr., and Malcolm X. King was a Baptist minister, and he believed that Christianity was essentially about freedom; he saw it as fundamentally supportive of civil rights for African Americans. When he wrote one of his most eloquent pleas, his "Letter from the Birmingham Jail," he modeled it, in part, on the letters of St. Paul. Malcolm X, on the other hand, believed that Christianity had been corrupted by racist assumptions, which could be observed over a century of post-Civil War American history. During this era, so-called "Christians" advocated and carried out segregation, Jim Crow laws, and lynchings. Malcolm X eventually put his views into practice by converting to Islam—a faith that he considered much more appropriate for peoples of African descent.

The debate between "Martin and Malcolm" was not only about religious faith. It was also about the strategies for changing racial attitudes. Both sides agreed on the need to rethink and redefine all sorts of societal structures, including economic opportunity, education, criminal justice, and politics. However, they differed about how to achieve those goals. Some leaders, such as King, argued for slow, measured change, in close collaboration with white leaders (who held most of the power). Others, such as Malcolm X, argued that blacks should take charge of their own liberation and should seek to throw off the burden of racial oppression by whatever means necessary. This approach eventually became known as the Black Power movement. Would Christianity always be attached to King's vision of slow, collaborative change? Or was it equally compatible with Black Power?

In 1969, a new PhD graduate published his doctoral dissertation, which argued for a radical reinterpretation of Christianity—one that was allied very firmly with the Black Power movement. The author was James H. Cone, and his book was entitled *Black Theology and Black Power*. One year later, Cone wrote a somewhat more scholarly treatment of the same issues, published as *A Black Theology of Liberation*. Together, these two books have been enormously influential in shaping the movement known as black theology. Black theology works from the presupposition that African Americans are among the most marginalized people in American culture today. Brought to this country against their will, completely cut off from the structures of power for centuries, and only recently beginning to attain some measure of equality, they are the modern-day "underdogs" who receive God's favor. Thus, black theology makes considerable use of the Bible, pointing to God's tendency to side with the underdog—the slaves (such as Israel in Egypt), the powerless (such as the poor, the widow, and the orphan), and all those who are marginalized by their society. In particular, it appeals to stories about Jesus's ministry to the blind, the sick, prostitutes, tax collectors, and other "undesirables" of his own culture.

James Cone on the Task of Black Theology

The task of black theology, then, is to analyze the nature of the gospel of Jesus Christ in the light of oppressed blacks so they will see the gospel as inseparable from their humiliated condition and as bestowing on them the necessary power to break the chains of oppression. This means that it is a theology of and for the black community, seeking to interpret the religious dimensions of the forces of liberation in that community.

There are two reasons why black theology is Christian theology. First, there can be no theology of the gospel which does not arise from an oppressed community. This is so because God is revealed in Jesus as a God whose righteousness is inseparable from the weak and helpless in human society. The goal of black theology is to interpret God's activity as related to the oppressed black community.

Secondly, black theology is Christian theology because it centers on Jesus Christ. There can be no Christian theology, which does not have Jesus Christ as its point of departure. Though black theology affirms the black condition as the primary datum of reality to be reckoned with, this does not mean that it denies the absolute revelation of God in Jesus Christ. Rather it affirms it. Unlike white theology, which tends to make the Jesus-event an abstract, unembodied idea, black theology believes that the black community itself is precisely where Jesus Christ is at work. The Jesus-event in twentieth-century America is a black-event—that is, an event of liberation taking place in the black community in which blacks recognize that it is incumbent upon them to throw off the chains of white oppression by whatever means they regard as suitable. This is what God's revelation means to black and white America, and why black theology is an indispensable theology for our time. (Cone 1986, 5)

Black theologians argue that racism should be understood within the theological category of sin. Racism can be seen in individual racist acts (just as sin can be seen in individual sinful acts); but more importantly, racism can be structural. It can be "built in" to particular systems, just as sin seems to be "built in" to the human race. God's act of redemption through Jesus Christ not only frees us from sin in the ordinary sense, it also frees us from our racist behavior and sets us on a path toward ending racism. For Christianity to operate in racially polarized America, it must recognize God's special care for African Americans, and it must fight the sin of racism with the same kind of energy that it gives to fighting other moral ills.

Black theology is closely related to both feminist theology and liberation theology. In fact, it is sometimes combined with these approaches in an attempt to recognize the special circumstances of those who are marginalized by society in more than one way—by being black and female, for example, or being black and poor. Since the days of Cone's pioneering work, black theology has expanded and developed in highly sophisticated ways. Its advocates include James Evans, who has written a systematic theology from an African American perspective; Cornel West, who has provided considerable philosophical support (and pure inspiration) to the movement; Katie Geneva Cannon, who has developed a distinctive African American feminist perspective (sometimes called Womanist theology), and Cain Hope Felder, who has examined how racial assumptions affect biblical interpretation. The movement has also been inspired by the development of theological themes in the work of African American novelists, such as Alice Walker and Toni Morrison.

RESPONSES OF CHRISTIAN CHURCHES TO POSTMODERNISM

As one might expect, the responses of Christian churches to postmodernism are as wide ranging as the churches themselves and as the people who comprise them. We will comment on two: the emerging church movement and the Catholic restorationist movement.

The Emerging Church Movement

The Emerging Church Movement is the name given to a phenomenon that has been gaining attention over the past decade mostly among Protestant churches—Christian communities who seek to live the gospel by reaching out to people who embody a postmodern worldview, especially those who never were or are no longer affiliated with a particular church. Their goal is to foster a sense of church that is in and of today's world by adopting more decentralized models of organization and more casual forms of worship than those of traditional Christianity. Typically, religious services take place in a home or "coffee house" setting, with regular opportunities for people to engage in conversation and share their spiritual journey with others. Less emphasis is placed on hierarchy of leadership and strict adherence to doctrinal teachings, and more attention is given to personal interaction around a wide variety of religious perspectives. It also makes ample use of multimedia arts and the internet as avenues of inspiration and communication. Solomon's Porch in Minneapolis, Minnesota, is an example.

Although the Emerging Church Movement has been extremely successful in many circles, among both evangelical churches and other Protestant traditions, it also has its critics. Opponents say that its willingness to accommodate theology to the demands of culture results in religious **relativism**. This term refers to the view that all theological positions are equally valid and that truth is not absolute but is relative to individuals' experience. When all views are accepted without regard for the foundational doctrines of the church, they argue, Christianity has no theological center and no authority to speak on moral issues of the day. Those who consider sacred scripture as the sole authority for prayer and life are also concerned about the emerging church movement's openness to a wide range of spiritual practices (e.g., Eastern meditation, labyrinths, rituals of anointing or candle lighting, poetry readings), which they view as a threat to the position of authority that the Bible has traditionally held within their churches.

The Restorationist Movement

The opponents of the emerging church movement are not the only ones who worry about the dangers of relativism and secularism. Within the Roman Catholic Church there is a movement, which some call restorationist, though others call it the "Second Spring" or the

"New Advent" of the church, suggesting that the success of the movement will bring about the rebirth of the Catholic Church in America. Sociologist Joseph Varacalli, who has written several books and essays on the topic, cautions about the use of the term *restorationist* because it can be misunderstood to mean that the movement wants to restore the church to something whose time has past. However, he thinks the term is accurate, if one correctly understands its goals, which he describes as "bringing a dynamic orthodoxy back into the Church and of having it serve as a leaven in the larger society" (Varacalli 2006, 50).

In his assessment of the situation of the American Catholic Church today, Dr. Varacalli goes back to its early years in the United States, when the church consisted mostly of immigrants, and when it suffered marginalization by the majority Protestant population. To serve its people, the bishops and other leaders of the American Catholic Church developed a comprehensive system of institutions (e.g., parishes, schools, orphanages, hospitals), which served the physical needs of church members and also created a strong sense of Catholic identity. According to Varacalli, this network of Catholic institutions finally had become strong enough in the mid-twentieth century to significantly influence American culture. However, in the aftermath of the Second Vatican Council, because of a variety of factors both within and outside of the church, the American Catholic Church assimilated itself to the dominant secular culture and became "internally secular" as well. As a consequence, the network of Catholic institutions was dismantled and American Catholicism lost its identity and its influence in society (Varacalli 2002, 11–19). Hence the need for the restorationist movement.

Supporters of the Catholic restorationist movement are careful not to specify what the "Second Spring" of the church might look like because its form and structure are not yet fully known. However, certain themes and strategies seem to dominate the conversation. We have already noted that the restorationist movement considers secularism to be the enemy of the church. But, in their view, secularism also makes it possible for religious relativism to dominate American culture. To combat both dangers, the restorationist movement advocates developing among its members a clear sense of religious identity, which sheds light on the moral and spiritual bankruptcy of secularism, and enforcing orthodoxy (right teaching) concerning the doctrines of the church. It also seeks to establish a public presence in politics, and in society as a whole, which makes it possible for the movement to influence change in American culture. Essential to accomplishing these goals are bishops and clergy who share this worldview and who are willing to assert their authority and make the difficult decisions that the movement deems necessary to bring about the "New Advent" of the American Catholic Church.

CONCLUDING REFLECTIONS

As the history of Christianity has demonstrated, every historical situation and cultural context presents new challenges and opportunities for the revelation of God's Word in the world. In each time and place, Christianity has had to redefine itself and adapt to changing circumstances. Church organization has changed radically since the rather charismatic and informal time of house churches and missionary preachers in the first and second centuries. In the American Christian churches, denominationalism has resulted in an intricate arrangement of churches that differ significantly in both doctrine and organization but still call themselves Christian. Likewise, Christian churches experience a wide diversity in worship styles and lifestyle expectations—both deriving from the churches' attempts to further refine their doctrine and practice for a changing world.

None of these changes happen in isolation from the wider culture in which Christianity exists. The challenges and opportunities that Christian churches face today are further heightened by rapid advances in technology, by the widening gap between those who have sufficient resources to live a life of dignity and those who do not, and by the pluralism of modern society that provides the opportunity for peoples of different religions, cultures, and worldviews to work together in shared ventures. The gospel message of Jesus continues to be relevant as the inspired Word of God even in this time. However, as in any other time, Christians recognize that the Word must be reinterpreted and appropriated in new ways. Thus, Christian communities continue to draw upon their tradition and look for the guidance of the Holy Spirit in discerning how they might fulfill their mission of Christ's presence in this ever changing, increasingly globalized environment.

Key Terms

postmodernism	Quest for the Historical	praxis
nihilism	Jesus	relativism
deconstruction	base Christian communities	

Questions for Reading

1. What is postmodernism, and how does it impact that way that the study of theology is conducted today?

2. How do postmodern approaches to the study of the Bible differ from earlier historical scientific approaches? What positive contributions do they make to our understanding and appreciation of the Bible today?

3. What do scholars who are engaged in the Quest for the Historical Jesus hope to accomplish? What are some of the obstacles they have encountered in their quest?

4. What is the relationship between theology and science, which makes it possible for scientists and theologians to research issues of common concern together?

5. What are some of the central themes of Catholic social teaching? What societal issues or concerns does Catholic social teaching seek to address? In what ways does it provide an opportunity for ecumenical and interfaith, or interreligious, dialogue?

6. What is liberation theology? In what way is it concerned with a preferential option for the poor? Why?

7. What are some of the contributions of feminist theology? In what ways does it challenge traditional religious understandings about God and the world?

8. What are some of the contributions of black theology? In what ways does it challenge traditional religious understandings about God and the world?

9. Describe the goals of the emergent church and restorationist movements. In what ways are they responses to the culture of our time?

Works Consulted/Recommended Reading

Abbott, Walter M., S. J., ed. *The Documents of Vatican II.* New York: Herder and Herder, 1966.

Adam, Andrew. "Postmodern Biblical Interpretation." In Knight, ed., *Methods of Biblical Interpretation,* 173–178.

Berryman, Phillip. *Liberation Theology: Essential Facts About the Revolutionary Movement in Latin America—and Beyond.* Philadelphia: Temple University, 1987.

Bokenkotter, Thomas. *A Concise History of the Catholic Church.* Rev. ed. New York: Doubleday, 1979.

Carlen, Claudia, ed. *The Papal Encyclicals. 1939–1958.* Wilmington, NC: McGrath, 1981.

Carlin, David. *The Decline and Fall of the Catholic Church in America.* Manchester, NH: Sophia Institute, 2003.

Carson, D. A. *Becoming Conversant with the Emerging Church: Understanding a Movement and Its Implications.* Grand Rapids: Zondervan, 2005.

Catholic Church. *Catechism of the Catholic Church.* New York: Doubleday, 1994.

Cone, James H. *Black Theology and Black Power.* New York: Seabury, 1969.

———. *A Black Theology of Liberation.* Maryknoll, NY: Orbis, 1986.

Congregation for the Doctrine of the Faith. *Instruction on Certain Aspects of the "Theology of Liberation,"* August 6, 1984. The Holy See–Vatican Web site; *www.vatican.va/roman_curia/congregations/cfaith/documents/rc_con_cfaith_doc_19840806_theology-liberation_en.html.*

Derrida, Jacques. *Of Grammatology.* Translated by Bayatri Chakravorty Spivak. Baltimore, MD: Johns Hopkins, 1976.

Flannery, Austin P., ed. *Vatican Council II: The Conciliar and Post Conciliar Documents.* Collegeville, MN: Liturgical, 1975.

Frambach, Nathan C. P. Emerging Ministry: Being Church Today. Minneapolis, MN: Augsburg Fortress, 2007.

Gremillion, Joseph, ed. *The Gospel of Peace and Justice: Catholic Social Teaching Since Pope John.* Maryknoll, NY: Orbis, 1976.

Gutierrez, Gustavo. *A Theology of Liberation.* Maryknoll, NY: Orbis, 1973.

———. *We Drink From Our Own Wells. The Spiritual Journey of a People.* Translated by Matthew J. O'Connell. Maryknoll, NY: Orbis, 1984.

John Paul II. "Ordinatio Saccrdotalis. Apostolic Letter on Reserving Priestly Ordination to Men Only." May 22, 1994. The Holy See–Vatican Web site; http://www.vatican.va/holy_father/john_paul_ii/apost_letters/documents/hf_jp-ii_apl_22051994 ordinatio-sacerdotalis_en.html.

Kelly, George A. *The Second Spring of the Church in America.* South Bend, IN: St. Augustine's Press, 2001.

Knight, Douglas A. *Methods of Biblical Interpretation.* Nashville, TN: Abingdon, 2004.

Lee, Archie. "The David-Bathsheba Story and the Parable of Nathan." In Sugirtharajah, ed., *Voices from the Margin: Interpreting the Bible in the Third World,* 189–204.

Madison, Gary Brent. "Coping with Nietzsche's Legacy: Rorty, Derrida, and Gadamer." *Philosophy Today* (1991): 3–19.

McFague, Sally. *Models of God: Theology for an Ecological, Nuclear Age.* Philadelphia: Fortress, 1987.

McKenzie, Steven L., and Stephen R. Haynes. *To Each Its Own Meaning. An Introduction to Biblical Criticisms and Their Application.* Louisville, KY: Westminster John Knox, 1999.

Meier, John P. "The Present State of the 'Third Quest' for the Historical Jesus: Loss and Gain." *Biblica* 80 (1999): 459–487.

National Conference of Catholic Bishops. *The Challenge of Peace: God's Promise and Our Response.* Washington, DC: National Conference of Catholic Bishops, 1983.

———. *Economic Justice for All: Pastoral Letter on Catholic Social Teaching and the U. S. Economy.* Washington, DC: National Conference of Catholic Bishops, 1986.

Nietzsche, Friedrich Wilheim. *The Gay Science: With a Prelude in Rhymes and an Appendix of Songs.* Translated by Walter Kauffman. New York: Vintage, 1974.

———. *Human, All Too Human.* Translated by R. J. Hollingdale. New York: Cambridge University, 1996.

Polkinghorne, John. "So Finely Tuned a Universe of Atoms, Stars, Quanta, and God," *Commonweal* 123 (August 16, 1996): 11–17.

Pontifical Council for Justice and Peace. *Compendium of the Social Doctrine of the Church.* Vatican City: Libreria Editrice Vaticana, 2004.

Ross, Susan, and Mary Catherine Hilkert, O. P. "Feminist Theology: A Review of Literature." *Theological Studies* 56 (1995): 327–352.

Sacred Congregation for the Doctrine of the Faith. *Instruction on Certain Aspects of the "Theology of Liberation."* Washington, DC: United States Catholic Conference, 1984.

Sanders, E. P. *The Historical Figure of Jesus.* New York: Penguin, 1993.

Sugirtharajah, R. S., ed. *Voices from the Margin: Interpreting the Bible in the Third World.* Maryknoll, NY: Orbis, 1991.

Theissen, Gerd, and Mertz Annette. *The Historical Jesus: A Comprehensive Guide.* Minneapolis, MN: Fortress, 1998.

United States Catholic Conference. *Renewing the Earth: An Invitation to Reflection and Action on Environment in Light of Catholic Social Teaching.* Washington, DC: Office for Publishing and Promotion Services, United States Catholic Conference, 1992.

United States Conference of Catholic Bishops. "Statement on Iraq," November 13, 2002. www.usccb. org/bishops/iraq.shtml.

Varacalli, Joseph A. *The Catholic Experience in America.* Westport, CT: Greenwood, 2006.

———. "Catholic Social Thought and American Civilization." *The Homiletic and Pastoral Review* (2002): 11–19.

Witherington, Ben. *The Jesus Quest: The Third Search for the Jew of Nazareth.* Downers Grove, IL: InterVarsity, 1995.

Chapter

CHRISTIANITY AND INTERRELIGIOUS DIALOGUE

As the world moves into the third millennium, dialogue among the world's religions is becoming ever more urgent and unavoidable. Dialogue is more *urgent* because we live in an age marked by explosive conflict in which religion is often involved, even if we can't always tell whether religion is actually the cause of a particular conflict or whether it is merely an incidental identifying "marker" of the parties at odds with one another. But dialogue has also become more *unavoidable* because globalization is bringing the world's religions into regular contact with one another, whether they like it or not. The speed and expansiveness of communication, the increase and ease of travel, the expansion of world trade, the migration of peoples forced to become refugees, economic needs and opportunities, all of these mean an increased level of exposure to peoples who are different from ourselves. Even for Americans, contact with members of non-Christian religions is becoming commonplace. As one analyst reported, "By now there are well over one million Asian Indians [in America] whose presence results from the Immigration Act of 1965, and a majority of these immigrants and their children are Hindus . . . The number is growing faster than the general population" (William 1998, 21).

This chapter will begin by summarizing some negative and positive examples of Christian approaches to other religions during two thousand years of Christian history. It will then explore the rapid changes in the development of Christian theologies of non-Christian religions, which took place in the twentieth century, including some examples of exclusivism and inclusivism. The final section will survey several official church documents that demonstrate current approaches to interreligious issues. Special attention will be given to two activities of the church—proclamation and dialogue—as they relate to relations between Christians and people of other faiths.

471

HISTORY OF CHRISTIAN ATTITUDES TOWARD NON-CHRISTIAN RELIGIONS

The apostles of Christ and many of his other followers believed that through him they had experienced an unprecedented reconciliation with God and with their neighbors. Hence, they traveled across the countryside, even across the Mediterranean Sea, spreading the news of his death and resurrection. A new, tightly knit community developed through these efforts which "was of one heart and soul," where "no one claimed private ownership of any possessions, but everything they owned was held in common" (Acts 4:32). St. Paul believed that this community, which he referred to as the *ekklesia* or "assembly," often translated as "church," was the true Israel and the true body of Christ: "For just as the body is one and has many members, and all the members of the body, though many, are one body, so it is with Christ. For in the one Spirit we were all baptized into one body—Jews or Greeks, slaves or free—and we were all made to drink of one Spirit" (1 Cor 12:12–13). Paul further stated that the church is Christ's "body, the fullness of him who fills all in all" (Eph 1:23).

In the first centuries of the Christian era, the belief in the church as the body of Christ gradually developed into a negative judgment on those outside it. This did not begin as a condemnation of non-Christians, but rather as a warning against those who endangered the unity of the church. As discussed in earlier chapters, there was a wide range of schisms in the early church over belief and practice. To counter these divisions, leaders like Ignatius of Antioch (died c. 110) warned that "anyone who follows a maker of schism will not inherit the Kingdom of God" (*Letter to the Philadelphians* 3:3). In the third century, Cyprian, bishop of Carthage, declared that "there is no salvation outside the Church" (*Letter* 73.21.2), and that "whoever is separated from the Church and is joined to an adulteress [*by which Cyprian means a false church*] is therefore separated from the promises of the Church, and one who leaves the Church of Christ will not arrive at Christ's rewards. He is an alien, someone profane, an enemy. Whoever does not have the Church as his mother cannot have God as his father" (*On the Unity of the Catholic Church,* 6).

In the fourth century, the dictum "no salvation outside the Church" came to be applied not only to those who endangered its unity but also to those Jews and pagans who did not accept Christian faith. Christianity grew even more rapidly after the conversion of Constantine, and by the end of the fourth century it was the official religion of the Roman Empire. Hence it was argued that there was no longer a reason for any sincere seeker after truth not to consider Christianity and to realize that it held the truth. As St. John Chrysostom wrote:

> You will find that such a one [*a pagan*] has not really been diligent in seeking the truth, since what concerns the truth is now clearer than the sun. How shall they obtain pardon who, when they see the doctrine of truth spread before them, make no effort to come to know it? For now the name of God is proclaimed to all, what the prophets predicted has come true, and the religion of the pagans has been proved false. (Cited in Dupuis 1997, 89)

During the Middle Ages the idea that there is no salvation outside the church became incorporated into formal documents of the Catholic Church. A culminating point was the Ecumenical Council of Florence, which in 1442 explicitly condemned Jews and pagans in its "Decree for the Copts." The council's goal was to reunite the Catholic Church and the separated Eastern churches (see Chapter 11). Summarizing the essentials of Catholic belief for the sake of the Coptic Orthodox Church, the document stated that the church "firmly believes, professes and preaches that 'no one remaining outside the Catholic Church, not only pagans,' but also Jews, heretics and schismatics, can become partakers of eternal life; but they will go to the 'eternal fire prepared for the devil and its angels'" (Cited in Dupuis 1997, 95).

Protestants shared the belief that there is no salvation outside the church, but the fragmentation caused by the Reformation raised the crucial question of *which* church could claim to be the means of salvation. For all their differences, Protestants agreed in saying that the Catholic Church had become corrupted under the leadership of the popes and that only a remnant of faithful Christians existed within it. But most Protestants were unwilling to make an exclusive claim for any particular visible church. Rather, they tended to hold that the "true church" was invisible and known to God alone, though it had existed since the coming of Christ and was composed of all those who have genuine faith in him. They believed that this faithful remnant is justified by grace through faith alone, and they contrasted it with those who seek salvation through works, such as Jews, Muslims, and those Christians who continued to remain loyal to the pope. In the words of Martin Luther: "But apart from Christ there can be no discussion or any hope in regard to God. This is the kind of religion the Jews, the Turks, and the papists have" (LW 7:253; WA 44,487). Such an exclusive concept of God's saving revelation grew in part from the Protestant Reformers' belief in God's transcendence and sovereign will and from their skepticism about how much unaided reason could know about God. Later, in the modern period, such exclusive ideas of revelation and salvation would be subjected to criticism and debate, and Protestants would try in various ways to envision how God relates to human beings *outside* the scope of the biblical revelation.

In spite of these negative judgments on non-Christian religions, there is also a long history of constructive borrowing from the non-Christian world. The men and women who converted often brought aspects of their prior identities into the faith. For instance, Justin Martyr, who was originally a student of pagan philosophy, continued to regard the Greek philosophers as eminently wise men. These philosophers contemplated the *logos* or "reason" evident in the cosmic order and harmony. Justin Martyr identified this *logos* with the *Logos* of the Gospel of John, the divine Word through whom the universe had been created and which became incarnate as Jesus Christ. Similarly, the third-century Christian philosopher Clement of Alexandria said that Greek philosophy was God's providential way to prepare the Greco-Roman world for the gospel, just as the Law had been the preparation for the Jews. By thus introducing rational inquiry into Christianity, the church fathers formulated classic Christian doctrines and gave birth to the discipline of theology (Chapter 8).

Constructive interactions between Christianity and non-Christian culture were not limited to the intellectual life of the church. The liturgical year, for instance, was partially shaped by the religious festivals of pre-Christian Europe. The church commemorates the communion of saints on November 1, All Saint's Day, a celebration that coincides with Samhain, the earlier Celtic festival when the souls of the dead were believed to return to their earthly homes. Certain customs of Christmas, such as the lighting of the Christmas tree, are believed to have originated in earlier customs that celebrated the return of light on the shortest day of the year, the winter solstice. At the Easter vigil, the Paschal candle, representing Christ, is lit in the darkened church. This custom and also the practice of hunting for Easter eggs may have originated with spring rituals attempting to ensure a fertile harvest and celebrating the rebirth of nature. Further, when Christianity was legalized in the fourth century, it borrowed much of the ritual, architecture, and structural organization of the Roman world. It thereby transformed itself from a confederation of communities meeting in homes to a highly organized, imperial religion that held elaborate rituals in ornate basilicas. Hence in many ways pre-Christian beliefs and practices were the fabric out of which Christianity grew and developed.

This process of borrowing had biblical precedent, for although the ancient Israelites believed that they had a unique and privileged relationship with God, they were deeply influenced by the religions and cultures of their neighbors. Their first patriarch, Abraham, participated in a ceremony of thanksgiving led by Melchizedek, a Canaanite priest. Much later, the Temple of Solomon, which became the center of Israelite worship in Jerusalem, followed the model of Syrian temples. One can find many instances of borrowing from the religious literature of foreign cultures. For example, the author of the book of Proverbs adopted proverbs from Egyptian literature, sometimes verbatim. Some of the Psalms of the Bible were influenced by the themes and styles of Egyptian hymns. Similarly, the Pentateuch reflects the literary traditions of the law codes in Mesopotamia, such as Hammurabi's Law Code. The theme of a Creator-God who triumphs over a watery chaos appears in both Babylonian religious literature and in the Psalms. Finally, an entire book of the Bible, the Book of Job, is devoted to the experiences of a man named Job, who was a non-Israelite.

Creative interaction with other cultures and religions continued past the biblical and early church eras into later ages. During the medieval period Muslim contacts in Sicily and Spain made the works of Aristotle available to Western Christians. These texts of Greek philosophy, as discussed in Chapter 15, exposed Christians to a rational, coherent explanation of the world that did not depend on the Bible. Some Christians repudiated Aristotle completely, but major thinkers of the era, such as Albert the Great and Thomas Aquinas, did not shut out this world. Rather, they engaged in a dialogue with Aristotelian thought, integrating the insights of Greek learning with Christian faith. This integration profoundly influenced the development of theology through the twentieth century and showed Christianity's ability to engage with other worldviews.

During the Age of Discovery (approximately the fifteenth through the seventeenth centuries) courageous and inventive missionaries like the Jesuit priests Matteo Ricci (1552–1610) and Roberto de Nobili (1577–1656) adopted the cultures of the Asian peoples with whom they lived. Ricci learned the Chinese language, dressed in the robes of a Confucian scholar, and endorsed the veneration of ancestors and the cult of Confucius, on the grounds that they were merely civic rituals that showed respect for ancestors and for a great teacher, but that did not involve actual worship. Roberto de Nobili (1577–1656), a Jesuit who worked in India, learned three Indian languages, read Hindu scriptures, dressed as a Hindu ascetic, and advocated working within the traditional Hindu caste system rather than against it. Through careful arguments he stressed the compatibility of specific aspects of Hindu culture with Christian religion.

The experiences of the Catholic Church during the Age of Discovery had a deep impact on its approach to non-Christian religions. Previous borrowing by Catholics was generally from the European culture in which they were immersed by birth; they were not borrowing something that was inherently different or foreign to them. However, in the Age of Discovery Western Christians came into contact with cultures radically different from their own. They often persecuted these cultures. At the same time the church laid the theoretical foundations for inculturation, for borrowing from non-Christian cultures, by distinguishing between Christian faith and the culture in which a people lives (see Chapter 21).

As Catholic theologians reflected on the place that these newly discovered peoples occupied in God's plan for humanity, a further development occurred in how they understood the classic dictum "no salvation outside the church." Confronted with the vast masses of people in Africa, Asia, Oceania, and the Americas, some could not believe that all people who did not belong to the Catholic Church were condemned to hell. **Robert Bellarmine** (1542–1621) formulated the concept of an **implicit desire**: In following one's conscience and attempting to live morally, one who has not heard the gospel is expressing an implicit desire to join the church. Through this desire one may be saved. This theological concept gradually gained currency in Catholic thought over the following centuries. It was not, however, an endorsement of non-Christian religions themselves, but only a statement that salvation outside of formal membership in the Catholic Church is not impossible. It would not be until the twentieth century that there would be a deep and widespread consideration of non-Christian religions by Catholics and Protestants.

TWENTIETH-CENTURY DEVELOPMENTS

The twentieth century saw an unprecedented amount of reflection, from members of a wide range of religions, on religious diversity. Thinkers who reflected on religious diversity in prior eras generally considered only those religions in close contact with each other, such as Christians considering Judaism or Buddhists concerning Confucianists. In the nineteenth century, however, religious pluralism emerged as a category of thought in its own right, independent of any particular religion. These developments were promoted by the unprecedented levels of contact and communication across the globe.

This increased contact between religions and their members often promoted a positive evaluation of non-Christian religions, which in many cases were flourishing rather than declining, and which sometimes possessed qualities that Christians could admire and wish to foster themselves. Influenced by this dawning appreciation of the non-Christian world, Popes Benedict XV, Pius XI, and Pius XII encouraged serious consideration of non-Christian thought and culture. For instance, in 1939 Pope Pius XII reversed the earlier prohibitions against participating in the "Chinese rites"(see Chapter 21), on the grounds that the rejected practices were no longer genuinely religious but now had only a civil or social meaning. Two years later he endorsed the concept of implicit desire in the encyclical *Mystici Corporis* ("Mystical Body"). In 1949 he condemned the teaching of the American Jesuit Fr. Leonard Feeney, the Catholic chaplain at Harvard University, who had caused a furor by maintaining that there is no salvation without formal membership in the Catholic Church. Finally, in 1951 he published *Evangelii Praecones* ("Preachers of the Gospel"), in which he stated,

> "Let not the gospel on being introduced into any new land destroy or extinguish whatever its people possess that is naturally good, just or beautiful. For the Church, when she calls people to a higher culture and a better way of life, under the inspiration of the Christian religion, does not act like one who recklessly cuts down and uproots a thriving forest. No, she grafts a good shoot upon the wild stock that it may bear a crop of more delicious fruit" *(Evangelii Praecones* §56).

Not only was inculturation revived in the twentieth century, but it was also given a distinct theological underpinning. In *Evangelii Praecones* Pius XII applied the Catholic theory of salvation not just to the human soul, but also to human culture. The terms *nature* and *supernature* are key to his discussion. Traditional teachings affirm that human nature, though tainted by original sin, is essentially good. Yet the grace of Christ brings humans to unprecedented levels of goodness and holiness, which they could not attain by their own strength. At these "supernatural" levels, one may comprehend God, who lies beyond human understanding, and one may become virtuous beyond one's strength. Thus, humans are good by nature, but through grace they may be brought to supernatural levels of holiness.

Pius XII applied these teachings regarding the human soul to human culture. Just as human nature is essentially good, many aspects of human culture are essentially good. Yet the grace of Christ may bring human culture to unprecedented levels of holiness. Speaking concretely, Christian religion can transform human culture into a new and greater thing:

> Although owing to Adam's fall, human nature is tainted with original sin, yet it has in itself something that is naturally Christian; and this, if illumined by divine light and nourished by God's grace, can eventually be changed into true and supernatural virtue. This is the reason why the Catholic Church has neither scorned nor rejected the pagan philosophies. Instead, after freeing them from error and all contamination she has perfected and completed them by Christian revelation. . . . By no means has she repressed native customs and traditions but has given them a certain religious significance; she has even transformed their feast days and made them serve to commemorate the martyrs and to celebrate mysteries of the faith. (*Evangelii Praecones* §§57–58)

This view of non-Christian culture may be categorized as a **theology of fulfillment**, for Christ is believed to *fulfill* the positive aspects and longings of non-Christian belief and customs. This approach is also known as **inclusivism**, according to which other religions are believed to be included in the mystery of God. The opposite view, which holds that no truth or grace lies outside of Christianity, is known as **exclusivism**.

An Example of Exclusivism

Although dialogue and tolerance are now promoted through the teachings and activities of many Christian denominations, exclusivism remains a prominent outlook, especially among conservative types of Protestant Christianity. Protestant missionary efforts, for example, tend to be dominated by evangelical and fundamentalist Christians, who are strongly committed to witnessing and evangelizing. A profound defender of exclusivism was the Swiss theologian **Karl Barth** (1886–1968), the most influential Protestant theologian of the twentieth century. Barth's radical view of the exclusivity of God's revelation in Jesus Christ requires some explanation if it is not to be misunderstood as a species of fundamentalism. His exclusivism stemmed not from a mere unwillingness to consider other religions but from a great disillusionment with the modern world.

The core of Barth's ideas took shape after World War I as a protest against the liberal Protestantism that had dominated prewar Germany. Liberal Protestantism thought that Christianity needed to be reshaped in order to be compatible with modern intellectual and cultural advances. In Germany it was also strongly patriotic and nationalistic, and gave an uncritical endorsement to Germany's participation in World War I. When Adolf Hitler and his Nazi party came to power in 1933, many Christians thought they could see the hand of God at work in a dynamic movement that promised to renew all of German life and to put the country back on its feet again. Some Christians even saw in the Third Reich an instance of divine revelation.

Barth regarded all of this as sheer idolatry. He felt drawn to the more pessimistic view of human nature and the uncompromising belief in God's sovereignty as taught by the original Reformers like Martin Luther and John Calvin. In 1934 Protestants who shared his views met at the German town of Barmen and organized a dissenting movement within the

Figure 26–1 Swiss theologian Karl Barth (1886–1968).

official Protestant church. It became known as the "Confessing" Church because of its confession of faith, the celebrated Barmen Declaration, the first article of which proclaimed: "We reject the false doctrine that the Church could and should recognize as a source of its proclamation, beyond and besides this one Word of God, yet other events, powers, historic figures and truths as God's revelation" ("Theological Declaration of Barmen" 8.12 in Cochrane 1962, 240).

Given Barth's theology of revelation and his experience of the dismaying German Christian sellout to Nazi ideology, it should not surprise us that he refused to see knowledge of God anywhere but in the Bible. He regarded all religions, including Christianity, as idolatrous and sinful expressions of humanity. The critical difference, however, between Christianity and other religions is that Christianity is rendered capable of salvation through the grace of Christ. Hence, like the Christian herself, Christianity is at once corrupt and redeemed. Other religions are simply corrupt.

At first glance Barth's theology appears wholly negative about other religions and equally negative about the place of other human beings in God's redemptive plan. The first assertion seems true enough, but not necessarily the second. Surprising as it may seem, Barth is known to have speculated about the possibility of universal salvation, even of those who did not profess or even know of Jesus Christ. He thought universal salvation might be justified on the basis of God's sovereign will and on Jesus Christ as both the subject *and the object* of God's election. Paul says in his letter to the Romans that just as God had condemned all in Adam, so he really and truly elected all in Jesus Christ (see Rom 5:12–21). Barth took this to mean that Christ absorbed in himself the entire salvation history of the human race, not just as its culmination but as its very substance: what Christ did and what happened to him truly is the fate of all. Barth apparently never denied the accusation that he was advocating universal salvation—though he never explicitly endorsed it either.

Some Examples of Inclusivism

In contrast to Barth's exclusivist theology concerning non-Christian religions, two Catholic theologians of the twentieth century—**Jean Daniélou** (1905–1974) and **Hans Urs von Balthasar** (1905–1988)—provide us with inclusivist theologies of fulfillment. Daniélou wrote in the 1940s of "cosmic religion," arguing that religions such as Hinduism and Buddhism impart a knowledge of God through the universe. This knowledge is completed and brought to fulfillment through Jesus Christ. In the 1960s Hans Urs von Balthasar wrote about the striving for God

Figure 26–2 Karl Rahner (1904–1984), Roman Catholic theologian and Jesuit priest.

present in the various religions, referring especially to the meditative practices of Hinduism and Buddhism. He concluded, however, that such practices are a human search for God, whereas the Judeo-Christian tradition is the story of God's search for humanity, of God's effort to reveal his person and presence. In this way, Balthasar argued that Christianity fulfills the longings of other religions.

A radical step forward was made in the 1950s by the influential Catholic theologian **Karl Rahner** (1904–1984), who concluded that non-Christian religions may actually mediate salvation, that the supernatural grace of God may be available through them. As a Christian, Rahner believed that grace comes to humanity through the death and resurrection of Jesus Christ. The fullness of this grace is present only in that religion historically bound with the life and death of Christ—the Catholic Church. However, he argued that the Holy Spirit carries this grace to all times and places, making it available in non-Christian religions, as well. Insofar as these religions are not opposed to the Christian message but are conformed to a message of love and self-surrender, they mediate the grace of Christ. Non-Christians who lead lives of love and commitment to other people may receive grace and may therefore be known as "anonymous Christians," even though they do not explicitly know Christ or profess him as the savior.

Rahner was building upon the idea of implicit desire. While agreeing with the fundamental idea, the doctrine as it was then formulated seemed very barren to him, for it did not explain *how* the grace of Christ came to be transmitted to the non-Christian. A fundamental belief of the Catholic tradition is that the grace of Christ is received through the rituals and community of the church. For Rahner, to be saved independently from contact with a living tradition fundamentally violates the Catholic vision. Thus he argued that the communities, rituals, and ethical codes of non-Christian religions might *themselves* be channels of the grace of Christ. This participation is, however, of a limited nature—the fullness of grace is present only in Christianity.

Rahner's ideas were a controversial development in theologies of fulfillment, but in the view of many people he did not go far enough. Pluralism, which is different from exclusivism and inclusivism, describes the position that any religion may be a direct route to God. One of the most prominent pluralists, the philosopher John Hick, began arguing in the 1970s that ideas such as Bellarmine's "implicit desire" and Rahner's "anonymous Christianity" are like the epicycles of the ancient astronomers. Attempting to preserve a geocentric (earth-centered) solar system, the astronomers had posited that the planets each have their own, secondary centers of orbit, in addition to that of the earth. They had thereby accounted for discrepancies between the predictions of a geocentric system and actual observations of the heavenly bodies. However, in the 1500s Copernicus posited the heliocentric (sun-centered) system, which matched observation well and eliminated the complexities of epicycles. Hick argued that theories like those of Bellarmine and Rahner are efforts to explain the existence of truth and goodness outside of Christianity while retaining Christianity at the center, just as epicycles were attempts to retain the earth at the center of the solar system. Hick argued that

Christians should drop their ecclesiocentrism and christocentrism, beliefs that the church and Christ are the center of salvation, in favor of theocentrism, a view that God is the center of salvation and that he directly saves non-Christians through their religions, not through the intervention of the church or of Christ.

Although Hick taught that all religions may lead directly to God, He was aware of the many contradictions in belief and practice among them. He resolved this issue by appealing to the traditional teaching, present in some form or other in many religions, that the ultimate reality is beyond human description. He argued that beliefs and practices are ultimately human constructs, and that the divine reality is beyond all of them. Religions should simply be regarded as pathways to the divine, not as ultimate in themselves.

The twentieth century closed with a broad range of reflection on interreligious issues, but little overall consensus among theologians. For instance, Hick's approach may seem to be the most tolerant and open, but many argue that it is actually very closed and narrow. If no religious beliefs, of any religion, have ultimate validity, then why bother to dialogue and share them? Instead of interacting, the religions will become closed and narrow worlds, just as they can be with the exclusivist approach. And yet if the religions are not considered as equally valid, as they are in Hick's approach, can there be a genuine dialogue between their members? In light of these and other bewildering problems, many scholars, like the noted Catholic theologian and scholar of Hinduism, Francis Clooney, are reserving judgment on these matters and are arguing that it is best, for the present, to focus on dialogue and comparison rather than on theories about non-Christian religions.

FORMAL CHURCH TEACHINGS ON INTERRELIGIOUS ISSUES

Given the great ferment in thought concerning non-Christian religions, the highest levels of authority in many Christian councils and denominations have issued formal statements on the topic. A wide range of approaches exist among Protestant denominations, some of which reaffirm the belief that salvation comes only through explicit acceptance of Christ as the savior, while others believe that Christ's grace may be active in the lives of non-Christians. A statement by the National Council of the Churches of Christ in the United States summarizes this range of positions:

> We [all] agree that it is not by any merit of our own, but by God's grace that we are reconciled. Likewise, Christians also agree that our discipleship impels us to become reconciled to the whole human family and to live in proper relationship to all of God's creation. We disagree, however, on whether non-Christians may be reconciled to God, and if so, how [sic]. Many Christians see no possibility of reconciliation with God apart from a conscious acceptance of Jesus Christ as incarnate Son of God and personal savior. For others, the reconciling work of Jesus is salvific [saving] in its own right, independent of any particular human response. For many, the saving power of God is understood as a mystery and an expression of God's sovereignty that cannot be confined within our limited conceptions. (National Council of Churches 1999, §33)

This document indicates that some Protestants accept the possibility of the salvation of non-Christians while agreeing with the doctrine that salvation is from Christ alone. Some argue that because salvation is from Christ alone, not from human effort, that the human act of accepting Christ as the savior may not be necessary. Rather, Christians and non-Christians are saved solely by God's gracious love. (This interpretation seems to resemble a hypothesis proposed by the great Protestant theologian Karl Barth, who is otherwise thought of as an exclusivist.) Also, some argue that the salvation of non-Christians, while possible, exceeds the ability of the human mind to grasp or understand.

The National Council of Churches, which consists of a wide range of Christian denominations, further makes it clear that no matter what one's belief about the salvation of non-Christians may be, members of all religions must be treated with respect: "All are made in the image of God (Genesis 1:27). When we meet a human being, no matter what her or his religion, we are meeting a unique creation of the living God. 'One is the community of all peoples, one their origin, for God made the whole human race to live on all the face of the earth.' All are equal in God's sight; each is equally the object of God's love . . . Community is itself a divine gift which we are called to make real in our lives" (ibid. §20).

The key moment in the Catholic Church was the Second Vatican Council (1962–1965), which was called by Pope John XXIII to reflect on the church and the modern world. In a crucial statement of the Catholic understanding of God's dealings with those who do not know God, the council document *Lumen Gentium* ("Dogmatic Constitution on the Church") affirmed the baptism of desire, making it formal church teaching:

> Nor is God Himself far distant from those who in shadows and images seek the unknown God, for it is He who gives to all men life and breath and all things, and as Saviour wills that all men be saved. Those also can attain to salvation who through no fault of their own do not know the Gospel of Christ or His Church, yet sincerely seek God and moved by grace strive by their deeds to do His will as it is known to them through the dictates of conscience. Nor does Divine Providence deny the help necessary for salvation to those who, without blame on their part, have not yet arrived at an explicit knowledge of God and with His grace strive to live a good life. Whatever good or truth is found amongst them is looked upon by the Church as a preparation for the gospel. (*Lumen Gentium* §16; Abbott 1966, 36)

The council also prepared a short document, *Nostra Aetate* ("Declaration on Non-Christian Religions"), which states that "she [the Catholic Church] looks with sincere respect upon those ways of conduct and of life, those rules and teachings which, though differing in many particulars from what she holds and sets forth, nevertheless often reflect a ray of that Truth which enlightens all men" (*Nostra Aetate* §2; Abbott 1966, 662). The passage employs the language of John 1:9, which refers to Christ as the "true light, which enlightens everyone," thereby affirming that the light of Christ is present in non-Christian religions.

By affirming a positive relationship between Christ and other religions, the Second Vatican Council endorsed the theology of fulfillment expressed by men such as Pius XII and Jean Daniélou. Some have even argued that *Lumen Gentium* and *Nostra Aetate* support the more radical position taken by Karl Rahner. In either case, the Second Vatican Council put the inclusivist position at the forefront, challenging the views of a great number of Christians and altering the landscape of Catholicism.

In addition to making a general statement about Christ and non-Christian religions, *Nostra Aetate* discusses specific traditions. It implies, for instance, that Christians and Muslims worship the same God: "Upon the Moslems . . . the Church looks with esteem. They adore one God, living and enduring, merciful and all-powerful, Maker of heaven and earth" (§3; Abbott 1966, 663). The document praises Buddhism for teaching its adherents that worldly objects do not bring true fulfillment and happiness. Hinduism is esteemed for seeking the divine through stories and philosophical systems. The document concludes by stating that religious differences must not be a basis for discrimination and that one cannot truly worship

God if one is prejudicial toward one's neighbor: "We cannot in truthfulness call upon that God who is the Father of all if we refuse to act in a brotherly way toward certain men, created though they be to God's image" (§5; Abbott 1966, 667). However, in practice, many Catholics depart from these teachings, just as there are departures from formal teachings in many other areas, such as sexual morality. One finds Catholics ranging from those who are openly hostile towards other religions to those who consider all religions to be equally valid.

The church's new attitude towards non-Christian religions may appear to support the popular presumption that there are no significant differences between religions. However, church leaders are not endorsing a relativist view of religious differences. Rejecting such a misunderstanding was a major focus of the Vatican declaration *Dominus Iesus* (2000), authored by Cardinal Joseph Ratzinger, who became Pope Benedict XVI in 2005. Christianity continues to be based on the claim that a unique union of the human and the divine took place in Jesus Christ and that this union is decisively significant for people in all times and places: "There is salvation in no one else, for there is no other name under heaven given among mortals by which we must be saved," presented as the words of Peter in Acts 4:12. And in his last words to his followers, the risen Jesus himself commanded them: "Go therefore and make disciples of all nations, baptizing them in the name of the Father, and of the Son, and of the Holy Spirit" (Matt 28:19). Faith in Christ and baptism into the church remain foundational claims.

Although *Nostra Aetate* was a great watershed, it was a very brief document. Since then other documents have been issued by the Roman curia that explore the issue of interreligious

Figure 26–3 Pope John Paul II and participants of World Day of Peace at Assisi, Italy, in 1986. Pope John Paul II has been intensely involved in interreligious dialogue throughout his long reign as pope.

relations in more depth. Two of the most significant to date are "The Church and Other Religions" and "Dialogue and Proclamation," issued by the Secretariat for Non-Christians. **Proclamation** is "the communication of the Gospel message . . . an invitation to a commitment of faith in Jesus Christ and to entry through baptism into the community of believers which is the church" (Arinze and Tomko 1991, 124). **Dialogue**, in turn, is "a manner of acting, an attitude and a spirit which guides one's conduct. It implies concern, respect and hospitality toward the other" (Arinze and Zago 1984, 260). The Christian is called to participate in both proclamation and dialogue: "Both are legitimate and necessary . . . The two activities remain distinct but, as experience shows, one and the same local church, one and the same person, can be diversely engaged in both" (Arinze and Tomko 1991, 133).

Some may regard the activities of dialogue and proclamation as opposed to each other. How, for instance, can one dialogue with another party when one believes that one knows the ultimate truth and should try to convince the other of that truth? However, "The Church and Other Religions" argues that dialogue and proclamation are closely linked. To dialogue with a party presumes that one has something to share. In the case of the Christian, this something is Jesus Christ. Thus dialogue is not separate from the proclamation of Christ. However, to wish to share one's message, Jesus Christ, with another party presumes that this party has value and merits one's respect. Moreover, the message of Christ specifically involves love and respect for people. Hence, the proclamation of Christ must involve a growing appreciation of the other party. This, in turn, involves dialogue: "Respect for every person ought to characterize the missionary activity of the Church today . . . The fact that the Christian mission can never be separated from love and respect for others is proof for Christians of the place of dialogue within that mission" (Arinze and Zago 1984, 258).

Further, although Jesus Christ is the fullest revelation of the divine, individual Christians are not in full possession of the truth. Rather, each Christian must continually seek the truth, becoming better conformed to it. In this quest, Christians can learn through members of other religions, for God is present in these religions. "A person discovers that he does not possess the truth in a perfect and total way but can walk together with others towards that goal" (Arinze and Zago 1984, 258). Dialogue can involve sharing one's hopes and joys, collaborating in practical projects which benefit humanity, sharing religious experiences, and exploring theological issues together. Through these activities, "mutual affirmation, reciprocal correction, and fraternal exchange lead the partners in dialogue to an ever greater maturity which in turn generates interpersonal communication. Religious experiences and outlooks can themselves be purified and enriched" (ibid., 258).

Key Terms

Robert Bellarmine	inclusivism	Karl Rahner
implicit desire	exclusivism	proclamation
nature	Karl Barth	dialogue
supernature	Jean Daniélou	
theology of fulfillment	Hans Urs von Balthasar	

Questions for Reading

1. Discuss several examples of non-Israelite influence on the Jewish scriptures.

2. Explain how the concept of the *Logos* played an important role in how early Christianity related itself to non-Christian ways of understanding reality.

3. Explain the ways the teaching "outside the church there is no salvation" has been understood over the course of the Christian tradition.

4. Define the categories of nature and supernature and explain how Pius XII applied these to human culture.

5. Concerning the relationship of Christianity and other religions, describe the view of Karl Barth, paying particular attention to Barth's understanding of religion and also of election.

6. What argument does Rahner give to show that grace is present in non-Christian religions?

7. What is the understanding of religious diversity proposed by John Hick? How has it been criticized?

8. What are some of the different approaches among Protestant denominations to the issue of the salvation of non-Christians?

9. Define the two activities of dialogue and proclamation. In what ways are these activities closely linked? Why are they not opposed to each other?

Works Consulted/Recommended Reading

Abbott, Walter M., ed., and Joseph Gallagher, trans. *The Documents of Vatican II.* Angelus Books. New York: Guild, 1966.

Arinze, Francis, and Jozef Tomko. "Dialogue and Proclamation." *Origins* 21 (1991): 121, 123–135.

Arinze, Francis, and Marcello Zago. "The Church and Other Religions: Reflections and Orientations on Dialogue and Mission by the Secretariat for Non-Christians (June 10, 1984)." *The Pope Speaks* 29 (1984): 253–265.

Cochrane, Arthur C. *The Church's Confession Under Hitler.* Philadelphia: Westminster, 1962.

Dupuis, Jacques. *Toward a Christian Theology of Religious Pluralism.* Maryknoll, NY: Orbis, 1997.

Gillingham, Richard. "Is Barth's Theology Necessarily Exclusivist?" *Quodlibet: Online Journal of Christian Theology and Philosophy* 5:2–3 (July 2003). www.quodlibet.net/gillingham-barth.shtml.

Knitter, Paul F. *No Other Name? A Critical Survey of Christian Attitudes toward the World Religions.* American Society of Missiology, no. 7. Maryknoll, NY: Orbis, 1985.

Luther, Martin. *D. Martin Luthers Werke: Kritische Gesamtausgabe.* 73 vols. 1883. Reprint, Weimar: H. Böhlaus Nachfolger, 2000–2007.

Luther, Martin. *Luther's Works.* Edited by Jaroslav Pelikan and Helmut T. Lehmann. 56 vols. Philadelphia: Fortress; St. Louis: Concordia Publishing House, 1955–1986.

National Council of Churches in the U.S.A. "Interfaith Relations and the Churches." 1999. www.ncccusa.org/interfaith/ifr.html.

Pius XII. *Evangelii Praecones. Encyclical of Pope Pius XII on Promotion of Catholic Missions,* June 2, 1951. The Holy See–Vatican Web site; www.vatican.va/holy_father/pius_xii/encyclicals/documents/hf_p-xii_enc_02061951_evangelii-praecones_en.html.

Shorter, Aylward. *Toward a Theology of Inculturation.* Maryknoll, NY: Orbis, 1988.

William, Raymond B. "Immigrants from India in North America and Hindu-Christian Study and Dialogue." *Hindu-Christian Studies Bulletin* 11 (1998): 20–24.

Glossary

Aaron—according to the Exodus story, Moses' brother and assistant.

abbot—the spiritual leader who governs an organized community of monks.

Abraham—the first patriarch of the Israelite people (lived mid-nineteenth to mid-eighteenth century B.C.E.), with whom God formed an everlasting covenant; claimed as an ancestor by Jews, Christians, and Muslims.

absolution—forgiveness for the guilt associated with sin.

Adeotatus—meaning "Gift of God," the son of Augustine of Hippo (A.D. 354–430); born of Augustine's relationship with a concubine whose name we do not know.

Afonso the Good (A.D. 1482–1543)—Catholic king of the Congo who tried unsuccessfully to oversee the conversion of his people to Catholicism, while holding back the greed of the Portuguese colonists who were enslaving them.

agent of God—drawn from the analogy of a king and his messenger, this phrase is used by biblical scholars to describe how first-century people might have understood the relationship between God and Jesus, who acts on God's behalf in the world.

aggiornamento—meaning "a bringing up to date." This term describes the spirit of the Second Vatican Council as it attempted to reinterpret the church's doctrine and reform its practice in a way that was suitable for the present.

agnostic—someone who is unsure about the existence of God or gods.

Albigensians—see *Cathars*.

Ali Ibn Abu Talib—Muhammad's cousin and son-in-law, the fourth caliph of the Islamic people, assassinated in A.D. 661. Shi'a (meaning "partisans of Ali") Muslims take their name from his.

alienation of property—during the early medieval period, the practice of deeding church goods as the private inheritance of bishops' or priests' children.

Allah—the Muslim name for God; the one and only God.

allegorical—term used to describe a method of interpreting scripture; it involves looking for a hidden spiritual meaning beneath the bare literal or historical meaning of the text.

Ambrose of Milan (c. A.D. 339–397)—bishop and former provincial governor whose sermons inspired the young Augustine to take Christianity seriously.

Amos—an eighth-century B.C.E. prophet who condemned the social injustice of the northern kingdom of Israel and foresaw its destruction by the Assyrians.

anchorite/anchoress—a hermit who pledges his or her life to prayer and contemplation. During the Middle Ages, they lived in small enclosed rooms attached to a church, where they could be spiritual counselors for the people of the area.

animism—worship of the forces of nature.

Anselm of Canterbury (A.D. 1033–1109)—Benedictine monk and archbishop of Canterbury, Anselm is known for his "debt satisfaction" theory of atonement and for his ontological argument for the existence of God.

anthropocentric—human centered.

anthropology—the study of human beings or a particular view about the nature of human beings, based on various philosophical, cultural, and scientific methods; theological explanations concerning humanity's relationship to God, the human condition, and the promise or potential of a renewed humanity.

anthropomorphism—attributing human-like characteristics to God.

anticlericalism—antagonism toward priests and clergy.

Antony of Egypt (A.D. 251–356)—the father of Christian monasticism. Antony felt that Christ's teachings called him to sell all of his possessions and devote himself completely to following the gospel through a life of prayer in isolation from the world. Many Christians—early, medieval, and modern—have been inspired to follow his example.

apocalyptic—from a Greek word meaning "to reveal" or "to uncover," referring to revelations of the heavenly realms or the destiny of this world. It can also be used to describe a person, group, or text that expresses the beliefs that the present world is evil and that God will soon bring an end to it, destroying the evildoers and rescuing the righteous.

apocrypha—name given to the seven books that are included in the Old Testament by Catholics and Orthodox Christians but excluded from the scriptures by Protestants and Jews. The term is also used more broadly to refer to certain Jewish and Christian religious texts written during the same time as the biblical books and considered inspired by some, but not included in the Bible itself.

Apollinaris of Laodicaea (d. A.D. 390)—a Christian theologian who solved the problem of the dual nature of Christ (human and divine) by saying that Christ had a human body but not a human soul. His views came to be regarded as heretical.

apologist—meaning "defender." The apologists of the early church attempted to respond to pagan criticisms of Christianity by explaining what Christians believed and how they lived their lives in terms that made sense to outsiders.

apostasy—falling away from the faith or renunciation of the faith under threat of persecution.

apostle—from the Greek word *apostello*, which means "to send out." It is used by Christians to refer to "one who is sent out by Jesus to preach the word about him."

apostolic tradition—the witness of the apostles and early disciples of Jesus.

Aquinas, Thomas (A.D. 1224/5–1274)—Catholic theologian and saint; author of the *Summa Theologiae*, a comprehensive overview of Christian theology; best known for his integration of the philosophy of Aristotle into Christian faith, his view of the compatibility of reason and revelation, and his "proofs" for God's existence.

Aristotle—Greek philosopher and scientist of the fourth century B.C.E.; his ideas were seen as a challenge to religions like Christianity because without any access to divine revelation he had developed an account of reality that seemed more complete, more sophisticated, and more coherent than that of Christianity.

Arius (c. A.D. 250/56–336)—a fourth-century priest in Alexandria who taught that only God the Father was God in the true sense; the Son (Jesus Christ), though also divine, was created by the Father and therefore was less than him. His teaching was rejected at the Council of Nicaea (A.D. 325) and the Council of Constantinople (A.D. 381).

Ark of the Covenant—(1) a container for sacred objects of the Israelites, including the tablets of the Ten Commandments; (2) the "throne" on which Yahweh's invisible presence sat.

article—the basic unit of many medieval theological works, such as the *Summa Theologiae* of Thomas Aquinas. Each article considers one question and contains the following elements: a statement of the question, a review of the arguments for and against the proposition, the author's own view on the question, and finally a reply to the arguments with which the author ultimately disagreed.

asceticism—the training or discipline of the passions and the appetites (e.g., abstaining from food and sexual activity, denying the body comfort). In the case of hermits and monks, the practice was designed to foster spiritual development.

Athanasius (d. A.D. 373)—bishop of Alexandria and staunch opponent of Arianism.

atheist—someone who disbelieves or denies that God or gods exist.

Augsburg Confession—a statement of faith drafted by Philip Melanchthon, representing the Lutheran position, at the Diet of Augsburg (A.D. 1530). The diet, which was called to resolve differences between Protestants and Catholics, failed, but Lutherans signed Melanchthon's statement, making it one of the most important documents of Lutheran doctrine even today.

Augustine (A.D. 354–430)—theologian and bishop of Hippo; his conversion is described in the autobiographical work *Confessions;* best known for his opposition to Donatism and Pelagianism, his theological doctrines of grace, original sin, and predestination, and his solution to the problem of evil.

Averroes (A.D. 1126–1198)—medieval Muslim scholar known for his learned commentaries on the works of Aristotle.

Avicenna (A.D. 980–1037)—medieval Muslim scholar noted for medical commentaries on the classical Greek physician–scholars Galen and Hippocrates, mathematical commentaries on the classical Greek mathematician Euclid, and philosophical commentaries on Aristotle.

Avignon Papacy (A.D. 1309–1377)—referring to a period in the Late Middle Ages when the pope moved his court to Avignon, France. Before the papacy returned to Rome, the church leadership would be involved in an even greater struggle for power called the Great Schism.

Babylonian Exile—the period during the sixth century B.C.E. when the Judeans were held captive in Babylon by the Babylonians.

Balthasar, Hans Urs von (A.D. 1905–1988)—Swiss theologian and Jesuit priest, he is perhaps best known for his research on the topic of revelation and his theological reflections on beauty.

Baptism—a Christian rite of initiation, which brings about the forgiveness of sins, makes the person a member of the Christian community, and confers the Holy Spirit on the person. *Baptize* means "to plunge." Immersion into the water symbolizes entry into Jesus' death from which one is raised to new life.

Baptism, believer's—see *believer's Baptism.*

Baptist churches—a family of Christian churches that have their roots in the Puritan movement in England. They were also influenced by the Dutch Mennonites and millennialist movements who looked to the books of Daniel and Revelation, seeking "signs of the times" and a proper way of life for Christian believers. They hold conservative views on the authority and inspiration of the Bible, but otherwise they are committed to religious liberty and church independence.

baptistery—in the early church, a Christian building used for Baptism; later, a place in the church set aside for Baptism. The baptisteries of the early church had a centered design, and the focus was on the baptismal font into which the candidate stepped.

Baroque—an ornate style of art and architecture that was especially popular in Roman Catholic churches and among Roman Catholic artists during the Catholic Reformation. The baroque style was designed to dramatically illustrate the truths of Catholic orthodoxy but also to involve the viewer in the experience of faith by appealing to their emotions and overwhelming them with a sense of awe.

Barth, Karl (A.D. 1886–1968)—Protestant theologian and member of the Confessing Church, which was founded in 1933 to oppose the growing Nazi control over the churches in Germany.

base Christian communities—small groups of poor and disenfranchised people and/or their advocates, who meet together to study the Bible, discuss issues of common concern, and strategize about how to remedy or respond to social injustices. These groups are often associated with liberation theology.

Basil of Caesarea (A.D. 330–379)—one of the Cappadocian Fathers; known as the father of Eastern monasticism.

basilica—a style of Christian church architecture, distinguished from other churches by its adaptation of the standard rectangular layout of royal audience halls and public buildings in Roman cities. The Christian version of a basilica was conceived as an audience hall for Christ, the heavenly king.

Batuta, Ibn (A.D. 1304–1368)—an Arab scholar and traveler who was partly responsible for the European colonization and missionary efforts in Africa, because he revealed the presence of gold in that region.

beatitude—meaning "blessed" or "happy," a statement of blessing to be conferred on a person (for example, "Blessed are you . . .").

Beguines—independent communities of laywomen that first emerged in Europe in the High Middle Ages. They had no rule or permanent religious vows, but they shared a form of common life and engaged in contemplative prayer or ministries of caring for the sick and poor.

believer's Baptism—the idea, popularized by the churches of the Radical Reformation, that since Baptism involves entering into a covenant with God, it requires an act of conscious, active belief on the part of the person being baptized. Since only adults are old enough to formulate such belief and make such a decision, infant Baptism is ruled out.

Bellarmine, Robert (A.D. 1542–1621)—A Roman Catholic theologian and Jesuit priest who formulated the concept of implicit desire to explain how people who did not know Christ could be saved.

Benedict of Nursia (A.D. 480–547)—founder of the Benedictine monastery at Monte Cassino and author of the *Rule for Monasteries,* which eventually became the primary rule of monasticism in the West.

benevolence—good will.

Bernard of Clairvaux (A.D. 1090–1153)—a Cistercian monk who wrote and preached extensively on the spiritual life.

Bible—meaning "the books," Christianity's sacred and inspired literature.

biblical inerrancy—for faith communities who accept the verbal inspiration of the Bible, this means that the Bible is completely accurate in all respects and contains no mistakes whatsoever. See *inerrancy*.

biblical studies—a study of the written documents found in the Bible, how these documents were formed, how they were selected to be part of the Bible, what they meant to the original "authors" and "audience," and what they might mean for contemporary belief and practice.

bishop—meaning "overseer." In early Christianity, bishops were overseers of local churches, chiefly responsible for teaching and presiding at the Eucharist. Later, the bishop is an overseer of a group of churches known as a diocese.

Boniface VIII (reigned A.D. 1294–1303)—the pope who published *Unam Sanctam*, perhaps the most famous medieval statement on church and state, which asserts the authority of the papacy over the emerging nation kingdoms of that time.

breviary—a prayer book containing the Liturgy of the Hours, the official prayer of the church, regularly prayed by priests, monks, and religious sisters. It is composed of psalms and readings from the Bible and other religious literature.

bull, papal—see *papal bull*.

Byzantium—see *Constantinople*.

Caesaro-papism—term applied by some Western writers to the Byzantine political theory, which held that the civil ruler ("Caesar") also served as head of the church ("pope").

caliph—meaning "successor," i.e., of Muhammad. This title was given to a succession of leaders of the young Muslim movement after the death of Muhammad in A.D. 632. In theory there was only one, though competing ruling dynasties claimed it at various times; the title was abolished by the Republic of Turkey in 1924.

Calvin, John (A.D. 1509–1564)—the French reformer and theologian who led the Swiss city of Geneva through the Reformation. Calvin is known especially for the doctrines of election and double predestination and for grappling with the problem of church authority after the Protestant rejection of the authority of Rome. His teachings are most influential in the Christian Reformed Church and the Presbyterian Church.

canon—(1) the collection of authoritative writings of a particular religious group; (2) the "rule" or norm of religious truth in the Christian tradition; (3) church law as defined by councils or other church authorities.

canonization—a process by which the church designates certain persons as saints and therefore

models of the Christian life; also the process by which the canon of the Bible took shape.

Cappadocian Fathers—a group of Christian priests, including Basil of Caesarea (A.D. 330–379), his brother Gregory of Nyssa (A.D. 331/40–c. 395), and Basil's friend Gregory of Nazianzus (c. A.D. 329–390), whose theological advances and appropriation of Greek philosophical thought are reflected in the clarifications of the Nicene Creed adopted at the Council of Constantinople (A.D. 381).

Capuchins—a reform branch of the Franciscan movement, this religious order was officially recognized in 1528 during the Catholic Reformation. Members got their name from the unique four-pointed hood that they wore with their brown habit.

Casas, Bartolomé de las (A.D. 1474–1566)—the Spanish Catholic bishop in the territories of the New World who argued that the enslavement of the native peoples was immoral and should be stopped.

catechism—from a Greek word meaning "to instruct." A catechism is a manual of Christian doctrine used to instruct believers in the Christian faith. They were especially popular in the sixteenth century among both Protestant and Catholic reformers, because of the emphasis on religious instruction for ministers as well as laity.

catechumen—a candidate for Baptism who is undergoing instruction in the Christian religion.

Cathars—meaning "pure ones," this anticlerical, Christian reform movement emerged in the twelfth century A.D., teaching that the world and the flesh were the work of an evil god. Thus they practiced severe asceticism. Catharism was widespread in southern France, where they came to be known as the Albigensians.

cathedral—a bishop's church. It gets its name from the bishop's chair, his *cathedra*, which is the symbol of his teaching authority.

Catherine of Siena (c. A.D. 1347–1380)—a mystic of the late medieval period, she was a Dominican tertiary and was influential in bringing an end to the Avignon Papacy, only to see it affected by the Great Schism. Catherine's prayer life had led her into a vision of mystical marriage to Christ. Her visions often were of the nourishing and cleansing blood of the sacrifice of Christ on the cross.

catholic (or **catholicity**)—meaning "universal." The term *Catholic* is also used in a restrictive sense to refer to a tradition within Christianity, namely, the Roman Catholic Church or to describe those churches that claim a continuity of leadership that goes back to the early Christian churches (for example, Eastern Orthodox Christians, Anglicans, and Episcopalians).

Catholic Reformation—a term given to the efforts of those Roman Catholics who wanted to bring about the internal rebirth of Catholic sensibility—in theology, spirituality, religious piety, and morality—in the sixteenth century, during the time of the Protestant Reformation.

cenobitic monasticism—a form of monasticism in which monks live together in a community, rather than as hermits.

Chalcedon—see *Council of Chalcedon*.

Christ—from a Greek word meaning "anointed one." Christians use it to refer to Jesus as God's anointed, the fulfillment of the prophecy made to David concerning an heir who would be an eternal king (2 Sam 7).

Christ, cosmic—a term used in theologies of world religions to describe how Christ who is present throughout the universe can be present in non-Christian religions.

Christendom—a term that modern historians have given to the thorough merging of Christianity and culture, which took place in Europe during the twelfth and thirteenth centuries, also known as the High Middle Ages.

Christology—meaning "words or teaching about the Christ." A study concerned with who Jesus is as the Christ (Messiah) and what his role is in God's relationship with humanity.

Church of Jesus Christ of Latter-Day Saints—also known as the Mormons, who take their name from the Book of Mormon, which their founder Joseph Smith (1805–1844) claimed to have translated from golden plates revealed to him in 1827 by an angel named Moroni. This American church was founded in 1830.

Cistercians—a group of monks who, in the twelfth century A.D., sought religious reform by returning to the primitive Benedictine life in wilderness areas. They are named for their first house at Cîteaux in France.

College of Cardinals—originally the "cardinals" were local Roman clergy who assisted the pope in his work as bishop of Rome; in the Middle Ages they gained exclusive responsibility for electing a pope and for advising him on matters pertaining to the operation of the Roman Catholic Church. Today they come from all over the world and represent, along with the college of bishops, the universality of the church.

communion of saints—the ancient belief, enshrined in the creeds, that deceased holy ones share a relationship with the living members of the church.

comparative theology—comparison of the views of various religious traditions on theological themes like revelation, the nature of God, and sin and salvation.

conciliarism—a theory of church authority advanced by certain theologians and bishops of the Roman Catholic Church intended to resolve the Great Schism of the papacy (A.D. 1378–1417). According to this theory, the bishops, when they were gathered together in an official council in time of crisis, had the right to make binding decisions independent of the pope.

concubinage—during the early medieval period, the practice among some clergy of maintaining concubines in a relationship something like marriage.

confessors—in early Christianity, those who were arrested during persecution and stood firm in their faith but who were not put to death. Confessors enjoyed great prestige in the churches, and some claimed the right to forgive sins.

congregationalist—a model of church organization based upon the style of the earliest Christian communities. Its leaders are part of the local community and their authority comes from within the local community.

consistory—the governing council of the Calvinist Geneva, consisting of members from the city government, the church leadership, and the laity.

Constantine (reigned A.D. 306–337)—the first Christian emperor of Rome. He paved the way for the establishment of Christianity as the sole legal religion in the Roman Empire and began the practice of calling ecumenical councils to resolve urgent issues affecting the whole church.

Constantinople—a major city in what is modern-day Turkey; formerly the capital of the Eastern Roman Empire, founded by Constantine c. 330 on the site of the ancient city of Byzantium; historically, one of five patriarchal sees (along with Rome, Alexandria, Antioch, and Jerusalem) from which Christianity was governed; today, the seat of the foremost of the four patriarchs (along with the bishops of Alexandria, Antioch, and Jerusalem) who govern the Eastern Orthodox Church. See also *Council of Constantinople*.

contrition—sorrow for sin.

Copernicus, Nicholas (A.D. 1473–1543)—Polish astronomer who proposed that the earth and other planets revolved around the sun.

cosmology—the study of the nature and structure of the universe; a particular model ("picture") of the structure of the universe.

Council of Chalcedon—an ecumenical council held in A.D. 451, which considered the question of Christ's human and divine natures and taught that the incarnate Jesus Christ possessed a complete human nature and a complete divine nature united in one person.

Council of Constantinople—an ecumenical council held in A.D. 381 that affirmed the Nicene Creed and added clauses about the co-equal divinity of the Holy Spirit.

Council of Ephesus—an ecumenical council held in A.D. 431 that taught that Mary, the mother of Jesus, should be venerated as *Theotokos* ("Mother of God" or "Godbearer"). This safeguards the unity of Jesus Christ as one human–divine person.

Council of Nicaea—an ecumenical council held in A.D. 325, which maintained the true divinity of the Son (Jesus Christ) against the teaching of Arius.

Council of Trent—declared by Roman Catholics to be an ecumenical council, this church council met over a period of eighteen years (1545–1563) to address doctrinal and practical issues of reform, both within the Catholic Church and in response to the Protestant Reformation.

Counter-Reformation—a term given to the efforts of those who, during the Protestant Reformation, were loyal to the pope and supportive of the customary practices of the Roman Catholic Church in order to counter (go against) the teachings and practices of the Protestant reformers.

covenant—a sacred or formal agreement between two parties.

Cranmer, Thomas (A.D. 1489–1556)—archbishop of Canterbury for most of the early years of the English Reformation. He is recognized for his contributions to the *Thirty-Nine Articles*, which sets out the specific similarities and differences between the Church of England and the Roman Catholic Church, and the 1549 and 1552 versions of *The Book of Common Prayer*, a hugely popular and influential liturgical document.

creed—a short summary of belief; the earliest creeds originated as teaching instruments to prepare catechumens for Baptism; they later became formal instruments by which churches defined themselves.

crusades—in the narrow sense, a series of military campaigns from Christian Europe, between A.D. 1095 and 1291, aimed at recapturing the Holy Land (Palestine and Syria) and protecting the Eastern Byzantine Empire from Turkish Muslim encroachment. From the eleventh to the seventeenth centuries, crusades were also directed against other internal and external enemies of Christendom.

curia—the pope's court staffed by the college of cardinals, a papal advisory team of bishops and clergy.

Daniélou, Jean (A.D. 1905–1974)—French theologian and Jesuit priest, he is best known for his research and writing on the early church Fathers.

Darwin, Charles (A.D. 1809–1882)—an English scientist who developed the theory of evolution and the principle of natural selection.

David (reigned 1000–961 B.C.E.)—the greatest of the kings of Israel, known for his military genius, musical abilities, love of Yahweh, and his occasional moral failures.

Dead Sea Scrolls—the collection of Jewish religious writings and biblical texts that were preserved at Qumran and discovered only in the past century (1947–1960).

deconstruction—applied first to philosophical texts and later to other literature, including religious writings, this approach to reading reveals how the text might not mean what it appears to mean and ultimately how its central message will always elude the reader.

Deism—a view popular during the Enlightenment that God created the world but does not thereafter intervene in its operation. According to this view, the world is like a watch or clock that runs on its own without the help of the watchmaker, God.

denomination—a religious group within the Christian faith that has a particular tradition, a common doctrine and a specific organizational structure.

denominationalism—according to this principle, the individual Christian churches, with their particular forms of worship and their unique organizational structures, are understood to be denominations of the one true church, which is Christianity, and not separate churches; in America it became the classic way Christianity adapted to the separation of church and state.

Descartes, René (A.D. 1596–1650)—French philosopher, known for his skepticism about the value of tradition. He began his philosophical method by doubting everything he had been taught—all tradition—and by believing only what could be shown by reason to be absolutely certain.

desire, implicit—see *implicit desire*.

deuterocanonical—meaning "second canon," the term refers to certain Old Testament books and parts of books whose canonical status has been disputed over time. Christians who do not accept them as canonical call them *apocryphal*.

Deuteronomist tradition—according to the Documentary Hypothesis, the third of four sources that make up the Pentateuch; it dates to the seventh and sixth centuries B.C.E.

Deuteronomistic Historian—author(s) of a series of books of the Old Testament/Hebrew Bible, whose agenda was to show how Israel's fortunes were correlated to her obedience to the terms of the covenant with God.

Deuteronomistic History—name given to a series of books of the Old Testament written by the Deuteronomistic Historian, books that emphasized the necessity of Israel adhering strictly to its covenant with God.

dialogue—mutual discussion between parties who hold differing views on a particular topic. The term is often used of theological discussions between members of different faith traditions.

Diaspora—the dispersion of Jewish people outside the traditional Jewish homeland in Palestine.

Didache—meaning "teaching," the term refers to the title of an early church document, *The Teaching of the Twelve Apostles*. It is a church order, that is, a document describing how the Christian ought to live and how the sacraments ought to be celebrated.

diet—a governmental assembly or meeting, such as the imperial congresses or parliaments of the Holy Roman Empire.

Discalced Carmelites—a reform branch of the Carmelite order founded by Teresa of Avila and John of the Cross. It became a separate order in A.D. 1593. The term discalced means "unshod," referring to the spiritual practice of going barefoot in order to fulfill Jesus's mandate to provide themselves with nothing for the journey, not even sandals for their feet (Matt 10:9–10).

disciple—a learner or a follower. Christians use the term to refer to those who followed Jesus.

dispensationalism—a method of interpreting biblical prophecy; it divides the scriptural narrative of God's dealings with humanity into seven stages called dispensations. Each stage moved God's plan for humanity forward toward its completion. Especially important interpretive method in modern fundamentalism.

docetism—from a Greek word meaning "to seem" or "to appear to be." The belief of some early Christians that Jesus Christ did not really become flesh but only seemed to have a body. In reality he was a spiritual being who could not suffer or die.

Doctor of the Church—an honor reserved for those whose teaching and scholarship have reflected Catholic Christian beliefs and been important in the lives and faith of others.

doctrine—the official teachings or principles of a religion.

Documentary Hypothesis—the theory that the Pentateuch was produced by combining four strands of tradition (the Yahwist, the Elohist, the Deuteronomist, and the Priestly traditions) over a long period of time (ninth to fifth centuries B.C.E.).

dogma—doctrines or teachings that have been proclaimed authoritatively by a given religion or church.

Dominic Guzman (d. A.D. 1221)—founder of the Dominican order of mendicants, also called the Order of Preachers.

Dominicans—an order of beggar friars founded by Dominic Guzman, also called the Order of Preachers. Known for their radical understanding of the vow of poverty, their primary vocation was to preach and hear confessions.

Donatists—a group of Christians (primarily in North Africa) that split from the main body of the church in the fourth century A.D. in a dispute over whether priests or bishops who collaborated with Roman persecutors of Christianity could retain their offices or administer the sacraments. Donatists maintained that clergy needed to be free from any serious sin to administer the sacraments validly. They were vigorously opposed by Augustine.

double predestination—the Calvinist idea that God has already chosen some people for salvation and others for damnation, a result of emphasizing God's sovereignty and knowledge over human free will.

dualism—(1) in gnosticism, a way of looking at reality as divided between two hostile divine powers, one representing good and the other evil; (2) a way of looking at reality in terms of polar opposites (belief/unbelief; darkness/light; truth/falsehood).

ecumenical—meaning "worldwide"; (1) term applied to a general council or synod of church leaders supposedly attended by representatives of Christians throughout the world; (2) term applied to efforts designed to bring unity and cooperation between divided Christian churches or between Christians and non-Christians.

ecumenical council (or **general council**)—a universal (or worldwide) gathering of Christian bishops called to resolve urgent issues affecting the whole church.

Edict of Worms (A.D. 1521)—the statement issued by the emperor of the Holy Roman Empire of the German Nation that declared Martin Luther an outlaw and a heretic.

Elect—meaning "chosen." Although the term is used widely in Judaism and Christianity, the Manichees used it to refer specifically to their leaders.

election—the biblical idea, emphasized most strongly by John Calvin, that God mysteriously chooses to enter into special relationship with some persons and groups, but not with others.

Elohist tradition—according to the Documentary Hypothesis, the second earliest of the four sources that make up the Pentateuch; it dates to the eighth century B.C.E.

encomienda-doctrina **system**—a cooperative effort between the *encomendero* (conquistador or his descendant) and the *doctrinero* (usually a mendicant friar) to build a sound economic and spiritual base in the Spanish territories of the New World.

enculturation—a term used to describe the process by which an individual learns to live and act within a particular culture in such a way that the culture's particular pattern of actions and thought becomes second nature to the person.

Enlightenment, the—an intellectual movement dating from about A.D. 1700–1789 which emphasized reason, science, the goodness and rights of humanity, religious toleration, progress, and human freedom.

Ephesus—see *Council of Ephesus.*

episcopacy—government by bishops. The adjectival form of the word is *episcopal* (for example, episcopal authority is the authority of the bishop).

Episcopal Church—the American branch of the Anglican communion, meaning those churches that trace their roots to the Church of England and regard episcopacy as a biblically mandated ministry of the church.

Erasmus, Desiderius (c. A.D. 1466–1536)—a scholar of the Renaissance period, learned in the writings of both the Latin and Greek early church writers. His reconstruction of the New Testament text became the basis for many subsequent translations into the vernacular (language of the people).

Essenes—a Jewish group of the first century B.C.E. and first century C.E. whose members withdrew into the desert, perhaps in protest of the activities of the Jerusalem Temple leadership. They shared an apocalyptic worldview, awaiting the end of the world.

Eucharist—meaning "to give thanks," the Christian ritual reenactment of Jesus' Last Supper with his disciples. According to Catholic doctrine, when the bread and wine is consecrated, it becomes the body and blood of Jesus Christ.

Eusebius of Caesarea (c. A.D. 260–340)—an early Christian historian whose *Ecclesiastical History* preserved for later generations excerpts from a number of ancient Christian documents no longer available to us.

evangelical—having to do with the gospel or the Bible; sometimes used as a synonym for *Protestant.* In the fundamentalist–modernist controversy of the early twentieth century, it describes some of the more traditional forms of Protestant Christianity, especially those that stress the importance of personal conversion or being "born again."

evangelist—one who preaches the "good news." This term is also used to refer to the gospel writers.

evolution—a theory advocated by Charles Darwin about the development of species. The theory of evolution claims that species emerge by natural processes alone (for example, natural selection) rather than by the miraculous creation of God.

exclusivism—an attitude or disposition of exclusion; in theologies of world religions, the belief that truth resides only in Christianity and that there are no meaningful similarities between Christianity and other religions.

Exile, Babylonian—see *Babylonian Exile.*

Exodus—(1) the second book of the Hebrew Bible/Old Testament; (2) the mass departure of the Israelites from slavery in Egypt through the saving action of God.

Ezekiel—the sixth-century B.C.E. prophet who counseled the Judeans who were in exile in Babylon that, with renewed faithfulness to the covenant, God would allow them to return to their land.

faith—(1) a relationship of trust in God; (2) personal insight or knowledge-in-action about God; (3) belief in a set of propositions about God, humanity, and the created order that carry a claim to be true.

Fall, the—the theological doctrine that holds that human beings were originally created in a state of perfection but lost that state when they sinned against God.

feudal system—in the early medieval period, the organization of society on the basis of bonds of personal loyalty between a lord and his vassal, based on mutual duties and benefits (*feudal* is from Latin *foedus*, meaning "treaty" or "agreement"). Feudalism provided security and protection at a time when central political authority was weak. Wealthy landlords deeded large tracts of land to vassals who, in return, agreed to provide certain services like military assistance for the landlords. The vassals, in turn, required serfs or peasants to work the land.

filioque—meaning "and the Son," the term refers to a phrase which Western Christians centuries later added to the Nicene Creed without the approval of Eastern Christians: "We believe in the Holy Spirit who proceeds from the Father and the Son." Orthodox Christians opposed the addition because they believe that the Father is the sole source of being in the Trinity, and because the creed was amended without their consent.

First Vatican Council (A.D. 1869–1870)—the first Catholic ecumenical council since the Council of Trent. It was convened to rally the Catholic world around Pope Pius IX, when the Papal States were threatened by a nationalist movement that sought to unify the Italian peninsula. The council declared that the pope had a primacy of jurisdiction (legal governing authority) over the whole church that was universal, ordinary, and immediate.

five pillars of Islam—the most basic obligations of Islam: profession of faith, prayer, fasting, almsgiving, pilgrimage to Mecca.

Former Prophets—also known as Deuteronomistic History; the biblical books of Joshua, Judges, 1–2 Samuel, and 1–2 Kings, which tell the stories of legendary early prophets like Samuel, Nathan, Elijah, and Elisha.

Fourth Lateran Council (A.D. 1215)—urged reform of the clergy and defined the dogma of transubstantiation, concerning the real presence of Christ in the Eucharist.

Francis of Assisi (c. A.D. 1182–1226)—founder of the Franciscan order of friars.

Francis Xavier (A.D. 1506–1552)—a companion of Ignatius of Loyola, the founder of the Jesuit order, and the leader of the Catholic mission to India, Japan, and China.

Franciscans—the community founded by Francis of Assisi, also known as the Friars Minor ("the lesser brothers"). Known for their radical understanding of the vow of poverty, their primary vocation is to preach the gospel and to witness to it in action.

friar—from a Latin word meaning "brother," the term refers to a person who belongs to a mendicant order.

fulfillment, theology of—used to explain how human (non-Christian) customs and beliefs that do not explicitly contradict Christ and Christian belief can be brought to a greater level of perfection through Christ.

fundamentalist movement—a movement that began as a militant reaction to liberal Protestantism and to developments in modern science and the historical study of the Bible. The name comes from a series of pamphlets called "The Fundamentals" published in 1910–1915 by conservative Protestants, which stressed that there were certain fundamental Christian beliefs that could not be changed or watered down.

Galilei, Galileo (A.D. 1564–1642)—astronomer and scientist who attempted to prove the Copernican theory that the earth revolves around the sun. He was disciplined by the church for advocating views that were contrary to the Bible and church teaching.

glossolalia—a Greek term meaning "speaking in tongues," one of the gifts of the Holy Spirit.

gnosticism—from the Greek word *gnosis*, meaning "knowledge." Gnostics claimed to have access to a special kind of knowledge known to them alone and by which they could be saved. They believed that there were two gods: one who was the supreme godhead of the divine realm (representing good) and who was unknown until Jesus came to reveal him; and the other the creator of the physical universe (representing evil), whom they equated with the God of the Old Testament. Gnostics believed that they belonged to the divine realm and their goal was to return there unharmed by this physical world.

God-fearers—From Acts of the Apostles, people who were attracted to Judaism but who were uncertain whether to become fully Jewish (perhaps because of other Jewish requirements, such as circumcision and the kosher dietary restrictions). Biblical scholars believe that some of the early Jesus followers came from among these people.

gospel—meaning "good message" or "good news;" (1) a written account of the life of Jesus Christ; (2) a proclamation of the Christian message.

grace—free, unmerited assistance given to human beings by God for their salvation. It is participation in the life of God.

Great Awakening—a great religious renewal that swept the American colonies in the 1740s. Marked by powerful preaching and intense emotional experiences, the movement sought to awaken people whose faith was spiritually dead or who had no faith at all.

Great Schism—this may refer to two different events: (1) the severing of relationships in A.D. 1054 between the pope and the patriarch of Constantinople or (2) the split *within* the Roman Catholic Church from A.D. 1378 to 1417, when European Catholicism was evenly divided between the competing claims of two different popes (and from 1409 to 1414 of a third pope). The schism of 1054 has never been healed. The split within the papacy was resolved by the Council of Constance (1414–1418).

Gregorian chant—a repertoire of music consisting of chants used in the city of Rome together with the native chants of the Frankish churches, mandated by Charlemagne to be used as church music throughout the empire.

Gregory I (reigned A.D. 590–604)—also known as "Gregory the Great." Statesman, theologian, and prodigious writer, his wise and pastoral leadership made him a model for subsequent popes. Among his accomplishments was his decision to sponsor a mission to convert the Anglo-Saxons in England.

Gregory VII (reigned A.D. 1073–1085)—a reform pope, he attacked abuses such as simony, alienation of property and lay investiture. He also declared the pope to be the supreme judge under God, holding the absolute powers of absolution and excommunication.

Gregory Palamas (A.D. 1296–1359)—an Orthodox Christian monk of Mount Athos in Greece whose work *The Triads* defended the hesychast spirituality and used the distinction between God's essence and God's energies to explain how people participate through grace in a union of love with the divine.

Guadalupe, Our Lady of—see *Our Lady of Guadalupe*.

hadith—reports concerning the sayings and deeds of Muhammad, six major collections of which were compiled during the first 300 years of Islamic history. Their status and authority is second only to the Qur'an.

Hagia Sophia—the great "Church of Holy Wisdom" in Constantinople, where the patriarch of Constantinople held services and the Byzantine emperors were crowned, until A.D. 1453, when the city of Constantinople was conquered by the Muslims and the church became a mosque.

haj—pilgrimage to Mecca. The fifth pillar of Islam is pilgrimage to Mecca, an obligation for Muslims whose resources and personal circumstances allow.

Hanukkah—the Jewish holiday celebrating the rededication of the Jerusalem Temple following the victory over Antiochus IV in the Maccabean revolt (167–164 B.C.E.).

Hearers—the name given to the members of the Manichees who did not have leadership roles. Augustine was a Hearer for a time prior to his conversion to Christianity.

Hebrews—referring to the ethnic group to which Abraham belonged, the term is sometimes used interchangeably with the terms *Israelites* and *Jews*.

Hellenization—in the wake of the conquests of Alexander the Great the spread of Greek language, cultural ideals, and political institutions throughout the ancient Near East.

Henry VIII (reigned A.D. 1509–1547)—the king of England who led his country through the Reformation. At first a supporter of Catholicism against the reformers, Henry eventually broke with the pope and the Catholic Church and established the Church of England with himself at its head, at least in part in a dispute with Rome over Henry's desire to divorce his wife.

Henry the Navigator (A.D. 1394–1460)—the Portuguese prince who explored and colonized Africa, spreading Christianity along the way.

heresy—false teaching, or teaching that goes against orthodoxy (correct teaching) in the eyes of the church.

hesychia—meaning "inner stillness" or "silence of the heart," the term is used by Eastern Orthodox Christians to describe this state of deep meditation.

hijra—an Arabic term meaning "migration." The migration of Muhammad and his followers from Mecca to Medina in A.D. 622 marks the beginning of the Muslim calendar, because it corresponds with the establishment of the first Muslim community.

historical criticism—(1) a development of the Renaissance movement, the use of historical knowledge to evaluate ancient writings, as well as existing traditions and institutions; (2) a modern approach to the study of the Bible, whereby the Bible is subjected to scientific scrutiny and the critic attempts to discover the historical circumstances of the biblical text and the intended meaning of its author.

historical theology—a study of the development of the Christian faith in the various periods of history after the biblical era.

Holiness movement—a family of Protestant churches who seek perfection in the world by developing a lifestyle of personal holiness and following a rigid code of behavior. It includes the Free Methodist Church, the Church of God, the Holiness Christian Church, and the Church of the Nazarene.

Holy of Holies—the innermost part of the Temple in Jerusalem, where God's presence is believed to have dwelled. Entrance was restricted to once per year by the high priest.

Hosea—an eighth-century B.C.E. prophet of Israel who used the imagery of marital infidelity to characterize Israel's relationship with Yahweh.

humanism—Renaissance humanism was a literary and historical movement to recover the Latin and Greek classics, and with them to discover a more secular and individualistic view of humanity. Modern humanism is a philosophy that focuses on and exalts humanity.

Hus, Jan (A.D. 1372–1415)—a reformer of the late medieval period. Like his contemporary, John Wycliffe, he preached against abuses in the church and challenged some of the church's doctrines. He was eventually executed as a heretic.

icon—a painted image of Christ, his mother, angels, or saints (tempera on wood). This religious art form is usually associated with Eastern Christianity.

iconoclasm—meaning "image breaking." Hostility to images derives from the biblical condemnation of idolatry (Exod 20:4–5). There were two major iconoclastic episodes: (1) the efforts of Eastern Orthodox opponents of images to abolish devotion to icons thrust the Byzantine Empire into constant turmoil from c. 725 to 843; and (2) during the Protestant Reformation, some reformers forcibly entered churches and removed or destroyed statues, stained glass, and paintings containing images.

iconoclast—one who is opposed to the veneration of icons.

iconodule—one who supports the veneration of icons.

iconostasis—meaning "icon screen," a wall bearing icons arranged in a prescribed order, which divides sanctuary from nave in Orthodox Christian churches.

Ignatius of Loyola (A.D. 1491/95–1556)—founder of the Society of Jesus, also known as the Jesuits. A Spaniard, Ignatius was trained as a knight, but he took up a life dedicated to the church after reading devotional books, including a life of Christ and lives of the saints, during a long convalescence.

imam—a leader of an Islamic community; an Islamic scholar; a Muslim religious leader who is regarded as a direct descendant of Muhammad or Ali.

imperial cult—in the Roman world, a partly political and partly religious ceremony in honor of the emperor who was recognized as a superhuman or divine figure.

implicit desire—a concept formulated by Robert Bellarmine (A.D. 1542–1621) that is used to describe how a person who attempts to live a moral life but who has not heard the gospel of Christ might be expressing an implicit desire to join the church.

incarnation—meaning "enfleshment"; the Christian doctrine that asserts that God became human, specifically, that the divinity called the Word (*Logos*) or the Son became human, or took on flesh, in the person of Jesus of Nazareth.

inclusivism—an attitude or disposition of inclusion; in theologies of world religions, the belief that Christ fulfills the longings and aspirations of other religions and that the good qualities in these religions are included within the scope of Christianity.

inculturation—a term used to describe the process by which a religion "learns" to live and act within a culture different from the one in which it began, so that the religion gradually comes to act naturally within that culture's pattern of actions and thought.

indigenization—the church policy that the native people of a country in which missionary work is being done should eventually take charge of the church in that country.

indulgences—a practice popular in the medieval church in which the church would cancel all or part of the penance (punishment) due to an individual who had sinned, when the individual had completed certain devotions, acts of charity, or services for the church, as substitutes.

inerrancy—the belief that the Bible is "without error." For faith communities who accept the verbal inspiration of the Bible, this means that the Bible is completely accurate in all respects and contains no mistakes whatsoever. For other faith traditions, it means that the Bible is a trustworthy guide to salvation.

infancy narratives—stories about the birth and early childhood of an important personality. The gospels of Matthew and Luke contain infancy narratives concerning Jesus.

Innocent III (reigned A.D. 1198–1216)—pope of the Roman Catholic Church, perhaps best known for his political involvements. The Fourth Lateran Council took place during his reign.

Inquisition—a legal body set up to investigate and punish heretics. Although the Inquisition itself was usually under the jurisdiction of church officials, civil leaders were often called upon to execute whatever punishments were assigned.

inspiration—in Christian theology, the belief that the Bible was written under the influence of the Holy Spirit and that it contains the Word of God. Christian churches have differing understandings about how inspiration took place.

inspiration, verbal—the theory that God (or the Holy Spirit) directed the biblical authors to write what is contained in the Bible without any input from the human author.

interdict—a kind of "strike" in which the church shuts down the sacramental system (Eucharist, Baptism, Penance, etc.). It was used in the medieval period by popes who wished to discipline civil leaders (kings, princes, etc.).

Irenaeus of Lyons—a late second-century bishop of the church at Lyons, he wrote *Against Heresies,* primarily in response to gnosticism.

Isaac—son of Abraham (by his wife Sarah) and patriarch of the Israelite people, with whom the covenant with the Israelites is continued and through whom the promises to Abraham are fulfilled.

Isaiah—an eighth-century B.C.E. prophet, who reassured the people of Judah that a Davidic king and possession of the Temple would protect them from harm.

Isaiah, Second—see *Second Isaiah*.

Ishmael—son of Abraham by his wife's maid Hagar, who was sent away into the desert but was rescued by God; claimed by the Muslims as the son of Abraham through whom they are descended.

Islam—meaning "submission" to the one God. One of the three major religions that trace their roots back to Abraham. A person who practices Islam is called a Muslim, that is, one who has submitted to God.

Israel—(1) the Israelite people, so named after their common ancestor Jacob, who was renamed Israel by God; (2) the country in which the Israelites dwelled; (3) the name of the northern kingdom of the Israelites, from 922 B.C.E. until it was conquered by the Assyrians in 721 B.C.E.; (4) the modern Jewish state, founded in 1948.

Israelite—one of the people who claimed Jacob, also known as Israel, as their ancestor. The term is sometimes used interchangeably with the terms *Hebrew* and *Jew*.

Istanbul—see *Constantinople*.

Jacob—son of Isaac and patriarch of the Israelite people, renamed *Israel* by God. Jacob migrated from Canaan to Egypt with his twelve sons.

Jehovah's Witnesses—an American Christian church that has its origins in the International Bible Students Association founded by Charles Taze Russell (1852–1916). The church is intensely focused on eschatology and on the imminent return of Christ in the end time.

Jeremiah—a sixth-century B.C.E. prophet who warned the people of Judah of their coming destruction by the Babylonians and counseled them to rely on faith and justice rather than on their possession of the Temple and a Davidic king.

Jerusalem—the capital city of Israel, and later Judah; site of Israel's Temple.

Jerusalem Conference—a meeting of Christian leaders held in Jerusalem in 48 or 49 C.E. According to the Acts of the Apostles, it was attended by Paul and Barnabas and the leaders of the Jerusalem church, and its purpose was to determine whether Gentile converts to Christianity needed to follow all of the requirements of Judaism.

Jesuits—see *Society of Jesus*.

Jesus Prayer—a brief meditation prayer, usually "Lord Jesus Christ, Son of the living God, have mercy on me, a sinner," which a person repeats again and again in order to enter into a state of deep meditation or stillness.

Jew—the term originated with the return of the people of Judah from the Babylonian Exile in the latter part of the sixth century B.C.E. It is sometimes used interchangeably with the term *Israelite*.

jihad—considered by some Muslims to be a sixth pillar of the faith, it involves inner striving to purify oneself of the forces of evil and to follow the way of Allah. A *jihad* might also consist of corporate attempts to purify the Islamic community of anti-Islamic features or warfare to defend Islamic land or spread Islamic territorial jurisdiction.

John Cassian (A.D. 360–435)—known as the "father of Western monasticism," he sought to establish a standardized form of monasticism for the Western Roman Empire based upon the ideals of Eastern monasticism.

John of the Cross (A.D. 1542–1591)—a follower of Teresa of Avila, the cofounder of the Discalced Carmelites, a reform branch of the Carmelite order, and a Spanish mystic. His writings include the *Ascent of Mount Carmel* and the *Dark Night of the Soul.*

Joseph—favorite son of Jacob and founder of one of the twelve tribes of Israel, he was sold into slavery in Egypt but eventually ascended to become a high government official.

Joshua—the successor to Moses, who led the Israelites into the promised land of Canaan and conquered the peoples who dwelled there.

Judah—the name of the southern kingdom of the Israelites, from 922 B.C.E. until it was conquered by the Babylonians in 597 B.C.E.

judge (Hebrew *shofet*)—in ancient Israel, a military and political leader who was chosen by God to rescue the Israelites from oppression brought about by their sin.

Julian of Norwich (c. A.D. 1342–after 1417)—an English mystic of the Late Middle Ages; author of *Showings,* which includes a series of visions she received during a brief illness and her theological reflections on those mystical experiences. She also reflects on the motherhood of Christ, the meaning of sin, and the question of why God allows sin and evil to exist.

justification—(1) generally, making straight that which is crooked or ragged; (2) in theology, being set in right relationship with God. Justification is closely related to the notion of sin as a severing of humanity's relationship with God.

justification by faith—the belief that humans cannot achieve right relationship with God through their own actions but that humanity is justified by God as a free gift to those who trust in Jesus Christ.

justification by works—the belief that right relationship with God can be achieved by avoiding sin and atoning for any transgressions with good deeds. In Paul's writings, the phrase is shorthand for *justification through observance of works of the Law.*

Justinian (A.D. 527–565)—the Byzantine emperor best known for compiling the *Codex Juris Civilis* (Code of Civil Law) and for rebuilding the great Church of Holy Wisdom (or *Hagia Sophia*) in Constantinople.

Ka'ba—a pilgrimage site located at Mecca. Muslims are encouraged to make a pilgrimage or *haj* to the *Ka'ba* once during their lifetime (health and finances permitting) to commemorate the key events from the founding era of Islam and from the time of Abraham.

kingdom of God—the reign of God, which is manifested in the coming of Jesus Christ, in the Spirit's continued presence in the world, and in the conviction that God will triumph over the forces of evil.

kosher—in Judaism, the special dietary restrictions required by the Torah, whereby certain foods are prohibited (for example, pork) and other foods must be prepared according to certain guidelines.

Law, the—(1) the first five books of the Hebrew Bible, also known as the Pentateuch or Torah; (2) the first major grouping of books in the Hebrew Bible or Old Testament, the other groupings being the Prophets and the Writings; (3) the Israelites' obligation to the Mosaic covenant.

Latter Prophets—comprised of the Major Prophets (Isaiah, Jeremiah, and Ezekiel) and the Minor Prophets (Hosea, Joel, Amos, Obadiah, Jonah, Micah, Nahum, Habakkuk, Zephaniah, Haggai, Zechariah, Malachi), also called the Book of the Twelve.

lay investiture—during the early medieval period, secular rulers (emperors, kings, nobility) took upon themselves the right to appoint bishops, abbots, and other church officials; the right of appointment was expressed ritually in the ceremony in which the secular ruler "invested" the official with the spiritual symbols of his office.

legend—stories that are situated in human history and involve characters and events that are part of the historical memories of the people who preserved them, but their purpose is to edify their readers and provide examples of the traditions, values, and ideals that these people hold sacred.

Lent—a period of forty weekdays in which Christians fast and do penance in anticipation of the feast of Easter, commemorating the resurrection of Jesus Christ.

Logos—a Greek word meaning "word" or "reason." John's gospel uses this term to describe Jesus as the revelation of God.

Maccabees—the family who led the revolt by the Jews against Antiochus IV in the second century B.C.E.

madrasa—literally, "a place of study." A traditional Muslim school of advanced study of the Qur'an and other subjects.

magisterium—the teaching office of the Roman Catholic Church, made up of the pope and the bishops.

Maimonides, Moses (A.D. 1135–1204)—medieval Jewish scholar; author of the *Guide of the*

Perplexed, in which he synthesized rabbinic Judaism and the Muslim form of Aristotelian philosophy. He also wrote some influential works on medicine and Jewish law.

Manichees—a strongly dualistic religion deriving its name from Mani, a third-century A.D. prophet and visionary. Like the gnostics before them, they believed in a dualism of evil matter and good spirit. They taught that people could liberate spirit from matter through the strict practice of asceticism.

manifest destiny—a term used to describe the Pilgrims' belief that their call to come to the New World was a divinely granted second chance for the human race and that God was making a new covenant with them.

Marburg Colloquy—the debate between Martin Luther and Ulrich Zwingli held in A.D. 1529. Zwingli and Luther did not resolve their differences, but Zwingli convinced Luther to see that reconciliation with the Catholic Church was not really possible.

martyr—from the Greek term meaning "witness," someone who, under persecution, dies rather than give up his or her faith.

Marx, Karl (A.D. 1818–1883)—philosopher and economist who advocated the socialist economic system and on whose ideas communism is built. Marx was an outspoken critic of religion, calling it the "opium of the people," because he believed that it was like a drug that kept the lower classes passive and resigned in their economic oppression.

Mecca—one of the most holy cities in Islam. It is the location of the *Ka'ba,* or pilgrimage site, where Muslims go to commemorate the key events from the founding era of Islam and from the time of Abraham. It is also revered as the birthplace of Muhammad and, according to Muslim tradition, the site of Ishmael's rescue.

Medina—the city in which Muhammad founded the first Islamic community in A.D. 622.

memoria—a type of church building built to honor the tomb of a saint or martyr, or a holy site. *Memoriae* had a centered design, focusing attention on the place of honor.

mendicants—from a Latin word for "begging," a type of religious order that emerged in the High Middle Ages. Unlike monks, mendicants lived in towns and cities, begged for their livelihood, and performed whatever ministry needed to be done.

merit, treasury of—see *treasury of merit.*

messiah—meaning "anointed one"; a term used in Judaism and Christianity for the one "anointed" by God to rescue or save God's people.

Messianic Secret—a term used to describe the apparent commands to silence concerning the identity of Jesus contained in the Gospel of Mark.

methodism/Methodist Church—an independent Protestant church founded by John Wesley, which began as a reform movement within the Church of England. It differed from the Church of England in its greater emphasis on personal spirituality, Bible study, evangelistic preaching, and lively services.

monasticism—from the Greek word *monos,* meaning "one," "unique," "solitary," or "alone." A rule and way of life for Christian men or women dedicated to holiness by separating from existing society, either by withdrawing into unpopulated areas or by living within a cloister (walled enclosure).

Monica—Augustine's mother. He writes about her in his *Confessions.*

monk—from the Greek word *monachos,* meaning a single or a solitary person, the word *monk* was coined in the fourth century A.D. as a name for the many men and women who had begun to withdraw to secluded desert regions to lead lives of prayer and spiritual discipline. Later it would come to refer to anyone who abandoned life in the everyday world to devote himself or herself completely to religion.

monophysite—from the Greek words for "of one nature"; one who holds that Jesus did not have two natures—one human and one divine—but only one. Eutyches, for example, believed that the humanity of Christ had been absorbed into his single divine nature. Dissenters against the two-natures definition of the Council of Chalcedon went into schism as separate Christian churches in Armenia, Syria, Egypt, and Ethiopia; though unfairly stigmatized as monophysite, they held and still hold that Jesus Christ was fully human, while rejecting Chalcedon's two-natures terminology.

monotheism/monotheistic—belief in only one God.

moral theology—a study of the values arising from Christian beliefs and the behaviors that are congruent or incongruent with these values.

Mormons—see *Church of Jesus Christ of Latter-Day Saints.*

mortal sin—sin that is committed willfully and deliberately and with the understanding that it is serious wrongdoing.

Moses—the greatest prophet of Israel, who led the Israelites out of slavery in Egypt and into the promised land of Canaan, and who received from God on Mount Sinai the Law on which the Israelite covenant with God is based.

mosque—Arabic term meaning "place of prostration" or "place of prayer." Ordinarily, mosques have an open space where the daily prayer is performed. On one wall is a niche that indicates the direction of Mecca. It also contains a pulpit with a staircase from which the imam (the leader of prayer) presents the sermon at Friday noon prayers.

Muhammad (A.D. 570–632)—the first leader and greatest prophet of Islam. According to Muslim tradition, the one god Allah sent the angel Gabriel to deliver messages to Muhammad to be recited aloud as guidance to the followers. The revelations were later collected and recorded in the Islamic scriptures known as the Qur'an.

Muslims—followers of the Islamic faith.

mystery religions—in the Greek and Roman religious world, secret cults that conducted ritual initiations into the mysteries of a particular god or goddess. Their celebrations usually involved purification rituals and sacred meals.

mysticism—a spiritual phenomenon that expresses itself in direct, intense experiences of union and oneness with God. Generally, the mystical journey consists of three phases: purgation (cleansing from sin), illumination (an attraction to all the things of God), and union (the state of oneness with God).

myth—a story that articulates, in symbolic words and images, a people's most profound sense of themselves and their world, their destiny, and their relationship to the deity.

Nathan—an Israelite prophet during the reign of King David, known for prophesying about the everlasting dynasty of David and for exposing the sin of David with Bathsheba.

natural selection—a principle of the theory of evolution, which holds that individuals in a species who have characteristics that are advantageous for survival in their environment will survive, while individuals without these characteristics will perish. Gradually, this transformation of the character of individuals in a species will lead to the development of new species.

nature—usually referring to human nature and the limitations of the human condition. In traditional Catholic teachings about salvation, human nature is said to be essentially good, though tainted by original sin.

neo-scholasticism—a renewal of Catholic theology that took place between the First Vatican Council and the Second Vatican School. It involved an endorsement of Thomas Aquinas' philosophy and theology—and the scholasticism that attended his writings—as the way in which Catholic theologians should engage the modern world.

neo-Thomism—the application of Thomas Aquinas' thought to distinctively modern conditions and problems.

nepotism—the practice of allowing dispensations from church law for the advancement of one's relatives.

Nestorian—one who accepts the Christology promoted by Nestorius, who held that Jesus had two separate natures (one the perfect man without sin who is son of Mary in the flesh, the other the divine word of God or *Logos* settled within him); a term sometimes applied to the Ancient Assyrian Church of the East.

Nestorius (c. A.D. 386–451)—a fifth-century A.D. patriarch of Constantinople, who taught that it was inappropriate to call Mary the Mother of God (*Theotokos)* on the grounds that God could not be said to have been born; at best she was only the Mother of Christ, the man. His views were condemned at the Council of Ephesus in 431, on the grounds that he divided Christ into two separate persons.

Newman, John Henry (A.D. 1801–1890)—one of the leaders of the Oxford Movement, which fostered a revival of the Catholic elements of English (Anglican) Christianity. He later converted to Roman Catholicism and eventually was named a cardinal.

Newton, Isaac (A.D. 1642–1727)—mathematician and scientist who was able to explain the motion of the planets by means of natural laws (for example, the law of gravity) rather than the will of God, and hence was a major contributor in the development of the mechanistic view of the universe.

Nicaea—see *Council of Nicaea.*

nihilism—the belief that there is no objective basis for truth and that human values are worthless.

nominalism—a late medieval philosophical movement that addresses issues of human knowledge. It argues that knowledge can be derived only from the experience of individual things. Universals such as humanity or truth do not really exist.

omnipotent—all powerful.

omniscient—all knowing.

oracles—pronouncements that come from God and are delivered through the voice of prophets.

Origen of Alexandria (c. A.D. 185–251)—an early Christian theologian, he wrote a number of works including *Against Celsus*, a response to a non-Christian critique of Christianity, and *On*

First Principles, an exposition of Christian doctrine as it was understood at that time.

original sin—the idea that human nature is wounded and deprived of original holiness and right relationship with God because of the sin of Adam and Eve. As a result of original sin, human nature is subject to suffering and has an inclination to sin. Western Christianity traditionally holds that all human beings also inherit the guilt as well as the consequences of the sin of Adam and Eve.

orthodox—a term formed from two Greek words meaning "right praise" or "right opinion." Orthodox Christians consider themselves to be a single church in the sense that they share a single faith and the same Byzantine liturgical, canonical, and spiritual heritage.

orthodoxy—meaning "right teaching" or "right opinion." The term is often used to describe doctrine or teaching that is declared by the church (or any religious authority) to be correct and binding for believers; it is contrasted with heresy.

Our Lady of Guadalupe—(1) title given to Mary, the mother of Jesus, based on her miraculous appearance to Juan Diego at Tepeyac, Mexico, in A.D. 1531; (2) a painted image of Mary as she appeared to Juan Diego.

Oxford Movement—a nineteenth-century group of teachers in Oxford who rallied against England's interference in the workings of the Irish church. John Henry Newman was one of its leaders.

pagan—a term used (especially in Roman times) to describe those persons who are neither Christians nor Jews.

papacy—referring to the reign of a pope or the office of popes in general.

papal bull—a formal document issued by the pope.

papal primacy—referring to the pope's status as first among the other bishops. In Roman Catholic teaching the pope's primacy gives him jurisdiction (legal authority) over the universal church. In Eastern Orthodox teaching his primacy is only honorary and not jurisdictional.

parousia—meaning "coming," the term is used of the second coming of Christ at the end time.

passion narrative—a term used to describe the gospel stories of the arrest, trial, crucifixion, and death of Jesus.

passive or alien righteousness—Martin Luther (A.D. 1483–1546) used this phrase to explain that God is the one who justifies people. Salvation does not depend on a person's own goodness or righteousness, but on God's righteousness, which is imputed or credited to believers because of the merits of Christ's atoning death.

Passover—the Jewish holiday that celebrates the event when God rescued the Israelites from captivity in Egypt by killing the firstborn sons of the Egyptians but "passing over" the houses of the Israelites (c. 1250 B.C.E.).

pastoral theology—education and formation for people who minister to communities of faith through activities like preaching, teaching, spiritual direction, and counseling and advocacy for persons in need.

patriarch—(1) an early father of a people or (male) founder of a group, like Abraham, Isaac, and Jacob; (2) bishop of one of the leading seats of early Christianity: Rome, Constantinople, Alexandria, Antioch, and Jerusalem, though the title has since been extended to bishops of other important churches as well.

patriarchal sees—the head or leading seats of early Christianity, originally five in number (see *patriarch*); the word comes via the Latin word for "chair," because the bishop's chair symbolized his authority to teach.

patristic—an adjective describing a period in Christian history, roughly the second century to the fifth or sixth century A.D. in the West, though the East traditionally extends it as far as the ninth century. The period is so named because the major writers of the time are known as the "fathers" (*patres* in Latin) of the church.

Paul—a first-century C.E. Jew who embraced belief in Jesus Christ after a visionary experience on the way to Damascus. He became a missionary for the Christian way, establishing churches throughout Asia Minor. Several of his letters are preserved in the New Testament.

peace churches—descended from the Anabaptists ("re-baptizers") of the Radical Reformation, these churches practice believer's Baptism and live a simple way of life intended to set them apart from the larger secular society. They include the Mennonites, Amish, Hutterites, and Church of the Brethren.

Pelagius—a Christian monk (mid-fourth to early fifth century A.D.) who introduced the Pelagian notion that original sin did not seriously damage the human capacity to do good, that human nature remained essentially good, and that human beings could lead holy lives if they exerted sufficient effort; these notions were opposed by Augustine and eventually condemned as heretical by the Catholic Church.

penance—(1) actions that show repentance for sin (e.g., praying, fasting, giving alms, making a pilgrimage); (2) the sacrament of forgiveness of sin, which consists of the penitent's acts of repentance, confession of sin, the intention to make reparation, and the priest's absolution of sin.

penitent—a person who is denied communion because of serious sin such as murder, adultery, or apostasy and who is doing penance (a penalty) for that sin.

Pentateuch—the first five books of the Hebrew Bible or Old Testament, also known as the Torah or the Law.

Pentecost—(1) a Jewish harvest festival that came to mark the fifty days separating the Israelites' escape from Egypt and God's gift of the Law on Mt. Sinai; (2) a Christian feast celebrated fifty days after Easter, commemorating the day on which the Holy Spirit came down upon Jesus' disciples when they were in hiding after his death and resurrection. According to Acts of the Apostles, this happened during the Jewish feast of Pentecost—in Luke's account the gift of the Spirit is thus intended to parallel and transcend the gift of the Law.

Pentecostalism—a family of Protestant churches whose members demonstrate their Christian faith through the gifts of the Holy Spirit, in particular, healing, wisdom to discern spirits, prophecy, and speaking in tongues (*glossolalia*). It includes the Assemblies of God, the Church of God, the Pentecostal Holiness Church, the Apostolic Faith Church, the Church of God in Christ, and the Full Gospel Fellowship.

People of the Land—in ancient Judaism, the poor and uneducated peasant farmers who comprised the majority of the Jewish population.

Pharisees—Jewish religious leaders and scholars of the Torah (second century B.C.E. through the first century C.E.) who were experts on the written Law and its interpretation.

Philistines—enemies of ancient Israel, who used their monopoly on iron weapons to defeat the Israelites prior to the reign of King David.

pietá—artistic representations of Mary holding the dead body of her son Jesus after he had been taken down from the cross. These were especially popular in the late medieval period.

pietists/pietism—a family of Protestant churches that was established out of a Bible-centered revivalism and a desire to fight against religious indifference by focusing on sharing the experience of God in their lives. It includes the Methodists, Scandinavian evangelical churches, and Moravian Christians.

Pilgrims—the English Puritan settlers who arrived on the Mayflower in A.D. 1620 to establish the Massachusetts Bay colony. The name *pilgrim* (a reference to Heb 11:13–14) was given to these founders a decade later and was formally adopted in 1798.

Pius XII (reigned A.D. 1939–1958)—head of the Roman Catholic Church during World War II and the first decade of the Cold War, he wrote several encyclicals for which he is well known, including *Mystici Corporis Christi* (The Mystical Body of Christ) and *Divino Afflante Spiritu*, which opened the way for Catholic scholars to use modern biblical critical methods in the study of scripture.

pluralism—the presence of different religious or cultural groups within a single society.

Polo, Marco (A.D. 1254–1324)—an Italian traveler who visited the lands of the Far East and returned to Europe to spread the news, sparking European interest in exploration for commercial gain and missionary expansion.

polyglot Bible—a single Bible in which the text was presented in several languages. Polyglot Bibles were especially popular in the sixteenth and seventeenth centuries A.D.

polytheism/polytheistic—belief in many gods.

pope—the bishop of the church in Rome and the head of the Roman Catholic Church.

postmillennialism—the eschatological (end-time) doctrine that Christ's second coming would not take place until after the gospel had been preached to the whole world and human history was fully developed and ready for his return; in this view the promised millennial (thousand year) reign of Christ (see Rev 20:1–10) tends to be interpreted symbolically and optimistically as the progressive improvement of the world or the universal spread of the church.

postmodernism—a cultural and intellectual movement that emerged out of modernism and therefore builds upon or provides a corrective to modernism. For example, if modernism is characterized by reliance on reason and scientific methodology as the measure of human progress, postmodernism calls attention to the limits of reason and offers a critique of the assumption that scientific methodology and reason, by themselves, can produce certitude.

practical theology—an examination of the relationships between abstract theological concepts and particular concrete situations encountered by individuals and communities of faith through a process of theological reflection.

praxis—activity that is reflected upon and consciously chosen to produce a particular effect; the practical application of a theory.

predestination—the idea that God has chosen in advance that certain events will come to pass (e.g., God has decided beforehand that some people would be saved and others damned).

predestination, double—see *double predestination*.

premillennialism—the eschatological (end-time) doctrine that Christ's return would happen *before* the millennial (thousand year) reign of Christ promised in Revelation 20:1–10 would take place. Premillennial eschatology tends to be pessimistic about the state of the world and of the church. Allied with *dispensationalist* biblical interpretation, it has been a powerful force in modern fundamentalism.

Priestly tradition (Priestly writer)—according to the Documentary Hypothesis, the latest of the four sources that were combined to form the Pentateuch, written around the fifth century B.C.E. or later.

priests—(1) in ancient Judaism, people who were specialists in conducting sacrifices; (2) in Christianity, ordained clergy, meaning a group set apart from the laity (the rest of the baptized community) by the ritual of the laying on of hands (ordination). Only Catholic, Orthodox, and Anglican forms of Christianity have priests (the word comes from Greek *presbyteros*, "elder") in the biblical sense of the word—someone whose duty is the offering of sacrifice—because Protestant Christianity generally rejected sacrificial understandings of the liturgy.

proclamation—the act of publicly declaring or affirming a statement of faith.

prophet—a spokesperson for God, chosen by God to reveal his will to people.

Prophets, the—the second major group of books of the Old Testament consisting of historical narratives (the Former Prophets) and books bearing the names of actual prophets (the Latter Prophets). The other two major groups are the Law and the Writings.

Prophets, Former—see *Former Prophets*.

Prophets, Latter—see *Latter Prophets*.

Protestant—a term used to describe members of the churches that trace their ultimate origin to the Reformation of the sixteenth century A.D. It derives from an incident in the early period of the Reformation in which six German princes protested a declaration of the Second Diet of Speyer (1529) designed to suppress Lutheranism.

Protestant Reformation—a term given to the sixteenth-century A.D. reform efforts initiated by Martin Luther, which eventually led to the separation between Roman Catholics and Protestants.

Pseudo-Dionysius the Areopagite—the pseudonym of an anonymous Syrian monk of the early sixth century A.D. who authored several important and influential theological works. He is perhaps most famous for his *via negativa* ("negative approach") in which all affirmations concerning God must be denied since the divine reality so far supersedes any word that can be said about it.

pseudonymity—the practice of writing a document with a false name attached to it. Pseudonymous writings were quite common in the ancient world, in part as a way of honoring famous people in a particular culture or religious tradition and in part as a way of increasing the authority of the document.

purgatory—a place or state following death in which sinners destined for heaven undergo the punishment still remaining for forgiven sins and thereby are "purged" or made ready for heaven.

Q—representing the German word *Quelle*, meaning "source." A hypothetical written document or documents, mostly containing parables and sayings of Jesus, used as a source for the Gospels of Matthew and Luke.

Quest for the Historical Jesus—an area of modern scholarly research that seeks to uncover what can be known about the actual historical person, Jesus of Nazareth, and to reconstruct his story based upon verifiable historical and scientific evidence.

Qur'an—the sacred writings of Islam. The Qur'an consists of the revelations that the angel Gabriel delivered to Muhammad from the one God, *Allah*, for the guidance of the followers.

rabbis—(1) in ancient Judaism, teachers (especially of the Torah); (2) in modern Judaism, the leader of a Jewish synagogue or a scholar qualified to interpret Jewish law.

Rahner, Karl (A.D. 1904–1984)—A Roman Catholic theologian and Jesuit priest, he authored numerous books and articles on topics of systematic theology. Although he believed that the fullness of grace was available only within Christianity, he argued that the Holy Spirit carries grace to all people in every time, including those in non-Christian religions.

rationalism—the belief that reason alone can provide us with a knowledge of all reality. It is opposed to the belief that there are some dimensions of reality (for example, God) that are beyond reason and that can only be known through revelation.

recapitulation—a doctrine about redemption taught by Irenaeus, a second-century A.D. bishop.

Irenaeus said that the redemption effected by Jesus Christ was a "doing over again" of all that had gone wrong in human history.

redemption—having been bought back for God and thus ransomed from our sinfulness.

Reformation, Catholic—see *Catholic Reformation*.

Reformation, Protestant—see *Protestant Reformation*.

relativism—the view that all theological positions are equally valid and that truth or moral goodness is not absolute but is relative to individuals' experiences.

relics—the bodily remains of martyrs or other saints.

religion—a comprehensive worldview that involves belief in some god or power beyond human existence, together with actions or teachings that support that belief (ritual, stories, doctrine, organizational structure, and ethical conduct).

religious studies—an umbrella term that encompasses a variety of social-scientific, historical, comparative, and philosophical approaches to questions concerning humanity's engagement with religion and religious phenomena.

Renaissance—meaning "rebirth," a cultural movement that began in Italy approximately A.D. 1350 and spread to other European countries by the time it came to a close in 1600. It involved a renewed interest in the Latin and Greek classics, a focus on the individual person and the natural world, and a more scientific approach to history and literature. It was accompanied by a burst of creative activity in art and architecture.

ressourcement—meaning "going back to the origin," a French term that was used to describe a common desire of several theological renewal movements of the late nineteenth and early twentieth centuries to rejuvenate theology by recovering older sources in scripture and tradition.

restorationism—the idea that the way to reform and renew Christianity was to "restore" the church to the original structures, beliefs, and practices that prevailed during the time of Jesus and the apostles. The Radical Reformers of the sixteenth century held this belief. In early nineteenth century America, the Second Great Awakening (religious revival) inspired new restorationist churches that called themselves simply "the Christian Church" and also the "Disciples of Christ."

revelation—(1) God's act of disclosing God's self to believers; (2) that which has been revealed by God through nature and human conscience, but also through the Bible, mystical experience, and worship, about God and God's relationship to creation.

revival—a religious meeting designed to awaken in people an awareness of their sin and their need for forgiveness. Revival meetings were part of the Great Awakening, an eighteenth-century A.D. spiritual renewal movement in the English colonies.

revivalism—an American Christian movement sometimes described as born-again Christianity, which is based on the experience of a personal conversion to Jesus Christ as one's Lord and savior.

Ricci, Matteo (A.D. 1552–1610)—an Italian Jesuit known for his successful missionary work in China, especially his efforts to make Catholic Christianity intelligible in Chinese cultural terms.

righteousness, passive or alien—see *passive or alien righteousness*.

Romanesque architecture—the style of buildings developed during the Carolingian and Ottonian dynasties of early medieval Europe. The structures featured stone vaulted ceilings, heavy walls and piers, and small openings for light, creating a fortress-like impression.

Roman rite—the primary form of liturgy for the Roman Catholic Church, which was standardized by Charlemagne in the second half of the eighth century. Some of its prayers are thought to have been composed by Pope Gregory I.

sacrament—a symbolic ritual consisting of words and visible gestures or material substances (bread, wine, water, oil, etc.) which, when properly performed for a recipient disposed to its action, becomes the means of transmitting the grace of God. Traditionally, it has been defined as an outward sign instituted by Christ to give grace.

sacramental theology—the study of Christian worship; also called liturgical theology.

sacramentals—a term used to describe certain religious practices and objects that are similar to sacraments in the fact that they have tangible qualities (water, oil, the rosary, etc.), but they are different from sacraments in the fact that they are not publicly celebrated and are not considered to be instituted by Christ.

sacramentary—a book containing the prayers needed by a priest to celebrate the Eucharist and (sometimes) other sacraments.

sacrifice—referring to the practice of offering gifts (animals, grains, etc.) to God or the gods as a way to make a request of the deity or to give thanks for favors received.

sacrificial atonement—making up for one's sins with a sacrificial offering; specifically in Christianity, the idea that our sins are forgiven through the death of Jesus Christ on the cross.

Sadducees—members of the Jewish aristocracy, consisting mostly of the priests who ran the Jerusalem Temple (second century B.C.E. through first century C.E.).

Salafism—sometimes called Wahhabism, from the name of its founder, a movement within Islam that argued for a return to the strict observation of Islam as lived by the Prophet and his first companions.

salah—The second pillar of Islam, "prayer," which obliges Muslims to perform a series of ritual actions five times in each twenty-four-hour period, namely at dawn, noon, afternoon, sunset, and nightfall.

salvation—a theological term referring to the process of being saved or rescued from harm.

Samaritans—Israelites who were left behind in the northern kingdom, when Israel was taken over by the Assyrians in the eighth century B.C.E.

Samuel—an Israelite prophet and last of the judges, he appointed Saul as king of Israel (reigned 1020–1000 B.C.E.).

sanctification—the idea of someone or something being made holy for God.

sanctuary—the principle that all who take refuge from civil authority in a church or on church land cannot not be removed without the permission of the abbot or bishop; a holy place within a church or temple.

Sanhedrin—the highest Jewish council in first-century Judaism. According to the gospels, Jesus was put on trial before this body.

satisfaction, vicarious—see *vicarious satisfaction*.

satisfaction, works of—see *works of satisfaction*.

Saul (reigned 1020–1000 B.C.E.)—the first king of Israel who was replaced by David when God found him unworthy to be king.

sawm—the third pillar of Islam, "fasting," which requires Muslims who are healthy and of age to abstain from all food and drink from sunrise to sunset during the holy month of Ramadan.

scholasticism—medieval theology that took the truths uncovered by philosophers like Aristotle and showed how they were compatible with Christianity. In general, scholastic theology, so-called because of its setting in medieval schools and the new universities, tried to harmonize faith with reason.

scientism—the claim that the only valid method of knowing is science and that what cannot be known by science does not exist.

scribes—(1) in ancient Judaism, the class of people who could read and write and who made their living from these skills. They are portrayed in the gospels as enemies of Jesus and associates of the Pharisees; (2) in the ancient and medieval world, people whose occupation involved the copying of manuscripts.

scriptures—sacred writings or texts.

Second Isaiah—a sixth-century B.C.E. prophet and the author of chapters 40 to 55 of the book of Isaiah, who foretold the Jews' return from exile.

Second Temple—the Temple in Jerusalem that was built following the destruction of Solomon's Temple by the Babylonians; destroyed by the Romans in 70 C.E.

Second Vatican Council (A.D. 1962–1965)—a gathering of Catholic bishops, abbots, and theological experts called by Pope John XXIII to renew the religious life of the church and to bring it into the modern world.

secularism—from Latin *saeculum*, meaning "world" or "age"; the belief that religion has no place in the public or political realm; sometimes criticized as "the religion of no religion at all," though its defenders argue that a neutral public space is the only alternative to some form of religious preference or establishment.

seminary—a school of theology especially designed for the training of priests. The Council of Trent (A.D. 1545–1563) ordered that every Roman Catholic diocese establish a seminary for the training of its priest candidates. Many dioceses still retain their own seminaries today.

separationism, strict—see *strict separationism*.

Septuagint—a Greek version of the Hebrew scriptures, created in the centuries before Christ by Greek-speaking Jews, but differing from the Hebrew Bible in the order of the books and in its inclusion of the apocrypha or deuterocanonical books; appropriated by Greek-speaking Christian Jews, it became the dominant version of the Christian bible for hundreds of years, and remains so for Orthodox Christians.

Seventh-Day Adventists—an American church that emerged out of the millennial expectation that accompanied the second Great Awakening, a spiritual renewal that spread across the United States and its territories toward the beginning of the nineteenth century A.D. They observe Saturday as the proper day for worship and view a literal reading of the Bible as the only rule of faith.

shahada—the first pillar of Islam, the profession of faith: "There is no god but God and Muhammad is the Prophet of God."

Shari'a—the Islamic law code that is based upon the Qur'an and the *sunna,* or way of the prophet, together with human reason and community consensus.

Shi'a—meaning "partisans of Ali," Muhammad's cousin and son-in-law. This Muslim group arose soon after the death of Muhammad, as a consequence of a dispute over how the position of caliph (Muslim ruler) ought to be filled. Today, it continues to be a minority group within the Islamic faith.

shofet—the Hebrew term for a judge, a military and political leader who was chosen by God to rescue the Israelites from oppression brought about by their sin.

simony—the buying and selling of spiritual things, including church leadership positions.

sin, mortal—see *mortal sin.*

Society of Jesus—also known as the Jesuits, this religious order was founded by Ignatius of Loyola in A.D. 1540. Dedicated to the service of the pope, they played an important role in the Catholic Reformation both as missionaries and teachers. Today they are the largest Catholic religious order, with a large and respected system of high schools, colleges, and universities.

Solomon (reigned 961–922 B.C.E.)—successor to his father David as king of Israel, known for his wisdom, excessive wealth, and the building of the Temple in Jerusalem.

soteriology—the study of, or teachings about salvation. Christian soteriology is primarily concerned with the saving work of Jesus Christ.

Spiritual Exercises—developed by Ignatius of Loyola, this month-long spiritual examination allows the individual to participate in the drama of sin and salvation, leading to a turning over of everything, especially the will, to obedience to one's religious superior, to the teachings of the church and its traditions, for the spread of the faith.

spirituality—describes various forms of prayer and religious practice that orient persons toward God (or the divine) and that direct the way they live in the world.

strict separationism—the view that the First Amendment of the U.S. Constitution erects "a wall of separation between church and state" and requires total religious neutrality on the part of the state.

studia humanitatis—meaning "humane studies" or liberal arts, including Latin and Greek literature, history, and ethics. In studying Latin, students learned to read, write, reason, and speak well—skills that were especially necessary for civic leaders and scholars.

Suffering Servant—a figure in the book of Isaiah who suffers on behalf of the whole people and wins forgiveness for their sins (see Isa 52:13–53:12).

Sufism—a movement within Islam that stresses the way of the heart. It originated in the late ninth and early tenth centuries as a reaction against the legalism and intellectual rationalism of *Shari'a.*

sultan—meaning "holder of power," the Turkish tribe known as the *Seljuks* used this title for their leaders.

Summa Theologiae—literally a "summary or compendium of theology." Perhaps the most famous *Summa* was written by Thomas Aquinas.

sunna—the "way of the prophet"; sayings of the prophet Muhammad and reports of his deeds, as recorded in the *hadith.*

Sunnis—meaning "those who followed the example or custom of Muhammad." In the dispute concerning who was qualified to assume the position of leader of the Muslim community, this group argued that it should be someone who best exemplified Muhammad's thought and way of life, rather than someone who was related to Muhammad by blood. Today, it is the main body of the Islamic faith, comprising approximately 85 percent of Muslims worldwide.

supernature—used by Pope Pius XII in *Evangelii Praecones* to describe the condition brought about by the grace of Christ whereby humans can comprehend God and become virtuous in ways that exceed the limitations of human nature.

sura—an individual chapter of the Qur'an.

Syllabus of Errors—a document issued by Pope Pius IX in 1864 consisting of eighty condemned propositions concerning topics like freedom of religion, separation of church and state, and the temporal power of the pope. It provided an overture for the First Vatican Council.

Symeon the New Theologian (A.D. 942–1022)—an Eastern Christian mystic and theologian, representative of the spirituality and theology of the early medieval period.

synagogue—a Jewish place of worship where the Torah is read and interpreted.

synoptic gospels—from a word meaning literally "seeing together." The term is usually used with reference to the Gospels of Matthew, Mark, and Luke, which tell the same general story of the life and teaching of Jesus.

synoptic problem—the question concerning the literary relationship between the Gospels of Matthew, Mark, and Luke, which are so similar that it is almost universally believed that one or more of their authors used another gospel as a source.

systematic theology—a study of the basic formulations of Christian belief (called dogmas or doctrines) and their relationship to one another.

Tanakh—an acronym for *Torah* ("Law"), *Nevi'im* ("Prophets"), and *Khetuvim* ("Writings"); a term used to refer to the Jewish scriptures.

temple—(1) any building dedicated to the worship of a god or gods, at which sacrifices are usually performed; (2) the building in Jerusalem in which Israelites performed sacrifices and where God was said to dwell; first built by Solomon in the tenth century B.C.E., destroyed by the Babylonians in 587 B.C.E., rebuilt later in the sixth century B.C.E. after the return from the Exile, refurbished by King Herod in the first century B.C.E., and then destroyed by the Romans in 70 C.E.

Teresa of Avila (A.D. 1515–1582)—a Spanish mystic and founder of the Discalced Carmelites. Her writings include the *Life,* an autobiographical account of her life, and the *Interior Castle,* a description of her method of prayer.

tertiary—referring to a layperson who follows an adapted rule of a founder of a monastery or a friar movement and the ideals or charisms of that group, but does so outside of the convent or monastery. Examples include the third order Dominicans and the third order Franciscans.

testament—a synonym for covenant, this term is applied by Christians to the two major collections of books of the Bible.

theocentric—God centered.

theocracy—literally "the rule of God," a system of government that has as its worldview a common set of beliefs about God and God's relationship with their community, whose civil laws are governed by its religious agenda and in which religious authorities have the ultimate power to govern.

Theodosius I (reigned A.D. 379–395)—emperor of Rome who established Christianity as the sole legal religion in the Roman Empire and who affirmed the Nicene Creed as the benchmark of orthodox (correctly taught) Christian faith.

theology—an intellectual discipline that explores (religious) reality from a particular perspective, namely God as ultimate ground and goal of all reality; in the words of Anselm, it is "faith seeking understanding."

theology of fulfillment—see *fulfillment, theology of.*

Torah—(1) the Hebrew scriptures as a whole; (2) the first five books of the Hebrew Bible or Old Testament, also known as the Pentateuch or the Law; (3) the Jewish Law, or system of laws, believed to have been revealed by God to Moses and set down in writing in the first five books of the Old Testament.

tradition—the accumulated wisdom of the church and its leaders, whereby the faith derived from the scriptures, contained in the creeds, and expressed in the liturgy is interpreted for contemporary believers.

tradition, apostolic—see *apostolic tradition.*

transubstantiation—a teaching about how the bread and wine of the Eucharist become the body and blood of Jesus Christ: after consecration (blessing) by a validly ordained priest, the accidents (physical appearance) remain as bread and wine, but the substance (or essence) changes and becomes the body and blood of Jesus Christ.

treasury of merit—in the late medieval period, a treasury of surplus good works of the saints and of Christ. The pope could draw from this treasury and transfer excess merits to a repentant sinner in the form of an indulgence.

Trent, Council of—see *Council of Trent.*

Trinity—a theological term used to describe the relationship of the three "persons" of Father, Son, and Holy Spirit in one Godhead; as defined at the fourth century ecumenical councils of Nicaea and Constantinople, the dogma of the Trinity affirms that the three persons are co-eternal and share equally in the same divine nature.

Two-Source Hypothesis—a theory that explains the literary relationship among the synoptic gospels by suggesting that the writers of the Gospels of Matthew and Luke used the Gospel of Mark and a hypothetical source Q (a written document or documents mostly containing parables and sayings of Jesus) as sources for their gospels.

Tyndale, William (c. A.D. 1494–1536)—an admirer of Martin Luther, he was the first to publish an English translation of major parts of the Bible.

ulama—"those who are learned," referring to the Sunni class of religious and legal scholars trained in the great mosque-colleges or madrasas.

ultramontanism—a nineteenth-century tendency to exalt the authority of the papacy "beyond the mountains," referring to Rome's location south of the Alps.

umma—an Arabic term meaning "community."

university—originally the "guild" or association of teachers and students united in the "craft" of teaching and learning. By the thirteenth century, universities began to develop into institutions of higher learning with permanent faculties and offered basic degrees in the "arts" and more advanced degrees in various fields of specialization.

verbal inspiration—see *inspiration, verbal.*

vernacular—language of the common people.

vicarious satisfaction—the possibility that someone could pay the debt of another person's sin.

voluntarist principle—popularized by the churches of the Radical Reformation, the idea that becoming a Christian (and a member of a church) always requires an active decision. It never occurs simply because of where people live or because of their parents' beliefs.

Vulgate—a Latin translation of the Bible, containing also the books of the apocrypha, widely used in the West at least from the sixth century A.D. and declared by the Council of Trent to be the only authoritative translation of the Bible.

Waldensians—named for their founder Valdes, these twelfth-century A.D. Poor Men of Lyons sought to return to the apostolic life of the early church. Their hostility toward the clergy (because of clerical abuses) eventually led to their condemnation by the Council of Verona in 1184.

Wesley, John (A.D. 1703–1791)—an English theologian and reformer, Wesley was originally a member of the Church of England. He and his followers eventually broke away to form the Methodist Church.

works of satisfaction—prayers, fasting, pilgrimages, or works of piety assigned to a person in the sacrament of penance to remove the penalties or consequences of sin.

Wycliffe, John (A.D. 1330–1384)—a reformer of the late medieval period. He preached against abuses in the church and challenged some of the church's doctrines. He also advocated the translation of the Bible into English, the language of the people.

Yahwist tradition—according to the Documentary Hypothesis, the earliest of the four sources that make up the Pentateuch; it dates to the ninth century B.C.E.

YHWH (Yahweh)—the name for God that is most commonly used in the Hebrew Bible/Old Testament.

Yom Kippur—the "Day of Atonement," a Jewish holiday in which people reflect upon their sins. In ancient Judaism, this was the only day of the year in which the high priest would enter the Holy of Holies to offer a sacrifice.

zakat—the fourth pillar of Islam, almsgiving, which obliges Muslims to give of their wealth, whether it be great or small, to sustain those in need.

Zealots—a Jewish group of the first century C.E., who advocated the violent overthrow of the Romans and were major players in the disastrous revolt of 66–70 C.E.

Zwingli, Ulrich (A.D. 1484–1531)—Swiss reformer and theologian, known especially for his emphasis on justification by grace alone, his "spiritual" understanding of the Eucharist, his exclusive reliance on the Bible rather than church traditions and proclamations, and his opposition to priestly celibacy and the use of images in worship. Zwingli was killed defending Zurich, the city he led through the Reformation, against attack by Catholics.

Copyright
Acknowledgments

Index

A

Aaron, 51, 81
Abbasids, 218–19
Abbot, 174
Abel, 39
Abortion issues, 413, 414–15
Abraham, 43–47
Absalom, 64–65
Absolution, 319
Abu Bakr, 216, 217
Acts of the Apostles, 92, 120, 122–23
Adam and Eve, 34–36
Addai, 133
Address to the Christian Nobility of the German Nation
    (Luther), 321
Adeodatus, 184
Adiabene, Christianity in, 133
Admonition to Peace, An (Luther), 325
Aeneid, The (Virgil), 311
Aeterni Patris, 426
Afonso the Good, 366–67
Africa, missionaries in, 366–67
African Americans
    religions of, 409, 410–11
    theology, 463–66
African Methodist-Episcopal (A.M.E.) Church, 410
Against Apion (Josephus), 22
Against Celsus (Origen), 156
Against Heresies (Irenaeus of Lyons), 153–54
Against the Robbing and Murdering Hordes of Peasants
    (Luther), 325
Agent of God, 109
Aggiornamento, 432
Agnosticism, 1
Al-Aqsa Mosque, 218
Alberti, Leon Battista, 311
Albert the Great (Albertus Magnus), 279
Albigensians, 259, 263
Albrecht of Mainz,
    archbishop, 319

Alexander VI, Pope, 367
Alexander the Great, 82
Alexandria
    Catechetical School, 155–56
    Christianity in, 131
    scholarship in, 155
    school of, 169–70
Ali, 217–18
Alien righteousness, 318
Al-Kamil, Malik, 257
Allah, 213
Allegorical method, 156
Allen, Richard, 410
Alves, Rubem, 458
Ambrose of Milan, 186, 187
Ambulatories, 270–71
American Baptist Churches USA, 409
Americas, missionaries in the, 367, 369
Amish, 341, 342, 343, 408
Amnon, 64
Amos, 61, 69
Anabaptists, 341, 408
Anaphora, 201
Anchoress/anchorite, 299
Andalus, 218
Anglican Church, 349, 401
Anselm of Canterbury, 9, 249
"Answering the Question, 'What is Enlightenment?'"
    (Kant), 384
Anthropocentric, 311
Anthropological theories, 6–7
Anthropology, 15
Anthropomorphism, 32
Anticlericalism, 263, 384, 423–24
Antioch
    church at, 130–31
    school of, 169, 170
Antiochus IV, 82
Antony of Egypt, 173–74, 239
Apocrypha, 23
Apocalyptic messiah, 80

Apollinaris of Laodicaea, 169
Apollos from Alexandria, 131
Apologia Pro Vita Sua (Newman), 428
Apologists, 149–50
Apostasy, 149
Apostles, 100
    See also names of specific
        apostles.
    Acts of the, 92
    defined, 124
    missions, 118–34
Apostolic tradition, 100
Apostolic Tradition (Hippolytus of Rome), 157
Aquila, 130
Aquinas, Thomas, 38, 262, *274*
    biblical commentaries, 284–85
    Doctor of the Church, 286
    influences on, 275
    life of, 278–79
    major themes, 281–82
    poetry and mysticism, 285–86
    scholasticism and, 275–77
    Summa Theologiae, 279–80, 282–84
    thirteenth-century world and, 274–75
    Thomist revival, 426–27
Architecture
    Baroque, 359–60, *360*
    Carolingian Renaissance, 246, *246*
    early church, 175–79, *176, 177, 178*
    Gothic, 270–71, *270*
    Islamic, 226–28, *227, 228*
    postmodernism, 442–43, *442*
    Reformation, 359–60, *360*
    Renaissance, 312
    Romanesque, 246, *246*
    Vatican Council II and, 433, *434*
Aristotle, 275
    cosmology, 380
Arius, 165–66
Ark of the Covenant, 62, *63*, 64
Armenian Apostolic Church, 205
Art
    Baroque, 359, *359*
    Carolingian Renaissance, 245, *245, 247*
    icons, 198–200, *199*
    Islamic, 226–28, *227, 228*
    medieval, 304
    Middle Ages, Late, 293, *293*
    postmodernism, 442–43, *443*
    Reformation, 358–60,
        359, 360
    Renaissance, 312, 314–15
Articles, in *Summa Theologiae*, 283–84
Ascetical movement, 173–75
Asceticism, 173
Asia, missionaries in, 372–74

Assemblies of God, 406
Assyrian Church of the East, 206–8, 209
Assyrian period, in Israel, 68–70
Athanasius of Alexandria, 95, 155, 166, 173–74
Atheism, 1, 382
Augsburg Confession, 327
Augustine, Saint, 150, 156, 175, *191*, 197
    as bishop, 187–92
    conversion of, 182, 186–87
    Donatist schism, 188–89
    early life, 182–87
    Manicheism, 184–85
    neoplatonism, 186–87
    Pelagian controversy, 189–92
Averroes, 275
Avicenna, 275
Avignon Papacy, 260, 290–91

B

Babylonian Captivity, 290
Babylonian creation stories, 30–31, 393
Babylonian Exile, 70–71
Babylonia period, in Israel, 70
Bacon, Francis, 381
Balthasar, Hans Urs von, 428, 477–78
Baptism
    believer's, 341
    Calvin and, 338
    Luther and, 321–22
    Middle Ages, High, 264
    origins of, 115–16
    Paul and, 115, 128–29
    Radical Reformers and, 341
    Zwingli and, 335
Baptist churches, 336, 409
Baptistery, 177–78, *178*
Baptists, 403, 409
Barlaam the Calabrian, 202
Barnabas, 121, 122, 130
Baronius, Cardinal, 380
Baroque art and architecture, 359–60, *359, 360*
Barth, Karl, 476–77, *477*, 480
Base Christian communities, 458
Basel, Council of, 292
Basilica, 175–76, *176*
Basil of Caesarea, 168, 174, 239
Bathsheba, 64, 448–49
B.C.E. (Before the Common Era), 21
Beatitudes, 106
Beguines, 262–63, 268
Believer's baptism, 341
Bellah, Robert, 416
Bellarmine, Robert, 475
Benedict XV, Pope, 475

Benedict XVI, Pope, 231, 426, 481
Benedictine monasteries, 240
Benedict of Nursia, 13
    Rule for Monasteries, 237, 239–40, 261
Benevolence, 38
Benjamin, 49
Berger, Peter, 8
Bergson, Henri, 8
Bernard of Clairvaux, 254, 261, 266
Bible
    See also New Testament; Old Testament;
        names of specific books.
    Aquinas' commentaries on, 284–85
    defined, 19
    genealogies, 48–49
    inspiration for, 25–27
    polyglot, 352–53
    scientific interpretation of, 392–93
Bible, translations
    Erasmus, 314
    Greek and Latin, 314
    King James, 305
    Luther, 305, 314, 328
    Tyndale, 345
    vernacular, 295, 314, 353
    Vulgate, 353, 356
    Wycliffe, 295
Biblical inerrancy, 25
Biblical studies, 11
    postmodern, 447–55
    Vatican Council II
        and, 431
Big Bang theory, 453–54
Bishops
    authority of, 152, 164
    church government, 171–73
Black Death, 289, 292–94
Black theology, 463–66
Black Theology and Black Power (Cone),
    464, 465
Black Theology of Liberation, A (Cone),
    458, 464
Bond, Helen, 3
Boniface VIII, Pope, 242, 260–61, 290
Bonino, José Míguez, 458
Book of Common Prayer
    (Cranmer), 346, 347, 349
Books of hours, 269
Booths, festival of, 76
Bora, Katherine von, 326–27, *326*
Borg, Markus, 452
Borromeo, Charles, 357
Breviary, 356
Bris or *brit mila,* 47
Bubonic plague, 289, 292–94
Buddhism, Vatican II and, 480

Burke, Edmund, 387
Byzantine Empire, 164

C

Cabal, Opero, 367
Caecilian, 188
Caelestius, 190
Caesaro-papism, 197
Cain, 39
Calendar designations, 21
Caliphs, 216
Calligraphy, 228
Calvin, John, 137, *337*
    beliefs of, 337–38
    early life of, 337
    in Geneva, 339–40
Calvinism, 403
Campbell, Alexander, 405
Campbell, Joseph, 4
Canaan, 44, 45, 48, 62
Canisius, Peter, 357
Cannon, Katie Geneva, 466
Canonicity, criteria for, 95–96
Canonization, 268
Canon, 19
    defined, 93
    Hebrew Bible (Tanakh), 24–25
    New Testament, 93–96
    Protestant Bible, 24–25
    Roman Catholic Bible, 24–25
Cappadocian Fathers, 168
Capuchins, 354, 372, 375
Cardinal, origin of term, 258
Carlstadt (priest), 324
Carmelites, 354, 357–58
Carolingian Renaissance, 237, 244–46,
    245, 246
Carolingians, 236–38, *238*
Carroll, John, 412
Cassian, John, 239
Cassirer, Ernst, 383
Catechetical School, 155–56
Catechisms
    Luther's, of 1529, 328–29
    Roman/Catholic, 357
Catechumens, 177–78
Cathars, 259, 263
Cathedrals, 176
Cathedral schools, 276
Catherine of Genoa, 294
Catherine of Siena, 293,
    297–98
Catholic, use of term, 151

Catholicism
  after the French Revolution, 422–24
  in the United States, 411–15
*Catholicism: A Study of the Corporate Destiny of
    Mankind* (De Lubac), 429
Catholic Reformation
  art, 358–60, *359, 360*
  Council of Trent, 352, 355–57
  defined, 352
  mysticism in Spain, 357–58
  pre-Tridentine reform, 352–54
Catholic Worker Movement, 415
C.E. (Common Era), 21
Celibacy
  Luther and, 326
  monastic, 241
Celtic monasticism, 239
Cenobitic monasticism, 174–75
Cerularius, Michael, 204
Chalcedon, Council of, 168–71, 198, 205
Chaldean Catholic Church, 209
Challenge of Peace, The, 414
Charlemagne, 202, 237, 245
Charles V, Holy Roman emperor, 323, 327, 355
Chenu, M. D., 429
China
  Christianity in, 395
  missionaries in, 372–74
Chi-Rho, 162, *162,* 163
Christ
  See also Jesus of Nazareth.
  church as the body of, 128
  Eastern Orthodoxy and nature of, 198
  portrayals of, in art, 146, *146, 147,* 293, *293*
  resurrection of, 114–15, 143
  second coming of, 115
  suffering, 266
Christendom, defined, 253
Christian Church (Disciples of Christ), 336, 341, 405
Christianity
  See also Eastern Orthodox Christianity; Middle
    Ages, early; Middle Ages, High; Middle Ages,
    Late; Modern period.
  church government, 171–73
  Constantine, 162–65
  dogma, development of, 165–71
  genealogy of, 138, *139*
  historical divisions, 136–38
  incarnation, doctrine of, 151, 168–71
  monasticism and ascetical movement, 173–75
  scripture and tradition, 135–36
  Trinity, doctrine of, 151, 168
Christianity, early (patristic period)
  apologists, 149–50
  apostolic missions, 118–34
  break with Judaism, 142–43
  Constantine, 162–65
  dates for, 142
  doctrine, development of, 150–52
  gnosticism, 152–54
  Jesus Movement, 87–88, 98
  life and community, 157–58
  persecutions, 148–49
  in Roman Empire, 130, 147–49, 162
  spread of, 129–34, *133,* 142–46, *144*
  summary of, 137
  theology, birth of, 154–57
Christianity, medieval period. *See* Middle Ages,
    early.
Christian Liberty (Luther), 323
Christian–Muslim dialogue, 230–32
Christian Reformed Church, 340
Christian theology, subdivisions of, 11–12
Christology, 103–9
Chrysoloras, Manuel, 310
Chrysostom, John, 275, 472
Church(es)
  See also Architecture.
  as the body of Christ, 128
  corruption, 164–65, 291, 294–96
  Eastern Orthodox, 196–205
  government, 171–73
  non-Chalcedonian, 205–9
  as people of God, 434–36
Church and state, United States and separation of,
    400–1
Church of England, 349, 401
Church of God in Christ, 406
Church of Jesus Christ of Latter-Day Saints (LDS),
    407–8
Church of the Brethren, 341, 408
Cicero, 183–84
Cistercians, 261, 268
Civil Rights movement, 464
Clare of Assisi, 262
Classical (pagan) Greek
  stream, 275
Claudius, Roman emperor, 130
Clement III, Pope, 244
Clement V, Pope, 260, 262, 290
Clement VII, Pope, 291
Clement XI, Pope, 374
Clement of Alexandria, 94, 155–56
Clooney, Francis, 479
Clovis, 236
Cluniac reform movement, 240–41
Codex Juris Civilis (Justinian), 197
Colet, John, 345
College of Cardinals, 258, 354
Collegium Urbanum, 374
Colonization. *See* Globalization; Missionaries.
Columbus, Christopher, 304, 312, 367

Commerce, during the Renaissance, 308
Common good, 455
Communion of saints, 265
Communion rite, 349
Communism, 394–95
Communist Manifesto, The (Marx), 394
Comparative theology, 13
Compostela, 269
Comte, Auguste, 8
Conciliarism, 291–92
Concordat of Worms, 244
Concubinage, 241
Condorcet, Marquis de, 385
Cone, James, 458, 464, 465
Conferences, The (Cassian), 239
Confessions (Augustine), 150, 175, 182, 183, 184,
    185, 186, 187, 189
Confessors, 149
Confraternities, 269
Confraternity of Christian Doctrine, 357
Confucius, 374
Congar, Yves, 429
Congregationalists, 401
Congregation for the Propagation of the Faith, 374,
    459
Congregation of the Mission, 353
Consistory, 339
Constance, Council of, 291–92
Constantine
    "Donation of Constantine," 313
    impact on the development of Christianity,
        163–65
    rise to power and religious policies, 162–63, 195
Constantinople
    Council of, 167–68
    formation of, 163, 164, 195
Constitution on the Sacred Liturgy, 433
Contrition, 319
Conventuals, 262
Copernicus, Nicholas, 380
Coptic Orthodox Church, 205
Corpus Christi, 265
Cosmology, 380–81
Councils
    See also Ecumenical councils.
    of Basel, 292
    of Constance, 291–92
    Fourth Lateran, 259–60
    of Pisa, 291
    of Trent, 95, 352, 355–57
    of Verona, 263
    of Vienne, 262
Counter-Reformation, defined, 352
Covenant
    Abraham, 43–47
    defined, 19–20, 43

Hittite, 55–56
    ritual enactment of, 57–58
    at Sinai, 55–57
Cranmer, Thomas, 346, *346,* 347
Creation
    Big Bang theory, 453–54
    impact of the theory of evolution, 389–92
Creation of the Heavenly Bodies, 15
Creation stories
    Egyptian and Babylonian, 30–31
    Genesis, 29–30, 32–34
    God's role in, 32
    goodness of humanity, 33–34
    Mesopotamian, 36
Creeds, 151
    Nicene, 166, 167
    Nicene–Constantinople, 167–68, 203
Criticism, historical, 313
Critique of Practical Reason, The (Kant), 384
Crusades, 219–20
    First, 253, *254,* 256, 265
    Fourth, 203, 259, 269
    Holy Wars against Muslims, *254,* 255–57
    Wendish, 253–54
Cunctos Populos, 166–67
Cur Deus Homo (Anselm), 249
Curia, 258
Cyril of Alexandria, 170, 171, 205
Cyrus, 71

D

Daniel, book of, 114–15
Daniélou, Jean, 429, 477
Dante, 304
Darwin, Charles, 389–91, 453
David, 64–65, 448–49
Day, Dorothy, 415, *415*
Day of Atonement, 76
Dead Sea Scrolls, 81, 85
Decius, Roman emperor, 148–49
*Declaration on Religious
    Freedom/Liberty,* 388, 414
*Declaration on the Relationship of
    the Church to Non-Christian Religions
    (Nostra Aetate),* 436–37, 480–81
Deconstruction, 445–46
Decree on Eastern Catholic Churches, 209
Decree on Ecumenism, 436
De ecclesia (On the Church) (Hus), 296
Degrees of Knowledge, The (Maritain), 427
Deism, 382–83
de las Casas, Bartolomé, 370
De Lubac, Henri, 429–30
Democracy, 305

Denominationalism, 403–4

Derrida, Jacques, 443, 445–46

Descartes, René, 2, 381, 382

Descent of Man, The (Darwin), 391

d'Este, Isabella, 311–12, 313

Deuteronomist, 21

Deuteronomistic Historian, 61

Deuteronomistic History, 61
    See also Former Prophets.

Dialogue
    See also Interreligious dialogue.
    Christian–Muslim, 230–32
    defined, 482

Dialogue, The (Catherine of Siena), 298

Diaspora, 75

Dictatus Papae, 244

Dictionnaire Philosophique (Voltaire), 384

Didache (The Teaching of the Twelve Apostles),
    130–31, 155, 157

Diderot, Denis, 383, 385, 386

Diego, Juan, 370

Diet of Speyer, 327

Diet of Worms, 323–24

Dinkha IV, Mar, 206, 207–8

Diocletian, Roman emperor, 162, 175,
    188, 195

Discalced Carmelites, 354, 357

Disciple, defined, 124

Discipleship, 112–14

Disciples of Christ, 336, 341, 405

Dispensationalism, 410

Disputes, as a teaching method,
    277–78

Divine Comedy (Dante), 304

Divino Afflante Spiritu, 431

Docetism, 95, 153

Doctor of the Church, 286, 298

Doctrines, 9
    development of Christian, 150–52

Documentary Hypothesis, 21

Dogma
    defined, 165
    development of, 165–71

*Dogmatic Constitution on Divine
    Revelation (Dei Verbum)*, 438–39

*Dogmatic Constitution on the Church (Lumen
    Gentium)*, 231, 434–36, 480

Dome of the Rock, 218

Dominicans, 257, 262, 278–79

Dominus Iesus, 481

"Donation of Constantine," 313

Donatist movement/schism,
    162, 188–89

Double predestination, 338

Douglas, Mary, 7, *7*

Durkheim, Emile, 7, 8

E

Earth, stewardship of the, 456

Eastern Catholic churches, 208–9

Eastern Orthodox Christianity, 164
    Byzantine context, 195–96
    churches, 196–205
    crusades and, 203
    ecumenical councils, 198–99
    filioque, 203
    Heyschast spirituality, 202
    icons, 198–200, *199*
    Jesus, nature of, 198
    liturgy, 200–202
    non-Chalcedonian churches, 205–9
    papal primacy, 203–4
    separation of West and, 202–5
    Trinity, nature, 198

Eck, John, 320–21

Economic liberalism, 388–89

Ecumenical councils
    Chalcedon, 168–71, 198, 205
    Constantinople, 167–68
    development of, 163
    Eastern Orthodox Christianity, 198–99
    Ephesus, 168–71, 198
    Florence, 208
    Lyons, 208
    Nicaea, 165–66, 198, 203

Ecumenical movement and interreligious dialogue,
    Vatican II and, 436–37

Edessa, Christianity in, 133

Edict of Milan, 163

Edict of Worms, 323

Education
    of clerics, 356
    encomienda-doctrina system, 369, 370–71
    humanism, 310–13

Education of the Christian Woman, The (Vives), 311

Edward VI, king of England, 346

Edwards, Jonathan, 404

Egypt
    Christianity in, 131
    creation stories, 30–31
    cult of Isis, 144–45
    Jacob and Joseph in, 49
    Moses in, 49–58

Elect, 185

Election, doctrine of, 337–38

Eliade, Mircea, 5

Elijah, 67

Elisha, 67

Elizabeth I, queen of England, 244, 312,
    347, *347*, 349

Elohist, 21

Emerging Church Movement, 466

Encomienda-doctrina system, 369, 370–71
Enculturation, 375
England
   colonies, 412
   Reformation in, 344–47, 349
Enlightenment, 2
   criticism of, 387–88
   freedom and religious toleration, 386–87
   human nature and progress, 385–86
   rationalism, 383–85
   writers of, 383
Enuma Elish, 30, 31, 393
Ephesus, Council of, 168–71, 198
Episcopacy, 152
Episcopal Church, 349
Erasmus, Desiderius, 314, 345
Esau, 47
Essay in Aid of a Grammar of Assent, An (Newman),
   428
Essay on the Development of Christian Doctrine
   (Newman), 428
Essenes, 85–86, 142
Ethiopia, Christianity in, 131, *132*
Ethiopian Orthodox Church, 205
Eucharist, 94
   Calvin and, 338
   Hus and, 296
   Justin and, 151
   Luther and, 321, 322
   Middle Ages, High, 265
   origins of, 115–16
   Paul and, 116, 128–29
   Prayer, 201
   Wycliffe and, 295
   Zwingli and, 335
Eugene IV, Pope, 292
Eusebius of Caesarea, 94, 95, 130, 131, 133, 156,
   163, 164, 196
Evagrius, 174–75
Evangelical, use of term, 401
Evangelical Lutheran Church, 232
Evangelii Praecones, 475–76
Evangelists, 92
Evans, James, 466
Evans-Pritchard, E. E., 7
Evolution, theory of, 389–92
Exclusivism, 476–77
Exile, Babylonian, 70–71
Exodus, book of, 49–58
Exodus, route of, *55*
Explaining Religion: Criticism and Theory from
   Bodin to Freud (Preus), 3
Exploration/explorers, 304, 312,
   364–66
   See also Missionaries.
   map of, *368*

Expulsion of Adam and Eve, 35
Ezekiel, 61, 71
Ezra, 71

F

Faith
   defined, 11
   justification by, 125–26, 355–56
   justification by, and Luther, 318–19
Fall, the, 34
Falwell, Jerry, 409
Feeney, Leonard, 475
Felder, Cain Hope, 466
Feminist theology, 461–63
Ferdinand, king of Spain, 305, 309
Festal Letter (Athanasius of Alexandria), 95
Feudal system, 240
Filioque, 203
Fiorenza, Elizabeth Schüssler, 452
First Vatican Council. *See* Vatican Council I.
Five pillars of Islam, 222–24
Five Wounds of Christ, 266
Flagellants, 293
Florence, Council of, 208
Folklore, 269
Former Prophets, books of, 21, 61
Foucault, Michel, 445
Fourth Lateran Council, 259–60
France, missionaries from, 375, 411–12
Francis I, king of France, 305
Franciscans, 257, 262, 268
Francis of Assisi, 13, 257, 260, 262, 266
Francis Xavier, 372
Franklin, Benjamin, 383, 385–86, 416
Frazer, James, 7
Frederick II, Holy Roman emperor, 259
Frederick the Wise of Saxony, 323, 324, 325
Freedom, Paul's views on, 127
French Revolution, 387
   Catholicism after the, 422–24
Freud, Sigmund, 4, *4*
Fulfillment, theology of, 476
Fundamentalism
   in the United States, 409–10
   use of term, 401

G

Galileo Galilei, 380, 381
Gallicanism, 425
Gama, Vasco da, 304, 367

Gay Science, The (Nietzsche), 444
Genealogies, 48–49
    of Christianity, 138, *139*
General councils. *See* Ecumenical councils.
Genesis
    Abraham, 43–47
    creation stories, 29–30, 32–34
    evolution, theory of, 389–92
    genealogies, 48–49
    God of Israel, 36–39
    human sin, 34–36
    Jacob, 47–49
Geneva, Calvin in, 339–40
Gentiles, 120, 122
Gilgamesh, 36, 393
Gilson, Étienne, 427
Globalization, 304–5, 364–66, 411–12
    See also Missionaries.
Glossolalia, 127–28, 406
Gnosticism, 152–54
God
    attributes of, 37–39
    gender of, 38
    of Israel, 36–39
    names for, 36, 38–39
God-fearers, 120
Gonzaga, Elisabetta, 311–12
Gospels
    See also names of specific gospels.
    Christology, 103–9
    description of, 92, 94
    origin of, 99–103
    origin of term, 92
    parables and miracle stories, 110–16
    synoptic, 92, 101–2
    Two-Source Hypothesis, 102–3
Gothic architecture, 270–71, *270*
Grace, 125
    justification by, through faith and Luther,
        318–19
    Middle Ages and the seven sacraments, 264–66
Great Awakening, 404
Great Schism (1054), 204
Great Schism (1378–1417), 291–92
Greek patristic stream, 275
Greek studies, humanism and revival of, 310–12
Gregorian chant, 245
Gregory I, Pope, 242–43, 248–49
Gregory VII, Pope, 243, 258
Gregory XI, Pope, 291
Gregory XV, Pope, 374
Gregory of Nazianzus, 168, 169
Gregory of Nyssa, 168
Gregory Palamas, 202
Guide of the Perplexed
        (Maimonides), 275

Guilds, 269
Gutierrez, Gustavo, 458, 460
Guzman, Dominic, 262

H

Habakkuk, 61
Hadith, 222, 223
Hadrian I, Pope, 245
Haec Sancta, 292
Hagar, 45
Haggai, 61
Hagia Sophia, 197, *197,* 227
Hagiography, 155
Hail Mary prayer, 268
Haj (pilgrimage), 223–24
Handbook of the Christian Soldier (Erasmus), 314
Hanukkah, 82
Hasideans, 85
Hearers, 185
Hebrew Bible/Scriptures. *See* Old Testament.
Hebrews, use of term, 22
Hellenistic Age, 82
Hellenization, 82
Henry I, Holy Roman emperor, 237
Henry IV, Holy Roman emperor, 238, 243–44
Henry VII, king of England, 305, 309
Henry VIII, king of England, 137, 305, 309, 344,
        344, 345, 346
Henry the Navigator, 366
Herbert of Cherbury, lord, 382
Heresy
    defined, 152
    docetism, 95, 153
    in England, 347
    gnosticism, 152–54
    Inquisition, 264, 309
    Middle Ages, High, 263–64
Herod the Great, 76
Hesychia, 202
Hexapla (Origen), 156
Hesychast spirituality, 202
Hick, John, 478–79
Hijira, 214
Hildebrand. *See* Gregory VII, Pope.
Hinduism, Vatican II and, 480
Hippolytus of Rome, 157
Historical criticism, 313
Historical Jesus, quest for, 450–52
Historical theology, 12
Hittite covenants, 55–56
Hoffman, Melchior, 343
Holbach, Baron d', 382
Holiness movement, 406
Holy of Holies, 76–77

Holy Roman Empire, 236–38, *238*
Holy Spirit
    Eastern Orthodoxy and nature of, 203
    Paul's views, 127–28
Holy wars (crusades), *254,* 255–57
Holy water, 269
Homilies on Ezechiel (Gregory I), 248–49
Homilies on the Gospels (Gregory I), 249
Horsley, Richard, 452
Hortensius (Cicero), 183–84
Hosea, 61, 69
Hospitallers, 257
Human dignity, 455
Humani Generis, 391, 430
Humanism, 310–12
Human nature
    Enlightenment and, 385–86
    nominalism, 289–90
Humbert, Cardinal, 204
Hume, David, 383, 384
Hus, Jan, 295–96, 321
Hussites, 296
Hutterites, 341, 408
Hymnbook, Lutheran, 329

I

"I am" sayings, 108–9
Ibn Batuta, 365
Iconoclasm, 324–25, 335
Iconoclasts, 198
Iconodules, 198
Iconostasis, 199–200
Icons, 198–200, *199*
Ignatius of Antioch, 135
Ignatius of Loyola, 353–54, 372
Imams, 216
Immaculate Conception, 423
Imperial cult, 147–48
Implicit desire, 475
Incarnation, 107
    doctrine of, 151, 168–71
Inclusivism, 476, 477–79
Inculturation, 375–76
Indigenization, 365
Individualism, 305
Indulgences, 265, 291, 296
    Council of Trent and, 356
    Luther and controversy over, 319–21
Infancy narratives, 105
Ingoli, Francesco Cardinal, 374
Innocent III, Pope, 203, 254, 258–59
In Praise of Folly (Erasmus), 314
Inquisition, 264, 309

Insight (Lonergan), 428
Inspiration and the Bible, 25–27
Institutes, The (Cassian), 239
Institutes of the Christian Religion (Calvin), 337
Integral Humanism (Maritain), 427
Interdict, 259
International Church of the Four Square Gospel,
    406
Interreligious dialogue
    exclusivism, 476–77
    formal church teachings, 479–82
    history of Christian attitudes toward
        non-Christian religions, 472–75
    inclusivism, 476, 477–79
    twentieth-century developments, 475–79
    Vatican II and, 436–37
Investiture conflict, 243–44
Iqbal, Muhammad, 225–26
Irenaeus of Lyons, 94, 153–54
Isaac, 45
Isabella, queen of Spain, 305, 309
Isaiah, 61, 70
Ishmael, 45
Islam
    art and architecture, 226–28, *227, 228*
    challenges of the modern world, 228–30
    Christian–Muslim dialogue, 230–32
    crusades, *254,* 255–57
    defined, 212
    expansion of, 216–20, *219*
    five pillars of, 222–24
    law, life, and spirituality, 222–26
    map of Arabia, *215*
    Muhammad, 212–16
    Qur'an and the Sunna, 213, 220–22
    Vatican II and, 480
Israel
    Assyrian period, 68–70
    Babylonian Exile, 70–71
    Babylonia period, 70
    Jacob and the twelve tribes of, 47–49
    Lost Tribes of, 71
    Solomon and the division of, 65–66, *66*
Israelites
    God of, 36–39
    passage through the Red Sea, 54
    judges and tribal system, 62–63
    use of term, 22–23

J

Jacob, 47–49
James, apostle, 121, 122, 129
James, William, 4

Jehovah's Witnesses, 407
Jefferson, Thomas, 383–84, 400, 416
Jeremiah, 61
Jerusalem
    church in, 129–30
    Conference, 122–23
    as David's capital, 64
Jesuits, 353–54, 356, 372–74
Jesus Movement, 87–88, 98
Jesus of Nazareth
    See also Christ.
    Christology, 103–9
    Eastern Orthodoxy and nature of, 198
    life and death of, 98
    Quest for the Historical, 450–52
    resurrection of, 114–15, 143
Jesus Prayer, 202
Jesus Seminar, 451–52
Jewish stream, 275
Jewish War, 88
Jews
    expelled from Rome, 130
    in the High Middle Ages, 255
    in Spain, 309
    use of term, 23, 65
    Zealots, 88
Jihad, 224
Joao III, king of Portugal, 366, 367
Joel, 61
John, apostle, 122, 131
John, Gospel of, 92, 101, 103
    Christology, 107–9
John XII, Pope, 238
John XXIII, Pope, 430, 432, 432, 435, 480
John Mark, 100
John of the Cross, 357–58
John Paul II, Pope, 203, 205, 208, 231, 380, 381,
        389, 391, 411, 415, 423
John the Baptist, 115
Joint Declaration on the Doctrine of Justification,
        126, 436
Jonah, 61
Joseph, son of Jacob, 49
Josephus, 22
Joshua, 61
Joyful Science, The (Nietzsche), 444
Judah, 49
    Solomon and the division of, 65–66, 66
Judaism
    Christianity's break with, 142–43
    Essenes, 85–86
    Hellenistic Age, 82
    Jesus Movement, 87–88
    in New Testament times, 82–86
    People of the Land, 86
    Pharisees, 84–85

Sadducees, 83–84
scribes, 86
Second Temple, 71–72, 74–82
use of term, 23
Judges, 62–63
Julian of Norwich, 298–300
Julius II, Pope, 314
Jung, Carl, 4, 4
Justification
    defined, 124–25
    by faith, 125–26, 355–56
    by grace through faith and Luther, 318–19
    by works, 125
Justinian I, Roman emperor, 195, 196–97, 242
Justin Martyr, 94, 143, 150, 151, 473

K

Ka'ba, 212–13
Kant, Immanuel, 2, 383, 384, 427
Kempe, Margery, 298
Kerr, Fergus, 430
Kharijites, 217, 218
Khomeini, Ayatollah, 226
King, Martin Luther, Jr., 417, 464
Kingdom of God, 112–14
Kings, Old Testament, 63–66
Knights of St. John, 257
Knights Templar, 257
Kosher, 78
Kristensen, W. Brede, 5
Kunin, Seth, 3, 5

L

Laban, 48
Lagrange, Marie-Joseph, 431
Laissez faire, 388–89
Lamentabili, 426
Latin America
    base Christian communities, 458
    liberation theology, 457–60
    structural violence, 458–59
Latter Prophets, books of, 21–22, 61
Law. See Torah.
Lay investiture, 240
Lazarists, 353
Lectura (lecture), 277
Lee, Archie C. C., 448–49
Legends, 43
Leipzig debate, 320–21
Lent, 178
Leo I, Pope, 171, 172–73
Leo III, Pope, 202, 237, 277

Leo IX, Pope, 204
Leo X, Pope, 319
Leo XIII, Pope, 389, 426, 427, 455
Leonardo da Vinci, 305, 312
Letter to the Duke of Norfolk (Newman), 428
Lévi-Strauss, Claude, 7
Lévy-Bruhl, Lucien, 7
Liberalism, 388–89
Liberation theology, 457–60
Licinius, Roman emperor, 163
Life and Morals of Jesus of Nazareth, The (Jefferson),
    383–84
Life of Antony (Athanasius of Alexandria), 155,
    173–74, 175
Lincoln, Abraham, 416
Liturgical theology. *See*
    Sacramental theology.
Liturgy
    Eastern Orthodox, 200–202
    Luther, 329
    Vatican Council II and, 430, 432–34
Locke, John, 385, 386
Logos, 107, 150, 473
Lollards, 295, 296
Lombard, Peter, 277
Lonergan, Bernard, 427–28
Lost Tribes of Israel, 71
Louis XIV, king of France, 386
Louis the Pious, 237
Love, Paul's views, 127
Luke, Gospel of, 92, 100, 101–3
    Christology, 106–7
*Lumen Gentium (Dogmatic Constitution
    on the Church),* 231, 434–36, 480
Luther, Martin, 137
    Bible translation, 305, 314, 328
    death of, 329–30
    Diet of Worms, 323–24
    early life, 317–18
    excommunication, 321
    exile and return, 324–25
    indulgence controversy, 319–21
    justification by grace through faith, 318–19
    Leipzig debate, 320–21
    marriage, 326–327, *326*
    Ninety-Five Theses, 320
    Peasants' Revolt, 325
    writings of, 321–23
Lutheranism
    Bible, 328
    catechisms of 1529, 328–29
    church, formation of, 328
    hymnbook, 329
    Joint Declaration on the Doctrine of Justification, 126
    liturgy, 329
Lyons, Council of, 208

M

Maccabees, 82
Machiavelli, Niccolo, 310
Madrasas, 222
Magellan, Ferdinand, 367
Maimonides, Moses, 275
Malachi, 61
Malankara Orthodox Syrian Church, 205
Malcolm X, 464
Man and the State (Maritain), 427
Mani, 184
Manicheism, 184–85
Manuel I, king of Portugal, 366, 367
Marburg Colloquy, 335
Marcion, 94
Maritain, Jacques, 427
Mark, Gospel of, 92, 100, 101–3
    Christology, 104–5
Maronite Christians of Lebanon, 208
Martel, Charles, 236–37
Martin V, Pope, 292
Martyrdom of Perpetua and Felicity, 155, 158, 266
Martyrs, Roman Empire 149
Marx, Karl, 8, 393–95
Marxism, 394–95
Mary (mother of Jesus/God), 170, 198
    Middle Ages, High, 266–68, *267*
    Our Lady of Guadalupe,
        370, *370*
Mary, Queen of Scots, 312
Mary I, queen of England, 312, 346–47
Mater dolorosa, 267
Mathematical Principles of Natural Philosophy
    (Newton), 381
Mathematics, revival of Greek, 310
Matthew, Gospel of, 92, 100, 101–3
    Christology, 105–6
Matthew of Bascio, 372
Maurin, Peter, 415
McFague, Sally, 461–62
McPherson, Aimee Semple, 406
Mecca, 212–13
Medieval period
    See also Middle Ages, early.
    characteristics of, 303–4
Meier, John P., 452
Melanchthon, Philip, 327
Memoria, 176–77
Memphite Theology, 30, 31
Mendicants, 261–62
Mennonites, 164, 341, 342,
    343, 408
Merovingians, 236–37
Mesopotamian creation stories, 36
Messianic Secret, 104

Messiah
   Essenes and, 86
   Jesus Movement and, 88
   Judaism, 75, 78–82
   Pharisees and, 85
   Sadducees and, 84
Method in Theology (Lonergan), 428
Methodism, 404
Methodist Church, 349
Methodist Episcopal Church, 404
Methodists, 403
Micah, 61
Middle Ages, early
   Carolingians, 236–38, *238*
   cultural contributions, 244–46
   Holy Roman Empire, 236–38, *238*
   monasticism, development of, 239–41
   papacy, development of, 242–44
   scholars/theology, 246–50
   summary of, 137
Middle Ages, High
   Christ, Mary, and the saints, 266–68
   crusades, *254*, 255–57
   Gothic architecture, 270–71, *270*
   heresy, 263–64
   intellectual climate, 274–75
   Jews, 255
   monasticism, 261–63
   paganism, 253–54
   papacy primacy, 258–61
   religion of lay people, 269
   sacraments, 264–66
   scholasticism, 275–77
   teaching and learning,
      methods of, 277–78
Middle Ages, Late
   Avignon Papacy, 290–91
   Black Death, 289, 292–94
   Great Schism, 291–92
   mysticism, 296–300
   nominalism, 289–90
   revolts against church and state, 294–96
Millennialism, 406–7
Miller, William, 407
Miracles of the Virgin, 268
Miracle stories, 110–16
Mishnah, 84–85, 142
Missionaries
   in Africa, 366–67
   in the Americas, 367, 369, 411–12
   apostolic, 118–34
   in Asia, 372–74
   Congregation for the Propagation
      of the Faith, 374
   French, 375, 411–12
   inculturation, 375–76

   royal patronage and, 369–71
   Spanish, 367, 369, 411–12
Mithraism, 144, 145
Modern period
   See also Renaissance; Reformation.
   Bible, scientific interpretation of, 392–93
   characteristics, 304–6
   cosmology, 380–81
   Deism, 382–83
   democracy, 305
   Enlightenment, 383–88
   evolution, theory of, 389–92
   globalization and pluralism, 304–5
   individualism, 305
   liberalism, 388–89
   Marxism, 393–95
   nationalism, 305
   nature and science, 305–6
   science, 381–82
   scientific history, 392
   summary of, 137
Monasticism
   Augustine and Pelagian
      controversy, 189–92
   defined, 239
   development of, 173–75
   Middle Ages, early, 239–41
   Middle Ages, High, 261–63, 276
   schools, 276
Monica, mother of St. Augustine, 183
Monk, 173
Monophysites, 171
Monotheism, 1
Moral Majority, 409
Moral Man and Immoral Society (Niebuhr), 418
Moral Teachings from Job
      (Gregory I), 249
Moral theology, 12
Moravian Brethren, 342, 404
More, Thomas, 345
Mormons, 407–8
Morrison, Toni, 466
Mortal sin, 266
Moses, 49–58
Mosques, 227, *227*
Mount Sinai, covenant at, 55–57
Mu'awiyya, 217, 218
Muezzin, 223
Muhammad, 212–16
Mujathids, 222
Muratorian canon, 94–95
Murphy, Francesca Aran, 3
Murray, John Courtney, 413–14, *414*
Music
   Gregorian chant, 245
   Lutheran hymnbook, 329

Muslims
    See also Islam.
    stream, 275
Mystery religions, 143–45
Mystical Theology, The (Pseudo-Dionysius
        the Areopagite), 247–48
Mysticism
    Aquinas and, 285–86
    defined, 248
    Middle Ages, Late, 296–300
    in Spain, 357–58
Myths
    creation, 30–31
    defined, 30

N

Nahum, 61
Nathan, 64
National Baptist Convention USA, Inc., 409
National Council of the Churches
        of Christ, 479–80
Nationalism, 305
Nation-states, 308–9
Native Americans, 370–71, 411–12
Naturalistic approach, 3
Natural selection, 390
Nature, 305–6
    Surnaturel (Supernatural)
        (De Lubac), 429–30
*Nature and Destiny of Man,
        The* (Niebuhr), 418
Near East, map of, *68*
Nehemiah, 71
Neoplatonism, 186–87
Neo-scholasticism, 426–27
Neo-Thomism, 427
Nepotism, 291, 356
Nestorian, 207
Nestorius, 170, 207
Newman, John Henry, 349, 428
New Testament
    canon, 93–96
    division of, 91–93
    use of term, 20
Newton, Isaac, 381
Nicaea, Council of, 165–66, 198, 203
Nicene-Constantinople Creed, 167–68, 203
Nicene Creed, 166, 167
Nicholas I, Pope, 204
Nicholas V, Pope, 314
Nicholas of Myra, 269
Niebuhr, Reinhold, 418
Nietzsche, Friedrich, 443–45
Nihilism, 444

Ninety-Five Theses (Luther), 320
Nobili, Roberto de, 474
Nominalism, 289–90
Northumberland, duke of, 346
*Nostra Aetate (Declaration on the Relationship of the
        Church to Non-Christian Religions),*
        436–37, 480–81

O

Obadiah, 61
Of Grammatology (Derrida), 445–46
Old Testament
    See also names of specific books.
    genealogies, 48–49
    Hebrew Bible (Tanakh) canon, 24–25
    origins of, 20–23
    Protestant Bible canon, 24–25
    Roman Catholic Bible canon, 24–25
    use of term, 19–20
Omnipotence, 37
Omniscient, 65
On Consulting the Faithful in Matters of Doctrine
        (Newman), 428
On First Principles (Origen), 156–57
On Prayer (Origen), 156
On the Babylonian Captivity of the Church
        (Luther), 321, 322
On the City of God (Augustine), 156, 183, 197
On the Origin of Species by Means of Natural Selection
        (Darwin), 389–91
On the Revolutions of the Heavenly Spheres
        (Copernicus), 380
Oracles, 69
Oratories, 353
Oratory of Divine Love, 353
Order of Preachers, 262
Origen of Alexandria, 94, 95, 156, 158,
        182, 275, 429
Original sin, 189–91
Orthodoxy
    See also Eastern Orthodox Christianity.
    defined, 196
    development of Christian, 150–52
Otto I, Holy Roman emperor, 237–38
Ottoman Empire, 229
Our Lady of Guadalupe, 370, *370*
Oxford Movement, 349, 428

P

Pachomius, 239
Paganism, Middle Ages and, 253–54
Pagans, 143, 149

Paine, Thomas, 383
Palestine, 75
    map of, in New Testament times, *98*
Paley, William, 453
Papacy
    See also names of specific popes.
    Avignon, 260, 290–91
    development of, 171–73
    development of, in early
        Middle Ages, 242–44
    personalization of, 423
    primacy, 203–4, 258–61
    reforms, 354
    Renaissance, 314
Papal bull, 321
Papal States, Italian unification
        and, 388
Papias, 100
Parables, 110–16
Parham, Charles, 406
Parousia, 115
Pascal, Blaise, 387
Passive righteousness, 318
Passover, 53, 76
Pastor Aeternus, 424
*Pastoral Constitution on the Church in the Modern
        World (Gaudium et Spes)*, 437–38, 457
Pastoral theology, 12
Patriarch, 44, 171
    hereditary, 206
Patriarchal sees, 129
Patristic period. *See* Christianity, early
        (patristic period).
Paul
    authority of, 124
    baptism and, 115, 128–29
    church as the body of
        Christ, 128
    Eucharist and, 116, 128–29
    freedom and love and, 127
    Holy Spirit, 127–28
    Jerusalem Conference,
        122–23
    letters of, 92, 123
    life of, 119–24, *121*
    living the good Christian life, 126–29
    map of his journeys, *122*
    message of, 124–26
    pseudonymity, 123
Paul III, Pope, 354, 355, 371
Paul VI, Pope, 435
Pauline churches, 128–29
Peace churches, 408–9
Peasants' Revolt (1381), 296
Peasants' Revolt (1524 and
        1525), 325

Pelagian controversy, 189–92
Pelagius, 190
Penance, 178
    elements of, 319
    Middle Ages, High, 265
Penitents, 178
Pentateuch, 21, 61
Pentecost, 76, 178–79
Pentecostalism, 406
People of the Land, 86
Persian period, in Israel, 71–72
Personal revelation, 10
Peter, 119, 130, 131
    confession, 173
    gospel of, 95
    Jerusalem Conference, 122–23
    letter of, 93–94
Peter II, king of Aragon, 258
Pharisees, 84–85
Phenomenological approaches, 4–6
Philip (apostle), 131
Philip IV, king of France, 260, 290
Philistines, 63, 64
Philo of Alexandria, 107
Photius, 204
Pietà, 293
Pietism, 404
Pilgrimages, 269
Pippin III, 237
Pisa, Council of, 291
Pius II, Pope, 292
Pius V, Pope, 244
Pius VI, Pope, 412
Pius VII, Pope, 423
Pius IX, Pope, 388, 423, 424
Pius X, Pope, 426
Pius XI, Pope, 475
Pius XII, Pope, 391, 423, 430,
        431, 475–76
Plagues, ten, 52–53
Plato, 149, 186, 310
Pliny the Younger, 149
Plotinus, 150, 186
Pluralism, 8, 304–5
Poetry, Aquinas and, 285–86
Polkinghorne, John, 454–55
Polo, Marco, 365
Polyglot Bibles, 352–53
Polytheism, 1
Poor Clares, 262
Pope
    See also Papacy; *names of
        specific popes.*
    bishop of Rome as, 172
Porphyry, 186
Portuguese missionaries in Africa, 366–67

Postmillennialism, 407
Postmodernism
    African American/black theology, 463–66
    art and architecture, 442–43, *442, 443*
    Biblical studies, 447–55
    defined, 442, 443–46
    feminist theology, 461–63
    liberation theology, 457–60
    responses of churches to, 466–67
    social issues, dealing with, 455–57
    theology, 446–47
Post-Reformation period, summary of, 137–38
Practical theology, 12
Praxis, 458
Predestination, 191
    double, 338
Premillennialism, 407
Presbyterian Church, 340
Presbyterians, 401, 403
Pre-Tridentine reform, 352–54
Preus, Samuel, 2–3
Priestley, Joseph, 383
Priestly, 21
Priests, in Second Temple period, 76
Principia (Newton), 381
Printing, 309–10
Priscilla, 130
Proclamation, 482
Property, ownership of private, 455–56
Prophets
    Assyrian period, in Israel, 68–70
    development of, 21–22, 66–67
    Former, 21, 61
    Latter, 21–22, 61
    Moses, 50–53
Proslogion (Anselm), 249
Protestant Bible canon, 24–25
Protestantism, in the United States, 401–11
Protestant Reformation
    art, 358–60, *359, 360*
    Calvin/Calvinism, 336–40
    in England, 344–47, 349
    Luther/Lutheranism, 316–31
    map of, *348*
    Radical, 340–44
    summary of, 137
    Swiss, 333–36, *336*
Protestants, use of term, 327
Pseudo-Dionysius the Areopagite, 247–48

Pseudonymity, 123
Psychological theories of, 3–4
Psychology and Religion (Jung), 4
Ptolemy, Claudius, 380
Purgation and Purgatory (Catherine of Genoa), 294
Purgatory, 266
Puritans, 401, 416

Q

Q (gospel source), 102
Quakers, 164, 343, 401, 408
Quanta Cura, 388
Quest for the Historical Jesus, 450–52
Qumran, 81, 85
Quodlibetal debates, 278
Qur'an, 213, 220–22

R

Rabbis, 84
Rachel, 48, 49
Radcliffe Brown, A. R., 7
Radical Reformation, 340–44
Rahman, Fazlur, 222
Rahner, Karl, 427, 478, *478*
Rashi, 255
Rationalism, 383–85
Reagan, Ronald, 415
Rebekah, 47
Recapitulation, 154
Red Sea, Israelites' passage through, 54
Reformation. *See* Catholic Reformation; Protestant Reformation.
Reformed Christians, 403
Rehoboam, 65
Reinhart, Anna, 334
Relativism, 466
Relics, 149, 269
Religion
    anthropological theories of, 6–7
    defined, 1
    phenomenological approaches to, 4–6
    psychological theories of, 3–4
    Smart's dimensions of, 5–6
    sociological theories of, 7–8
Religious freedom and toleration, 386–87, 413–14
Religious studies
    as an academic discipline, 3–8
    defined, 2–3
    reasons for studying, 13–14

Religious Studies and Theology: An Introduction
    (Kunin, Bond, and Murphy), 3
Renaissance
    art, 314–15
    beginnings of, 308–10
    commerce, 308
    defined, 308
    education and criticism, 312–13
    humanism, 310–12
    nation-states, 308–9
    papacy, 314
    printing, 309–10
    southern and northern,
        313–14
    view of the world, 312
Reply to Sadoleto (Calvin), 339–40
Rerum Novarum, 455
Resourcement, 428–30
Restorationism, 342, 466–67
Resurrection of Jesus,
    114–15, 143
Reuther, Rosemary Radford, 462
Revelation
    Abraham and, 44
    book of, 93
    defined, 9–11
    general versus special, 9–10
    personal, 10
    Vatican II and, 438–39
Revivalism, 404–5
Ricci, Matteo, 372–73, *373,* 474
Richelieu, Cardinal, 375
Righteousness, passive or
    alien, 318
Riley, William B., 410
Roberts, Oral, 406
Roman Catholicism
    See also Catholicism; Catholic Reformation.
    Bible canons, 24–25
    Joint Declaration on the Doctrine of Justification, 126
    separation of Eastern Orthodoxy and, 202–5
Roman Empire
    Christianity in, 130, 147–49, 162
    Constantine, 162–65, 195
    decline of, 195
    Jewish War, 88
Romanesque architecture, 246, *246*
Roman Rite, 245
Rood screen, 271
Rorty, Richard, 445
Rousseau, Jean-Jacques, 383, 385, 386
Rufinus, 131
Rule for Monasteries (Benedict), 237, 239–40, 261
Rule of St. Augustine, The
    (Augustine), 187
Rumi, Jalal ad-din, 225, 226

Russell, Charles Taze, 407
Russian Orthodox Church, 394
Russian Revolution, 394

S

Sacramentals, 269, 356
Sacramental theology, 12
Sacramentary, 245
Sacraments
    Augustine and Donatist schism, 188–89
    Calvin and, 338
    Council of Trent and, 356
    Luther and, 321–22
    Middle Ages and the seven, 264–66
    Zwingli and, 335
Sacrifice
    Essenes and, 85
    Jesus Movement and, 87
    Jewish Second Temple period, 75–76
    Pharisees and, 84
    ritual enactment of the covenant, 57–58
    Sadducees and, 83
Sacrificial atonement, 126
Sadducees, 83–84, 142
Sadoleto, Cardinal, 339–40
Sagan, Carl, 395
St. Peter's Basilica, 314, 319
Saints
    canonization, 268
    communion of, 265
    Middle Ages, High, and the veneration of, 268
Salafism, 229
Salah (prayer), 223
Sallust, 392
Salvation
    Calvin and, 337–38
    Luther and, 318
    Radical Reformers and, 342
Samaritans, 71
Samuel, 63–64
Sanctuary, 364
Sanders, E. P., 452
Sanhedrin, 83
Sankore Mosque, 227, *227*
Sarai (Sarah), 45
Saul, 64
Sawm (fasting), 223
Schisms
    Donatist, 162, 188–89
    Great (1054), 204
    Great (1378–1417), 291–92
Scholars, Middle Ages, early, 246–50
Scholasticism
    Middle Ages, High, 275–77

Middle Ages, Late, 289–90
    neo-, 426–27
School of Alexandria, 169–70
School of Antioch, 169, 170
Science, 305–6
    religion and, 381–82
    theology and, 453–55
Scientism, 396
Scofield Reference Bible, 410
Scribes, 86
Scripture and tradition, 135–36
Second Coming of Christ, 115
Second Great Awakening, 405
Second Isaiah, 71
Second Temple Judaism, 71–72,
        74–88, 77
Second Vatican Council. *See* Vatican Council II.
Secularism, 8, 400
Secularization, 437–38
Seljuks, 219
Seminary, 356
Sentences (Lombard), 277
Separation of church and state, U.S., 400–1
Septuagint, 23
Serapion of Antioch, 95
Sermon on the Mount (Plain), 107
Serra, Junipero, 411–12
Seventh-Day Adventists, 407
Seymour, William, 406
Sforza, Caterina, 312
Shahada (faith), 222
Shari'a, 222–25
Shi'a, 213, 216, 218
Shrines, 269
Simony, 240, 291, 356
Simplicianus, 186
Sin
    Augustine's views, 189–91
    Genesis' stories on, 34–36
    mortal, 266
    original sin, 189–91
Sinai, covenant at, 55–57
Sixtus IV, Pope, 309
Slavery, 370–71, 463–64
Smart, Ninian, 5
Smith, Adam, 388–89
Smith, Joseph, 407–8
Social Contract, The
        (Rousseau), 385
Social issues, dealing with, 455–57
Society of Friends. *See* Quakers.
Society of Jesus, 353–54
Sociological theories, 7–8
Solomon, 65–66
Soteriology, 15
Sources chrétiennes, 429

Southern Baptist Convention (SBC), 409
Spain
    explorations in the Americas, 367, 369, 411–12
    mysticism in, 357–58
Speyer, diets of, 327
Spirit of Medieval Philosophy, The (Gilson), 427
Spiritual Exercises, 354
Spirituality, 12–13
Spirituals, 262
Stations of the Cross, 266
Stephen, early Christian, 120
Stephen II, Pope, 237
Stone, Barton, 405
Strict separationism, 400
Sublimis Deus, 371
Subsidiarity, 456
Suffering Servant, 81
Sufism, 225–26
Sultan, 219
Summa Doctrinae Christianae
        (Canisius), 357
Summa Theologiae (Aquinas), 279–80, 282–84
Sunna, 220–22
Sunnis, 213, 216, 217, 218
Surnaturel (Supernatural) (De Lubac), 429–30
Sura, 220
Swiss Reformation, 333–36, *336*
Syllabus of Errors, 388, 424
Symeon the New Theologian, 248
Synagogues, 75
Synod of Orange, 191
Synoptic gospels, 92, 101–2
Synoptic problem, 101
Syria, church at Antioch, 130–31
Syriac Orthodox Church, 205
Systematic theology, 12

T

Taj Mahal, 227, *227*
Talmud, 85, 142
Tamar, 64
Tanakh, 20–21, 78
    canon of, 24–25
Teaching of the Twelve Apostles, The (Didache), 130–31,
        155, 157
Temple of Solomon
    first, 65–66
    second, 71–72, 74–88, 77
Ten Commandments, 56–57
Teresa of Avila, 357, 358, *360*
Tertullian, 95
Testament
    See also New Testament; Old Testament.
    defined, 19–20

Tetzel, Johann, 320
Teutonic Knights, 254, 257
Theatines, 353
Theocentric, 311
Theodosius I, 163, 166, 167
Theology
    as an academic discipline, 9–13
    African American/black theology, 463–66
    birth of, 154–57
    Calvin and, 337–38
    defined, 2, 9
    feminist theology, 461–63
    of fulfillment, 476
    liberation, 457–60
    Middle Ages, early, 246–50
    Middle Ages, High, 275–77
    Middle Ages, Late, 289–90
    postmodern, 446–47
    reasons for studying, 13–14
    scholasticism, 275–77
    science and, 453–55
    subdivisions of, 11–12
Theology of Liberation, A (Gutierrez), 458
Thirty-Nine Articles (Cranmer), 346
Thomas, 131, 133
Thomist revival, 426–27
Tocqueville, Alexis de, 8
Toleration, religious freedom and, 386–87
Torah, 21, 61
    Essenes and, 85–86
    Jesus Movement and, 87
    Pharisees and, 84–85
    Sadducees and, 83
    Second Temple period, 77–78
Tradition
    apostolic, 100
    defined, 14
    scripture and, 135–36
Transubstantiation
    Calvin and, 338
    defined, 260
    Luther and, 321
    Wycliffe and, 295, 345
    Zwingli and, 335
Treasury of merit, 319
Tremblay, Joseph Leclerc du, 375
Trent, Council of, 95, 352, 355–57
Triads, The (Gregory Palamas), 202
Trinity
    Cappadocian Fathers and, 168
    doctrine of, 151, 168
    Eastern Orthodox Christianity and, 198
Twelve Articles, The, 325
Two-Source Hypothesis, 102–3
Tylor, Edward, 7
Tyndale, William, 345

U

Ukrainian Catholic Church, 208–9
Ulama, 222
Ultramontanism, 424
Umar, 217
Umayyad Mosque, 227
Umayyads, 218
Umma, 214
Unam Sanctam, 260–61
Uniate churches, 208–9
United Church of Christ, 336
United Nations Declaration of Human Rights, 427
United Pentecostal Church International (UPCI), 406
United States
    African Americans, religions of, 409, 410–11
    Catholicism in, 411–15
    civil religion question, 416–17
    colonial period, 401, *402*
    denominationalism, 403–4
    First Amendment, 400–1
    fundamentalism, 409–10
    Great Awakening, 404
    Holiness movement, 406
    immigrants and assimilation, 412–15
    millennialism, 406–7
    peace churches, 408–9
    Pentecostalism, 406
    Protestantism in, 401–11
    revivalism, 404–5
    separation of church and state, 400–1
U.S. Conference of Catholic Bishops, 457
Unity of Philosophical Experience, The (Gilson), 427
Universities, in Middle Ages, 275–77
Urban II, Pope, 256
Urban VI, Pope, 291
Urban VIII, Pope, 374
Urban College, 374
Uriah, 64
Ursulines, 353
Ussher, James, 389
Uthman, 217, 220

V

Valdemar II, Danish king, 254
Valdes, 263
Valla, Lorenzo, 313
Varacalli, Joseph, 467
Vatican City, 237
Vatican Council I
    purpose of, 424–25
    theology trends between Vatican II and, 425–31
Vatican Council II
    church as people of God, 434–36

Declaration on Religious Freedom/Liberty, 387, 388, 414
Declaration on the Relationship of the Church to Non-Christian Religions (Nostra Aetate), 436–37, 480–81
Decree on Eastern Catholic Churches, 209
Decree on Ecumenism, 436
Dogmatic Constitution on Divine Revelation (Dei Verbum), 438–39
Dogmatic Constitution on the Church (Lumen Gentium), 231, 434–36, 480
ecumenical movement and interreligious dialogue, 436–37
liturgy, reforms, 432–34
Pastoral Constitution on the Church in the Modern World (Gaudium et Spes), 437–38, 457
purpose of, 431–32
revelation, theology of, 438–39
secularization, 437–38
theology trends between Vatican I and, 425–31
war and peace, 457
Vatican Library, 314
Verbal inspiration, 25–26
Vergerio, Pietro, 313
Vernacular Bible translation, 295, 314, 353
Verona, Council of, 263
Vicarious satisfaction, 265
Victor Emmanuel II, king of Italy, 388
Victorines, 255, 276
Vienne, Council of, 262
Vincent de Paul, 353
Vincentians, 353
Virgil, 311
Vives, Juan Luis, 311
Voltaire, 383, 384
Voluntarist principle, 341
Vulgate, 353, 356

W

Wahhabism, 229
Waldensians, 263
Walker, Alice, 466
War, Vatican II and, 457
Wealth of Nations (Smith), 388–89
Weber, Max, 8
We Hold These Truths: Catholic Reflections on the American Proposition (Murray), 413
Wesley, John, 349, 404
West, Cornel, 466
White, Ellen, 407
White, James, 407
Whitefield, George, 404
William of Ockham, 289–90
William the Pious, 240
Windows for Understanding: Jewish Muslim-Lutheran Relations, 232

Winthrop, John, 415, 416
Women
    Beguines, 262–63
    Catherine of Genoa, 294
    Catherine of Siena, 293, 297–98
    Day, Dorothy, 415, *415*
    d'Este, Isabella, 311–12, 313
    equality of, in churches, 462–63
    feminist theology, 461–63
    Gonzaga, Elisabetta, 311–12
    Islam and, 230
    Julian of Norwich, 298–300
    Kempe, Margery, 298
    medieval period, 303
    ordination issues, 462–63
    Renaissance and, 311–12, 313
    Sforza, Caterina, 312
    Teresa of Avila, 357, 358
    Ursulines, 353
Workers, living wages for, 456
Works
    justification by, 125
    of satisfaction, 319
World Council of Churches, 231
World Methodist Council, 232
World's Christian Fundamentals Association, 410
Worms
    Diet of, 323–24
    Edict of, 323
Writings, books of, 22
Wycliffe, John, 295, 313, 345

X

Xi'an monument, 206, *207*
Ximenes, Cardinal, 352

Y

Yahwist, 21
YHWH, 22
    Abraham, 43–47
    God of Israel, 36–39
    Moses, 49–58
Yom Kippur, 76
Young, Brigham, 408

Z

Zakat (almsgiving), 223
Zealots, 88
Zechariah, 61
Zephaniah, 61
Zwingli, Ulrich, 137, 333–36, *333*